BEYOND EQUALITY

Labor and the

Radical Republicans,

1862-1872

BEYOND EQUALITY

Labor and the
Radical Republicans
1862-1872

DAVID MONTGOMERY

Vintage Books

A DIVISION OF RANDOM HOUSE
NEW YORK

To Marty

who made it possible

Preface

The central political issues of the Reconstruction era were the future integrity of the United States of America and the future political and social status of the newly emancipated Negroes. At long last the writings of LaWanda and John Cox, W. R. Brock, James M. McPherson, Eric L. McKitrick, Kenneth M. Stampp, John Hope Franklin, and David Donald have established a respected status in American historical circles for this elementary proposition. That so much splendid scholarship had to be expended in order to demonstrate that the "real" subjects involved in the debate over Reconstruction were just what its leading participants always declared them to be testifies to the peculiar resiliency of the contrary viewpoint advanced earlier by such figures as Howard K. Beale and Charles A. and Mary R. Beard.

To Beale and the Beards the questions of guaranteeing integrity of the Union and Negro rights were smoke screens masking efforts by the Northeastern business community to secure its hegemony in the federal government against the threat of a hostile coalition of Southern and Western agrarian interests. Early in the 1960's their assumption that a unity of economic interests existed within Northeastern business was attacked almost simultaneously by Stanley Coben, Irwin Unger, and myself. The obverse of this assumption, that the foes of Radical Reconstruction manifested "agrarian radicalism," was challenged by Robert P. Sharkey's study of the currency question. When Unger demonstrated that no coherent interest group was able to gain effective political hegemony in the decade following the Civil War, the circle of revisionist assault on Beale and the Beards was complete.

Yet echoes of the vanquished doctrine persist, not just in obsolete textbook chapters but often in the writings of revisionists themselves. Stampp, for example, portrayed Andrew Johnson as the same "agrarian . . . backward-looking Jacksonian Democrat" Beale and William A. Dunning had envisioned, and, more important, deemed this characterization sufficient explanation of the President's policies. Similarly, John Hope Franklin, in the midst of his effort to focus attention on the central question of Negro rights, spoke of a war-spawned "industrial plutocracy that was seeking to keep a stranglehold on government in order to maintain its entrenched position."

There are two cogent reasons for the persistence of the Beale-Beard thesis. The first is that the revisionists have devoted themselves primarily to exposing flaws in the older theory or scrutinizing isolated, if important, strands in the complex web of Reconstruction politics. Although McKitrick and the Professors Cox have analyzed Washington political relationships between 1865 and 1868 with great skill, although Sharkey and Unger have traced the currency dispute through the Reconstruction period, and Franklin, Stampp, and McPherson followed controversies over the status of Negroes down to 1877, none of these scholars has integrated the many strands of development into a meaningful whole. None has offered today's readers a new interpretation of Radical Republicanism to take the place of Beale's.

Secondly, there is no escaping the suspicion that the interests and aspirations of Northern businessmen had something to do with the terms in which Reconstruction controversies were cast and the manner in which basic decisions were reached. The effective debate over the future of the South, after all, was carried on among Northerners, for they alone had access to the machinery of government. The social elite of Northern communities, furthermore, was composed at least in part of businessmen. Their approval or disapproval of a politician's course of action weighed heavily in determining its (and his) success or failure. Such considerations suggest that, for all the flaws in their conclusions, Beale and the Beards were not pursuing an altogether erroneous set of problems.

What is needed, then, is to reassemble the scattered fragments of this epoch's historical interpretation in a new fashion. As a contribution to the achievement of this goal, I have undertaken in this book to identify and analyze the various Northern groups participating in the Reconstruction debate by examining their responses to issues which arose in their home communities. Viewed from the mainstream of national life—that is, from the standpoint of the Union and Negro rights—these local questions were peripheral. No attempt is made here to claim they were the "real issues" of the times, as Beale and the Beards said of tariffs, currency, and economic penetration of the South. But the towns and cities where these questions arose supplied the social base of Republican strength. State legislators who expressed their endorsement of congressional policies toward the South enacted their own measures to change life in the North. These communities and these measures reveal the general ideological inclinations with which Republican congressmen approached the Southern question.

In other words, at the very time Radical Republicans were wrestling enthusiastically with the extension of legal equality to Negroes, they were facing other problems, often less to their liking. Prominent among them was the insistence of labor's spokesmen that social reconstruction be extended northward. "So must our dinner tables be reconstructed," demanded the Boston Labor Reform Association in 1865, "our dress, manners, education, morals, dwellings, and the whole Social System." Here was a challenge from the flank, which both exposed the social roots of Radical ideology and contributed to the abrupt decline of Radical power and influence from its zenith of 1867 and 1868. Confrontation between labor and the Radicals produced a maddening imbroglio from which emerged a new style of politics, typified by the famous Republican Stalwarts, a peculiar ideology inherited from radicalism by the labor movement itself, and a genteel critique of Radicals, Stalwarts, and labor, which styled itself liberalism.

The labor question, therefore, is used here as a prism with which to study the political spectrum of Reconstruction America. To use it in this way presupposes a thorough understanding of its configuration in the thought and practice of the time. Such awareness has been blocked from one side · by widespread acceptance of the Beale-Beard thesis among historians of labor, and from the other by the acquiescence of political historians in the terms of analysis employed by John R. Commons, Selig Perlman, and Gerald N. Grob. Their bifurcation of types of labor leaders into wage-conscious trade unionists and antimonopoly reformers has obscured both the ideological affinity between the then-prominent trade unionists and the Radicals and the great strides made by wage earners between 1862 and 1875 in creating effective bargaining and lobbying institutions. Thinking of these labor leaders as anti-industrial romantics renders one incapable of appreciating their impact on contemporary economic and political life. On the other hand, isolating their conflicts with employers from their other social activities artificially divorces their efforts from the mainstream of national development. Workers were not purely economic men but were in every sense members of their local and national communities, and it is in this setting that their efforts to improve their lot should be studied.

Equality before the law within a securely unified nation, then, was the political goal toward which Radicals aspired. But beyond equality lay demands of wage earners to which the equalitarian formula provided no meaningful answer, but which rebounded to confound the efforts of equality's ardent advocates. Class conflict, in other words, was the submerged shoal on which Radical dreams foundered. Since the clearest manifestations of this conflict were found in the industrial towns of America, rather than in congressional debates, the task of this book will be to indicate the national patterns embedded in a mosaic of local histories.

Preparation of this study would not have been possible without the generous support of a grant from the American Philosophical Society. The unstinting assistance of several library staffs lightened the burdens of research. Among them are those of the American Antiquarian Society, the Bapst Library of Boston College, the Carnegie Library of Pittsburgh, the Chicago Historical Society, the Manuscript Division of the Library of Congress, the Baker Library of Harvard University, the Newberry Library of Chicago, the Historical Society of Western Pennsylvania, the Dinand Library of the College of the Holy Cross, the University of Minnesota library, the New York Public Library, the National Archives, and the Archives of Industrial Society at the University of Pittsburgh. Special appreciation is reserved for the cooperative personnel of the University of Pittsburgh library, the Joseph A. Labadie Collection at the University of Michigan, and the State Historical Society of Wisconsin. To Professors David W. Noble, William R. Stanton, Seymour Drescher, and Julius Rubin I am profoundly grateful for their criticisms and discussions of various portions of the manuscript.

DAVID MONTGOMERY

Pittsburgh, Pennsylvania

Over all pg is.

the creation of effective bargaining institutions

- class conflict the school on which Rads dreams founded

Contents

BEYOND EQUALITY

Labor and the

Radical Republicans,

1862-1872

CHAPTER I

Entrepreneur and Wage Earner

The decade preceding the Panic of 1873 resembled a classical economist's description of the close of a long upswing in the business cycle. Since the late 1830's, per capita income in the United States had risen on a secular average of more than 1.62 per cent annually. In somewhat more than three decades the national economy had wrenched itself loose from the condition of stable, or even declining, per capita income which had characterized it since the Revolution, and especially since the end of the War of 1812. Its growth was now self-generating, so that despite all fluctuations of trade and employment, the increase of industrial output consistently surpassed that of population. In the 1860's, however, although total commodity production continued to rise, the rate of growth fell off. The demands of the Civil War generated more inflation than production, and a last-minute outburst of productive energy between 1869 and 1873 served only as a prelude to the great crash.[1]

The nodal point of the long escalation had come between 1847 and 1854, when, in the words of Alfred D. Chandler, Jr., "the simultaneous widespread adoption of the railroad, the telegraph, and the ocean-going steamship" opened the way for both factory mass production and "the use of the corporation as an administrative device for the managing and controlling of large amounts of men, money, and materials."[2] But use of the corporation in production, as distinct from transportation or banking, remained in its infancy through the sixties—a possibility, rather than a reality in widespread use. Despite many technological innovations in production during the forties and fifties, furthermore, as late as 1869 nearly half of America's manufacturing was still powered by water rather than steam.[3] The increasing value of manufacturing output between 1862 and 1873, therefore, represented not a revolution in technology or forms of business organization, but the flowering of the industrial economy cultivated during the two previous decades.

Of four major sectors of the economy, only mining enjoyed a rate of increase higher in the 1860's than the general average for the epoch 1839 to 1899. The others, manufacturing, construction, and agriculture, all grew, but at rates that were retarded by nineteenth-century American standards. Value added by manufacture rose only 26 per cent during the decade ending in 1869, as compared with 152 per cent and 76 per cent for those ending in 1849 and 1859, respectively, and

---

[1] George Rogers Taylor, "The National Economy Before and After the Civil War," in *Economic Change in the Civil War Era,* ed. David T. Gilchrist and W. David Lewis (Greenville, Del., 1965), pp. 11–22 (hereafter cited as *Economic Change*); Taylor, "American Economic Growth Before 1840: An Exploratory Essay," *Journal of Economic History,* Vol. XXIV (Dec. 1964), pp. 427–44; Robert E. Gallman, "Commodity Output, 1839–1899," in Conference on Research in Income and Wealth, *Trends in the American Economy in the Nineteenth Century. Studies in Income and Wealth* (Princeton, 1960), XXIV, 13–67.
[2] Alfred D. Chandler, Jr., "Organization of Manufacturing and Transportation," in *Economic Change,* pp. 137–8.
[3] Stuart Bruchey, *The Roots of American Economic Growth, 1607–1861. An Essay in Social Causation* (New York and Evanston, 1965), pp. 129–33, 139–40.

82 per cent, 112 per cent, and 51 per cent for the remaining decades of the century.[4] Nor was the growth of the 1860's smooth or uniform. Unemployment was heavy during 1861 and again between the last quarter of 1865 and the first quarter of 1868. Even the years of greatest expansion (1869–73) found some industries sluggish. Geographical variation in the tempo of growth was also remarkable. Not only were the former Confederate states largely omitted from its benefits, but of the leading industrial states of 1860—New York, Pennsylvania, Massachusetts, Ohio, and Connecticut—all but Pennsylvania had rates of increase in manufacturing and mining output below the national average.[5]

There was remarkable economic dynamism within two broad zones, one in the Ohio River Valley between Pittsburgh and Louisville, and the other along the lower Great Lakes region from Buffalo to Milwaukee. The upsurge in mining and the 100 per cent increase in pig-iron production in the last half of the 1860's provided much of the impetus in both areas. Pittsburgh and its cluster of satellite towns at the head of the Ohio set the pace, buttressing their well-established iron-fabricating and glass industries with basic pig-iron smelting and oil refining. In Ohio five sixths of the manufacturing and mining was in the lower half of the state, especially in and around Cincinnati, but at the decade's end coal, iron, oil, and railroads were elevating Cleveland to prominence. In both Ohio and Michigan the value of manufactured products well exceeded that of agricultural goods by 1870, and even in Wisconsin farm produce held but a negligible lead. The Ohio

---

[4] Gallman, 24. See also Thomas C. Cochran, "Did the Civil War Retard Industrialization?" *Mississippi Valley Historical Review*, Vol. XLVIII (Sept. 1961), pp. 197–210; Victor S. Clark, "Manufacturing Development during the Civil War," *The Military Historian and Economist*, Vol. III (April 1918), pp. 92–100.

[5] My calculations from raw figures in U.S. Congress, Senate, *A Compendium of the Ninth Census*, 42d Cong., 2d Sess., Senate Document, 1872, pp. 796–7 (hereafter cited as *Ninth Census*); U.S. Congress, House, *Preliminary Report on the Eighth Census*, 37th Cong., 2d Sess., House Exec. Doc. 190, 1862, p. 190. By these figures the total value of manufacturing and mining production rose 123 per cent for the U.S. as a whole, 107 per cent in New York, 113 per cent in Massachusetts, just under 100 per cent in Connecticut, 121 per cent in Ohio, and 145 per cent in Pennsylvania.

River and Great Lakes belts of progress converged across Illinois to meet in St. Louis. A 262 per cent increment to Illinois' total manufacturing and mining output over the decade placed it sixth among the industrial states of the nation. Even this performance was dwarfed by that of Missouri where, although the population remained predominantly agricultural, production in the nonfarm sectors soared 394 per cent, allowing it to replace Connecticut briefly as the country's fifth-ranking industrial state. State-encouraged railroad building and the mining of coal, iron, copper, lead, zinc, and tin were the mainstays of Missouri's growth.[6]

In this decade external economies—those reductions in unit production costs related to transportation, the urban environment, and governmental encouragement to suppliers of raw materials—clearly played a larger role in fostering growth and in the thinking of most entrepreneurs than did economies of scale or organization within the plant. The proprietor of the typical family firm, with its unimaginative productive and accounting techniques, cast his eye more frequently toward the government than toward his own concern when wondering how to improve his position. Men of speculative bent, and above all those in coal and iron, hungered for state promotion of economic growth. They longed to break the economic circuit through which the escalation of the previous decades had taken place—the relationship in which American agricultural goods and raw materials were traded for Europe's fabricated wares and capital.[7] By using the government as both a source of capital and an obstacle to imports, they aspired to build urban industrial centers rapidly so that the fruits of America's soil might be exchanged for the produce of her own mills.

[6] Pittsburgh and Allegheny County Almanac, Being a Business Directory . . . for 1867 (Pittsburgh, 1867), pp. 7, 8; Eugene H. Roseboom, The Civil War Era, 1850–1873 (Vol. V of History of the State of Ohio, ed. Carl Wittke; Columbus, 1944), pp. 11–14; Ninth Census, pp. 796–7; Eighth Census, p. 190; Clarence Lee Miller, States of the Old Northwest and the Tariff, 1865–1888 (Emporia, Kansas, 1929), p. 78; American Annual Cyclopaedia, VIII (1868), 517–18.
[7] See Harry H. Pierce, "Foreign Investment in American Enterprise," in Economic Change, pp. 41–52, for an excellent description of this relationship.

While the tapering off of growth encouraged such thinking, the sorry state of business profits lent it a sense of urgency. In manufacturing and mining as a whole, the value added per gainful worker actually fell 13 per cent between 1859 and 1869. By way of contrast, the average decade between 1839 and 1899 witnessed a 12 per cent increase in value added per worker.[8] Intense competition among manufacturers drove the prices of their wares steadily down after the war's end, while the costs of raw materials and transportation remained relatively stable. To be more precise, the aggregate cost of raw materials consumed in manufacture rose 145 per cent during the decade, while the total selling price of all goods manufactured rose only 123 per cent (using raw census figures of current dollars in both cases).[9] Ironmaster Abram Hewitt, who doubted he could "point to 10 families in the United States which have been successful" in his business, argued that "the employers generally are very uneasy because manufacturing has not been profitable in America." To him, "all this immense development of manufacture is to-day without advantage either to the proprietor or . . . to the workman, though perhaps the world has gained by the cheap rate at which they get the commodities."[1]

Here lay the heart of the entrepreneurial crisis of the 1860's. Production continued to rise on the basis of established business methods, so that profits lagged or even fell. By the eve of the Panic of 1873 a new generation of industrial leaders was coming to the fore, men such as Andrew Carnegie, Thomas A. Scott, Gustavus Swift, and Franklin P. Gowen, who were to introduce new institutional forms for production, marketing, and the financing of costly new technology. But their heyday came after the great crash. The sixties and early

---

[8] Gallman, p. 30.

[9] *Eighth Census*, p. 190; *Ninth Census*, pp. 796–7.

[1] U.K., *Parliamentary Sessional Papers, 1867*, xxxii, c 3952, "Fourth Report of the Commissioners Appointed to Inquire into the Organization and Rules of Trades Unions and Other Associations" (London, 1867), pp. 20, 24; *ibid.*, xxxii, c 3893, "Second Report of the Commissioners . . ." (London, 1867), p. 8. Hereafter these reports will be cited as *Royal Comm. on Trades Unions*, with page number. Pagination is continuous for the two reports.

seventies marked the close of American industry's "take-off" period.

THE MANUFACTURING ELITE

Except for those in the textile industry, American manufacturing firms were seldom limited liability corporations in the 1860's. Indeed, the spread of this form of business organization was one of the important innovations of the era. Prior to the Civil War only enterprises "clothed with a public interest" —specifically, banking and transportation—had commonly been legally incorporated. In other words, the privileges of limited liability were traditionally considered as belonging to quasi-public undertakings. Manufacturing and mining were the realms of private enterprise in the narrowest sense of the term—the domains of the individual entrepreneur.[2] The typical firm was so small that in 1869 the average number of wage earners per establishment was 8.15.[3] But large or small, it was owned and operated by one man or by partners. Many entrepreneurs were active members of several companies, and in larger firms the partner in charge of sales often had some personal connection with a mercantile establishment. The Lewis, Oliver, and Phillips Company, for example, Pittsburgh's leading manufacturer of nuts, bolts, and bar iron, in its partnership papers made Henry W. Oliver, son of a prominent saddle merchant, head of sales, while each of the other four associates (including two of Oliver's sons) directed a division of production.[4]

In manufacturing, corporations were known primarily in textiles, where the major establishments had been founded by

---

[2] George H. Evans, Jr., *Business Incorporations in the United States, 1800–1943*, Publications of the National Bureau of Economic Research, No. 49 (New York, 1948), pp. 20–1; Clifton K. Yearley, Jr., *Enterprise and Anthracite: Economics and Democracy in Schuylkill County, 1820–1875* ("Johns Hopkins University Studies in Historical and Political Science," Series LXXIX, No. 1; Baltimore, 1961), pp. 86–7, 133–9, 212; Edward C. Kirkland, *Industry Comes of Age. Business, Labor, and Public Policy, 1860–1897* (New York, 1961), pp. 196–8.

[3] H. A. Logan, "Labor Costs and Labor Standards," in *Labor in Canadian-American Relations*, ed. H. A. Innis (Toronto, 1937), p. 86.

[4] Articles of Agreement of Co-partnership, Sept. 11, 1867, in Oliver Iron and Steel Papers, Box 1; unidentified clippings, Henry William Oliver Scrapbook, *ibid.*

associations of export-import merchants; in mining they were found in those anthracite areas (such as the Wyoming and Lehigh regions of Pennsylvania) where mining privileges had been included in the charters of canal companies.[5] It is noteworthy that such joint stock companies had generally been chartered before the 1840's, so their officers did not form part of the new industrial elite crowding to the fore after the Civil War. To be sure, unusual forms of enterprise could be found. The Fall River Iron Works of Massachusetts, for example, was chartered as a corporation in 1825, with privileges of owning land and water rights as well as manufacturing iron. Using its control of the local water supply as a springboard, the company developed by 1850 into a holding company which operated cotton and woolen mills, print works, a railroad, and a steamship line, as well as its iron factory.[6]

Far more typical was the form of the nation's largest fabricator of iron rails, the Cambria Iron Works. After a poor beginning, this firm was reorganized in 1862 by Daniel J. Morrell, with John Fritz, a talented engineer, and Edward Townsend, a dry-goods merchant, as his partners. Though a decade later the company owned 40,000 acres of mineral land, 4 blast furnaces, 42 puddling furnaces, and a Bessemer converter, and employed 6,000 men and boys,[7] it remained a partnership, as dependent on the personal resources, supervision, and business contacts of its owners as any local family workshop. In fact, Pennsylvania law did not extend even qualified privileges of limited liability to iron and steel manufacturers until 1872.[8] Itemized records of production costs,

[5] George R. Taylor, *The Transportation Revolution, 1815–1860* (New York, 1962), pp. 230–8; Yearley, *Enterprise and Anthracite*, pp. 25–6, 30; "Coal in the United States," *Hunt's Merchants' Magazine and Commercial Review*, Vol. LIV (June 1866), pp. 418–23.

[6] Memorandum by J. T. Lincoln, Fall River Iron Works Papers.

[7] William H. Barnes, *The Fortieth Congress of the United States: Historical and Biographical* (New York, 1869), I, 251–4; Fritz Redlich, *History of American Business Leaders: A Series of Studies*, Volume I, *Theory, Iron and Steel, Iron Ore Mining* (Ann Arbor, Mich., 1940), 86–7; Herbert G. Gutman, "Two Lockouts in Pennsylvania, 1873–1874," *Pennsylvania Magazine of History and Biography*, Vol. LXXXIII (July 1959), pp. 307–9.

[8] *Debates of the Convention to Amend the Constitution of Pennsylvania* (Harrisburg, 1873), V, 480–1.

Andrew Carnegie discovered in the mid-sixties, were never kept by iron manufacturers. Until stock was taken at the year's end, the entrepreneur was "in total ignorance of results."[9] Rough accounts in the ledger books, or even in the head of the owner, sufficed. It was his firm, his property, his toil, his success or failure.

As some partnerships waxed fat in the sixties, a swarm of tiny replicas of these key concerns grew up around them. The building trades, which employed more labor than any other urban occupation, were carried on by very small firms. This industry boomed right though the lean years of 1865–8, creating such a demand for lumber that both the sawmill output of 1870 and the number of sawmills and planing mills in operation that year were larger than in any other decennial year during the century.[1]

In coal the picture was similar. Although the expansion of bituminous production during the decade from 2.7 million tons to 6.6 million spurred the rapid growth of a few major companies, the average establishment at mid-decade employed only 20 men.[2] By 1873 the Chicago, Wilmington and Vermillion Coal Company employed 900 men in Braidwood, Illinois, more than half the local miners and almost 150 per cent of the total number it and the other two mines of the area had employed in 1869.[3] Yet Allegheny County, Pennsylvania, producer of as much bituminous as the rest of the nation

---

[9] Andrew Carnegie, *Autobiography of Andrew Carnegie* (New York, 1920), p. 135.

[1] U.S. Census Office, *The Statistics of the Population of the United States. Ninth Census* (Washington, 1872), I, 704 (hereafter cited as *Stat. of Ninth Census*); Harry C. Bates, *Bricklayers' Century of Craftsmanship* (Washington, 1955), pp. 31–2; Frederick S. Deibler, *The Amalgamated Wood Workers' International Union of America* ("Bulletin of the University of Wisconsin, Economics and Political Science Series," VII; Madison, Wis., 1912), pp. 26–7; George B. Engberg, "Labor in the Lake States Lumber Industry, 1830–1930," unpublished doctoral dissertation (Univ. of Minnesota, 1949), pp. 185–210.

[2] Edward A. Wieck, *The American Miners' Association: A Record of the Origin of Coal Miners' Unions in the United States* (New York, 1940), pp. 55, 73, 95–6.

[3] Herbert G. Gutman, "The Worker's Search for Power, Labor in the Gilded Age," in *The Gilded Age, A Reappraisal,* ed. H. Wayne Morgan (Syracuse, N.Y., 1963), pp. 48–9, for 1873 figures. For 1869 data see *Stat. of Ninth Census,* III, 774.

combined, had 66 mines averaging fewer than 100 hands apiece.[4] In the anthracite fields of Schuylkill County, where a score of collieries provided the stable elements of the economy, more than 1,000 operators sank shafts between 1830 and 1875, of which less than half survived a single year of operation, while 78 per cent failed within five years.[5]

Pig-iron output rose 100 per cent between 1865 and 1870, and the number of blast furnaces, rolling mills, and iron and steel works in operation in 1869 reached the highest level in the history of the country, when 808 such firms employed 77,555 hands. A decade later only 792 companies would employ 140,798 workers, with almost twice the earlier capital investment, indicating a trend of concentration which has continued steadily until the present.[6] According to Fritz Redlich, the military orders of the war, "large from the viewpoint of the small-sized American iron business of that time," provided "some farseeing and active business leaders" the opportunity "to build up capital and develop a larger business. But in fact hardly more than half a dozen of the iron masters who were in business at that time grasped this opportunity and reaped a real harvest."[7]

Here was an industry suspended between the era of iron and the era of steel, beckoned forward by the great demand for rails and bridges provided by government-subsidized railroad promotion, but restrained by the fact that the new and necessary techniques in refining and rolling were expensive— far too expensive to be financed by individual industrialists.[8] The same problem existed in the Schuylkill County coal fields, where the easily available red-ash coal had been exhausted, and financing the sinking of shafts to reach the deeper beds of white-ash coal was beyond the means of private operators.[9] Employers in these fields, therefore, were extremely sensitive to the price of loan capital. High, sustained demand for their

[4] *Stat. of Ninth Census*, III, 785.

[5] Yearley, *Enterprise and Anthracite*, pp. 57–62.

[6] Cochran, p. 200; Harold U. Faulkner, *American Economic History*, 6th ed. (New York, 1949), p. 427.

[7] Redlich, p. 95.

[8] Clark, pp. 95–6; Kirkland, *Industry Comes of Age*, pp. 165–6; Carnegie, pp. 114–32, 184–7.

[9] Yearley, *Enterprise and Anthracite*, pp. 73–5.

wares and low interest rates were indispensable if they were to continue to expand their enterprises in the manner to which they had become accustomed.

Furthermore, the market of the entrepreneur of the sixties was seldom local, but regional or national. Even given adequate demand for his wares, he could reach potential customers only through the intervention of transportation companies and "jobbers," who bought and moved wholesale lots of goods.[1] In other words, interposed between the vigorous new manufacturing elite and both their capital and their customers was the established "old elite" of businessmen engaged primarily in commerce, shipping, finance, and real estate. It was these captains of commerce to whom the title "capitalist" was then customarily applied, for they had at their disposal the large sums of money and credit needed to move both producer and consumer goods to the point of usage. "Morris K. Jessup, Elliot C. Cowdin, William E. Dodge, Abiel A. Low, Simeon Chittenden, Jonathan Sturges, and William Aspinwall, to name the best known, were men of national prominence and repute," argues Irwin Unger, "often more influential than the contemporary industrialists and promoters we now identify as the great business movers of the era."[2]

The relationship between manufacturing and the old elite was not the same everywhere. The textile industry, for example, was already in its third generation of large-scale operation in New England and Pennsylvania and had originally been organized by merchants of fabrics, such as Francis C. Lowell and his associates in the Boston Manufacturing Company. Not only was there no conflict between commercial and manufacturing capital here (both being in the same hands), but the scale of organization of labor was on a level far above that of any other industry. The Pepperell Manufacturing Company at Biddeford, Maine, employed 1,600 women, the Androscoggin Mills at Lewiston, Maine, 1,000. The Wamsutta

---

[1] John R. Commons *et al.*, *History of Labour in the United States* (New York, 1918–35), II, 3–7, 14; Fred Mitchell Jones, *Middlemen in the Domestic Trade of the United States, 1800–1860* (Urbana, Ill., 1937), pp. 13–32.
[2] Irwin Unger, *The Greenback Era, A Social and Political History of American Finance, 1865–1879* (Princeton, 1964), p. 148.

Mills in New Bedford, Massachusetts, had 1,050 employees, and 3,000 signatures were collected on a petition circulated within the rooms of the Pacific Mills at Lawrence. In Massachusetts the average capital investment per manufacturing establishment in 1870 was $17,536, as compared with $10,936 in Pennsylvania and a national average of only $8,400. The high degree of concentration of manpower within the industry of Massachusetts is illustrated by the fact that the capital invested per worker in that state was only $830 that year, as compared with $1,273 in Pennsylvania, where the high overhead of the coal and iron industries carried the figure well over the national average of $1,031. In short, the looms of Lowell, so prominent in the interpretations of such historians as Beale, Parrington, and the Beards, represented a very untypical situation, not the norm of American manufacturing, and their proprietors belonged to the old, not the new, business elite.[3]

In the states of the Old Northwest, on the other hand, the typical scale of production was especially small. Ohio had 22,773 manufacturing establishments in 1870, over 9,000 more than Massachusetts, yet employed just under one half the number of factory hands used in the Bay State. Illinois had 12,579 firms, less than 7,000 fewer than Massachusetts, yet had only one third the number of factory workers. Within Illinois itself Cook County had one half the workers of the state, but only one ninth of the establishments.[4] Equally important for this area is the fact that most of the loan capital for industrial development in cities such as Chicago and Cleveland had to come from the East, because local capital was mostly involved in railroads, real estate, and dealings in land and farm produce.[5]

[3] Stanley Coben, "Northeastern Business and Radical Reconstruction: A Re-examination," *Mississippi Valley Historical Review,* Vol. XLVI (July 1959), pp. 69–71; Boston *Daily Advertiser,* Jan. 15, 23, 1868; *Daily Evening Voice,* Feb. 20, 25, 1867; *Ninth Census,* pp. 796–7.
[4] *Ninth Census,* pp. 796–7; Arthur C. Cole, *The Era of the Civil War* ("The Centennial History of Illinois," ed. Clarence V. Alvord, Vol. III; Springfield, Ill., 1919), p. 365. Ohio had 137,202 factory hands; Massachusetts, 279,380.
[5] Bessie Louise Pierce, *A History of Chicago* (New York, 1940), II, 148–9; Roseboom, p. 24.

The peculiar relationship of the manufacturers to the leaders of finance and commerce was reflected in the ambivalent rhetoric of the period. At times the new elite spoke of themselves as "capitalists" and described disputes with their employees as conflicts between labor and capital. More frequently, they referred to themselves as part of the "producing classes," or as "labor," or even as "workingmen," as distinct from the "capitalists" (i.e., the old elite). A generation later conventional American symbolism would term the employers "middle class," and William Jennings Bryan would seek to ennoble the worker, farmer, and corner grocer by calling each of them, like the industrialist, "a business man."[6] But in the 1860's the phrase "middle class" was such a novelty that, when it appeared at all, it was enclosed in quotation marks.[7] The speaker who valued precision might term the wage earners the "mechanical interests" or "industrial classes" or even "working classes" (always plural), but common practice indiscriminately spoke of "labor" as a group of which employers at times were a part and at times were not.[8] Thus the nation's economic system was not called "capitalism" but the "free-labor system."

Central to this vague rhetoric was the cult of the "self-made man," according to which the employer was but a successful workingman. All this phraseology was employed by Abraham Lincoln in his speech to Congress on the war aims of the Union. The President pronounced labor "prior to, and independent of, capital" and "the superior of capital." He made this remark while praising as the "just, and generous, and prosperous system" that in which the "prudent, penniless beginner in the world, labors for wages awhile, saves a surplus with which to buy tools or land for himself; then labors on his own account another while, and at length hires another new beginner to help him." It was the political rights and power of

---

[6] "Bryan's Cross of Gold Speech," in *Documents of American History*, ed. Henry S. Commager, 3d ed. (New York, 1947), II, 175.

[7] *Eg.*, editorial in *Daily Evening Voice*, July 17, 1867, mentioning "the intelligent 'middle classes'—speaking, to be understood, after the fashion of the day . . ."

[8] *Eg.*, Rev. A. S. Twombly, *A Thanksgiving Plea for Free Labor, North and South* (Albany, N.Y., 1864).

such men as these which the rebellion threatened, said Lincoln. "No men living," he concluded, "are more worthy to be trusted than those who toil up from poverty. . . ."[9]

Because it played such a significant role in American ideology, the myth of the self-made man in industry deserves critical examination. A study by Frances W. Gregory and Irene D. Neu of 303 leading figures in the textile, railroad, and iron and steel industries in the decade following 1870 concludes "most—perhaps 90 per cent—of the industrial leaders in our group were reared in a middle- or upper-class milieu."[1] Of the one hundred iron and steel entrepreneurs studied, 48 were sons of businessmen, 16 of professional men, 27 of farmers, and 11 of industrial wage earners. Only 14 of the iron leaders were immigrants, and at least 6 of them were from "substantial middle-class backgrounds" in Europe. Interestingly, all of the businessmen in all three fields studied were Protestants.[2]

These findings are substantiated by Clifton K. Yearley's study of the Schuylkill County anthracite fields. Despite the constant turnover of petty operators in the mines, about twenty "master operators" provided stability, leadership, and about one half the production of the area. Yet it is crucial to note that these "master operators" were themselves heads of individual or partnership concerns. Furthermore, it was precisely these men who consistently led the battles of the local colliers against the Schuylkill Navigation Company and the Philadelphia and Reading Railroad, sparked the high tariff and soft money crusades, and organized the Anti-Monopoly Convention of 1867.[3]

All these efforts were conducted in the name of the "producers" defending themselves against the "monopolizing capitalists." Real conflicts of economic interest between manufacturers and commercial capitalists, in other words, were rationalized in (and perhaps intensified by) an ideology which

9 *The Collected Works of Abraham Lincoln,* ed. Roy P. Basler (New Brunswick, N.J., 1953), V, 52. (Hereafter cited as Lincoln, *Works.*)
1 Frances W. Gregory and Irene D. Neu, "The American Industrial Elite in the 1870's," in *Men in Business, Essays in the History of Entrepreneurship,* ed. William Miller (Cambridge, Mass., 1952), p. 202.
2 *Ibid.,* pp. 197–202.
3 Yearley, *Enterprise and Anthracite,* pp. 65–70, 197–8.

allowed them to be verbalized only in a vague and shadowy manner. But despite the failure of contemporary rhetoric to express such antagonisms clearly, they were not imaginary or rhetorical only. Northern business was not a harmonious or cohesive economic unit.

It was not difficult to fabricate from the warp of such economic conflicts and the woof of contemporary ideology the image of a conspiracy of the capitalists to retard the growth of industry. Since trade and finance, in the words of James Russell Lowell, had "no fatherland but the till,"[4] while promoters of industry identified themselves with the nation, the victim of the plot was the country itself. This idea was expressed sharply in 1868 by John Magwire, a wealthy rolling-mill owner and shipbuilder of St. Louis, who charged the financial interests with retarding the growth of America's capacity to manufacture its own iron rails, thus helping England. Although Magwire's doctrinaire adherence to greenbackism as the solution to the difficulties of which he spoke set him apart from many manufacturers, the intellectual framework of his analysis was both commonplace and revealing. Stating that a day's production of a ton of iron cost the labor of ten men in England and only eight in Missouri, he explained the reason less railroad iron was produced in Missouri as follows:

Here is Mr. McCarty makes up his mind to go into the iron business, and he brings thirty or forty families down to Missouri, and determines to sink $100,000 in the business. When he is about to set to work, the capitalists says [*sic*], "What are you going to sink all this money in such a business for?" He replies, "Because I can get 10 per cent. on my capital." Then they tell him that he will have a great deal of labor and trouble to carry on the enterprise; whereas, if he likes, he can get 20 per cent. for his money with no risk and no trouble at all. So they persuade Mr. McCarthy [*sic*] to invest half of it in bonds which bring him $8,400, and the other half in a national bank which brings in $9,000 more. But he says, "What am I to do with all those people that I have brought out here

---

[4] J. R. Lowell to John L. Motley, July 26, 1864, in *Correspondence of John Lothrop Motley*, ed. George William Curtis (New York and London, 1900), III, 34.

to give employment to?" They reply, "Let them look to that themselves. . . . Let the women sell their virtue." These are facts. . . . Those men in England make iron for us, while we could make better iron than they, if it were not for the high rates of interest that money will fetch here. This money should find its way into business and employment.[5]

How to bring that "money . . . into business and employment" was the issue of the hour for the entrepreneur. The most ingenious manufacturers of the period, those best remembered by posterity, at that very time were beginning to find such solutions as use of the limited liability stock company and direct participation of a railroad company in the firm which produced the iron it used or the coal it hauled. But most industrialists, ardently attached to their private enterprises— "the family business"—and disdaining, as even Carnegie did throughout his life, to become the hireling of a corporation,[6] instead turned for help to the government. Let the state "promote the general welfare" by lending all possible assistance to the growth of America's industry, was the essence of the economic philosophy of Henry Carey.[7] And so prominently was Carey identified with the economic aspirations of the new elite that he was the unchallenged choice of the Pennsylvania constitutional convention of 1873 to speak for its Committee on Industrial Interests and Labor.[8]

To the question of what help the state could provide, several answers were forthcoming. One in particular deserves mention here, both because its outcome gave warning of some hazards inherent in governmental aid to business, and because it roused the wrath of organized labor in a way its initiators never anticipated. This was the attempt to import to the United States the national finance doctrines of the Saint-Simonian advisers of Napoleon III of France.

Early in the century Henri, comte de Saint-Simon had

---

[5] *Workingman's Advocate,* Oct. 18, 1868. For sketch of Magwire see below, pp. 402–3.
[6] Carnegie, p. 142.
[7] Henry C. Carey, *Miscellaneous Works of Henry C. Carey, LL.D. With a Memoir by Dr. William Elder* (2 vols., Philadelphia, 1895).
[8] *Debates of the Convention to Amend the Constitution of Pennsylvania,* V, 470.

sought a formula by which the creative energy of industrial society might be reconciled with the order of the Middle Ages. His disciples converted Saint-Simon's doctrines into an effort to eliminate exploitation and economic crisis from society through the *"organization of work."*[9] The first step in this task was to be the creation of a social institution which might put the land and capital owned by society's wealthy idlers and needed for production into the hands of the "worthiest industrialists."[1] Banks executed this function in embryonic form, but their role was limited by their inability to envision the needs of society as a whole and their tendency to tax industry for their private profit.[2] Banks were thus necessary, but posed a dilemma:

> The advantage that would follow from an intervention of bankers between the idle [capitalists] and the *travailleurs* [note—"laborer" used as embracing both proprietor and worker] is often balanced, or even annulled, by the opportunities offered by our disorganized society to Egoism, which may manifest itself in various forms of fraud and charlatanry. The bankers often come between the idle and the *travailleurs* for the purpose of exploiting both of them to the injury of society.[3]

Thus the coordination of the banking system with the machinery of state was proposed as the means by which financiers could take direct command of the movement of production without the danger of exploitation and could distinguish themselves "through the number and usefulness of the organized establishments and of the promoted works."[4] In France, under the regime of Louis Napoleon, these theories bore fruit in the creation of the *Crédit Mobilier* for industry

---

[9] *The Doctrine of Saint-Simon: An Exposition. First Year, 1828–1829,* trans. and ed. by George C. Iggers (Boston, 1958), p. 13.

[1] *Ibid.,* p. 98.

[2] *Ibid.,* pp. 90–112.

[3] *Doctrine de Saint-Simon, exposition, première année, 1828–1829,* quoted in Karl Marx, *Capital: A Critique of Political Economy* (Chicago, 1909), III, 711. The same passage in the Iggers translation is in a footnote (p. 103), but Marx's rendition of the passage is far more clear than Iggers's.

[4] *Religion saint-simonienne, Economie et Politique,* quoted in Marx, *Capital,* III, 714.

and the *Crédit Foncier* for agriculture. The former, a joint stock company headed by the brothers Emile and Isaac Péreire, financed the construction of the Paris Gas Company, the Paris Omnibus Company, and the Maritime Company of Clippers, as well as railroads in several foreign countries. The *Crédit Foncier* was organized by the House of Rothschild.[5] It was through these practical examples that Saint-Simon's influence crossed the ocean four decades after his death. Both projects were imitated in America, names and all, and they also inspired several smaller enterprises.

The Crédit Mobilier of America was chartered by the legislature of Pennsylvania in 1859 under the name Pennsylvania Fiscal Agency, with authority to "become an agency for the purchase and sale of railroad bonds and other securities, and to make advances of money and credit to railroad and other improvement companies, and to aid in like manner contractors and manufacturers. . . ."[6] Despite this bold warrant, the corporation remained dormant until 1864 when two circumstances gave it a sudden burst of life. One of these was the inability of the newly chartered Union Pacific Railroad to raise the funds it needed to begin construction. The other was the return to the United States from Europe of the tempestuous Fenian, Peace Democrat, and pioneer in urban street transportation, George Francis Train, who considered Louis Napoleon "the best statesman in Europe, and the best financier in the world."[7] Train persuaded his friend Thomas C. Durant, the vice-president of the Union Pacific, to allot the construction contract for his railroad to the Pennsylvania Fiscal Agency and to change the name of the latter to the Crédit Mobilier of America. Actually, the Crédit Mobilier constructed only 247 miles of road and realized very little

[5] Robert S. Binkley, *Realism and Nationalism, 1852–1871* (*The Rise of Modern Europe,* ed. William L. Langer; New York and London, 1935), p. 97; J. B. Crawford, *The Crédit Mobilier of America: Its Origin and History, Its Work of Constructing the Union Pacific Railroad and the Relation of Members of Congress Therewith* (Boston, 1880), pp. 14–15; Rowland Hazard, *The Crédit Mobilier of America* (Providence, R.I., 1881), pp. 15–16.

[6] Crawford, pp. 17, 18.

[7] C. F. Train to C. H. McCormick, Sept. 29, 1865, in William T. Hutchinson, *Cyrus Hall McCormick* (New York, 1930, 1935), II, 136.

profit. In 1867 the contract was transferred jointly to Representative Oakes Ames of Massachusetts and the trustees of the Union Pacific, who meanwhile had also made themselves the stockholders of the Crédit Mobilier. Through this means the Crédit Mobilier became practically synonymous with the Union Pacific.[8] Train's grandiose scheme for establishing the Péreire system in America evaporated, and his Saint-Simonian dream of banker's initiative without "Egoism" became the most widely renowned symbol of predatory business activities of the decade.

Undaunted, Train persuaded Cyrus McCormick and George Bemis to help him establish the Crédit Foncier of America to develop land along the Union Pacific line. Despite the presence of an impressive array of prominent politicians on its board of directors and the lure its prospectus offered stockholders of owning "the towns and cities at every station on the line of the Pacific Railway,"[9] nothing more came of the scheme than the purchase of eighty acres of land and the erection of a few houses in Omaha.[1] Train still refused to surrender his hopes. In 1868, when he founded the journal *The Revolution*, edited by Susan B. Anthony and Elizabeth Cady Stanton, he included in its platform a demand for "The Credit Foncier and Credit Mobilier system, or Capital Mobilized to Resuscitate the South and our Mining Interests, and to People the Country from Ocean to Ocean."[2]

Train's efforts might be taken lightly if they were unique. After all, not only did he soon return to Ireland, where a British jail cell rewarded his solitary efforts to free the Emerald Isle, but in 1870 he took an eighty-day trip around the world which he alleged inspired Jules Verne's famous novel, and during which he later claimed he had established the Commune of Marseilles.[3] The fact remains that among his

---

[8] Hazard, pp. 17–18, 20–4; Hutchinson, II, 134–41.
[9] Hutchinson, II, 136.
[1] *Ibid.*, II, 137.
[2] *Revolution*, I (Jan. 8, 1868), 1.
[3] *Ibid.*, II (Oct. 8, 1868), 218; II (Oct. 15, 1868), 234; obituary in *The Truth Seeker*, undated 1904 clipping in Joseph A. Labadie Collection (hereafter cited as JAL), in the file marked: Anarchism –Train, George Francis.

colleagues in the railroad ventures of 1864–6 were some of the most prominent businessmen and politicians of the land.

Jay Cooke also envisaged a Crédit Mobilier plan for the physical reconstruction of the South, but the intense political debates of 1866 frustrated the efforts of John Sherman to introduce a bill for federal participation in the plan.[4] At that time a private concern for the same purpose was founded by Duff Green, an original director of the Pennsylvania Fiscal Agency, and his son Benjamin C. Green. Entitled the American Industrial Agency, the Greens' organization advertised itself as ready to provide land, capital, and labor for undertakings in all branches of industry, transportation, and agriculture through "corporate powers and franchises more extensive and valuable than those of the CREDITS FONCIER AND MOBILIER of France. . . ."[5] Benjamin Green went to great lengths to enlist the National Labor Union in his scheme.[6]

Aside from the Crédit Mobilier, the only effort to create a central directing body for economic promotion which succeeded in linking itself with governmental activities was the American Emigrant Company. Henry Carey himself interested a number of Philadelphia wholesale iron merchants in pooling their efforts with those of a group of New England speculators in Western lands to create a single development agency which could provide entrepreneurs with both land from the public domain and labor from Europe. After the company was chartered by Connecticut in 1863, it turned to the federal government for funds to help move European workers to the United States.[7] A special committee of the House under Elihu B. Washburne studied the problem and issued a recommendation in 1864 based largely on the advice of Secretary of State William H. Seward. The Secretary argued that the country stood in desperate need of labor, while the Old World was

---

[4] Ellis Paxson Oberholtzer, *Jay Cooke, Financier of the Civil War* (Philadelphia, 1907), II, 23–4.

[5] Advertisement in pamphlet, *National Labor Congress, Baltimore, Md., August 20, 1866. Letter and Remarks by Ben E. Green* (New York, 1866), p. 13.

[6] See below, pp. 113, 224–5.

[7] Charlotte Erickson, *American Industry and the European Immigrant, 1860–1885* (Cambridge, Mass., 1957), pp. 7–11.

crowded with potential emigrants who could not afford to come. The obvious solution, government payment for their transportation, was out of the question because the costs of the current war prohibited it and because European governments would take it as a hostile act. Thus indirect methods had to be used. Let merchants, farmers, and miners advance the money, Seward advised, while the government assisted their search for labor and in some way underwrote the private risks.[8]

Congress passed "An Act to Encourage Immigration" in July 1864. The measure established a commissioner of immigration and set him up in an office which he shared with the American Emigrant Company. American consuls in Europe were authorized to act as hiring agents for employers in the United States. Instead of providing the funds the company had wanted, Congress declared valid contracts made by immigrants in foreign countries pledging their wages for a term not to exceed twelve months, to repay the cost of transportation to America. This contract was to be registered with the commissioner and to operate as a lien upon any land or other property acquired by the immigrant until the obligation was liquidated. Upon the recommendation of both the Washburne committee and President Lincoln, such immigrants were specifically exempted from the wartime draft.[9]

In this particular effort at "the organization of work," moving labor rather than capital to the points where industry needed it became the point of emphasis. Abiel Abbot Low, president of the New York Chamber of Commerce, reported to that body at the beginning of 1865 on the work of the American Emigrant Company. Arguing that the war and the tariff had provided the "protection and encouragement which our manufacturers needed," he predicted a vast national demand for labor. Ecstatically, he heard the "call for labor" wafted "on every breeze, from the Rocky Mountains and the Sierra Nevada, from the mountains and valleys of Pennsyl-

---

[8] U.S. Congress, House, *Report of the Special Committee on Foreign Emigration.* 38th Cong. 1st Sess., House Rept. 56 (Washington, 1864).
[9] Erickson, pp. 11–13; John R. Commons *et al.*, *Documentary History of American Industrial Society* (Cleveland, 1910–11), IX, 74–6. (Hereafter cited as Commons, *Doc. Hist.*)

vania and Michigan, from California, Oregon, Idaho, Colorado, Iowa, Ohio, Illinois, and other States, where lie buried the gold and silver, lead, iron, copper and vast beds of coal, underlying the rich prairie lands and mountains of the West; where, too, are found subterranean deposits of petroleum, enough to illuminate a world."[1]

But like the Crédit Mobilier, the Emigrant Company was designed as a collective effort of businessmen with government aid. In more than half a dozen European states it established agencies which contracted with workmen and assisted others who were able to pay their own way, at a fee to prospective employers of ten dollars apiece for skilled artisans, six dollars for railroad and agricultural labor, and five dollars for boys and women who would work as domestics and farm workers. American consuls in Europe, at the urging of the Secretary of State, aided this work. During the law's first two years of operation, the commissioner of immigration registered 311 contracts, but the agents of the company inspired many more laborers who emigrated with their own resources.[2]

The company soon roused the anger of several trade unions, not because it effected a mass influx of newcomers to the American labor market, but because it directed Europeans to the scenes of several important strikes to replace men who had walked out. Commissioner of Immigration E. Pershine Smith wrote to Henry Carey in 1866 that he was disturbed by the "continued success of strikes by workmen of almost all kinds," and wished to use his office to correct this trend.[3] The company dispatched British ironmolders under contract to break strikes in St. Louis in 1864 and in Chicago in 1865. Coal miners were imported to the Belleville fields of Illinois under the same circumstances early in 1865.[4] Prussian and Belgian ironworkers were poured into Pittsburgh by the hundreds during the strike of 1867, with the result that delegates to the National Labor Congress of that year denounced the Ameri-

---

1 *Daily Evening Voice*, Jan. 9, 1865.
2 Erickson, pp. 13–21; Commons, *Doc. Hist.*, IX, 74–8; Daniel Creamer, "Recruiting Contract Laborers for the Amoskeag Mills," *Journal of Economic History*, Vol. I (May 1941), pp. 42–56.
3 E. Pershine Smith to Henry Carey, May 4, 1866, quoted in Erickson, p. 13.
4 Erickson, pp. 50–4; Wieck, p. 111.

can Emigrant Company for breaking strikes, bribing European trade unions to participate in its schemes, and devouring western public lands.[5]

The next year Congress repealed the act of 1864. Although contracting immigrant labor in Europe remained legal for almost two decades more, and United States consuls continued to assist emigration, both the one-year indenture and the office of commissioner of immigration were thereby abolished. The protests of labor probably had little to do with the 1868 action of Congress. More persuasive to the legislators, as Charlotte Erickson has shown, were the reluctance of the legislators to pay the cost of maintaining the commissioner's office, the eagerness of state immigration agencies to pre-empt the field, and the difficulties of enforcing the lien contracts made by the immigrants.[6] Of 44 weavers brought from Britain under contract in 1868 by the Amoskeag Mills of New Hampshire, for example, ten left the company without repaying the transportation funds it had advanced them.[7] The repeal of the act of 1864, in other words, simply meant that the federal government had yielded its part in the effort to direct the flow of immigration in favor of purely private and state efforts. Even Henry Carey concluded that high tariffs and expansionist monetary policies alone would suffice to attract from the Old World all the workmen America could employ.[8] Carey still believed the state should play a major developmental role, but he had lost his interest in a quasi-public agency to direct factors of production to the point of social need.

In one sense the Saint-Simonian scheme fell victim in America to the very "Egoism" and disorganization of society which it was intended to remedy. The work of the American Emigrant Company was chronically hamstrung by lack of

---

[5] *Workingman's Advocate*, Aug. 31, 1867. The only significant land acquisition of the company was the Cherokee Neutral Tract in Kansas, which it was soon forced to surrender. Paul Wallace Gates, *Fifty Million Acres: Conflicts over Kansas Land Policy, 1854–1890* (Ithaca, N.Y., 1954), pp. 155–67.

[6] Erickson, pp. 28–31.

[7] Creamer, p. 54. Cf. Erickson, pp. 46–50.

[8] *Debates of the Convention to Amend the Constitution of Pennsylvania*, V, 474–6.

funds. Private employers proved as tight-fisted as the federal government when it came to contributing money, for, sighed one company leader to Carey: "You *know* how hard it is to get the *iron men* to pay *anything*."[9] To make matters worse, scandal dogged the tracks of the Crédit Mobilier, as federal grants were siphoned off into private pockets. Three or four decades later, the movement of capital to "worthy industrialists" would be highly organized by a handful of investment banking houses. But before finance capital could come to play a directing role in industry it was necessary that the corporation mature as an institution in manufacturing—that the banker might be able to sit on the board of directors of the factory or the holding company. The individualistic entrepreneurs of the 1860's, however, looked askance at both the corporation and the banker. To preserve the family factory, they sought help from the state in the form of tariff protection, low interest rates, cheap transportation, and sustained demand. The appeal of Louis Napoleon's economic methods to American manufacturers, however, had evaporated by the end of the decade.

THE LABOR FORCE

In 1869 the *New-York Times* featured a series of articles surveying the condition of "Our Working Classes."[1] Seeking to explain the proliferation of trade unions and strikes, the author of the series noted that little workshops were "far less common than they were before the war," and that "the small manufacturers thus swallowed up have become workmen on wages in the greater establishments, whose larger purses, labor-saving machines, &c., refused to allow the small manufacturers a separate existence."[2]

At first blush this statement seems to contradict the observation of the preceding section that small manufacturers flourished during the 1860's. The key to the paradox lies in the definition of the concept "small manufacturer" implicit in the

---

[9] John Williams to Henry C. Carey, May 25, 1866, quoted in Erickson, p. 16.
[1] *New-York Times,* Feb. 22, 24, March 2, 5, 17, 24, 1869.
[2] *Ibid.,* Feb. 22, 1869.

usage of the *Times*. The article which described their eclipse continued: "One capitalist employs five men now where he employed one twenty years ago. . . ."[3] Five employees hardly describes a trust. In fact, this figure is even lower than the national average of the time. What the *Times* depicted, therefore, was not the waxing of "big business" but the descent of the independent mechanic to the status of wage earner. This loss of independence was characterized by the article as "a system of slavery as absolute if not as degrading as that which lately prevailed at the South. The only difference is that there agriculture was the field, landed proprietors were the masters and negroes were the slaves; while in the North manufacturers is the field, manufacturing capitalists threaten to become the masters, and it is the white laborers who are to be slaves."[4]

Here was an economic development which left Americans in a quandary. A brief statistical survey will reveal both emerging social patterns and the lack of correspondence between the new society and the rhetoric of the "free-labor system." In the first place, the number of Americans engaged in nonagricultural production was rapidly approaching that of those devoted to farming. Note the following figures on the distribution of the total labor force:[5]

	agricultural		nonagricultural	
Year	Workers Employed	Per Cent of Total Labor Force	Workers Employed	Per Cent of Total Labor Force
1860	6,207,634	58.9	4,325,116	41.1
1870	6,849,772	53.0	6,075,179	47.0

The growing importance of nonfarm occupations, however, did not mean that the society had become largely urban. On the contrary, despite the rapid pace of city growth,

---

[3] *Ibid.*

[4] *Ibid.*

[5] U.S. Department of Commerce, Bureau of the Census, *Historical Statistics of the United States, 1789–1945* (Washington, D.C., 1949), p. 63. (Hereafter cited as *Hist. Stat. 1945*.)

scarcely a quarter of the American population was to be found in places of 2,500 or more inhabitants, as the following comparisons reveal.[6]

Year	Rural Population	Per Cent of U.S. Total	Urban Population	Per Cent of U.S. Total
1860	25,266,803	80.3	6,216,518	19.7
1870	28,656,010	74.4	9,902,361	25.6

In other words, although the rate of increase of the urban population far exceeded that of the rural, the absolute growth was about the same. The figures suggest that a great deal of American manufacturing took place in country areas—that industrial growth and city growth are *not* two different measures of the same phenomenon. Furthermore, much of the resident laboring population of the great cities consisted of day laborers in commerce and transportation, while many skilled mechanics in such areas as Boston and Philadelphia commuted to work daily or weekly from homes outside the city. The ubiquitous American boardinghouse catered as much to such artisans as to newly arrived immigrants.[7] At the other extreme, as late as 1878 a Three-Little-Pigs-type morality story about "typical workingmen" in New England could depict a shoe worker, a carpenter, and a quarryman all living in rustic surroundings.[8] Between these poles were many small factory towns, or clusters of towns, often adjacent to major cities, such as Manchester, Birmingham, East Birmingham, Monongahela, Lawrenceville, and the other communities ringing Pittsburgh and Allegheny City. Even in Massachusetts, where half the population inhabited towns of more than 10,000 by 1870, the

6 *Ibid.*, 25.

7 E. H. Rogers, dissenting report, in Massachusetts House of Representatives, *Report of the Commissioners on the Hours of Labor*, House Document 44, 1867 (Boston, 1867); letter of iron molder's wife, *Daily Evening Voice*, Nov. 9, 1866; [James D. Burn], *Three Years among the Working Classes in the United States during the War* (London, 1865), pp., 5–9; Charles J. Kennedy, "Commuter Services in the Boston Area, 1835–1860," *Business History Review*, Vol. XXXXVI (Summer 1962), pp. 153–70.

8 [*Anon.*], "Three Typical Workingmen," *Atlantic Monthly*, Vol. XLII (Dec. 1878), pp. 717–27.

most formidable growth was evident in the interior towns like Worcester, Lowell, Holyoke, Lynn, and Fall River.[9] These phenomena of rural or quasi-rural residence among workmen and industrial growth removed from the great cities profoundly influenced both the shape of the labor movement and local reactions to it. The labor-reform association which banded workingmen of diverse trades into a single body was a natural outgrowth of the dispersal of industry itself. So too, as Herbert Gutman has argued, "the social environment in the large American city after the Civil War was more often hostile toward workers than was that in the smaller industrial towns. . . . The ideology of many nonworkers in these small towns was not entirely hospitable toward industrial, as opposed to traditional, business enterprise."[1]

With these considerations in mind, it will not be difficult to grasp the fact that the America of 1870, largely rural though it remained, was already predominantly a nation of employees. Insights into the changes taking place in society may be gleaned from the ninth census of the United States. This study, directed by the pioneer statistician Francis A. Walker, was itself a landmark in American intellectual history, being the first national survey to pay close and detailed attention to the occupations of the people.[2] Because the census of 1860 was extremely crude and vague in comparison to that of 1870, it is not possible to draw a meaningful picture of trends over the decade. Even in the ninth census employers and employees are by no means clearly distinguished. A category such as "blacksmiths" or "draymen, hackmen, teamsters, &c." em-

---

9 [Charles F. Adams, Jr.], "The Butler Canvass," *North American Review,* Vol. CXIV (Jan. 1872), pp. 158–9.

1 Gutman, "Worker's Search for Power," p. 41.

2 Walker wrote in the introduction to his report: "The habits of a people, their social tastes, and moral standards, would be more truthfully depicted in a complete list of their daily occupations, than ever was done in any book of travels or of history." (*Stat. of Ninth Census,* I, xxxiii.) He was the son of the eminent economist Amasa Walker and an able economist in his own right. See Joseph Dorfman, *The Economic Mind in American Civilization* (New York, 1946–9), III, 101–10; James Leiby, *Carroll Wright and Labor Reform: The Origin of Labor Statistics* (*Harvard Historical Monographs,* Vol. XLVI; Cambridge, Mass., 1960), pp. 124–5.

braced many self-employed artisans as well as many hirelings. Director Walker himself complained that the flexibility of occupations in America and the multiplicity of dual listings in the returns, such as "blacksmith and miner," made precise classification impossible.[3]

Still more difficulties are inherent in the census figures. First, one must not (as is all too often done) identify industrial wage earners with the census category "manufactures, mining, and mechanical industries." On one hand, of the 2,707,421 who fell into that classification at least 62,766 were clearly employers. On the other hand, among the 2,684,793 people in "professional and personal services" were 1,031,666 "laborers, (not specified)" and an equal number of other wage earners, mostly domestic servants.[4] Secondly, a review made of the ninth census data at the time of the 1940 census discovered grave errors in the work of Walker's staff. More than a million Southerners were never counted at all, and since most of them were involved in agriculture, this oversight led to a severe underestimate of the farm sector of the work force. The error was compounded by the fact that almost 60 per cent of those classed "laborers, (not specified)" turned out to have been farm laborers.[5]

Despite these impediments, it is possible to draw a crude outline of the 1870 American social structure from the census figures. Careful perusal of each category in the revision made in 1940 discloses some remarkable social patterns. Of the 12.9 million people in all occupations, only 1.1 million (8.6 per cent) can be listed as nonagricultural employers, corporation officials, and self-employed producers or professionals. Thus the business and professional elites, old and new, totaled less than one tenth of the nation's economically active population. In agriculture there were just over three million farmers, planters, and other independent operators—not quite one

---

[3] *Stat. of Ninth Census,* III, 797–805.
[4] *Ibid.,* I, 682, 674.
[5] U.S. Bureau of the Census, *Sixteenth Census of the United States: 1940. Population. Comparative Occupation Statistics for the United States, 1870 to 1940* (Washington, D.C., 1943), pp. 141–56. (Hereafter cited as *Compar. Occ. Stat.*)

fourth of the gainfully employed. When these groups are combined it is seen that during this age which held the independent entrepreneur to be the typical American, only 4.24 million (32.9 per cent) were actually employers or self-employed. More than 4.9 million men, women, and children (38.4 per cent) were wage earners in industry, transportation, and service occupations. Of this group, 387,559 were office clerks, salesmen, saleswomen, and others who would now be called "white-collar workers." Another 3.7 million Americans (28.7 per cent) were agricultural wage earners, located mostly, though by no means entirely, in the South. In short, 67 per cent of the productively engaged Americans were dependent for a livelihood upon employment by others. Industrial manual workers, or what would now be called "blue-collar labor" (manufacturing, transportation, and service wage earners minus white-collar workers and domestics), numbered just over 3.5 million souls, or 27.4 per cent of the gainfully employed.[6]

The fact that two out of three productively engaged Americans were hirelings posed an ideological dilemma for the free-labor system. Americans associated liberty with the ownership of productive property. Its opposite—lack of property—was thus a form of slavery, and in fact the phrase "wage slavery" enjoyed widespread and respectable use at mid-century.[7] But what a paradox for the "free-labor system" to generate "wage slavery"! It could be resolved only on the supposition that all wage earners were free to escape that status. Such an event was that escape for young Andrew Carnegie that he still recalled the ecstasy of the moment half a century later: "From the dark cellar running a steam engine at two dollars a week, begrimed with coal dirt, without a trace of the elevating influences of life, I was lifted into paradise, yes, heaven, as it seemed to me, with newspapers, pens, pencils, and sunshine about me. . . . I felt that my foot was upon the ladder and that I was bound to climb."[8] Climb he did, to the

---

[6] *Ibid.*, pp. 104–12. For explanation of this data, see Appendix A.
[7] Norman J. Ware, *The Industrial Worker, 1840–1860* (Chicago, 1924), xv.
[8] Carnegie, p. 39.

ultimate success fifteen years later when he could proudly declare: "Thenceforth I never worked for a salary."[9]

Americans believed that the workman contracted his hire of his own free will, and by inference, was at liberty to reject unsatisfactory terms. The master-servant relationship of the eighteenth century which had made breach of contract by the hireling a criminal offense had long since been abandoned in the United States. Abram Hewitt, speaking as an employer, told Parliament that he considered such legislation "very undesirable."[1] No man could or should be assigned by law to a position of dependence upon another, went the doctrine of the free-labor system, for that was the essential crime of slavery. This was Lincoln's argument when he praised the social order which offered every man hired "to help" another the opportunity to rise to the position of employer. Extending this reasoning, Lincoln declared: "If any continue through life in the condition of the hired laborer, it is not the fault of the system, but because of either a dependent nature which prefers it, or improvidence, folly, or singular misfortune."[2]

The failure of the dominant American ideology to come to grips with the fact that the growth of manufacturing necessarily creates far more employees than it does employers led, in other words, to an ambivalent attitude toward the workingman himself. On the one hand, the "honest mechanic" was still regarded as a virtuous figure. On the other, since it was assumed that a "free" system rewards honorable toil with advancement, something evidently was lacking in the character of those who failed to rise. Labor reformer Ira Steward put the question rhetorically: "Are Abraham Lincoln, Andrew Johnson, and N. P. Banks honored because they once toiled with their hands, or because they were fortunate enough to lift themselves into a position where it was no longer necessary?"[3] Few Americans could bring themselves to dismiss the "wage slaves" as *canaille* or *Pöbel* in the fashion of the contemporary European *bourgeoisie*, but many could agree with Horace Greeley that the "crushers" of the workmen were not the

---

[9] *Ibid.*, p. 142.
[1] *Royal Comm. on Trades Unions*, p. 10.
[2] Lincoln, *Works*, III, 479.
[3] Commons, *Doc. Hist.*, IX, 299.

capitalists but drink, prostitution, and gambling.[4] And many more imputed these vices especially to Negroes or Irishmen, attributing to these groups a congenitally "dependent nature."

The belief that "manual labor is disreputable," argued a New Yorker, skewed the urban economy by placing a special premium on white-collar positions. Craftsmen had to be imported from Europe, he declared, because Americans all wanted to be clerks, professionals, or bosses, or to drive something. Thus, despite the fact that masons earned more than twice as much as clerks, his city had four times as many clerks as masons.[5] The complaint was echoed from Philadelphia, where the *Public Ledger* editorialized: "As there are but few thorough workers, so there are but a few thoroughly learning a trade compared with the demand; but our young men 'take up' this or that 'genteel' occupation while the lives and comforts of the whole community are wrecked by all sorts of incompetence."[6] And from Boston came agreement: "Our shops are full of stalwart young men, retailing gimp and taffeta, while our young women are ruining themselves . . . [in] the cotton mill. A lower grade of the sex masculine, disgusted with the duration and low esteem of labor, crowd every easy means of living without work, from rum selling to peddling pins and needles."[7]

While these statements accurately describe the values of the period, they leave the misleading impression that all manual labor was performed by women or immigrants. In the

---

[4] Glyndon G. Van Deusen, *Horace Greeley, Nineteenth Century Crusader* (Philadelphia, 1953), pp. 331–2. *Cf.*, "Three Typical Workingmen"; Anita Shafer Goodstein, "Labor Relations in the Saginaw Valley Lumber Industry, 1865–1885," *Bulletin of the Business Historical Society*, Vol. XXVII (1953), pp. 203–4.

[5] [*Anon.*], "Is Labor a Curse?" *Galaxy*, Vol. VI (Oct. 1868), pp. 537–48. Quote on p. 539. *Cf.* Burn, pp. 294 ff.; *Royal Comm. on Trades Unions*, p. 6; Pennsylvania, *First Annual Report of the Bureau of Statistics of Labor and Agriculture . . . 1872–3* (Harrisburg, 1874), pp. 406–7. (Hereafter reports of this bureau and its successors will be cited as *Pa. BLS*.)

[6] Philadelphia *Public Ledger*, June 13, 1867.

[7] *Daily Evening Voice*, June 11, 1867. These sentiments were echoed in 1868 by the Milwaukee *Sentinel* and the Chicago *Republican*. Frederick Merk, "The Labor Movement in Wisconsin during the Civil War," *Proceedings of the State Historical Society of Wisconsin, 1914* (Madison, Wis., 1915), p. 176.

country as a whole there were more native-born American men working at the building trades alone than all the men and women, native-born and foreign-born, working as clerks, bookkeepers, sales personnel, and peddlers.[8] On the other hand, women did play a major role in the urban-industrial economy. In 1870 one out of every four wage earners in nonfarm occupations was a woman. To be sure, 70 per cent of these women were domestic servants, but the 368,266 women among the industrial manual workers constituted over 10 per cent of the group. More than four fifths of the women in industry worked for firms which fabricated wearing apparel. This complex of enterprises (spinning, weaving, tailoring, sewing, shoemaking, glovemaking, hatmaking, and so on) employed 19.3 per cent of the manual wage earners, and 45.4 per cent of these were women.[9] They enjoyed the lowest wages and often the harshest conditions on the American industrial scene.

The supply of working women remained abundant, however, because in New England and the middle states, women between the ages of fifteen and thirty so far outnumbered men of the same age that, despite the surplus of males under fifteen and above thirty, there were some 250,000 mature women who had to support themselves.[1] Having already been assigned by society to make clothing at home, they readily swarmed into the clothing workshops. But the hundreds of thousands who became mantua-makers, milliners, and sewing-machine operators found their produce facing competition from the weekly wagonloads of needlework put out by contractors to the wives and daughters of neighboring farmers.[2]

The low wages paid women were often justified on the grounds that a woman had only herself to support, in contrast to the man, who presumably supported a family. In textiles, however, few families could enjoy a subsistence income unless every member worked. Thus in Massachusetts mills 13 per cent of the labor force consisted of children under sixteen years of age, while in Pennsylvania the proportion of children

---

[8] See Appendix B.
[9] *Compar. Occ. Stat.*, pp. 122–39. See Appendix B.
[1] "Our Working Classes," *New-York Times*, March 17, 1869.
[2] *Ibid.*; Sinclair Tousey, *A Business Man's Views of Public Matters* (New York, 1865), p. 8.

in that industry rose to 21.8 per cent, and in South Carolina to 29 per cent.[3] The following items culled from the Help Wanted columns of a leading Philadelphia newspaper would indicate that family hiring was commonplace in textiles:

> Wanted—THREE FAMILIES WITH AT least four members each who are skilled workers in a Cotton Spinning Mill where the "Danforth" Spinning Frame is used. Good new stone Houses, with gardens, furnished at moderate rent. Apply to RICHARD THATCHER, Darby, Penna.[4]

> SPINNERS, WITH FAMILIES—WANTED—One or two good Jack Spinners, with large families, suitable for work on worsted spinning frames, cards, spooling, or twisting machines, to work in a woolen mill in the country, seven miles from the city. Spinners without such families need not apply. A widow woman would find employment for such a family. . . . E. HEY & BROS'. MILLS, on the Darby creek, Delaware county, Pa.[5]

Alternative sources of employment for women were scarce and seldom attractive. The famous department store of A. T. Stewart in New York employed 800 women by the late 1860's. At first, Stewart, like most "respectable employers" of the age, secluded his women employees from the view of passers-by, but gradually, with daring spirit, he began to employ "American ladies of refinement and culture" selling behind counters right out in public.[6] Other pioneering women made their way into print shops, telegraph offices, and light manufacturing to compete with male clerks and artisans, but their numbers were tiny compared to those in the metropolitan lofts sewing hoop skirts or shirts, or laundering and dyeing clothes. The introduction of the cigar mold, eliminating the need for both skill and strength in twisting and breaking filler leaves, opened the way for the number of women cigar makers to leap, between 1860 and 1870, from 731 to 21,409 (eight times the number of

---

[3] U.S., Congress, Senate, *Report on the Condition of Woman and Child Wage-Earners in the United States in 19 Volumes. Volume VI: The Beginnings of Child Labor Legislation in Certain States: A Comparative Study,* 61st Cong., 2d Sess., Senate Doc. 645 (Washington, 1910), p. 46.
[4] Philadelphia *Public Ledger,* Nov. 26, 1866.
[5] *Ibid.,* May 16, 1866.
[6] "Our Working Classes," *New-York Times,* March 17, 1869.

men in the trade). The kitchen, the great textile mill, and the sweatshop, then, were the sponges soaking up the women in the labor force; but they represented a substantial proportion of national production in the 1860's.[7]

Immigrants constituted only one third of the nation's industrial workers in 1870. More than 3.3 million of the society's nonfarm wage earners (66.6 per cent of the total) were native-born Americans. Even excluding white-collar and domestic workers, the proportion of natives remains about the same (65.1 per cent). To identify workman with immigrant, therefore, is incorrect. In a typical sample of 20 industrial workers drawn from the nation as a whole, one would have found 13 born in the United States, two or three in Ireland, two in German states, one in England or Wales, and one or two in Sweden, British North America, France, Scotland, China, or some other land. By and large, the two million German and Irish peasants who had flocked to the United States between 1847 and 1856 were found in the bottom strata of unskilled labor. Yet there was no simple promotional ladder in industry bearing different ethnic groups on successive rungs. The majority of common laborers in the country as a whole were native-born, while New York City had 12 immigrant laborers for every American counterpart. Although the foreign-born outnumbered the natives in the woolen and cotton mills of Massachusetts, the proportions were sharply reversed when such manufacture in the rest of the nation was considered. In fact, of the 35 occupational categories showing foreign-born majorities, only mining was among the large industries (152,107 miners, of which 94,719 were foreign-born), and only three others had more than 20,000 workers apiece—bakers, cigar makers, and marble and stone cutters.[8]

The Irish were scattered too broadly over the face of American manufacturing to be the majority group in any major industry. Although most of them were common laborers,

[7] *Ibid.*; Virginia Penny, *Five Hundred Employments Adapted to Women* (Philadelphia, 1868), pp. 180–209, esp. pp. 190, 301–11, 331–4; F. E. Wolfe, *Admission to American Trade Unions* ("Johns Hopkins University Studies in Historical and Political Science," Series XXX, No. 3; Baltimore, Md., 1912), p. 80.
[8] *Stat. of Ninth Census*, I, 704–20, 793. See Appendix B.

a large proportion had learned trades in America. Starting as helpers in rolling mills or laborers in mines and construction, they had become puddlers, miners, and carpenters. The Germans were somewhat different. Clustered together in a smaller range of occupations, they equaled or surpassed the numbers of native workmen in bakeries, bronze shops, copper works, fur shops, upholstering firms, and piano-making companies, not to mention breweries. In short, Germans provided both laborers and large numbers of artisans in traditional handicrafts. The Englishmen and Welshmen were the industrial immigrants par excellence, possessing critical skills in the most modern of industries. They could mine anthracite faces, be the best iron puddlers and mule spinners, operate the new machine tools, and frequently act as foremen over native American operatives. Few in number compared to natives, Irishmen, and Germans, the Britons remained key men.[9]

The massive influx of Europeans during the late forties and early fifties fanned the furious pace of American industrial growth. Although the years of economic hardship and war between 1856 and 1865 had slowed the pace of immigration, the earlier tempo was revived with the restoration of peace. Already in the year between October 1, 1866, and September 30, 1867, the commissioner of immigration reported that 327,183 people had crossed the Atlantic or Pacific to America.[1] Immigrants tended to cluster in cities along the lines of water transportation, following in reverse the routes of commercial export. More than two thirds came through the receiving station at Castle Garden, New York, and the majority of those landing there in the first half of 1867 settled within the boundaries of New York State. Others flowed through Quebec,

---

[9] *Ibid.*, I, 704–15; *Royal Comm. on Trades Unions*, pp. 6, 25; Yearley, *Enterprise and Anthracite*, p. 166; Clifton K. Yearley, Jr., *Britons in American Labor: A History of the Influence of the United Kingdom Immigrants on American Labor, 1820–1914* ("Johns Hopkins University Studies in Historical and Political Science," Series LXXV, No. 1; Baltimore, Md., 1957), pp. 87,166, and *passim*; Rowland T. Berthoff, *British Immigrants in Industrial America, 1790–1950* (Cambridge, Mass., 1953), pp. 30–87.
[1] Cochran, p. 202; U.S. Congress, House, *Report of the Commissioner of Immigration for the Year Ending Sept. 30, 1867*, 40th Cong., 2d Sess., House Exec. Doc. 18 (Washington, 1867), pp. 41–2.

Boston, Baltimore, Chicago, and the New Orleans–St. Louis route.[2]

The abundant supply of cheap labor attracted manufacturing to these centers of commerce. Thus, among the New York City workers in manufacturing were 93,160 immigrants and only 52,125 native Americans. Similarly, in Chicago, where 34 per cent of the native-born were employed in trade and only 26 per cent in manufacture, the immigrants in the factories and mills outnumbered the natives by more than two to one. In Cleveland two fifths of the population had come from abroad. The foreign-born fifth of Baltimore's inhabitants were converting that city into a manufacturing center for the first time. In St. Louis more of the workingmen had been born in Germany than in the United States. There, as in Chicago, Germans provided the bulk of the craftsmen. Of the nation's six largest cities only Philadelphia had more native-born workmen than immigrants in manufacturing. It was, therefore, from the vantage point of the big city that the working classes appeared to be made up overwhelmingly of foreigners.[3]

Adjustment to the new country could be a bewildering experience. Unscrupulous boardinghouse runners, confidence men, "crimps," and (during the war) recruiting agents swarmed Castle Garden ready to relieve the greenhorn of his scanty savings, entrain him for a distant job which often turned out to be a mirage, lure him into the care of a "friendly" boardinghouse keeper, or ship him off to a southern battle-front, of course pocketing a share of the immigrant's enlistment bounty. Some Europeans, like Anton Probst, defendant in a celebrated Philadelphia murder trial, enlisted and deserted more than once, wandered from job to job in both town and country, and ultimately became ensnared in crime.

---

[2] *Ibid.*, p. 125; Philadelphia *Public Ledger*, July 24, 1867; Erickson, pp. 89–94; Marcus Lee Hansen, *The Atlantic Migration, 1607–1860* (Harper Torchbook edition, New York, 1961), pp. 179–98, 280–306.

[3] Oscar Handlin, *Boston's Immigrants: A Study in Acculturation* (Revised ed., Cambridge, Mass., 1959), pp. 70–87; *Stat. of Ninth Census*, I, 772; Pierce, II, 151–2; Roseboom, pp. 8–9; Charles Hirschfeld, *Baltimore, 1870–1900; Studies in Social History* ("Johns Hopkins University Studies in Historical and Political Science," Series LIX, No. 2, Baltimore, Md., 1941), pp. 23–4, 32–7.

Others in time became homesick and returned to their native lands. John Wilson, a skilled British coal miner who eventually became the leader of the Durham Miners' Association and Labour Member of Parliament, was a case of this type. Wilson successfully evaded the Castle Garden "crimps"; clung resourcefully to his assets of fifty dollars; moved from one coal field to another, following the work; took part in one strike (his English upbringing had not prepared him to see pistols used to ward off strikebreakers); but never failed to obtain work for long. Yet despite the fact that he considered American mine conditions preferable to the British pit rows, eventually he simply wanted to go home. The English hatter and author John Burn reacted more vehemently to America: he was disgusted with everything in the country.[4]

Most immigrants, however, not only remained in their new homeland, but blended into the scenery with amazing rapidity. British craftsmen, often mere boys when they arrived, struggled side by side with their American fellow workmen to establish trade unions, cooperatives, and friendly societies, many of them closely modeled on those in the old country. John James of Scotland, for example, was twenty-six years old when he came to the United States, but he already had sixteen years' experience as a coal miner and trade unionist. Arriving at his first job only to find the men on strike, he moved immediately on to Illinois, where he helped found a union, a chapter of the Good Templars, and a temperance society.[5]

German and Irish nationalists unhesitatingly embraced American nationalism. As early as 1846 German newcomers, led by Hermann Kriege, had rallied to the banner of "Manifest Destiny" and marched off to fight Mexico with an enthusiasm equal to that demonstrated by their brothers two years later in

---

[4] Burn, pp. 274–5; Philadelphia *Public Ledger,* June 8, 9, 1866 (Probst trial); John Wilson, *Memories of a Labour Leader: The Autobiography of John Wilson, J.P., M.P.* (London, 1910), pp. 148–55, 181–2, 194–9; Oscar Handlin, *The Uprooted: The Epic Story of the Great Migrations that Made the American People* (Boston, 1951), pp. 7–36.

[5] Yearley, *Britons,* 84–152; biographical sketch of John James, *Workingman's Advocate,* Nov. 29, 1873.

the cause of German unification. The latter, fleeing Prussian reaction in their turn, gradually gave up all hope of returning home and plunged into the political and economic life of their adopted country.[6] "Your greatest handicap," Frederick Engels admonished Joseph Weydemeyer, who hoped to activate his fellow refugees in New York, "will be the fact that the useful Germans who are worth anything are easily Americanized and abandon all hope of returning home. . . ."[7]

The Irishman commonly found a new orientation for himself to fit the New World. Patrick A. Collins was but four years old when his mother sold the Irish farm and moved to Massachusetts. He dreamed in vain of becoming a machinist, but his companions in a Boston upholstery shop taught him loyalty to the trade union, Irish independence, and the Democratic party, while a fortunate opportunity to learn law opened the door to fame and wealth.[8] These elements of the career which carried Collins to the office of mayor of Boston belonged to America, not the Emerald Isle. Yet even the sophisticated Irish political refugee blended into his new surroundings as readily as did his German counterpart. Fenian leaders from Ireland enlisted with gusto in the Union army, and even recruited nationalists in the old country to fight in America.[9] One such *émigré* advised a colleague who had just arrived in the United States to hold himself aloof from Fenians here and to "Go into business, old man, don't lose one day about it. . . ."[1] Small wonder John Burn called the naturalized foreigners

---

[6] Hermann Schlüter, *Die Anfänge der deutschen Arbeiterbewegung im Amerika* (Stuttgart, 1907), pp. 11–48; Wilhelm Kaufmann, *Die Deutschen im amerikanischen Bürgerkriege* (*Sezessionskrieg 1861–1865*) (Munich and Berlin, 1911), p. 107.

[7] Frederick Engels to Joseph Weydemeyer, Aug. 7, 1851, in Karl Marx and Frederick Engels, *Letters to Americans, 1848–1895, A Selection* (New York, 1953), p. 26.

[8] Patrick A. Collins, "Obituary written by himself," c. 1893, in Patrick A. Collins Papers.

[9] Florence E. Gibson, *The Attitudes of the New York Irish toward State and National Affairs, 1848–1892* (New York, 1951), pp. 162–4. On enlistments of immigrants in the Union army, see Benjamin A. Gould, *Investigations in the Military and Anthropological Statistics of American Soldiers* (New York, 1869), pp. 14–29.

[1] John Boyle O'Reilly to John Devoy, Feb. 13, 1871, in *Devoy's Post Bag*, ed. William O'Brien and Desmond Ryan (Dublin, 1948), I, 31.

"the most bounceable men in the country," and remarked that "Irishmen or the sons of Irishmen are often more American than the natives, who trace their genealogies back to the pioneers."[2]

Despite this tendency of the new American to blend with the old, American labor was anything but a homogeneous unit in the 1860's. It is worth noting that the phrases "working classes" and "industrial classes" were always used in the plural, and rightly so. Workmen were profoundly divided by income, trade, nationality, religion, and politics. Some important groups of wage earners even hired other workmen and paid the latter out of their own earnings. Iron puddlers and coal miners, for example, were both customarily paid by the ton (bituminous miners usually by the bushel) and in turn paid a fixed rate to their helpers. In both industries it was the craftsmen who developed the trade union. Thus, in the iron mills, puddlers customarily opposed their employers over puddling rates but assisted them in demands on Congress for higher tariffs, while the bosses fixed a minimum scale for helpers (usually one third the puddler's tonnage) to shield them from exploitation by the artisans. Both the puddler and the miner often went home after some eight hours of work, leaving their helpers behind with another two hours of toil to complete.[3]

Even where such intermediate relationships were absent, the range of incomes between one worker and another was vast. In the woolen mills of the Hamilton Manufacturing Company of Massachusetts, for example, the payroll for January, 1867, shows the highly skilled and hard-drinking English mule spinners averaging between $42 and $48 compensation, while the 20 men in the print room earned up to $88 and their foreman $132 for the month. Piecework earnings for the women weavers, however, ranged from $36 for the month down to $5. Women scrubbers and sweepers were paid six cents an hour, so that steady work let them take home $15.42

2 Burn, p. 46.
3 *Royal Comm. on Trades Unions*, pp. 2–3; Joseph F. Patterson, "Reminiscences of John Maguire after Fifty Years of Mining," *Publications of the Historical Society of Schuylkill County* (Pottsville, Pa., 1907–14), IV, 305–36. (Hereafter cited as *Schuylkill Hist. Pubs.*)

for the month.[4] Irish and Swedish hands building the Union and Titusville Railroad in Pennsylvania in 1870 received a standard $2 a day, but some put in seven days in a month, others twenty-four days. Carpenters on the same job worked steadily at $3.50 daily—a standard rate east of the Mississippi.[5]

The *New-York Times* survey of 1869 clustered the workmen of the Empire State into three income groups. The most select class, composed of building tradesmen and printers on daily papers, averaged over $26 a week. Below them stood those paid around $20 per week, a group equal in size to the first. Included here were blacksmiths, book printers, and painters, among others. The bottom group, three times the size of the other two combined, was composed of those earning a meager subsistence wage or less, ranging from boiler makers at $18 a week through iron molders at $15 to shoemakers and waiters at $12 and $7, respectively.[6] Their families crowded the slum apartments and boardinghouses of the cities, and even the middle bracket found the comforts of life eluding them. What was true of New York was true of Boston, where, said the commissioner of labor statistics, "there are no places within the settled portions of the city . . . where the low-paid toiler can find a home of decency and comfort."[7]

The testimony of Massachusetts spinners and ship joiners, on the other hand, indicates that in the smaller industrial town these middle-income workmen owned or rented tidy homes in decent surroundings.[8] A ship joiner who complained of walking five miles to a horse car and then riding another ten to work could at least boast that the trim homes of his neighborhood were "all occupied by respectable American

[4] Payroll, Jan. 1867, Hamilton Manufacturing Company Papers. On character of mule spinners, see Massachusetts General Court, Senate, *Report of the Bureau of Statistics of Labor . . . March 1, 1870, to March 1, 1871*, Senate Doc. 150 (Boston, 1871), pp. 469–70. (Hereafter cited as *Mass. BLS, 1870–1871*.)

[5] J. S. and D. T. Casement Payroll, Union & Titusville Railroad, Sept. 1870–Jan. 1871, Historical Society of Western Pennsylvania, Box MSS, BB.

[6] "Our Working Classes," *New-York Times*, Feb. 24, 1869.

[7] *Mass. BLS, 1869–1870*, p. 182. On New York conditions, see Robert Ernst, *Immigrant Life in New York City, 1825–1863* (New York, 1949), pp. 48–60.

[8] *Mass. BLS, 1869–1870*, pp. 317–37.

families, and about one-quarter (mostly clerks) own their houses."[9] A leather cutter averaging less than $3 a day lived in five rooms of a sixty-year-old house outside of the small town in which he worked, but even that was worlds apart from Boston's ghastly Half Moon Place or Burgess Alley.[1] The conditions of life of the working classes, in short, encompassed extraordinary variety from trade to trade and from place to place.

Ethnic divisions cut diagonally across all the industrial classes. With them came barriers of language and culture and the imported hostilities of the Old World supplementing the nativism of the New. Irish urchins delighted in pelting Germans parading to their grandiose *Schützenfesten* in New York's parks. A German labor paper in turn heaped the worst possible insult on the Irish, calling them no better than Russian peasants, and summoned its readers to break with Tammany Hall so as to free New York from *"der Herrschaft des irischen Pöbels. . . ."*[2] But the most ardent, inveterate foe of the Irish Catholic was the Orangeman who had emigrated with him. In 1870 and 1871 New York City witnessed fierce riots involving these two groups.[3]

The deepest line of division within the working classes, in fact, was that of religion. Fraternal orders such as the Odd Fellows, Sons of Temperance, Knights Templar, Masons, and (after the Civil War) the Grand Army of the Republic, Knights of Pythias, and Ancient Order of United Workmen enrolled tens of thousands of workingmen in search of mutual insurance. The secrecy and quasi-religious trappings of these societies brought them all under the ban of the Roman Catholic Church. The Baltimore Council of the clergy in 1866 repeated its warning to the flock against such organizations and pointed out that close association among men of different faiths put the Catholic in peril of corruption.[4] Convinced,

---

9 *Ibid.*, p. 320.

1 *Ibid.*, pp. 333–7; Handlin, *Boston's Immigrants*, pp. 102–14.

2 Editorial, New York *Arbeiter-Zeitung*, Sept. 10, 1864.

3 [Anon.], *Civil Rights. The Hibernian Riot and the "Insurrection of the Capitalists." A History of Important Events in New York, in the Midsummer of 1871* (New York, 1871).

4 Fergus Macdonald, *The Catholic Church and the Secret Societies in the United States* (New York, 1946), pp. 8–27, 64–74; Henry J. Browne,

furthermore, that public schools gave a Protestant slant to education, the Catholic Church bent every effort to promote parochial schools for children of immigrants. The poverty of America's Catholics made public financial assistance to such schools sorely needed, and their attempts to tap school tax funds roused Protestants to ardent defense of "secular education" and "separation of Church and State."[5]

Protestant workmen, in turn, were infected by the perfectionist evangelism which captured America's urban centers. So popular had interdenominational prayer and revival meetings become in 1858 that enthusiasts called it the "Year of Pentecost."[6] Four years earlier an uglier form of religious self-assertion had gripped them. Young Patrick Collins, then a boy in a workmen's town east of Boston, watched his Protestant neighbors burn and smash their way into the Catholic section under the leadership of the "Angel Gabriel" (John S. Orr). The ten Catholic boys in his school were so hounded by their classmates that one by one they all dropped out.[7] No single task, therefore, loomed larger before the would-be organizer of a labor movement than to overcome the barrier of denominational antagonism. At every turn labor reformers found themselves ensnared, for better or for worse, in the religious life of America.

Finally, the ethnic divisions among the working classes both shaped and were reinforced by partisan loyalties. Raphael Pumpelly wrote in 1869: "The prejudice of race is, with us, a part of the foundation of politics . . . the moral characteristics of various nationalities become important parts of the framework on which parties are constructed . . . the opposing armies which fight with the ballot, and at times threaten the

The Catholic Church and the Knights of Labor (Washington, D.C., 1949), pp. 13–14.
[5] John W. Pratt, "Boss Tweed's Public Welfare Program," *New York Historical Society Quarterly*, Vol. XLV (Oct. 1961), pp. 400–4.
[6] Timothy L. Smith, *Revivalism and Social Reform in Mid-Nineteenth Century America* (New York and Nashville, 1957), pp. 45–79; Arthur C. Cole, *The Irrepressible Conflict* (*A History of American Life*, ed. Arthur M. Schlesinger and Dixon Ryan Fox, Vol. VII; New York, 1934), pp. 253–5.
[7] Collins, "Obituary." Cf. Ray Allen Billington, *The Protestant Crusade, 1800–1860. A Study of the Origins of American Nativism* (New York, 1938), pp. 305–6.

sword, are, to a large extent, massed by race. . . ."[8] The Know-Nothing heritage was deeply entrenched in the Republican Party, and politicians as popular with workmen as Henry Wilson and Nathaniel P. Banks had found their way to that party via the nativist movement.[9] On the other hand, one of the rare Irish Catholics who was also a Republican complained of his countrymen: "Democrats they profess themselves to be from the start—the instant the baggage-smashers and cut-throat lodging-house-keepers lay hands on them—and Democrats they remain until the day of their deaths, miserably and repulsively regardless of the conflicting meanings that name acquires through the progressive workings of the great world around them."[1] Two molders in the same shop, moaned the nation's leading labor journal, would oppose each other at the polls. Political parties, it concluded, were "the curse of the workingmen."[2]

Intensely competitive as individuals and as groups, the workers thus shared their employers' commitment to the ideology of the free-labor system, which the maturing industrial order had already rendered anachronistic. Also like their employers, workmen sought remedies for their problems from the machinery of state. This search involved them directly in the complex politics of Reconstruction.

---

[8] Raphael Pumpelly, "Our Impending Chinese Problem," *Galaxy*, Vol. VIII (July 1869), pp. 23–4.
[9] Fred Harvey Harrington, *Fighting Politician, Major General N. P. Banks* (Philadelphia, 1948), pp. 22–31; Elias Nason, *The Life and Public Services of Henry Wilson* (Boston, 1881), pp. 119 ff.
[1] Gen. Thomas F. Meagher to Col. Patrick R. Guiney, Oct. 7, 1863, in Patrick R. Guiney Papers.
[2] Editorial, *Workingman's Advocate*, Feb. 15, 1868.

CHAPTER 2

Democrats, Conservatives, and Radicals

Out of the controversies of the war years, and especially from the exigencies of national election campaigns in 1862 and 1864, the semblance of a two-party system had emerged to replace the multiparty politics of the 1850's. Arrayed against the battered Democratic party, withal still powerful and proud of its venerable traditions, stood the dominant, but new and makeshift, Union party. Not even the rehabilitation of the name Republican in the latter's ranks, however, could resolve postwar debates into two sides. On the contrary, four distinct political tendencies could be discerned by the end of 1865: the old-line Democrats, the Conservatives, the Radicals, and the labor reformers.

Two warnings should be kept in mind in defining these groups. First, their names identify the poles around which political developments pivoted. The ideological spectrum of the period exhibited many shadings which served to blend the fringes of each group into those of the next. Both the former

Whigs of the South and the broad Republican center, led by
Jay Cooke, John Sherman and James G. Blaine, were to play
crucial, independent roles after 1868, but in 1866 the course of
events drew them into the wake of one or another of these
polar groups. Secondly, from the moment the first Confederate
shot hit Fort Sumter, political developments in America
moved at such a rapid pace that the Radical position of one
day easily became the Conservative stand of a year, or even a
few months, later. Thus the Southern Whig leaders who
played a dominant role in Andrew Johnson's provisional governments not only championed tariff protection and government aid to transportation but accepted the abolition of
slavery. In other words, they espoused goals the Radical wing
of the Republicans had advocated in 1860.[1]

Four steps taken by the federal government during the
war had fundamentally changed its character. Three of them
were identified by the brilliant banker and Republican leader
from Buffalo, New York, Elbridge G. Spaulding:

> Three great measures were adopted by the Government,
> which, in my judgement, were necessary to crush the
> rebellion and maintain the national unity, viz.:
>
> 1. The *legal tender act,* by which the credit of the
> Government was brought into immediate action in the
> most available form.
>
> 2. *Emancipation,* by which 4,000,000 slaves became
> intensely interested in the Union cause.
>
> 3. The *draft,* by which the army was speedily rein-
> forced at the turning point of the rebellion.[2]

The fourth measure may be summarized in a word: taxes.
Through the 1850's the expenses of the federal government
had been met by tariffs and land sales. Right down to the war
Americans could echo Thomas Jefferson's proud boast of 1805:
"What farmer, what mechanic, what laborer ever sees a tax-

---

[1] Thomas B. Alexander, "Persistent Whiggery in the Confederate South,
1860–1877," *Journal of Southern History,* Vol. XXVII (August 1961),
pp. 311–15.
[2] E. G. Spaulding to Hugh McCulloch, Dec. 9, 1868, in E. G. Spaulding,
*History of the Legal Tender Paper Money Issued during the Great
Rebellion. Being a Loan without Interest and a National Currency*
(Buffalo, N.Y., 1869), Appendix p. 35.

gatherer of the United States?"[3] What nostalgia these words must have evoked in 1866! For four years in both North and South an impost had been levied on everything taxable.[4] In his final message to Congress, Andrew Johnson depicted dramatically the change in the scale and cost of governmental activities. From the inauguration of George Washington as President of the nation to the end of June 1861, he said, the entire expenditures of the federal government totaled some $1,700,000,000. In this sum were included the expenses of war with England, Mexico, and countless Indian tribes, and the purchase of Louisiana, Florida, and the Mexican Cession. Then came the War of the Rebellion. In four subsequent fiscal years—July 1, 1861, to June 30, 1865—federal expenditures reached $3,300,000,000. Although the next four fiscal years covered a period of peace, federal disbursements were $1,600,000,000, or, commented the President, "nearly as much as was expended during the seventy-two years that preceded the rebellion. . . ."[5]

A government-controlled currency, the end of legal subordination of one man to another so that all Americans became direct subjects of the government, universal obligation for military service, and direct taxation to sustain the bureaucratic and military machinery of the central government—these were the products of four years of civil war. In brief, the United States had become a state in the full meaning of the word. This was the change which the first section of the Fourteenth Amendment translated into law. It is by their attitudes toward

---

[3] James D. Richardson, ed., *A Compilation of the Messages and Papers of the Presidents, 1789–1908* (Washington, D.C., 1909), I, 379.
[4] On wartime internal taxes see F. W. Taussig, *The Tariff History of the United States*, 5th ed. (New York, 1892), pp. 161–7; Allan Nevins, *The War for the Union*, Vol. II, *War Becomes Revolution, 1862–1863* (New York, 1960), pp. 213–14; Wilfred Buck Yearns, *The Confederate Congress* (Athens, Ga., 1960), pp. 197–217.
[5] Richardson, VI, 675. The largest single item in the federal budget after 1865 was repayment of the principal of the public debt. This sum is omitted from all Johnson's figures because to include it would mean listing the same expended sum twice—once when the borrowed money was spent, again when it was repaid. Interest on the debt, however, is included in the sums above. For an analysis of the budgets of 1861–8 see Edward McPherson, *The Political History of the United States of America during the Period of Reconstruction* (Washington, D.C., 1875), p. 375.

this new situation that the political alignments of the time must be identified.

OLD-LINE DEMOCRATS

All four of the revolutionary measures had been adamantly opposed by the Democratic party. From Buchanan's administration to the New Departure of 1872 this party stood forth as the ultraconservative organization in American politics. Around the standard of the national party now rallied all those who found the trends of the times repugnant and desired a return to the Good Old Days. Its following was strong indeed: in every election from 1864 to 1868 the Democrats polled between 44 and 49.5 per cent of the votes cast in the states which had remained with the Union.[6] Among the party leaders were old Democrats, Whigs, and Know-Nothings —and some ex-Republicans like the Blairs—ranging in outlook from men who had rejected the very fundamentals of political democracy, through pristine Jacksonians like Clement C. Vallandigham, grotesquely out of date but drawing support from the farmers of the backward "butternut" districts of Ohio, to men like Samuel Tilden of New York and Governor Joel Parker of New Jersey, who actually were Conservatives.

The old-line Democrats naturally embraced most of those ante-bellum southern Democrats who remained active in politics after the war. Hence they included at one extreme men like the Virginian who wrote Cyrus McCormick in 1867 that the experience of the decade had "verified the lesson of all past history that man is incapable of self-government, and the sooner we run the race of mobocracy the better for the whole country. . . ."[7] But the mainstream sprang from the Peace Democrats of the war years. In New York their center was Mozart Hall, headed by Fernando Wood and James Brooks. Prominent among the Pennsylvania leaders was the chief justice of the state supreme court, George W. Woodward, who had advocated that his state secede in 1860, ruled conscription unconstitutional, and in 1867 upheld segregation on streetcars

---

[6] Charles H. Coleman, *The Election of 1868; the Democratic Effort to Regain Control* (New York, 1933), p. 381.

[7] T. J. Massie to C. H. McCormick, quoted in Hutchinson, II, 279.

in the state despite the fact that the legislature had just outlawed it. In the Middle West the focal point was the "butternut" Democracy of Vallandigham and "Gentleman George" Pendleton. In the Mississippi Valley it was Henry Clay Dean and Marcus Mills ("Brick") Pomeroy who hurled anathemas at everything that had happened in the land since 1860, from emancipation and the issuance of greenbacks to the attempt to recall the greenbacks. All these men had been real powers in the land before the war.[8]

The specters of Negro equality, Puritanism, and the growing power of government jarred the basic traditions in which the Democratic party was rooted. In the Jacksonian heritage, majority rule did not imply popular use of the machinery of state so much as control of society by the predominant customs and mores without interference from the state. Alexis de Tocqueville observed that the American "majority claims the right not only of making the laws, but of breaking the laws it has made."[9] For Brick Pomeroy the foe of the common man was basically the state itself, for its laws, regulations, taxes, bonds, and special privileges were simply too much for him to cope with. Pomeroy depicted his archenemy, the Radical congressman controlled by "New England money," as welcoming the "age of progress. New ideas, new Constitution, new amendments, and new bureaus for the niggers, and labor and taxation for the poor white men."[1]

---

[8] Wood Gray, *The Hidden Civil War: The Story of the Copperheads* (New York, 1942), pp. 213–15; Gustavus Myers, *The History of Tammany Hall*, 2d ed. (New York, 1917), pp. 181–93; *Proceedings of the Great Peace Convention Held in the City of New-York, June 3d, 1863* (New York, 1863), pp. 4–13 and *passim;* David Montgomery, "Radical Republicanism in Pennsylvania, 1866–1873," *Pennsylvania Magazine of History and Biography*, Vol. LXXXV (Oct. 1961), pp. 449–50; Kenneth M. Stampp, *And the War Came, The North and the Secession Crisis, 1860–1861* (Baton Rouge, La., 1950), p. 49; Henry Clay Dean, *Crimes of the Civil War and Curse of the Funding System* (Baltimore, 1868). Horace Merrill considers these men the "progressive Democrats" of the age, who unfortunately allowed themselves to be dominated by the Bourbons. Merrill, *Bourbon Democracy of the Middle West, 1865–1896* (Baton Rouge, La., 1953), pp. 8–9.
[9] Alexis de Tocqueville, *Democracy in America*, trans. Henry Reeve (New York, 1838), p. 242.
[1] [Marcus Mills] "Brick" Pomeroy, *Soliloquies of the Bondholder, the Poor Farmer, the Soldier's Widow, the Political Preacher, the Poor Mechanic, the Freed Negro, the "Radical" Congressman, the Returned*

Partner in crime to the agitating office-holder was the "political preacher" who had deserted salvation in favor of abolition, sectional hatred, and war. "We *do not* believe in Puritanism," thundered Pomeroy. "We *do not* believe in the religion which stirs up hate, strife and discord."[2] This blend of antistate political conservatism and antiperfectionist religious conservatism went over well in the rural "butternut" areas of the Middle West. Since 1840 these predominantly Lutheran, Baptist, and Presbyterian farmers had shunned the new currents of revivalism which sought simultaneously to bring new souls to the mourners' bench and to regenerate society. Strict adherence to Calvinist predestination and a corresponding hostility toward evangelism prevailed among both the Baptists of Ohio, Tennessee, Georgia, and Alabama and the Old School Presbyterians of the Ohio Valley, who more than doubled their numbers between 1850 and 1870.[3] Personal salvation, not social reform, was the business of the church, they believed. Hence Cyrus McCormick ardently devoted his time and money to the cause of bolstering the Old School Presbyterian Church and the Democratic party (in his eyes the twin bastions of the Union) and was supported by the Democratic press of Chicago when he sought to block the conversion of the seminary erected with his money into "a manufactory of political preachers of the Jacobin persuasion."[4] In the same vein, Brick Pomeroy contrasted his meddling Radical congressman, a "shining light for the God and Morality party," with the Democrats who had led a once-happy country in a policy of "minding our own business."[5]

Soldier, and Other Political Articles (New York, 1866), p. 16. Note the similarity of Pomeroy's analysis of the Radicals (esp. pp. 21–2) to that of the Beard-Beale School. For a view of Pomeroy as basically a pacifist, see Frank Klement, " 'Brick' Pomeroy: Copperhead and Curmudgeon," *Wisconsin Magazine of History*, Vol. XXXV (Winter 1951), pp. 106–13, 156–7.

[2] Pomeroy, pp. 10–12, 28.

[3] Smith, *Revivalism and Social Reform*, pp. 25, 45–62, 92, 186–7; Hutchinson, II, pp. 8–24, 208–73. *Cf.* Lee Benson, *The Concept of Jacksonian Democracy, New York as a Test Case* (New York, 1964), esp. pp. 198–207, where Democratic politics are correlated with absence of piety.

[4] Hutchinson, II, 8–24, 42–7, 215–55. Quotation is on p. 235, from *Chicago Evening Post*, Dec. 4, 1868.

[5] Pomeroy, pp. 16–17, 29.

This amalgam of political and religious conservatism was seconded by the hierarchy of the Roman Catholic Church, whose flock in America provided massive voting support to the Democratic candidates. The Second Plenary Council of the American clergy (1866), called to consider the problems inherited from the war, could not find a good word for the abolition of slavery. Regretting that emancipation had been so abrupt, the council warned of "the evils which must necessarily attend upon the sudden liberation of so large a multitude with their peculiar dispositions and habits. . . ."[6] Two years earlier Pope Pius IX had listed the rationalist, nationalist, and liberal tendencies of the age in a *Syllabus of Errors,* which he found so widespread that he concluded with a plenary indulgence—a spiritual general amnesty—for all Catholics in the hope that they might begin anew. Exclusion of the Catholic Church from civil society, he contended, was the basic error from which all others flow. Protestant evangelists and Republican politicians alike not only shouted for such exclusion, but went on to embrace most, if not all, of the specific "false doctrines" outlined by the Papal Secretary of State in his letter accompanying the encyclical.[7] Advocacy of popular sovereignty, secular public education, toleration of secret societies, and restriction of Church prerogatives were "errors" essential to the Republican philosophy. How could a devout Catholic vote for such a party?

Uncomfortable bedfellows of these Democrats were the leaders of the southern provisional governments who had formerly been Whigs. These men despised Democrats both from tradition and because the Democrats of the South had led the disastrous secession movement which so many of them had opposed. Benjamin H. Hill told his fellow Southerners in 1866:

> We will not go to the democracy, because if secession was wrong the democratic party instigated it; and if secession

---

[6] Rev. Peter Guilday, ed., *The National Pastorals of the American Hierarchy, 1792–1919* (Washington, D.C., 1923), p. 221.
[7] Anne Freemantle, ed., *The Papal Encyclicals in Their Historical Context* (New York, 1956), pp. 135–52. The letter *Quanta Cura* of Cardinal Antonelli (*ibid.,* pp. 135–43) was especially relevant to American conditions.

was right, the democratic party of the North joined in the war to put it down. In no event, therefore, should we of the South trust the democratic party. . . .[8]

The revival of strength on the part of the old Whigs and antisecession Douglas Democrats had already begun in the elections for the Confederate Congress in 1863. Significantly, it was not their prewar backers, the great planters and town merchants and bankers, who now swept the Whigs into office, but primarily the poor-white farmers on whom the brunt of the war had fallen. The Whigs of the South after 1863 thus bore a distinct resemblance to the Midwestern groups which had launched the Republican party in the fifties. In the Southern elections of the summer and fall of 1865 former Whigs carried almost every national office presumably open to them. "The Whig party," as Governor William L. Sharkey of Mississippi testified, "were clear of the odium of secession."[9]

What, then, moved them into the Democratic column? Benjamin Hill explained: "Congress came in, lumped the old Union democrats and whigs together with the secessionists, and said that they would punish us all alike; would put us all alike under the negro. That naturally created a sympathy between us and the secession democrats."[1] Here was the key: opposition to the Radicals drove the old Whigs into alliance with the Democrats of the North, and since only the latter had a voice in the government in 1866, the Democrats were in the leading position of the coalition. And, as Hill's statement indicates, only one slogan could hold together a group as motley as the old-line Democrats then were: "White supremacy."

The platform of the old-line Democrats enjoyed its most

---

[8] Walter L. Fleming, *Documentary History of Reconstruction: Political, Military, Social, Religious, Educational, & Industrial, 1865 to the Present Time* (Cleveland, 1906, 1907), II, 92.

[9] Yearns, pp. 42–59, 224–35; Charles G. Sellers, "Who Were the Southern Whigs?" *American Historical Review*, Vol. LIX (Jan. 1954), pp. 335–46; Alexander, pp. 311–15; U.S., Congress, *Report of the Joint Committee on Reconstruction at the First Session Thirty-Ninth Congress* (Washington, 1866), Part III, p. 136. (Hereafter cited as *Committee on Reconstruction.*) For a case study of the shifting base of Southern Whigs, see the account of Absalom M. West, below, pp. 403–4.

[1] Fleming, II, 92.

dignified presentation from Senator Reverdy Johnson of Maryland. Johnson was truly an appropriate figure to speak on behalf of the old America against the new. Born during the Presidency of George Washington, Johnson had entered politics as a National Republican, supported Andrew Jackson during his rise to power, then turned Whig, entered the Senate, and later became President Taylor's Attorney General. Strong loyalty to the Union induced the aged Marylander to return from retirement to the Senate in 1862. His course after that time was one of general opposition to the actions of the Lincoln administration, though he did vote for the Thirteenth Amendment. In 1866 he was the most prominent spokesman for the Johnson administration on the Joint Committee on Reconstruction.[2]

Reverdy Johnson argued that the purpose of the authors of the Constitution was "to secure to each State a government of like form with that which each possessed at that time." This did not mean universal franchise—first, because the founders were familiar from Roman history with the "dangers of an unrestrained, tumultuous democracy," and secondly, because suffrage is not a right, but a privilege to be extended and limited by the state as it sees fit. The Constitution, furthermore, had left the states sovereign in domestic activities and the federal government sovereign only in external affairs. The recent rebellion could neither alter this relationship nor extinguish the position of the Confederate states within the Union. Finally, the supreme question of the postwar period, he said, was the "determination of the white men of the North, the East, the West, and the far Pacific, to have the Constitution respected, and to continue the governments, State and national, exclusively in the hands of men of their own race."[3]

Southern spokesmen appearing before the Joint Committee on Reconstruction echoed these views. Alexander H. Stephens, for example, argued that the Southerners' view of their "constitutional liberties" had not changed—not even on the "abstract principle" of the right of secession. Even the

[2] Barnes, I, 119–22.
[3] [Reverdy Johnson], *A Further Consideration of the Dangerous Condition of the Country, The Causes which Have Led to It, and the Duty of the People. By a Marylander* (Baltimore, 1867), pp. 5, 8, 21, and *passim.*

Southern Whigs had not disputed the *right* of a state to secede; they had believed secession was a foolish *policy*. Now, said Stephens, the majority of Southerners agreed they had been misguided in 1861. "They have come to the conclusion that it is better to appeal to the forums of reason and justice, to the halls of legislation and the courts, for the preservation of the principles of constitutional liberty, than to the arena of arms."[4]

This outlook ignored, or defied, the recent changes in the character of the American government. Stephens felt that the former Confederate states should immediately resume their "practical relations with the Government" as they had existed before the war. True, they had already made significant concessions. Under the prodding of President Johnson—in Wade Hampton's words, to "the echoes of Mr. Seward's 'little bell' "—the Southern leaders had annulled or repealed the ordinances of secession, ratified the Thirteenth Amendment (thus setting a precedent for ratification of a constitutional amendment as a condition of readmission), and more or less repudiated the Confederate debt. That done, they felt they had made concessions enough.[5]

It was precisely at this point that important divergences appeared between the viewpoints of the old-line Democrats and the Conservatives. In the first place, for the former, the fact that a man had opposed the policy of secession was more than adequate proof of his loyalty to the Union. To the eyes of Governor Sharkey of Mississippi it was an impressive demonstration of good faith that "not one of our delegation [to Congress in December 1865], I think, had any connexion with secession; they were all opposed to it."[6] In the eyes of men who had been loyal throughout the war, on the other hand, these same men were those who had fought against the

---

[4] *Committee on Reconstruction*, Part III, pp. 158–66, esp. p. 159.
[5] *Ibid.*, Part III, pp. 158–66 (Stephens's testimony), pp. 132–7 (William L. Sharkey's testimony); Wade Hampton to Andrew Johnson, 1866, in Fleming, I, 195–6. President Johnson was especially adamant on the subject of the Confederate debt. Philadelphia *Public Ledger*, Oct. 21, 30, 1865. Both Mississippi and South Carolina balked at this demand. Eric L. McKitrick, *Andrew Johnson and Reconstruction* (Chicago, 1960), pp. 166–7.
[6] *Committee on Reconstruction*, Part III, p. 136.

government. Surveying the Southern pretenders to congressional seats, the Republican clerk of the House counted four former Confederate generals, four rebel colonels, six ex-members of the Confederate Congress, and the vice-president of the Confederacy himself.[7]

The second, and perhaps the most crucial, gulf separating the old-line Democrat from the Conservative developed over the position of the Negro in postwar America. The main reason for secession, Alexander Stephens testified, had been the anxiety of Southerners for "their constitutional liberties," particularly "in their internal social polity, and their apprehension from the general consolidating tendencies of the doctrines and principles" of the Republican party. Asked by Congressman George Boutwell what features of their social polity the Southerners believed to be in danger, Stephens replied bluntly: "Principally the subordination of the African race, as it existed under their laws and institutions."[8] Although most of the old-line Democrats now repudiated the policy of secession, by no means did they repudiate the main objective of that policy, "the subordination of the African race."

The Southern state governments elected during 1865 had replaced (or to some extent continued) the laws of chattel slavery by new Black Codes. In essence, these codes tied the freedmen to the land by law. Furthermore, they placed obstacles in the path of Negroes seeking to change jobs, even from one plantation to another, so the freedmen would have little choice but to accept whatever wages were offered them. The Black Code of Mississippi, enacted in November 1865, required every Negro to have a lawful employment by the second Monday in January 1866, and each year thereafter. Similarly, in Louisiana a Negro was obliged to have a labor contract by the tenth of January and not to leave for the following year. Refusal to work or absence from work after the deadlines subjected the Negro to arrest for vagrancy and, with conviction, to being rented out as convict labor for private or public projects. The code of South Carolina required a Negro

---

[7] McPherson, *Reconstruction*, pp. 107–9.
[8] *Committee on Reconstruction*, Part III, p. 160.

to pass an examination and pay a fee ranging from $10 to $100 in order to hold any job other than farm laborer or domestic servant.[9]

Not all the codes were equally severe. Governor R. H. Patton of Alabama vetoed the harshest laws in his state in 1865. Patton the next year was to go so far as to recommend that Alabama ratify the Fourteenth Amendment (to the disgust of Andrew Johnson) and even to endorse Negro suffrage, in hopes of avoiding poor-white control of the legislature. After an electoral victory for former Confederate leaders in Virginia that state adopted the most stringent code of all, but General A. H. Terry prohibited its application. The code of Mississippi went so far as to forbid freedmen to own real estate, a restriction which Governor Sharkey said had never existed in the days of slavery. In general, the codes adopted the earliest—those of Mississippi, Louisiana, and South Carolina—were the most stringent. The indignant reaction among even Conservatives in the North led Georgia and Alabama to be more circumspect in the laws they finally enacted. After President Johnson vetoed the Freedman's Bureau Bill in February 1866, however, Florida and North Carolina reversed the trend toward leniency and established codes of the earlier pattern.[1]

It was not only in the South that the old-line Democrats made "white supremacy" the key to their efforts to restore the Good Old Days. All the advantages of tradition were on the side of the Democrats at this point, and it was around this slogan that the Democrats rallied the greatest portion of their mass support. Between the mid-1830's and 1860 every Northern state outside of New England had not only disfranchised

---

[9] Fleming, I, 273–314; McPherson, *Reconstruction*, pp. 29–44.

[1] McPherson, *Reconstruction*, pp. 21, 33–4, 38–42; *American Annual Cyclopaedia*, VI (1866), 12; W. E. B. Du Bois, *Black Reconstruction in America, 1860–1880* (New York, 1935), pp. 167–79, 385–6, 434, 488–9, and *passim*; Charles H. Wesley, *Negro Labor in the United States, 1850–1925* (New York, 1927), pp. 119–23; *Committee on Reconstruction*, Part III, p. 133. For the view that the Black Codes involved no special intent to subordinate Negroes, see Francis B. Simkins, *A History of the South* (New York, 1956), pp. 266–7; Commager, *Documents*, II, 2; William A. Dunning, *Reconstruction, Political and Economic, 1865–1877* (Harper Torchbook edition, New York, 1962), pp. 54–9.

its Negro population, but segregated it in schools, streetcars, housing, and employment. From Ohio westward legislation made it hazardous or even impossible for a Negro to enter the state. By 1857, when Justice Roger B. Taney, in the Dred Scott decision, defined the American political community as excluding Negroes, in a very real sense he was speaking for the entire nation. The Democratic party of Ohio carried the elections for the state legislature in 1857 with Taney's idea as its platform, repealed the state personal liberty law, and passed a "visible admixture" law to bar from the polls anyone who seemed to the local election officials to reveal a trace of Negro ancestry. An Illinois law of 1855 and the Indiana constitution of 1851 prohibited the entrance of Negroes into those states. By the end of the war much of this legislation was under fire from the Republicans: the Illinois Black Laws had been repealed, the Ohio legislation had become the center of stormy controversy, and the Indiana supreme court had ruled void the section of the state's 1851 constitution barring the entry of Negroes. In response the Democrats made Negro-baiting the central plank of their platform.[2]

There was no lack of opportunities for them to advance their views. The Northern states in the mid-sixties were still operating under constitutions framed in the Jacksonian spirit. In states such as Ohio, Pennsylvania, and Vermont a new legislature was elected every year. In Connecticut and Massachusetts all offices were renewed annually. In short, the nation seemed to be engaged in one endless election campaign, in which the Democrats ceaselessly called from the stump for preserving the "subordination of the African race." The Democratic party of Pennsylvania, in the campaign of October 1865 (at that time declaring its opposition to President Johnson), called itself the party of a "white man's country." Its speakers asked the citizens of Philadelphia: "Do you remember that every Republican Senator and Representa-

---

[2] W. E. B. Du Bois, *The Philadelphia Negro, A Social Study* ("University of Pennsylvania Series in Political Economy and Public Law," No. 14; Philadelphia, 1899), pp. 25–57; Richard Hofstadter, *The American Political Tradition* (New York, 1957), pp. 110–14; Roseboom, pp. 327–8, pp. 341 ff.; Cole, *Era of the Civil War*, pp. 333–6; *American Annual Cyclopaedia*, Vol. VI (1866), p. 404.

tive in Harrisburg now before you for re-election, that was present at the time, voted to compel you, your wives and children to ride in the cars with negroes?"[3] In the same month the voters of Connecticut, at the urging of the Democrats, had voted down Negro suffrage for that state; and to honor Connecticut's achievement guns were fired and the Stars and Stripes flown in front of Tammany Hall in New York. [4]

During the campaign of 1866, the Illinois Democrats focused their fire on the threat of Negro equality. In Pennsylvania the Democrats charged that if the Fourteenth Amendment were to be ratified, the Negro "may by *law* force himself into our company in the cars, in the hotels, and in the lecture rooms." A pamphlet circulated nationally during that campaign under the frank of Senator Reverdy Johnson charged that under the Civil Rights act any white father who deprived a Negro of the opportunity of marrying his daughter could be jailed. During the Ohio elections of 1867, says Roseboom, "Democratic processions featured wagons occupied by girls dressed in white who bore banners with such inscriptions as this: 'Fathers, save us from Negro equality.'"[5]

In short, the old-line Democrats of 1866 were the uncompromising opponents of all the nationalizing tendencies in the American government unleashed by the war. Adamantly hostile to greenbacks, the draft, the swelling of the central government machinery in both size and cost, and especially to any change in the subordinate position of the Negro, this party focused its attention on the last point as the one with the greatest popular appeal: "White supremacy" became institutionalized in the party, giving it a mass following, but also crippling its ability to move with the new currents of public opinion. Even in 1866 some Democrats were urging their party to abandon its rigid position. The Chicago *Times,* for example, warned that the Democratic party must cease to be a "conservative party . . . and become what it was in its palmy days, a progressive and aggressive party." But reports from Demo-

[3] Philadelphia *Public Ledger,* Oct. 7, 1865.
[4] *Ibid.,* Oct. 4, 1865; McPherson, *Reconstruction,* p. 120.
[5] Cole, *Era of the Civil War,* pp. 400–3; Philadelphia *Public Ledger,* Sept. 27, 1866 (Democratic paid advertisement); *Daily Evening Voice,* Oct. 5, 1866; Roseboom, p. 460.

cratic circles in both New York and Chicago indicated that the proposal of the *Times* had been firmly rejected.[6]

CONSERVATIVES

The Conservatives, unlike the old-line Democrats, were reconciled to the fact that the prewar social and political structure of the United States had been irretrievably destroyed. In the words of the New York *Herald,* they stood apart from "the blockheads of the democratic party [who] will have it that we are still living under the regime of poor Pierce and Buchanan."[7] Having accepted the four war measures as steps that had been necessary to preserve the Union, they now sought to stem the nationalization tide which the war had loosed—to find some formula by which the old and the new in America might be reconciled and their own ascendancy assured.

The Conservatives embraced most Northern members of the prewar social and economic elite. Close personal ties among the export-import merchants, shippers, and bankers who, together with prominent politicians, Eastern academicians, and noted Congregationalist and Episcopalian clergymen, constituted this old elite, made the Conservatives the most compact and homogeneous of the country's three major political groups. Although most of them had opposed the election of Lincoln in 1860 and had subsequently thrown their weight behind the Crittenden Compromise, the outbreak of civil war brought them firmly to the side of the Union. In New York, for example, such men as Hamilton Fish, William Astor, Moses Grinell, William Evarts, and Edwards Pierrepont, who in 1860 had mobilized a coalition of all political groups of the city save the Republicans in a vain effort to bar Lincoln from the White House, reassembled the next year as the Union Defense Committee to aid the war effort.[8] From this point

---

[6] Chicago *Times,* Nov. 12, 1866; Philadelphia *Public Ledger,* Nov. 15, 17, 1866.

[7] New York *Herald,* July 10, 1868.

[8] Philip S. Foner, *Business and Slavery* (Chapel Hill, N.C., 1941), pp. 169–207, 248–74; Stampp, *And the War Came,* pp. 122–58; Allan Nevins, *Hamilton Fish: The Inner History of the Grant Administration* (New York, 1936), I, 80–1, 93–4, 100.

their power grew steadily, until by 1865 they were "tempted by a vision of practically unchallenged political control, of a fusion in the name of national unity so embracing that effective opposition would be impossible for a generation or two."[9]

The power of the Conservatives had grown because they alone could fill two needs: that of both the Treasury and the political parties for money, and that of the Lincoln administration for votes to abolish slavery. The Treasury crisis was both elementary and staggering. In the three fiscal years of really serious fighting (1863, 1864, and 1865), federal expenditures, including current redemption of the mounting debt, totaled some $4,091,600,000. Despite the unprecedented growth of both internal taxes and tariffs, revenues (exclusive of note and bond issues) netted only $711,000,000 during those years.[1] In other words, 82 per cent of the funds needed to sustain the war were borrowed in some form or other. Down to 1863, Jay Cooke's famous sales campaigns to draw the funds of the "little people" into 5-20 bonds (bonds bearing 6 per cent interest payable in five years and due in twenty) actually brought the Treasury as much as a million dollars a day. But in these last years the war devoured more than $3,730,000 daily, and such sums could be obtained nowhere but in the financial houses of the coastal cities and Europe and from the new national banking associations. Under these circumstances the bond, banking, and currency enactments of 1863 to 1865 were not so much legislated by Congress as negotiated between the government and the bankers. As spokesmen for the money supply, Conservatives held the whip hand in debates. Above all, after the resignation of Salmon P. Chase, the Secretary of the Treasury had to be a man in whom the banking community had confidence—and such were both Fessenden and McCulloch.[2]

---

9 LaWanda and John Cox, *Politics, Principle, and Prejudice, 1865–1866: Dilemma of Reconstruction America* (New York and London, 1963), pp. 32–3.
1 These figures are based on data in McPherson, *Reconstruction*, p. 375.
2 See Spaulding, pp. 167–99; Oberholtzer, I, 235–358, 387–476; Charles A. Jellison, *Fessenden of Maine, Civil War Senator* (Syracuse, N.Y., 1962), pp. 183–90. For a detailed analysis of banks, bonds, and currency, see below pp. 340–56.

This direct influence of the commercial classes over affairs of state by way of the Treasury was supplemented by their role in the machinery of the nation's political parties. Money was the lifeblood of American politics. In fact, to some observers it appeared that the broader the extension of the franchise, the greater in turn became the political influence of men with substantial liquid wealth.[3] In every election campaign, parades, barbecues, poll-watchers, electioneering tours, pamphlets, ballots, and voters (single and repeating) all had to be paid for. More than one contest in a state legislature over the selection of a United States Senator became the occasion for large quantities of cash to change hands, for the Senator selected controlled the patronage from his state, and hence the careers of party workers.[4] As stated concisely by William Seward, a political party was "a joint stock association, in which those who contribute most direct the action and management of the concern."[5]

On the other hand, the power of money in determining party decisions was far from absolute, for the business of this particular type of "joint stock association" was to win elections and provide jobs for the faithful. Hence the function of party management consisted of adopting such campaign issues and candidates as would attract both voters and funds. The party as an institution, in other words, provided both a lever and a limit to the political influence of accumulated wealth.

Conservatives, therefore, were found in the high councils of both parties. In the Democratic party the "New York Central Railroad Group," led by Dean Richmond, Samuel J. Tilden, Horatio Seymour, and Erastus Corning, and with the intermittent support of Tammany Hall, opposed the open Peace Democrats during the war and was among the first segments of the party to rally around President Johnson.[6] Edwards Pierrepont, a Grand Sachem of Tammany, stood in

---

[3] [Rowland G. Hazard], "Hours of Labor," *North American Review*, Vol. CII (Jan. 1866), p. 206.

[4] Burn, pp. 247–53; Alexander K. McClure, *Old Time Notes of Pennsylvania* (Philadelphia, 1905), II, 179–80, 224–6, 263–4, 269, 413–18.

[5] Quoted in Matthew Josephson, *The Politicos, 1865–1890* (New York, 1938), p. 13.

[6] Gray, p. 215; Coben, pp. 87–9; Cox, *Politics*, pp. 16, 21, 35, 64–71.

Conservative ranks, as did Samuel J. Randall, prominent Philadelphia Democrat whose political expenses were faithfully provided by Anthony J. Drexel, George W. Childs, and other businessmen.[7]

Within Republican ranks Henry J. Raymond, editor of the *New-York Times* and chairman of the National Union Executive Committee, and the veteran Whig Thomas Ewing of Ohio were key Conservative figures. James R. Doolittle, James W. Grimes, and Edgar Cowan upheld their views in the Senate, but until his death in 1869 their most consistent and capable leader there was Maine's William Pitt Fessenden, whose ability to meet the demands of the times without surrendering his principles made him a spokesman well loved in commercial circles.[8] In 1865, however, two cabinet members were the most prominent Conservatives in public office: Secretary of the Treasury Hugh McCulloch and Secretary of State William H. Seward.

Seward assumed special prominence during Lincoln's efforts to obtain the two-thirds vote needed in the House of Representatives to pass the constitutional amendment abolishing slavery. As LaWanda and John Cox have shown, slavery was still a legal and functioning institution in the United States at the beginning of 1865, and the Republicans lacked the votes in Congress necessary to pass a constitutional amendment to prohibit it. Enactment of the Thirteenth Amendment became possible, however, when sixteen Democrats (all but two of them lame ducks) joined its supporters. The task of finding these Democrats fell to a coterie of business lobbyists, Border State Whigs, and New York Democrats organized by Seward. In return for this group's support against slavery, Seward pledged the administration to a speedy peace and immediate restoration of the Confederate states. In other words, the activities of the Seward lobby both

[7] Edwards Pierrepont to Alexander T. Stewart, Oct. 10, 1868, open letter in unidentified newspaper clippings, A. A. Lawrence Papers; McClure, II, pp. 23–4.
[8] Henry J. Raymond obituary, *New-York Times,* June 19, 1869; Roseboom, p. 444; William A. Dunning, "More Light on Andrew Johnson," *American Historical Review,* Vol. XI (April 1906), pp. 574–9; Francis Fessenden, *Life and Public Services of William Pitt Fessenden* (Boston and New York, 1907), *passim* and esp. II, 228–9; Jellison, pp. 167–259.

made possible the final abolition of slavery and left the new Johnson administration heir to the pledges of its Secretary of State that with slavery abolished and the Confederacy destroyed, the Southern states would quickly resume full status in the Union without further demands from the federal government.[9]

To put it another way, in contrast to the old-line Democrats, who persistently carped against the administration's war effort, the Conservatives became a power to reckon with in national politics precisely through their support for the causes of union and emancipation. But while endorsing the wartime revolutionary measures, they also hoped to curb the revolution. In 1865 they sought domestic peace, economic stability, and a reorganization of national political alignments that would guarantee their own ascendancy. These aspirations were summarized by John Quincy Adams II, when he wrote:

> My grandfather used to predict that when the great slavery struggle which he saw impending closed, there must come a great constitutional party or anarchy, and today it seems to me high time for calm and patriotic men to be gathering around the organic law.[1]

A "great constitutional party"—and how bright the prospects for developing such a party appeared during the summer and fall of 1865. Within the cabinet sat Seward, McCulloch, and Gideon Welles to be its midwives.[2] Conservatives in both parties hailed the administration as their own. As the Union party savored sweet triumph in all state elections that year, both the Republican *New-York Times* and the Democratic *World* hailed the returns as a popular endorsement of the President's policies. The *Times* agreed with Johnson that if

---

[9] Cox, *Politics*, pp. 1–30, 40.

[1] John Quincy Adams II, to Andrew Johnson, Sept. 1868, quoted in Coleman, *Election of 1868*, pp. 281–2.

[2] John H. Cox and LaWanda Cox, "Andrew Johnson and His Ghost Writers: An Analysis of the Freedman's Bureau and Civil Rights Veto Messages," *Mississippi Valley Historical Review*, Vol. XLVII (Dec. 1961), pp. 460–9. *Cf.* Beale's position that Johnson's administration represented "agrarian radicalism" and Dunning's view that Johnson sought to build a leadership of true "Jacksonian Democrats." Howard K. Beale, *The Critical Year, A Study of Andrew Johnson and Reconstruction* (New York, 1930); Dunning, "More Light on Andrew Johnson."

only the Southern states would nullify their ordinances of secession, ratify the Thirteenth Amendment, and repudiate the Confederate debt, the Union could be fully restored. An editorial in Philadelphia's leading mercantile organ, the *Public Ledger*, owned by Anthony J. Drexel, called upon the Congress to readmit the Southern representatives, end the income tax, limit the national banking system, and reduce the size of the army. It added, however, that some troops should remain in the South to preserve order and industry, and felt that, although Johnson was the best friend of the Southern states, "instead of supporting him they embarrass him."[3]

The following January the *Ledger* argued in an editorial entitled "Business and Politics" that the status of the South should be settled immediately:

> Especially is it in the interest of those who, like us in Philadelphia, desire to open up new commercial relations with the Southern seaboard, to support and advance the earliest restoration of those states to their places in the Union, so that their people shall be able to plant and produce and trade with a knowledge that they can manage their own affairs as we of the rest of the country do. . . . Therefore the nation should endorse the common sense policy of President Johnson.[4]

Conservatives devoted close attention to governmental economic policies. With the end of the war they sought reduction of both internal taxes and the tariff, and a return to a specie basis for the currency. The captains of commerce, especially in New England and New York, were no friends of the high protective tariff. They had supported several increases in duties as a means of augmenting government reve-

[3] Georges Clemenceau, *American Reconstruction, 1865–1870, and the Impeachment of President Johnson* (New York, 1928), pp. 35–9; *New-York Times*, Nov. 8, 9, 13, 15, 1865; Philadelphia *Public Ledger*, Dec. 5, 1865; James Albert Woodburn, *The Life of Thaddeus Stevens* (Indianapolis, 1913), p. 334; McKitrick, pp. 10, 178, 209.
[4] Philadelphia *Public Ledger*, Jan. 23, 1866. See also the editorials of Aug. 9 and Dec. 4, 1866, and a letter from an English merchant to his partner regarding conditions in Louisiana, stating that despite the fact that "A No. 1 plantations are to be had fabulously low," foreign capital is not moving in because "there is the danger of Washington legislation." *Ibid.*, Jan. 18, 1867.

nues during the war, but after 1865 most of them were again seeking a reduction of schedules. As early as 1857 New England's votes had largely been cast against tariff protection. In 1866 a mild reform bill prepared by Commissioner of Revenue David A. Wells and backed by Secretary McCulloch passed the Senate 27 to 10 and obtained a majority support in the House, though it failed to receive the two-thirds vote necessary to suspend the rules and bring it up for final action. Only in Pennsylvania did almost all sections of the business community and both parties agree to a high tariff.[5]

Secretary McCulloch expressed the prevailing Conservative view on the currency question when his report to Congress in December 1865 termed the legal tender acts emergency war measures which "ought not to remain in force a day longer than would be necessary to enable the people to prepare for a return to the gold standard," and expressed the hope that the work of retiring greenback notes would be "commenced without delay, and carefully and persistently continued until all are retired."[6] A bill designed to expedite the contraction process recommended by the Secretary passed Congress in the spring of 1866. In the House vote on this measure all Democrats but one supported the bill, while the Republicans divided 56 to 52. The heart of the opposition in Republican ranks came from the Radicals.[7]

The fact that supporters of the administration's Reconstruction policy also tended to endorse its fiscal policy would hardly be worthy of comment were it not for the fact that historians of the school of Howard K. Beale attempted to place Andrew Johnson in one political camp and his Secretary of the Treasury in another.[8] Such an effort must be made if Johnson is to appear as a spokesman of "agrarian radicalism," and it is true that Democratic proponents of the Pendleton Plan tried to draw such a distinction. The fact remains that this stand is

[5] J. W. Grimes to Edward A. Atkinson, Sept. 4, 1867, Atkinson Papers, Box 2; Coben, pp. 69–77; Taussig, pp. 159–67; McPherson, *Reconstruction*, p. 126; Philadelphia *Public Ledger*, July 19, 1866.
[6] Quoted in Spaulding, p. 202.
[7] Robert P. Sharkey, *Money, Class, and Party: An Economic Study of Civil War and Reconstruction* (Baltimore, 1959), p. 75.
[8] Beale, *Critical Year*, pp. 243–4.

completely untenable. On the one hand, McCulloch endorsed Johnson on Reconstruction to the point that he did not "see how the President in the exercise of his duty could pursue any other policy than the one he has determined upon."[9] During the summer of 1865 he led the cabinet in efforts to destroy the "iron-clad oath" requirements for federal office-holders by appointing assessors in the South who could not take that pledge.[1] In January 1866, McCulloch advocated immediate seating of the Tennessee representatives barred by Congress, and in October he denounced the Fourteenth Amendment and shared the President's hope that congressional Radicals would be replaced at the polls by men "of broader views."[2] Simultaneously, Johnson backed McCulloch's currency policy without the slightest sign of hesitation, at least until the spring of 1868. In his message to Congress of December 1867, a time of intense national debate over the greenbacks, Johnson defended both the policy of his Secretary and the gold standard as dogmatically as any Conservative could have desired:

> The proportion which the currency of any country should bear to the whole value of the annual produce circulated by its means is a question upon which political economists have not agreed. Nor can it be controlled by legislation, but must be left to the irrevocable laws which everywhere regulate commerce and trade. . . . The law of demand and supply is as unerring as that which regulates the tides of the ocean; and, indeed, currency, like the tides, has its ebbs and flows throughout the commercial world.[3]

Clearly, in 1865 and early 1866 there was enough affinity between the stands of the Conservatives and the Democrats to

---

[9] Hugh McCulloch to Edward A. Atkinson, June 30, 1865, Atkinson Papers, Box 1.
[1] Harold M. Hyman, *The Era of the Oath, Northern Loyalty Tests during the Civil War and Reconstruction* (Philadelphia, 1954), pp. 53–82.
[2] Hugh McCulloch to Edward A. Atkinson, Jan. 10, 1866; McCulloch to Atkinson, Oct. 8, 1866, Atkinson Papers, Box 2.
[3] Richardson, VI, 571. The identification of Johnson as a Greenbacker is based solely on his last annual message to Congress, in which he denounced the bond-holders. But Johnson was then a lame-duck President, without political base or significance, and even in that message he reiterated this paragraph verbatim. *Ibid.*, VI, 677, 679.

make a coalition between the two groups a real possibility. The support both factions lent to Johnson's administration provided a focal point around which such a coalition could become a permanent—and dominant—political bloc. By the time Congress disbanded in the summer of 1866, however, that possibility was dead, and a very different alignment appeared in national politics. The reason for this development is that two crucial issues divided the ranks of the Conservatives themselves, and ultimately pitted the bulk of them against the Democrats. Those issues were: the rights and status of the Negroes and the return of former Confederates to office.

Initially, Conservatives commonly agreed that the Thirteenth Amendment had settled the status of the Negro, or at least had exhausted the role of the federal government in the matter. Indeed, thanks to the efforts of the Seward lobby, it was precisely with the understanding that this was to be the case that many Conservatives had given their support to that amendment. When a delegation of Negroes visited the President to seek his help against the Black Code pending in the Virginia legislature, Johnson rebuffed it with the reply: "Gentlemen . . . you *are free,* and the vainest Virginian shall not only acknowledge your freedom, but your equality, if you are true to yourselves."[4] Two months later, the Reverend Henry Ward Beecher, in an audience with the President, offered his support for the policy of quick restoration of the Southern states. Railroad promoter John Murray Forbes, who privately advocated Negro suffrage, agreed that the subject was best left up to the returning Southern states.[5]

The Black Codes, therefore, came as an unexpected blow to the Conservatives. Not sharing the intransigent "white supremacy" sentiments of the old-line Democrats, the Conservatives were prepared to accept the fact that the war had

[4] *Colored Tennessean,* Aug. 12, 1865. Johnson was much more openly hostile to the Negroes in his interview with the delegation led by Frederick Douglass. See McPherson, *Reconstruction,* pp. 52–6.
[5] Philadelphia *Public Ledger,* Oct. 24, 1865; John Murray Forbes to Edward A. Atkinson, Feb. 19, 1865, Atkinson Papers, Box 1. On the broad public support to Johnson, see Laurence Oliphant, *On the Present State of Political Parties in America* (Edinburgh and London, 1866), p. 9.

ended the "subordination of the African race," made the Negroes citizens, and put the personal and property rights of all citizens on the basis of legal equality—even though they shrank from admitting the freedmen to full political participation. Even Secretary of State Seward believed that "freedmen who were emancipated by the nation as a means of suppressing the civil war are entitled to national protection until the country shall have resumed its normal and habitual condition of repose." His drafts for Johnson's veto messages on both the Freedmen's Bureau bill and the Civil Rights bill recommended that the President endorse the general policy of the measures and confine his attacks to specific objectionable features. He contended that a law was necessary "to secure all persons in their civil rights without regard to race or color."[6] James Doolittle and Henry J. Raymond, loyal supporters of Johnson, both voted in favor of the Freedmen's Bureau. The Civil Rights and Freedmen's Bureau bills, in fact, gained general endorsement from Conservatives as a necessary consequence of emancipation. Fessenden and Reverdy Johnson consulted with the President at length after the passage of the two measures and came away with the impression he would approve them. Reverend Beecher now urged the President to sign the Civil Rights measure. Johnson's veto of these bills split the Conservative forces, left men like Raymond and Doolittle voting to uphold the vetoes only out of loyalty to the President, and effectively destroyed the possibility that this group might play the leading role in the process of Reconstruction.[7] Conservatives were left with the choice of following the old-line Democrats or following the Radicals.

Many Conservatives, furthermore, found themselves increasingly at odds with Johnson over the leadership of the former Confederate states. Two basic problems were involved here. The first was the question already noted of what constituted "loyalty." In the same man, Southern eyes could see a unionist (meaning an opponent of secession) and Northern

---

[6] Cox, "Johnson and His Ghost Writers," pp. 465, 472–4.
[7] James Ford Rhodes, *History of the United States from the Compromise of 1850* (New York, 1893–1906), V, 571; McKitrick, pp. 279–81; McClure, II, 192; Cox, *Politics*, pp. 196–208, 227–8; George S. Merriam, *The Life and Times of Samuel Bowles* (New York, 1885), II, 21–7.

eyes could see a rebel (a Confederate officer).[8] Secondly, as Eric McKitrick argues, Johnson saw secession only as the work of wicked individuals, for he was totally unable to grasp the meaning and significance of social institutions. For him all that was required to restore the South was to punish the sinners, or to make them confess their sins to him in person and ask forgiveness. For such an approach the pardon power of the President alone was an adequate instrument on which to build Reconstruction policy.[9] It was precisely this characteristic of the President which first led many Radicals to believe he stood with them; no one could talk more vehemently about hanging rebels and making treason "odious" than Johnson—and he continued such talk throughout his career.[1] It soon became evident to many Conservatives, as well as to the Radicals, that the hanging-and-pardoning policy of Johnson was totally inadequate. To secure the Union, they felt, a new leadership had to be brought forward in the South which had had no connection, early or late, with the Confederacy. The last article of the Fourteenth Amendment was shaped with this end in mind. Significantly, in the Conservative stronghold of Philadelphia even Democratic pronouncements against the amendment conceded that the disfranchisement provisions, like those prohibiting repayment of the Confederate debt, "may be proper in themselves," but rejected them as "sugar coating to the negro pill."[2] In short, the early possibilities of a coalition between the Conservatives and the old-line Democrats were shattered by the inflexibility of the latter.

As Johnson widened the gulf between himself and Congress, to the distress of his cabinet and many of his Conservative followers, the Democrats cheered him on. News of the Ku Klux Klan, the Schurz Report, the tales of social and economic pressures against Northerners in the South, and then the terrible Memphis and New Orleans riots indicated to the

---

[8] See above, pp. 54–5.

[9] McKitrick, pp. 142–52.

[1] A splendid analysis of Johnson's personality may be found in James G. Blaine, *Twenty Years of Congress: From Lincoln to Garfield. With a Review of the Events which Led to the Political Revolution of 1860* (Norwich, Conn., 1884–6), II, 5–13.

[2] Democratic campaign advertisement in the Philadelphia *Public Ledger,* Sept. 27, 1866.

captains of commerce that their dream of peace, stability, and order was fading like a will-o'-the-wisp. The *Public Ledger* in Philadelphia was deeply distrubed, for example, by the Memphis riots and news of mob action in Kentucky against planters who hired Negroes. After the New Orleans riot, it lamented: "All such disgraceful outbreaks add strength to those who favor postponement of Southern restoration."[3]

It was in this setting that the Radicals painstakingly worked out the terms of a common platform for themselves and the conservative Republicans: the Fourteenth Amendment. This addition to the Constitution did more than merely place the Civil Rights Act in the Constitution. It codified the nationalizing effects of the war, while evading the divisive question of Negro suffrage. The first section gave legal expression to the national citizenship created by the war. That meant both that the rights of citizens were drawn directly from the federal government, rather than exclusively from the states, and that no legal subordination of some citizens to others was to be allowed. Dred Scott was buried.[4] The subsequent sections made an awkward compromise on Negro suffrage, guaranteed the permanent repudiation of the Confederate debt, and transferred control of rebel pardons to Congress in an attempt to stimulate the development of new leadership in the South. Here was a program on which the Radicals attracted the bulk of the Conservatives away from Andrew Johnson and into the Republican party, which, for the moment, could embrace all the nationalist and reform trends of the country. The response of the electorate was an overwhelming endorsement.

In August those Conservatives who remained loyal to Johnson made a final effort to fuse with the Democrats at the National Union Convention in Philadelphia. Together they resolved that the war had affirmed the end of slavery and the supremacy of the national government, but that it had given

---

[3] *Ibid.*, May 3–13, Aug. 1, 1866.
[4] The Supreme Court rejected the full implications of this interpretation of the amendment in the Slaughterhouse cases. Commager, *Documents*, II, 71–5. But this decision came during the upsurge of the Liberal movement and represented one phase of that movement's retreat from the nationalism of 1866.

the federal government no new powers and that Congress had no right to interfere with the franchise qualifications of the states. Any amendments to the Constitution, it asserted in a strange doctrine, must conform to the spirit of the document and not change its meaning. In an emotional climax, the Massachusetts delegates, led by General Couch, entered the hall arm-in-arm with those of South Carolina, led by Governor J. L. Orr, while the band played "Dixie."[5]

When President Johnson began his "swing 'round the circle," he still enjoyed evident support among the old elite. He was greeted in Philadelphia by the banker Anthony Drexel. In New York City his welcoming committee included Alexander T. Stewart, Henry Clews, Edwards Pierrepont, and August Belmont. His policies were publicly endorsed by William H. Aspinwall, Cornelius Vanderbilt, John J. Cisco, and Henry Grinnell. Indeed, one Wall Street reporter declared that the day after the $45,000 dinner given for the President at Delmonico's business was very dull on the Street, because many "merchants and stock brokers" were still recuperating from the affair and "did not come downtown at all."[6]

Despite such auspicious beginnings, the campaign begun at Philadelphia failed to recreate the massive support Johnson had enjoyed only a year earlier. Outside of Massachusetts the congressional candidates put in the field under its banner were for the most part not Conservatives but old-line Democrats.[7] The movement thus appeared to many, indeed most, of the voters as merely a mechanism by which Copperheads and Confederates were seeking a return to power. Johnson,

---

5 Philadelphia *Public Ledger*, Aug. 9, 14, 15, 17, 1866; Roseboom, p. 454; Coben, p. 88; McPherson, *Reconstruction*, pp. 118–19. Earle Dudley Ross sees in this convention the origins of the Liberal Republican movement. Ross, *The Liberal Republican Movement* (New York, 1919), p. 2. Thomas S. Barclay placed the origin somewhat later, at the Planters House meeting in St. Louis after the election of 1866. Barclay, *The Liberal Republican Movement in Missouri, 1865–1871* (Columbia, Mo., 1926), pp. 109–11. Both dates are premature. These meetings were ancestors of liberalism, but not the whole genealogy. Both the Radicals and the Democrats contributed to Liberalism, as did the Conservatives. See below, pp. 379–83.
6 Philadelphia *Public Ledger*, Aug. 29, 31, 1866; Coben, 88. Jay Cooke's position in the campaign was ambivalent. Oberholtzer, II, 59.
7 Beale, *Critical Year*, pp. 344–70.

furthermore, hardly offered the Conservative image of an ideal President. Judge David Davis spoke for many Conservatives when he said: "I believe the President to be an honest man and a true patriot, but with qualities totally unfitting him to be the ruler of a people in the fix we are in."[8] After his bout with hecklers in Cleveland even the Philadelphia *Public Ledger* began to cool visibly toward him.[9]

The National Union movement, in short, turned out not to be a genuine Conservative movement at all. Conservatives who took part in it found themselves, like the Southern Whigs before them, riding reluctantly in a train with Democratic engineers. The Fourteenth Amendment won the endorsement of more and more of the old elite. Just before Election Day the New York *Herald* abandoned the Johnson camp. Summing up the campaign after Election Day, the *Herald* said:

> In a word, Mr. Johnson forgets that we have passed through the fiery ordeal of a mighty revolution, and that the pre-existing order of things is gone and can return no more—that a great work of reconstruction is before us, and that we cannot escape it.[1]

RADICALS

The Radicals approached the "great work of reconstruction" with enthusiasm, not hesitation. They had not only supported the four decisive war measures but generally had provided their authors and congressional floor leaders.[2] When Thaddeus Stevens endorsed the proposed Fourteenth Amendment, he was reluctant only over the concessions to which he had agreed in order to win Conservative support. All his life, Stevens mused, he had dreamed that "when any

---

[8] Davis to Rockwell, April 22, 1868, in Willard L. King, *Lincoln's Manager: David Davis* (Cambridge, Mass., 1960), p. 260.
[9] Philadelphia *Public Ledger*, Sept. 19, 1866. See also Merriam, II, 24-7.
[1] New York *Herald*, quoted in Philadelphia *Public Ledger*, Dec. 5, 1866.
[2] David Donald, *Lincoln Reconsidered* (New York, 1961), Chap. 6. *Cf.* T. Harry Williams, *Lincoln and the Radicals* (Madison, Wis., 1941), which depicts a Civil War without rebels, fought between Lincoln and the Radicals. Williams ignores all questions of war policy but emancipation and fails to see that without the consistent aid of Radical congressmen the policies Lincoln adopted from the fall of 1862 on would never have become law.

fortunate chance" might release the nation from the grip of slavery and break up "for awhile the foundations of our institutions," the occasion would see "the intelligent, pure and just men of this Republic" remodel "all our institutions" in such a way as to free them from "every vestige of human oppression, of inequality of rights, of the recognized degredation of the poor, and the superior caste of the rich." Here was the dream of Radical reconstruction, and its realization would lie in the fact "that no distinction would be tolerated in this purified Republic but what arose from merit and conduct."[3]

While the Radicals expressed this egalitarian ideal in the name of "the people," they saw the people's needs and desires through the eyes of the vigorous new elite of manufacturers and promoters. With a few exceptions like Stevens, Daniel J. Morrell, John A. Griswold, and John Covode, however, Radical politicians were not entrepreneurs. In general, they were lawyers and editors, men who made their careers in politics. Many, such as William D. Kelley, John Conness, and Henry Wilson, were of very humble origins, the vocations of law and politics being far easier routes of social mobility than were industry and commerce. Like the entrepreneurs, they envisaged the "self-made man" as the most trustworthy and proper spokesman for the community as a whole. James Russell Lowell expressed their disdain for "the mercantile classes" when he concluded: "All our foreign trading population have no fatherland but the till. . . ."[4] That the hireling masses at the other end of the social spectrum were equally unfit to lead the nation was stated emphatically by Radical ideologists Karl Heinzen and Elisha Mulford. Only men of property could possess the free will, the intelligence, and the disposition to be true revolutionaries, they argued.[5] But they assumed, of course, that in a "purified Republic" of equal

---

[3] Quoted in Thomas F. Woodley, *Great Leveler: The Life of Thaddeus Stevens* (New York, 1937), p. 375.

[4] J. R. Lowell to John L. Motley, July 26, 1864, in Motley, *Correspondence*, III, 34.

[5] Karl Heinzen, *Teutscher Radikalismus in Amerika. Ausgewählte Abhandlungen, Kritiken und Aphorismen aus den Jahren 1854–1879*, ed. Karl Schmemann (Milwaukee, 1890–8), II, 611–12; Elisha Mulford, *The Nation: The Foundations of Civil Order and Political Life in the United States* (Boston, 1870), p. 212.

opportunity, "merit and conduct" alone would determine who rose to acquire property.

Radical politicians, in other words, were more likely to be aspiring advocates of the manufacturers than actual members of that group, and their views influenced more by an effort to win and retain the approval of their clients than by direct economic interest. To be sure, many established politicians of all stripes invested some of their earnings in manufacturing. Many more invested in commerical enterprises for the compelling reason that the latter were more likely to offer stock for sale, and the investor was not obliged to assume the risks of a partner. Correspondingly, entrepreneurs were unlikely to be vociferous—or even very articulate—on major political questions.[6] Silence on issues other than those which immediately affected their business interests was often deliberate. "I am now in business," wrote a friend to Benjamin Butler, "so it is now to my interest to stay out of politics."[7] On the other hand, foolish indeed would have been the politician who neglected to court the most prominent figures in the economy of his constituency. Explaining the power and influence of his colleague Henry L. Dawes, George F. Hoar wrote: "There was in every factory village in Massachusetts some man of influence and ability and wealth, frequently a large employer of labor, who had been in the habit of depending on Mr. Dawes for the security of his most important interests, so far as they could be affected by legislation."[8]

The political antecedents of the Radicals covered the prewar spectrum. Men like Leonard Myers of Pennsylvania, Samuel Pomeroy of Kansas, and Charles Sumner of Massachusetts had begun their careers with the Republican party or such antislavery forebears as the Liberty and Free Soil parties. Many Radicals stemmed from the ranks of the Whigs: Timothy Howe of Wisconsin, George Julian of Indiana, Governor Richard Oglesby of Illinois, and his predecessor

---

[6] Edward C. Kirkland, *Dream and Thought in the Business Community, 1860–1900* (Chicago, 1964), p. 2.

[7] William W. Hinkley to Benjamin F. Butler, Sept. 15, 1868. Butler Papers, Box 56.

[8] George F. Hoar, *Autobiography of Seventy Years* (New York, 1903), I, 228.

Richard Yates, who together with his colleague Governor Oliver P. Morton of Indiana had held the two keystone states of the Old Northwest in pro-Union hands by the most draconic measures during 1862 and 1863. Other former Whigs were Frederick A. Pike, a diligent watchdog for the lumber, fishing, and shipping interests of Maine, Benjamin F. Wade, who had once been a construction worker on the Erie Canal, and Henry Wilson, the "cobbler of Natick," who never lost his following among the working class.[9]

From the ranks of the Democratic party, some Radicals had come to the Republicans during the Kansas crisis and some not until the Civil War was well under way. John Farnsworth of Illinois, for whom impeachment of Andrew Johnson was something of a psychological fixation, had cut his ties with the Democrats as early as the Mexican War. William D. "Pig Iron" Kelley at that time had been an active campaigner for Polk. He quit his party over Kansas. Oliver P. Morton, something of a latecomer to Radical ranks during Reconstruction but full of the ardor of the convert, had also joined the Republicans in 1854. Among the Radicals who had abandoned the Democratic fold only during the war were Senator Charles D. Drake of Missouri, who had been a Douglas Democrat, and Senator John Conness of California, who had run for governor of his state as a Union Democrat in 1861. Both Benjamin F. Butler and John A. Logan had been Negro-baiting Buchanan Democrats right down to secession, then had rebuilt their political careers and moved into the Radical camp by way of the army.[1]

Not only leaders but many voters who supported the Radicals had come over from Democratic ranks. Although some counties of rural northern Illinois and the Ohio Western

---

[9] Barnes, I, 261–4, 69–74, 29–34, 147–52, 345–50, 103–8, 167–75, 23–8, II, 369–74; *Dictionary of American Biography*, ed. Robert L. Schuyler (New York, 1958), XIII, 648–9, hereafter cited as *D.A.B.*; H. L. Trefousse, *Benjamin Franklin Wade, Radical Republican from Ohio* (New York, 1963); Nason, *Wilson*.

[1] *D.A.B.*, VI, 284–5, X, 299–300; Barnes, I, 51–4, 109–14, 167–75, II, 351–6; Hans Louis Trefousse, *Ben Butler; The South Called Him "Beast"* (New York, 1957); Evarts Boutell Greene, "Some Aspects of Politics in the Middle West, 1860–1872," *Proceedings of the State Historical Society of Wisconsin, 1911* (Madison, Wis., 1912), pp. 68–9.

Reserve had moved from the Whig to the Republican columns, in Pennsylvania the stronghold of Republican votes during the sixties lay in the counties of the northern and western portions of the state which had once been Andrew Jackson's bastion.[2] Simon Cameron stressed the change in Pennsylvania when he invited Benjamin F. Butler, as a fellow former Democrat, to tour the northern part of the state on behalf of Republican candidates in 1866. Wrote Cameron: "The whole tier of counties from the Delaware to Lake Erie now all intensely republican, formerly gave very large democratic majorities, need to be roused, and we think no one can do it so well as you."[3]

Similarly, in Missouri, says Thomas S. Barclay, the Germans provided but one third of Radical strength at the 1865 Constitutional Convention, while a "majority of the most radical of the delegates represented the northern, western and southwestern border counties" of the state and "regarded the Missouri River counties where the conservative Whig tradition was strong, as the stronghold of rebellion. . . ."[4]

These largely rural and rapidly developing areas dominated by farmers and small entrepreneurs, whether their past was Whig or Democrat, were now Radical bastions. By contrast, Democratic predominance persisted in similar districts mainly when they were not sharing in the rapid economic growth of the times—the "butternut" areas of central Ohio and northern Indiana and the southern counties of Illinois, for example. Without pretending to provide a sufficient explanation of political behavior, these considerations do seriously contradict the thesis of Howard K. Beale that radicalism represented "New England bred economic and social standards" in combat with "those of the frontier and plantation."[5] Quite the contrary interpretation was made in 1867 by *Harper's Weekly* when it reported that "some warm Radicals"

[2] Cole, *Era of the Civil War*, pp. 60, 125–53; Roseboom, pp. 279–82, 295; Montgomery, "Radical Republicanism in Pennsylvania," pp. 442–3.
[3] Simon Cameron to Gen. B. F. Butler, June 22, 1866, in *Private and Official Correspondence of Gen. Benjamin F. Butler during the Period of the Civil War*, privately issued by James A. Marshall (Norwood, Mass., 1917), V, 707. (Hereafter cited as Butler, *Correspondence*.)
[4] Barclay, pp. 28, 126.
[5] Beale, *Critical Year*, p. 1.

considered all the New England senators but Sumner "fossil Conservatives," and concluded:

> The maturer civilization of New England, the soberer temperament, the hallowed traditions of peaceful obedience to law, the solution of strife by ballot, and the general intelligence in a certain degree incapacitate its sedate Senators from a vivid conception of the actual situation. They have not been brought face to face with the rebels. . . . They have forgotten how surely the STUART and the BOURBON under some form return. But the men of the border and of the West understand more truly that a BOURBON never learns; and it is upon the border and in the West that Radicalism prevails.[6]

Finally, centers of Radical politics tended also to be strongholds of religious radicalism (evangelical Arminianism, to be exact). The mass revivalism which swept out of the urban centers across the nation in the "Pentecostal Year" of 1858 marched hand in hand with Republican triumph. Replacing predestination with the doctrine of grace freely available to all who chose the path of faith and righteous conduct, preachers of "holy living" such as Charles G. Finney castigated any "loss of interest" in good government, temperance reform, abolition of slavery, and relief of the poor as evidence of a "backslidden heart."[7] The most prominent Arminian denomination of the land, the Methodists of the North, lent ardent and public support to the Reconstruction program of Congress. While former circuit rider William G. "Parson" Brownlow built a Radical political organization among the Methodists of eastern Tennessee, the General Conference of the church wrote off the remaining Methodist Episcopal Church, South, as guilty of treason as well as slavery, and resolved to proselytize worthy souls in the South only among Negroes.[8] Massachusetts's most prominent Methodist clergy-

---

[6] *Harper's Weekly*, XI (Sept. 21, 1867), p. 594. See below, pp. 117–26, on the peculiar character of Massachusetts radicalism.

[7] Smith, *Revivalism and Social Reform*, pp. 45–79, 148–62. Quotations from Finney are on pp. 60–1.

[8] William A. Russ, Jr., "The Influence of the Methodist Press upon Radical Reconstruction (1865–1868)," *Susquehanna University Studies*, Vol. I (Jan. 1937), pp. 51–62; Russ, "The Failure To Reunite Method-

man, Gilbert Haven, predicted at the end of the war that the grace of Christ would now "renew the land in holiness and love," end the liquor traffic, bring universal education, and end the "luxurious absorption by a few families of the people's wealth."[9]

Radicals, in short, shared an entrepreneurial orientation, stemmed generally from areas enjoying heady economic progress, drew upon both Whig and Democratic traditions, and were supported by the revivalist's faith in the possibility of human perfection. Precisely what, then, was radicalism? As a political schema it boiled down to two concepts: nationalism and utilitarianism. As the sentiment which bore the Union cause through the war was devotion to preserving the nation intact, and as the main effect of the war had been to nationalize a great federation of states, so the Radicals were those who had welcomed both developments unequivocally. The Radicals, furthermore, had not the least desire to curb the tendencies thus unleashed. On the contrary, as Thaddeus Stevens said, the process of erecting a "purified Republic" of equality and virtue had only begun. In the words of Leonard Myers in 1865:

> Republican institutions have stood the trial. The sovereignty of the people—the right of the majority to rule, asserted in the beginning, has been vindicated to the end, even through rivers of blood. The flag was shibboleth; but on its starry folds, in storm and sunshine, still floated "the Union,"—"the People!"[1]

Whatever theory of the Constitution Radicals held, it leaned in the direction of the supremacy of the nation. Sumner

---

ism after the Civil War," *ibid.*, Vol. I (Sept. 1936), pp. 8–16; E. Merton Coulter, *William G. Brownlow, Fighting Parson of the Southern Highlands* (Chapel Hill, 1937), pp. 1–34 and *passim*. On radicalism and religion, see also George L. Austin, *The Life and Times of Wendell Phillips* (new edition, Boston, 1901), pp. 370–87; James Leiby, *Carroll Wright and Labor Reform: The Origin of Labor Statistics* (Cambridge, Mass., 1960), pp. 23–6; Cole, *Irrepressible Conflict*, pp. 253–5; Hutchinson, II, 8–25, 206–55; Hodding Carter, *The Angry Scar, The Story of Reconstruction* (Garden City, N.Y., 1959), pp. 79–89.
9 Smith, *Revivalism and Social Reform*, p. 235.
1 Quoted in Barnes, I, 262.

spoke of "state suicide," Stevens of "conquered territories," and Samuel Shellabarger, in the doctrine which became most common among both Radicals and Conservatives (and was used by the Supreme Court in *Texas* v. *White*), spoke of "forfeited rights," meaning that the Confederate states remained as political entities but had forfeited their political rights by the rebellion.[2] The most extreme stand on the Constitution was offered by Isaiah Weir on behalf of Negro Radicals. Weir contended that a state is merely "an organized community within the jurisdiction and under the supervision of the Government of the United States." Neither secession nor suffrage is a matter for the states to regulate, said he—in fact, "there can be no middle ground between sovereign and subject in any one government."[3] But common to all these doctrines was the premise that neither the vested rights of states nor the vested rights of one group of men in the subordination of another was to withstand the "sovereignty of the people."

From this integral view of the nation there flowed two logical consequences. The first, in the words of Elisha Mulford, was "the right of every person born in the nation, to be and to remain in its citizenship. The nation cannot arbitrarily determine who shall or shall not exist in it as members of it." And, he emphasized: "This is irrespective of ancestry, and consists with a national not a racial principle."[4] The second logical result was that the powers of popular government were and should have been unlimited. Sinclair Tousey, the radical and articulate president of the American News Company, argued that it was ridiculous to circumscribe the power of democratic government in the name of safeguarding liberties. "By whom will those liberties be destroyed?" he asked. "This central power, styled the Federal Government

---

[2] McKitrick, pp. 113–19.

[3] *Proceedings of the National Convention of the Colored Men of America, Held in Washington, D.C. on January 13, 14, 15, and 16, 1869* (Washington, 1869), Appendix pp. IV–V.

[4] Mulford, p. 100. Elisha Mulford was a Hegelian whose doctrine offered the Radicals the most systematic available rationale for their stand. Probably, however, few contemporaries understood or appreciated him. Hence he scarcely merits the title "philosopher of Reconstruction" awarded him by John Higham. Higham, *Strangers in the Land: Patterns of American Nativism, 1860–1925* (New York, 1963), pp. 20–1.

. . . being of and from the people . . . cannot destroy its (or their) own liberties." Were the United States a monarchy or had it privileged classes, Tousey continued, placing too much power in federal hands might indeed create a danger, "but formed as our institutions are, framed as our Constitution is, educated as our people are, there can be no fear of having the central power of the general Federal Government too strong, or its authority supreme."[5]

Radicalism thus united the Jacksonian Democratic belief in the unlimited rule of the majority with the Whiggist conception of an active state. As the people were sovereign, furthermore, so the good of the people was the only criterion by which the activity of the state could be measured. Utilitarianism emerged as the corollary of radical nationalism.

Edwin L. Godkin's new magazine, the *Nation,* which initially championed the Radical cause, presented a striking exposition of this relationship in its review of a new book by Charles A. Bristed, *The Interference Theory of Government.* Bristed's work was in line with Conservative thought; it warned that the trend in the world was toward increasing strength of and "interference" by the state, a development stemming in Europe from the suppression of the revolutions of 1848 and in America from "the Puritan element" which advocated liquor laws, tariffs, and extinction of states' rights. The *Nation* counterposed the proposition that the trend of progress was not necessarily toward either stronger or weaker states, but toward the spread of utilitarianism. The doctrine, which the review claimed had been widely disseminated in America by "John Stuart Mill's writings, *in spite of* the essay 'On Liberty,' " was defined as follows:

> That government being simply the whole community organized for action, its business is to do whatever the good of the community requires, and what the good of the community requires is to be ascertained by reflection and discussion, and, in certain cases, by experiment. . . . The end of government is neither liberty nor restraint, but the common weal. Liberty is, after all, but a means to an end. If the effect of prohibitory legislation be worse

---

5 Tousey, *A Business Man's Views,* p. 38.

than the effect of free liquor, let it be swept away; if not, not; but this has to be shown. Do not, therefore, prove the Maine-law men to be wrong by a mere deduction from a principle of your own manufacture, such as, "That government is best which governs least," or, "The proper function of government is the protection of life and property." This is simply "high *priori*" nonsense.[6]

For the European observer, therefore, American politics were something of an enigma. The British Liberal Laurence Oliphant, who saw in the United States the specter of authoritarian democracy, was perplexed by the paradox of Radicals advocating centralization of power and Conservatives upholding the claims of local governments.[7] The future Tiger of France, Georges Clemenceau, in 1867 a young and ardently democratic journalist, was disturbed by Congress's repressive measures against former Confederate leaders but clearly recognized America's Radicals as his ideological kin.[8] The United States, he cried, is the "center of the world's attention,"[9] and the Radicals of England agreed. John Bright and Richard Cobden endorsed the Reconstruction legislation of Congress warmly, as did John Stuart Mill, who added that compared to the questions of civil rights and Negro suffrage, "free trade is but a secondary matter."[1] Bright concluded that the march of democracy on both sides of the Atlantic would create in the present generation "something of 'a new heaven and a new earth.'"[2]

The perfectionist hopes of the Radicals evoked only scorn from Conservatives. Scribbling vitriolically in his diary,

---

[6] *Nation*, Vol. V (Nov. 7, 1867), p. 372. This review may have been written by the *Nation*'s literary editor, Wendell Phillips Garrison, but Godkin clearly endorsed both this philosophy and congressional legislation proposed by the Radicals from 1865 to 1867. See *Nation*, Vol. I (Aug. 31, 1865), pp. 261–2; Alan Pendleton Grimes, *The Political Liberalism of the New York Nation, 1865–1932* (Chapel Hill, N.C., 1953), VII, 3–9.

[7] Oliphant, pp. 6–7, 26–8.

[8] Clemenceau, pp. 77, 83–7, and *passim*.

[9] *Ibid.*, p. 82.

[1] Richard J. Hinton, "John Bright at Home," *Galaxy*, Vol. V (March 1868), pp. 293–4; J. S. Mill to John Lothrop Motley, May 6, 1866, in Motley *Correspondence*, III, 101–3.

[2] John Bright to John Lothrop Motley, July 31, 1865, in *ibid.*, III, 83.

Edward Bates noted that the noun "Radical" means "a rooter" or "digger," with the comment that the " 'Digger' Indians are the lowest and vilest upon the continent." Continuing in this vein, he offered a definition of political radicalism which, for all its sarcasm, is substantially accurate. A Radical, wrote Bates, was "always dealing with the *root*—the origins and foundations, of society," appealing in all things to "the primitive principles of man's nature, *as he understands them.*" Claiming to "act in the name of the *Sovereign People,*" he was "above all constitutions and laws," for to him " 'the good of the people is the *Supreme law,*' and *he* is the only judge of what is good for the People!"[3]

From the Radical outlook arose significant consequences with regard to Negro rights. The integral nationalism of the Radicals left no place for a subordinate race. The Conservative *New-York Times* in 1867 warned its readers that plans for Negro suffrage in the South would result in forcing "universal negro enfranchisement upon all the states." Recent Democratic victories in Maryland and Kentucky, said the *Times,* had given rise to a "plea for reconstructing the whole North as well as the whole South upon the Radical basis. The movement is wild as well as mischievous."[4] But Radical spokesmen had called for full citizenship and suffrage for Northern and Southern Negroes well before the Democrats captured Kentucky and Maryland. George S. Stearns and some abolitionist colleagues in Massachusetts opened an organized drive to promote the cause of Negro suffrage in February 1865.[5] Three months later George Julian raised the issue in a Republican congressional caucus, only to find his proposal downed by cries that public opinion was not yet ready.[6] "Pig Iron" Kelley espoused Negro suffrage as early as January 1865. In the summer of that year he placed his position squarely before a Philadelphia audience:

---

[3] U.S., Congress, House, *The Diary of Edward Bates, 1859–1866,* ed. Howard K. Beale, 71st Cong., 3d Sess., House Doc. 818 (Washington, 1933), pp. 431–2.
[4] *New-York Times,* May 7, 1867.
[5] Edward A. Atkinson to [John Murray Forbes], Feb. 17, 1865, Atkinson Papers, Box 1.
[6] George W. Julian, *Political Recollections, 1840–1872* (Chicago, 1884), pp. 263–4.

The enemy that we are grappling with is *pride of race, unchristian and antirepublican prejudice against all races of men save our own*. He sits enthroned in our Northern hearts. He controls every hour of the day in every street of Philadelphia; and if we cannot conquer him, we cannot maintain our own freedom, or transmit the real safeguards of personal liberty to our immediate posterity.[7]

Radicals assaulted racial segregation everywhere it confronted them. In 1865 the Republicans of Wisconsin—and in 1866 those of Minnesota and Iowa—urged universal manhood suffrage for their states, and Kansas Republicans agreed, adding women's suffrage as well. The next year the Republicans of Ohio, California, New Jersey, Michigan, and New York followed suit. In Illinois the Black Laws were repealed in 1865. Radicals in Pennsylvania struck down streetcar segregation, and those in Rhode Island ended segregated schools. During the elections of 1866, Negro candidates were elected for the first time to state offices in both Wisconsin and Massachusetts. Success in these states was neither easy nor uniform—in fact, where put to a referendum, Negro suffrage inevitably lost in 1866.[8]

These struggles cast doubt on the common contention that the Radicals "used" the issue of Negro rights for party advantage or as a smoke screen for economic interests, or both.[9] Note, first, that the Radicals did press the question of Negro rights in the North as well as in the South. Second, and more important, to have used Negro rights as a smoke screen to hide Republican advantage or economic questions would have been the worst type of party management—it would have meant advancing the *least* popular issue at the expense of more congenial ones. In 1866 more Americans wanted a high

---

[7] Quoted in Ira V. Brown, "William D. Kelley and Radical Reconstruction," *Pennsylvania Magazine of History and Biography*, Vol. LXXV (July 1961), pp. 322–3.

[8] *South Carolina Leader*, Dec. 9, 1865; Philadelphia *Public Ledger*, April 16, 26, March 20, 1866, June 20, 21, July 20, 25, 27, 1867; McPherson, *Reconstruction*, pp. 257–8, 354; Cole, *Era of the Civil War*, 335; *Daily Evening Voice*, April 28, 1866; Montgomery, "Radical Republicanism in Pennsylvania," pp. 449–51; *Colored Tennessean*, March 31, 1866.

[9] *Eg.*, Beale, *Critical Year*, pp. 145–6.

tariff than favored civil rights for Negroes. More Americans identified the cause of the Republican party with the cause of the Union than wanted Negroes to vote. It was for this latter reason that the Democrats were the party which talked incessantly about the Negro; the Republicans talked first about the Union.

The key to Republican triumph in 1866, therefore, was Northern sympathy—not for the Negro, but for the Fourteenth Amendment. This measure not only united Radical and Conservative Republicans but offered the nation a codification of the wartime evolution of government and a legal guarantee of the stability of the new Union. For the Radicals this amendment could not be accepted as the end of the Reconstruction process, but it did secure the gains made up to that point. Rallying the voters to the proposal, the Pennsylvania Republicans asserted in their platform: "The most imperative duty of the present is to gather the legitimate fruits of the war, in order that our Constitution may come out of the rebellion purified, our institutions strengthened, and our national life prolonged."[1]

Every step beyond this point required intense struggles. Not only did the Radicals have to contend with the well-entrenched conviction that American equals white, they also had to overcome in Northern minds as well as Southern what the Radical novelist Albion Tourgée was to call the "Juggernaut of American politics," the doctrine of states' rights.[2] Frederick Douglass correctly said that the idea of "the right of each state to control its own local affairs [is] more deeply rooted in the minds of men of all sections of the country than perhaps any one other political idea."[3]

The Radicals, in short, were middle-class political innovators, dragging the voters as well as their party behind them. As Thaddeus Stevens said: "Some of the papers call me 'the

---

[1] McPherson, *Reconstruction*, p. 123. *Cf.* the first inaugural address of Governor John W. Geary of Pennsylvania, *Pennsylvania Archives*, Fourth Series, VIII, 957.
[2] [Albion Tourgée], *A Fool's Errand, by One of the Fools* (New York, 1879), p. 347.
[3] Philip S. Foner, *Life and Writings of Frederick Douglass* (New York, 1950–5), IV, 199.

leader of the House.' I lead them, yes; but they never follow me or do as I want them until public opinion has sided with me."[4] Stevens's sublime certainty that democracy and progress inevitably coincide, and that he was the voice of both, is shown in his use of the word "until"—rather than "unless"— the people sided with him. But in fact, on the subject of civil and political rights for Negroes, at least, popular sentiment did change dramatically between 1857 and 1870. This fact was noted by President Grant when he promulgated the Fifteenth Amendment. He quoted from the Dred Scott decision of the earlier year and said that by contrast with that ruling the universal suffrage amendment "is indeed a measure of grander importance than any other act of the kind from the foundation of our free government to the present day."[5] The crowning tribute to the work of the Radicals in this area came two years later when both Presidential candidates espoused equal rights and equal suffrage regardless of race.

"The tendency of the modern period of society," rejoiced E. L. Godkin, "is toward nationalization, and against either a feudal federation or a despotic centralization."[6] In this tendency, labor reformer H. H. Marsh commented, the Republicans represented "the party of political progress."[7] Once Radicals diverted their attention from political to economic questions, however, the cohesion of their group disintegrated, for economic policy was a matter of means, rather than of ends. Edward A. Atkinson, an early and principled advocate of Negro suffrage, endorsed McCulloch's Treasury policies so warmly that he was glad the Secretary's views on Reconstruction allowed him to stay in the cabinet and continue his good work.[8] Charles Sumner agreed with Atkinson, and leaned heavily on him for advice on economic matters.[9] While most of Sumner's New England Senate colleagues of all political

---

[4] Interview published after the death of Stevens, Philadelphia *Public Ledger,* Aug. 19, 1868.
[5] Richardson, VII, 55–6.
[6] Quoted in Grimes, p. 5.
[7] Letter of H. H. Marsh, *Workingman's Advocate,* Oct. 5, 1867.
[8] E. A. Atkinson to Hugh McCulloch, Oct. 12, 1866, Atkinson Papers, Box 2.
[9] Charles Sumner to E. A. Atkinson, Jan. 3, 1868; *ibid.,* Feb. 21, 1868, Atkinson Papers, Box 2.

shades shared this view, Radicals from Pennsylvania westward, and even a number of New England Radicals in the
House, ardently dissented from the Secretary on both the tariff
and the currency.[1] In fact, the doctrines of tariff protection
and expansionist monetary policy were embraced by so many
Radicals and blended so harmoniously with nationalism and
utilitarianism that they may meaningfully be described as
economic corollaries.

That many Radicals favored protective tariffs is well
known; indeed, this tenet was to become the cornerstone of the
Beard-Beale interpretation of them.[2] Not so familiar are the
arguments advanced on behalf of the tariff and the connection
of tariff protection to nationalism. The most influential figure
among the Radicals as far as economic policy was concerned
was Henry C. Carey.[3] In his report to Pennsylvania's Constitutional Convention of 1873, Carey stated that the true interests
of labor and capital were identical and that supply and
demand "naturally" balanced each other. He noted, however,
that "markets are glutted" and much labor was unemployed.
The source of the problem, he continued, was the effort of the
leading nations of western Europe to monopolize world industry and trade. To this end the Europeans had driven down
the wages both of their own workers and of their competitors'.
Their policies prevented the economic diversification of less
advanced countries and attracted capital in America into the
least remunerative branches of production, the extraction of
raw materials, forcing down the prices of the raw materials
themselves and effectively diminishing domestic demand, thus
channeling the flow of these resources to Europe. Fortunately,
said Carey, the United States was large and resourceful
enough to change this pattern of trade. By its economic
policies of the last decade America had both achieved un-
paralleled prosperity at home and, by means of inducing
emigration from Europe, raised wages in the older centers of
industry. The key to this change was the protective tariff.
Behind its shelter iron production had tripled between 1860

[1] Sharkey, pp. 107–24, 130–4, 276–311.
[2] Howard K. Beale, "The Tariff and Reconstruction," *American Historical Review*, Vol. XXXV (Jan. 1930), pp. 276–94.
[3] Dorfman, III, 6.

and 1872, and nine tenths of the iron had gone into the fabrication of machinery. The abolition of slavery, furthermore, had created a vast new market for American products among the freedmen. The economic boom had led employers to increase substantially the wages of workingmen; in fact, total consumption per capita had risen from $65 in 1860 to $130 in 1872. Thus the tariff was the key to economic independence and progress.[4]

Underlying Carey's arguments, obviously, were a nationalistic challenge to the supremacy of the Old World and the utilitarian approach to the promotion of the "common good." Similar reasoning led those Radicals who were the most ardent protectionists to be also the foremost opponents of McCulloch's policies of contracting the greenbacks.[5] Conservative Republicans, following Elbridge Spaulding, the "father of the greenbacks," looked upon the government-issued paper currency only as an emergency war measure and heartily endorsed Secretary McCulloch's call for gradual but steady recall of the notes after the end of the war. Most prominent among McCulloch's opponents at this point were Thaddeus Stevens, John A. Bingham, George Julian, William D. Kelley, and John A. Griswold.[6]

This is not to say that all, or any, of the Radicals were Greenbackers in the full sense that term was soon to assume. But some form of expansionist fiscal policy, such as continuation of the wartime legal tender notes, new greenback issues to redeem bonds, or free banking—or some combination of these —was advocated by most Radicals as well as by Carey himself. In this stand they enjoyed abundant business support. "Soft money," Irwin Unger argues, "became the hallmark of industrialists, promoters, and speculators because they believed it would encourage continued economic buoyancy and meet the demands of a capital-scarce nation."[7] The wealthy Abram Hewitt stood almost alone among the prominent iron-

---

[4] *Debates of the Convention to Amend the Constitution of Pennsylvania*, V, 470–7. See also Henry C. Carey, *Reconstruction: Industrial, Financial, and Political. Letters to the Hon. Henry Wilson, Senator from Massachusetts* (Philadelphia, 1867).

[5] Sharkey, pp. 66–80.

[6] *Ibid.*, p. 77.

[7] Unger, *Greenback Era*, p. 59.

mongers of the land as a conservative Democrat. Most of them followed his crusty father-in-law, Peter Cooper, who loudly championed protection and soft money and who presided at a New York reception for "Southern loyalists" called in answer to the National Union Convention.[8] Especially intriguing is the case of John Griswold of New York. This prominent iron manufacturer entered Congress as a Democrat in 1862. His ardent support of the war effort led the Democrats to repudiate him in 1864 and the Republicans to place him on their ticket. From this point on Griswold moved toward an unequivocally Radical stand on Reconstruction, tariffs, and currency.[9]

These economic issues, finally, served to some extent to distinguish between those who were Radicals in the fullest sense of the word and the large, amorphous Republican center, which moved in the period around 1866 so closely in the tracks of the Radicals that it is often hard to identify, but which was to become very prominent during the Grant administration and among the "Half-Breeds" later in the century. The central figure of this group in the late sixties was Jay Cooke, who was never consistently Conservative or Radical. After the election of 1866, his brother Henry held "a regular levee" of Jay's followers in Washington. Among those attending were John Sherman (who was practically Jay Cooke's personal representative in the Senate), Schuyler Colfax, James K. Moorehead, and Elihu Washburne.[1] Cooke and his group endorsed McCulloch's policy in 1866, turned against him the following year, then swung around again to support the cause of specie when the center of attention in the greenback debate became the repayment of the 5-20 bonds, then at the close of the decade called again for currency expansion.[2] The actions of the center tend to obscure the consistency of the Radicals, and also serve to distinguish the center from the

---

[8] Allan Nevins, *Abram S. Hewitt, with Some Account of Peter Cooper* (New York, 1935); Dorfman, III, 6; Peter Cooper, *Ideas for a Science of Good Government in Addresses, Letters and Articles on a Strictly National Currency, Tariff and Civil Service* (New York, 1883), pp. 1-3, 9-15, 345; *Daily Evening Voice*, Sept. 12, 1866.

[9] Barnes, II, 435-40.

[1] Oberholtzer, II, 25.

[2] *Ibid.*, II, 4-68; Unger, *Greenback Era*, 46-7.

Conservatives, who never swerved in their devotion to a return to specie payments.

The unassuming carpetbag has long been used by historians as the symbol of Radical rule and corruption. The same symbolism was used, but with very different connotations, by J. T. Trowbridge, who called his carpetbag his "emblem of enterprise and patriotism."[3] Such a badge does indeed typify the nationalistic reformers who grouped themselves under the label "Radical." Their spirit of political innovation matched the entrepreneurs' devotion to innovation in technology, and the parallel advances on the two fronts in the postwar years demonstrated the supreme self-confidence of the new elite. The Radicals challenged both the obsolete ideas of the Democrats and the constitutionalist hesitancy of the Conservatives, with full faith that economic and political progress must occur in simple harmony. But at the very moment this faith was in full bloom and the "party of political progress" was triumphantly sweeping aside the older ruling groups of the land, a fourth political force appeared from the ranks of the working class to challenge radicalism. Perversely, the labor reformers adopted the nationalism and utilitarianism of the Radicals only to hurl them against the needs of the new industrial elite itself. By this act they upset the confidence of the manufacturers that they had nothing to fear from unlimited democracy, and drove the Republican party to repudiate its own handiwork. This is the story in the pages to come. Its beginnings lie in the wartime stirrings of the labor-reform movement.

---

[3] J. T. Trowbridge, "A Carpet-Bagger in Pennsylvania," *Atlantic Monthly*, Vol. XXIII (April 1869), p. 449.

CHAPTER 3

The War
and the Worker

On the evening of November 2, 1865, thousands of working-men from the Boston area were gathered in Faneuil Hall to hear speeches by local trade-union leaders, Wendell Phillips, and Congressman Benjamin F. Butler. At the close of the rally the plump, heavily bearded machinist Ira Steward stepped to the podium to read a lengthy series of resolutions which concluded:

> RESOLVED, that with grateful hearts we praise our Heavenly Father that He has permitted his angel of peace once more to wave her silver wand over our recently distracted land. That we rejoice that the rebel aristocracy of the South has been crushed, that we rejoice that beneath the glorious shadow of our victorious flag men of every clime, lineage and color are recognized as free. But while we will bear with patient endurance the burden of the public debt, we yet want it to be known that the workingmen of America will in future claim a more equal

share in the wealth their industry creates in peace and a more equal participation in the privileges and blessings of those free institutions, defended by their manhood on many a bloody field of battle. . . .[1])

The fledgling labor-reform movement for which Steward spoke was the child of civil war. The political debates of that conflict provided the basic elements of the workingmen's ideology, the alignments of political and social groups effectuated by the war created the framework within which their movement unfolded, and the economic pressures the great struggle engendered spurred them into action. For most wage earners the war had been a nightmare that had given them little reason to endorse the revolutionary measures of the Republicans. The burden of taxation fell heavily on them, greenbacks were associated with severe inflation, and conscription not only gave the state a claim upon their very lives but discriminatorily provided the wealthy citizen with an escape through commutation for cash. Emancipation, though long advocated by a minority of workers, appeared to most as a threat to unleash from the plantations hordes of Negro laborers who would depress industrial wage levels. But the fact that toilers disliked the war measures does not prove the contention of some historians that the Peace Democrats were able to rouse "the mass opposition of the working classes" against the war effort.[2]

It is certainly true that in any war there is a constant ebb and flow of the will to fight, and this is especially true of a civil war in which, to a much greater extent than an international war, the questions of whether or not to continue the carnage and even of which side to support are always live issues.

---

[1] *Daily Evening Voice*, Nov. 3, 1865; Commons, *Doc. Hist.*, IX, 304–5.
[2] DuBois, *Black Reconstruction*, p. 102. See also Emerson D. Fite, *Social and Industrial Conditions in the North During the Civil War* (New York, 1910), pp. 183–211; Brother Basil Leo Lee, *Discontent in New York City, 1861–1865* (Washington, D.C., 1943), pp. 195–227; Gray, pp. 212, 213. A more balanced treatment may be found in Philip S. Foner, *History of the Labor Movement in the United States* (New York, 1947–65), I, 321–7. See also Williston H. Lofton, "Abolition and Labor," *Journal of Negro History*, Vol. XXXIII (July 1948), pp. 249–83; Lofton, "Northern Labor and the Negro during the Civil War," *ibid.*, Vol. XXXIV (July 1949), pp. 251–73.

Lincoln's administration had to win battles and votes simultaneously, and often the election campaigns were more important to the ultimate outcome of the struggle than the military encounters. Varied as the views of Northern workers may have been, however, toward Lincoln, slavery, the draft, and the various military leaders, one fact remains clear: they were ardently devoted to the cause of preserving the Union intact. In fact, the same could be said of the industrial laborers, at least, of New Orleans, Louisville, Covington, and St. Louis in the slave states. This devotion was rooted in the intense nationalism of the working classes—their commitment to the world's only political democracy.

The secession crisis roused this devotion.[3] "Come, then," called Daniel Weaver to his fellow coal miners in January 1861, "and rally around the standard of union—the union of States and the unity of miners. . . ."[4] Simultaneously, the mechanics of Louisville, Kentucky, under the leadership of Robert Gilchrist (later an officer of the National Labor Union) and the molder William Horan, requested fellow trade unionists to convene on Washington's Birthday in Philadelphia to consider steps to preserve the Union. Denouncing both the "traitors in Washington" and the militant antislavery men, they endorsed the proposed Crittenden Compromise. Significantly, this meeting, the decade's first national assembly of labor leaders, was held in response to political, not economic, problems, and its resolutions expressed the belief that workingmen would make better legislators in the crisis than would "party politicians." To promote the election of workmen to office it established the Committee of Thirty-Four. The leaders of the movement included such Douglas Democrats as Gilchrist, Horan, and William H. Sylvis, and such Republicans as Uriah S. Stephens. Finally, it is noteworthy that both the most famous president of the future National Labor Union (Sylvis) and the founder-to-be of the Knights of Labor (Stephens) played prominent roles in this effort.[5]

---

[3] See Foner, *Labor*, I, 298–306.
[4] Quoted in Chris Evans, *History of United Mine Workers of America from the year 1860 to 1890* (Indianapolis, 1918–20), I, 7.
[5] Foner, *Labor*, I, 302–3; Hermann Schlüter, *Lincoln, Labor and Slavery: A Chapter from the Social History of America* (New York,

Rebel bombardment of Fort Sumter transformed the workers' nationalism from a call for compromise to a call for arms. Symbolically, twelve-year-old Terence V. Powderly, son of a stanch Democrat of Carbondale, Pennsylvania, attached an American flag sewn by his mother to a sapling he had cut and nailed the crude banner to the side of his house. Two of his brothers enlisted early enough to serve at Antietam. The nearby town of Port Carbon sent 518 men to war, one fourth of its population, including the miners of the Petersburg crater in 1864. Across the state, in the hamlet of Cherry Tree, sawmill operator Robert Hughes discovered that the April enlistments had robbed him of all of his twenty-two hands save one old man.[6]

Military enthusiasm wrought havoc on the little trade unions of the time. A Philadelphia union closed its books with the words: "It having been resolved to enlist with Uncle Sam for the war, this union stands adjourned until either the Union is safe or we are whipped."[7] William Sylvis, then secretary of the Philadelphia ironmolders, raised a company which soon disbanded because the men disliked the colonel placed over them; he later enlisted in the Pennsylvania militia. Coal miners of central Illinois made up several companies, drastically depleting union rolls, and elected their paid lecturer, Martin Boyle, a captain. In some small Western towns like St. Paul, Minneapolis, and St. Anthony, enlistments closed down all existing trade unions. The hardiest of the national organizations, the National Typographical Union, doubly stricken by military recruitment of one third of the members of its key New York local and the loss of its large Southern membership,

---

1913), pp. 129–33; James C. Sylvis, *The Life, Speeches, Labors and Essays of William H. Sylvis, Late President of the Iron-Moulders' International Union: and also of the National Labor Union* (Philadelphia, 1872), pp. 42–4; Norman J. Ware, *The Labor Movement in the United States, 1860–1890: A Study in Democracy* (New York, 1929), pp. 26–7.

[6] Terence V. Powderly, *The Path I Trod*, ed. Harry J. Carman, Henry David, and Paul N. Guthrie (New York, 1940), pp. 16–17; Daniel F. Bausum, "Personal Reminiscences of Sergeant Daniel F. Bausum, Co. K, 48th Regt., Penna. Vol. Inf., 1861–1865," *Schuylkill Hist. Pubs.*, IV, 248; Vincent Tonkin Lumber Papers, Misc. Papers, Box 2.

[7] Quoted in Terence V. Powderly, *Thirty Years of Labor, 1859 to 1889* (Columbus, Ohio, 1890), p. 57.

held no convention at all in 1861, and the next year its president, future Congressman John M. Farquhar, joined the army himself.[8]

In all, 37 per cent of the males of military age in the loyal states were or had been in the federal armed forces by May 1865. State militia calls aside, 2,653,062 men had entered the national army. Benjamin A. Gould concluded that of every 1,000 U.S. soldiers, 421 belonged to the working classes (mechanics and laborers), 487 to agriculture, 16 to the professions, 35 to commerce, and the remaining 41 to miscellaneous other or unidentified occupations. Skilled mechanics made up an especially large number of Union volunteers. Only the professional classes (who flocked to the colors in 1861 and 1862) provided more soldiers in proportion to their numbers than did the workingmen.[9]

Foreign-born workmen matched the enthusiasm of the natives. Ten regiments of Germans were raised in New York State alone, one of them exclusively members of the *Turnverein* and another (the "Frémont" Regiment) commanded by the Prussian Marxist Rudolph Rosa. In fact, the *Turnverein,* a combination athletic and mutual insurance society that was the largest secular German organization in the nation, practically turned itself into a recruiting agency. Three fourths of its members enlisted in the army, providing the battalion in Washington that boasted of being the first volunteer group mustered in the national crisis, three companies of the First Missouri Regiment, and almost the whole Seventeenth Missouri. German manpower, organizations, and ideas were transplanted to the fields of battle. The Forty-third Illinois Regiment was constituted almost exclusively of German youth from Belleville, a center of trade unionism and free thought labeled by Wilhelm Kaufmann *"ein kleines deutsches Athen in Amerika."* The Thirty-second Indiana was frequently assem-

---

[8] Sylvis, pp. 46–7; Wieck, pp. 113–14; George B. Engberg, "The Rise of Organized Labor in Minnesota, 1850–1890," unpublished Master's thesis (Univ. of Minnesota, 1939), pp. 12–13; George A. Stevens, *New York Typographical Union No. 6: Study of a Modern Trade Union and Its Predecessors* (Albany, N.Y., 1913), pp. 577–8, 604, 652; *Biographical Directory of American Congress,* pp. 875–6.

[9] Gould, pp. 5, 10–14, 209–10, 215, 217.

bled by its commander, brevet Major General August Willich, for lectures on Marxism, which he delivered in German.[1]

The Irish were not to be outdone by Germans. Despite their traditional loyalty to the Democratic party and hatred of Negroes, James Burn found Irish workmen in the New York–Philadelphia region ardently loyal to the Union. They supplied more than 144,000 soldiers, a larger proportion of their number of military age than the natives in service. New York's famous Sixty-ninth Regiment and Irish Brigade, and the Ninth Massachusetts were Irish units which fought from Bull Run to Appomattox, their standard-bearers carrying the green flag beside the Stars and Stripes. Indeed, the Irish pennant of the Sixty-ninth was sewn in Tipperary and shipped to New York, where General George McClellan ceremoniously presented it to Colonel James Cavanaugh of the regiment.[2] For the Irish, after all, America was *their* country, the land where, quipped John O'Leary, they fear neither law nor landlord, but "fancy themselves growing smart almost with the air they breathe, and feel as if they had become free by that declaration of independence which is forever floating about the moral atmosphere." On the Old Sod, they believed, the only Confederate sympathizers were Englishmen and Orangemen.[3]

In the opening months of 1864 the tenacity of this nationalism was put to the acid test. At the very moment General Grant was preparing to mount his May offensive on all fronts, the enlistment terms of his indispensable, battle-hardened three-year volunteers of 1861 began to expire. The War De-

---

[1] Kaufmann, pp. 185, 543–4, 481–2, 474, 496 (quotation is on p. 482); Schlüter, *Deutsche Arbeiterbewegung*, pp. 162, 189–98; Schlüter, *Lincoln, Labor and Slavery*, pp. 78–81. See also Morris Hillquit, *History of Socialism in the United States* (New York, 1903), pp. 170–1; Richard T. Ely, *The Labor Movement in America* (New York, 1886), p. 223; Karl Obermann, *Joseph Weydemeyer, Pioneer of American Socialism* (New York, 1947), pp. 114–40.

[2] Burn, p. xlv; Ella Lonn, *Foreigners in the Union Army and Navy* (Baton Rouge, La., 1951), pp. 116–24, 578; Sister M. Jeanne d'Arc O'Hare, "The Public Career of Patrick Andrew Collins," unpublished doctoral dissertation (Boston College, 1959), p. 32; John Devoy, *Recollections of an Irish Rebel* (New York, 1929), p. 312.

[3] John O'Leary, *Recollections of Fenians and Fenianism* (London, 1896), I, 109–10, 152–97; Frank Roney, *Frank Roney, Irish Rebel and California Labor Leader, An Autobiography*, ed. Ira Cross (Berkeley, Cal., 1931), pp. 93–5.

partment estimated that as early as December 31, 1863, 455 out of 956 volunteer infantry regiments and 81 out of 158 volunteer batteries would simply go out of existence. Many more of the three-year men were scattered as cadre among the raw recruits. Under the terms of the conscription law these veterans could not be drafted. There was no way the government could compel them to stay in the army; yet without them there could be no effective offensive.[4]

The three-year men were offered a $400 bounty, a thirty-day furlough, and a special chevron designating them "veteran volunteers," but these inducements alone could hardly have enticed men who had known three years of death to return for more. In this critical hour 136,000 of the veterans re-enlisted. The weakest returns were in the Army of the Potomac, where General Meade found that almost one half the veterans had gone home, leaving him with 26,000 re-enlistments. Even this force, however, was enough to supply the core of experienced cadre for the advancing army. Down in Georgia whole regiments of Sherman's veterans signed up *en masse*.[5] As those soldiers advanced toward Atlanta in the following months, James Russell Lowell exulted: "I believe the people are more firm than ever."[6]

This loyalty was sorely taxed. The cost of the war rose daily, and the Union party's war measures confronted the working classes with issues far more complex than secession. The will to defeat the Rebels was nearly unanimous, but not so the readiness to bear mounting taxes and inflation, much less to welcome conscription and emancipation of the Negroes. The cost of living rose abruptly, Wesley Mitchell's index based on 100 for 1860 standing at 156 by 1864 and 168 in 1865. Wages inevitably lagged in their upward race with prices, the wage index being 130 for 1864 and 150 for 1865.[7] But even the

[4] U.S. War Department, *The War of the Rebellion: A Compilation of the Official Records of the Union and Confederate Armies* (Washington, 1900), Series iii, V, 649–55. (Hereafter cited as *O.R.*)
[5] *Ibid.*
[6] J. R. Lowell to John L. Motley, July 26, 1864, in Motley, *Correspondence*, III, 34.
[7] Sharkey, p. 146. *Cf. Fite*, 183–6; U.S. Congress, Senate, *Wholesale Prices, Wages and Transportation. Report by Mr. Aldrich from the Committee on Finance, March 3, 1893*, 52d Cong., 2d Sess., Senate

wage index reveals little, because the income of craftsmen whose skills were in short supply kept abreast of the cost of living rather well in 1864, while those of the unskilled and the women workers fell woefully behind. Pathetically, some seamstresses of Cincinnati appealed to President Lincoln to be paid directly for their work rather than through merchants. "We are unable to sustain life for the prices offered by contractors, who fatten on their contracts by grinding immense profits out of the labor of their operatives," the women wrote. "We are in no way actuated by a spirit of faction, but desirous of aiding the best government on earth, and at the same time securing justice to the humble laborer."[8]

Skilled and semi-skilled tradesmen, on the other hand, incessantly demanded higher "prices" for their work and put down tools without hesitation when they were refused. Some of their strikes were led by unions, others, perhaps many more, involved no unions at all. James Burn, the English hatter, remarked that at his trade in New York he found "a constant struggle between the men and their employers about prices. I have seen as many as four shop-calls [work stoppages] in the course of a day on as many different kinds of work." When the workers, led by "a set of headstrong young men," did "turn out . . . should any man with a proper sense of right and wrong attempt to defend the employer . . . he would surely be branded as a traitor, as well as being made the butt of ridicule by every fool in the shop who chooses to raise a laugh at his expense. . . ."[9]

A similar picture was drawn by an office clerk in the McCormick reaper plant in Chicago in April 1864: "Our molders are going on their fourth strike for an advance of wages since last fall. They now want 25 per cent more!!! Manufacturers will have to shut up shop if things go much farther in this line. . . . We wish we could help it but we are powerless."[1] Determined employers could resort to long and

Rept. No. 1394 (4 parts, Washington, 1893), I, 9, 13, 180 (hereafter cited as *Aldrich Report*); report of Commissioner David A. Wells, *American Annual Cyclopaedia*, VIII (1868), 258–9.

[8] Commons, *Doc. Hist.* IX, 72–3.

[9] Burn, pp. 186–7.

[1] The McCormick Company to G. Monser, April 11, 1864, quoted in Robert Ozanne, "Union-Management Relations: McCormick Harvesting

costly lockouts, such as those of the piano makers and unionized daily newspapers of New York.[2] In both these instances the employers could not pass increased costs on to the government or an expanding market; yet even the publishers balked only when their typographers (already paid far above those of nonunion competitors) demanded their second raise of the year.[3] In at least one instance common laborers were able to duplicate the success of the tradesmen. New York's longshoremen staged a series of strikes in the spring of 1863, culminating in the massive June walkout of every worker in and around the docks, which converted an attempted wage cut into a substantial wage increase.[4]

Harassed employers turned to the government for help in resisting the wartime demands of their workers. Ascribing labor's effectiveness in advancing wages to a "labor shortage" they enlisted United States consuls in Europe to step up the flow of immigrants and asked army officers at Southern forts to send "contrabands."[5] Since neither of these steps was adequate to cope with the power of skilled workmen, the manufacturers sought more direct state aid through antistrike legislation and military suppression of strikes. All these measures in turn stimulated the political awareness of the working classes.

A series of strikes in the coal fields around LaSalle, Illinois, in 1863 prompted the legislature of that state to pass an act making it a criminal offense to interfere with another person's going to work, to combine to deprive the owner of property of its lawful use, or to enter a coal mine with the intention of inducing others to leave it. Known as the LaSalle Black Laws, this legislation was the product of bipartisan action. The Democrats who then controlled the Illinois legislature had just passed resolutions condemning the Emancipation Proclamation and were maneuvering to remove control of

---

Machine Company, 1862–1886," *Labor History*, Vol. IV (Spring 1963), p. 134. See also Hutchinson, II, 89, for same letter.

[2] U.S. Commissioner of Labor, *Third Annual Report of the Commissioner of Labor, 1887, Strikes and Lockouts* (Washington, 1888), pp. 1048–9. (Hereafter cited as *Strikes and Lockouts*.)

[3] Stevens, pp. 278–95, 397–8.

[4] Albon P. Man, Jr., "Labor Competition and the New York Draft Riots of 1863," *Journal of Negro History*, Vol. XXXVI (Oct. 1951), pp. 394–9.

[5] *Foreign Emigration*, pp. 1–3; Man, pp. 382–9.

the state militia from the hands of Republican Governor Yates. The day after the antistrike act was signed by Yates the legislature was adjourned for want of a quorum because Republican members absented themselves to prevent the passage of Democratic peace resolutions.[6]

Similar legislation was proposed in Massachusetts and Minnesota, and in Ohio a bill to prohibit anyone's preventing another person from going to work became law. But the greatest controversy arose over a measure introduced in March 1864, in the New York Senate by Frederick R. Hastings, which exempted from conspiracy prosecution all associations of workmen or employers to establish wages, hours, or rules, but provided fine and imprisonment for the use of any coercive means by these groups. Thus, to interfere with employees' going to work, to force anyone to join a union, or to fine anyone for breaking the rules of the body would be an indictable offense. The bill was quickly identified by the public with Senator Charles J. Folger, chairman of the Senate Judiciary Committee, to which it was referred, and a leading contender for the Republican gubernatorial nomination that year. The fledgling Workingmen's Union (New York City's central body of English-language trade unions) mobilized massive demonstrations against the bill. The sustained campaign against this proposal, led by William Harding, president of the Workingmen's Union and of the Coachmakers' International Union, inspired the establishment of both a central body of German-language unions in the city (the *Arbeiter-Bund*) and a state Workingmen's Assembly, which quickly became a formidable lobby in Albany. So furious was the storm roused by the workers that Senator Hastings himself saw to it that his bill died in committee and the Republican party passed over Folger to select Reuben Fenton as its standard-bearer for the governorship.[7]

More successful—and more sensational—than these legis-

---

[6] *Statutes of Illinois 1818–1868* (Chicago, 1868), pp. 189–90; Earl R. Beckner, *A History of Labor Legislation in Illinois* (Chicago, 1929), pp. 9–10; Wieck, pp. 128–30.
[7] *Fincher's Trades Review*, April 22, 1865 Schlüter, *Lincoln, Labor and Slavery*, pp. 212–14; Stevens, pp. 585–90; *Arbeiter-Zeitung*, Feb. 24, 1865; Lee, pp. 224–5.

lative efforts was the use of the army to break strikes. In March 1864, the operatives of the R. P. Parrott Works in Cold Springs, New York, laid down their tools to support their demand for wage increases. Citing its need for the famous Parrott guns, the army sent two companies of troops to the town, proclaimed martial law, and jailed four strike leaders in Fort Lafayette, where they remained seven weeks without trial. Yielding before this show of force, the workers resumed operations at the old wages. At the same time the Machinists' and Blacksmiths' Union and the Tailors' Union went on strike in St. Louis. A month after the strike began, General William S. Rosecrans issued orders prohibiting refusal to work, meetings, and picketing. Perhaps because St. Louis was a major hub of the riverboat operations, indispensable to all military endeavors in the Western theater of war, the petition of the workers for a revision of the order was spurned. In May, General Stephen G. Burbridge took similar action to break a strike of machinists in Louisville.[8]

As the year 1865 opened, employers in many industries, anticipating a fall of demand and prices with the impending end of the war, undertook vigorous efforts to reduce wages. The simultaneous demands of workers for wage increases and their employers for cuts provoked a rash of bitter strikes.[9] In the coal fields around Blossburg in northern Pennsylvania a struggle occurred which manifested all the tendencies of the period in bold relief. In 1863 these miners had affiliated themselves with the American Miners' Association, through which they won raises ranging from 35¢ to $1.10 a ton. Worse yet, from the standpoint of the employers, the union embraced every miner, mechanic, mule driver, and laborer in and around the pits, enforced a closed shop, and regulated hours and output per man. The colliers determined to rid themselves of this "tyranny."[1] In December 1864 the Fall Brook Coal Com-

---

[8] Sylvis, pp. 133–8. On the role of riverboats, see Nevins, *War Becomes Revolution*, pp. 70–4.
[9] *Strikes and Lockouts*, p. 1049; Wilson, pp. 181–7; Wieck, pp. 107–11; Roger W. Shugg, *Origins of Class Struggle in Louisiana, a Social History of White Farmers and Laborers during Slavery and After, 1840–1875* (Baton Rouge, La., 1939), p. 301.
[1] James Macfarlane, Gen. Agt. Blossburg Coal Co., to Thomas J. Bigham, Jan. 15, 1874, in *Pa. BLS, 1872–1873*, pp. 500–3.

pany and two other firms posted notice that henceforth they would establish all prices unilaterally, that company houses should thereafter "be occupied only by well disposed people, who, without exception, will be required to enter into a special agreement specifying the conditions upon which he or they will occupy," and that the companies would "put down" any resistance to their decrees and decide without interference from a union who was to be hired or fired. When the union members refused to work on such terms, the colliers directed all work to be suspended until the conditions were agreed to and all company houses to be evacuated. In May a sudden raid on company towns by three hundred soldiers, plus a sheriff's posse of equal numbers, took the strikers by surprise. Their leaders were arrested, and miners and families totaling some four thousand persons were evicted and dumped with their household goods in the town of Blossburg. Work was then resumed with wages cut in half and an ironclad oath not to join a union imposed on all rehired miners. The state legislature legalized the action of the operators after the fact by passing the so-called Tioga County Law, which permitted mining companies to evict striking miners from company houses at any time. "Shame!" cried Jonathan Fincher, president of the Philadelphia Trades Assembly. "Eternal shame on the men who can be guilty of such an outrage on honest labor!"[2]

WORKERS AND COPPERHEADS

Labor's involvement in politics and legislation entailed more than simply the effort to free trade unions from statutory or military interference. Spokesmen of the working classes could not avoid orienting their movement in relation to the major political alignments of the day. All major factions, furthermore, assiduously courted the votes of the workingmen. Three important results stand out. First, in every election the votes of the workers were well divided between the parties. Second, despite intense efforts by the Peace Democrats to woo urban workmen, few of the latter—and none of their organiza-

---

[2] *Ibid.; Fincher's Trades Review*, March 18, 25, April 8, 1865; Wieck, pp. 162–72, 277–83; *Pennsylvania Session Laws* (1865), 6; Evans, I, 12.

tions or leaders—"went Coppery." Third, in several important respects the most aware and active spokesmen of the working classes found themselves drawn into close-functioning relations with the Radicals.

The wartime grievances of the working classes mounted at the very time the enactment of the revolutionary Republican measures threw important sections of the Democratic party into open opposition to the war. The fact that protests from labor and from the Copperheads swelled simultaneously gave the impression in some areas that the workmen were swinging into the camp of the Peace Democrats; and the latter, of course, sought to bring just such a development to pass. The Copperheads, furthermore, enjoyed a formidable advantage: the major grievances which sparked labor protest were all related to the growing power and centralization of government, and opposition to that tendency was the very essence of old-line democracy. Military suppression of strikes, greenback inflation, the specter (for it was never more than that) of liberated Negroes flocking North, and the ubiquitous draft—what could have been better grist for the Coppery mill? Their campaign against the war reached a fever pitch in the spring of 1863. In New York City it was spearheaded by Mozart Hall, the Democratic society of ex-Mayor Fernando Wood, who had been quite a hero to foreign-born laborers during the fifties.[3] As Lee's troops marched north into Pennsylvania and the Lincoln administration prepared to issue the first federal draft call, Wood's organization mounted a series of protest meetings, culminating in a massive Peace Convention at Cooper Institute on June 3 and a Fourth of July rally against conscription. From the rostrum Copperhead orators pounded home the themes that the government's war effort was undermining the Constitution, that conscription claimed the lives of the poor in a rich man's war, and that emancipated Negroes were flooding the North.[4]

---

[3] Carl Neumann Degler, "Labor in the Economy and Politics of New York City, 1850–1860; A Study of the Impact of Early Industrialism," unpublished doctoral dissertation (Columbia Univ., 1952, University Microfilms, No. 4174), pp. 183–9, 315–20.
[4] *Proceedings of the Great Peace Convention;* Gibson, pp. 147–59; Man, pp. 375–405.

Simultaneously, rising rents and higher food prices triggered such a wave of trade organizing and strikes that *Fincher's Trades Review* headlined a June column on New York events "The Upheaving Masses in Motion!"[5] Early that month the entire Manhattan waterfront suspended work in sympathy with the newly unionized longshoremen, and by June 18 the latter triumphantly announced both a 60 per cent raise in daily wages and exclusion of all nonunion members from the docks.[6] Ominously, the aroused workers echoed some Copperhead themes. Among the scab longshoremen violently driven from work by the union were all the Negroes employed on the docks. Even the ardently loyal Jonathan Fincher of Philadelphia, leader of the Machinists' Union and dean of the labor press, begged the national government to prevent an influx of freedmen to the North and, while endorsing the draft act itself, denounced the $300 commutation provision as an "unpardonable crime."[7] On the other hand, his paper warned the New York workers to devote more attention to perfecting their unions and not to be intoxicated by mass rallies and outside speakers. "Already we see the shadowy fingers of politicians, place hunters and capitalists laying hold of the movement for their own selfish ends," the veteran Philadelphia unionist wrote. He concluded with the warning: "Weed out the unworthy ones among you."[8]

Too late! On the morning of Saturday, July 11, the great wheel began to spin in the Enrollment Office in midtown New York. By evening 1,236 names had been drawn and posted. The task of selecting the remainder of the 2,000-man quota was postponed to the following Monday. New Yorkers passed a hot Sunday reading and discussing the names of the elect. On Monday morning longshoremen, railroad trackmen, iron workers, blacksmiths, and others put down their tools to parade in protest against the draft. Members of Fire Engine Company Number 33 (the "Black Joke" Company) learned that among the names drawn from the wheel were some of their own. Such fire companies ranked with the saloons and

---

[5] *Fincher's Trades Review*, June 20, 1863.
[6] *Ibid.*, June 27, 1863; Man, pp. 394–9.
[7] *Fincher's Trades Review*, two editorials, June 13, 1863.
[8] *Ibid.*, editorial, June 27, 1863.

police force as one of the three pedestals on which the city's Democratic organization rested. The Black Joke men therefore had little difficulty rousing a crowd of supporters and sacking the Enrollment Office itself. This attack ignited rioting in many parts of the city. Near the burning office a Virginian named Andrews, a familiar figure at earlier Mozart Hall rallies, exhorted the crowd to frustrate conscription physically. Some of his audience then stormed an armory on Second Avenue and in the ensuing chaos burned the building with hundreds of their comrades trapped inside, where they were gathering arms.[9]

The rioting thus begun on Monday raged through the city until Thursday night, and a few outbursts were reported even Friday morning as police undertook a city-wide search for loot and participants involved in the earlier debacle. An estimated twelve to fifteen hundred people lost their lives in those four days. To detail the carnage of that week is unnecessary here.[1] The patterns of destruction do deserve attention, however, because the rioters' choice of targets upon which to unleash their spleen reveals some basic social attitudes of the city poor. The reaction of the organized workmen, furthermore, indicates their own conception of their position in society.

The draft act itself was more than simply the first quarry of the turmoil, quickly forgotten in the quest of loot, as some Republican accounts alleged. True, by Monday afternoon the process of conscription had been brought to a complete halt. But on Friday when Archbishop John Hughes addressed a huge crowd urging them to peace, he was continuously interrupted with cries of "Stop the draft."[2] The archbishop's audience was composed of people who were not, or at least no longer, rioting; yet they took up the chant of those who were still battling police many blocks away. Jonathan Fincher, who

---

9 [William Osborn Stoddard], *The Volcano under the City. By a Volunteer Special* (New York, 1887), pp. 19–22, 25–59; *Fincher's Trades Review*, July 18, 1863. On the role of fire engine companies in the Democratic party, see Ernst, pp. 162–5.
1 For useful accounts of the riot, see Stoddard; Joel T. Headley, *The Great Riots of New York, 1712–1873* (New York, 1873), pp. 136–288; Lee, pp. 97–109; Schlüter, *Lincoln, Labor and Slavery*, pp. 209–10; Man, pp. 375–405.
2 Stoddard, p. 290.

hurled anathemas at the rioters, attributed the first wrong to
the authors of the draft act. Exempt men with families, he
demanded, and repeal the $300 commutation privilege.[3] Simi-
larly, Tammany aldermen in the City Council, although they
spurned the antidraft agitation, hastily enacted a hefty appropriation of municipal funds to provide the commutation fee
for poor men—only to see the measure vetoed by Mayor
George Opdyke.[4]

On the other hand, conscription was by no means the only
prey of the crowd. As the women of the slums poured into the
streets urging on the men and all the declassed criminal and
vagrant population of the sprawling port city joined the mob,
it quickly directed its attention primarily to Negroes. Any
black man, woman, or child who chanced within the reach of
the rioters was put to death, often through hideous tortures.
Similar wrath was vented upon captured police officers,
though seldom on soldiers. A relatively small band did march
on a hospital sheltering wounded soldiers, but it was easily
dispersed by armed civilians. Homes of the wealthy were
subjected to sack unless they were heavily guarded. In such
cases, hatred of the rich was well complemented by the urge
to loot. The crowd also singled out for vengeance some
symbols of industrialism—in particular, railroad tracks and the
city's newly purchased street-sweeping machines. A Protestant
mission in the dismal Five Points area was destroyed on the
first day of the riots. One detachment even descended on
Columbia College. It would seem, however, that anti-intellec-
tualism was not as strong a motive in the crowd as was hatred
of Negroes, police, labor-saving machines, and Protestants, for
a single priest on the steps of the college convinced the rioters
to spare that seat of learning.

By Wednesday morning President Thomas C. Acton of
the Police Board was certain the tide had turned against the
rioters. Through that day and the next his police, now rein-

---

[3] *Fincher's Trades Review,* editorial, July 18, 1863. *Cf. ibid.,* July 25,
1863.
[4] Sidney David Brummer, *Political History of New York State during
the Period of the Civil War* ("Columbia University Studies in History,
Economics, and Public Law," Vol. XXXIX, No. 2; New York, 1911),
pp. 325–6; Stoddard, p. 259.

forced by five battle-hardened regiments of the Army of the Potomac, confined the rioters to the worst slum areas. Clearing streets with howitzers loaded with grapeshot and chains used at point-blank range, the forces of order then invaded the heartland of their enemy. At this point reports reaching police headquarters mentioned a desperate, revolutionary quality emerging among the rioters, many of whom exhibited fierce heroism defending their barricades. To complete the new picture, on Wednesday night crowds raided and closed houses of prostitution, in the standard tradition of revolutionary mobs.[5] In the dying embers of a race riot were grotesque reflections of Paris's Bloody June Days.

It was also clear by Wednesday that the workingmen whose activities were channeled through organized social institutions were becoming an important segment of forces opposed to the riot. The fire companies, for example, though one of their number had sparked the whole turmoil, were braving rioters' missiles as well as raging flames as they worked tirelessly to keep down conflagrations. After Monday most factories and shipyards resumed operation, despite attacks on their employees by the crowd. Among the troops who assaulted the rioters as ruthlessly as they recently had Lee's forces at Gettysburg was New York's own all-Irish Sixty-ninth Regiment. Civilian volunteers bolstered the predominantly Irish professional police, among them a patrol of a thousand German members of the *Turnverein*. Trade unions of the city took great pains to dissociate themselves from the rioters, and the organized hatters, typographers, carpenters, and cabinetmakers founded the Democratic-Republican Workingmen's Association of New York to propagandize for the Union cause.[6] President Patrick Keady of the New York Practical House Painters' Association gloried in the discovery that no arrested rioters were painters and requested members of his union to use their influence "to prevent recurrence of such disgraceful scenes as were then enacted . . . [by] thiev-

---

[5] Stoddard, *passim;* Cf. George Rudé, *The Crowd in History: A Study of Popular Disturbances in France and England, 1730–1848* (New York, 1964), Ch. 14.
[6] Stoddard, pp. 134–5, 201–2, 275, 279–81, 317–18; Foner, *Labor,* I, 323–4.

ing rascals . . . who have never done a day's work in their lives. . . ."[7]

In a word, workingmen's organizations of all kinds, hostile though they were to the discriminatory impact of the draft on the poor, rallied to the banner of the government—in fact, to the established social structure—in the face of the draft riots. Blaming the outbursts on unemployed foreign-born in the port cities, "professional thieves," heartless speculators, and designing partisan politicians, Fincher editorialized: "The people have too much at stake to tolerate any action beyond the pale of the law. Every mob has been put down. . . . No improvement can be made by popular outbursts upon the great superstructure created by the wisdom of our fathers."[8]

A second test of attitudes among the working classes was offered by the national elections, a little more than a year after the draft riots had shaken the country. The intensity of current political conflicts brought many more voters to the polls than had gone in 1860. Much of the increase went to George McClellan. Schuylkill County, Pennsylvania, where conscription had met violent resistance, moved from the Union to the Democratic column in the gubernatorial election of 1863, and it remained there in 1864 (and until Grant recaptured it in 1872). In the Middle Atlantic States taken as a whole (New York, New Jersey, and Pennsylvania), Lincoln's percentage of the popular vote fell from 54 per cent in 1860 to 50.6 per cent in 1864. On the other hand, the Republican share of the total vote in free states, excluding the newcomers Kansas, Nevada, and West Virginia, rose from 53.8 to 54.9 per cent. The loyal slave states, Missouri, Maryland, and Kentucky, where wartime upheavals created wild fluctuations in voting patterns, are also omitted from these figures. Although Lincoln's acquisition of 63.2 per cent of the New England votes surpassed his 1860 showing of 61.5 per cent, the figure was considerably below the combined Lincoln-Bell vote of that year (67.8 per cent). Thumping victories in the Old Northwest and across the Mississippi offset the losses in the East to give the President his slight over-all gain. In the Illinois, Indiana,

---

[7] *Fincher's Trades Review*, July 25, 1863.
[8] *Ibid.*, editorial, July 25, 1863.

Michigan, Ohio, Wisconsin area, where Democrats had scored impressive gains in state legislatures in 1862 and 1863, McClellan actually won fewer votes than the combined Douglas-Breckenridge total of 1860, and Lincoln's majority rose from 52.7 to 55 per cent.[9]

More pertinent to an examination of the attitudes of the working classes was the outcome in the cities. Of the 20 largest urban centers all but New Orleans took part in the voting. Lincoln carried 12 of them to McClellan's seven. In 1860 Lincoln had won a majority of the votes in but eight of these cities, while Democrats or fusion tickets carried six, and the others gave no candidate a majority. The following table shows the percentage of votes won by Lincoln in the county in which each of these major cities is situated. For Baltimore, city figures are shown. The counties are ranked in order of the percentage of votes cast for Lincoln in 1864. To complete the picture, the party which controlled that county in 1852, 1856, and 1868 is also indicated (D-Democrat, W-Whig, A-American, R-Republican).[1]

It is evident from these figures that Lincoln lost control of only one city which could not be called "normally Democratic," and that was Buffalo. It seems safe to say that both race riots and draft-dodging—of which the town was a major center—played roles in this result. In both Detroit and Milwaukee, Lincoln polled substantially fewer votes in 1864 than in 1860 (not just a smaller percentage), but in both cases 1860 appears to be the abnormal year. On the other hand, his gains

---

[9] The calculations in this and the two following paragraphs are based on data in W. Dean Burnham, *Presidential Ballots, 1836–1892* (Baltimore, 1955), pp. 245–88, and Erwin S. Bradley, *The Triumph of Militant Republicanism, A Study of Pennsylvania and Presidential Politics, 1860–1872* (Philadelphia, 1964), pp. 424–34. Zornow argues that the 1864 Lincoln vote was roughly equivalent to the combined Lincoln-Bell votes of 1860. For the free state area I have examined this is almost the case. In 1860 Lincoln and Bell garnered 56.1 per cent of the vote, in contrast to Lincoln's 54.9 per cent in 1864. William Frank Zornow, *Lincoln and the Party Divided* (Norman, Oklahoma, 1954), pp. 208–14. But this method of analysis leads to more confusion than clarity in most particular counties or states.

[1] Data in the table are calculated or taken from Burnham, pp. 231–84. The table was inspired by one in Zornow, p. 209, but mine is designed to reveal trends.

Voting in 19 Major Cities, 1860 and 1864 (County Vote)

City	Lincoln Percentage				
	1852	1856	1860	1864	1868
Baltimore (city)	D	A	45.3	83.8	D
Boston	D	R	48.8	63.7	R
Pittsburgh	W	R	68.0	63.4	R
Cleveland	D	R	62.4	63.0	R
St. Louis	D	A	40.2	61.2	R
Providence	D	R	59.6	60.3	R
San Francisco	D	D	47.5	60.2	D
Cincinnati	D	D	42.6	57.8	R
Chicago	D	R	59.3	56.7	R
Philadelphia	D	D	50.7	55.8	R
Rochester	W	R	59.6	52.8	R
Newark	W	D	47.5	50.4	R
Buffalo	W	D	53.3	49.4	R
Brooklyn	D	D	43.5	44.7	D
Albany	D	D	46.8	44.1	D
Detroit	D	D	51.3	42.9	D
New York	D	D	34.7	33.2	D
Milwaukee	D	D	41.5	31.6	D
Louisville	D	A	1.1	24.4	D

in Newark stemmed from an absolute loss in Democratic votes. The remarkable advance in San Francisco came with the accession of John Conness's machine of Douglas Democrats to the Union party,[2] while in St. Louis and Boston many Constitutional Unionists had clearly entered the administration fold. All in all, wartime grievances brought no stampede of workingmen to the Democratic ticket, though Lincoln's strength slipped in several cities. Most remarkable is the fact that his tally rose impressively in Cincinnati, the scene of fierce race riots in 1862, and advanced in Newark and Brooklyn, both of which experienced riots in 1863.

More significant even than the failure of the war issues to augment the Democratic vote among the working classes much beyond its 1860 level was the outcome of wartime factional struggles in New York City among Democratic poli-

[2] Winfield J. Davis, *History of Political Conventions in California, 1849–1892* (Sacramento, 1893), pp. 101–207.

ticians whose power rested on the labor vote. Republicans
were so few in the city that the crucial political contests of the
war were those between Fernando Wood's Mozart Hall and
Tammany Hall, of which William Marcy Tweed emerged as
Grand Sachem early in 1864. Mozart Hall whipped up enthusiasm for the great riots of 1863 and was represented in
Congress at that time by four ardent peace advocates, including Wood himself. Quite different was Tweed's stand.
Tammany, wrote Sidney D. Brummer, "prided itself upon its
patriotic record, and therefore could not endorse the peace
idea. . . ."³ Its leaders were conspicuously absent from
Wood's peace conventions, and Tweed himself was a member
of the county volunteering committee.⁴

During the electoral maneuvers of early 1864, Tammany
ardently endorsed General McClellan while Mozart Hall and
the Albany Regency raised the peace banner and excluded the
Tweed forces from the party's state convention. In response,
Tammany rallied War Democrats to its fold. A public circular
written by Tweed's lieutenant, Peter B. Sweeny, called the
issue of the hour successful prosecution of the war or surrender, and even went so far as to argue that "slavery, as a
subject of political agitation, has passed from the politics of
this country. . . ."⁵ Although McClellan certainly did not go
as far as Sweeny, the tone of his campaign in the city was that
set by Tammany. When the general addressed a rally with an
estimated attendance of 100,000, the German-language labor
paper of the city remarked on the failure of Peace Democrats
to show themselves. The favorite theme of Democratic orators
at the affair was denouncing Rebel atrocities at Andersonville
and elsewhere.⁶ While that paper in turn endorsed neither
Presidential candidate (as was the case with every bona fide
trade-union journal) and locally preferred the German-based
"McKeon Democracy" of Mayor C. Godfrey Gunther to both
Tweed and Wood, it clearly identified the Copperheads with

---

³ Brummer, p. 316.
⁴ *Ibid.*, pp. 26–7, 306–19; Myers, pp. 194–210; Gray, pp. 213–14; Croswell Bowen, *The Elegant Oakey* (New York, 1956), pp. 37–54; *Proceedings of the Great Peace Convention, passim.*
⁵ Brummer, pp. 371–4, 398–439. Quotation from Sweeny is on p. 374.
⁶ *Arbeiter-Zeitung*, Sept. 24, 1864.

the "gold clique" on Wall Street, August Belmont, and, by implication, with a conspiracy of the House of Rothschild to destroy the United States.[7]

In other words, the close identification of Fernando Wood with the Copperhead cause weakened, rather than strengthened, his popularity with the workers. In 1864, John Winthrop Chanler alone among the Peace Democrats of the city was returned to Congress. The Wood brothers, James Brooks, and Anson Herrick were defeated by candidates of the Union party. On the other hand, Tammany's tactic of critical but consistent support of the Union war effort left it the beneficiary of Wood's decline. In 1865, Tweed's candidate, John Hoffman, won the mayor's office in a four-way race in which he received three times the vote of the Mozart Hall nominee. The next year James Brooks and Fernando Wood were returned to Congress (Wood from a new constituency), but both were opposed by the labor press. The seats which the two Woods had occupied in the Thirty-eighth Congress, however, were won by Tammany men: labor-endorsed John Morrissey and John Fox, who handily defeated both Benjamin Wood and labor's choice, Horace Greeley.[8]

Elsewhere, genuine labor leaders were equally adamant in their hostility toward the Copperheads. When the Chicago *Times* commended the workers of that city for opposing the draft and called on them to rid the country of all Lincoln's war policies, Editor Andrew Cameron of the *Workingman's Advocate* responded by castigating the *Times*'s editor as "a traitor to his countrymen, to his God, and to the workingmen."[9] Jonathan Fincher of Philadelphia conceded that the workingmen sorely needed peace if they were not to be driven to eating clay, and would not quarrel over whether slavery was abolished now or later ("as it must be eventually"). But he added: "One thing to which all else must assume a subordi-

---

[7] Editorial in *ibid.*, Oct. 1, 1864. For the *Arbeiter-Zeitung* stand in municipal politics, see editorial of Sept. 10, 1864, and news article on Citizens' Association rally, same issue.

[8] Myers, p. 208; *Civil List and Forms of Government of the Colony and State of New York . . . Edition of 1870* (Albany, 1870), pp. 583–4; *Daily Evening Voice*, Oct. 20, 1866.

[9] Quoted in Zornow, p. 206.

nate position is, the 'United States' must forever be a fact; we can tolerate no division."[1] The same year Fincher sailed for England on the *George Griswold,* a relief ship dispatched by American admirers of the pro-Union British workingmen, and he spoke at rallies for the American cause all over the island.[2]

On the other hand, many employers readily identified resistance to themselves with opposition to the national cause. At times this identification was a product of confused observations, at times it was deliberate. In the mine regions of Schuylkill County, for example, forceful resistance to conscription appeared as early as the state draft of 1862.[3] The next year Charles Albright, a Mauch Chunk proprietor, wrote President Lincoln that "a large majority of the coal operatives" were defying the draft and "making unsafe the lives and property of Union men." Continuing his description of a reign of terror imposed by Irish "Buckshots," Albright protested: "They dictate the prices for their work, and if their employers don't accede they destroy and burn coal breakers, houses, and prevent those disposed from working."[4]

In other words, to Albright defying conscription and striking for higher wages were one and the same crime. Although his request for a "military force of several thousand men" to deal out "summary justice . . . to these traitors"[5] was not granted by the President, Albright was to enjoy his hour of vengeance thirteen years later when he assisted the prosecution at the Molly Maguire trials.[6] His definition of loyalty was shared by mine owners and Republican newspapers in central Illinois who baited miners' leader John Hinchcliffe as a Copperhead and had him dismissed from a military position when he ran for Congress on the Democratic ticket in 1862. Yet then and afterward, Hinchcliffe was a familiar speaker at

---

[1] *Fincher's Trades Review,* Aug. 20, 1864.
[2] Yearley, *Britons,* p. 195.
[3] McClure, I, 537–51, II, 81, 431.
[4] Chas. Albright to A. Lincoln, Nov. 9, 1863, in *O.R.,* Series iii, III, 1008–9.
[5] *Ibid.*
[6] Victor R. Greene, "The Molly Maguire Conspiracy in the Pennsylvania Anthracite Region, 1862–1879," unpublished Master's thesis (Univ. of Rochester, 1959), p. 80; Wayne G. Broehl, *The Molly Maguires* (Cambridge, Mass., 1964), pp. 272–4, 295.

patriotic rallies.[7] Symbolically, a worker's promise not to join a union, later called a "yellow dog contract," was then known as an "ironclad oath," just like the Southerner's pledge that he had never aided the rebellion.

In short, the burdens placed on the working classes by the war roused them to economic and political protest actions. These actions did not signal the accession of labor to the old-line Democrats, but rather the vitalization of an entirely new political force—the labor-reform movement. Nowhere was the distinction more clear than in the workingmen's reaction to the efforts of Benjamin E. Green to convince them through speeches, pamphlets, and newspapers that the Southern planter was their natural ally against the common enemy, the Yankee capitalist. The abolition of slavery, argued Green, had left white and black labor "two poor *divorced* widows" who could be rescued only by resurrecting their stricken husband and protector, the slaveholder.[8] Andrew Cameron denounced Green as an impostor and declared: "The ghost of negro superiority which haunts the peace of Mr. Green has no terrors for us."[9] Green in turn concluded that trade unions offered the workers "a poor and vain reliance" and that "egotism, selfishness, was their only motive."[1]

Workingmen could not and did not yearn with the Copperheads for the dying past. Rather, while bidding slavery and rebellion farewell, labor reformers raised the next question on the agenda. The *Daily Evening Voice* of the Boston Trades Assembly editorialized that the "oligarchy at the South" was "from the very nature of things, antagonist to free labor," but it added that the emerging "question of the day" was: "Have the laboring men of the country any rights which capital is bound to respect?"[2]

[7] Wieck, pp. 113–14, 195.
[8] Benj. E. Green, "Translator's Preface" to Adolphe Granier de Cassagnac, *History of the Working and Burgher Classes* (Philadelphia, 1871). Quotation is on p. lxiii. See also Green, *Letter and Remarks . . . National Labor Congress.*
[9] Editorial, *Workingman's Advocate,* April 11, 1868. See also editorial on Green, *ibid.,* May 30, 1868.
[1] Green, "Translator's Preface" to Granier de Cassagnac, pp. lxii, lxiii.
[2] Editorial, *Daily Evening Voice,* Dec. 10, 1864.

WORKERS AND RADICALS

As labor reformers formulated an ideology and a course of action for their nascent movement, they found themselves drawn toward alliances with the Radicals at several significant points, despite the devotion of the latter to the manufacturers with whom the trade unions were in conflict and despite labor's qualms over the great war measures. This tendency is best illustrated by developments in Louisiana and Massachusetts during and immediately following the war. It would be difficult to find two cities less similar at first glance than New Orleans and Boston, yet they shared not only comparable political movements, but even some of the same cast of characters, thanks to the fortunes of war.

The working classes of New Orleans found themselves the favored members of the population during that city's long occupation by federal troops. They provided that loyal 10 per cent of the adult white male population with which Lincoln dreamed of creating a new state government. Before the war Louisiana's constitution permitted the rural population far greater representation than that accorded the metropolis, and the city itself was governed by an unspeakably corrupt machine dominated by Mayor John T. Monroe and his Know-Nothing "pug uglies."[3] General Benjamin Butler disposed of Monroe and his colleagues summarily and courted the sympathies of the workers, most of whom he knew had been antisecession Douglas Democrats.[4] In 1863 the mechanics organized the Working Men's Union League under the approving eye of Butler's successor, General Nathaniel P. Banks. Its platform, reminiscent of the prewar Republican outlook, called for "the abolition of slavery, the removal of every Negro from Louisiana by colonization, and the admission of all white men to suffrage without restrictions as to residence."[5]

In the 1864 state elections the league and other rapidly growing labor organizations supported the Free State party,

---

[3] Shugg, pp. 146–8; Harrington, pp. 98–9; Henry Clay Warmoth, *War, Politics and Reconstruction: Stormy Days in Louisiana* (New York, 1930), pp. 271–3.
[4] Trefousse, *Butler*, pp. 107–21.
[5] Shugg, pp. 198–9.

which nominated Michael Hahn for governor and called for an entirely new constitution to shift the balance of power in the state away from the planters and to the city. A new organic law was needed, said Hahn, to abolish both slavery and "the power of the aristocrat," and to give "the poor man that which he has never had—an equal voice in the State."[6] Although a Conservative candidate, J. Q. A. Fellows, entered the race, Hahn's foremost opponent was Radical Benjamin F. Flanders, who also supported labor's demands but favored limited Negro suffrage and confiscation of the estates of rebels.[7]

At the state Constitutional Convention, which sat from April through July 1864, "two steamboatmen, a few clerks, a tailor, decorator, fireman, and several mechanics and laborers" were among the delegates.[8] Lincoln's ironclad oath, the fact that most upstate parishes were still held by Confederate troops, and General Banks's ruling that only the white population should be counted in apportioning representatives all combined to give the New Orleans Unionists, particularly the Free State party, a preponderant voice in the convention. The assembly produced a constitution which abolished slavery, and while restricting suffrage to whites, nevertheless gave the vote to all whites who had resided one year in the state, based representation exclusively on population (ending the prewar subordination of New Orleans in the state legislature), and empowered the legislature to grant limited Negro suffrage if it chose to do so. The influence of the workingmen carried the convention beyond even these measures; the new organic law established a progressive income tax, opened public schools to every white and Negro child, and proclaimed a nine-hour day and a minimum daily wage of two dollars for all laborers employed on public works. The article on the working day was passed in response to a petition signed by 1,500 workingmen.[9]

The power of the Free State party proved short lived. The constitution had established no guarantees to preserve the new regime: it neither disfranchised Confederates nor enfranchised the Negroes. The new order, therefore, crumbled under blows

[6] *Ibid.*, p. 199.
[7] Harrington, pp. 100–3, 144–6; Warmoth, pp. 34–7.
[8] Shugg, p. 200.
[9] *Ibid.*, pp. 201–10; Rhodes, V, 52–3; Blaine, II, 39–40.

from both sides. When Michael Hahn was sent to the United States Senate in March 1865, Charles Sumner was joined by Reverdy Johnson and Thomas Hendricks in denying Hahn his seat. More important, the political divisions evident within the state in 1864 hardened into three contending parties. Hahn's successor as governor, J. Madison Wells, declared himself in favor of Johnson's policy and headed up a Conservative Union party. His bid for re-election in October was seconded by a group of returning Confederates who styled themselves the Democratic party and nominated their own slate for all positions below the office of governor. The Radicals, headed by B. F. Flanders and Thomas J. Durant, refused to take part in the election, but anticipated Congress by almost two years when they begged it to ordain "territorial status" and Negro suffrage for Louisiana. Democrats used returning Confederate veterans to mobilize the resurrected planter and farmer vote in October and were swept into office with huge majorities.[1]

The triumph of old-line democracy proved a disaster for Conservatives, Radicals, and workingmen alike. The new legislature enacted a Black Code and sought to abolish the 1864 constitution. John Monroe himself was re-elected mayor of New Orleans in the summer of 1866. Desperate in the face of the reactionary tide, Conservative Governor Wells tried to reconvene the Constitutional Convention that July, but Monroe's police, supplemented by a mob, descended on the convention and scattered it, killing forty-eight people in the process.[2] Louisiana had returned to the Good Old Days.

Yankee reaction to these events contributed significantly to the Republican victory in the national congressional elections in the fall, and as a result of that victory Congress itself assumed responsibility for the future of Louisiana. Among the legislators present in Washington to act on the subject were both Butler and Banks—now representatives of Massachusetts and ardent suitors of labor's election-day favors in that state. Also in Washington, as a lawyer, was the Louisiana Radical Thomas J. Durant, who had gone into exile from his native

---

[1] Warmoth, pp. ix–x, 37–45; McPherson, *Reconstruction*, p. 107; Shugg, pp. 210–12; Rhodes, V, 53–7; Harrington, pp. 114–16, 140–50, 164–9.
[2] Warmoth, pp. 35–40.

state after the New Orleans riot and was shortly to appear as a prominent Greenbacker in the New England Labor Reform League.[3]

That Butler and Banks, as Massachusetts congressmen, should sit in judgment on Louisiana emphasizes the divergent courses of development of the two states. But the story of these two figures also symbolizes the wartime convergence of progressive forces in the Bay State which momentarily gave the labor reformers a remarkably strong voice in its Republican councils.

The unique politics of Massachusetts were fashioned by the early growth of great textile corporations and the intellectual heritage of the state. The former, by installing commercial wealth directly in a commanding position in the state's manufacturing, created a phalanx of Conservative strength against which the more radical intellectuals and small manufacturers had to contend. Simultaneously, the textile corporations placed in the very heart of the state's labor force a large body of unskilled or semiskilled operatives, largely women, who were chronically unsuccessful in attempts to wring concessions from their employers by means of trade unions. Consequently, as early as the 1830's and 1840's these operatives looked primarily to the legislature for relief.

Thus, parallel to the trade unions of the craftsmen there developed a quite distinct movement of textile operatives aimed mainly at the reduction of working hours by legislative action. To influence the legislature they utilized frequent massive conventions and great petition campaigns. Such efforts readily attracted middle-class intellectuals, who often dominated the conventions, and ambitious politicians who championed the cause of the working girls against the "soulless corporations." As an overseer, probably from the Atlantic Mills, explained this phenomenon, the few young men in the mills (he should have excepted the mule spinners) aspired to become foremen, a goal which was usually reached only by "good conduct and obedience to the will of their employer." The rest of the help consisted of women. "Hence the element that asserts its right and insists upon it, is not there," the

---

[3] On Durant see *D.A.B.*, V, 543–4.

foreman concluded, "and it is only by outside pressure brought to bear upon the subordinate help, oftentimes by demagogues, that the thing [shorter hours] can be agitated, or anything accomplished in this direction." Thus, although the operatives, "with scarcely an exception," desired a ten-hour day, the overseers looked upon their efforts "with distrust, as designed more to advance the interest of some political aspirant than to benefit the operative or laboring classes."[4] The prototype of this political spokesman was Benjamin F. Butler.[5]

Finally, in the decades preceding the Civil War the native American workman of Massachusetts had imbibed deeply of the intellectual's culture of transcendentalism, abolitionism, and millennialist reform. Thomas Wentworth Higginson recalled that among the Transcendentalists in the early 1840's were both "the more refined votaries, who were indeed the most cultivated people of that time and place," and "a less educated contingent, known popularly as 'Come-Outers.'" These workmen, consumed with "the Second Advent delusion just then flourishing," were, said Higginson, the very heart of the antislavery movement, "which was not, like our modern civil service reform, strongest in the educated class, but was predominantly a people's movement . . . far stronger for a time in the factories and shoe-shops than in the pulpits or colleges."[6] The Free Soil party in Massachusetts institutionalized the bond between the reformist professional or businessman and the native-born workman. Skilled workers in industrial towns like Worcester and shoe towns like Lynn and Abington provided the main base of support for that party.[7] Henry Wilson, the "cobbler of Natick," so typified the political leader who emerged in these towns that Higginson could assert: "Radicalism went with the smell of leather. . . ."[8]

---

[4] *Mass. BLS, 1870*, pp. 125–6.

[5] On prewar movement among textile operatives, see Ware, *Industrial Worker*, pp. 125–62; Trefousse, *Butler*, pp. 28–41; Commons, *Labour*, I, 536–41.

[6] Thomas Wentworth Higginson, *Cheerful Yesterdays* (Boston and New York, 1898), p. 115. *Cf.* David Donald's view of abolitionism as a reassertion of traditional values by a once-dominant social class. *Lincoln Reconsidered*, pp. 19–36.

[7] Hoar, I, 156; Boutwell, I, 119.

[8] Higginson, *Cheerful Yesterdays*, p. 115.

Simultaneously, the great migration of Irish filled the bottom rungs of labor with immigrants and the textile mills with Irish women. The newcomers quickly allied themselves with the Democrats, but a fusion of the Free Soil and Democratic tickets in 1850 blended the causes of antislavery, trade unionism, and factory legislation. Benjamin Butler, Nathaniel Banks, Henry Wilson, George Boutwell, William S. Robinson, and Charles Sumner emerged as leaders of a coalition aimed at redistricting the state to diminish the conservative influence of Boston, making the ballot secret, and establishing by legislation a ten-hour day. But the coalition was soon shattered. From one side the Pierce administration, aided by the Boston Democrats, who feared a loss of influence under the proposed constitution, brought pressure on the Democrats to break ranks. From the other, nativism waxed increasingly strong among the Free Soilers until many found themselves in the Know-Nothing movement as allies of the very conservative Whigs they had formerly been fighting.[9]

The mid-1850's were thus the time of Know-Nothing dominance. During this period the state's labor movement was thoroughly destroyed by the pitting of native trade unionist against immigrant factory hand and the divorcing of both from middle-class reformers. Democrat Butler and Know-Nothings Banks and Wilson became political enemies. To be sure, the reformist momentum from the coalition period was sufficient to give even the Know-Nothing-dominated legislature an impressive record of minor accomplishments,[1] and the ultimate effect of the period was, in the words of labor reformer Edward H. Rogers, the "maturing of opinion among the leading workmen in the direction of the Republican Party."[2]

---

[9] William S. Robinson, *"Warrington" Pen-Portraits: A Collection of Personal and Political Reminiscences from 1848 to 1876, from the Writings of William S. Robinson,* ed. Mrs. W. S. Robinson (Boston, 1877), pp. 30–86; Charles E. Persons, "The Early History of Factory Legislation in Massachusetts: From 1825 to the Passage of the Ten Hour Law in 1874," in *Labor Laws and Their Enforcement, with Special Reference to Massachusetts,* ed. Susan M. Kingsbury (New York, 1911), pp. 55–90; Handlin, *Boston's Immigrants,* pp. 192–206.

[1] Handlin, *Boston's Immigrants,* p. 202; Nason, *Wilson,* p. 119; Harrington, pp. 8–15.

[2] Edward H. Rogers, "The Auto-Biography of Edward H. Rogers of Chelsea, Mass., Reformer in Religion, Education, and Labor," unpub-

But the movement for shorter hours was immediately side-tracked in favor of investigations of nunneries, blocking a charter for Holy Cross College, and imposing literacy and residence requirements on the suffrage.[3]

Most serious of all, this period isolated the Catholic Irish from Protestant society and all its reform currents. Abused, hounded, attacked by their neighbors in the name of saving the land from "Catholic bigotry," the Irish (especially in the factory towns outside Boston)[4] withdrew as far as possible from the community around them and dealt with it only through the mediation of the priest and the Hunker Democrat. Thus the Catholic Boston *Pilot* concluded: "Co-operation for any length of time in important matters between *true* Catholics and *real* Protestants is morally impossible."[5] The Baltimore Plenary Council of the hierarchy offered a special caution to Catholics attracted to trade unions. Though there was no ban on societies aimed only at "mutual help," warned the council, the faithful should beware "lest workers, who join these societies, be induced by the deceitful wiles of evil men to give less work than is due from them, against the laws of justice, or in any way injure the rights of those to whom they are subject."[6]

No mass labor movement was possible in Massachusetts until this chasm of ethnic suspicion was bridged. The war provided the setting for this task,[7] but the men who opened the way for Protestant and Catholic workingmen again to find a common cause were the Radical Republicans and the Fenians.

The operative center of Radicalism in the state was the "Bird Club," a group of ten to twenty political, intellectual, and business leaders who met each Saturday afternoon for

---

lished manuscript, completed in 1902, in Edward H. Rogers Papers, Ch. 10, p. 7 (hereafter cited in this form: 10:7).

[3] Handlin, *Boston's Immigrants*, pp. 199–204; Billington, pp. 316, 412–15. For information on the College of the Holy Cross I am indebted to the Rev. W. A. Lucey of that institution.

[4] O'Hare, pp. 41–2.

[5] Boston *Pilot*, July 29, 1854, quoted in Handlin, *Boston's Immigrants*, p. 176.

[6] Quoted in Macdonald, p. 66.

[7] Handlin, *Boston's Immigrants*, pp. 207–11; Higham, pp. 12–14.

dinner under the auspices of Frank W. Bird, a successful paper manufacturer of East Walpole. The Bird Club included such figures as Sumner, Wilson, John A. Andrew, Charles Francis Adams, Henry L. Pierce, Franklin B. Sanborn, Samuel G. Howe, Frank P. Stearns, and Elizur Wright. William S. Robinson, author of the "Warrington" columns in the Springfield *Republican,* was its favorite mouthpiece. At the close of the war, Butler was admitted to the charmed circle very briefly, prior to becoming its most prominent enemy. These men led the "Straight" Republicans, who opposed Banks's fusion with the Know-Nothings in the fifties, emerged (in Sanborn's phrase) as an "unrecognized cabinet" during Governor Andrew's administration, dominated the state during the 1860's, and went *en bloc* to the Liberal Republican movement in 1872.[8]

The Bird Club came to power with the election of John Andrew as governor in 1860. "The 'Straights' had it all their own way . . ." crowed Warrington, "a complete and glorious victory over Banks and the Know-Nothings, old Boston conservatism, and everything bad."[9] More moderate than his closest political associates, the new governor quickly made his administration acceptable, even admired, in Boston commercial circles, while he relentlessly insisted on the major Radical demands: emancipation, arming of Negroes, civil rights. Astutely, he appointed prominent Democrats to military commands, among them Butler himself. Not only did Andrew insist that the legislature charter Holy Cross College, he dramatically attended commencement at the Catholic institution just as he did at Harvard. And when Patrick Guiney became the state's first prominent Irish Catholic Republican, the governor quickly appointed him an assistant district attorney, over the vehement protests of his party's nativists. Labor reformers were delighted to see W. S. Robinson, among the most prominent champions of factory legislation in Coalition days, given a sinecure as clerk of the House and elected secretary of the Republican State Committee, and his ally

---

[8] Frank Preston Stearns, *Cambridge Sketches* (Philadelphia, 1905), *passim* and esp. pp. 162–79; Robinson, *Pen-Portraits,* pp. 86–136; F. B. Sanborn, Introduction to *ibid.,* p. x.
[9] *Ibid.,* pp. 92–3.

Alexander H. Bullock made Speaker of the House.[1] During his three terms, Andrew soothed the antagonisms of the previous decade in the name of national unity and mobilized Conservative, Radical, and labor-reform forces in the state into an apparently harmonious phalanx, far more formidable than the Coalition had been.

The meaning of the change for the workers is apparent in the career of Edward H. Rogers, a ship joiner in the Charlestown navy yards. This Medford-born artisan had taken part in the trade unionism, Know-Nothingism, and Republicanism which swept through the native workmen of the Boston area in the 1850's. He entered the navy yard during the war, when employment in the yards increased from a low of 245 men in June 1860 to 3,339 in February 1862. Rogers found grievances mounting among the workmen during 1863 and 1864 over both the administration of the draft and problems at work. The log of the yard records three work stoppages during 1863 and one instance (July 15) when the authorities "kept a force under arms to quell an expected riot." Wages were actually reduced after the initial surge of war production—a ship carpenter, for example, receiving $5.00 per day in April 1863, $4.00 in December 1864, and $3.50 (on "new work") in early 1865.[2]

At the request of some of the yard workmen, Rogers ran for the state legislature in 1864 and was elected. In effect, he appeared in the capitol as spokesman for some 4,000 shipyard workers. To his delight, Rogers found the legislature to which he had been elected "largely comprised of men who had been engaged for twenty years in urging the various phases of Reform, all the way from the most intense Abolitionism, up through Free Soil, and Republicanism, to the triumph in which we all unanimously joined, of voting for the national

[1] Stearns, pp. 242–61; Robinson, *Pen-Portraits*, pp. 92–107, 406–15; the Rev. W. A. Lucey, "How Strange Has Been My Fortune. The Civil War Letters of Patrick R. Guiney, Colonel of the Massachusetts Ninth," unpublished manuscript in possession of the Rev. Lucey, College of the Holy Cross, pp. 281–2; Persons, p. 103.

[2] Rogers, "Auto-Biography," Chs. 9, 10, 14; Commodore George H. Preble, U.S.N., *History of the Boston Navy Yard in Charlestown, Mass., from 1797 to 1875, with an Historical Introduction and Appendix* (1875, Film Microcopies of Records in the National Archives, No. 118, Washington, 1947), pp. 431, 365–6, 372, 379.

constitutional step which finally abolished slavery." Because there were but six "Copperheads" in the lower house, Rogers considered the soil ideal for the planting of labor reforms.[3]

Meantime, Boston's labor leaders had determined that reduction of the hours of labor was the foremost reform on their agenda. In September 1863 the Machinists' and Blacksmiths' International Union in convention in Boston adopted a resolution proposed by Ira Steward pledging it to campaign "until *over-work*, AS A SYSTEM, is prohibited. . . ." When Steward and two fellow machinists approached the Boston Trades Assembly for help in this effort, the latter responded by establishing its own committee of three, appropriating $400 to match that already put up by the Machinists and Blacksmiths, and resolving that "a reduction of the number of hours for a day's work, be the cardinal point to which our movement ought to be directed. . . ."[4]

Labor's new agitation fell on soil well prepared by the developments of the preceding decade and a half. Boston's delegates to the Radical German Convention of 1863, with Karl Heinzen as their spokesman, urged that assembly vigorously, if unsuccessfully, to demand a legal limit of eight hours to the working day.[5] Prominent abolitionists endorsed the cause in the following three years, among them William F. Channing, Josiah Abbott, Rufus Wyman, and Ezra Heywood.[6] From New York, Gerrit Smith sent Ira Steward a check annually to help his work.[7] William Lloyd Garrison also sent a contribution and wrote in 1866 that he supported the labor reformers on "the same principle which has led me to abhor and oppose the unequalled oppression of the black laborers of the South."[8] In short, the widely accepted notion that among

---

[3] Rogers, "Auto-Biography," 14:4–6.
[4] Ira Steward to Boston Trades Assembly, Nov. 17, 1863; note on resolution of Boston Trades Assembly, both in Ira Steward Papers, Box 3.
[5] Hermann Schlüter, *Die Internationale in Amerika: Ein Beitrag zur Geschichte der Arbeiter-Bewegung in den Vereinigten Staaten* (Chicago, 1918), p. 450.
[6] Persons, p. 103; *Daily Evening Voice*, Jan. 2, 1866 (on Wyman).
[7] Ira Steward to F. A. Sorge (dated only "Tuesday"), Steward Papers, Box 3.
[8] W. L. Garrison to Ira Steward, March 20, 1866, in *Daily Evening Voice*, May 2, 1866. This position was a complete reversal of the stand

the antislavery men of the Bay State Wendell Phillips alone
was sympathetic to labor's cause is pure myth.[9] For most of
these doughty warriors the emancipation of the slaves meant
simply that they took time off for one lusty cheer (or fervent
prayer of thanks) before plunging back into the work of
improving the world. Their spirit was typified by Abby Kelley
Foster, whose farm was confiscated when she was quite elderly
because she refused to pay taxes to a government which
would not let her vote. This lady wrote her daughter in 1870:
"Your father went to a County temperance meeting in Webster
yesterday and this evening is to be at a debate on the labor
question in town. We are all on the go. . . ."[1]

The agitation bore fruit in March 1865 when John W.
Mahan, a Boston lawyer who had served as a captain under
Patrick Guiney in the Ninth Massachusetts, moved in the state
House that the legislature establish a committee to investigate
the hours of labor and the propriety of legislation on the
subject. When the proposal passed, Speaker Bullock called
Edward Rogers to his chamber and asked him to select the
members of the committee. Senator Martin Griffin chaired the
group, and Rogers and Mahan were among the members, as
was Charles McLean, a millwright turned legislator who was
to represent the State Labor Union of Massachusetts at the
National Labor Congress of 1870.[2]

In May the committee issued its report. Not only did all
the workingmen interviewed want an eight-hour day, it declared, but such a change would not hurt industry. In fact, the
shorter day would increase both the quantity and quality of
production, thus benefiting the community as a whole. The
issue, furthermore, involved a moral question higher than this
economic one, namely, "the protection, preservation and ad-

Garrison had taken in 1831 when he denounced the labor movement.
Schlüter, *Lincoln, Labor and Slavery*, p. 41.
[9] *Eg.*, Hofstadter, *American Political Tradition*, pp. 157–8; Foner, *Labor*,
I, 394; Oscar Sherwin, *Prophet of Liberty, the Life and Times of
Wendell Phillips* (New York, 1958), pp. 574–5; Donald, pp. 29–33.
[1] Abby Kelley Foster to Alla W. Foster, Dec. 9, 1870, in Stephen S.
Foster Papers. On the Foster family's eviction see W. L. Garrison to
Abby K. Foster, Feb. 16, 1874; John T. Sargent to Abby K. Foster,
Feb. 25, 1874, *ibid.*
[2] Rogers, "Auto-Biography," 14:4–15, 15:2–3; John W. Mahan to *Boston
Journal*, Sept. 27, 1864, clipping in Guiney Papers.

vancement of man." Stating that "evidence presented almost challenged belief" and revealed the growth of "cringing servility and supineness . . . want of confidence and growing ignorance" among the working classes, who once had been characterized by "manly and sturdy independence," the report concluded: "The state is composed of *men,* and the interest, progress, and advancement of man is the foundation upon which the state rests."[3]

The committee did not recommend any legislation. It merely proposed that the governor appoint a commission of five unpaid members to make a thorough study of hours of labor and conditions in industry and submit its findings to the next legislature.[4] But the ideological significance of the report is immense. The foremost demand of labor reform had been given a clear sanction in terms of the nationalist and utilitarian formulas of the Radicals themselves. The eight-hour day was endorsed for the community good and to be advanced by state action for that end. Reducing hours of labor would hurt no one, help everyone. Thus there would be no need for one class to fight another over the subject. The state could act for the common weal.

For labor reformers the legislative report had an added significance. It provided them for the first time with an official document with which to support their case, and the fact that the report was unanimous lifted their spirits still higher. Ira Steward mailed a copy to Jonathan Fincher, inscribed with his own joyful couplet:

Let all now cheer, who never cheered before,
And those who always cheer, now cheer the more.[5]

Thus by 1865 the Bay State's labor movement had emerged stronger than ever and once again made a common front with middle-class reformers. This relationship, as seen from the standpoint of the workingmen, was underscored by the prospectus of Boston's excellent labor paper, the *Daily*

[3] Massachusetts House of Representatives, *Report of the Joint Special Committee on the Apprentice System, to whom was referred the Order of March 8th, Instructing the Committee to Inquire as to the Propriety of Reducing the Hours of Labor,* House Doc., 1865, No. 259 (Boston, 1865), pp. 3–5. (Hereafter cited as *Mass. Labor Report, 1865.*)
[4] *Ibid.,* p. 7.
[5] *Fincher's Trades Review,* May 13, 1865.

Evening Voice. The journal proclaimed its political position "RADICAL BUT INDEPENDENT" and explained: "It advocates the cause of the working classes, believing that the claims made in their behalf are not only consistent with, but conducive and essential to, the GENERAL WELFARE." The "independence, intelligence, and moral development of the masses," it continued, "are the only sure foundation of our Republican System of Government." For this reason, the prospectus concluded, the *Voice* was "friendly" to all causes tending toward these ends, especially "EQUAL SUFFRAGE," and it "recognizes no distinctions or preferences founded on RACE OR COLOR."[6]

Simultaneous with these dramatic developments among basically Protestant Radicals and labor reformers was a remarkable intellectual awakening among the Irish Catholics. A labor movement as effective as that produced by Massachusetts in the 1860's and 1870's could never have been created by the Protestant workers alone—and it was not. By the late sixties increasing numbers of Catholics were emerging from behind the psychological walls of the ghetto to join, at times even to lead, labor organizations. The new and significant Irish figure in America was not the Ribbonman or Molly Maguire, for his mentality was simply anti-Protestant. His dividing line between friend and foe was ethnic, not political or class. Thus the most eloquent of Fenian writers remarked that "it was easier both in 1848 and in the Fenian times to make a rebel of an Orangeman than of a Ribbonman."[7] The new figure was exemplified by William McLaughlin, leader of the huge shoemakers' union in 1869; his successor, Thomas Ryan; John Siney, guiding light of the anthracite miners' union; or Hugh McLaughlin of Chicago, president of the iron puddlers' national organization after 1871.[8] These men were leaders not of ethnic organizations but of workers' organizations. By the 1880's the majority of American labor unions would be headed by Catholics of Irish descent, but in the sixties this role was

---

[6] Prospectus, *Daily Evening Voice,* eg., April 3, 1867.
[7] O'Leary, I, 111. See also Roney, pp. 77, 95–100.
[8] See on W. J. McLaughlin, *Workingman's Advocate,* June 19, 1869; on Siney, Charles Edward Killeen, "John Siney: The Pioneer in American Industrial Unionism and Industrial Government," unpublished doctoral dissertation (Univ. of Wisconsin, 1942); on H. McLaughlin, *Workingman's Advocate,* Dec. 13, 1873.

new for them. Furthermore, the new role of trade unionist subjected the traditional role of Catholic-Democrat to severe stress.[9]

The battering ram that first breached the walls of ethnic isolation, however, was not labor reform, but the Irish nationalist movement. The confluence of the struggles for preservation of the American Union and for separation of Ireland from Britain roused the ardor of America's immigrants from Eiren as had (and could) no other issue, bringing them into conflict with their Church and party leaders here, and making them henceforth contributors, rather than obstacles, to the Radical and labor-reform trends of the decade.

The Fenian Brotherhood, founded in 1857, had four characteristics that set it apart from earlier, or later, separatist movements in Ireland. First, it was a secret society whose aim was, by use of armed force, to "make Ireland an independent Democratic Republic," in the words of the Fenian oath.[1] Thus it rejected not only the parliamentary methods employed earlier by Daniel O'Connell's "Repealers" but also any home rule solution, which would have meant retaining either a tie to England or a monarchy.

In this respect they were similar to the Young Irelanders, who led the uprising of 1848. In fact, their leader, James Stephens, and many prominent Fenians on the American side of the ocean were erstwhile Young Irelanders, such as John O'Mahoney and John Savage.[2] But, secondly, they differed from the insurrectionists of '48 in that, while the latter were almost exclusively middle class, student, or gentry in background, the great strength of the Fenians was among industrial workers. The movement was purely nationalist in ideology and objectives, with scarcely a trace of awareness of "labor issues," but its recruits were workingmen and soldiers, and its strength was urban.[3] Thus in the revolutionary history

---

[9] See George E. McNeill, *The Labor Movement: The Problem of To-Day* (New York, 1887); Browne, *Catholic Church and the Knights of Labor;* Edward and Eleanor Marx Aveling, *The Labour Movement in America* (London, 1888); Marc Karson, *American Labor Unions and Politics, 1900–1918* (Carbondale, Ill., 1958).

[1] Oath reproduced in O'Leary, I, 120.

[2] *Ibid.,* I, 15.

[3] *Ibid.,* I, 30–2, II, 141, 238; Devoy, *Recollections,* pp. 118–20, 160–84;

of Ireland it stands as a halfway house between the Liberals of
1848 and the Socialists of 1916. Third, the Fenians operated
from bases on both sides of the Atlantic. The brotherhood was
founded in America, but its founders sent emissaries to James
Stephens asking him to take command in the Old Country.
During the Civil War, an Irish Republican government was
established in New York. America's Irish, operating from their
sheltered sanctuary, were to supply the men, money, and
materials to free the mother country.[4]

Finally, the Fenians belonged to the same Western intellectual current of nineteenth-century nationalism as the Radical Republicans. Fenianism and Ribbonism, John O'Leary
explained, had nothing in common but illegality. "Ribbonism
is purely agrarian and religious . . . while Fenianism is
purely national, i.e., anti-English."[5] In fact, the fatal weakness
of the Fenians (before their "New Departure" of the late
1870's) was that they were totally oblivious to the agrarian
question in Ireland, expecting an armed and enlightened
vanguard to carry the revolution alone—Blanqui style. But the
crucial point is that since Ireland, like America, was a nation
with several ethnic heritages, the Fenian doctrine of nationalism was necessarily akin to that of Elisha Mulford. It embraced men of all historical or ethnic backgrounds within the
physical boundaries of the island as part of the nation. Thus
Fenians boasted of their Protestant leaders in Belfast, or their
Mormon organizer in Dublin. Symbolic of the whole movement was the fiery young Patrick "Pagan" O'Laoghari, who
dubbed Christianity the curse of Ireland as it set brother
against brother, and adopted for himself a pre-Christian
"Irish" faith.[6]

Inevitably, such a movement came into conflict with the

Cole, *Immigrant City*, pp. 45–6; Roney, pp. 33–65; J. Dunsmore Clarkson, *Labour and Nationalism in Ireland* ("Columbia University Studies
in History, Economics and Public Law," Vol. CXX, No. 266; New York,
1925), pp. 159–62.
[4] This point is stressed in the antinationalist Philip H. Bagenal, *The
American Irish and Their Influence on Irish Politics* (Boston, 1882),
pp. 105–236.
[5] O'Leary, I, 111.
[6] Devoy, *Recollections;* Roney, pp. 53–75, 86–100. On O'Laoghari see
Devoy's Post-Bag, I, 65–6.

clergy. "Hell is not hot enough nor eternity long enough to punish the Fenians," Bishop David Moriarity of Kerry is alleged to have cried,[7] while the charge that James Stephens had enrolled in the French *Carbonari* echoed from pulpits all over the island.[8] The congress of the brotherhood held in Chicago in 1863 responded to these attacks by resolving to "protest against, repudiate and resist all interference with the legitimate exercise of our civic and social privileges as freemen under the American constitution on the part of those who may claim to represent or to receive instructions from any foreign potentate or foreign official whatsoever," for to submit would render them "unworthy" of American citizenship.[9] The Church saw red! Not only did this resolution express the basic error from which, said Pius IX, all others were derived (liberty of conscience), but its language resembled that of a Know-Nothing. The next year Archbishops Martin J. Spaulding of Philadelphia and J. B. Purcell of Cincinnati, and Bishops James Wood of Philadelphia and Duggan of Chicago all warned their flocks to avoid the Fenians. And in 1870 came the official denunciation from the Inquisition in Rome.[1]

The most rapid growth of Fenian circles in America took place quite naturally inside the Union army. Colonel John O'Mahony, the American "Head Centre" of the organization, and Brigadier General Thomas Smith, head of the circles inside the army, pursued a policy of close collaboration with Lincoln's administration, which in turn encouraged Fenians to recruit among the soldiers as a counterweight to Democratic influence.[2] Every Irish soldier was seen by O'Mahony as a trained recruit for the coming struggle in Ireland itself. Although the Fenian dream of 200,000 war veterans led by Philip E. Sheridan disembarking under arms in Cork was never to come to pass, by early 1866 there were in Ireland 150 former American army officers, ready to fight. James Stephens's military staff there consisted of five former captains and colonels of the United States Army, the most famous of

---

[7] Devoy, *Recollections*, p. 120.

[8] *Ibid.*, p. 118. For a pro-Church version of the conflict, see Macdonald, pp. 33–47.

[9] Quoted in Macdonald, pp. 35–6.

[1] *Ibid.*, pp. 36–47; O'Leary, II, 12, 140–41; Roney, pp. 69–75, 149.

[2] Gibson, pp. 174–80; Clemenceau, pp. 42–7.

whom were Colonel William G. Halpin, commander of a Kentucky regiment, and Colonel Richard O'Sullivan Burke of Meagher's Brigade.[3]

Some Irish nationalists went so far as to become Republicans. Although both General Thomas F. Meagher and Colonel Patrick Guiney were Republicans and nationalists, neither was a member of the brotherhood. On the other hand, ardently Republican Colonel Richard O'Sullivan Burke headed a Fenian circle in the army, and S. B. Conover, who had served as a surgeon in the army, later became a carpetbagger United States senator from Florida and offered his Fenian colleagues the use of his state for prisoner rescue operations. The *Irish Republic*, put out in Chicago by Michael Scanlan and Reverend David Bell (a former Presbyterian minister from Ireland), was pro-Republican. Among Fenians who had never left the Old Sod, sympathy to the Republicans was practically unanimous, and all the exiles who crossed the Atlantic in the late 1860's and early 1870's promptly identified themselves with Grant's party.[4] In 1867, Scanlan utilized such new arrivals as the nucleus for an Irish Republican Club in New York, presided over by Thomas J. Masterson, who was also prominent in the shoemakers' union and was later secretary of the Workingmen's Union of the city.[5]

But party affiliation is not the crucial consideration here. Most American Fenians voted Democratic, and all welcomed the journalistic support given them by John Mitchel, a former Young Irelander who had become intensely pro-slavery and pro-secession in America. At least two veterans of the Confederate army served the Fenians in Ireland: Ohio-born John McCafferty and Irish-born Thomas F. Bourke, who at the outbreak of war was a resident of New Orleans.[6] The important point is that during and immediately following the war, Irish

---

[3] Devoy, *Recollections*, pp. 92–6, 116–17. For examples of active Fenians who served in the U.S. Army, see *Devoy's Post-Bag*, I, 12, 24, 25, 28, 35, 45, 49, 80, 125, 155.

[4] Gen. Thomas Francis Meagher to Col. Patrick R. Guiney, Oct. 7, 1863, Guiney Papers; Devoy, *Recollections*, 347–52; *Devoy's Post-Bag*, I, 155; Roney, pp. 95, 173–9.

[5] Roney, p. 179; *New-York Times*, July 8, 1871.

[6] Gibson, pp. 174–80; *Devoy's Post-Bag*, I, 27, 37. Bourke later apologized to his Fenian comrades for his "mistake" in aiding the Confederacy. Devoy, *Recollections*, pp. 353–4.

soldiers and workmen in the United States flocked into the brotherhood. In Lawrence, Massachusetts, $5,200 and a hundred stands of arms were raised for the cause. Patrick Collins, organizing for the Fenians in the industrial towns of the state where the Irish population had been tightly repressed and withdrawn since the fifties, helped establish seventy-five circles by June 1865.[7]

The massive surge of men and money into the organization created both pressure for quick action and intense factional competition for leadership of the movement. Head Centre O'Mahony found himself challenged in 1865 by a faction led by William B. Roberts, a wealthy New York dry-goods merchant, which drew considerable support from the more committed Democrats in the movement, who feared the partisan drift of the men around O'Mahony. It was the Roberts (or "Senate") faction that sponsored the plan to invade Canada and hold it hostage for the liberation of Ireland. While Stephens and his staff in Ireland protested in anguish against this diversion of funds and energy, two attacks on Canada were mounted, one on June 1, 1866, by the Roberts group, and the second six days later by supporters of the Head Centre, who dared not be left out of the action. Both were handily routed by the Canadian militia, and their participants interned by either Canadian or American authorities.[8]

The comic-opera character of the Canadian fiasco tempts the historian to regard it, in Oscar Handlin's terms, as "a distraction for a time."[9] It was certainly disastrous to the revolutionary schemes. British police raids in September 1865 had already crippled the conspiracy in Ireland. Their effectiveness made Stephens disregard the advice of his staff of Americans to strike in the Old Country early in 1866, and his failure to act in turn opened the way for advocates of the Canadian plan to come to the front, then for his own replacement in 1867 by Colonel Thomas J. Kelly, a veteran of Missionary Ridge. Kelly's effort to resuscitate the revolt in the Emerald Isle by bringing eight thousand Springfield rifles and a hand-

[7] Cole, *Immigrant City*, p. 46; O'Hare, pp. 36–46.
[8] Gibson, pp. 180–8; Rhodes, VI, 214; *American Annual Cyclopaedia*, VI (1866), 286–8; O'Leary, II, 213–33.
[9] Handlin, *Boston's Immigrants*, p. 218.

ful of experienced military men of several countries from New York aboard the *Erin's Hope* was frustrated by a watchful British coast guard. The futility of all this expenditure of lives and energy plunged the Fenians into hopeless factional bickering.[1] On the other hand, Gustave-Paul Cluseret, a French participant in the uprising, significantly saw the Fenians' assault on Canada as the "last act of the War of Secession."[2]

Certainly, for the Irish-American, the dual struggle against secession and against England left an important legacy. First, it offered the Republicans a marvelous opportunity to solicit Irish votes. The task of enforcing the neutrality laws against the invaders of Canada fell upon the Johnson administration. Despite the fact that General George G. Meade, who was sent to seal the border, carried out his task with a minimum of zeal,[3] the commander of the Fenians in Buffalo blamed his defeat on "the extreme vigilance of the Government of the United States."[4]

In the election campaign of 1866, Democrats often advocated Irish independence from the stump, but they had been boxed into the position of advising caution and apologizing for the actions of the President. Republican leaders, on the other hand, lionized the nationalists who had been imprisoned in Canada, and led by N. P. Banks and Robert Schenck, called upon the administration to recognize a lawful state of war between Ireland and England. In September the Fenian Congress responded by adopting resolutions of praise for the congressional Radicals and openly aiding their election campaign. Governor Oglesby of Illinois and even former Know-Nothing Schuyler Colfax were provided with speaking platforms at Fenian picnics. In New York the Fenian organ *Irish American* opposed the National Union candidate for governor, John A. Dix, and helped swing Irish votes to Republican Reuben Fenton.[5] So alert did New York's Democrats become

---

[1] Devoy, *Recollections*, pp. 238–9, 275–6; O'Hare, pp. 46–64; Bagenal, pp. 134–48; General [Gustave-Paul] Cluseret, "My Connection with Fenianism," *Fraser's Magazine*, New Series VI (July 1872), pp. 31–41.

[2] Cluseret, p. 31.

[3] Devoy, *Recollections*, pp. 116–17.

[4] Quoted in *American Annual Cyclopaedia*, VI (1866), 288.

[5] Beale, *Critical Year*, pp. 301–4; Gibson, pp. 188–92; *American Annual Cyclopaedia*, VI (1866), 288; Cole, *Era of the Civil War*, pp. 345–7;

to the perils of this issue that their paper *Irish Citizen* in 1868 busily scotched rumors of new Fenian attacks on Canada, advised Irish voters that neither party would actually aid the independence of their homeland, and urged them to vote Democratic "on American grounds."[6]

Secondly, the labor-reform press threw its support behind the Fenians. The *Daily Evening Voice* of Boston linked Ireland with America's Manifest Destiny, stating that "Americans fully endorse" the independence of Ireland and that the country was full of "combustible Irishmen" and "acquisitive Yankees" who might, if provoked (for instance, by the execution of captured Fenians), come to consider Canada a desirable "speculation in real estate."[7] Labor's nomination of Irish nationalist Patrick Guiney for Congress that fall symbolically sealed the new alliance.[8] Simultaneously, the International Workingmen's Association both in London and in New York made Irish independence a major demand. The subjugation of Ireland, explained Karl Marx, was the bulwark of England's landed aristocracy, the foremost source of cheap labor for England's *bourgeoisie*, and the root of national hostilities not only within the English working class but also between workers in England and those in the United States. Since England was the only country in the world where industry had matured sufficiently to make it ripe for socialism, he conti.1ued, "to hasten the social revolution in England is the most important object of the International Workingmen's Association. The sole means of hastening it is to make Ireland independent." In conclusion, he advised two organizers for the I.W.A. in New York: *"A coalition of the German workers with the Irish* (as well as with those English and American workers who are ready to do so) is the most important job you could start at the present time."[9]

Willard H. Smith, *Schuyler Colfax, The Changing Fortunes of a Political Idol* (Indianapolis, 1952), pp. 240–2; McPherson, *Reconstruction*, pp. 113–14; Cole, *Immigrant City*, p. 46.

[6] *Irish Citizen*, July 11, 1868 (two editorials).

[7] Editorial, *Daily Evening Voice*, Oct. 30, 1866.

[8] See below, pp. 271–3.

[9] Karl Marx to [Siegfried] Meyer and [August] Vogt, April 9, 1870, in Marx, *Letters to Americans*, pp. 77–80; F. A. Sorge, "Die Arbeiterbewegung in den Vereinigten Staaten, 1866–1876," *Die Neue Zeit*, X, 1st Band (1891–2), pp. 393–4. (Hereafter cited as Sorge, "1866–1876.")

Finally, although many Irish workers became disillusioned or even disgusted with Fenianism per se,[1] they had been drawn into the mainstream of national life. Irish votes were not by definition Democratic in 1866 or in the following six years, and the Grant administration courted them avidly.[2] More important, new intellectual horizons had been opened for thousands of Irishmen, who had found themselves ignoring the priest and viewing the Democrat with suspicion. No longer were the Irish the *Vendée* of labor reform in Massachusetts. They were now free to meet the reactivated Protestant workers on common grounds. How far the results could go was demonstrated in the spring of 1869 when lodges of the Knights of St. Crispin held first-anniversary celebrations all over the state. Shoe towns everywhere halted all work for a day of picnics, parades, and speeches by local dignitaries. A report from Abington noted that Crispin banners bearing the flexed arm holding a shoemaker's hammer flew beside "American and Irish flags, typical of the unity of race and feeling on the occasion."[3]

The Crispin celebrations, furthermore, made it unmistakably clear that the labor-reform movement had established itself by the end of the Civil War decade as a force to be reckoned with in American political and economic life. More than a thousand members of Whittier Lodge proudly bore their regalia past their new $16,000 union building to Haverhill's City Hall, where they were greeted by their district's representative in the state legislature. Trains bore fraternal delegations from all parts of the state to enjoy speeches, poetry, concerts, and a grand ball lasting late into the evening.[4] The organized power represented by such workers was destined to exert a significant influence on the social upheaval of the 1860's—one which had not been anticipated by Conservatives, Democrats, or Radicals.

---

[1] John Boyle O'Reilly to John Devoy, Feb. 13, 1871, in *Devoy's Post-Bag*, I, 30-2.
[2] See below, pp. 374-6.
[3] *American Workman*, July 3, 1869.
[4] *Ibid.*, May 1869.

CHAPTER 4

Labor-Reform
Organizations

The war-inspired efforts to improve the social and economic
plight of the working classes produced a vast array of reform
societies. Among them can be distinguished four major types
of organizations: reform associations, trade unions, sections of
the International Workingmen's Association, and labor
parties. These groups are most meaningfully differentiated,
not in terms of ideology or membership—in these areas each
overlapped significantly with each other—but rather in terms
of structure and function. All were constituent parts of the
labor-reform movement. All were at least partially represented
in the National Labor Union at the epitome of its career,
1869–70.

Reform associations were primarily educational and agita-
tional in purpose, and they admitted to membership anyone
who subscribed to their principles. Some—like the Ten Hour
Leagues that met in nearly every New England mill town, or
the New Democracy, in which colleagues of the late George

Henry Evans continued to preach his land-reform doctrines—
were rooted in the ideas, methods of work, and personnel of
prewar movements. Typical of such bodies was the Ten Hour
League of Lowell, whose spokesman declared that in the six
years following its establishment in 1866 the group's working-
class membership had sometimes numbered in "hundreds, and
had a controlling influence over legislative elections," while at
other times "it has dwindled to a mere handful in numbers
and to zero in influence." The sustaining influence in the
league derived from "certain energetic spirits, who have risen
from the wage-labor class, but have retained a generous
sympathy from [sic] the class from which they have sprung.
. . . "[1]

Boston's Eight Hour Leagues and Workingmen's Institute
(and its successor, the Labor Reform Institute) brought
craftsmen together with legislators and professional or propertied men and women under the ideological leadership of Ira
Steward. When Steward's associate George McNeill became
deputy director of the Massachusetts Bureau of Statistics of
Labor in 1869, these groups acquired both an official voice and
close institutional ties with the state's Republican administration.[2] These and other reform associations of the area, several
major trade unions, and Boston sections of the International
were all represented after 1869 in at least some of the sessions
of the New England Labor Reform League. Ezra H. Heywood, a Worcester anarchist who listed his occupation as
"lecturer," was the guiding spirit of these conventions, which
gathered shoemakers and legislators, craftsmen and clergymen, Heywood and McNeill—whose careers in labor reform
were only beginning—and such honored veterans of the turbulent forties as William H. Channing and Stephen S. Foster.[3]

The membership of such New England groups resembled
that of the Industrial Congresses of the 1840's, but newer
reform associations were made up almost exclusively of skilled

---

[1] Charles Cowley, quoted in *Mass. BLS, 1873*, p. 287.
[2] On the Labor Reform Institute, see *American Workman*, May 1869.
On the Eight Hour League, see below, pp. 369, 413. On the origins of
the B.L.S., see *Mass. BLS, 1873*, pp. 5–41.
[3] *American Workman*, June 5, 1869; letter of W. G. H. Smart, *Labor
Leader*, March 6, 1897.

workmen. The Workingmen's Union and Independent Order of Friendship, for example, launched in Nashville, Tennessee, late in 1867, was a society of craftsmen who stood for "cutting loose from existing parties" and entering labor politics. Prominent among them was William Saffin, who was to become president of the Iron Molders' International Union in 1869.[4] Similarly, the Labor Reform Association of St. Louis, established the same year, was headed by O. B. Daley, who went on to succeed Jonathan Fincher as president of the Machinists and Blacksmiths.[5] The largest such organization was the Supreme Mechanical Order of the Sun, a secret society with an elaborate ritual and several degrees of membership, which had been founded during the war. Its representative at the 1868 National Labor Congress was John J. Junio of Syracuse, who was then also president of the Cigar Makers' International Union.[6] At the time of its origin in 1869 the Noble Order of the Knights of Labor was simply another secret society of this type.[7]

In 1868 the National Labor Union undertook to integrate this profusion of workingmen's societies into its permanent structure. Constitutional revisions of that year empowered the vice-presidents of the N.L.U. to organize workingmen in their states into labor-reform parties and to charter organizations of friends of the N.L.U. "who have no international or national unions. . . . " Furthermore, any seven workers could obtain a charter for their group from the N.L.U., provided there was no local union of their trade in the vicinity. Such bodies were to be known as "labor unions." Carefully hedged against infringing on the jurisdictional claims of trade unions, the labor

---

[4] Letter from Nashville, *Workingman's Advocate*, Sept. 7, 1867; letter of H. N. Cramer, *Revolution*, I, 411 (July 2, 1868). John Andrews calls Saffin "primarily" a trade unionist, in contrast to the reformer Sylvis, but note the origins of Saffin's labor career. Commons, *Labour*, II, 152.

[5] *Daily Evening Voice*, May 27, 1867. Daley's name was often spelled *Dailey*.

[6] McNeill, *Labor Movement*, p. 125; Frank T. Carlton, "Ephemeral Labor Movements, 1866–1889," *Popular Science Monthly*, No. 85 (Nov. 1914), p. 493; *Proceedings of the Second Session of the National Labor Union, in Convention Assembled, at New York City, Sept. 21, 1868* (Philadelphia, 1868), pp. 3–4.

[7] Ware, *Labor Movement*, pp. 23–5.

unions were the predecessors of the more famous mixed assemblies of the Knights of Labor. By the 1869 Congress twenty-seven of them had been chartered; another 124 formed the following year. A few established associations, such as the Workingmen's Union and Independent Order of Friendship, which became Labor Union No. 1 of Nashville, sought the charters offered by the N.L.U. Many more continued to send delegates to the labor congresses while they remained structurally independent. At both the 1869 and 1870 congresses nine labor unions were represented, while fourteen autonomous societies—ranging from the National Guard of Industry in Washington through the Excelsior League of Stoneham, Massachusetts, to the National Improvement Association of Millstown, Pennsylvania—sent their delegates.[8]

The new labor unions proved especially effective in enlisting mechanics, professionals, politicians, and frequently farmers of the South and West into the labor movement. The group in Black River Falls, Wisconsin, listed as the occupations of its officers: grain miller, blacksmith, cooper, gunsmith, farmer, and mason.[9] Those in Vicksburg and Water Valley, Mississippi, were made up primarily of foundry and railroad workers, but supplied platforms from which conservative politicians attacked their state's Republican regime.[1] The State Labor Union of Kansas, under which twenty-one subordinate bodies were chartered, grew out of a violent dispute between settlers on the Cherokee Neutral Tract and the federal government over railroad land grants. Its foremost spokesman was Hugh Cameron, who had come to "Bleeding Kansas" through the Emigrant Aid Company, later served as a lieutenant colonel in the Union cavalry, and was still active as a member of the General Co-operative Board of the Knights of Labor in the mid-eighties.[2] Less rural in composition was the State

---

[8] N.L.U. Proceedings, 1868, p. 26; Workingman's Advocate, Sept. 24, 1869, Aug. 27, 1870.

[9] Weekly American Workman, June 26, 1869.

[1] Workingman's Advocate, Jan. 11, 1868. See also below, pp. 403–4 on A. M. West and the N.L.U. in Mississippi.

[2] Workingman's Advocate, Aug. 27, 1870; Daniel W. Wilder, Annals of Kansas (Topeka, Kansas, 1875), pp. 52, 283, 507–32; Journal of United Labor, V (Oct. 25, 1884), 826; ibid., VI (Oct. 25, 1885), 1112.

Labor Union of Nebraska, which drew its members primarily from Omaha, where it was led by Frank Roney, secretary of the local molders' union, and Clinton Briggs, former abolitionist, then an elderly and prosperous lawyer and railroad promoter.[3] The Kansas and Nebraska arms of the N.L.U. served historically as instruments through which labor's currency-reform doctrines reached the farmers of the Great Plains.

Side by side with the reform associations grew the trade unions. Although the two types of organizations often shared members and proclaimed similar ultimate objectives, their functions were quite different. The trade union was an organization of workers in a given occupation which sought through the establishment of work rules and standard wages to regulate the conditions under which its members worked.

Education, mutual insurance, and agitation to influence the conduct of government were always part of the trade-union program. Union lodges often provided reading and music rooms for their members and offered them lectures on diverse topics. A single meeting of Carpenters' and Joiners' Union No. 88 in Boston, for example, heard guest speakers on currency reform, health, the menace of Chinese immigration, and efforts to shorten the working day.[4] Similarly, although few national unions provided effective mutual insurance schemes in this decade (such as the $5 weekly disability benefits and $30 burial payment given by the Workingmen's Benevolent Association), many if not most local unions had some such funds—at least enough to buy a coffin for a deceased member.[5] But fraternal activities were peripheral, and education followed the close of the regular order of business. Above all, union practice everywhere banned divi-

[3] *Workingman's Advocate*, Sept. 4, 11, 1869; Roney, pp. 198–205.
[4] *Weekly American Workman*, Aug. 21, 1869. On reading rooms, etc., see testimony on the K.O.S.C. in *Mass. BLS, 1870*, p. 357.
[5] Killeen, p. 143; Vidkunn Ulriksson, *The Telegraphers: Their Craft and Their Unions* (Washington, D.C., 1953), pp. 15–18; Edwin Clyde Robbins, *Railway Conductors, A Study in Organized Labor* (New York, 1914), p. 20. For examples of local union benefit funds in Ohio, see *Third Annual Report of the Bureau of Labor Statistics Made to the General Assembly of Ohio for the Year 1879* (Columbus, 1880), pp. 259–62. (Hereafter cited as *Ohio BLS, 1879*.)

sive partisan issues. "No subject of a political or religious nature shall at any time be entertained," proclaimed the typical union constitution.[6] Regulation of the terms under which workers in particular trades sold the use of their strength and skills was what distinguished the union from other forms of labor organizations and determined the evolution of its structure.

It is probably safe to say that a larger proportion of the industrial labor force enrolled in trade unions during the years immediately preceeding the depression of 1873 than in any other period of the nineteenth century. At the end of 1872 the Massachusetts Bureau of Statistics of Labor, in answer to an inquiry from Senator Sumner on the state of labor organizations in America, turned for information to William J. Jessup, head of the Workingmen's Assembly of New York State. Jessup listed twenty-one national and international unions then in operation. He indicated further that there were hundreds of trade unions which operated on a local level only and had no affiliation with any national group. In all, he reckoned "fully 1,500 Trades Unions existing in the United States at the present time."[7] Jessup did not attempt to estimate the total number of trade-union members; but the previous year Richard J. Hinton had put the figure at 300,000. Despite the facts that there were eight national unions of which Jessup knew and Hinton did not, and that William Sylvis had put the number of trade unionists at 600,000 already in 1868, Hinton's oft-quoted figure is plausible. Known membership of trade unions then ranged between 20 and 2,000, so that an average membership of 200, which Hinton's calculation implies, is certainly credible. In fact, the conclusion reached by a *New-York Times* survey in January 1870 that the sixteen major

---

[6] *Constitution and By-Laws of Erie Typographical Union No. 77* (Erie, Pa., 1869), p. 16. *Cf. Constitution, By-Laws, and Rules of Order of Scranton Typographical Union, No. 112* (Scranton, Pa., 1870), p. 34; *Constitution and Rules of Order of the Iron Molders' Union of North America* (Cincinnati, 1876), p. 45.

[7] *Mass. BLS, 1873*, pp. 251–8. (The quotation is on p. 256.) For a general evaluation of trade-union strength at various points in the nineteenth century, see Lloyd Ulman, *Rise of the National Trade Union: The Development and Significance of Its Structure, Governing Institutions, and Economic Policies* (Cambridge, Mass., 1955), p. 19.

national and international unions of the land alone had an aggregate membership of 184,121 suggests that Hinton's 300,000 figure was on the conservative side.[8]

But the reason estimates of membership vary widely is that while thousands enrolled in unions, only hundreds, at best, consistently paid dues and took part in their mundane daily activities. American unions operated then as now on the theory that once a worker in a given trade joins the union, he may never leave it except by expulsion or by quitting the trade.[9] Thus one may never pay the initiation fee twice in a lifetime. The "lapsed" member must either redeem all unpaid dues or be forgiven them by special dispensation. This assumption led in the 1860's to wildly misleading claims of membership. The Massachusetts Grand Lodge of Knights of St. Crispin, for example, when seeking a charter from the state legislature in 1870, boasted of 40,000 members, but its income for that year indicated that its dues-payers could not possibly have exceeded 8,400. The membership book of Unity Lodge No. 23 in Lynn reveals that almost 2,000 lasters paid the initiation fee of one dollar (two dollars starting in 1872) between May 1868 and August 1872, but few if any of them consistently kept up their dues payments. Yet, as John P. Hall argues, "the whole 2,000 thought of themselves as Crispins, because only acceptance of the order's purposes was considered obligatory."[1] Small wonder that calculations of national Crispin membership varied from 30,000 to 80,000.[2] With some validity, therefore, Hinton could call the K.O.S.C. the "largest trades union in the world," but its membership was certainly not comparable to the 33,600 workmen enrolled in England's Amalgamated Society of Engineers at that time,

---

[8] Richard J. Hinton, "Organization of Labor: Its Aggressive Phases," *Atlantic Monthly*, Vol. 27 (May 1871), p. 558; *N.L.U. Proceedings, 1868*, p. 56; *New-York Times*, Jan. 18, 1870.

[9] Ulman, pp. 92–107.

[1] John Philip Hall, "The Knights of St. Crispin in Massachusetts, 1869–1878," *Journal of Economic History*, Vol. XVIII (June 1957), pp. 161–2; Membership Book, Unity Lodge No. 32 K.O.S.C., in Lynn Lasters' Union Papers, Baker Library.

[2] *Cf.* Hinton, "Organization of Labor," p. 558; Don D. Lescohier, *The Knights of St. Crispin, 1867–1874* ("Bulletin of the University of Wisconsin," Economics and Political Science Series, VII; Madison, Wis., 1912), pp. 7–8; McNeill, *Labor Movement*, p. 200.

for the systematic bookkeeping and dues collection of the latter set a standard no American labor organization could then duplicate.[3]

In fact, the central feature of trade-union evolution during the 1860's was the emergence of embryonic organizational controls over the membership. Such controls derived necessarily from the function of the trade union as an institution, a function well described in the preamble to the Crispin's constitution: "Recognizing the right of the manufacturer or capitalist to control his capital, we also claim and shall exercise the right to control our labor, and to be consulted in determining the price paid for it—a right hitherto denied us. . . ."[4]

In contrast to the manufacturer's control of his capital, which rested upon individual property, the workers' control of their labor could be exerted only through concerted action. The term "collective bargaining" cannot be applied to trade unionism in the sixties, however—not because working-class action was not collective, but because it involved precious little bargaining. Negotiations between the two contending parties were almost unknown before 1866. In the typical strike of craftsmen, union members in a particular trade met and decided among themselves what price they would charge for their labor. They then announced that after a given date no member might be employed by anyone for less than the wage decided upon. When the deadline arrived, any employer who paid the union scale kept his men and went on with his work. An owner who refused to pay the scale was placed on a "rat list," and the union then undertook to keep all workers away from the "rat shop." The union considered itself victorious if all (or the bulk) of its members were soon employed somewhere at the union scale. Thus, at the end of a successful strike of carpenters in New York City, the strike committee reported that its desk "has for two days been covered with cards of employers wanting journeymen at $4 a day, and not a solitary carpenter was unemployed."[5]

If, on the other hand, the employers effectively resisted or

---

[3] Hinton, "Organization of Labor," p. 558; *Royal Comm. on Trades Unions,* p. 28.
[4] Lescohier, p. 60.
[5] *Daily Evening Voice,* May 6, 1867.

replaced the strikers, the union was shattered, at least for the
time being. Having declared its price, or "rule," the union was
forced either to rescind the rule and accept the owners' terms
or to keep the rule and watch the members desert union ranks
in order to find the only work available—work at a wage rate
below union scale. Occasionally, long strikes were sustained
by the workers: 348 molders in Philadelphia, for example,
closed the city's iron foundries for several months in 1863 by
finding other jobs (97 of them went into the army) and
ultimately won acceptance of their rule.[6] Most trade unionists
in the country, however, would have concurred with the
"axiom" Frederick Merk applied to Wisconsin: "A strike lasting longer than three days was lost."[7]

The tactics of the early sixties, in short, were dangerously
brittle. Often unions were compelled to declare amnesties for
former members who had "ratted," allowing them back into
the ranks despite the fact that they had violated the rules,
because such rats had come to outnumber the stalwarts.[8] At
other times a strike might ultimately be abandoned as futile.
The thirty-three molders of Brent's foundry in New York, for
example, all had new jobs after three months of striking, so the
union paid a committee of three to watch the shop and warn
off members, while the company simply continued in operation with new personnel.[9]

Union methods based on the unilateral adoption of rules
to control the sale of their labor were peculiarly appropriate
for the workmen who had progressed but partway down the
path from journeyman artisan to factory-wage labor. Not only
did their conduct resemble the behavior of a modern trade
association more closely than that of a modern labor union;
these patterns of action had been adopted by skilled craftsmen
in America as early as the end of the eighteenth century.[1] A
large measure of independence was preserved for each union
member, as each agreed to vend his commodity (his particular

---

[6] Sylvis, p. 55.
[7] Merk, p. 174.
[8] For examples of typographers', molders', and cigar makers' amnesties,
see Philadelphia *Public Ledger*, Sept. 7, 1868; Wolfe, pp. 158–9.
[9] Philadelphia *Public Ledger*, Aug. 26, 1868.
[1] See the testimony in *Commonwealth* v. *Pullis*, in Commons, *Doc. Hist.*,
III, 60–248, esp. 72–126.

skill) in accordance with rules adopted by the majority. No submission to the decisions of elected leaders was involved, and no delegation of authority to make rules was made to such leaders. For unskilled laborers, however, such practices were clearly impossible. Because these men had no peculiar training of which they were the exclusive merchandisers, they used different tactics. An example of their methods is provided by a strike of some fifteen hundred to two thousand New Jersey iron miners early in 1867. Led by a local political aspirant, they closed eighteen mines within two days by marching in a body from pit to pit, stopping teamsters from hauling ore, and, when the owners tried shipping ore by canal boat, filling in large sections of the canals. When state militia arrived to escort the boatmen, the strike was broken. It is noteworthy that even amidst this undisciplined action there was no violence, and the strikers allowed stationary engineers to continue working so that the mines would not be flooded. The miners sought to raise their wages from $1.65 to $2.00 a day, but, said proprietor Abram Hewitt: "They struck first without making any demand."[2]

A newspaper story from Boston in the same year told of similar labor tactics. Sailors in the city had organized a Seaman's Protective Union and passed a rule determining union wages. One shipowner, however, was provided with a crew by a waterfront boardinghouse keeper named Tom Bennett, who had been expelled from the union for his alleged part in a murder some six months earlier. A committee from the union went aboard the ship to persuade her captain not to sail without paying the union scale. At the call of the captain, fifty police went to Bennett's boardinghouse and escorted the "rat" crew to the ship in a wagon. A large crowd gathered and pelted the policemen and Bennett generously with bricks and rocks. After four participants in the crowd had been arrested, the ship sailed, manned by her nonunion crew.[3]

In a word, the unskilled workers relied on massive solidarity supplemented by intimidation of dissenters through

---

[2] *Royal Comm. on Trades Unions*, p. 6; New York *Daily Tribune*, April 11, 1867.
[3] *Daily Evening Voice*, Sept. 18, 1867.

social ostracism, threats, or riots. Their actions were more frequently community-based than workshop-based, all inhabitants of a residential neighborhood becoming involved in the strike action. Within the factory, the craftsmen usually were the only organized groups, but their trade organizations provided leadership to all employees in the industry. From 1862 through 1886, for example, Local 23 of the Iron Molders' Union acted in practice as spokesman for all the employees of the McCormick Harvesting Machine Company in Chicago, despite the fact that only some 10 per cent of the company's work force belonged to it. A study of this local has revealed that "the bargaining gains of this small band of skilled molders were immediately passed along to the unskilled foundry workers (equal in number to the molders), and usually to the entire plant, within a week or two."[4] The strong bond of common interest which this relationship fostered between skilled and unskilled was largely duplicated by the ties between the organized iron puddlers and the other mill hands in Pittsburgh.[5] In coal-mining towns skilled miners and laborers belonged to the same union, so that craft, work place, and community solidarity all combined to the advantage of the miners. "This was the best strike there had ever been in this country," wrote a miner of St. Clair County, Illinois. "We had support from the shopkeepers, farmers, and everyone else to stand out against our oppressors."[6]

Not always was this harmony evident, however. The mule spinners of New England formed a national union in 1866 and notified owners of the cotton mills that after April 1, 1867, no union member would work more than ten hours daily. These craftsmen ignored the aspirations of the tens of thousands of unskilled hands who toiled in the same mills, and the unskilled reciprocated the treatment. While some 60 union spinners were locked out in Manchester, 100 in Lowell, and 150 in Lawrence, all other departments of the mills continued to operate with full complements. By the end of two weeks the

4 Ozanne, p. 133.
5 See below, pp. 389–92.
6 Charles Evans to Editor, *Y Gwladgarwr*, Oct. 4, 1868, in Allan Conway, ed., *The Welsh in America. Letters from the Immigrants.* (Minneapolis, 1961), p. 181.

union spinners had either been replaced by the corporations or returned sheepishly to work.[7]

The first prerequisite of union success, therefore, was to enroll as members all workmen of the same trade seeking employment in any given local market—in other words, to establish a closed shop. Two methods were employed to secure union control of workshops. One was for the union to fine any members who worked beside nonunion men. The bricklayers' unions of New York, for example, charged members who worked with "rats" one dollar a day.[8] The second means, often used in conjunction with the first, was for union men to quit work and banner the shop if a worker was paid less than union scale, or perhaps even if a nonmember was hired.[9]

Such practices readily brought trade unions afoul of state conspiracy laws. The supreme court of New York held in 1867 that for journeymen to fix their own wages by a rule was perfectly legal, but for them to demand obedience from employers or journeymen who were not parties to the adoption of the rule was an indictable offense.[1] New Jersey courts ruled more broadly when they declared an effort by patent-leather workers to compel their employer to discharge nonunion members an "unwarrantable interference with the conduct of his affairs, a threat that they would disarrange his business," and hence a criminal conspiracy.[2] In short, the notion that *Commonwealth* v. *Hunt* put an end to conspiracy convictions of trade unions in 1842 is thoroughly misleading. William H. Jessup reported three conspiracy cases pending in the vicinity of New York City in the summer of 1868. These cases, like the famous Massachusetts ruling, all involved union efforts to exclude nonmembers from employment.[3] Thus one must con-

---

[7] *Daily Evening Voice*, March 7, April 1, 3, 5, 6, 9, 13, 16, 1867; Persons, pp. 111–12; *Strikes and Lockouts*, p. 1050.
[8] Philadelphia *Public Ledger*, July 16, 1867.
[9] See, for example, *Mass. BLS*, 1871, p. 119.
[1] *Master Stevedore's Association* v. *Peter H. Walsh*, 2 Daly 1.
[2] *State v. Donaldson and others*, 3 Vroom 151. Compare the similar New Jersey cases involving Newark coachmakers and hatters. Philadelphia *Public Ledger*, June 7, 1867; *Daily Evening Voice*, June 15, March 11, 1867.
[3] *N.L.U. Proceedings*, 1868, p. 12.

clude that it was not Justice Shaw's decision of 1842 that made conspiracy indictments of unions subside during the next two decades, but the absence of union activity.

No aspect of the trade-union effort to control the labor market caused organizations of the time more trouble than the easy entry into the market of untrained or partly trained workmen. One New York labor reformer considered the abundance of workmen knowing no more than the rudiments of their trades the foremost obstacle to the growth of trade unions. Having to pay such men union scale compelled employers to give them more than they were worth, "and the result is they are repeatedly discharged and kicked around."[4] Hostility toward the union was thus fanned both among such workmen and among their masters. On the other hand, to tolerate their employment at a rate below union scale would have undermined the scale and discouraged proprietors from hiring union men.[5] Unions, consequently, sought to control access of untrained or partially trained workmen through the enforcement of rules on apprenticeship, a subject which Sylvis said "has given us more trouble than all others combined."[6] Furious strikes, among them the lockout of Sylvis's molders in Troy, were initiated because of employer efforts to evade union rules by hiring large numbers of apprentices.[7] But the growing division of labor that attended the growth of the factory system made apprenticeship daily less desirable for many employers. "Each class of labor devotes itself to a speciality," the Massachusetts Bureau of Statistics of Labor reported of shoemaking in Lynn. "The use of machinery has virtually swept away the old race of shoemakers who could make up an entire shoe. . . . You can put into a shop a farm laborer from New Hampshire, and in three days he will learn

---

[4] Letter of J.T.C., *Workingman's Advocate*, June 26, 1869.
[5] See Robert F. Hoxie, *Trade Unionism in the United States* (New York, 1917), pp. 10–14, 279–95.
[6] *Proceedings of the Eighth Annual Session of the Iron Molders' International Union, in Convention Assembled, at Boston, Mass., January 2, 1867* (Philadelphia, 1867), p. 13. (Hereafter proceedings of this union will be cited thus: *I.M.I.U. Proceedings,* 186~)
[7] Jonathan P. Grossman, *William Sylvis, Pioneer of American Labor* ("Columbia University Studies in History, Economics, and Public Law," No. 516; New York, 1945), pp. 85–6, 94–9.

to do a part. There is comparatively nothing to learn, and so no apprenticeship is required."[8] In reply, the shoemakers attempted the ultimate in job control. The constitution of the Crispins provided: "No member of this order shall teach or aid in teaching any part or parts of boot or shoe making," except to his own son, without permission of a three-fourths vote of the lodge.[9]

The apprentice question involved New York's Bricklayers' Union in a sensational conspiracy trial in 1868, a case which revealed just how far both sides were prepared to carry their efforts. The case was heard during the time of New York City's great strike of bricklayers for an eight-hour day in 1868 and cast a pall over that struggle, but it did not arise out of that conflict. Henry B. Dawson, a lawyer of Weschester County, asked a building contractor named Peter Dunham to take on Dawson's eighteen-year-old son William and teach him the construction business. When the youth was set to laying bricks at one dollar a day, the Morrisania Bricklayers' Union notified Dunham that unless the boy was duly apprenticed according to union rules, none of the other men would work with him. In fact, only one man left the job—Dunham's foreman, a union member, who declared he could not afford the $15 fine the union would charge him for working with a rat. Dunham then fired the boy, and with the elder Dawson as his advocate, sued the union in a court of oyer and terminer for conspiracy to obstruct trade and commerce. Despite the fact that the overt act of the union consisted of one man's quitting his job, the union was found guilty and seven of its officers fined $25 to $50 apiece. The embattled master masons in New York City joyfully wired congratulations to Dunham and Dawson on their victory for the principle of free contract.[1]

Here, then, lay the problem that spurred the rapid evolution of trade-union structure and practices during the sixties. To control the labor supply by union rules was conceivable only if employer resistance was ineffective or if all workers

---

[8] *Mass. BLS, 1871*, pp. 242–3.
[9] Lescohier, p. 76.
[1] [Anon.], "Law and Labor," *Galaxy*, Vol. VI (Oct. 1868), pp. 566–7; Philadelphia *Public Ledger*, Aug. 28, 29, 1868; *Irish Citizen*, June 20, 1868.

who could enter the particular labor market in dispute were
reliable union members, or both. Although the former was
often the case, the latter never was.

Weakness of employer opposition was frequently the
secret of trade-union success. The secretary of an Ohio miners'
local boasted during the war: "If the masters do not give us
the wage we want, the consequence is a strike, and we have
been victorious every time."[2] Abram Hewitt explained such
concessions simply: "The capitalist yielded, and if the government was his customer, he made the government suffer for his
yielding."[3] Toward the close of the war many employers'
associations were organized to cope with trade unions, but the
competitive relationships among the many small employers
made their organizations even more unstable than those of
their workers. Between 1863 and 1865 the Louisville iron
founders, New York boss plasterers, and Buffalo ship owners
and builders all formed such leagues, and in Michigan a
general employers' association was established. All of them
were failures except the Buffalo organization, which was
backed by the Erie and New York Central railroads.[4] In the
Pittsburgh area coal jobbers sought without success to organize the pit operators through the Pittsburgh Coal Exchange,
but they did compel the American Miners' Association to
accept a regional wage reduction in 1865 by importing miners
from Europe through the American Emigrant Company.[5]
Here, as in Buffalo, the commercial capitalists were the organizers: the manufacturers simply had no solidarity.

The Piano Makers' Association in New York City met with
a sad fate. When the German Piano Makers' Union closed the
shop of one member of the association for a 10 per cent raise
in pay, the other employers proclaimed that they would fire all
union officers and hire no union members while their fellow
manufacturer was faced with the strike. The union responded
by striking all the shops, putting some 700 workers out on the
streets. Within four days, six firms repudiated the resolution of

[2] Thomas and Mary Ann Jones to their parents, Oct., 1864, in Conway,
p. 171.
[3] *Royal Comm. on Trades Unions*, p. 8.
[4] Commons, *Doc. Hist.*, IX, 89–114.
[5] Wieck, pp. 107–11, 146–58.

their association and even granted their men raises. Seven days later only the original shop and its 17 workmen remained in the fight.[6] Even in the great 1872 New York strike for the eight-hour day, as Reuben Carroll—who was then treasurer of one of the employers' groups—later testified, the proprietors failed to stand by their resolutions. They did not even pay their $20.00 dues: Carroll had to hire an agent at $3.50 a day to collect the society's fees and still made up a $200.00 deficit out of his own pocket.[7]

Still, unions could not gamble their fate on the assumption that the manufacturers would always prove weak and divided. As prices fell following the war, employer resistance to wage demands stiffened remarkably. Still less could unions assume that all workers in any given trade would be reliable supporters of union rules. In St. Louis, to take an extreme case, the heavy volume of river traffic resulted in a chronic labor surplus adequate to break any strike, and a union official complained that the German majority among the workers, "with very few exceptions . . . take no part whatever in trade organizations."[8] Everywhere there were at least some workmen ready to ignore union rules, and a prolonged strike might persuade many hungry union members to do the same. They might be turned away from the works by force. "Revolvers are ready weapons here with the ordinary people," wrote a Schuylkill County miner, explaining the hazardous position of local "turncoats."[9] At the other end of the state two hundred miners came armed with their guns to chase scabs from a struck pit at Pine Run. One man lay dead and five wounded after the proprietor, his son, and his foreman had exchanged shots with the strikers.[1] But violence was certain to bring the

---

[6] Philadelphia *Public Ledger*, Nov. 9, 1868.

[7] U.S., Congress, Senate, Committee on Education and Labor, *Report of the Committee of the Senate upon the Relations between Labor and Capital* (Washington, D.C., 1885), II, 1120–21. (Hereafter cited as Senate, *Labor and Capital*.)

[8] Letter of an officer of the St. Louis Workingmen's Union to William Jessup, in *Daily Evening Voice*, June 6, 1867.

[9] John J. Powell to Editor, *Y Gwladgarwr*, May 12, 1865, in Conway, pp. 175–6. *Cf.* Wilson, pp. 181–2.

[1] Pittsburgh *Daily Post*, June 26, 27, 1868.

law down upon the workers, just as it alienated many of the union men themselves.

ARBITRATION AND BUREAUCRACY

The alternative force was for trade unionists to perfect their own organizations: to develop more effective machinery for treating with employers and for controlling the workmen in the trade. This necessity led to the simultaneous development of arbitration, bureaucratization, and centralization in trade unions. The word "arbitration" was used so broadly and vaguely in the 1860's that it could encompass any form of organized negotiation of grievances between trade unions and employers. At the first National Labor Congress a committee composed exclusively of leaders of national unions agreed that "strikes . . . have been productive of great injury to the laboring classes," often "ill-advised, and the result of impulse," and recommended that labor "discountenance them except as a *dernier* resort, and when all means for an amicable and honorable adjustment have been exhausted."[2] In place of traditional rule-making, Jonathan Fincher had proposed the previous year that unions try "conferring committees, and friendly negotiations . . . before labor assumes a hostile attitude toward capital."[3] This suggestion was echoed in the official address issued by the National Labor Union in 1867, which urged upon unions "the appointment, where practicable, of a conference committee, whose duty it would be to lay the nature of the grievance before the employer, and ask redress for the same."[4]

Introduction of such an innovation did not come quickly or easily. Three unions of New York bricklayers resolved that after July 1, 1868, none of their 2,800 members would work more than eight hours a day and were forced to undertake a massive work stoppage to enforce their rule. Not until the strike had been in progress a month and a half did the Joint Committee of the striking unions seek to hold a conference

---

[2] Commons, *Doc. Hist.*, IX, 131.
[3] *Fincher's Trades Review*, Jan. 7, 1865.
[4] Commons, *Doc. Hist.*, IX, 155.

with the Master Masons' Association. So successful had the strike been up to that point that union negotiators actually obtained an offer from the masters conceding union demands in full, provided the unions allow their employers four apprentices each instead of the two formerly permitted. At that point some bricklayers furiously challenged the authority of their committee to negotiate, or to do anything but collect and disburse strike funds. When a group of dissident unionists visited the masters' association and notified it that no union committee held any warrant to bargain, the efforts toward a settlement collapsed. The building season closed with the issue unresolved: master masons claimed they could obtain all the bricklayers they needed for ten hours a day, and the unions boasted most of their members were working eight-hour schedules. In December the bricklayers did amend their constitutions to allow masters an unlimited number of apprentices, provided they were duly indentured for four-year terms. But it was then too late to achieve by rule what had been within the workers' grasp by negotiation the previous summer.[5] The price of rank and file conservatism was high.

More successful were the cigar makers, led by the energetic John J. Junio. In the fall of 1868 this union reached an agreement with an association of thirty New York manufacturers who employed twelve hundred journeymen that neither side would undertake to change the price list for cigar-rolling without notifying the other through a joint committee. A union demand for an increase of two to three dollars per thousand cigars resulted in a conflict in which the workers unveiled a new strategy, the "rolling strike," closing a few shops at a time while workers in other establishments gave financial support to those who had walked out. In November the employers

[5] "Is Labor a Curse?" pp. 537–48; Bates, pp. 27–30; *Workingman's Advocate*, July 11, 1868; New York *Herald*, July 7, 1868; *Irish Citizen*, June 20, 1868; Philadelphia *Public Ledger*, June 23, July 1, 3, 4, 18, 23, 25, 29, Aug. 3, 7, 10, 11, 12, 13, 17, 24, 29, Sept. 10, 18, 29, Oct. 5, 28, Nov. 17, Dec. 4, 11, 25, 1868; *New-York Times*, July 17, 1868. For a full account of this strike, see David Montgomery, "Labor and the Radical Republicans: A Study of the Revival of the American Labor Movement, 1864–1868," unpublished doctoral dissertation (Univ. of Minnesota, 1962), pp. 532–7.

offered to raise rates one dollar on January 1, 1869, and
another dollar on May 1, provided the state of the trade held
up. The union would agree only if the employers also accepted
a closed shop. This point the masters refused to concede,
declaring instead they would hire no union men at all. A brief
city-wide strike ended with the union accepting the earlier
wage offer and the manufacturers rescinding their exclusion of
union members. Although the closed shop was not won, there
did emerge from the dispute a "joint committee of arbitration"
on which spokesmen of both groups hoped to work out future
problems. In short, the union obtained both a wage increase
and recognition as bargaining agent for the city's cigar
makers.[6]

As "arbitration" implied adjustment of disputes through
union delegates prepared to "treat" with the proprietors, it led
logically to written contracts. Wages for iron puddlers in the
Pittsburgh area were fixed in February 1865 by a sliding scale
which pegged the payment for iron boiling to the price of bar
iron received by the manufacturers. The scheme was suggested by ironmonger Benjamin Franklin Jones and elaborated
into an agreement terminable only after ninety days' notice by
either side, which was signed by five manufacturers, headed
by Jones, and ten representatives of the Sons of Vulcan,
headed by Grand Master Miles Humphreys. Although tum-
bling prices quickly led to the breakdown of the agreement, a
new and more durable scale was negotiated in 1867.[7]

The Workingmen's Benevolent Association reached a verbal agreement on a sliding scale of wages with Schuylkill
County's Anthracite Board of Trade in 1869. The following
year a written contract between the two bodies formalized
wages, conditions for discharge of miners, and machinery for
the processing of grievances that might arise during the one-
year life of the pact. No other contract of the period was as
comprehensive in its terms as this: it even committed both
parties to what had formerly been union rules regulating the

---

[6] Philadelphia *Public Ledger,* Oct. 28, 31, Nov. 9, 13, 17, 24, 26, 30,
1868.
[7] *Pa. BLS, 1880–1881,* pp. 282–4; *ibid.,* 1887, pp. 2–16; McNeill, *Labor
Movement,* p. 273.

output and equalizing piece-rate earnings of its members.[8] Another significant agreement was reached in Lynn, Massachusetts, between the shoe manufacturers of that city and the K.O.S.C. A brief strike in 1870 produced a negotiated price list for lasters and other shoemaking crafts. The next year a general contract was negotiated peacefully by a Crispin committee representing all branches of the trade. Although the masters repudiated the contract and defeated the union in 1872, the very fact that the order undertook such negotiations showed how far it had advanced from its original purpose simply to exclude "green hands."[9]

Finally, the term "arbitration" was used in rare instances to mean settlement of disputes by a neutral third party. This notion was clearly a British import. What popularity it enjoyed appeared primarily in the 1870's as news of A.J. Mundella's arbitration boards in England reached this side of the Atlantic.[1] Aside from the rapture with which the American Social Science Association and other upper-class reform groups greeted the idea, its influence was felt primarily among workers who were themselves British immigrants. Thus the Workingmen's Benevolent Association submitted its disputes with the Anthracite Board of Trade to adjudication by Judge William Elwell in 1871. Three years later the Miners' National Association presented its grievances in Ohio's Tuscarawas Valley to a panel for decision. In both cases the rulings were severely detrimental to union interests.[2] The only other union which seriously committed itself to arbitration in this sense was the Iron Molders' Union, when it was led by William Saffin and H.J. Walls. A provision was inserted in that organization's constitution in 1872 banning strikes over any dispute which had not first been referred to an "arbitration committee" consisting of two union spokesmen, two representatives of the

---

[8] *Pa. BLS, 1872–1873,* pp. 335–7; Killeen, pp. 215–18. The text of the contract may be found in Andrew Roy, *History of the Coal Miners of the United States* (Columbus, Ohio, n.d.), pp. 82–3.

[9] John Philip Hall, "The Gentle Craft: A Narrative of Yankee Shoemakers," unpublished doctoral dissertation (Columbia Univ., 1953), pp. 306–17.

[1] Yearley, *Britons,* pp. 171–2.

[2] *Ibid.,* pp. 172–6; Killeen, pp. 238–52, 295–300; *Pa. BLS, 1872–1873,* pp. 355–9.

employers, and a fifth individual "of good character" to be selected jointly by the other four. Only if that committee failed to reach a settlement within five days could a strike be sanctioned by the International. The flaw on which this scheme collapsed is obvious: there was no way for the union to bind employers to such a procedure.[3]

Generally, trade unionists excluded such third-party involvement from the meaning of the arbitration which they advocated. Fincher, the ardent proponent of conference committees, denounced impartial arbitration as "a humbug, a delusion, and a snare."[4] In the midst of the Mundella rage of the early seventies, Andrew Cameron argued that quasi-judicial procedures of the type then being developed in England could not be transplanted to the United States because "the disinterested arbiter . . . is a *rara avis* on American soil. The substitution of a monied for a titled aristocracy—anomalous as the assertion may seem—militates against its success."[5] More emphatically, at the behest of Henry Keating of New York's bricklayers, the National Labor Union in 1868 struck from its platform a clause which linked the appeal for negotiations with the assertion that the N.L.U. "deprecates" strikes.[6] Trade unionists wanted to make it clear that they considered arbitration a means to regulate strikes and make them more effective, not to eliminate them; that they were not repudiating strikes per se, but the traditional method of governing the labor market by unilateral rules.

Seen in this light, the use of conferences to adjust disputes becomes part of the larger evolution of trade-union bureaucracy. Local and national unions were transferring the power to deal with employers from the whole membership—who dealt with their antagonists through the establishment and rescinding of trade rules—to select committees authorized to haggle with the employers and subject only to ultimate ratification of their work by the membership. Inseparable from

---

[3] *Ohio BLS, 1877,* pp. 273–4.

[4] *Fincher's Trades Review,* April 22, 1865.

[5] *Workingman's Advocate,* April 19, 1873. Terence V. Powderly was an enthusiastic advocate of impartial arbitration and wrote his meaning of the phrase into his account of the 1860's, where it did not belong. Powderly, *Thirty Years,* p. 68.

[6] *N.L.U. Proceedings, 1868,* pp. 21–2.

this process was the transfer to elected officers of effective power to call and terminate strikes and to accumulate and safeguard strike funds. National unions began to require that local strike actions be approved by two thirds of the other locals (or, in some cases, by a majority of all members of the national union) before strike benefits might be sent to the local involved. Unions that had previously relied on emergency voluntary subscriptions to support striking members now sought to create national funds through regular assessments.[7]

The establishment of national and international unions and the transfer of powers from locals to these nationals were but part of a much broader process of bureaucratization. Indeed, in the pre-1873 period the formal powers gained by national unions were usually confined to the authority to charter new locals and to dispense of strike funds. Few if any were able to regulate the level of local dues, local disciplinary actions, or local apprenticeship regulations, let alone determine local wage policies. Throughout the period many unions remained aloof from national organizations of their trades. Even within the national unions rank-and-file members felt only a remote attachment to the national body. Delegates and (in some organizations) former delegates to national union conventions in a real sense *were* the national union, for they alone were eligible to hold office in it, they chose the officers, they determined its policies—in short, they constituted something of a closed corporation vis-à-vis the remaining members.[8] On the other hand, power gravitated toward elected officers on *all* levels of union operation.

The salaried functionary became especially significant. Initially, it was usually the secretary, burdened with the keeping of union records and correspondence, who first left the workshop and became a union functionary by occupation. New York Typographical Union No. 6, finding its enrollment had almost quadrupled over the previous two years, began to

---

[7] Philadelphia *Public Ledger*, Oct. 29, 1868; Commons, *Labour*, II, 52; *I.M.I.U. Proceedings*, 1865, p. 11; McNeill, *Labor Movement*, p. 13.
[8] This point is discussed well in Ulman, pp. 213–16. Ulman's whole focus, however, is on the national union and thus encompasses only a portion of my conception of bureaucratization.

pay its secretary $1,200 per year in 1869.[9] The Sons of Vulcan started paying Miles Humphreys and other traveling organizers the trade wage plus traveling expenses in 1866, while they rewarded their Grand Master by taking up a collection for him among the delegates to the annual convention. In 1867 the Grand Secretary was provided with a $700 annual salary, and in 1872 the Grand Master was placed on a fixed pay of $1,200 a year. The second innovation proved more of a financial burden than the union could bear, so two years later the offices of Grand Master and Grand Secretary were merged and the single official was paid $1,500.[1] Lloyd Ulman has argued that as salaries rose, so did the length of incumbency in office. The tenure of national union officers averaged one to two years from the 1860's through the 1880's, but the highly paid presidency of the Iron Molders ($1,600 in 1867) had only five incumbents from 1862 to 1903.[2]

Bureaucratic controls reached a higher level of development among coal miners than among any other group of workmen. The Workingman's Benevolent Association was born during a strike of miners at the Eagle Colliery in St. Clair, Pennsylvania, in January 1868. Its membership remained less than twenty until July of that year, when thousands of anthracite miners abandoned their jobs in the hope of forcing their employers to comply with a recently enacted state law which made eight hours a day's work. Although the workers failed to achieve the shorter day, they did return to their jobs in mid-August with both a wage increase and a strong organization. A rally called by the W.B.A. in Mahanoy City had attracted more than 12,000 people and marked the real origin of effective trade unionism in Schuylkill County. In the spring of 1869, delegates from seventeen miners' unions met in Hazelton to form a general council, commonly known as the "Executive Board of Schuylkill County," which became the bargaining agency for the 35,000 members of the union. Its chairman,

---

[9] Stevens, pp. 420, 470–1.
[1] McNeill, *Labor Movement*, pp. 274, 276; Jesse H. Robinson, *The Amalgamated Association of Iron, Steel and Tin Workers* ("Johns Hopkins University Studies in Historical and Political Science," Series XXXVIII, No. 2; Baltimore, 1920), pp. 12, 14.
[2] Ulman, pp. 221–3.

elected by the membership at large and paid $1,500 a year, was the famous John Siney, who held the office from the time it was established until he resigned late in 1873 to head the Miners' National Association.[3]

The administrative powers of the Executive Board derived from its efforts to resolve two crucial problems: a surplus of miners in the region and a chronically glutted market for the coal they produced. The output of coal in the region's anthracite fields had grown but little during the war. In 1860 some 8.5 million tons were dug; five years later the production had only risen to 9.7 million tons. Yet in the same five years the number of miners and mine laborers in Schuylkill County alone increased from 10,000 to 17,000, because of the good war-time wages and the lure isolated rural towns had as places in which to escape the draft. At the end of the war, however, the introduction of the Allison Cataract Steam Pump, which could carry steam directly to engines and fans at the bottom of shafts, made it feasible for collieries to tap deep veins of white-ash coal. At the same time, the development of the diamond drill, the power-drilling machine, and air-compressing equipment vastly augmented the productivity of companies that had enough capital to introduce them. By 1870 the state's output of anthracite had risen to sixteen million tons.[4]

These changes created a crisis for both the workers and their employers. "There are too many men in the country connected with coal mining," explained an immigrant. "They are almost treading on each other in these parts. . . ."[5] Even after union organization, miners on contract were only averaging $572 a year net income; inside laborers received $299, and breaker boys, $122.[6] On the other hand, the hundred or so Schuylkill County proprietors were themselves frequently

[3] Killeen, pp. 102–3, 107–10, 121–7; *Pa. BLS, 1872–1873*, pp. 335–7.

[4] Yearley, *Enterprise and Anthracite*, pp. 125–66; Killeen, pp. 69, 74–5; Robert Allison, "Early History of Coal Mining and Mining Machinery in Schuylkill County," *Schuylkill Hist. Pubs.*, IV, 151–2; Philadelphia *Public Ledger*, Jan. 10, 1867, July 22, 1868; Hendrick B. Wright, *A Practical Treatise on Labor* (New York, 1871), *passim* and esp. pp. 132–56, 381–405.

[5] Thomas Morris to his brothers and sisters, July 20, 1866, in Conway, p. 180.

[6] *Pa. BLS, 1872–1873*, p. 345.

faced with a satiated market and always pressed by competition from the corporation-owned northern fields.

The W.B.A. grappled with all aspects of this crisis simultaneously. It opened up continuous discussions with the county's Anthracite Board of Trade, culminating in the sliding scale contract of 1870. To level out the highly divergent incomes which a standard tonnage rate returned on a wide variety of coal faces, it adopted an "equalization rule," fixing maximum and minimum incomes, and in 1870 included this rule in the contract. For several years the union was even able to accomplish what the operators had never been able to do for themselves: reduce chronic overproduction. First, the W.B.A. by its own rules restricted the tonnage each union member could mine daily. After the establishment of the sliding scale, it initiated the practice of annual suspensions of work when the market price of coal fell too low to allow the miners an adequate income. Such suspensions bolstered the earnings of the proprietors as well as the workers.[7] Siney, furthermore, openly favored the individual colliers in their conflicts with corporate competitors of the Northern fields, where the union was always weak, and the Philadelphia and Reading Railroad, and this devotion to the small producer drew him and his union into greenback politics. At the 1869 National Labor Congress, Siney sat on the committee on mining which reported that the three great enemies of mine workers, colliers, and consumers were the "great mining monopolies," the "transportation monopolies," and the "city speculators."[8]

Discipline, cohesion, instantaneous action by thousands of miners at the call of a singler officer, and, last but not least, a vigilant attentiveness to the health of the industry in which they worked—these characteristics for which American coal miners have become famous were all apparent in the W.B.A. From it they were carried to the Miners' National Association,

[7] *Ibid.*, pp. 335–41; Killeen, pp. 125–7, 140–1, 365–8; Yearley, *Enterprise and Anthracite*, pp. 182–93; Joseph F. Patterson, "Old W.B.A. Days," *Schuylkill Hist. Pubs.*, II, 357–9; Evans, p. 16; Terence V. Powderly, "A Man and a Stone: The Same Being a Little Journey with John Siney," *United Mine Workers' Journal*, May 11, 1916, pp. 6–7; May 18, 1916, pp. 8, 25; May 25, 1916, pp. 8, 25.

[8] *Workingman's Advocate*, Sept. 4, 1869; Broehl, pp. 109–20.

which spread through the bituminous fields in the seventies. The M.N.A. Executive Board had unqualified authority to call and halt strikes, levy special assessments, and hire organizers, and at its head stood Siney himself.[9] Even when the W.B.A. was ultimately crushed in the Long Strike of 1875 by the superior resources and organizational strength of the Philadelphia and Reading Coal and Iron Company, there was no demoralized drift of hungry workers back to the job. The Executive Board officially furled the union banners and in a public circular ringing with proud defiance "recognized the necessity of putting back into" the hands of the miners "the privilege of breaking the deadlock as Union Men." The decree concluded: "You are hereby authorized . . . not as an organization, to bind yourselves for any length of time to the unfair terms of the Coal Exchange's proposition—but to accept the situation 'under protest,' each branch to have the right to resume under the law of the Union at its pleasure, and upon the best terms that can be secured."[1]

CENTRALIZATION

A development running parallel with the bureaucratization of trade unions was the centralization of union controls, as the practice of mutual assistance among related unions led to the formation of new authoritative bodies on city, state, and national levels. Although national and so-called international trade unions played a major role in the government of such trades as iron molding, iron puddling, and coal mining by the early seventies, the major focal points of coordination of local unions were the city trades assemblies. These bodies of delegates from various trade unions of a single municipal area were successors of the city Trades' Unions, which had been the main center of labor activity in the Age of Jackson, and the few central bodies of the early fifties, such as New York's Industrial Congress.[2] The formation of Rochester's Trades Assembly in 1863 marked the revival of this institution. By the

---

[9] Killeen, pp. 289–90.
[1] Marvin W. Schlegel, *Ruler of the Reading: The Life of Franklin B. Gowen, 1836–1889* (Harrisburg, 1947), p. 74.
[2] Commons, *Doc. Hist.*, V, 203–392, VI, 21–190; Degler, pp. 57–61.

end of the war these assemblies could be found in Boston, New York, Chicago, Albany, Buffalo, Troy, Philadelphia, Cincinnati, Detroit, St. Louis, Pittsburgh, and San Francisco.[3]

The vigorous Chicago Trades Assembly exemplified the functions of such bodies. It lent assistance to the city's trade unions, of which there were some thirty-three by 1869, in their efforts to control the markets for the labor of their members. Although it had no regular strike funds or authority to call or halt work stoppages, the assembly could and did raise subscriptions to aid strikes by member unions, undertake to adjust disputes between unions and employers in particular trades, and promote boycotts of employers who violated rules of constituent unions. This last function, the "bannering" of "rat" employers, is one of the two historic pedestals of trade-assembly power. The other is political activity. From the outset the city bodies devoted much of their attention to influencing city ordinances and state and federal legislation.[4] The Chicago body used the occasion of a mass rally to support striking printers on the Chicago *Daily Times* to proclaim its own election platform, to which candidates for state and federal office were asked to adhere as early as 1864.[5] Thereafter, it regularly endorsed candidates friendly to its program, especially for the city council. It could boast in the spring of 1866, for example, that in seven of the city's sixteen wards the elected aldermen had pledged themselves to a municipal ordinance making eight hours a day's work for city employees, and by June the desired measure had been enacted.[6]

Some of the most important labor-reform journals were sponsored by trades assemblies. Often their origins lay in strikes or lockouts of typographical unions. During the strike on the Chicago *Times,* for example, some of the printers

[3] Commons, *Labour,* II, 21–6, 58–60; *Fincher's Trades Review,* June 6, 1863, Feb. 11, 1865; *Daily Evening Voice,* Dec. 2, 1864.

[4] Editorial on Trades Assemblies, *Workingman's Advocate,* May 16, 1868. Data on Chicago trade unions and Trades Assembly is drawn from Chicago City Directories (Bailey's for 1865–7 and Edwards's for 1868–9).

[5] *Workingman's Advocate,* Sept. 7, Nov. 5, 1864; Pierce, II, 162–3; Hutchinson, II, 46–7.

[6] Editorial, *Workingman's Advocate,* April 21, 1866; *Daily Evening Voice,* Sept. 17, 1866; Pierce, II, 175.

involved established the *Workingman's Advocate,* which they placed under the editorship of Andrew C. Cameron. The city's trades assembly, of which Cameron became president in 1866, adopted that journal as its official organ. The *Daily Evening Voice* of Boston, Detroit's *Daily Union,* and the *Daily Press* of St. Paul had similar careers. The most influential such paper at the close of the war was *Fincher's Trades Review,* organ of the Philadelphia assembly, which was edited by Jonathan Fincher, a thoughtful and cautious leader of that city body and of the Machinists' and Blacksmiths' International Union. By December 1865 this paper claimed 11,000 subscribers spread over nearly every state and territory of the United States, as well as England and continental Europe. Many important weekly or monthly journals were established and maintained by national unions, such as the *Anthracite Monitor* of the W.B.A., the *Iron Molders' Journal,* the *Belleville Miner* of the American Miners' Association, the *Machinists' and Blacksmiths' International Journal,* and the *Brotherhood of Locomotive Engineers' Monthly Journal.* Although the relatively reliable dues structure of national unions made such organs less prone to financial failure than was the press of the city bodies, the latter provided their readers with a breadth of subject matter and a range of opinion (through editorials, articles, and letters) rarely equaled by the press of the national unions.[7] Such periodicals as the *Workingman's Advocate* and the Boston *Voice* were, in fact, among the most important institutions of the labor movement. Constantly short of funds, sustained by the fifty-cent or dollar contributions of their supporters and the tireless efforts of individual workers who gathered the subscriptions of their shopmates and neighbors, such labor papers offered workmen both sympathetic reporting of their activities and a forum for theoretical discussion and guidance of the movement.[8]

The most effective city central bodies appeared in New

---

[7] Commons, *Labour,* II, 15; Yearley, *Britons,* p. 196; David A. Boyd, "The Labor Movement of Detroit" (unpublished manuscript in JAL), pp. 11–12; Evans, I, 10–12; Cole, *Era of the Civil War,* p. 369; Foner, *Labor,* I, 349; Grossman, *Sylvis,* p. 118.

[8] See *Daily Evening Voice,* Dec. 17, 20, 1864, for lists of contributors, and letter of "iron molder's wife" in *ibid.,* Nov. 9, 1866.

York City, where the large German element in the labor force led to the creation of both English- and German-language trades assemblies; and the close contact of the great port city with the Old World gave the First International an influence it enjoyed in no other American municipality. Both the Workingmen's Union and the *Arbeiter-Bund* were founded in 1864. By no means were all trade unions of the city adherents of the Workingmen's Union, any more than was the case in other cities. In fact, in 1867 only 22 of 86 known workingmen's societies in New York City sent delegates, but their 15,000 members represented about half the union members of Manhattan Island. The two largest unions, the Longshoremen's and the Laborers' United Benevolent Society, whose combined following of 9,000 workmen was overwhelmingly Irish, remained aloof from the city central.[9] Craft organizations of the building trades, printers, and shipyard workmen provided the leadership of the Workingmen's Union.[1]

The issue that sparked the growth of the Workingmen's Union was the eight-hour day. An 1866 strike of shipyard workers, although itself a failure, both made this the central question for the city's trades and elevated to the leadership of the Workingmen's Union one of the most impressive labor leaders of the decade, William J. Jessup.[2] This Connecticut-born ship joiner had received a rural elementary education, then taught school briefly before coming to New York to work as a clerk. The war made wages in the shipbuilding industry sufficiently attractive to Jessup, then in his mid-thirties, for him to learn the joiner's trade. By 1866 he had helped organize his fellow joiners into a union and been sent by them to the Baltimore Labor Congress, where he was elected vice-president of the National Labor Union for New York State. During

---

[9] New York *Daily Tribune*, April 30, 1867.
[1] See reports of officers elected by the Workingmen's Union, *Workingman's Advocate*, July 17, 1869, Jan. 14, 1871; *New-York Times*, July 2, 1870, July 8, 1871.
[2] F. A. Sorge, "Die Arbeiterbewegung in den Vereinigten Staaten, 1860–1866," *Die Neue Zeit*, IX, 2 Band (1890–1), p. 441 (hereafter cited as Sorge, "1860–1866"); Massachusetts, House of Representatives, *Report of Commissioners on the Hours of Labor*, House Document, 1867, No. 44 (Boston, 1867), pp. 60–1. (Hereafter cited as *Mass. Labor Report, 1867*.)

the following year, Jessup threw himself tirelessly into strengthening the structure of trade unionism in both the city and the state. While representing the N.L.U. in New York he became recording secretary of the Workingmen's Union, and during the next five years he consistently served as either president or corresponding secretary of that body. Simultaneously, he was elevated to the presidency of the New York Workingmen's Assembly, the state-wide organization of trade unions which functioned primarily as the labor lobby in Albany. Between 1867 and 1872, in other words, Jessup was a professional trade unionist—leading a national union, a city central, and a state assembly.[3] Prominent among his lieutenants in the city were Thomas J. Masterson, the Irish nationalist and Republican party activist who represented the Crispins in the Workingmen's Union, and English-born Robert Blissert, a leader of the International who was to reappear in the early 1880's among the founders of the new Central Labor Union of the city.[4]

Several unions of German craftsmen, among them tailors, waiters, silver-platers and bookbinders, established their own central body in 1864, calling it the *Arbeiter-Bund*. Neither wage demands nor political activity absorbed much of the attention of this group, however, for its leaders, among them G. Kahl and Friedrich L. Roell, were devoted followers of Prussia's Hermann Schulze-Delitzsch. In accordance with their mentor's philosophy of self-help, these artisans hoped to pool their meager funds toward the establishment of their own bank and hospital, home-building societies, and producers' cooperatives. They appealed to the members of German unions to contribute ten dollars apiece toward the construction of a great labor hall to serve both as a meeting place and as a warehouse for groceries and coal to be sold through consumers' cooperatives. By late 1865 the *Arbeiter-Bund* was selling potatoes, tea, sugar, and coffee at cost and providing its

---

[3] There is no biography of Jessup save an unidentified typescript, "William J. Jessup," in the Labor Collection, Biography and Papers, WSHS.
[4] On Masterson, see *New-York Times*, July 8, 1871; Roney, p. 179. On Blissert, see *Workingman's Advocate*, July 17, 1869; Samuel Bernstein, *The First International in America* (New York, 1962), p. 141; Senate, *Labor and Capital*, I, 841.

members with a $200 death benefit, which kept the organization perpetually on the verge of bankruptcy.[5]

By this time, however, enthusiasm for the eight-hour day had captured the organized German workers, just as it was sweeping through the ranks of English-speaking workmen. Columns of their journal, *Arbeiter-Zeitung*, carried more news of the eight-hour movement almost every week. Initially, its editorials stressed the righteousness of Schulze-Delitzsch's cause, but made no direct comment on the movement for the shorter day. In September, however, the unions of waiters and capmakers seceded from the *Arbeiter-Bund*, denouncing it as useless. Two months later the German Joiners invited several other unions to convene with them in Germania Hall to debate the subject of the hours of labor. So ardently did the assembly endorse the eight-hour day that President Kahl of the *Arbeiter-Bund* found himself compelled to join President Michael Stevens of the Workingmen's Union on the rostrum of Cooper Institute at a grand rally for the eight-hour day. Desperately, editorials of the *Arbeiter-Zeitung* cautioned its German readers against the path they were now taking. First through reprinting without comment editorials to this effect from other German papers, and ultimately by openly asserting themselves, the editors warned that for workers to seek by law to shorten the working day would make them the pawns of political demagogues and create the politics of bread and circuses. But this warning came at the end of December 1865, as part of an editorial in which the *Arbeiter-Zeitung* bowed off the stage. Self-help no longer excited the organized German craftsmen of New York, and both the paper and the *Arbeiter-Bund* expired from lack of support.[6]

On the ruins of this original German trade-union assembly a second arose in little more than two years, but the ideological orientation of the newcomer, the *Arbeiter-Union*, was toward the International Workingmen's Association. Two main streams of thought flowed into this new group: Lassallean and Marxist. Despite all the strictures of the *Arbeiter-*

[5] *Arbeiter-Zeitung*, Sept. 26, Oct. 4, 28, Nov. 25, 1864, May 26, Sept. 1, Nov. 3, 1865.
[6] *Ibid.*, Oct. 13, Nov. 3, 10, 17, Dec. 1, 15, 29, 1865.

Zeitung that Ferdinand Lassalle represented *"der französich-socialistischen Lehren,"* which was theoretical and centralizing in tendency, in contrast to the *"deutsche Methode"* of Schulze, which was practical and decentralist,[7] it was the Lassallean current that was then in ascendancy among the workers in Prussia—and hence among German workers in America. Siegfried Meyer and August Vogt arrived in New York in 1866, bringing with them years of leadership experience in the Lassallean *Allgemeine deutsche Arbeiter-Verein.* They were soon joined by Edward Grosse, erstwhile private secretary of Lassalle's successor, Johann Baptist von Schweitzer. Their voices from New York were echoed by Edward Schlaeger in Chicago, leader of the city's *Arbeiterverein* and associate editor of Cameron's *Workingman's Advocate.*[8] The *Deutsche Arbeiter,* published in 1869 and 1870 by Chicago's central body of German unions, pursued a thoroughly Lassallean line.[9]

But influential as Lassallean teachings were among German immigrant craftsmen, they were profoundly modified by contact with American conditions. Lassalle taught that it is impossible for workingmen under capitalism to raise their wages above the bare minimum necessary to sustain life. The only escape from poverty and bondage for the workers, therefore, was to establish their own cooperative enterprises. But, unlike Schulze, Lassalle insisted that laborers could never finance such undertakings without the support of the state. The first task of labor, therefore, was to take control of the state away from the capitalists, through the use of universal suffrage. Once the "Fourth Estate" had captured governmental power, it could utilize that force to care for labor's welfare, promote a cooperative economy, and establish a harmonious, morally ordered community. Such a doctrine necessarily underwent a drastic transformation in the United States. The successful strikes of trade unions made a mockery of Lassalle's "iron law of wages," and the fact that all white males could already vote made pointless his stress on extension of the

---

[7] Editorial in *ibid.,* Oct. 4, 1864.
[8] Schlüter, *Die Internationale,* pp. 404–7; Stevens, pp. 543–4; Pierce, II, 171–2, 187–8; Cole, *Era of the Civil War,* pp. 123, 166–7.
[9] See editorials, *Deutsche Arbeiter,* March 26, 1870.

suffrage as the first revolutionary objective of the workers. Adapting themselves readily to the new scene, the Lassalleans entered trade unions in America, but brought with them ideas concerning cooperatives and state aid which were to blend nicely with American greenbackism. In New York they created a miniature replica of the *Allgemeine deutsche Arbeiter-Verein,* and ultimately formed Section 6 of the International.[1]

Distinct Marxist organizations had all but disappeared from the American scene by the end of the Civil War. The Communist Club, founded in New York by refugee forty-eighters in 1857, had dwindled to some twenty members, few of them workers. The most influential Marxists of the 1850's, having concluded that at the moment America's *bourgeoisie* were more revolutionary than her inert proletariat, allied themselves closely with the Republican party. Military service during the war completed the process of drawing many such Marxists away from labor activity, for some met their deaths, like Joseph Weydemeyer, and others, like Fritz Anneke, simply exchanged the Marxism of their younger days for a Radical Republican outlook.[2] Still others turned their attention at the war's end to organizing aid to the expected revolution in Germany. Both Adolph Douai and Friedrich A. Sorge, who were to play prominent roles in the International by the end of the decade, were on the Executive Committee of the *Bund für deutsche Freiheit und Einheit,* until the Austro-Prussian War made it clear to them that German unification was not going to come through revolution.[3]

The founding of the International Workingmen's Association in 1864, however, not only opened the way for a revival of Marxist influence, but also linked Marxist thought (and Marx's personal activity) directly with the trade-union movement.[4] The "final object" of the workers' movement, Marx emphasized

---

[1] Ferdinand Lassalle, *The Workingman's Programme* (*Arbeiter Programm*) (London, no date); *Deutsche Arbeiter,* March 26, 1870; Sorge, "1860–1866," pp. 438–9; Foner, *Labor,* I, 413–15.
[2] Schlüter, *Die Internationale,* pp. 413–14; Obermann, *Weydemeyer.* Data on Anneke is drawn from Fritz Anneke Papers.
[3] Schlüter, *Die Internationale,* pp. 414–16.
[4] See Royden Harrison, "The British Labor Movement and the International in 1864," in *The Socialist Register, 1964,* ed. Ralph Miliband and John Saville (New York, 1964), pp. 293–308.

to his New York disciple Friedrich Bolte, is "the conquest of political power," but such an accomplishment presupposes "a previous organization of the working class developed up to a certain point, which itself arises from its economic struggles." For this reason both the economic movements of the workers (trade-union efforts to wring concessions directly from particular employers) and their political movements (efforts to achieve their "interests in a general form" such as an eight-hour law) deserved full support, said Marx, because both were "a means of developing this organization."[5]

Despite the fact that Marxists enthusiastically embraced trade unions, while American Lassalleans partook in them only by compromising their doctrine, both concurred in the ringing challenge of Marx's *Inaugural Address of the Working Men's International Association:* "To conquer political power has therefore become the great duty of the working classes."[6] It was to promote this common aim that activists of both the Communist Club and the *Allgemeine deutsche Arbeiter-Verein* formed the Social party in January 1868. Its catchall platform reflected the fusion character of the party. Among the demands were a progressive income tax, an eight-hour day by law, a greenback currency, equal rights for all men and women, and governmental protection of the weak against the strong. The party even offered an Executive Committee seat to the venerable pioneer of German socialism, Wilhelm Weitling.[7] Although the electoral influence of the Social party was nil, the merger of Lassalleans and Marxists it represented proved the beginning of a new orientation for the German trade unions of the city. Its first target, in fact, was not the polling booth, but the editorial office of the new trade-union newspaper *Arbeiter-Union,* then occupied by Dr. W. G. Landsberg, a follower of Schulze. In the summer of 1868 the Social party

---

[5] Karl Marx to F. Bolte, Nov. 23, 1871, in Marx, *Letters to Americans,* pp. 93–4.
[6] *Documents of the First International. The General Council of the First International, 1864–1866. The London Conference 1865. Minutes* (Moscow, n.d.), p. 286.
[7] Bernstein, p. 37; Schlüter, *Die Internationale,* pp. 417–18; *Revolution,* Vol. II (July 30, 1868), p. 61; Sorge, "1866–1876," pp. 390–2; Carl Wittke, *The Utopian Communist: A Biography of Wilhelm Weitling, Nineteenth Century Reformer* (Baton Rouge, La., 1950), pp. 289–90.

succeeded in replacing Landsberg with Adolph Douai, a noted
Texas abolitionist of the fifties who was quite new to the
Socialist cause but an able journalist and firm devotee of
political action.[8]

After Election Day the Social party reconstituted itself as
Section 1 of the International Workingmen's Association in the
United States, with F. A. Sorge as its secretary. Simultaneously,
this section was chartered as Labor Union No. 5 of New York
by the N.L.U., providing the Internationals with their first
official credentials to the national labor congresses. More
significantly, Douai's journal was converted into a daily and
manifested a growing concern for trade-union affairs, which
reflected a similar trend in the European congresses of the
I.W.A. The very name *Arbeiter-Union* was adopted by the
new trades assembly formed by twenty-three German trade
unions in June 1869, and the paper was made the official organ
of that assembly. At the head of this new body stood Socialists
who were outstanding spokesmen of the new trends in trade-
union organization, such as Conrad Kuhn of the Cigar
Makers' Union, an idol of Samuel Gompers's youth, and Henry
Lucker of the Tailors' Union. Both these men also held office
in the Workingmen's Union and the National Labor Union, of
which Kuhn was a vice-president in 1869 and 1870 and Lucker
temporarily president after the death of Sylvis in 1869.[9]

A bilingual organization of New York City's trade unions
was now operative, and the International was a significant
force within that structure. The partial success of the bricklayers' strike for eight hours in the summer of 1868, furthermore, whetted the appetite of the city's labor force for the
shorter day. Trade-union efforts toward this goal were soon
supplemented by those of newly-formed Building Trades
Leagues, which enlisted construction workers of all types,

---

[8] Sorge, "1866–1876," 390–1; Commons, *Labour*, II, 229; Bernstein,
pp. 38–9; letter of William J. Jessup, *Workingman's Advocate*, May 23,
1868.
[9] Bernstein, pp. 37–9; Schlüter, *Die Internationale*, 417–21; *La Première
Internationale. Recueil de documents publié sous la direction de Jacques
Freymond* (Geneva, 1962), I, 265–90; on strikes and unions, II, 19–28
(hereafter cited as *Prem. Int.*); *New-York Times*, June 22, 1869, July 8,
1871; *Workingman's Advocate*, June 26, July 17, 1869; *American Workman*, July 3, 1869. Kuhn's name was often spelled *Kuhm*.

including many who belonged to no union, on a quasi-industrial basis for the sole purpose of winning the eight-hour day. A stone cutters' strike in 1871 provided the occasion for a grand parade organized by the Workingmen's Union to rally all Manhattan's labor to the cause. The next spring nearly 100,000 workmen left their jobs in unison, in a city where the 1870 census had counted 52,125 native-born and 93,160 foreign-born workers in manufacturing.[1] Quite accurate was the estimate of Greeley's *Tribune:* "All the trades have been convulsed, and altogether three-fourths of all the journeymen in the city have been on strike for more time."[2] Although, like all general strikes, this effort proved no more than partially successful and raised the specter of social revolution that soon rent the city's labor movement asunder,[3] the Workingmen's Union of New York represented in May of 1872 the very pinnacle of trade-union centralization.

NATIONAL ORGANIZATIONS OF LABOR

Inevitably, the centralization of trade-union controls led to some organization on a national level. Three types of national bodies appeared—the International Industrial Assembly of North America, the various national and international unions of trades, and the National Labor Union. Although none of the three exerted an influence comparable to that of city assemblies, the National Labor Union was the most grandiose in conception and, at least between 1868 and 1870, held the greatest promise of providing an institution that could centralize labor-reform efforts on a national scale.

The earliest effort to found a national labor congress came directly from the city central bodies and represented, in effect, an attempt to recreate the organizational form of the National Trades' Union of the 1830's. The trades assembly of Louisville, Kentucky, led by the very Robert Gilchrist who had been prominent in the peace efforts of 1861, issued a call in 1864 to similar assemblies throughout the land asserting (quite opti-

---

[1] *Mass. BLS, 1873,* p. 258; Commons, *Doc. Hist.,* IX, 367–8; Schlüter, *Die Internationale,* pp. 470–80; *Stat. of Ninth Census,* I, 772.

[2] New York *Daily Tribune,* June 24, 1872, quoted in McNeill, *Labor Movement,* p. 143.

[3] See below, pp. 326–34.

mistically) that there were 200,000 members of unions in the United States and Canada and asking their representatives to convene in Louisville in September. When opening day of the convention arrived, however, only twelve delegates were on hand, the most important of whom were Gilchrist and Richard Trevellick of Detroit. Undaunted, those men launched the International Industrial Assembly of North America. This organization was to be composed of the delegates of city centrals, with each city accorded one vote. The program, although it doffed its hat toward the needs of unskilled laborers, focused its attention on the claims of mechanics "to be the judges of the value of their labor" and on promoting "consultation with employing capitalists, with a view to the adoption of a scale of wages which may be mutually satisfactory to both parties."[4]

The I.I.A. of N.A. never met again, for it suffered from two fatal flaws. First, its program offered no great unifying issue around which to mobilize labor as a whole. Although the question of shorter hours which was to supply this need in 1866 was already being widely debated, it received only minor attention at Louisville. Secondly, its structure was anachronistic. True, the trades assembly was currently the most vigorous center of working-class activity, but an effective national congress of labor in the 1860's had to find a place for the emerging national organizations of particular trades and for the multitudinous reform associations, in addition to the city centrals. That the Louisville conception of a national assembly of trades assemblies was too narrow was realized by such men as William Sylvis and Jonathan Fincher (national presidents of the iron molders and the machinists and blacksmiths, respectively), both of whom were leaders of the Philadelphia central body. Both advocated the formation of a national labor congress; in fact, in January 1864 their national unions agreed to cooperate in creating a "National Trades

---

[4] Commons, *Doc. Hist.*, IX, 121. See also *ibid.*, IX, 118–23; Commons, *Labour*, II, 33–9; *Michigan, A Centennial History of the State and Its People*, ed. George N. Fuller (Chicago, 1939), II, 269; Norman J. Ware, "The History of Labor Interaction," in *Labor in Canadian-American Relations*, ed. H. A. Innes (Toronto, 1937), 13–14.

Assembly." But neither they nor anyone else from Philadelphia went to Louisville.[5]

The first effective national cooperation of trade unions, therefore, came through the process of drawing unions of the same trade (or closely related trades) together into a national union. Only three of the national unions formed in the fifties had survived the 1857 depression and the outbreak of the war: the National Typographical Union, the Machinists' and Blacksmiths' International Union, and the Iron Molders' International Union—and the two last named had come into existence only in 1859. Even the Molders' Union was too badly disintegrated in 1862 to hold a convention, but the following year Sylvis did gather twenty delegates at Philadelphia to revitalize it. The iron puddlers revived their defunct Sons of Vulcan the same year. The next year the American Miners' Association held a congress in LaSalle, Illinois, which marked its expansion from a local to a national scale, and the Brotherhood of the Footboard began its national career. The year 1864 saw national organizing conventions held by cigar makers, ship carpenters, plasterers, and curriers. During the year of Appomattox, seven new national unions were launched, those of the carpenters and joiners, bricklayers, painters, iron heaters, tailors, dry-goods clerks, and coach-makers.[6]

Two of these organizations illustrate the variety of courses of evolution a national union might follow. The Brotherhood of the Footboard was established in 1863 at a series of conventions organized by William D. Robinson, an engineer on the Michigan Central who had been secretary of a short-lived

---

[5] Commons, *Labour*, II, 33–9; *I.M.I.U. Proceedings, 1864*, pp. 12, 25; *Fincher's Trades Review*, Oct. 15, 1864.

[6] Commons, *Labour*, II, 8–10; Charlotte Todes, *William H. Sylvis and the National Labor Union* (New York, 1942), p. 60; Powderly, *Thirty Years*, p. 28; Wieck, pp. 25–8, 84–5, 135–43. Todes includes a national union of wool-hat finishers in her list, but I can find no record of this union as early as 1865, and McNeill says the national union was founded in 1869. McNeill, *Labor Movement*, pp. 394–5. The Dry Goods Clerks' Early Closing Association is mentioned in none of these works and was primarily a New York organization, but it did send its president to a meeting of national union leaders in March 1866. Commons, *Doc. Hist.*, IX, 126.

union of engineers in 1855. Initially, the union was quite aggressive in its dealings with railroad corporations, and for the first year of its existence it welcomed firemen and machinists as well as engine drivers into its fold. Having been discharged by the Michigan Central, Robinson became a full-time organizer and traveled widely through the North—somewhat mysteriously, since he had no money, and many lines posted notice that any engineer or conductor who let him travel free would be dismissed. By the time of the convention of August 1864, the brotherhood had fifty–four lodges and had weathered several strikes against major railroads.[7]

Two portentous changes were made in the brotherhood at this meeting. Charles Wilson was elected Grand Chief Engineer of the union (now renamed the Brotherhood of Locomotive Engineers) when Robinson declined the nomination. Wilson immediately set about to consolidate his control over the brotherhood and to orient its activities away from disputes with railroad corporations and toward mutual insurance schemes. At the 1865 Boston Convention, held in the wake of a severe strike on the Michigan Central, Wilson's cohorts refused to allow Robinson the delegate's seat to which he had been elected. They proceeded to enact strike controls which were practically prohibitive, instituted an elaborate system of insurance benefits, and spent the rest of their time making a grand tour of local factories, listening to eulogies on their profession, and honoring Waltham watches.[8] The logical conclusion of the new trend was reached the following year when the brotherhood's convention approved and placed in its official proceedings a letter from a superintendent of the Erie Railroad instructing them on the proper purposes of their organization. The letter concluded: "Any attempt on the part of your members [or] your organization to place your body in antagonism to your employers . . . should be promptly and

---

7 *Workingman's Advocate*, May 2, 1874 (biography of W. D. Robinson); *Locomotive Engineers' Monthly Journal*, Vol. I (Feb. 1867), pp. 1–3; Allan Pinkerton, *Strikers, Communists, Tramps and Detectives* (New York, 1878), pp. 101–10.
8 *Locomotive Engineers' Monthly Journal*, Vol. I (Feb. 1867), pp. 1–3; *Daily Evening Voice*, Nov. 16, 22, 23, 1866.

immediately checked, and such evil disposed persons cured of their error, or summarily expelled from your deliberations. . . ."[9]

Wilson told the Boston meeting that the brotherhood should be "a school for engineers," so that membership would be a badge of competence and reliability. There were still unworthy men in the organization, he continued, and "managers of railroads would confer a great favor by assisting us to rid both the company and the Brotherhood of all such men."[1] The next year another officer summed up the new outlook by declaring: "Let our motto be *pro bono publico,* and ere long our Brotherhood will gain the approbation of the travelling world."[2]

As Wilson and his followers spurned strikes in order to husband the union's funds for benefit payments, they found themselves anticipating the "higher strategy of labor" which the A.F. of L. was to enunciate in the 1920's: build the trade union by demonstrating its worth to the employers and the public. They retained cultural peculiarities of the 1860's, however, by giving their sessions and their *Journal* the flavor of revival meetings. Each month a list of expulsions of unworthy members appeared in the *Journal.* Among them were A. C. McDonald, ejected for "leaving his lawful wife, and living with another woman," and E. M. Spencer, ousted for "being beastly drunk and running ten minutes on Express trains time." The mood of Wilson's brotherhood was epitomized by Brother Peter Swisher when he wrote: "In union there is strength; but in whiskey and prostitute society there is shame and remorse, and the evils deriving therefrom, very often resulting in death."[3]

More typical was the career of the national organization of bricklayers. A complex dispute between the Bricklayers' Union of Baltimore and both that city's contractors' association and the Baltimore and Ohio Railroad led to a strike in the spring of 1865. At the urging of President Fincher, the Philadelphia Trades Assembly contributed funds to the

[9] Quoted in Commons, *Labour,* II, 65.
[1] *Locomotive Engineers' Monthly Journal,* Vol. I (Feb. 1867), p. 3.
[2] *Ibid.,* p. 18.
[3] *Ibid.,* Vol. I (April 1867), pp. 7, 23; I (Feb. 1867), p. 24.

Baltimore strikers, helping them weather the storm intact.[4]
Fincher drew from the controversy the moral that bricklayers
needed an institution of their own to guarantee mutual support by all local unions in the trade. At his urging, leaders of
the Baltimore group met with their Philadelphia counterparts
in October to establish the Bricklayers' International Union of
the United States of North America. To a convention called by
the new organization in January 1866 came the delegates of
seven bricklayers' unions, with some 1,750 members. Two
years later, the 47 subordinate unions represented at the
convention claimed 5,736 members. Among all the significant
unions of the trade only the Chicago bricklayers held aloof
from the International—and they remained mavericks until
1899. The appointment of professional organizers salaried by
the International and concerted efforts to make the eight-hour
day the rule of the trade were the keys to this organization's
growth.[5]

The Bricklayers' Convention of 1866 did not confine its
attention to the peculiar problems of the craft, but joined the
swelling chorus of labor demands for "a law making eight
hours a legal day's work," and endorsed the proposals of
Fincher and Sylvis for the establishment of a national center of
all labor organizations.[6] It was, in other words, the search for
an institution to coordinate the efforts of the new national
unions that led directly to the founding of the National Labor
Union. The actual initiative was provided by Sylvis and
William Harding, the president of the Coachmakers' International Union and ex-president of the Workingmen's Union
of New York. At their summons, officers of nine national
unions, all of them residents of the New York area, met in
New York City late in March 1866. This group resolved to call
a National Labor Congress to meet in Baltimore in August and
to make the eight-hour question the principle business of the
meeting. Because of objections raised by the Workingmen's
Union that it and other trades assemblies were being slighted
in the preparations by this handful of officials of national

---

[4] Bates, pp. 18–19.
[5] *Ibid.*, pp. 19–29; *Workingman's Advocate*, Jan. 25, 1868; Ulman, pp.
142–5.
[6] Bates, pp. 19–22; Ely, pp. 63–4.

unions, the final call for the Baltimore Congress, issued jointly
by a committee established at the New York meeting and the
Baltimore Trades Assembly, included in its invitation all
national unions plus all "Trades Assemblies, Workingmen's
Unions, eight-hour leagues, and Labor Organizations throughout the United States."[7]

THE NATIONAL LABOR UNION

Baltimore's large, gloomy Front Street Theater was the
birthplace of the National Labor Union. From August 20
through August 25, 1866, some 65 delegates from local or
national unions in 20 different trades, 12 trades assemblies,
and four eight-hour leagues threshed out a program and a
constitution for an institution which they hoped might represent and guide the labor-reform movement in all its various
manifestations. This was a meeting of workers. Although but
two of the 18 national unions then in operation sent official
delegates, 55 of the participants were sent from local unions or
city bodies, and most of the remainder from eight-hour
leagues. The congress, furthermore, bore no evidence of any
dichotomy between "social theorists" and "hard-headed craftsmen . . . indifferent to utopias and primarily concerned with
matters of fact" such as Charles and Mary Beard ascribed to
the labor movement of that day.[8] Wage earners experienced in
the daily efforts of their class constituted the overwhelming
mass of the personnel, dominated the crucial committee structure, and filled the organizational offices both at Baltimore and
at the following year's congress in Chicago—the two sessions
at which the N.L.U. assumed the organizational form and the
theoretical orientation that controlled its entire career.[9] At
Baltimore the prime objective announced was the establish-

---

[7] Commons, *Doc. Hist.*, IX, 126–7; Sylvis, pp. 64–5; Commons, *Labour*,
II, 95–96. Andrews mistakenly says all national unions but two sent
representatives to the New York meeting. *Ibid.*, II, 96.
[8] Charles A. Beard and Mary R. Beard, *The Rise of American Civilization* (New York, 1928), II, 214–15. This dichotomy is repeated in
Gerald N. Grob, *Workers and Utopia. A Study of Ideological Conflict
in the American Labor Movement, 1865–1900* (Northwestern Univ.,
1961), p. 12.
[9] See Montgomery, "Labor and the Radical Republicans," pp. 240–3,
459–62.

ment by law of the eight-hour day, and the recommended means toward this goal—political action. At Chicago the greenback doctrine made its first appearance in the program of the N.L.U. These early decisions cast the die; from them the subsequent history of the organization flowed logically.

The desires of the assembled workingmen were spelled out in their many resolutions, and were subsequently recast in systematic form by a five-member committee to which was assigned the task of drafting *The Address of the National Labor Congress to the Workingmen of the United States*.[1] The work of the committee was dominated by Andrew C. Cameron of Chicago and Thomas A. Armstrong of Pittsburgh, two printers prominent in their respective city-central bodies. Cameron was already a leading labor journalist and Armstrong was on his way to becoming one. They were assisted by three men who never again appeared at national labor congresses: Gilman Rand of Massachusetts; William Iles, an iron molder from Georgia; and J. R. Bolan, a New York ship carpenter. Although the Baltimore Congress allowed the committee two weeks after the meeting's close to compose the *Address*, the committee did not complete its task for eleven months. Nevertheless, the pamphlet which appeared on the eve of the 1867 Chicago Congress made no mention of the currency reform proposals that were to loom so large in the *Declaration of Principles* adopted at Chicago.

The "all-absorbing subject of Eight Hours" keynoted the *Address*. Shortening the working day was presented as the pivotal concept in a program for remolding American social realities to a shape consistent with American political ideals. In the name of "the producing classes" the pamphlet argued "that the success of our republican institutions must depend on the virtue, the intelligence and the independence of the working classes; and that any system, social or political, which tends to keep the masses in ignorance, whether by unjust or oppressive laws, or by over-manual labor, is injurious alike to the interests of the state and the individual."[2] This "much desired reform" was to be realized, furthermore, not through

---

[1] Reprinted in Commons, *Doc. Hist.*, IX, 141–68.
[2] *Ibid.*, IX, 145.

the philanthropic endeavors of educated or elite groups in society, but rather through "the co-operation of the working-men of America" in promoting their own cause.[3] Through their efforts, expended with "a proper energy," an eight-hour law would be enacted "by an almost unanimous vote" at the next session of Congress and "eight hours will shortly become, by legal enactment, a day's work in every state in the American Union."[4]

Labor's pursuit of virtue, intelligence, and independence led the authors of the *Address* from concern over the eight-hour day to the traditional remedy of preserving the public domain for homesteaders and the somewhat newer recourse of promoting consumers' and producers' cooperatives. Both objectives were embraced by the motto: "The tools to those that have the ability and skill to use them, and the lands to those who have the will and heart to cultivate them."[5] Although the pamphlet warned that land grants to corporations threatened to promote a system of concentrated land ownership which was "not of American, but rather of British origin,"[6] it had only praise for British cooperative efforts, such as those of the Rochdale Pioneers. In both cases the evil to be combatted was "monopoly"—the concentration of control over land or capital in the hands of small groups of men. Most significantly, the lengthy argument in favor of workers' ownership of the means of production they employ contained not the slightest hint of an attack on profits or private property. Rent and interest were conceived as the fruit of exploitation; profit was not. Hence the *Address* contended that the high returns to capital from "bank stock, railroad bonds, federal securities, or loaned out on mortgage" attracted it away from manufacturing and housing construction, thus retarding economic growth, to the injury of the workingman. Against this evil he had no remedy "but to combine with his brother in labor and build his own house, manufacture his own goods, and supply his and his family's needs with his own provisions."[7]

---

3 *Ibid.*, IX, 147.
4 *Ibid.*, IX, 148.
5 *Ibid.*, IX, 164.
6 *Ibid.*, IX, 163.
7 *Ibid.*, IX, 148–51.

Such cooperative endeavors, furthermore, were envisaged as "intimately associated with" the struggle for the eight-hour day, for they would help make the workers "masters of their own time." Through their use, industrial growth could become an unmitigated boon to labor. The national future hopefully predicted by the *Address* was no arcadian paradise. On the contrary, it blended the aspiration for wide diffusion of economic power with an enthusiasm for the machine worthy of Henry Carey: "We confidently look forward to a period not remote when the co-operative principle will carry on the great works and improvements of the age. It will build all our cities, dig our ores, fill the land with the noise of the loom and the spindle."[8]

The third pedestal for the new society proposed by the *Address* was the thorough organization of workingmen and workingwomen into trade unions. Undeserving of the calumny which had been heaped upon them, these organizations, the *Address* argued, were "purely defensive in character." The unions insisted, "and justly so, that the employee shall have, at least, an equal voice with the employer in determining the value of the labor performed," and through this function they reduced poverty, fostered self-respect, and educated leaders among the workers. Effectively organized they created a barrier against "strife, anarchy and confusion."[9] But, the pamphlet concluded, trade unionists themselves had to introduce two reforms if this goal was to be reached. The first was the institution of a comprehensive apprentice-training system so as to make it impossible for employers to use "botches to thwart the claims of competent workmen." The second was the use of strikes only "as a *dernier* resort." The authors contended that "by the appointment, where practicable, of a conference committee, whose duty it would be to lay the nature of the grievance before the employer, and ask redress for the same, many, if not all, of the difficulties complained of could be satisfactorily removed."[1]

Finally, the *Address* drew labor's attention to its stake in

---

[8] *Ibid.*, IX, 151–2.
[9] *Ibid.*, IX, 153–4.
[1] *Ibid.*, IX, 154–5.

organizing Negro workers. "Unpalatable as the truth may be to many," it declared, the Negroes were now in a new position in America, and the actions of the white workingmen would determine whether the freedmen became "an element of strength or an element of weakness" in the labor movement. "What is wanted then," it concluded, "is for every union to help inculcate the grand, ennobling idea that the interests of labor are one; that there should be no distinction of race or nationality; no classification of Jew or Gentile, Christian or Infidel; that there is but one dividing line—that which separates mankind into two great classes, the class that labors and the class that lives by others' labor."[2]

This was labor's Baltimore Program—a synopsis of the labor-reform aspirations of the day. In addition to formulating common goals, however, the workers assembled in the Front Street Theater also designed and set in motion the National Labor Union as the institution to lead the way toward realization of these goals.

At the outset, the N.L.U. was, in fact, nothing more than a series of annual congresses at which each trade union, trades assembly, national union, eight-hour league, and other association striving for "the amelioration of the condition of those who labor for a living" was entitled to send representatives. The delegates were duty-bound to carry out the decisions of the congresses, but no real administrative center was created. A president was elected—J. C. C. Whaley, a prominent figure in the typographical union of the nation's capital—and Edward Schlaeger of Chicago's German *Arbeiter-Verein* was designated vice-president at large. Neither was appropriated a salary. These two officers headed an Executive Board which also included a recording secretary, a corresponding secretary, and a treasurer, together with the vice-presidents who represented each state.[3] The primary function of the vice-presidents, as it turned out, was to keep the various segments of the organization informed as to what others were doing. In the ensuing year William Jessup, the vice-president from New

---

[2] *Ibid.*, IX, 158-9.
[3] *Ibid.*, IX, 174; *Workingman's Advocate*, Sept. 1, 1866; Philadelphia *Public Ledger*, Aug. 24, 1866.

York, labored tirelessly to strengthen the N.L.U. and promote its program. Many of his counterparts in other states satisfied themselves with occasional letters to labor papers.

Furthermore, although the N.L.U. was founded by leaders of trade unions as a result of convention decisions of their unions, it never became a congress of trade unions. During the ten years (1866–75) in which annual gatherings were held—first under the name National Labor Union, then under the title Industrial Congress—a total of 34 national and international unions appeared on the American scene. Many of these were ephemeral, and in some cases one union was the successor of another in the same field (such as the American Miners' Association and the Miners' National Association), so that the number in existence at any one time never exceeded 20 during the 1860's, though it probably rose above 25 by early 1874. The largest number of national unions represented by official delegates or their presidents at any time in this series of ten congresses appeared in 1867 at Chicago. There, ten national unions of the 18 then in operation were represented. This figure was never again even approached until the Cleveland Industrial Congress of 1873, when nine of the existing 24 national unions sent delegates. Although all the congresses except those of 1871, 1872, and 1875 were attended by officials of subordinate unions affiliated with anywhere from eight to 13 nationals, the attendance of delegates holding credentials directly from the latter declined to five in 1868, rose to six the next year, fell to four in 1870, and stood at only one (the ever-loyal W.B.A.) in 1871. Similarly, the nine national unions attending the Industrial Congress of 1873 dwindled to six the next year and two in 1875 (among them still the anthracite miners).

To put the picture another way, nine unions, among them the Brotherhood of Locomotive Engineers and the telegraphers, never sent a representative of the national body to a national labor congress. Six others often had members attending, but those members held credentials from locals only. Among them were the American Miners' Association, the journeymen painters, and the ship joiners. Eighteen national unions sent their delegates to at least one labor congress, and among them were ten groups which deserve to be called the mainstays of the N.L.U., those whose representatives sat consistently at three or more congresses. Significantly, the same national unions lent such support to the congresses whether they went under the name N.L.U. or Industrial Congress. The only exception to this rule was the Coopers' International Union, which was not formed until 1872, and was represented for the first time that year. Only one national union had delegates at six congresses: the iron molders. Three of them, the W.B.A., the cigar makers, and the Typographical Union, were represented at five. The remainder of the mainstay group was made up of the bricklayers, the carpenters and joiners, the Crispins, the tailors, the machinists and blacksmiths, and the coopers. By and large, delegates or presidents of these organizations took part in the congresses of 1867, 1868, 1869, 1873, and 1874.[4]

Except for the sessions of 1871 and 1872, therefore, the national labor congresses drew heavy representation from these ten trades. On the other hand, the number of city trades assemblies directly represented declined abruptly—from twelve in 1866 to three the next year, remaining near that low figure at all succeeding congresses. The dominant weight among the delegates always lay with those dispatched directly from subordinate or unaffiliated local unions. Among them, as indeed among all delegates, the cost of rail transportation was clearly the most significant factor determining which were and which were not represented. At Baltimore the delegates from the convention city and the District of Columbia together constituted some 43 per cent of the total number attending. The next year at Chicago, workingmen from Illinois and Michigan enjoyed an absolute majority (forty out of seventy-two), while those from Maryland and the capital district had been reduced to six. Similarly, the following year in New York City, the states of New York and New Jersey provided a majority.[5] When the congress was moved to St. Louis in 1871, trade-union representation of any kind almost disappeared.[6]

What is striking, then, is that these trade-union leaders

---

[4] See Appendix C.
[5] Montgomery, "Labor and the Radical Republicans," pp. 240–1, 459–60, 589.
[6] *Workingman's Advocate*, Aug. 19, 1871.

did not set up a federation based on their own trades' organizations, but rather created an entirely new body more along the lines of a city trades assembly for the whole nation. Since, however, the trade unions refused to grant it the boycott, strike support, and arbitration functions typical of the city assembly, the N.L.U. from the outset was primarily a political organization.

After the Baltimore Congress, Whaley appointed President William Harding of the coachmakers; Alexander Troup, then secretary-treasurer of the National Typographical Union; and James Reed of the Washington House Carpenters' Union to draft a permanent constitution for the N.L.U. When Harding brought the proposals of his committee to Chicago, he met adamant opposition from the floor of the congress. He planned to create a trade-union congress with centralized controls. He proposed to base representation at congresses directly on affiliated membership, and he suggested that a Board of Directors conduct the activities of the N.L.U. between conventions. The provision for such a board was stricken out after a stormy debate in a committee of the whole. Sylvis was among those warning against the transfer of excessive power to a group of officers. Many other delegates expressed fear that numerical representation would lead to domination of the N.L.U. by New York City's unions. Consequently, a new committee chaired by Isaac J. Neale of the Cincinnati Trades Assembly, and including Sylvis, Jessup, Harding, and Daniel Evans of the Illinois Anti-Monopoly Association, was selected to formulate another draft constitution.[7]

The handiwork of Neale's committee was adopted as the new constitution of the N.L.U. It created a dual structure of representation from national unions and labor-reform organizations of all types, grouped by states. Each national union was entitled to three delegates and a vice-president at large; and local bodies, unions and others, were allowed one delegate apiece. Provision was also made for state unions, each of which might send two delegates. The last category remained quite amorphous in 1867, but two years later the N.L.U.

---

[7] *Ibid.*, Aug. 24, 1867; *Chicago Daily Tribune*, Aug. 21, 1867.

directed its president to appoint an executive officer in each state whose duty it was to call a state convention and charter a state labor union, so as to provide the N.L.U. with a geographical structure of federalism appropriate to the tasks of lobbying in legislatures and conducting electoral campaigns.[8] Again, the point to be emphasized is that the 1867 constitution and the 1869 revision were made at sessions heavily dominated by active trade unionists. They envisaged the N.L.U. as their political arm.

On the other hand, the trade-union leaders of the 1860's were no more willing to cede control over their trade affairs to a central labor body than their successors were to be twenty years later. When Conrad Kuhn, the formidable advocate of New York's German cigar makers, moved in 1869 that the N.L.U. coordinate and direct the efforts of the trade unions to "enforce" state hour laws by having trades centralized on a state basis so that they might conduct state-wide general strikes, his plan was studiously ignored by the other delegates.[9] Kuhn's suggestion took the line of the International Workingmen's Association, which sought to conduct both direct action and electoral maneuvers from the same labor centers. His comrade F. A. Sorge the next year sought to commit the N.L.U. to directing its constituent unions to bend "all their energies to obtain the general carrying out of the eight-hour rule, even going so far as to punish laborers who violate it."[1] The motion was referred to a committee, where it died.

Efforts to create a strike fund in the hands of the N.L.U. fared little better. Motions to provide mutual assistance in case of strikes were often made and sometimes passed, but the funds were never created. The Cleveland Industrial Congress of 1873 did promise its "hearty co-operation" to any labor organizations engaged in a "just" struggle that was brought to the attention of the congress.[2] Although many a bitter strike took place in the following two years, none received financial

---

[8] *Workingman's Advocate*, Aug. 24, 31, 1867, Sept. 4, 1869; *Chicago Daily Tribune*, Aug. 21, 1867.

[9] *Workingman's Advocate*, Sept. 4, 1869.

[1] *Ibid.*, Aug. 27, 1870.

[2] *Ibid.*, July 26, 1873.

aid from the Industrial Congress. In fact, the National Labor Congress of 1868 met in New York in the very midst of that city's great bricklayers' strike for the eight-hour day. Orators from the striking unions had toured the East raising money for their cause. The National Labor Congress resolved its sympathy and adopted a ringing defense of the right to strike, all for the sake of the bricklayers, but it offered them no money.[3] It should be kept in mind, however, that the jealousy with which unions treasured their trade autonomy did not extend only to the N.L.U. In 1872 the New York Workingmen's Union, at the urging of the Internationalists, instituted a plan of scrutiny of trade grievances in the city and a plan to raise funds through a tax on member unions to support authorized strikes by other members, whereupon Typographical Union No. 6 immediately seceded. Only the pledge that it would not be taxed induced that union to return to the city assembly.[4]

Here lies one of the several paradoxes in the life of the N.L.U. In conformity with the wishes of the leaders of national trade unions, it guaranteed each of those organizations absolute autonomy in trade affairs. But it went so far in their direction that it had nothing positive to offer national unions in the conduct of those affairs. Consequently, in the very years 1868 through 1870, when attendance of workingmen at the congresses was steadily swelling, one national union after another stopped sending official delegates. Although representatives of subordinate unions from all but one of the nationals that had demonstrated consistent loyalty to the N.L.U. were present at Cincinnati in 1870, only the Crispins, typographers, molders, and the W.B.A. bothered to dispatch representatives of their national bodies.[5] As the N.L.U. had seen to it that national unions had nothing to lose by their participation, so it guaranteed that they had nothing to gain. By 1870 the participants in the N.L.U. had already become the individual labor reformers who were committed to its political program, irrespective of the type of organization they led.

---

[3] *N.L.U. Proceedings, 1868*, pp. 25, 39–40, 47.
[4] Stevens, pp. 592–3.
[5] *Workingman's Advocate*, Aug. 27, 1870.

THE NATIONAL LABOR REFORM PARTY

The subsequent evolution of the structure of the N.L.U. was thus set by its political program and the limits already set by trade autonomy. Although agreement that the organization was to be labor's national political arm was easily reached, one tactical question flowing from that commitment stirred furious controversy: whether or not to found a labor reform party. The N.L.U. made the decision formally as early as 1866, and made it in the affirmative. The time had come, read a resolution adopted at Baltimore, "when the workingmen of the United States should organize themselves into a National Labor Party, the object of which shall be, to secure the enactment of a law making 'eight hours' a legal day's work by the national congress and the several state legislatures, and the election of men pledged to sustain and represent the interests of the industrial classes."[6]

That resolution, however, was adopted by the rather close margin of 35 to 24. The fact that the record of nay votes is incomplete (only 17 of the 24 negatives having been recorded) makes it difficult to analyze the tally precisely. The votes available and the hot debate which surrounded the adoption of the motion make it evident, however, that the delegates of the Philadelphia Trades Assembly adhered to the consistent stand of Jonathan Fincher, that body's leader: adamant hostility toward all talk of a labor party. The only Philadelphian to favor the party was I. D. Ware, editor of the *Coachmakers' International Journal*, who stood in agreement with President Harding of his union. The large core of the negative vote was cast by Virginians and Marylanders; the latter explained to their fellow delegates that they concurred with the labor party in principle, but wished first to help their Governor Swann and his allies remove the Radicals from control of the state legislature. "When we acquire our rights," pledged Baltimore carpenter William Cathers, "we are with you." Cathers proved true to his word. After the state elections of 1867 had ratified a new state constitution which abolished all test oaths (thus leaving only Negroes disfranchised), installed

---

[6] *Ibid.*, Sept. 1, 1866.

a legislature without a single Republican member, and launched an era of unspeakably corrupt railroad-ring politics, Cathers and James Hyland, both of whom had voted against the new party in 1866, went to work vigorously to promote a labor party in their state.[7] Almost all delegates from outside the Baltimore-Richmond-Washington-Philadelphia quadrangle favored the formation of the party. In deference to the dissenting minority, however, the question was reopened one day after the original ballot, and with but one opposing voice the proposal was carried once more—this time with the proviso that the party should be formed *"as soon as possible."*[8]

Four years passed without further progress toward the goal set at Baltimore. When delegates to the 1868 Congress in New York adopted a report which stated that "the very existence of the National Labor Union depends upon the immediate organization of an independent labor party,"[9] the only protests came from Fincher and from John LeBarnes, who was not a worker but a Republican veteran of the antislavery fighting in Kansas. Still, the congress did amend the report so as to remove the N.L.U. from the Presidential campaign, and, more important, it took no steps whatever to create the machinery of a party.[1]

President Whaley was, at most, a lukewarm supporter of the proposed party, and possibly even an opponent who disguised his true sentiments with guarded and diplomatic phrases. His successors, Sylvis and Trevellick, on the other hand, devoted themselves tirelessly to the task of realizing the pledge made at Baltimore. They supplemented their organization of state labor unions with encouragement to those bodies to form state labor parties. Under authorization from the 1869 congress, Trevellick appointed both a standing Executive Council of the N.L.U. and seventeen state executive officers,

---

[7] *Ibid.* On the political situation in Maryland in 1866, see Frank Richardson Kent, *The Story of Maryland Politics* (Baltimore, 1911), pp. 5–10; Harrington, pp. 56–60; DuBois, *Black Reconstruction*, pp. 564–5. On developments in 1867 and 1868, see Kent, pp. 19–30; *American Annual Cyclopaedia*, VIII (1868), 453–5; *Workingman's Advocate*, Dec. 7, 1867, Jan. 25, Feb. 1, 1868.

[8] *Workingman's Advocate*, Sept. 1, 1866. Italics in the original.

[9] *N.L.U. Proceedings, 1868*, pp. 22–3.

[1] *Ibid.*, pp. 23–4.

all of them devotees of the labor party idea. By the time the 1870 Congress assembled in Cincinnati, labor parties were functioning in states as disparate as Massachusetts, New York, and Nebraska. During the previous year, Trevellick had toured shoe towns, mine fields, farm communities, and industrial cities from the prairie to Cape Cod exhorting labor reformers toward the electoral arena. Now he asked the Cincinnati Congress to consider the proposition that the N.L.U. "declares itself a distinct political party, denominated as the Labor Reform Party." He suggested a national convention to choose a Presidential nominee and state conventions to nominate state candidates. "I consider this to be the only true basis . . . for ultimate success," argued Trevellick. As if to underscore his point, he had already sent an official letter to men he considered Presidential timber requesting their views on the N.L.U. platform, and he appeared at Cincinnati armed with replies from Governor John W. Geary of Pennsylvania, Generals Thomas Ewing, Jr., and C. W. Morgan of Ohio, and Congressman George W. Julian of Indiana.[2]

One formidable obstacle loomed in the path of Trevellick's plan. Trade unions almost universally prohibited the discussion of partisan subjects within their halls, and many of their leaders were reluctant to have such topics aired at any gathering to which they were accredited union delegates—city assemblies, state bodies, or the N.L.U. On the other hand the same leaders frequently endorsed the proposal to form a party. The question, therefore, seemed to be one of finding an organizational form which would separate the party from the congress of trade unionists.

The feasibility of such a step had already been demonstrated in New York, where the 350 trade organizations in operation made the state the nation's foremost center of trade unionism. Quite in contrast to the widely accepted notion that New York's trade unionists were antireformist or antipolitical, the labor leaders of both New York City and upstate had committed themselves enthusiastically to electoral activity in 1869. A rally held in Cooper Institute early in October to

2 *Workingman's Advocate*, Aug. 27, Sept. 3, 1870.

denounce the old parties and promote a Labor party had generated the highest level of cooperation yet witnessed among the unions of the city. The 26 unions then affiliated with the Workingmen's Union, 15 from the *Arbeiter-Union* and some 22 unions with no ties to any city body, among them the great Irish organizations of the waterfront trades, all participated in the rally. When the grand meeting took place, however, rank-and-file attendance proved very disappointing. These unions, which among them led between 70,000 and 100,000 workers, failed to fill more than two thirds of the hall. Many of the leaders quickly lost interest in the cause. Others rallied around the efforts of the *Arbeiter-Union* to set up a Joint Committee of unions to nominate a slate for county and legislative offices. Heading their ticket was Nelson W. Young, then president of the Workingmen's Union, who was put up for coroner and quickly endorsed by anti-Tammany Democrats, the Republicans, and the *New-York Times*.[3]

The International was clearly prominent in this movement. German woodworkers, heavily influenced by the I.W.A., were well represented in the Joint Committee by leaders like John Bossong and Fred Homrighausen. Robert Blissert and Conrad Kuhn were regular speakers at election rallies, and they often shared the limelight with Thomas Connally, a visiting spokesman of English labor. On the other hand, the facts that the Joint Committee in practice chose its candidates from among nominees of existing parties, that the *Arbeiter-Union* editorially advised workingmen to vote for any opponent of Tammany where no labor nominee was on the ballot, and that President Lucker of the Tailors' Union at one rally admonished his listeners to vote for the Republican candidate for Secretary of State (General Franz Sigel) led a number of devotees of the N.L.U. program to protest that the Labor party effort was being sabotaged. Foremost among these

---

[3] Excerpts from Proceedings, Workingmen's Assembly, State of New York, 1870 (Labor Collection, Misc. General Labor Organizations & Conventions, Box 2, W.S.H.S.), p. 14; *Workingman's Advocate*, Oct. 9, 23, 1869; "Report of the Executive for the State of New York," *Workingman's Advocate*, Sept. 3, 1870 (hereafter cited as Troup Report); *New-York Times*, Oct. 11, 16, 19, 26, 30, 31, Nov. 2, 1869, Jan. 18, 1870.

critics were Alexander Troup of the Typographical Union and
John W. Browning of the Bricklayers'.[4]

On Election Day, Tammany swept the polls, as usual.
Young received about one third of the votes cast for coroner,
while few of his running mates polled more than one seventh
of the votes.[5] Suspicion in many union halls that the Workingmen's Union had been made the plaything of ambitious politicians led to a serious decline in the number of delegates
attending its meetings. On the other hand, the frustrated
enthusiasm for a Labor party was offered new encouragement
by Trevellick. He designated as state executive for the N.L.U.,
not Jessup, the president of the state Workingmen's Assembly,
but Troup, its secretary. In his capacity as chairman of the
N.L.U.'s Committee on Obnoxious Laws, Browning went to
Albany to form a lobby for his own four-point legislative
program, with the aid of Troup and Assemblyman William G.
Bergen (a New York bricklayer). Although Jessup protested
that his leadership of the state was being usurped, Troup and
Browning were joined in their efforts by Kuhn and Young.
When this foursome suggested to the January session of the
Workingmen's Assembly that it set up a state Labor party,
they received such an enthusiastic response that even Jessup
felt obliged to include himself among the sponsors of the
party.[6]

The stumbling block to Troup's plan was that the constitution of the Workingmen's Assembly prohibited the discussion of partisan topics at its meetings. To circumvent this
obstacle, Troup invited the delegates to a private gathering to
be held after the close of the Workingmen's Assembly sessions.
When Troup's meeting took place, it was inspired by the
eloquence of Trevellick to form a state labor union (headed by
Troup and Browning), organize a grand rally to introduce it

---

[4] *New-York Times,* Oct. 11, 13, 25, Nov. 2, 1869; Troup Report;
Samuel Gompers, *Seventy Years of Life and Labor* (New York, 1925),
I, 48–9. *Cf.* Selig Perlman's conception of the International as unin-
terested in electoral activities. Commons, *Labour,* II, 204–7.

[5] *New-York Times,* Nov. 27, 1869.

[6] Letter of John W. Browning in *Workingman's Advocate,* Oct. 19, 1872;
letters of Browning, *ibid.,* Jan. 8, 29, Feb. 5, 1870; Troup Report. At
the Cincinnati Labor Congress Jessup and Troup clashed over Browning's program. *Ibid.,* Aug. 27, 1870.

to the workers, and charter local labor unions under its auspices
in every electoral district. Strictly local issues provided the
platform for the new labor union—enforcement of the eight-
hour law, repeal of conspiracy laws, mine and factory safety
legislation, prohibition of contract convict labor, and so on—
and it summoned the workers to abandon the Republicans and
Democrats. Within two weeks its leaders were making their
appeal for a Labor party explicit.[7] The crucial point, however,
is that through the creation of a state branch of the N.L.U.,
with its own structure peculiarly oriented toward electoral
activity, the political and trade-union functions of the state's
labor movement had been organizationally separated.

Here was a model for the N.L.U. to duplicate on a
national scale. At the Cincinnati Congress the proposal was
made by the prominent Massachusetts Crispin S. P. Cummings that the president of the N.L.U. be authorized to
appoint a committee whose task it would be to call an
immediate convention to establish a National Labor Reform
party. His objective, Cummings explained, was to create "a
distinct movement in both the political and industrial world"
—that is, to convene a separate body so that it might create a
party without "offending the prejudices of any connected with
this organization."[8] Troup seconded the motion, arguing the
importance of separating trade unions and politics. As trade
unions were necessarily "composed of men of all existing
parties," he declared, it was necessary to make the Labor
party distinct from the congress of trade unions so that
workers could participate in the party "without interfering
with their loyalty to their trade unions."[9]

When debate on Cummings's proposal was resumed after
the lapse of a day, the motion carried by the overwhelming
margin of 60 to 5. By the time the vote was cast, however, the
focus of the delegates' discussion had shifted away from
Cummings's central theme of divorcing the trades and electoral functions to the desirability of a Labor party per se.
Because Isaac Myers, leader of Baltimore's Negro workers,

---

[7] Letter of Browning, *ibid.*, Feb. 5, 1870; *ibid.*, Feb. 12, 1870; *Deutsche Arbeiter*, Feb. 19, 1870; Troup Report.
[8] *Workingman's Advocate*, Aug. 27, 1870.
[9] *Ibid.*

had opposed the projected Labor party with the contention that all labor's needs could and would be won through the Republican party, one worker after another (Cameron, Gilchrist, Trevellick, Troup, and so on) stormed to the floor to denounce existing parties and call for a new one. The debate was climaxed by a rousing oration against monopoly from the Reverend H. O. Sheldon, a venerable Oberlin abolitionist who participated in every industrial congress from 1869 through 1875. Amidst the "deafening cheers" that followed Sheldon's speech, the favorable vote was cast.[1]

Pursuant to the Cummings's resolution, Trevellick appointed a committee headed by two experienced politicians, Austin M. Puett and Alexander Campbell, both of whom were active in the N.L.U. but neither of whom had any trade-union connections. This committee issued a call for a convention to meet in Columbus, Ohio, in October 1871 to found a National Labor Reform party and to nominate candidates. Although the sitting of the Columbus Convention was subsequently postponed until February 1872—and at that time fell under the absolute control of professional politicians whose primary objective was to influence the impending convention of the Liberal Republicans—the fact remains that the party was at last a fact, and did surge energetically ahead.[2] It was the Industrial Congress, the trades segment of the N.L.U. structure, which collapsed. As the character of the debate over Cummings's motion had revealed, all attention at Cincinnati had been focused on giving life to the long-awaited party. No thought had been given to the proper character and role of the Industrial Congress now that its political function was being taken from it.

Although Andrew Cameron editorially assured trade unionists that the creation of the party meant that "future sessions of the Congress will partake exclusively of an INDUSTRIAL character," as "seems to be the desire of a large portion of the trades unionists,"[3] the situation was in fact by no means

---

[1] *Ibid.*
[2] *Workingman's Advocate*, Feb. 4, 1871; Call for a National Labor Party Convention, *ibid.*, July 8, 1871. For political developments in 1872, see below, pp. 400–9.
[3] Editorial, *Workingman's Advocate*, July 8, 1871.

so clear. For one thing, the state labor-union structure, into which the N.L.U. had by now been cast, was of value only for political purposes. At the allegedly "industrial" congress of 1871 there was not a single delegate with credentials from a national union. John Siney was present, to be sure, but as part of the Pennsylvania delegation. Many trade organizations, including the New York Workingmen's Assembly, declined to send delegates on the grounds that the congress was "political." Furthermore, the congress was called for St. Louis, an open-shop town far removed from the centers of union strength. Even President Trevellick declared in confusion: "Some claim that we are a political, and others a purely industrial body," and asked the delegates to clarify the situation. Still no clarification was forthcoming. The twenty-four delegates passed four aimless days tinkering with the constitution and resolving against evils of various sorts. At one point, they even called upon workers in every congressional district to assemble and elect delegates to the pending party convention in Columbus, despite the vehement objection of John Siney that such a resolution was out of place at the industrial gathering.[4] To cap the climax, the city chosen as site for the next annual gathering was Nashville, which was even more remote from trade centers than St. Louis.

Clearly, the N.L.U. was dying. But while the party was the victim of the manipulations of ambitious politicians who invaded the labor-reform movement for their own purposes, the Industrial Congress was expiring from neglect and from lack of purpose. At this point, President John Fehrenbatch of the Machinists' and Blacksmiths' International Union issued a plea for the formation of a National Trades Assembly, at which only bona fide workers would be represented and from which "everything that has a tendency to give the organization a political complexion" would be excluded.[5] When this call was endorsed by Martin Foran, president of the newly established Coopers' International Union, Browning successfully persuaded Trevellick to change the site of the pending con-

---

[4] *Ibid.*, Aug. 7, 1871; *Ohio BLS, 1877*, p. 34; Commons, *Doc. Hist.*, IX, 355.
[5] *Machinists' and Blacksmiths' International Journal*, Vol. IX (Sept. 1872), p. 779.

gress to Cleveland, headquarters of both Fehrenbatch and Foran. The *Workingman's Advocate* editorialized that the Cleveland Congress would be "purely of an *industrial* character," and exhorted all trade unionists to come, "reason together, and have a good old-fashioned re-union similar to the Baltimore Congress of 1866—where harmony and brotherly feeling prevailed."[6]

The gathering at Cleveland was forlorn. Fewer than a dozen men were present, and they left without electing officers or fixing a date for another meeting. They did, however, select Foran, Cameron, and Trevellick as a committee to bring the leaders of state and national unions together with the officers of the N.L.U. for the purpose of "calling a *National Industrial Congress*, whose primary object shall be to discuss questions of a non-political character. . . ."[7] Although Cameron was the author of this move, he was at that time so thoroughly involved in the Labor party effort that he deliberately withdrew from the scene and held his silence—as did Trevellick— while Foran contacted top figures in the iron molders (Saffin and Walls), machinists and blacksmiths (Fehrenbatch), and typographers (Collins). Through their efforts, the Industrial Congress of 1873 was convened at Cleveland. National trade-union officials, represented there almost as well as they had been at Chicago in 1867, recreated their national organization and energetically debated both trade and legislative issues, but studiously shunned all mention of electoral activity.[8]

John Andrews has drawn a sharp contrast between the N.L.U. and the Industrial Congress that has commonly been accepted by subsequent historians. The Cleveland Congress, said Andrews, "was the first appearance of an organization similar in object and structure to the present American Federation of Labor."[9] Such a contrast is misleading. The Industrial Congress could better be described as a continuation of the N.L.U. They both had the same program, and the national

---

[6] Letter of John W. Browning, *Workingman's Advocate*, July 20, 1872; editorial, *ibid.*, Aug. 17, 1872.

[7] *Ibid.*, Sept. 21, 1872.

[8] *Ibid.*, Sept. 21, 22, Nov. 2, 16, 1872, Jan. 25, Feb. 1, May 3, 31, July 26, 1873.

[9] Commons, *Labour*, II, 157. *Cf.* Ware, *Labor Movement*, p. 12.

unions that had built the N.L.U. were those that reappeared at the 1873 and 1874 congresses. Both seated delegates from reform associations as well as trade unions. In fact, in 1874 and 1875 the Industrial Congress began to erect its own local and state structure, to give itself a membership and life independent of the trade unions, just as the National Labor Union had done between 1868 and 1870.[1] To treat the N.L.U. as an assembly of reformers and the Industrial Congress as a body of "job-and wage-conscious unionists" is to distort the characters of both organizations and to miss the intimate continuity between them.

The basic distinction between the electoral and the trades organizations was one of function, not one of personnel, ideology, or objectives. The N.L.U. did not fail, as Gerald Grob contends, because of "the opposition of the constituent unions to a *program* that came to emphasize reform and political objectives to the almost total exclusion of practical ones. . . ."[2] On the contrary, the leaders of the "constituent unions" were the authors of that program, and they were themselves men who, in the words of Samuel Gompers, "turned instinctively to political activity for reform."[3] The lesson drawn from the N.L.U. experience of 1870 to 1872 by the founders of the Industrial Congress was not to shun reform politics, but rather to segregate clearly the trade-union and electoral functions of the movement. Thus John Browning, while secretary of the Bricklayers' International Union, never ceased to believe that the highest form of labor activity was the political, but he warned that trade unions and labor parties "must be kept distinct" lest the unions be destroyed. "We have excellent trades' unionists, who are warm democrats and zealous republicans . . . and who are ready to point with suspicion to every movement on our part towards the formation of political organizations," he argued in 1872. "The only way we can be successful with our local and national trades unions is by excluding politics from them."[4]

---

[1] See *Workingman's Advocate*, April 25, 1874, April 24, 1875; letter of William J. Jessup, *ibid.*, April 11, 1874.
[2] Grob, *Workers and Utopia*, p. 31.
[3] Gompers, I, 48.
[4] Letter of John W. Browning, *Workingman's Advocate*, Oct. 19, 1872.

Such was the institutional anatomy of the labor-reform movement from the middle of the 1860's to the mid-seventies. Energetic, often exerting a significant influence on both the economic and legislative fronts, the movement of this epoch nevertheless failed to generate a national center which could effectively coordinate its activities on either front. The National Labor Union served primarily as a series of annual congresses where the common demands of labor reformers were formulated and the vague social philosophy behind them was expressed, and to some extent, refined. It never became the focal point of labor activity. That remained the city trades assembly, supplemented by national trade unions. Effective bureaucratic machinery developed primarily on these levels. The administrative mechanisms and energy of the N.L.U. were entirely absorbed by the National Labor Reform party, and that in turn was easily dominated by nonworking class leaders. The corollary to this conclusion is that the historian searching for effective manifestations of working-class reform aspirations in the 1860's must focus his attention on the local community, rather than the National Labor Union.

From 1867 to 1875, on the other hand, the constant element in the N.L.U. and the Industrial Congress remained the program, while important changes took place in personnel, structure, and tactics. It was a workers' program, drafted and fought for by industrial wage earners. Devotion to that program is what brought labor reformers year after year to labor congresses that offered their organizations no material reward for their participation. And it was this program which directly challenged the Radicals' claim to be the voice of the people. The labor-reform movement became in effect the persistent activity of a large number of individuals who were committed to that program and who worked for it through a variety of institutional channels—reform clubs, benevolent societies, trade unions, the International, and political parties. To understand the movement and its relationship to the Radicals, therefore, requires an analysis of the personal and social characteristics of the labor reformers themselves, as well as a grasp of the structural dynamics of their organizations.

CHAPTER 5

Labor Leaders

The plastic quality of workers' organizations in post-Civil War America allowed the personal stamps of prominent spokesmen to leave indelible imprints. In fact, the primitive nature of the institutional sanctions at the disposal of the organizational leader forced him to rely heavily on personal charisma to bolster his authority among the workingmen. Since his personality and values were, and had to be, those which his followers admired, they also provide indications of the social ideology of the workingmen attracted to his organization. It was the eloquence of John Siney, standing at the sight of the terrible Avondale, Pennsylvania, mine disaster and delivering a sermon on the plight of the coal miner, that drew young Terence V. Powderly into the labor movement.[1] The impact of Richard Trevellick on his audiences was described by Ralph Beau-

---

[1] Powderly, "A Man and a Stone," *United Mine Workers' Journal,* May 18, 1916, p. 8.

mont, who had been the twenty-three-year-old president of the Knights of St. Crispin lodge in Utica, New York, at the time:

> He was the first speaker that I had ever heard on the labor question outside of my own lodge room . . . I shall never forget it. . . . The idea that a mechanic should be able to stand up before a crowded hall full of people and entertain them for more than two hours on economic questions was considered marvelous, and it was the talk of the city for days afterward.[2]

Unfortunately, most of the prominent labor reformers of the time left little record behind them. Intellectual friends of labor reform whose own origins lay in the proprietary or professional classes usually can be traced with ease. They were active in various causes over a long period of time and literate to the point of being garrulous. Quite the contrary was the case with actual wage earners in the movement. William Jessup, after almost a decade of great prominence as leader in New York, simply passed into oblivion. Workers as eminent in their time as J. C. C. Whaley, Samuel P. Cummings, and Jonathan Fincher bequeathed future historians abundant information about their cause, but none about themselves.

Enough data is available on ninety-six labor leaders, however, to allow a meaningful characterization of the labor reformer as a personality. All these men and the two women among them were wage earners who were prominent in the labor movement between 1860 and 1875. Unfortunately, the sample is biased toward figures who were still prominent in the 1880's, for it was in that decade that most of the biographical information on labor personalities was first compiled. This means that workers who pursued successful political careers and those who were to lead the Knights of Labor or the A.F. of L. are represented all out of proportion to their actual numbers in the 1860's, while many of those who passed quietly from the national scene before the late seventies are omitted. This bias is partially offset by available sketches of cigar

---

[2] Ralph Beaumont to O. Hicks, July 18, 1896, in [Obadiah Hicks,] *Life of Richard Trevellick, The Labor Orator, or the Harbinger of the Eight Hour System* (Joliet, Ill., 1896), pp. 218–19.

makers' officers elected in 1872, none of whom remained long in the limelight. Again, some 60 per cent of the workmen in the sample were printers, tailors, miners, and shoemakers, not because other trades played smaller roles in the 1860's, but because organization in these occupations was subsequently continuous. For example, ten leaders of the Knights of St. Crispin appear because two decades later they were renowned in the Knights of Labor, while other Crispins, often more noteworthy in the sixties, remained too obscure to be included in the sample. Finally, such vital information as date and place of birth is available only for sixty-five and seventy-seven workers, respectively, not for all ninety-six in the sample.

Of the leaders in this group, 32 were born in the United States, 13 in England, 11 in Ireland, nine in Germany, five in Scotland, five in Wales, and two in France. In other words, of the 77 whose birthplaces are known, 42 per cent were native Americans. Lumping all Britons together, on the other hand, reveals that they constitute 44 per cent of the sample. Even omitting the 11 Irishmen fails to detract from the remarkable role of the United Kingdom in providing American labor leadership, for the remaining 30 per cent of the prominent workmen stemmed from British nativity groups that constituted about 4.7 per cent of the industrial working classes.[8]

The bulk of these labor reformers were rather young men in the 1860's. Only nine of them had been born before 1825. On the other hand, only seven had been born in 1846 or later. Most of their birth dates lay between these extremes: 20 were born between 1826 and 1835, and 29 in the years 1836 to 1845. Eighteen of these workmen, or 27.7 per cent of the sample, were born between 1842 and 1847. It is, therefore, not surprising that at least 20 of them served in the army during the Civil War, and three others saw duty in the armed forces before that time. More impressive is the fact that none of them had personal experience in American labor activity of the 1830's and 1840's. Surviving veterans of the Locofoco age who were

---

[8] The discrepancy between the figure 4.7 per cent used here to describe British nativity groups in the working classes and the figure 4.6 per cent used in Appendix B arises because the latter refers to English- and Welsh-born only, and in the present percentage some 34,000 Scots are included.

still busy in labor-reform circles in the sixties were by that time all employers or self-employed, and with one or two exceptions, all were land reformers of the George Henry Evans school, such as John Commerford, Joshua K. Ingalls, Lewis Masquerier, and John Windt. Although there were a few trade unionists like Samuel Leffingwell and Charles W. Colburn, both typographers, whose union activity had begun in the fifties, and several Britons, Germans, and French with organizational experience from the Old Country, none of the working-class leaders of the sample had taken part in the American labor upheavals of the previous generation. Labor reformers whose personal careers linked the new movement with that of Jacksonian times were all middle class. Working-class activity had to generate itself anew.[4]

The careers of some individuals in the sample reveal both the variety of routes through which one could become a labor reformer and the common ideology of these men. Edward H. Rogers was exclusively a political spokesman for the workers. He was born in 1824 in Medford, Massachusetts, the son of a ship carpenter who had worked his way up to the ownership of a Charlestown shipyard, then lost it in the depression of 1837. Rogers labored briefly in his father's yard, then became a dry-goods clerk and later a machine-builder. He turned to shipbuilding as a wage earner in the forties. His thinking on social questions was awakened when he found himself snubbed by his fellow members of the Winthrop Congregational Church in Boston, who were successful mill owners and merchants. He found that "the church was very unsocial . . . poor people were not wanted."[5]

This experience is significant—first, because it was a common one for Massachusetts Protestant workingmen. Surveys conducted by the state Bureau of Statistics of Labor in 1869 and 1870 revealed that most Protestant workingmen did not attend church. The reason, explained one middle-aged boot cutter, was that "the church is composed of moneyed men, and there is no place for a day laborer to show himself."[6] Other

---

[4] See Appendix D.
[5] Edward H. Rogers, "Reminiscences," unpublished MSS in Rogers Papers, pp. 37–8; Rogers, "Auto-Biography," 1:3–4:5.
[6] *Mass. BLS, 1871*, p. 606.

workers pointed to the cost of pews and generally snobbish atmosphere of the congregations as deterrents to attendance. Most concurred in the observation of the worker who argued that Catholics came to church while Protestants remained home, because the "Catholic Church is democratic; the Protestant Church is too aristocratic for the clothes they [working people] are able to wear."[7]

On the other hand, it would be very misleading to conclude that Protestant workmen had turned their backs on religion. Their children were regularly dispatched to Sunday school, and many who stayed away from church subscribed to religious periodicals. Rogers himself was profoundly devout. His notebooks are filled with scriptural quotations, sermons, and commentaries by theologians, and his "Reminiscences" are devoted mainly to the development of his religious thought. In one notebook he assembled in the 1880's the reader finds side by side notes from Edward Bellamy's *Looking Backward* and the text of a sermon by the Reverend L. C. Baker entitled "The Fire of God's Anger." More specifically, Rogers reacted to Congregationalist snobbery by turning Methodist. Since Methodism was the faith most commonly associated with radicalism, it is noteworthy that Rogers enrolled in Methodist classes in 1854, the very year he joined the Republican party.[8]

Only among German Socialists were atheist workingmen to be found in substantial numbers. The Lassallean-oriented *Deutsche Arbeiter* of Chicago criticized the National Labor Union in 1869 for opening its convention with a prayer. Such nonsense, it commented, keeps no wolves from the door. The following year the Marxist F. A. Sorge attended the National Labor Congress and moved that the opening prayer be eliminated from the proceedings. The motion was instantly tabled without discussion.[9] In this respect, the *Freidenker* attitudes of German workers reflected their ideological affinity with middle-class radicalism in their homeland, just as did the Methodist inclinations of Protestant American labor reformers.

---

[7] *Mass. BLS, 1870,* p. 306. See also *ibid.,* 586, 588–9, 593, 595, 601, 605, 606, 610, 618.
[8] Scrapbook, Rogers Papers; Rogers, "Auto-Biography," 10:7, 10:9.
[9] Chicago *Deutsche Arbeiter,* Aug. 28, 1869; *Workingman's Advocate,* Aug. 27, 1870.

Sorge had been active in the secret Order of Secularists in New York before he entered labor activity, and Karl Heinzen, the noted German Radical in Boston, warned German workers not to join trade unions lest the American workers force them to say prayers.[1]

But pray the Americans did. William Sylvis and Richard Trevellick were both ardent Methodists. Uriah Stephens, founder of the Knights of Labor, was educated for the Baptist ministry. Although church attendance seems to have been particularly low among English immigrants, those who adhered to any denomination were largely Dissenters.[2] Methodism was almost universal among the Welsh miners, for whom the trade union and the chapel were the basic pillars of social life.[3] A Bay State machinist, who proclaimed himself a reader of several religious periodicals, the Bible, the *American Oddfellow*, and the *Springfield Republican* made the connection between his religious beliefs and labor's cause explicit: "If all would labor eight hours, and spend the remaining sixteen rightly, this world would be a paradise."[4]

The logical link between the theological and social doctrines of such labor reformers lay in the Wesleyan notion of "free agency." As labor reformers shared the Radicals' devotion to free upward mobility in worldly station on the basis of merit alone, so were they attracted to religious beliefs that placed simple faith above doctrinal erudition and held saving grace free in all and free for all. John Jacob Astor, who climbed from humble origins to great wealth, emerged as a heroic figure in the speeches of Sylvis. In the pages of the Boston *Voice* the reader could find poetry by a struggling young Unitarian minister named Horatio Alger, Jr. One such poem began: "Work while the day lasts, for the night cometh when no man can work."[5] On the other hand, the editors of the *Voice* protested excessive glorification of earned wealth with the comment: "It is not the desire to be 'capitalists' with

---

[1] Schlüter, *Die Internationale*, pp. 411–21; Heinzen, II, 290–5.

[2] See *Mass. BLS*, 1870, pp. 465, 600; Yearley, *Britons*, p. 192; Berthoff, pp. 156–60.

[3] Conway, pp. 33–40, 285.

[4] *Mass. BLS*, 1872, p. 272.

[5] *Daily Evening Voice*, Jan. 12, 1865. On Alger's career at this period, see *D.A.B.*, I, 178.

which we must inspire the people. . . . It is the high and holy mission of labor reform to show men an object worthier than wealth."[6] And this mission was couched in unmistakably Wesleyan terms by Sylvis when he called upon the Iron Molders' Union in 1867 to

> rejoice that manly independence, blended with a just appreciation of individual rights, has given us strength and power to combat the wrong, and to assert and maintain the great principle of free agency, with which an all-wise Creator has endowed mankind.[7]

Hand in hand with the doctrine of free agency came the cause of temperance. Until the close of the career of the Knights of Labor, the war against "demon rum" remained a major aspect of labor reform. It was through the labor movement that Sylvis became a "cold water man," and in the last years of his career he wrote many articles for the cause. Trevellick had not only become a temperance advocate in his younger days in England, but had even joined a vegetarian society. Rogers defended the eight-hour day as a reform that would lead workingmen away from the bottle. Samuel F. Cary of Cincinnati, who after 1867 was known as "labor's Congressman," began his public career as a lecturer for prohibition.[8] Here again, the parallel with the Radicals is striking. Godkin, it will be remembered, discussed utilitarianism in terms of the value of prohibition laws. Henry Wilson and Nathaniel Banks both entered politics in the 1830's by making speeches to their fellow workmen on behalf of water. In the heyday of radicalism, 1867, Wilson, together with General Oliver O. Howard of the Freedman's Bureau and Senator Richard Yates, led a move to banish liquor from the halls of Congress, obtained a pledge of total abstinence from the capitol police and most Senate employees, and organized a Congressional Temperance Society.[9]

---

[6] Editorial, *Daily Evening Voice*, Sept. 20, 1867.

[7] Sylvis, p. 173.

[8] Sylvis, pp. 88, 141–3; Hicks, p. 15; [Edward H. Rogers], *Reasons for Believing that the People Will Use Leisure Wisely, With a Statement of the Character of the Eight-Hour Movement, by a Workingman* (Boston, 1866); Roseboom, p. 224.

[9] Nason, *Wilson*, pp. 378–81; Harrington, pp. 3, 4.

At first blush, the Irish labor leader would appear to be alien and immune to such an ideology. This was not the case, however, because the Irish-born labor reformer in America was culturally a far different figure from the Catholic peasant of the Old Country. To begin with, of the eleven Irish labor leaders in the sample, four were Protestants (Robert McKechnie of the Typographical Union, James L. Wright and Robert Calvin Macauley of the Knights of Labor, and John Pollock of the American Miners' Association). Among those Catholics of whom enough is known to place them in the sample, not one could be classified as a peasant immigrant. On the contrary, three were raised from childhood in industrial districts of England (Hugh McLaughlin, John Siney, and John Welsh). So thoroughly had Siney adapted himself to the ways of Lancashire that the Mauch Chunk *Coal Gazette* remarked: "He looks and talks like a Scotch-Irishman."[1] Two others, Patrick Collins and Hugh Dalton, had arrived in the United States at the ages of two and four, respectively, and spent their youths in American schools and industry, and John A. Heenan, a skilled cigar maker, could hardly have been older than fourteen when he reached America. The last, Frank Roney, had been a city-bred iron molder in Ireland and, more important, was an ardently anticlerical Fenian.[2] It is, therefore, not surprising to discover Siney an ardent apostle of the temperance cause; to find the Father Matthew Temperance Society as strong among Irish-American trade unionists as the Good Templars were among native-born members; or to read of speakers at meetings of the Catholic society arguing simultaneously the evils of drink and the virtues of producers' cooperatives.[3]

The ideological syndrome of "free agency," self-improvement, and temperance was capped by a commitment to a society in which all members were free to move upward on the

---

[1] Quoted in Berthoff, p. 92. For religion and early years of McKechnie, see Stevens, pp. 648–51; of Wright, see Ware, *Labor Movement*, p. 28; of Macauley, see McNeill, *Labor Movement*, p. 610; of Pollock, see Roy, pp. 127–8; of McLaughlin, see *Workingman's Advocate*, Dec. 13, 1873; of Siney, see Killeen, pp. 35–59; of Welsh, see *ibid.*, pp. 262–3.
[2] Collins, "Obituary"; Stevens, p. 666; Roney, pp. 2–54.
[3] See account of meeting of Father Matthew Temperance Society No. 3, New York *Daily Tribune*, April 26, 1867.

basis of their own talents. Although labor reformers and Radicals both viewed such a social order as the ideal, the former were far from convinced that it represented the actual state of American affairs. In fact, the rhetoric of the labor movement stressed the downward movement of the mechanic's social status. The organizational activity of Charles H. Litchman began too late to permit his inclusion in a sample of leaders of the sixties, but his career dramatized the type of downward social mobility which workers in the sixties frequently attributed to the growth of industrial capitalism.

Litchman's father was a shoe manufacturer in Marblehead, Massachusetts, and Litchman learned to "turn a shoe" while employed as a salesman by his father. In 1870 he established his own factory in partnership with a brother, and a few years later he took up the study of law. The outbreak of the depression in 1873 ruined both his shoe business and his law study and drove Litchman to seek employment as a journeyman shoemaker. Not only did he find himself a wage earner, he was now not even a full-fledged journeyman, for the advance of mechanization and division of labor left him only one of sixty-four men working on successive phases of the production of a single shoe. He was, to use his own phrase, "one sixty-fourth of a shoemaker."[4]

Here is the classic case of the alienation of the worker from the means of production. But how typical was it? Enough information is available on eighty-seven men in the sample to suggest an answer. In only five cases had the fathers of the labor reformers been employers or self-employed. Martin Foran was born to the family of an Irish immigrant who owned a farm and a small cooper shop, Sylvis was the son of a wagon maker, and Rogers of a onetime shipyard proprietor. George A. R. McNeir learned printing in the office of his father, who was state printer of Maryland. James Madison Hilsee, a founder of the Knights of Labor, was a sixth-generation American who initially cut garments in his father's tailor shop. Each of these men, furthermore, had pursued a variety of occupations before settling down as a wage earner in his trade. Three others grew up on family farms, though all left

---

[4] *Journal of United Labor,* June 15, 1880, pp. 17–19.

for industry or the army while still minors—John Devlin in
Pennsylvania, W. H. Harden in Massachusetts, and John R.
Pike in Maine. Trevellick and Thomas Phillips were born on
British farms.[5] James L. Wright had worked his way up to the
position of manager of a large Philadelphia clothing firm
before the 1857 depression sent him back to the tailor's bench,
and two others who helped him found the Knights of Labor
(Joseph S. Kennedy and Robert C. Macauley) at some time
operated their own tailor shops. Sylvis and Devlin had both
tasted and then lost success and independence in the business
world.[6]

The truly impressive fact, however, is that seventy-six of
the labor reformers (87.3 per cent of the sample) entered the
economy as wage earners in industry and apparently were
sons of wage earners. There was, in other words, no personal
loss-of-status crisis for most of these labor leaders. Only the
tailors among them, especially the little group who founded
the Knights of Labor in 1869, dwelt as a group in a world
where the line between small shopkeeper and journeyman was
still hazy. More impressive yet is the fact that only three had
in a meaningful sense come off American farms. In a word,
these leaders had overwhelmingly been born into the working
classes and grown up in the industrial world. A perusal of the
workingmen's responses to questionnaires of the Massachusetts Bureau of Statistics of Labor in the early seventies
strengthens this impression. In almost every case the respon-
dent had entered the mill or the trade in boyhood and spent
the rest of his life there.[7] The arcadia of the independent

---

[5] On Foran, see *Workingman's Advocate*, Sept. 27, 1873; *National
Cyclopaedia of American Biography* (New York, 1926), XIC, 156. On
Sylvis, see Sylvis, 19. On Rogers, see "Auto-Biography," 1:3. On McNeir,
see George G. Seibold, *Historical Sketch of Columbia Typographical
Union Number One Hundred and One (Known as Columbia Typo-
graphical Society from 1815 to 1867)* (Washington, D.C., 1915), pp. 28,
71, 72. On Hilsee, see McNeill, *Labor Movement*, pp. 608–9. On Devlin,
see *Journal of United Labor*, Vol. IX (Jan. 3, 1889), p. 2761. On
Harden and Pike, see *Labor Leader*, Jan. 15, 1887. On Trevellick, see
Hicks, p. 11. On Phillips, see Yearley, *Britons*, pp. 198–202.

[6] On Wright, see Ware, *Labor Movement*, p. 28. On Kennedy and
Macauley, see McNeill, *Labor Movement*, pp. 609–10. On Sylvis, see
Sylvis, p. 24. On Devlin, see *Journal of United Labor*, Vol. IX (Jan. 3,
1889), p. 2761.

[7] *Mass. BLS, 1871*, pp. 570–621.

mechanic and agrarian egalitarianism after which labor's rhetoric often hankered was already a generation dead.[8]

On the other hand, the urban-industrial world offered important career opportunities to the young worker of which labor leaders were quick to take advantage. Both Fred Turner and William Jessup voluntarily left clerical occupations for manual trades (gold beater and ship joiner, respectively) in the belief that they could improve their livelihoods by the change. Some rose directly through the ranks of industry. Andrew Roy became a mine superintendent even before entering labor-reform activity and Daniel McLaughlin closed his career as one, while John Jarrett became secretary of an employers' association. Shortly after they established the Knights of Labor, Robert Macauley and Uriah Stephens became partners in their own tailor shop. Just as their firm during its brief existence served as a headquarters for the Knights, so Arsene Sauva's tailor shop in New York was at the same time a meeting place for his fellow-refugee Communards. Only four figures in the sample, however, became successful employers in their own right: George Blair, who employed sixty men in his box factory by 1883; Alexander Troup, who published the New Haven *Daily Union* in the seventies; Homer L. McGaw, owner of a printing shop at the same time; and Henry George, who owned a mill in Detroit in the eighties. Interestingly, Blair, McGaw, and Troup all continued to be active in either the Knights of Labor or a greenback party after they had become employers. George was different—by 1887 he had earned himself a place on the Knights' unfair list.[9]

Still, labor reformers who moved upward through the

---

[8] *Cf.* Grob, *Workers and Utopia*, pp. 7–21; Samuel P. Hays, *Response to Industrialism: 1885–1914* (Chicago, 1957), pp. 32–5.

[9] On Turner, see *Journal of United Labor*, Vol. IV (July 1883), pp. 513–14. On Jessup, see unidentified biographical sketch "William J. Jessup," Labor Collection, Biography and Papers, WSHS. On Roy, see *Workingman's Advocate*, Jan. 17, 1874. On McLaughlin, see *Journal of United Labor*, Vol. I (Sept. 15, 1880), p. 56. On Macauley, see McNeill, *Labor Movement*, p. 610. On Sauva, see Bernstein, pp. 89, 144. On Blair, see Senate, *Labor and Capital*, II, pp. 37–8. On Troup, see Stevens, p. 432. On McGaw, see McNeill, *Labor Movement*, p. 611. On George, see Thomas Dolan reminiscences in *The Labor Leaf*, Jan. 7, 1885; Agnes Inglis, "Thomas Dolan," MSS in Trevellick Papers.

ranks of industry were few. More frequently, trade-union activity led a leader to lose his job against his will, and subsequently to enter the business or professional world. Thomas A. Armstrong of Pittsburgh and Andrew C. Cameron of Chicago were both working printers who undertook the editorship of labor papers during strikes in their trade. The two remained journalists even after their original papers had failed. Fred Turner and John James became grocers after they were blacklisted.[1] Similarly, Joseph Patterson was driven from Schuylkill County's anthracite fields after the defeat of his union in 1875, only to return at the end of the century as a prominent lawyer.[2] A similar tale was recounted by a Massachusetts shoemaker concerning four workmen who had led a strike in his trade in 1860 and been blacklisted for their pains: "All four went into the army as privates; two came home bearing the rank of Colonel, and one came home as Captain, and one was shot and killed in the Red River expedition. Of the three, one is an able lawyer, one a shoe dealer, and the third is in good business."[3]

THE LURE OF OFFICE

Beyond question, however, the most significant avenue of social advancement open to the workingman in this age was party politics. For labor leaders to become successful politicians was both easy and commonplace. Among the 96 labor reformers in the full sample were 44 who took part in the machinery of American party politics, a few as executives of greenback or labor-reform parties, but the bulk as candidates for public office. Of these 44 the largest number (18) participated in labor-reform parties, but 13 were active Republicans and nine functioning Democrats. No members of socialist parties who were not actually seeking electoral office are included in this group, and the party affiliations of four

---

[1] On Armstrong, see [anon.], *100 Years as a Chartered Union, 1852–1952: History of Pittsburgh Typographical Union No. 7* (n.p., n.d.), p. 30; *National Labor Tribune*, Jan. 31, 1874. On Cameron, see *D.A.B.*, III, 433–4. On Turner, see *Journal of United Labor*, Vol. IV (July 1883), pp. 513–14. On James, see Roy, p. 161.
[2] Joseph F. Patterson, "After the W.B.A.," *Schuylkill Hist. Pubs.*, IV, 168–84.
[3] *Mass. BLS, 1871*, p. 615.

members of the sample are unclear. More significant even than this extent of political participation is the degree of success these labor leaders achieved. Sixteen of them at some time in their lives held seats in state legislatures, three were city councilmen, three were mayors, and four became members of the federal House of Representatives. Fifteen of them (including several who gained elective office) earned patronage appointments. Seven of these were positions in state bureaus of labor statistics and eight were other sinecures, ranging from American consul in Birmingham, England, (Jarrett) to chief of the Pittsburgh Fire Department (Miles Humphreys).

Small wonder a Massachusetts woolen manufacturer asserted that he preferred workmen with no more than a common-school education, because "the more learned are endeavoring to fit themselves for Congress."[4] Small wonder too that Samuel Gompers found labor reformers in the sixties "looked at industrial problems from the point of view of American citizens and turned instinctively to political activity for reform."[5] Both power to achieve legislative reforms and a great potential future for the reformer lay in the working-class vote.

Thus Edward Rogers attached himself to the rising Republican party and won a seat in the Massachusetts legislature as the candidate of his fellow shipyard workmen at the age of forty-one. His work on the legislative committee investigating the hours of labor gained Rogers such prominence that, though he was defeated in his effort for re-election in 1866, Governor Bullock appointed him to a salaried commission to study the same question the next year. Rogers was returned to the legislature in the 1867 elections, and afterward remained stanchly loyal to his party. In 1869 he wrote a pamphlet urging the workingmen not to support the Labor Reform party, which entered the lists that year. By this point Rogers's career was clearly his prime concern. He hoped to become deputy chief of the state Labor Bureau in 1869, but he wrote:

> Wendell Phillips ruled the State, in matters of reform at the time. He decided in favor of General H. K. Oliver,

---

[4] Quoted in Kirkland, *Dream and Thought,* p. 69.
[5] Gompers, I, 48.

and my friend Geo. E. McNeill. I became satisfied that there would be no further promotion for me, and that I must begin, and follow up a course of pamphleteering, in order to keep myself and my cause before the public.[6]

The Republican party made good use of Rogers's pamphlet, but it soon lost interest in Rogers. All he earned for his efforts was a federal appointment to a clerical post—back in the navy yards. In 1872 he joined forces with T. Wharton Collens, a Catholic layman from New Orleans, and the Reverend Jesse H. Jones of North Abington, Massachusetts, to establish the Christian Labor Union, based on a social gospel doctrine. To this organization Rogers devoted his remaining years.[7]

A smoother path to political success was found by John Fehrenbatch. Born in Rochester, New York, in 1844, Fehrenbatch entered a woolen factory at the age of eight, but before he was able to educate himself through evening school and apprenticeship and become a machinist, the Civil War began. Moving west to Indianapolis, he was elected president of the local Machinists' and Blacksmiths' Union No. 4, while he pursued his trade by day and attended Purdue College by night. As leader of his state's Grand Eight Hour League he became an influential figure in state politics during the 1866 campaign. Four years later he became president of the International Union and editor of its journal. Nominated by the Republicans for the state legislature in 1873, he lost in a chaotic race. But three years later he won the desired seat, and after 1878 retired to a federal sinecure provided by the Hayes administration.[8]

The path from trade-union office to a seat in the state legislature was well traveled. In 1863, for example, Patrick Keady stood before the New York Practical Housepainters' Association as its president, denouncing the recent draft riot and glorying in the fact that no members of his union had participated. Five years later he sat upon the platform at the

[6] Rogers, "Auto-Biography," 15:13–14, 16:10; Rogers, *Is It Expedient to Form a Political Party in the Interest of Labor?* (Chelsea, Mass., 1869).

[7] Rogers, "Auto-Biography," 17:5–14.

[8] *Workingman's Advocate*, Nov. 15, 1873; Commons, *Labour*, II, 176.

Special Council of the National Labor Union as the Honorable Patrick Keady, Democratic assemblyman from Kings County.[9] Miles Humphreys, an iron boiler from South Pittsburgh, helped negotiate a historic sliding-scale agreement with Allegheny County manufacturers in 1865 when he was Grand Master of the Sons of Vulcan. Three years later his neighbors sent him to the state legislature on the Republican slate. After three terms in the state assembly and two in the state senate, Humphreys was appointed chief of the Pennsylvania Bureau of Industrial Statistics. Only in 1877 was his rise in power checked. Nominated by the Republicans to succeed William C. McCarthy (himself an erstwhile printer who enjoyed labor endorsement) as mayor of Pittsburgh, Humphreys met defeat when the city's chamber of commerce threw massive support to his Democratic opponent. Still, he never again boiled iron, but served on the Bureau of Industrial Statistics and could be found in 1911 as chief of the city's fire department.[1]

Among Humphreys's associates in the Pennsylvania legislature of 1874 was John W. Morgan, who had served as president pro tem of the W.B.A. (by then renamed the Miners' and Laborers' Benevolent Association) during the great strike of 1871. Welsh-born Morgan had been in the pits since childhood, excepting four years of service in the Union army. In 1873, at the age of forty-one, he received the nomination of both the Republicans and the Labor Reform party, launching him toward six years of life as a legislator. During his last year in Harrisburg he was joined by John F. Welsh, leader of the same union during the Long Strike of 1875. One year older than Morgan, Welsh had been born in Ireland but raised in British pit towns before he came to America and entered the mines and the army of the new country. Before he helped John Siney establish the Workingmen's Benevolent Association,

9 *Fincher's Trades Review*, July 25, 1863; "Grand Rally of Workingmen," *Workingman's Advocate*, July 3, 1868; *New York Civil List*, pp. 506, 508.
1 *Pa. BLS*, 1887, G 2; Allen Humphreys Kerr, "The Mayors and Recorders of Pittsburgh, 1816–1951: Their Lives and Somewhat of their Times" (unpublished MSS, Historical Society of Western Pennsylvania archives), pp. 174–83; John A. Fitch, *The Steel Workers* (Vol. III of *Pittsburgh Survey*, ed. Paul U. Kellogg; New York, 1909–14), pp. 20, 106; Pittsburgh *Gazette*, Oct. 17, 1868; *National Labor Tribune*, April 4, May 16, 1874.

Welsh belonged to a secret Pennsylvania branch of the Free Colliers of Scotland. The blacklist deprived him of his livelihood after his union was crushed in 1875, but his four years in the legislature on the Greenback-Labor ticket opened new vistas. In the eighties he became a mine superintendent, and his three sons were professional men.[2]

Among labor reformers who entered state legislatures in these years only Patrick A. Collins made the step from there to Congress. Collins was but four years old when his mother fled with him from the chaos of starving Ireland to the Boston region. At first his Chelsea boyhood was normal for a Catholic immigrant child. Driven from school at the age of eleven by his young Protestant classmates, who were excited by the Know-Nothing craze, he went to work in a fish shop. At this point, his life made a most unusual twist. Among the parishioners at his church was a Negro attorney named Robert Morris, who took a liking to the Irish lad and made him his office boy. Enjoying the "run of the court," Collins soaked up both literary and practical knowledge of the law and politics. His ambition at this point, however, was to become a machinist, but the Catholic boy could find no place for himself as an apprentice. After a brief trip westward with his family, Collins took a job in a furniture shop. Here he encountered still another world. Among his shopmates was Jeremiah W. Coveney, a Fenian who soon was to become a lieutenant colonel in the army and later a prominent Democrat in politics. Collins joined the brotherhood and was soon commissioned an organizer. During the war years he also helped establish the Upholsterers' Union of Boston. Although Collins was foreman of his shop by 1863, he was also president of his union and its delegate to the Boston Trades Assembly, and he led several strikes against the company where he worked.

In 1867 Collins became secretary of his Democratic ward club and was elected to the Massachusetts legislature. In all, he spent three years in the state House, then two in the state Senate, while he studied law and gained admission to the bar. At the close of his term as the first Irishman in the state upper house, a period he had devoted primarily to fighting for the

---

[2] Killeen, pp. 262–3, 277; Patterson, "Old W.B.A. Days," pp. 381–2; Harrisburg *Telegraph*, Feb. 10, 1904 (article on Henry W. Oliver).

rights and claims of Catholics, Collins committed himself full time to his law practice and to being boss of Boston's Democrats. He won election to Congress in 1882, 1884, and 1886. By the end of this time, this former Fenian and trade unionist had emerged as the archetype of the urban Democratic politician and defender of the Catholic Church. He was a director of the International Trust Company and admitted to the exclusive preserve of upper-class Democrats in New York City, the Manhattan Club. His career reached a climax in 1901 when he became the first Irishman to hold the office of mayor of Boston. He died in office, four years later.[3]

Three other trade unionists of the sixties sat in Congress with Collins in the eighties: John M. Farquhar, Frank Lawler, and Martin A. Foran. None of the three made their way through state legislatures. Farquhar's rapid rise to fame and wealth was based on his ability to utilize the ease with which printers still became editors or publishers, the ready access to the bar which America provided, and the great opportunities offered by a rapidly expanding army. Born in Ayr, Scotland, in 1832, Farquhar came to the United States as a boy and learned the printing trade. During the 1850's he studied law and engaged in some publishing ventures of his own, while he worked to build the new National Typographical Union. That union elected him president in 1860, but seeing his organization fall apart under the impact of the war, Farquhar joined the troops in 1862. Within a year he had risen from an infantry private to a major and judge advocate. Leaving the army with a Congressional Medal of Honor, he went to Buffalo to practice law. Although, like most typographers, Farquhar never severed his relations with his union, it was not as a trade unionist but as a prominent attorney that he was sent to Congress on the Republican ticket in 1885. In 1890 he declined to stand for re-election and retired to practice law privately (except for his service on the U.S. Industrial Commission from 1898 to 1902) until his death in 1918.[4]

---

[3] Collins, "Obituary"; O'Hare, pp. 22, 263–7, and *passim*.
[4] U.S. Congress, House, *Biographical Directory of the American Congress, 1774–1949*, 81st Cong., 2d Sess., House Document 607 (Washington, D.C., 1950), pp. 875–6; Stevens, p. 652; McNeill, *Labor Movement*, p. 191.

For Frank Lawler the route upward was considerably more difficult and devious. Lawler came from Rochester to Chicago with his parents in 1854 at the age of twelve. He had only a common-school education and went to work at several trades until he learned ship carpentry. During the war he joined the union being built up by Richard Trevellick and scrambled for its top positions, clearly viewing Trevellick more as a rival than as a comrade. In 1866, Lawler succeeded Trevellick as president of the Ship Carpenters' and Caulkers' International Union and simultaneously became corresponding secretary of the Chicago Trades Assembly. When that assembly contemplated offering Trevellick the position of full-time lecturer, to be compensated by a house and a salary of $1,000 a year, Lawler successfully protested that Trevellick should work in the shipyards like he did. In 1868, however, when Lawler lost the presidency of his union to William Graham, he convinced the trades assembly to urge the Grant administration to give him a job in the city post office. From 1869 to 1876 he carried mail, then he ran successfully for the city council. Until 1885 he remained a councilman, and during this time he opened a liquor store and declared himself a Democrat. On that party's ticket Lawler was elected to Congress in 1884, 1886, and 1888. Subsequent years were marked by a series of failures to gain office. Consequently, at his death in 1896 Lawler had little to show for his "vaulting ambition."[5]

Martin Foran, two years younger than Lawler, received a fine education in rural Pennsylvania, where his father owned a farm and cooper shop. At the age of twenty-one he entered the Fourth Pennsylvania Cavalry and served a year and a half in combat. The young veteran subsequently taught school briefly, then became an oil-field hand, saving his earnings to buy cooper's tools. In 1868 he moved to Cleveland and went to work as a journeyman cooper. Within two years he had assumed leadership of a demoralized local coopers' union, revitalized it, helped create the International Coopers' Union, and become its president. During the three years he held that office, Foran played a major role in organizing the Industrial

---

[5] *Ibid.*, p. 622; *Workingman's Advocate*, June 9, 1866; Hicks, p. 43; *Biographical Directory of the American Congress*, p. 1198.

Congress, attended law school, and was admitted to the bar. His political career began in 1873 when Foran was sent to Ohio's Constitutional Convention through the efforts of Cleveland workingmen. As the decade progressed, he aligned himself with the Democratic party and became prosecuting attorney for his city. The Democrats nominated him for Congress in 1882. Foran won the election and was re-elected twice before he retired to private law practice in 1889. He definitely made a more significant mark in the House of Representatives than did either Lawler or Farquhar. Most notably, he sponsored the act of 1885 barring the importation of contract labor. The devotion labor reformers of the seventies and eighties felt for Foran was well deserved. A gifted writer and capable organizer, Foran climbed high up the social ladder without abandoning his friendship to the labor movement from which he had sprung. At his death in 1921 he was a judge of the Cleveland Court of Common Pleas.[6]

The capacity of America's political structure to absorb talent from the working classes was perhaps the most effective deterrent to the maturing of a revolutionary class-consciousness among the nation's workers during the turbulent social conflicts of the late nineteenth century. The ability of working-class leaders to attain at least personal political success through the medium of the two major parties certainly militated against the successful development of a definite Labor party and kept the labor parties that frequently did appear distinctly local in scope. But there is another side to the matter. An English-born machinist, comparing the ease with which American workingmen entered elective office with the difficulties England imposed on such careers at the time, observed: "It is much easier to rise here, and nearly all who succeed, desert their class, leaving behind poorer leadership than in England, where it is forced to stay in the ranks. . . ."[7]

THE LABOR-REFORM COMMUNITY

Did labor leaders who tasted of political success "desert their class"? The question does not allow a simple answer. In

---

[6] *Workingman's Advocate*, Sept. 27, 1873; *National Cyclopaedia of American Biography*, XIC, 156; McNeill, *Labor Movement*, p. 619.
[7] *Mass. BLS, 1870*, p. 346.

the first place, the point cannot be overemphasized that the phrase "labor reformer" is not identical to "trade-union official." Leadership was provided the movement of the working classes in the 1860's by a vaguely defined aggregation of men and women who devoted themselves to the interests of those classes as they understood them. Among them were clergymen, lawyers, pamphleteers, workers who held no trade-union post, and political office-holders, as well as trade-union leaders and heads of reform associations. Not only was the movement in Massachusetts strongly influenced by middle-class figures such as Henry K. Oliver, Edwin M. Chamberlain, and Ezra Heywood, who devoted themselves unstintingly to the strengthening of labor organizations, but that in Pittsburgh bore the strong imprint of the school principal, Andrew Burtt, and that in the anthracite fields of Congressman Hendrick B. Wright. Such men are excluded from the present sample, despite the prominent role they played in the community of workers' leaders, solely because they did not belong economically to the working classes.

Leaders who did spring from the ranks of labor, furthermore, often provided direction from institutions other than trade unions. English-born Robert Bower, for example, went from the leadership of the Amalgamated Short Time Committee of Lawrence, Massachusetts, to the state legislature and the editorship of the Lawrence *Journal*. It was from these positions that Bower organized the National Labor Union in his city and led the campaign for a shorter working day.[8]

John R. Pike moved from one mill town to another seeking positions on their city councils. Born on a Maine farm in 1844, Pike joined the army after having worked a few years in a textile mill, and by 1868 was a mill hand in Biddeford, when he was elected to the city council. After ten years advocating workingmen's causes in that office, he moved to Saco and won a seat on its council. While there, he was elected president of the striking mill hands of Biddeford, and was subsequently blacklisted throughout Maine. Moving to Lowell, he was elected councilman and became a member of

---

[8] Donald B. Cole, *Immigrant City: Lawrence, Massachusetts, 1845–1921* (Chapel Hill, N.C., 1963), p. 135; Berthoff, p. 103.

the district assembly Executive Board of the Knights of Labor.[9] In other words, political success did not remove Bower or Pike from the labor movement, but provided them with valuable bases of operation.

The bituminous fields of St. Clair and Will counties, Illinois, were centers of both formidable trade unionism and labor politics during the 1860's and 1870's, and they illustrated clearly the type of labor-reform community which could then develop. John Hinchcliffe, the most prominent leader of the American Miners' Association during the war years, came to Illinois from the West Riding of Yorkshire by way of Pennsylvania. He was not a miner but a tailor who became a small employer in England. His first years in Illinois were spent as a tradesman, but by 1860 he was a newspaper editor and minor Democratic politician in Belleville. He was engaged by the Miners' Association to edit its journal, the *Weekly Miner*. So vital was the role of the paper in the life of the union that any miner who fell behind in his subscription was denied union clearance to work in organized pits. Although Hinchcliffe presided at the opening of the convention which founded the American Miners' Association and remained the most prominent spokesman of the state lodge of that organization throughout the decade, he was driven from the editorship of the *Weekly Miner* by Welsh-born William Bowen, who became agent (the salaried official) of the national union in 1865. Hinchcliffe's popularity with the state lodge was so great, however, that Bowen's coup only fractured the national union. Hinchcliffe soon became treasurer of the National Labor Union, then in 1870 was sent to the Illinois Constitutional Convention, where he fought successfully for a clause requiring the legislature to enact a mine-safety code. Two years later he became a state senator.[1]

So formidable was the resistance to his efforts to carry an inspection bill through the state Senate that Hinchcliffe had to fall back upon a measure to make the county surveyor ex-

---

[9] *Labor Leader*, Jan. 15, 1887.
[1] Wieck, pp. 193-8, 172-8; McNeill, *Labor Movement*, pp. 247-8; Yearley, *Britons*, pp. 124-6; *Workingman's Advocate*, Aug. 24, 1867, March 4, 1874; John Moses, *Illinois, Historical and Statistical* (Chicago, 1892), II, 821, 1173.

officio inspector of mines. This bill, which became law, was written by Walton Rutledge, an English-born miner also from St. Clair County, who was promptly elected surveyor there. For his assistant, Rutledge selected William Owens, leader of the A.M.A. and subsequently of the Miners' National Association in that district. These men—Hinchcliffe, Rutledge, and Owens—were the key figures in the early development of the state's mine-safety legislation, holders of elective office, and simultaneously directors of the miners' trade union.[2]

A similar group in Braidwood, Will County, worked toward the same objectives during these years. The local government there by the early seventies was in the hands of union miners, or businessmen sympathetic to the miners.[3] A union member named William Mooney was elected to the state legislature, where he helped prepare the safety legislation.[4] Although the A.M.A. in Braidwood was broken in a strike in 1868, many members took part in the formation of its successor, the Miners' National Association. John James, a Scotch-born miner and temperance advocate who was blacklisted in the 1868 strike and became a local grocer, sold his store and moved to Cleveland to assume the office of salaried secretary of the new organization.[5] His place in Braidwood was taken by Daniel J. McLaughlin, a fellow Scotsman, who became vice-president of the M.N.A. for Illinois. McLaughlin was elected mayor of the town in 1877, and subsequently a member of the Executive Board of the Knights of Labor. At one time or another during the eighties he was again mayor of Braidwood, a state legislator, and vice-president of the American Federation of Labor. At his death McLaughlin was superintendent of the Starkville Coal and Coke Company of Colorado. He could look back with equal pride on his role as champion of labor in elective office and his participation in the negotiation of the famous "Pittsburgh scale," covering all

---

[2] Roy, pp. 141–4; *Miners' National Record*, Vol. I (Feb. 1875), p. 57.
[3] Herbert G. Gutman, "The Braidwood Lockout of 1874," *Journal of the Illinois State Historical Society*, Vol. LIII (Spring 1960), pp. 5–28.
[4] *Miners' National Record*, Vol. I (April 1875), p. 90.
[5] *Ibid.*, Vol. I (Oct. 1875), p. 193; Wieck, p. 183; *Workingman's Advocate*, Nov. 29, 1873; Roy, pp. 160–1.

Midwestern bituminous wages in 1886—a landmark in the history of collective bargaining.[6]

In short, to look for—or to look at—labor leaders through blinders imposed by a preconception of "pure and simple trade unionism" distorts our understanding of these men. Tribunes of the working classes employed several forums and did not necessarily "desert their class" when they moved into legislative halls. On the other hand, the fact that successful trade unionists could realistically aspire to political careers gave them a stake in the political and social system which allowed such opportunities. Furthermore, the fact that active trade unionists pursued their organizational goals in a social setting that brought them into constant contact with politicians or other reformers, of both working-class and middle-class origins, and that these men were both locally eminent and friendly to the cause of labor reform meant that the latter became educators of the rising trade unionist. That is to say, the most active workingmen readily became the most thoroughly indoctrinated with the outlook of middle-class reformers. The labor-reform movement itself became an institutional funnel for the transmission of Radical ideas to the working classes.

In anger and frustration Marxist F. A. Sorge lashed out at the holders of elective offices who were active in labor circles as carpetbaggers in the North distracting the workers from their true class objectives. "They demand offices from the bourgeois parties by boasting of the influence they wield over the working class," Sorge charged, "and seek to build a following among the workers by appealing to their influence with the bourgeois party which is at the helm."[7] So saying, he presented the workingman's path to political success clearly, if cynically. But the crucial point is that it would have been

---

[6] *Journal of United Labor*, Vol. IV (June 1883), pp. 485–6; Roy, pp. 248–61; Ware, *Labor Movement*, pp. 212–13.
[7] Sorge, "1866–1876," p. 173 (my translation). Sorge's words were: *"Sie verlangen Aemter von den bürgerlichen Parteien, indem sie sich grossen Einflusses auf die Arbeiterklasse rühmen, und unter den Arbeitern suchen sie sich eine Gefolgschaft zu bilden unter Berufung auf ihren Einfluss bei der am Ruder befindlichen bürgerlichen Partei."*

impossible for men who had deserted their class to have utilized such a formula for success.

Martin Foran illustrated the ideology which emerged in this labor-reform community when he undertook in 1872 to write a labor novel. Enraged at the antitrade-union bias of an English romance published serially in the literary magazine *Galaxy*,[8] Foran wrote *The Other Side* to defend labor reform. In the issue of the *Workingman's Advocate* in which the first installment of his novel appeared, Foran explained that his story was designed to prove that the "struggle of classes constitutes the very fact of modern history," and that "while the world is cursed with the wages system, 'an irrepressible conflict'" must rage between capitalists and workingmen.[9]

Yet his novel belied the "irrepressible conflict," or at least indicated how easily the "wages system" could be abolished— simply by good will. Its hero, Richard Arbyght, is a farm-bred cooper like Foran. But unlike Foran, Arbyght's father was the scion of established wealth. Foul play, not the irresistible workings of economic law, deprived the hero of his birthright, for his father is murdered and robbed, and the villain escapes. Young Richard, thus reduced to toil, organizes his fellow workers, surviving both attempted assassination and frame-up by the capitalists. At the climax he discovers at last the murderer of his father—the antiunion capitalist himself! He then recovers the money stolen from his family a generation earlier, marries the daughter of a banker (who loved him even when he was poor, but marries him when he is rich), goes into business partnership with his brother-in-law, producing a useful commodity (unnamed, but obviously nothing speculative), and offers a profit-sharing plan to his hundred employees. Richard, it should be noted, enters the story wearing the purple and leaves wearing it again. All good people marry each other, and all evil people meet their doom. At the end, "Unionism flourishes in the city, and through its agency work-

[8] Charles Reade, "Put Yourself in His Place," *Galaxy*, Vol. VII (March 1869), pp. 309 ff.
[9] *Workingman's Advocate*, Sept. 28, 1872. Foran's explanation reveals the influence of B. E. Green's translation of Adolphe Granier de Cassagnac's *History of the Working and Burgher Classes* (Philadelphia, 1871).

ingmen are fast becoming more thoughtful, more industrious, more temperate, and are making rapid strides in mental and moral wealth and social elevation."[1] Here is the "free agency" syndrome in radiant attire. Corporate greed, political corruption, and socialism all are smitten as Arbyght moves to success through virtue.

Even those who spurned office, personal gain, and other social rewards for themselves shared this success-oriented ideology. It would be difficult for any man to be more consistently devoted to a cause than was Thomas Phillips, who labored for the workers' movement through almost every institutional form it manifested. Having learned chartism and cooperation in his native England, Phillips came to Philadelphia in 1852 and immediately joined the shoemakers' union. A fervent Methodist and adamant foe of slavery, he sought to lead workers out of the thralldom of the wages system into a world of cooperative enterprise by means of promoting functioning examples of such undertakings. The Union Co-operative Association he headed operated a successful retail store on the Rochdale Plan for four years, then collapsed. Returning to work in a shoe factory, Phillips received a circular describing the Knights of St. Crispin and quickly organized a lodge. As Grand Sir Knight of the lodge he helped incline the Crispins toward the principle of cooperative works both in his own city and in Massachusetts.

Early in the seventies Phillips joined Section 26 of the International Workingmen's Association and was its delegate to the convention of anti-Marxist sections in Philadelphia in July 1872. At this time he also entered the Knights of Labor, in response to the persuasion of his close friend James Wright, and became Sir Knight of Shoemakers' Local Assembly 64. During the Peter Cooper campaign of 1876, Phillips was a Presidential elector on the greenback ticket. But though he considered the Knights of Labor "the grandest conception of organized labor ever put into shape on this continent," he clashed violently with Terence V. Powderly, whom Phillips charged with directing the order "in the spirit of the Dark

---

[1] Martin A. Foran, *The Other Side. A Social Study Based on Fact* (Washington, D.C., 1886). The quotation is on p. 460.

Ages." In 1887 he openly defied the Grand Master Workman, first by ardently defending Albert Parsons after the Haymarket affair, next by running for mayor of Philadelphia on a coalition labor slate, and then by speaking at an agnostics' celebration of the birthday of Thomas Paine. He helped the shoemakers pull out of the Knights and organize the United Boot and Shoe Workers' International Union. As president of that union he entered the new A.F. of L., indulging "in the hope that the Old Guard of tried veterans will keep control and block out the spoilers." From first to last, Phillips had neither received nor sought personal gain. But always he was driven by the very vision of the good society that Foran portrayed in his novel.[2]

More romantic, but no more affluent, was the career of Richard F. Trevellick. Born in the Scilly Isles in 1830, the son of a Cornish farmer, he learned the trade of ship's carpenter in Southampton, England. While there Trevellick joined a debating society, most of whose members were middle class, took Methodist instruction, and became a temperance advocate and vegetarian. His aspiration for improved status showed in his always elegant dress and in his youthful search for a fortune to offer the woman on his home island he wished to marry. In quest of this fortune Trevellick embarked to Calcutta, to Australia, where he prospected for gold, then to New Zealand. In the latter colonies he participated in the movement for an eight-hour day, and he carried the memory of the 1857 legislative success of the Australians around the world with him. His career during the rest of the fifties would have provided appropriate material for a romantic novel. Shipwrecked off Peru, he enlisted in the Peruvian navy and saw some comic-opera action during a brief conflict between that country and Ecuador. After a sojourn in Panama, he moved to New Orleans.[3]

---

[2] Thomas Phillips, autobiographical sketch in Thomas Phillips Papers, Labor Collection, Biography and Papers, WSHS. All quotations are taken from this sketch. See also Yearley, *Britons*, pp. 198–216; *Journal of United Labor*, Vol. III (Jan. 1883), p. 395; *Proceedings of the First Congress of the American International Workingmen's Association, Held in Philadelphia, Pa., July 9 and 10, 1872* (New York, 1872).

[3] Hicks, pp. 11–32. Hicks stated that Trevellick fought with the Peruvian navy during a conflict with Chile. It was Ecuador, however,

In the Louisiana metropolis Trevellick first became active in American trade unions. His remarkable forensic abilities won him the presidency of both the local Ship Carpenters' and Caulkers' Union and a local temperance society within months of his arrival. His sweetheart in the Scilly Isles having tired of waiting for him and his chimerical fortune and married a butcher, Trevellick found work on a Mississippi riverboat and took his landlady's daughter for his wife. When the Confederacy pressed all riverboats into its service and offered him a commission as a boat captain, Trevellick took advantage of the services of the British consul to skip through the battle lines to New York, then went on to Detroit.[4]

In 1865 the Cornishman was president not only of the Detroit Trades Assembly but also of the Ship Carpenters' and Caulkers' International Union. He represented Detroit at the Louisville convention of the International Industrial Assembly of North America in 1864, but his life as a practicing ship carpenter ended that year. A city-wide strike of Detroit shipyards restored Trevellick to the job from which his employer had dismissed him; but the day he was reinstated Trevellick quit work to live the rest of his days as a professional labor leader. In 1869 he became president of the National Labor Union. After its demise he helped launch the Greenback-Labor party, which he served for years as an executive officer, though he was never nominated a candidate. From the late seventies until his death in 1895 he was a lecturer and organizer for the Knights of Labor.[5]

Certainly the most widely famous labor reformer of the decade, both among his contemporaries and among subsequent generations, was William H. Sylvis, whose career was remarkably different from those of Phillips and Trevellick, but whose basic values were quite similar to theirs. Sylvis was born in Armagh, Pennsylvania, in 1828, the son of the pro-

---

not Chile, which Peru fought in 1858. See Leon F. Sensabaugh, Jr., "The Ecuador-Peru Boundary Dispute," *Birmingham-Southern College Bulletin*, Vol. XXI (Dec. 1928), pp. 29–39.

4 Hicks, pp. 33–9.

5 *Ibid., passim;* Clifton K. Yearley, Jr., "Richard Trevellick: Labor Agitator," *Michigan History Magazine*, Vol. XXXIX (Dec. 1955), pp. 423–44; Sidney Glazer, "The Michigan Labor Movement," *ibid.*, Vol. XXIX (Jan.–March 1945), pp. 73–5.

prietor of a country wagon shop. When his father's business failed in the crisis of 1837, young Sylvis was apprenticed to a state legislator named Pawling, who carefully educated his young protégé. Here Sylvis developed his interest in politics and soon became a Whig like his master. He stood with the Whigs until the party disintegrated, named one of his sons Henry Clay Sylvis (the others being Oliver Perry and Lewis Clark Sylvis), and, like many former Whigs, was a Douglas Democrat in 1860.[6]

Even when Sylvis was advising labor to form a party of its own, he never really lost his preference for the Democrats over the Republicans. Like the Democrats, he lumped all Republicans under the label "Radical"; he believed that the Southern states had never left the Union; and he had nothing but contempt for the Freedman's Bureau.[7] His scorn for the Republican program increased in the last years of his life as Sylvis clearly fell under the influence of old Duff Green and his son Benjamin E. Green. Benjamin Green had made his way into the councils of the National Labor Union in 1867 with credentials from the Pattern Makers' Union of Baltimore, in order to promote his scheme for quick political restoration of the Southern states and their physical reconstruction through his American Industrial Agency. Although Green soon found both his plans and the editorial line of his newspaper, *People's Weekly*, under attack from Andrew Cameron and other labor spokesmen, he did capture Sylvis's fancy. By 1868, B. E. Green was praising Sylvis as a true adherent of "the Jeffersonian doctrine of strict construction of the constitution," and urging the Democratic party to make the iron molder its vice-presidential nominee on a ticket with George Pendleton.[8] When

---

[6] Sylvis, pp. 19–23, 45, 60; obituary of Sylvis, *Workingman's Advocate*, Aug. 21, 1869. There are four other biographies of Sylvis: Grossman, *Sylvis;* Todes, *Sylvis;* Charles A. Madison, *American Labor Leaders, Personalities and Forces in the Labor Movement* (New York, 1950), pp. 21–43; Reed C. Richardson, *Labor Leader, 1860's* ("New York State School of Industrial and Labor Relations, Cornell University, Bulletin 31," Ithaca, 1961).

[7] Sylvis, pp. 231–49.

[8] [B. E. Green], biographical sketch of William Sylvis in *Revolution*, Vol. I (July 2, 1868), p. 405. On Green's suggestion of Sylvis for vice-president, see Sylvis, p. 75. On relations between Green and Cameron, see above, p. 113.

Sylvis toured the South as president of the National Labor Union, he stopped first at the Baltimore home of his "old friend," Duff Green. His subsequent reports from Dixie combined condemnations of the Freedman's Bureau and social mixing of the races with optimistic speculation on the industrial future of the region and growing faith that all classes of the South represented potential allies of the Northern worker in his battles with capital.[9] These were precisely the basic doctrines that the Greens sought tirelessly but without success to convince other labor reformers to accept.[1]

Sylvis's activity in the labor movement, however, led him to depart at many points from the Greens's gospel-according-to-John C. Calhoun. While the Greens had only contempt for trade unions (father Green having gained considerable fame as an enemy of the Typographical Union while he was public printer under Andrew Jackson),[2] Sylvis had committed his life to organizing workers by the time he was thirty. He had learned iron molding in the 1840's and risen quickly from an apprentice to superintendent of the Forest Iron Works in Union County, Pennsylvania. But the works failed, and Sylvis became a journeyman molder in Philadelphia. In 1857 the members of the molders' union where he worked went on strike. He joined the walkout, became secretary of the picket committee, and afterward signed a union enrollment card. By 1859 he was secretary of the Philadelphia union and prominent in the efforts which founded the Iron Molders' International Union. The next year Sylvis, having been defeated in a race for president of the I.M.I.U. by Isaac J. Neale, was elected its treasurer. Subsequently, he took part in the Philadelphia Convention of the Committee of Thirty-Four and became briefly a first sergeant in the Pennsylvania militia. In January 1863, Sylvis reorganized the defunct I.M.I.U. and became its president, an office which he held until his death in 1869. The National Labor Union elected him its second president in 1868.[3]

[9] Sylvis, pp. 84, 329–48. See also Sylvis's speech at Sundbury, Pa., Sept. 16, 1868, on reconstruction of the South. *Ibid.*, pp. 231–49.
[1] Benjamin E. Green, "Translator's Introduction," to Granier de Cassagnac. On the Greens, see *D.A.B.*, VII, 538–9, 540–2.
[2] Stevens, pp. 192–4.
[3] Sylvis, pp. 24–54.

Sylvis did not equal Trevellick as an orator, never demonstrated the firm ideological consistency of Phillips, and never obtained or sought political office. As a union organizer and strike strategist, however, he had no peer in the 1860's. In 1866 and again in 1867 his generalship alone fended off disaster for the molders' union in bitter strikes. On both occasions he clearly distinguished basic goals from immediate grievances, drove reluctant local unions to sacrifice their momentary welfare for the general good of the organization, and rode roughshod over more parochially minded leaders within the international union.[4] Out of his efforts emerged a highly centralized organization directed by an effective administration caucus. By the 1868 convention of the I.M.I.U., Sylvis presided dictatorially, spoke at length on every significant point, and bent the delegates to his will.[5] By sheer force of personality he prevented his union from yielding to the centrifugal forces that so readily frustrated other national unions of the time. In 1863 he served the International without compensation. The next year he was appropriated the meager sum of $600, but in 1867 his salary of $1,600 made him the highest-paid labor official of the nation and reflected his pioneering role as full-time trade-union officer. The same energy, will power, and bureaucratizing role were manifested by Sylvis in the National Labor Union. He used the chair at the 1868 congress to silence debate antagonistic to his proposals, was elected president for the coming year, and enjoyed the congress' decision to pay him $1,500 plus expenses. He subsequently made himself joint proprietor with Andrew Cameron of the *Workingman's Advocate* and supplemented the N.L.U.'s amorphous Executive Committee of vice-presidents responsible only for and to their own states with a legislative committee of five members in Washington, D.C., appointed by himself—a body that was incorporated into the N.L.U. constitution the following year as a permanent Executive Board.[6] Small won-

[4] Grossman, *Sylvis*, pp. 94–9, 141–8, 169–79.

[5] *Neunte Sitzung der Eisen-Eiker Internationalen Union, in Convention zusammengetreten zu Toronto, Canada, am 8. Juli 1868* (title page missing, microfilm WSHS), pp. 4–35, 48–9, 52–7, 63–7, 76. (Hereafter cited as *I.M.I.U. Proceedings, 1868.*)

[6] Madison, p. 27; Sylvis, p. 331; *N.L.U. Proceedings, 1868,* p. 54 and

der Sylvis made bitter enemies within both the I.M.I.U. and the N.L.U. That was the personal price he paid for demonstrating to the American workers of the 1860's the meaning of organization.

His experience with strikes brought Sylvis to the conviction that they were futile and that the only hope of the working classes lay in creating their own producers' cooperatives and their own political party, through which a government-managed currency might be sought. He told a molders' convention that by late 1866 he was "fully convinced . . . that we had reached the end of all we could do, or hope to do" by strikes.[7] As he had arrived at a conclusion similar to Ferdinand Lassalle's "iron law of wages" and consequently endorsed cooperatives, it is understandable, though striking, that Sylvis also hoped for state aid to such enterprises. At the National Labor Congress of 1867 he introduced a resolution calling upon the federal Congress to appropriate $25 million "to aid in establishing the eight-hour system, co-operation and removal of such of the poor as wish to go to the public domain, and for the general benefit of laborers, without distinction of sex, color, or locality." The motion stirred up quite a storm, but Sylvis defended it with the ardent aid of several German delegates.[8] The next year he moved that the N.L.U. demand the establishment of a federal Department of Labor to distribute public land, regulate trade unions, and promote cooperatives. In defense of his motion Sylvis argued: "in Prussia they have a Labor Department, presided over by one of the ablest men of the day. The working class has the arm of the Government thrown around it, and are properly protected."[9]

Simultaneous admiration of Calhoun and Bismarck would seem to leave Sylvis, at the close of his career, a proponent of Tory democracy. He certainly could not adhere to the Republicans. A biographical sketch of him by B.E. Green contended that Sylvis believed "that the tendency of Red Republicanism in Europe, like Black Republicanism in America, is, through anarchy, to military despotism, to corrupt class legislation.

---

passim; "Proceedings of the National Labor Congress," *Workingman's Advocate,* Sept. 24, 1869.

[7] Sylvis, p. 267.

[8] *Workingman's Advocate,* Aug. 31, 1867.

[9] *Ibid.,* Oct. 10, 1868.

. . ."[1] In fact, Sylvis did write Green in 1868 that there was "no hope for the industry of the nation in the Republican party," and that its platform was an "INSULT TO EVERY WORKING-MAN IN THE COUNTRY."[2] Yet Sylvis made it clear again and again that his faith lay only in a labor party. Moreover, he challenged a fundamental tenet of Democratic doctrine by proposing that white workmen make common cause with the Negroes in such a party and in their unions. Despite his disgust at "mixed juries" in court and his revulsion at carpetbaggers who allowed their daughters to "entertain young negro gentlemen in their parlors,"[3] he warned the N.L.U. that "antagonism" between whites and blacks would "kill off the Trades' Unions, unless the two be consolidated," and that if white workmen "do not conciliate the blacks, the black vote will be cast against them."[4]

During his twelve years of arduous labor-reform activity, Sylvis came to embrace the whole reform syndrome of self-help, free agency, temperance, and the quest for upward social mobility. It was in this eventful climax of his life that he became an active Methodist, a Sunday-school teacher, and a militant cold-water man. Despite his unusual intellectual flirtation with the Greens and the Lassalleans, Sylvis's basic values conformed to those of his colleagues in the movement. On his deathbed Sylvis cried: "Glory to God, glory to God; I am going home to Christ; I *know* my sins are all forgiven."[5]

It was Sylvis, in fact, who provided the movement with the first comprehensive statement of its platform. In January 1865 the iron molders assembled at Chicago the largest trade-union convention America had yet witnessed. Here Sylvis sounded the tocsin for the workingmen in a speech which was reprinted in labor journals throughout the land:

> What would it profit us, as a nation, were we to preserve our institutions and destroy the morals of the people; save

---

[1] *Revolution*, Vol. I (July 2, 1868), p. 405.
[2] William Sylvis to *People's Weekly*, May 23, 1868, reprinted in Pittsburgh *Daily Post*, June 8, 1868.
[3] William Sylvis, letter from Mobile, Ala., March 8, 1869, in Sylvis, p. 344.
[4] "Proceedings of the National Labor Congress, Second Annual Session," *Workingman's Advocate*, Aug. 31, 1867.
[5] Sylvis, p. 88.

our Constitution and sink the masses into hopeless ignorance, poverty, and crime; all the forms of our republican institutions to remain on the statute books, and a great
body of the people sunk so low as to be incapable of
comprehending their most simple and essential principles? . . . Remember . . . that all popular governments must depend for their stability and success upon
the virtue and intelligence of the masses; that tyranny is
founded upon ignorance and liberty upon education; and
that while long hours, low wages, and few privileges are
the strength and support of the one, they are entirely
incompatible with the other. . . .⁶

The nation was on the brink of a violent battle between
labor and capital, he continued, pointing to recent military
strikebreaking and legislative efforts to prohibit strikes. The
injustice of these actions was magnified by the fact that "while
armed treason and rebellion threatened our institutions with
destruction, while the proud and opulent of the land were
plotting the downfall of our government, the toiling millions
stood like a wall of adamant between it and the destructive
elements of revolution, between the country and all its foes."⁷

The time had come, Sylvis declared, for the workingmen
to place their destinies in their own hands. "Combination, or
union among workingmen, may be looked upon as the first
step toward competence and independence," he argued, for
machinery, science, and immigration were bound to augment
the wealth of the nation, and workingmen had "a right to a
voice in the fixing" of their share of the increase.⁸ "Co-operation is the next step," he continued, for by that method
"we will become a nation of employers—the employers of our
own labor."⁹ But above all, he emphasized, no one could
wrench from life a better future for the working classes but
the workers themselves. *"It is not what is done for people,"* he
thundered in the best Wesleyan manner, *"but what people do
for themselves, that acts upon their character and condition."*¹

⁶ *Ibid.,* pp. 129–30.
⁷ *Ibid.,* pp. 130–40.
⁸ *Ibid.,* p. 164.
⁹ *Ibid.,* pp. 168–9.
¹ *Ibid.,* p. 169.

CHAPTER 6

The Hours of Labor
and the Question of Class

The ideals espoused by labor reformers were so similiar to those voiced by the Radicals that, on the basis of rhetoric alone, a good argument could be made for placing both groups under the single familiar heading "reformer." Both Radicals and labor reformers argued in terms of the nation, of the greatest good for the greatest number, and of the ideological syndrome of free agency, self-improvement, temperance, and the open society. It is, therefore, not surprising to find middle-class Americans who welcomed the advent of the labor movement. For example, a resident of a Massachusetts shoe town hailed the Crispins for stabilizing the local labor force so that "real estate has doubled in value," the earnings of workers were spent in the town, the shoemakers as "a class . . . are temperate," and their organization had "stimulated an interest in town affairs."[1] Even the Reverend Henry Ward Beecher,

---

[1] *Mass. BLS, 1871,* p .33.

who a decade later was to make the notorious declarations that "a man who cannot live on bread and water is not fit to live," and that "God intended the great to be great and the little to be little," was among the subscribers of the *Workingman's Advocate* in the sixties and sermonized that "the coming question is the mysteries of organized gigantic capital as offered to the unprotected individual, the laborer in the community."[2]

On the other hand, trade unions were patently coercive organizations that employed their peculiar sanctions and bureaucratic controls to promote the special interests of their members, challenged the employer's pretensions to exclusive control of his own property, and interfered in the affairs of workers who were not members. Such activities were fiercely resented by articulate bystanders as well as by manufacturers. A pamphlet on the labor question issued by a Chicago bank presented the argument that the very nature of the wage contract "implies a certain amount of deference to [the employer] as the ruling or managing power of the concern. . . . When workmen accept employment from such a person, they must be understood as surrendering their individual freedom to the extent which is necessary for enabling him to fulfill the responsibility of his position."[3] Abram Hewitt put the point more bluntly: "It is for the master to do the thinking."[4]

To Hewitt the "fundamental principles of social order" were "the security of capital, the security of person, and the right of free discussion." For this ironmonger of conservative Democrat persuasions, trade unions were obviously to be condemned, first because "capital is destroyed," and further since "personal freedom is also destroyed, because the trades unions will not permit the men to do what they would of their own free option."[5] Sinclair Tousey, on the other hand, was a businessman who stood with the Radicals in politics, yet he too denounced strikes and trade unions. They "destroy all

---

[2] *Workingman's Advocate*, June 26, 1869; *New-York Times*, July 23, 30, 1877.
[3] Merchants, Farmers & Mechanics' Savings Bank, Chicago, *The Labor Question* (Chicago, 1867), p. 84.
[4] *Royal Comm. on Trades Unions*, p. 8.
[5] *Ibid.*, p. 21.

individuality," he argued, and "blot out all those efforts by which a man works his way up and over the difficulties that meet him in the battle of life. All such combinations and societies are bad, bad, bad."[6]

On a more fundamental level, Radicals were wary of labor organizations because their very existence challenged the Radical tenet that the triumph of the nation eradicated class. Joseph Medill's Chicago *Tribune*, for example, had editorial fits over the N.L.U.'s *Address to the Workingmen:*

> The radical error which runs through the whole document is the distinction sought to be drawn between an employer and his journeymen. . . . The men who are rich, and who are the employers in all branches of industry, are those who commenced life as laborers, and who by industry and economy, and by their inventive genius, have accumulated the savings of their labor.[7]

Through the columns of his Boston *Pionier,* Karl Heinzen echoed and re-echoed the same theme. Radicalism knew no class- or corporation-consciousness, he declared, but carried reforms through the state by means of democratic majorities. By contrast, a working-class movement was inherently reactionary, for it revived the spirit of special interest. Hence the Baltimore Congress would quickly be forgotten because its efforts rested on false premises. Workmen, he preached, should abandon their pressure for wage increases and turn instead to the Radical's pursuit of equality before the law— *"allgemeine Herrschaft des Rechts, absolute Gleichheit vor dem Gesetz, nicht aber speziell um so und so viel Cents Lohnerhöhung. . . ."* Proof of the reactionary character of a labor movement he found in German labor's pleas for help from Bismarck and the N.L.U.'s requests to President Johnson to support its cause. The hopes of workmen, he insisted, could be realized only through the Radical party—the party of freedom.[8]

It followed from these Radical arguments that the proper route through which workmen should seek redress of griev-

---

[6] Tousey, *Business Man's Views,* pp. 9–10.
[7] Editorial, Chicago *Daily Tribune,* July 1, 1867. *Cf.* Samuel Johnson, *Labor Parties and Labor Reform* (Boston, 1871).
[8] Heinzen, II, 240–56, 290–5, 416–21, 539–40, 611–12. (The quotation is on p. 419.)

ances was the electoral process, and the proper agency for such redress was the state. The laborer of Massachusetts, said Wendell Phillips, "disdains to strike. That is not American. It is getting down upon his knees and acknowledging that he has no remedy but to bully." On the contrary, he continued, the workman asserted hs equality with the capitalist by saying: "I am a man . . . I can vote; I must be attended to."[9] The obverse of Phillips's thesis was presented by N. P. Banks in an argument which was especially impressive because it began with the explicit premise that the doctrine of "freedom of contract" in the relations between labor and capital was "a *monstrous absurdity.*" "Labor, in the eyes of the State," said Banks, "is a moral, social, and public interest. It is not an affair of absolutely private concern, but of paramount national importance."[1] His conclusion, however, was: "It is *to the State* that the rights of each should be referred, and to the State, which represents the people, the laboring classes should appeal, and may appeal with absolute certainty of protection."[2]

No class movements and no coercion, but rather invocation of the people's state acting for the general welfare—thus far Radical preferences were clear. But the Baltimore Program posed as labor's central task the pursuit of the legal eight-hour day through the political process. The program thus forced the Radicals to take a stand not simply on labor's means, but also on labor's foremost goal: to declare whether or not they considered a reduction in the hours of labor in "the common interest."

From the outset it was evident that no consensus existed among those most directly involved—that the attitudes of wage earners toward the proper length of the working day were diametrically opposed to those of their employers. There were, to be sure, scattered instances of manufacturers who believed shorter hours of labor would so increase output per hour as actually to result in an overall gain in production per man-day. The managers of both the American Twist Drill Company and the Atlantic Mills found that cutting back from

---

[9] *National Anti-Slavery Standard,* May 19, 1866, quoted in Irving H. Bartlett, *Wendell Phillips: Brahmin Radical* (Boston, 1961), p. 340.
[1] *Daily Evening Voice,* Nov. 12, 1866.
[2] *Ibid.,* Nov. 26, 1866. See also Banks's speech in *ibid.,* Nov. 28, 1866.

eleven and a half to ten hours a day had yielded them such a net gain.[3] George A. Brandreth, the young War Democrat who introduced the first eight-hour bill in the New York legislature, declared that he and his father had worked the one hundred hands in their patent-medicine factory no more than eight hours daily for three years and profited from the move. He cited a gutta percha mill in New York that had experienced similar benefits.[4] At least one businessman discovered potential profit in the movement for shorter hours, if not in the goal itself. Displaying the best Yankee initiative, he ran the following advertisement in the *Workingman's Advocate:*

> The Eight Hour League is very rapidly augmenting its numbers, and combining its strength, for a direct issue on the (to them) all important question of Eight Hours Labor as a day's work. Now, we are in favor of the movement, because we believe it is right. We are in favor of everything that will elevate and improve the condition of the laboring classes, either mentally or physically. They necessarily lose much time by reason of rheumatism, lame back, neuralgia, sore eyes, etc., caused by close application and exposure. We advise all such to use Morrell's Electric Magnetic Fluid, which will give you certain relief. All drug stores keep it. Smith & Dwyer, wholesale agents.[5]

In general, however, it is safe to say that employers who actually favored an eight-hour day for their own works were scarce as hens' teeth. The ten-hour day, a sixty-hour week, had become the norm for craftsmen and for most day laborers. Pieceworkers in most trades customarily evaluated their wage rates in terms of the weekly earnings sixty hours of work would bring them. In the textile factories, however, this ten-hour standard had not been reached, and hours ranging from eleven to thirteen daily prevailed. Some textile manufacturers

---

[3] *Mass. BLS, 1872,* pp. 223–4; Persons, pp. 112, 120; *Daily Evening Voice,* May 31, 1867.
[4] George A. Brandreth, *Speech of Hon. Geo. A. Brandreth, in Favor of the "Eight Hours Bill." Delivered in the Assembly of the State of New York, at Albany, March 15, 1866* (Albany, 1866), pp. 5–7. For biographical information on Brandreth, see *New York Civil List, 1870,* pp. 499–505; *Workingman's Advocate,* April 21, 1866; Brummer, p. 376.
[5] *Workingman's Advocate,* June 9, 1866.

were inclined to favor cutting their hours to ten, but they refused to make the change themselves unless and until it became national standard in the industry.[6]

Having been accepted in practice for upward of two decades, the ten-hour day came to be regarded by the employers as a natural law. The prevailing employer viewpoint was that sixty hours of work weekly did the average workman no physical injury, and anyone who disliked it or was unable to sustain such hours was free to quit the job. The scores of manufacturers who replied to the questionnaires of the Massachusetts Bureau of Statistics of Labor were unanimous on this point, and many justified still longer hours with the same type of argument.[7]

Employer respondents also utilized more elaborate arguments in opposing any reduction of hours. One was that "our men prefer to make 'longer days' and have more pay."[8] Closely related to this contention was this view: "Make the hours less and the production will be less, most assuredly, every time."[9] Both statements imply that reducing the hours of labor would reduce the income of the workers and thus be against their interests. Frequently, a more lofty posture was assumed by proprietors in their claims to be protecting the workman from himself. "I believe," declared a hardware manufacturer, *"that too much leisure is a detriment to his welfare."*[1] A producer of woolens concurred: "Licentiousness, gluttony, drunkenness, exposure, bad habitations, noisy and turbulent homes, will wear men out in half the time that steady labor in mills at usual hours of work will."[2] The correspondent of a guano firm added: "Especially would this apply to the foreign element, most of whom are under the control of forces which do not

---

[6] *Aldrich Report*, I, 178–9; Massachusetts, House of Representatives, *Report of the Special Commission on the Hours of Labor and the Conditions and Prospects of the Industrial Classes*, House Doc., 1866, No. 98 (Boston, 1866), *passim* (hereafter cited as *Mass. Labor Report, 1866*); *Mass. BLS, 1872*, p. 228.

[7] *Royal Comm. on Trades Unions*, p. 22; *Mass. BLS, 1870*, pp. 218–34; *Mass. BLS, 1872*, pp. 218–40.

[8] *Ibid.*, p. 223.

[9] *Ibid.*, p. 239.

[1] *Ibid.*, p. 222.

[2] *Mass. BLS, 1870*, p. 221.

encourage liberal education and general improvement."[3] And other masters presented themselves for the workers' emulation: "I have worked 11, 12, 14 and 15 hours a day, and have as yet felt no bad effects from it, but rather been strengthened. It is not the hours per day that a person *works* that breaks him down, but the hours spent in dissipation."[4]

Finally, there were manufacturers who spurned all this Protestant ethic and bluntly asserted that to satisfy the wishes of the workers would undermine the economy. "When they get easy in circumstances," said one, "they do not work constantly, but make lost time from visiting away from home, until their necessities compel them to return to labor."[5] A fabricator of shoddy agreed that "by *reducing* the *time* for a day's work, and *increasing* the *pay*, the employees have been less faithful, ever casting a longing eye at the sun."[6] As a woolen manufacturer summed up the case: "It would be very pleasant, doubtless, if we could get along without working at all. But as long as the present order of things exists, there will be poor men and women who will be obliged to work, and the majority of them will not do any more than necessity compels them to do."[7]

But among wage earners, support for reduction of working hours was as widespread and as firmly expressed as opposition to such reduction was among their employers. Worker respondents to questionnaires of the Massachusetts Bureau of Statistics of Labor often opposed strikes and trade unions, but never were content with the length of the working day. Of thirty-two workers' answers received by the bureau in 1870, for example, only one opposed shortening of the hours, and that was from a woman who feared it would mean a reduction of pay. Most of these replies came from textile workers who had personally experienced a reduction of hours early in the 1850's from thirteen and a half or fourteen daily down to eleven and a half or twelve and now favored a law to establish the ten-hour standard. Although the prospect of an

---

[3] *Ibid.*, p. 226.
[4] *Ibid.*, p. 221.
[5] *Ibid.*, p. 230.
[6] *Ibid.*, p. 228.
[7] *Ibid.*, p. 231.

eight-hour day was highly attractive to the respondents generally, many of them expressed skepticism that an eight-hour law would be obeyed by employers. This survey, it should be remembered, was made at a time when labor already had two or three years' bitter experience with such legislation.[8]

It is noteworthy that few of the workers favoring shorter hours suggested that such reduction would "spread the work" or would reduce industrial accidents—two of the favorite arguments of the early twentieth century. Many echoed the belief of a Lawrence mill hand (obviously an activist in the ten-hour movement) that the physical exhaustion brought on by long hours led him to lose a great deal of working time and hence of income. "I have never worked but *one whole* month in 10 years, and never took one week's continuous recreation in 10 years," he declared.[9] In fact, inspection of corporate payroll records from this period confirms the impression that few workers every put in full time week after week, though it is impossible to be certain whether the explanation lies more in absenteeism or in short-term layoffs. Advocates of the shorter day were quick to grasp at such lost time as proof that shorter hours would not mean less pay. A woman pieceworker, for example, noted: "The last hour is a very tedious drag; makes more bad work than any other hour, and is of little use to anybody."[1] Her attitude was shared by John Hanover, leader of the Wamsutta Mills workers, who declared: "As far as my experience goes, if a man works 12 hours a day all he gets is a living, and if he works eight hours a day he gets the same; and I do not see why we should not have a reduction of hours."[2]

PROPERTY, FREE CONTRACT, AND THE GENERAL WELFARE

Two other lines of argument were often employed by workmen and became those most frequently elaborated by the propaganda of the labor reformers. The first was phrased thus by "a reliable working man" writing the B.L.S.: "We ask for

---

[8] *Ibid.*, pp. 111–27, 288–98; *Mass. BLS, 1872*, pp. 241–8, 270–92.
[9] *Mass. BLS, 1870*, p. 112.
[1] *Ibid.*, p. 120. See payroll ledgers in Hamilton Manufacturing Company Papers and Fall River Iron Works Papers, Baker Library.
[2] New Bedford *Daily Mercury*, Feb. 19, 1867.

relief from Hours of Labor, which use up in the service of others, the whole day, leaving us no time to comply with the public duties which we are having thrust upon us, or for the exercise of any personal gifts or longings for refined pleasures."[3] This thesis—that shorter working hours would make the worker a more active and effective citizen of a democracy and would induce him to spend his free time at lectures and concerts instead of saloons—was the favorite line of debate for the eight-hour movement.[4] Its appeal lay in the grace with which it invoked the reform syndrome in support of the workingmen's aspirations.

The second familiar contention of labor reformers, on the other hand, violently jolted the basic assumptions of middle-class thought. A Massachusetts bootmaker made the point bluntly when he asserted that working eight hours made him feel "full of life and enjoyment" because "the man is no longer a *Slave,* but a man."[5] The struggle for shorter hours, in other words, was seen as a fight for the liberty of the worker. "EIGHT HOURS, A Legal Day's Work for Freemen" was emblazoned on the masthead of *Fincher's Trades Review.* The attractiveness of such a slogan is obvious, but as labor reformers elaborated its meaning they found themselves reluctantly drawn by their own logic into challenging the very concept of private property.

"Day labor," explained an Eight Hour League handbill issued in Philadelphia, "is the only important article of commerce which has no fixed standard, its length being determined by the necessities of the seller, or the generosity of the purchaser."[6] But if the commodity offered for sale by the worker (his strength and knowledge) had no fixed limit, and if he could deliver that commodity to its purchaser (the employer) only by placing himself at the latter's disposal, the worker, had in effect, delivered himself into a day's bondage

---

[3] *Mass. BLS, 1872,* pp. 246–7. *Cf.* letter of "T. G." in *Fincher's Trades Review,* March 4, 1865.
[4] *Eg.,* Rogers, *Reasons for Believing that the People Will Use Leisure Wisely;* Frederic A. Hinckley, *The Just Demand of Labor, A More Equal Distribution of Wealth* (Boston, 1871).
[5] *Mass. BLS, 1872,* p. 278.
[6] Handbill of the National Eight Hour Association (n.d.), in Thomas Phillips Papers.

for a day's wages. Here lay the very essence of the concept of "wage-slavery." The remedy proposed by labor reformers was to draw a clear delineation between that part of the workman's day which might be purchased for wages and that which remained inalienably his own. The symmetry of an even division of life's waking hours as expressed by some Pittsburgh workers emphasized this argument:

EIGHT HOURS FOR WORK
EIGHT HOURS FOR RECREATION, REST,
EIGHT HOURS FOR SLEEP.[7]

Pondering the absence of protection against wage-slavery in the otherwise excellent federal Constitution, Jonathan Fincher concluded that because the Founding Fathers were not wage earners but men "who spent their early and middle life amid the musty books of counting rooms or lawyer's office, or who *owned* a farm," they "overlooked the claims of that class upon whose existence the whole superstructure to which they gave their attention depended, the laborer." Hence they "failed to see the propriety of stating how many *hours* should be considered a legal day's work throughout the land."[8] This logic was carried to its ultimate outcome by an editorial favoring eight hours which appeared in the Philadelphia *Daily News:*

> The laws do not compel anyone to work a longer time than may be acceptable to him; but when a man is without means to subsist upon, his wants compel him to work, and he must ask for employment as a favor from someone who has the *property* required to carry on some kind of productive work. In plain language, *property is a tyrant, and the people are its slaves* . . . the penalty for resistance to its orders is starvation.[9]

Property a tyrant! Here surely was a conclusion as unpalatable to the Radical as it was to the Conservative or to the old-line Democrat. All three believed property the very root of

---

[7] "Hurrah! for the Working Men of New York!" handbill of Central Working Men's Society, Pittsburgh and Environs, May, 1872, in W.S.H.S. Labor Collection.

[8] *Fincher's Trades Review,* Sept. 17, 1864.

[9] Quoted in *Revolution,* Vol. II (Dec. 24, 1868), p. 395.

individual liberty. Reading Orestes Brownson's pronouncement "Property is communion with God, through the material
world," the Radical philosopher Elisha Mulford called the
definition "as profound as it is beautiful."[1] To be sure, some
Radicals were aware, with E. L. Godkin, that "when a man
agrees to sell his labor, he agrees by implication to surrender
his moral and social independence," and regretted that the
worker was "legally free while socially bound." Godkin even
feared that the employer often demanded and obtained "the
political support of his workmen," thus sapping the moral fiber
of democracy itself.[2] But Godkin and his fellow Radicals, who
hesitated to uphold the integrity of the freedmen's citizenship
and the independence of their ballots by distributing among
them the estates of the South, could hardly have been expected to render a like service to the wage earners by collectiv-
izing factories in the North.[3] At all times the Radical was
thoroughly bourgeois, and the reforms he espoused had to fall
within the limits that implied.

On the other hand, the citizenship-lectures-and-concerts
argument of the labor reformers could not fail to spark a
friendly response in the Radical mind. It became the main
theme of the favorable 1865 report of the Griffin Committee of
the Massachusetts legislature. It was picked up by George
Julian, one of the authors of the federal eight-hour measure,
who believed labor was "capital endowed with human needs,
and entitled to the special guardianship of the State. . . ."[4]
And it was pounded home by California's John Conness, who
battled for that bill in the Senate, declaring: "Let no man
forget, because his task is made easy in this world . . . the
hundreds of thousands who labor and toil for an ill-requited
compensation . . . scarcely sufficient to furnish bread, much
less to enable them to educate their children and bring them

---

[1] Mulford, p. 95.
[2] [E. L. Godkin], "The Labor Crisis," *North American Review*, Vol. CV
(July 1867), pp. 186, 188.
[3] See Wendell Phillips's reply in the symposium "Ought the Negro to
Be Disfranchised? Ought He to Have Been Enfranchised?" *North
American Review*, Vol. CLXVIII (March 1879), pp. 257–62, esp.
260–1.
[4] Julian, pp. 274–5. On the Griffin committee report, see above, pp.
124–5.

up fit to be citizens of this Republic. Make their paths as easy as you can by limiting their hours of labor. Give them time to think."[5]

Such Radical friendliness toward legislation to shorten hours provoked immediate and unanimous hostility among Conservatives. Former Conscience Whig Rowland Hazard conceded that workmen needed leisure time for the sake of education and citizenship, but held that it did not "comport with our notions of liberty" for the government to interfere with their individual efforts by "prescribing the terms or conditions upon which they may dispose of their labor."[6] Similarly, Senator Fessenden, opposing his fellow Republican Conness, attacked labor organizations for "fixing the hours of labor and all that and compelling everybody to come to them," with the effect of reducing "able men, men of capacity and ambition, to the level of the poorest."[7] Such arguments were effective in turn among the Radicals. Some of the older battlers against slavery, like Stevens and John F. Farnsworth, treated the whole controversy as an insignificant annoyance, and Charles Sumner openly opposed the federal bill in 1868, though he was converted to a supporter of the eight-hour movement by 1872.[8]

The debate over legislative limitation of the hours of labor, however, did not remain a Republican family squabble. At its first appearance in Massachusetts and in the congressional debates, the controversy for all practical purposes was intraparty. As labor reformers pressed their demands at various points around the nation, however, it was inevitable that the Democrats and the Johnson administration take their own

---

[5] *Congressional Globe*, 40th Congress, 1st Sess., 413 (March 28, 1867).
[6] [Rowland G. Hazard], "Hours of Labor," *North American Review*, Vol. CII (Jan. 1866), p. 198. This article is reprinted in Hazard, *Economics and Politics*, ed. Caroline Hazard (Cambridge, Mass., 1889), pp. 248–69. Remarkably similar reasoning and phraseology may be found in Amasa Walker, "Legal Interference with the Hours of Labor," *Lippincott's Magazine of Literature, Science, and Education*, Vol. II (Nov. 1868), pp. 527–33, as well as in Walker's majority report in *Mass. Labor Report*, 1867.
[7] *Congressional Globe*, 40th Congress, 1st Sess., 413 (March 28, 1867).
[8] On Stevens' attitude, see *ibid.*, 39th Congress, 1st Sess., 1969 (April 16, 1866). On Sumner, see *ibid.*, 40th Congress, 2d Sess., 3429 (June 24, 1868); *Charles Sumner, His Complete Works* (Boston, 1883), XI, 79.

initiatives on the subject. Neither party assumed any stand as a national organization on the question of the hours of labor during this whole period, though the Republicans in 1872 did issue some campaign literature that sought to identify the federal law with their national ticket.[9] During late 1865 and early 1866, however, a number of individual Democrats took up the banner of shorter hours. In Pennsylvania it was Representative Donnelly, leading a small band of fellow Philadelphia Democrats, who introduced the bill passed by the lower house of the state legislature in 1866 to make eight hours a legal day's work in the state. Party lines did not prevail in the vote, however, for the Republican-controlled House passed the bill 69 to 14. It subsequently died in the state Senate.[1]

In Indiana too it was the Democrats who first responded to the vigorous agitation of the state's Eight Hour League by placing a plank in their party's state platform favoring an eight-hour law. At the same time, Congressman William Niblack, who represented Indiana on the Democratic National Committee, introduced in the federal Congress a bill to make eight hours a day's work for mechanical employees of the United States. In reply, Republican George Julian sponsored a similar measure and proceeded to label himself the author of the whole idea. The Republicans swept the state elections in 1866, winning large majorities in both houses of the legislature and eight out of the eleven congressional seats. But since the Eight Hour League had disbanded after Election Day, the issue of a state eight-hour law was quickly forgotten.[2]

In other words, until late 1866 politicians of all stripes commonly regarded the proposition of a legal eight-hour day as a plaything, rather than as a serious political issue. Lip service was commonplace. Legislative action was at best in-

---

[9] See [John F. Meyers], *The Republican Party the Workingman's Friend*, and [anon.], *The Republican Candidate for Vice-President on the Eight-Hour Law* (pamphlets bound under title *Grant's Campaign of 1872*, University of Minnesota library).

[1] Philadelphia *Public Ledger*, Jan. 25, Feb. 7, 14, 15, March 30, April 13, 1866.

[2] *Workingman's Advocate*, Nov. 5, 1873 (biographical sketch of Fehrenbatch); *American Annual Cyclopaedia*, Vol. VI (1866), pp. 405–6; *Congressional Globe*, 39th Congress, 1st Sess., 1130 (March 1, 1866), 1331 (March 12, 1866).

conclusive. A sensational strike for the eight-hour day by ship carpenters and caulkers in New York City in April directed national attention to the question, primarily because the ship-yard workmen of Boston refused to handle a vessel transferred from New York to their city for repairs, and Negro caulkers were carried from Portsmouth, Virginia, to replace strikers in both New York and Boston.[3] Horace Greeley spoke loudly in defense of the strikers, and the flamboyant Democrat John Morrissey personally contributed $5,000 to their relief fund. Both men won labor endorsement in their congressional races that fall, as did the Radical Charles Spencer, though of labor's "Big Three" only Morrissey was elected.[4] Widespread, crude attempts of other aspirants for political office to associate themselves with the "sons of toil," however, gained them only the contempt of the labor press. Such candidates, wrote a correspondent of the Boston *Voice*, "bait their hooks with the eight-hour law for the workingmen, and stealthily sling the angle-worm of inflated currency in the mouths of the capital-ists. They teeter along the shore of popular prejudice like yellow-legged snipe. . . ."[5]

No one played the game of courting the workers' favor without taking meaningful action better than President Andrew Johnson himself. He was visited by a committee of delegates to the Baltimore Congress, headed by John Hinch-cliffe, who asked the President to institute shorter hours for federal employees by executive order, as Martin Van Buren had done in 1840. Unfortunately, Hinchcliffe also described to Johnson the stands taken by the labor congress on the public domain, contract labor importation, and convict labor. The President astutely seized upon the latter group of issues to show by his past record that he was a friend of the working-man. Having thus placed himself in a favorable light with his audience, Johnson glossed over the subject of the suggested eight-hour decree, calling the proper number of hours "a matter of expediency," and declaring himself in favor of "the shortest number possible, that will allow of the discharge of

[3] Sorge, "1860–1866," p. 441; *Mass. Labor Report, 1867*, pp. 60–1; *Workingman's Advocate*, June 16, 1866.
[4] See Montgomery, "Labor and the Radical Republicans," pp. 287–93.
[5] *Daily Evening Voice*, Oct. 20, 1866. See also *ibid.*, Oct. 8, 15, 1866.

duty and the requirements of the country." With that he shook hands all around and bade the committee adieu.[6] Yet word was sent out from Baltimore to many unions that "Andrew Johnson is with us." More than a year later, labor papers were still speaking of his "endorsement" of the eight-hour movement. In fact, however, the initiative for an eight-hour day for federal employees came from Congress, and Johnson played no role whatever in the reform.[7]

The actions of the various Democrats and the President made it evident that Radicals could not long fail to take a stand on the major demand of the labor movement. Nathaniel Banks, on his return from the army, initially refused to endorse the eight-hour proposal and won his nomination to Congress in 1865 only over the furious opposition of the Eight Hour League of Boston. But because his congressional district was a labor-reform stronghold, Banks understandably emerged by Election Day, 1866, as an ardent friend of the movement.[8] During the stormy session of Congress which opened in December 1865, hearings into the propriety of establishing the eight-hour day for federal employees were proposed by both Senator B. Gratz Brown of Missouri and Representative Ebon Ingersoll of Illinois. An effort by Ingersoll's fellow Radical John Farnsworth to table the House bill was defeated by a vote of 15 to 92. Such Radicals as James Ashley, William D. Kelley, Ignatius Donnelly, Charles O'Neill, and Robert Schenck opposed the tabling motion.[9] At the very least, they wished to give the proposal for a shorter workday a full hearing.

The next year a number of Radical senators of national

---

[6] *Workingman's Advocate,* Sept. 1, 1866; Richmond *Daily Dispatch,* Aug. 27, 1866.

[7] Letter of Ira Steward, *Daily Evening Voice,* Aug. 1, 1867; address of William Sylvis, *I.M.I.U. Proceedings, 1867,* p. 20. Philip Foner accepted the myth of Johnson's support so thoroughly that he gave Johnson the credit for the order countermanding pay reductions in the War Department following the federal eight-hour law, an order which was issued by President Grant. Foner, *Labor,* I, 393–4.

[8] Appeal of Boston Labor Reform Association, *Daily Evening Voice,* Oct. 26, 1865.

[9] *Congressional Globe,* 39th Congress, 1st Sess., 918 (Feb. 19, 1866), 1969 (April 16, 1866); Philadelphia *Public Ledger,* Dec. 1, 15, 1865, April 11, 1866.

prominence took up the cause of shorter hours. California's John Conness found his appeals seconded by his colleague Cornelius Cole, as well as by Henry Wilson and Benjamin F. Wade. Simultaneously, Governor Bullock of Massachusetts called on his legislature to limit the working day, and specific endorsement of the legal eight-hour day came from Governors Fairchild of Wisconsin, Oglesby of Illinois, and Fletcher of Missouri.[1] As usual, it was Wade who made sparks fly over the issue. During a speaking tour of Kansas, he called for both the promotion of cooperatives and the reduction of working hours. Now that the slavery question had been settled, he concluded, "that of labor and capital must pass through the ordeal." Denounced by the *New-York Times* for "agrarianism," Wade denied that he had advocated equal distribution of property, but he reasserted his demand for more leisure time for the workers.[2]

It may well be possible to account for the friendly attitude of these Radicals toward the eight-hour movement solely on the grounds that they were courting workingmen's votes. It is certainly true that the issue arose through the initiative of the labor reformers, not of the Radicals. It is even likely that many of the latter would have preferred to ignore the subject, as Thaddeus Stevens did or as Banks tried to do before he concluded such a course was hazardous. But too cynical an interpretation of the Radical response can be misleading. The fact of the matter is, in the first place, that elected officials who favored shorter hours faced a real risk of losing votes and campaign funds that manufacturers could influence. There was no position a politician might assume that might not jeopardize some significant group of voters. Secondly, even if Radical politicians favored legislation to shorten the working day only because they feared losing votes by failing to do so, they still had to rationalize their position in terms of their own ideology.

---

[1] *Congressional Globe*, 40th Congress, 1st Sess., 413–14 (March 28, 1867); *Journal of the House of Representatives of the Commonwealth of Massachusetts, 1866* (Boston, 1866), p. 208; Merk, p. 187; *Daily Evening Voice*, April 6, 1867; *New-York Times*, May 7, 1867.
[2] *Daily Evening Voice*, June 29, 1867; *Nation*, Vol. V (July 4, 1867), p. 11; Trefousse, *Wade*, pp. 286–9.

Here was the rub. The basic values inherent in the Radical outlook necessarily led to an ambivalent attitude toward legislation to shorten the hours of labor. This is evident especially in the mental anguish of Radical intellectuals who had no personal interest in political office. Edward Everett Hale, for example, fresh from the triumph of his patriotic novel, *The Man Without a Country,* wrote Ira Steward that he was greatly interested in "all movements for the reduction of the excessive daily labor" and enclosed ten dollars to help the Eight Hour League publish its tracts. Yet within the same year, Hale informed Edward H. Rogers that he opposed any legislation other than that which "tends to complete freedom in the sale by every man of this prime commodity, his labor." He explained: "No restriction,—even with the best motive, will help anybody. Complete freedom will in the end help us all."[3]

Others were disturbed by the timing of the eight-hour demand, and advised labor reformers, as they did advocates of women's suffrage, to wait their turn. Thus William F. Channing, who deemed the "employment or wages system . . . simple serfdom, nothing else," advised a labor reformer that "labor enfranchisement must await the settlement of the negro slavery question," and charged that President "Johnson, by impeding negro enfranchisement, has thrown back the eight hour movement for a year or more."[4]

A Radical editor of the *Watchman* of Erie, Pennsylvania, made an impressive case for the proposition that the Republicans were the natural friends of the eight-hour day, while Democrats must prove its opponents. His argument was that because the business enterprises of each state competed with those of others, state enactments to shorten the hours of labor must prove futile. Only federal legislation could obtain the desired end, and Democratic commitment to states' rights would bar them from supporting such national regulation of economic activity. Furthermore, the eight-hour day could succeed in America only if foreign competition were excluded. Hence a

[3] Edward Everett Hale to Ira Steward, in *Daily Evening Voice,* May 2, 1866; Hale to Edward H. Rogers, Dec. 20, 1866, Rogers Papers.
[4] William F. Channing to "a friend in the labor movement," Sept. 24, 1867, in *Daily Evening Voice,* Oct. 14, 1867.

protective, or even prohibitive, tariff was the necessary corollary of the law to shorten the working day. Again the Democrats would be found in the opposition. Free trade and slavery alike belonged to the past, concluded the *Watchman,* and in a land protected by tariffs, labor would have no need to be the slave of either the factory owner or the planter.[5]

But reluctance to interfere with freedom of contract—even for the sake of promoting the moral character and good citizenship of the workers—was the hurdle most intellectuals of Radical inclinations found hardest to cross. As E. L. Godkin first wrestled with the problem, he could not decide which way to turn. The dilemma was brought sharply to his attention by an article that appeared in the London *Spectator* in the summer of 1865, opposing the proposal of British reformers that their workers be allowed to vote. Of course, any Radical favored universal suffrage, but the line of argument taken by the *Spectator* particularly vexed Godkin. To illustrate the danger that universal suffrage would create a government in which workers voted *as a class* for their own interests and against those of the community at large, the article singled out the movement in Massachusetts to shorten the hours of labor by legislation. It thus confronted Godkin with three alternatives—repudiating democracy in the name of freedom of contract, continuing to champion democracy by proving that a shorter day *was* in the community interest, or adhering to both democracy and free contract by convincing the electorate that eight-hour laws were ill-advised for all concerned. Bewildered, Godkin wrote the eminent economist Edward Atkinson: "I was when I read this very anxious to have the point met, if it can be met & I intend to forward [the *Spectator*] to you for that purpose. I want to make the *Nation* a good exponent of democratic ideas abroad as well as here. If you can take this up, I should be glad to leave you do so. There is probably no one better fitted."[6]

About a month later the *Nation's* first editorial on the eight-

5 Quoted in "Stimmen der Presse über: Die Achtstundenbewegung," *Arbeiter-Zeitung,* Dec. 1, 1865.
6 E. L. Godkin to Edward A. Atkinson, Sept. 9, 1865, Atkinson Papers, Box 1.

hour movement appeared. The hand of Atkinson was evident in its argument that eight-hour laws would prove "unwise and injurious" political interference with the natural price of labor and would lessen production, which in turn "would be to diminish capital, the fund out of which labor is paid." This stand provoked a flood of letters from irate readers, so Godkin had to take up his pen anew to explain himself. Again his correspondence with Atkinson makes it clear he was drawing directly on the economist for ideas. The question, Godkin now editorialized, was one of economics, not morals. Conceding that the ten-hour laws of many states were beneficial to the community because a man could not work longer than that without injuring his body, he argued:

> There is, therefore, little or no violence done to the ordinary laws of trade by fixing ten hours as the legal working day. . . . But when it is proposed to force men to restrict their working to eight hours a day . . . [not on grounds of health], but on the ground that he needs the rest of his time for reading, society, and music, an entirely new class of considerations comes into play . . . [Such a measure tries to] nullify one of the natural economic laws by a law of the state . . . [and] the capitalist is of course launched at once on an ocean of uncertainty.[7]

In a word, Godkin accepted the businessman's vulgar assumption that ten hours constituted a "natural" day's work. In doing so he demonstrated that Radical utilitarianism could cut both ways when it came to the hours of labor—that conclusions favorable to shorter hours were not the only ones which could logically be drawn from the premises of nationalist-utilitarianism. He made it evident, furthermore, that just as labor reformers had to rely on their own initiative to make the shorter hours a political issue serious enough to capture the attention of the Radicals, so they needed an economic and social theory of their own to avoid the ambiv-

---

[7] Edwin L. Godkin, "The Eight Hour Movement," *Nation,* Vol. I (Oct. 26, 1865), pp. 517–18; *ibid.,* Vol. I (Nov. 16, 1865), pp. 615–16; "The Government and the Eight Hour Movement," *ibid.,* Vol. I (Dec. 21, 1865), pp. 775–6; E. L. Godkin to E. A. Atkinson, Jan. 26, 1866, Atkinson Papers, Box 2. For Atkinson's economic views, see E. A. Atkinson, *Labor and Capital Allies Not Enemies* (New York, 1879).

alence of radicalism on the labor question and provide a rigorous defense of the eight-hour day. In other words, they had to substitute a political economy of the working classes for the utilitarian economics of the Radicals. The man who created such a theory was Ira Steward.

IRA STEWARD

Steward was born in Massachusetts in 1831 and by 1850 was toiling twelve hours a day as a machinist's apprentice. In that year he was dismissed from a job for agitating on behalf of the eight-hour day, the cause to which he devoted himself unreservedly until his death in 1883. By the middle of the Civil War he had emerged as a prominent leader of the Machinists' and Blacksmiths' International Union and a founder of Boston's Eight Hour League.[8] His closest associates, George McNeill, Edward Rogers, George Gunton, and F. A. Sorge, knew, or at least revealed, little about Steward's personal affairs, but his letters to Sorge indicate that the labor movement was his life. The personality which arose from this total amalgamation of the man and his crusade was vividly portrayed in Rogers' memoirs:

> I have no doubt that [Steward] was a good workman, but there was nothing in his character, or appearance, indicating it. A mystery hung over his previous life, about which we had only hints that he was personally involved in the bloodshed which marked the admission of Kansas. He was highly intellectual; always scrupulously neat in person, and address, deferential in a high degree to all women. Inclining however to be discourteous, if not insulting at sight, to all men . . . [he] was wise in his purpose to magnify the Reduction of the Hours of Labor, but very injudicious in his personal bearing toward all who differed from him.[9]

The purposefulness of Steward easily became overbearing arrogance. Even when writing Edward Atkinson a personal

[8] Commons, *Labour*, II, 88–9; Foner, *Labor*, I, 364; Schlüter, *Internationale*, pp. 461–70. The *Encyclopedia of Social Reform*, ed. William D. P. Bliss (New York, 1897), p. 1290, mistakenly says Steward was born in England.

[9] Rogers, "Auto-Biography," 16:5–6.

request to use his influence with the Boston Board of Trade to obtain free use of its hall for the Eight Hour League, Steward could not restrain himself from commenting: "But whether our association, or we, are voted in or out, our ideas will take possession of you and all your boards, ultimately, *for we are right!*" Just for good measure, he added that it would be unfair "for a man of your position" to continue in ignorance of the eight-hour movement. "Of course I do'nt [*sic*] wish to be offensive," Steward concluded, "but we are becoming sore at"—here, at least, discretion prompted Steward to strike these last two words and continue—"impatient over the large number of responsible men who oppose us without knowing what we mean . . ."[1]

Perhaps this personal quality accounts in part for the consistency with which American intellectual historians (except Joseph Dorfman) have slighted Steward. He was utterly contemptuous of the greenback movement and thus found himself isolated from the mainstream of the labor movement by the 1870's. At the very peak of Wendell Phillips's popularity with labor reformers, Steward blasted the patrician for "quixotic and ill-considered utterances" and accused him of speaking "for applause rather than to give instruction."[2] In response, Greenbackers hung on Steward the label "eight hour monomaniac," and subsequent historians unfortunately have accepted the description.[3]

Because the machinist enjoyed no formal education above the elementary level, his writings remained crude and unsophisticated. Despite his many years of toil on a systematic treatise, he never published more than a few short pamphlets and allowed many of his most intriguing thoughts to lie fallow in the piles of manuscripts he had accumulated by the time of his death. His ideas were disseminated primarily through the Boston Trades Assembly, the Machinists' and Blacksmiths' Union, and the Massachusetts Bureau of Statistics of Labor, and they survived the nineteenth century through the efforts of his disciples McNeill and Gunton, who ultimately ground

---

[1] Ira Steward to Edward A. Atkinson, Feb. 14, 1872, Atkinson Papers, Box 3.
[2] Letter of Ira Steward, Boston *Commonwealth*, June 29, 1872.
[3] Commons, *Labour*, II, 88; Sharkey, p. 186; Dorfman, II, 980, III, 27–8.

out books and pamphlets for the A.F. of L.[4] In the last half century no one has had an interest in keeping his doctrines alive, so Steward has been safely relegated to the "monomaniac" niche.

There was in Steward's time, however, one man outside the ranks of his colleagues who considered him an oasis in the desert of American reformist quacks, and that was F. A. Sorge.[5] The reason is that in a decade when Marxist influence in American labor was at a very low ebb, Steward provided an American-born social philosophy that paralleled Marxism at remarkably many points. There is no indication, however, that Steward read any works by Marx until 1875 or 1876, when Sorge mailed him a manuscript copy of a translation of parts of *Das Kapital*. In fact, Steward remarked at that time that both he and McNeill were highly impressed by the book and wanted to make Americans familiar with it. "I shall quote from the Dr. several passages to help introduce and make his name more common to our readers," Steward wrote to Sorge. "I never knew how much he had said on the Hours of Labor."[6]

A comparison of the two writers can both aid in the understanding of Steward and underscore some peculiarities of American labor reform. From the first glance it is evident that Steward was the intellectual child of radicalism. His thought logically begins with a critique of the antislavery movement. "The anti-slavery *idea*," he wrote, "was, that every man had the right to come and go at will. The labor movement asks how much this abstract right is actually worth, without the power to exercise it." Because the laborer suffered from poverty and dependence, he "instinctively feels that something of slavery still remains, or that something of freedom is yet to come, and he is not much interested in the anti-slavery theory of liberty. He wants a fact, which the labor movement under-

---

[4] George McNeill, *The Eight Hour Primer* ("Eight Hour Series," No. 1, Washington, 1907); George Gunton, *Wealth and Progress: A Critical Examination of the Labor Problem* (New York, 1887); Gunton, *Principles of Social Economics* (New York, 1891).

[5] Sorge, "1866–1876," p. 179.

[6] Ira Steward to F. A. Sorge (dated only "Tuesday," but clearly written after the death of Gerrit Smith, Dec. 28, 1874, and before the establishment of the International Labor Union in 1878), Steward Papers, Box 3. See also Schlüter, *Internationale*, p. 461.

takes to supply."[7] The criticism to which labor subjected the doctrine of freedom as the absence of external restraints, therefore, was not philosophical—not the substitution of a new theory of freedom—but practical. Men must "handle *things*," wrote Steward, "before they can grasp thoughts. . . ." Just as men must build idols before they can understand an abstract God, he explained, so "there must be progress in *things, before* there can be progress in theory!"[8]

The "thing" to be attacked was the system of wage labor, for within it the "freedom of contract" which ostensibly existed between employer and employee was necessarily a sham. As George McNeill argued: "The laborer's commodity perishes every day beyond possibility of recovery. He must sell to-day's labor to-day, or never." The terms of such sale were thus set by the employer. "An empty stomach can make no contracts." The workers "*assent* but they do not *consent,* they submit but they do not agree."[9] In other words, the status of the laborer as factor of production contradicted the Radical idea of the laborer as citizen, and there was no solution to the dilemma within the wage system.

But in his search for a remedy, Steward, like the Radicals, turned to the democratic state. He heaped scorn upon the doctrine that little can be changed by legislation, pointing to the wonders accomplished by "the far-sighted Radicals" simply by insisting "that the single word 'white' shall be blotted out from all our legislatures. . . ." Their example, he believed, showed "the omnipotent power of the People when acting in their *collective capacity,* which is legislating."[1]

The first step in labor's attack on the wages system, Steward reasoned, should be the legislative enactment of the eight-hour day. While he argued hotly that all other reform demands were futile or diversionary until this goal had been obtained, he insisted with equal fervor that "the *idea* of eight

---

[7] Ira Steward, "Poverty," *Mass. BLS, 1873,* pp. 411–39. (The quotation is on p. 412.)

[8] Ira Steward, "Wealth and Progress" (manuscript probably written *c.* 1875, Steward Papers, Box 3), pp. 1–2.

[9] George McNeill, *Argument on the Hours of Labor. Delivered before the Labor Committee of the Massachusetts Legislature* (New York, n.d., *c.* 1874), pp. 13, 17–18.

[1] Letter of Ira Steward, *Daily Evening Voice,* Jan. 17, 1867.

hours isn't eight hours; it is *less poverty!* Eight hours is never put as an IDEA, or a panacea, but as a *first measure*."[2] In order both to explain why the shorter day was the indispensable first measure of labor reform and to convince workmen, and the electorate at large, that the state should enact legislation toward that end, it was necessary for Steward to develop an economic theory to counter the arguments of his opponents. To the elaboration of such an economic doctrine he devoted the major part of his literary efforts.

Orthodox economics in Steward's time rested on three basic tenets: the labor theory of value, Say's Law (for every product there is a consumer), and the wages-fund notion. Steward accepted the labor theory of value, but gave it no significant place in his system. Apparently unaware of the marginal utility theory Stanley Jevons was developing in the 1870's to replace that real cost concept, Steward simply treated the labor theory as axiomatic.

Say's Law and the wages fund, on the other hand, he subjected to severe criticism. Wages, according to economists from David Ricardo through John Stuart Mill and Henry Carey, are created out of invested capital: they are a portion of the gross product which the entrepreneur abstaining from personal consumption, reinvests in the employment of labor. The theory is a sophisticated version of the common assertion that the capitalist creates the job for the worker. For Ricardo and for Mill in the 1840's the fund was fixed, and from this concept sprang Lassalle's "iron law of wages." In his later years Mill conceived the fund as elastic, since technological improvement could increase output per worker, and argued that a rising standard of living for labor was possible. But, fixed or elastic, it was the entrepreneur's investment that created employment and hence the worker's income. Edward Atkinson carried the thesis still farther:

> Capital cannot be considered simply as a *wage fund;* it is a *wage force*, and the amount of wages that can be distributed depends as much on the skill with which capital is directed as it does on the amount used—perhaps more.[3]

---

[2] Letter of Ira Steward, Boston *Commonwealth,* June 29, 1872.
[3] Atkinson, *Labor and Capital Allies,* p. 20.

For Steward and Marx, on the other hand, both the level of wages and the level of employment are profoundly influenced by labor itself, though the routes by which the two thinkers reached this conclusion were different. Steward began with the thesis Joseph Dorfman traces to John Stuart Mill,[4] but which Steward might have learned from Malthus—that the standard of living of the masses can be increased only by changing their habits and wants. Here was an idea Radicals would certainly find congenial, but Steward turned it into an assault on the whole theory that the level of wages is fixed by the quantity of capital invested in the employment of labor. He did so by directing his attention to the determinants of labor's supply curve, rather than to the demand side of the question. Wage levels, he argued, are a function of the tastes, customs, and desires of the workers themselves. Men receive high wages only when they are accustomed to a high standard of living—when they insist on being paid high wages. Just as orthodox academic economic thought so frequently gave theoretical expression to commonplace notions of businessmen, so Steward here gave vent to a widespread assumption of American workers—the concept of an "American standard of living" or "white man's wages." But Steward related this notion immediately to the length of the working day, arguing that "men who labor excessively are robbed of all ambition to ask for anything more than will satisfy their bodily necessities, while those who labor moderately have time to cultivate tastes and create wants in addition to mere physical comforts." A reduction of the hours of labor was, therefore, a frontal assault on poverty because it would raise the supply function of labor—would leave the workers "stimulated to demand higher wages. . . ."[5]

Here was a view of social determination of wage levels remarkably similar to that of Marx, if not as thoroughly developed. Marx contended that wages (the value of labor power) must equal the value of the means of subsistence necessary for the laborer and his family, but he insisted that

---

[4] Dorfman, II, 980, III, 27.
[5] Ira Steward, *A Reduction of Hours Is an Increase of Wages* (Boston, 1865) reprinted in Commons, *Doc. Hist.*, IX, 284–301. (The quotation is on p. 285.)

this "necessary" level was not simply a matter of physical needs. On the contrary, the "number and extent of so-called necessary wants, as also the modes of satisfying them, are themselves the products of historical development, and depend therefore to a great extent on the degree of civilization of a country, more particularly on the conditions under which, and consequently on the habits and the degree of comfort in which, the class of free laborers has been formed."[6]

For both Steward and Marx, therefore, it was false to argue as Hazard, Godkin, Atkinson, Walker, and other opponents of eight-hour legislation did, that if the hours of labor were reduced, labor's income had to fall. This common-sense view of "less work, less pay" assumed that shorter hours would reduce the national product, while the proportions of its division would remain constant, so that workers would end up with less. Amasa Walker went so far as to argue that labor's share would fall drastically with shorter hours, for employers would defend their earnings so effectively that the rate of profit would increase.[7] Quite the contrary, argued Steward, labor's income would rise—first, because there is no fixed relationship between profits and wages; and secondly, because only with more leisure time would workers rid their minds of the layer of callous with which they had adjusted to poverty. Higher expectations and even higher expenditures could and must *precede* higher earnings and draw wages upward after them.[8] To prove his point, Steward had to demonstrate his own conception of both the relationship of wages to profits and the sources of economic growth.

Sharp debates with currency and land reformers after 1867 served to refine Steward's thinking on both these points. His view of profits approximated that of Marx, while his doctrine of economic growth anticipated the thinking of John Maynard Keynes. Greenback doctrines located exploitation in the process of *exchange* of commodities. Steward, like Marx, found it in the process of production itself. For the Green-

---

[6] Marx, *Capital*, I, 190.
[7] *Mass. Labor Report, 1867*, pp. 21–8.
[8] Steward, *Reduction of Hours*, pp. 289–94; Steward, "Wages and Wealth" (manuscript, c. 1870, in Steward Papers, Box 3), p. 5.

backer the concept "labor" embraced both the entrepreneur and the wage earner, and the "surplus value" exacted from labor consisted of the interest charged for loan capital over and above the real productive potential of that capital.[9] Steward responded that even with a just rate of interest, the wage earner would still suffer exploitation by his employer, and that the question of interest was merely a dispute between the entrepreneur and the financier over what the former had already withheld from labor. Just as the motive for "making a man a slave, was to get his labor, or its results, for nothing," so the "motive for employing wage-labor, is to secure *some* of its results for nothing; and, in point of fact, larger fortunes are made out of the profits of wage-labor, than out of the products of slavery."[1]

It followed for Steward that "the poverty of the masses" was the necessary obverse of the accumulation of capital, for without workers driven by their hunger to seek employment, capital would be "worthless."[2] Hence it was presumptuous, if not idolatrous, for Radicals to worship at the shrine of the self-made man. All wealth is created by society, not by individuals, he insisted, and the basis of its accumulation lies in what is withheld from the workers who create it. "If Robinson Crusoe had had an opportunity to profit by the labor and earnings of a hundred thousand Fridays, he might have been wealthy, and have called his fortunes his share of the work on his island."[3] It was, therefore, foolish to talk of "fair wages" and "fair profits." Wages were what labor could effectively demand. Profits were the difference between the day's wage bill and the product of the workers' day's toil. In other words, Steward found profits (and not wages) to be a function of the length of the working day:

> The Wages we receive, under the present system, are not a just equivalent for our Labor; and they will not be for what the Products of our Labor in the Eight Hour system will sell for, after allowing a liberal margin for every legitimate expense. . . . The Eight Hour system *may*

---

[9] See below, p. 432–3.
[1] Steward, "Poverty," p. 411.
[2] *Ibid.*, pp. 424–5.
[3] *Ibid.*, p. 422.

gradually reduce the profits or the "Wages" of the employers; but are not *our* Wages or "profits" reduced, now and then, when we work by the job or piece? From time to time Employers decide that *we* are making too much money. We have decided that THEY are making too much money! *They* cut down OUR Prices! We *shall cut down* THEIR *Hours!*[4]

In marked contrast, therefore, to the thesis that employer abstinence creates a wages fund, Steward reasoned that employer expropriation of the excess of labor's product above the wages paid created, in effect, a capital fund. Marx reached a similar conclusion: jobs are created by the reinvestment of a portion of "surplus value," at least after the first turnover of the initial accumulation of capital. But rather than develop this idea as Marx did, Steward moved his thinking into channels later to be claimed by Keynes. The increased wages that he believed must flow from shorter hours would stimulate both higher levels of employment and more rapid economic growth, by enhancing the demand for the products of industry. Only a small increment to the income of each workingman, he reasoned, would be enough to create a massive increase in aggregate purchasing power. "It is the function of laborers to create demands," he wrote, but the immediate problem was that while the industrialists were *"supplying* the world's demands, they are also engaged in the crime of *suppressing* them. In other words, their vast power is used to prevent laborers from *creating* demands."[5] High wages would both stimulate production through increasing demand and promote the use of machinery, thus lowering unit costs in two ways simultaneously. To translate Steward into Keynesian terms, a rising propensity to consume, not abstinence, is the foundation of an expanding economy.[6]

---

[4] Ira Steward, *The Meaning of the Eight Hour Movement* (Boston, 1868), pp. 6–8.
[5] Ira Steward, "Theory of Wages" (manuscript *c.* 1875–9, Steward Papers, Box 3), pp. 2, 4. *Cf.* Steward, "Poverty," pp. 427–8.
[6] Steward, "Wages and Wealth," pp. 2–3; John Maynard Keynes, *General Theory of Employment Interest and Money* (New York, 1935), pp. 177–9, 183–5; Dorothy W. Douglas, "Ira Steward on Consumption and Unemployment," *Journal of Political Economy*, Vol. XL (Aug. 1932), pp. 537, 540. *Cf.* H. J. Habakkuk's argument that in nineteenth-

One must beware pressing the Steward-Keynes analogy too far. There is a difference between the two men which at first glance appears somewhat petty, but which on closer examination unveils a remarkable lacuna in Steward's thought. Keynes was to argue that increased aggregate purchasing power would raise the level of production and employment *only* on the assumption that unemployment existed prior to the raising of wages. Given full employment, a wage increase would create only inflation. Steward disagreed, and the basis of his dissent was his belief that high wages promote the substitution of machinery for labor, thus increasing output, regardless of whether or not all workers were employed.[7] But once Steward introduced the element of rising productivity per worker, he opened up the possibility that economic growth might bring increases in *both* labor's income and employers' profits. This contingency, however, eluded Steward, who clung to the belief that progress based on rising wages had to reduce profits.

Viewing the same process another way, Steward produced a dialectical conception of progress. To date, he declared, social progress and the accumulation of wealth had moved hand in hand. On one side, "emancipation and popular progress have been possible, only because they were found to be more productive and profitable to the ruling classes than slavery and ignorance." On the other, that very advance of society had made the accumulation of wealth easier: demand was greater, inventors were no longer mobbed, contracts were widely respected, and so on. Hence, today's fortunes were social not individual products, giving society a legitimate claim to the wealth it produced. And it would make that claim, because the "intelligence and general conditions . . . that have accomplished so much, are the qualities that will ask for more. . . ."[8] Therefore, the educated and well-paid work-

---

century America, high wages were the cause of high productivity, not its result. Habakkuk, *American and British Technology in the Nineteenth Century* (Cambridge, 1962), pp. 13–15.

[7] Keynes, pp. 289–91; Steward, "Wages and Wealth."

[8] Steward, "Poverty," pp. 432–9. (The quotation is on p. 433.) Note the similarity of Steward's view here to the present-day conception of "human capital" as a major contributor to economic growth. See Theodore W. Schultz, "Human Wealth and Economic Growth," *The*

ing class was the gravedigger of capitalism. (Here the tone differed from that of Marx as remarkably as the thoughts were similar.) As hours fell and wages rose, profits would be extinguished, and the capitalist "as we understand him" would "pass away with the kings and royalty of the past." With the extinction of "one man power" in industry, the path would lie open to a cooperative era. "In America," dreamed Steward, "every man is king in theory, and will be eventually, and in the good time coming every man will be a capitalist."[9]

This conclusion reveals Steward's continued tie to the Radical intellect and sets his theory apart from that of Marx in two important respects. First, the two men disagreed on how much an eight-hour law could accomplish. For Steward the law would be the decisive step initiating a steady course of progress toward the raising of national economic standards and the withering away of the entrepreneurial class. For Marx such a law was no more than an important step in preparing the working class to undertake an eventual social revolution. It was desirable, not because society could "clear by bold leaps, nor remove by legal enactments, the obstacles offered by the successive phases of its normal development," but rather because by such laws capitalism could "shorten and lessen the birth-pangs" of socialism.[1]

Secondly, and more fundamental, for Marx the ultimate objective of the workers' movement was to seize state power and wield it against the capitalists. Steward, like all his contemporaries in the American labor movement, had no conception of an active role for the machinery of state. The sole function they attributed to government was that of enacting just and general laws applying impartially to all citizens. Within the framework of these laws, social development would take care of itself. Once the state had established a legal definition of the working day dividing the waking hours of the laborer equally between himself and the purchaser of

Humanist, Vol. XIX (March–April, 1959), pp. 71–81; Clark Kerr, John T. Dunlop, Frederick Harbison, and Charles A. Myers, *Industrialism and Industrial Man* (New York, 1964), pp. 230–9.
[9] Steward, *Reduction of Hours*, pp. 300–1; "Wages and Wealth," pp. 4–5.
[1] Marx, *Capital*, I, 15.

his work, Steward assigned it no further tasks. Subsequently, society would become harmonious by its own unaided evolution. Thus Steward departed from the Radical view of the world, only to return to it after the destruction of the practical obstacle which blocked its realization—the wages system. His future held "a republicanization of labor, as well as a republicanization of government."[2]

The workers' hunger for a shorter working day, then, loomed as their unique class aspiration, roused practically unanimous opposition among their employers, and created an agonizing dilemma for the Radicals. The length of the working day was not and could not be a bone of contention for the slave or the self-employed. It was the peculiar issue of the wage earner. To raise it was to carry the social debates of the day beyond Reconstruction, beyond equal rights for all citizens, beyond the limits of the Radical imagination. And from his investigation of this question, Ira Steward drew an economic doctrine tailored specifically to the needs of the working class. The Radicals, he implied, could never realize their own ideals. Only labor could do so, and to do this labor must assault the ramparts of private property, where the Radicals were among the defenders.

---

[2] Steward, "Poverty," p. 434.

CHAPTER 7

Workingmen
Outside the State House
and Legislators Inside

"The New Year opens with flattering auspices to the cause of labor reform," rejoiced the organ of New York's Workingmen's Union at the start of 1867. "Many governors of states and members of state legislatures have been elected upon the workingmen's tickets, as friends of the eight-hour system."[1] The fall elections of 1866 had vindicated Radical equalitarianism at the polls, and Radical leaders now used this popular endorsement and the whip of party discipline to goad their party toward federal reconstruction of the South. Simultaneously, labor reformers urged Republicans to include in their legislative program an eight-hour limit to the hours of work. The intersection of the two reform efforts, however, brought, not joint triumph, but a chaotic reaction that drove both Radicals and labor reformers to reappraise their methods and objectives.

---

[1] *National Workman*, Jan. 5, 1867, quoted in Carlton, pp. 494–5.

The ambivalence of Radical ideology toward the proposal for an eight-hour day was paralleled (and reinforced) by the paradoxical realities of political and economic life in 1866 and 1867. On one hand, the possibility that votes influenced by labor reformers might tip the uneasy balance in many close congressional and legislative districts tempted both Republican and Democratic candidates to be solicitous toward demands for eight-hour laws. Not only were endorsements of the principle forthcoming in abundance, there was no serious controversy even in legislatures where the desired bills were enacted—with the major exception of Massachusetts. On the other hand, the hostility of employers toward reduction of hours in their own works hardened into intransigence, because at this very time the economy was declining sharply. With the political front facing labor unusually soft and the economic front impenetrably hard, the confused outcome entailed, first, the easy passage of legislation which proved totally ineffective in practice; second, a rash of hotly-contested strikes; and third, the alienation from the Radicals of both labor reformers whose dreams were frustrated and businessmen who readily blamed radicalism for the turmoil of the times.

The gradual, uneven decline in the health of the economy was noticeable by May 1866, and degenerated during the winter of 1866–7 into a recession which reached its nadir the following winter. Although a sustained market for new housing kept the building trades busy throughout most of the land, and except for a single poor construction season in 1867, California suffered no noteworthy unemployment, sagging sales of manufactured goods in the urban centers of the Northeast and a financial crisis in England heralded the general approach of hard times.[2] By the spring of 1867 the *New-York Times* noted "an abundance of unemployed capital in Wall-Street," which it considered "favorable to speculative

---

[2] Bates, pp. 23–9; Ping Chiu, *Chinese Labor in California, 1850–1880. An Economic Study* (Madison, Wis., 1963), pp. 5, 48–54; Philadelphia *Public Ledger*, Nov. 27, 1866, Jan. 29, July 20, 1867; Boston *Daily Advertiser*, Jan. 23, 1868; [William B. Dana], "The London Financial Panic—Its Causes and Effects," *Hunt's Merchants' Magazine and Commercial Review*, Vol. LIV (June 1866), pp. 413–17.

activity," but "not indicative of a healthy business condition in the interior." Worse yet, the *Times* lamented, "complications of the labor question, and the probability of strikes in various trades, will not improve the prospect."[3] The Money Market column of Philadelphia's *Public Ledger* agreed that there was little demand for money in "legitimate business, those having the proper security to command it not having sufficient confidence in the future to put it to use. . . ."[4]

Prices of manufactured goods toppled during 1867, cottons dropping almost a third and woolens a fourth from their 1866 levels. The wholesale price index of Professor Mitchell, which had stood at the annual average of 185 in 1865, fell to 162 in 1867 and 158 the following year.[5] This abrupt decline in turn meant unemployment for many workers and wage reductions for many more. In Troy, the market price of shirts and drawers having fallen below the cost of production, 15 knitting mills closed down in the summer of 1867, throwing 2,000 people out of work. In January of that year the Washington Mills in Lawrence, Massachusetts, had stopped one fourth of their machinery, and neighboring mills reduced both hours and pay.[6] But it was not until a year later that the full impact of the industrial recession was felt. In January 1868 the directors of the Board of Poor in Pittsburgh reported more applicants for relief than at any time in the previous 13 years. The following month the Chicago *Times* asserted that there were 25,000 men out of work in that city and 19,000 receiving public and private charity. Similarly, in New York public want was compared with that of the winter of 1854–5, and police reported that for the first time in their experience "American mechanics" nightly sought shelter in station houses—by the dozens and with their families. In that city an estimated 50,000

[3] *New-York Times,* May 7, 1867.
[4] Philadelphia *Public Ledger,* June 7, 1867.
[5] Sharkey, p. 146; *American Annual Cyclopaedia,* VII (1867), 309; Harold F. Williamson, *Edward Atkinson, The Biography of an American Liberal, 1827–1905* (Boston, 1934), p. 33; Chicago *Daily Tribune,* Aug. 15, 1867.
[6] *Daily Evening Voice,* Dec. 29, 1866; Philadelphia *Public Ledger,* Jan. 26, 1867.

were jobless, cigar makers, longshoremen, shipyard workers, and iron workers being the hardest hit.[7]

Reduction of pay was a more common experience than total loss of employment. Instructing the manager of one of his Michigan logging camps to scale down payrolls despite loud protests from his workmen, H. W. Sage wrote that lumber is "slow of sale at *any price*—and wages *should be,* and *will be*—permanently lower before they are permanently higher. . . ."[8] Across the country in Massachusetts pay rates fell between 10 and 20 per cent in the Hebron Mills, the Pacific Mills, the Watson Car Works, the Atlantic Mills, and in the Leet ore beds in Stockbridge, where 3,000 workers futilely resisted with a strike. The Pennsylvania Railroad chopped wages 10 per cent, as did the Delaware-Lackawana, which also put the 1,800 men and boys in its coal mines on half time, with appropriate reductions. Rolling mills in Philadelphia agreed on a cut of one fifth for their employees' pay, Rhode Island quarrymen took a one-fourth reduction, and all Youngstown area employers cut wages one tenth.[9]

It would be a mistake to overestimate the industrial decline, despite all this very real hardship. The worst suffering of 1867 was in the South, where low cotton prices, a poor crop, and the continued federal cotton tax all accentuated the impact of the war's physical devastation.[1] Manfacturing was only experiencing only a postwar readjustment—albeit a severe one. Total industrial output continued to rise from year to year. Strong unions like the Iron Molders' successfully resisted employers' attempts to cut pay, and many building tradesmen, whose work remained plentiful, enjoyed raises. Wesley Mitchell's index of wages, which blended temporary reductions and increases alike into annual averages, even mani-

---

[7] *Ibid.,* Jan. 27, Feb. 12, 13, 1868; *Workingman's Advocate,* Dec. 21, 1867.

[8] H. W. Sage to J. G. Emory, July 12, 1867, quoted in Goodstein, p. 205.

[9] Boston *Daily Advertiser,* Jan. 1, 3, 14, 30, Feb. 3, 17, 1868; *Strikes and Lockouts,* p. 1051; *Workingman's Advocate,* Jan. 18, 1868.

[1] See E. Merton Coulter, *The South during Reconstruction* (Baton Rouge, La., 1947), pp. 10–12, 218–19; Rhodes, VI, 77–8; Vernon Lane Wharton, *The Negro in Mississippi, 1865–1890* (Harper Torchbook edition, New York, 1965), pp. 47–52, 69–70; *American Annual Cyclopaedia,* VII (1867), 546–8.

fested a seven-point rise for 1867, though it was scarcely able
to creep up one point for the 1868 average.[2] The crucial point
is that the slump guaranteed a maximum of employer resistance to the objectives which the Baltimore Congress had set
forth for labor. The mood of business was aptly expressed by
an editorial on the recession in *Hunt's Merchants' Magazine*,
which complained: "By one of those perverse freaks which
often deprive society of a much needed relief, the working
classes have organized influential combinations for exacting
unnaturally high wages, and, still worse, for curtailing the
hours of labor."[3] Many businessmen sought relief in fiat
currency and higher tariffs to raise their selling prices. All of
them—including the firmest advocates of deflation and free
trade—sought relief through lower production costs. Hence
their unanimous demand for the elimination of wartime domestic taxes, and hence their resistance to labor's appeals for
higher wages and shorter hours.

MASSACHUSETTS: FAILURE AT THE POLLS

Nowhere did labor's hopes fly higher in the summer of
1866 than they did in Massachusetts. Here the state legislature
had already sponsored an official report on the hours of labor
that not only favored labor's cause, but couched its endorsement in familiar Radical rhetoric.[4] Too, newly elected Governor Bullock was a proven friend of legislation to shorten the
working day, as were House Speaker James M. Stone and
House Clerk William S. Robinson. In some parts of the state,
like Lowell and the eighth ward of Boston, regular Republicans and workingmen's caucuses shared offices and libraries
and divided between them the seats on the party city committees. Especially heartening for labor reformers was the Republican State Convention, where the Radicals assumed full control of the proceedings and Benjamin Butler himself presided.
Already, Wendell Phillips had contributed his oratorical
talents to the cause of shorter hours, and he and Butler were

---

[2] Sharkey, p. 146. The wage index of the *Aldrich Report* (I, 13) rose
less than one point.
[3] *Hunt's Merchants' Magazine and Commercial Review*, Vol. LIX (Aug.
1868), p. 129.
[4] See above, pp. 124–5.

beginning to perfect their influential collaboration of the patrician and the politico.[5] In other words, the Republicans were solidly in power, Radicals were dominating Republican proceedings, and radicalism and labor reform seemed, if not married, at least betrothed.

But already the astute observer could discern signs that matters were not so simple as this. Pursuant to the recommendation of the 1865 Griffin Committee on the hours of labor, and the subsequent resolution of the legislature, outgoing Governor Andrew had appointed a commission of five unpaid members to undertake a more thorough study of the labor question than the Griffin Committee had been able to make, and to produce recommendations for specific legislation. The commission Andrew selected was indeed a bluestocking affair, including among its members Dr. Henry I. Bowditch, prominent physician and authority on public health; Elizur Wright, who was then making insurance history with his assaults on unsophisticated actuarial practices; and Franklin B. Sanborn, the former colleague of John Brown who was now editor of the Boston *Commonwealth*, head of the state Board of Charities, and secretary of the new American Association for the Promotion of Social Science. Not only were all three of these men old abolitionists, but they all moved in the charmed circle of the Bird Club, that informal headquarters of Massachusetts radicalism.[6] The report they submitted to the legislature in February 1866 was remarkably different from the previous year's Griffin report, and the importance of its authors made the difference ominous for labor reformers.

The committee documented at length the long hours and distressing conditions of toil prevalent in the state, noted the overwhelming demand for reduced hours among workmen, and listed the many arguments for and against the shorter day. Its conclusions, however, were not those of Ira Steward,

[5] *Daily Evening Voice*, Sept. 13, 14, Oct. 1, 2, 1866; Persons, pp. 60–3, 103; Trefousse, *Butler*, pp. 34–41; Bartlett, pp. 261–2, 265–6.
[6] Biographical data on commission members is taken from *D.A.B.*, II, 492–4; *ibid.*, XIV, 326–7; *ibid.*, XX, 548–9; Stearns, pp. 162–79, 286–308; F. B. Sanborn to E. A. Atkinson, Oct. 6, 1865, Atkinson Papers, Box 1; Robinson, *Pen-Portraits*, x.

but those of Atkinson and Godkin. No eight-hour law should be adopted by the legislature, advised Sanborn and his associates. If such a law effectively prohibited workers from spending more than eight hours on the job, they argued, "a very large portion of the industrial interests of the country *could not* observe it."[7] And if the law were so phrased as to provide only "moral countenance to the movement," by declaring eight hours a legal day's work while allowing contracts to be made for longer hours, "it would be rendered void by special contracts, and so add another to the dead laws that cumber the statutes."[8]

The commission did not restrict its objections to legislation for an eight-hour day; it also condemned any state action designed to interfere in "the bargain between [the worker] and the capitalist, and give him a larger share of the value that is or may be produced, than the capitalist is willing to agree to" as "subverting the right of individual property, and establishing communism."[9] No law can improve men, the commission concluded, for the "essence of law is nothing but force. If it undertakes to make men good, what becomes of its protection of the right of property?"[1] The welfare of the community would indeed be promoted by a reduction of working hours, especially in the textile mills, but it would not be enhanced by legislation to coerce the mill owners. "The Commission believe that the change desired can be better brought about by workingmen outside the State House, than by legislators inside."[2]

On this note Sanborn and his colleagues proceeded not only to advise the legislature on what it might do, but also to instruct the workingmen on objectives they should pursue. Both aspects of the report are remarkable in that, coupled with the comment on the inherent futility of making eight hours a legal day's work, while allowing workers to contract for longer hours, they provided a prediction of the evolution of labor-reform objectives over the coming two years which, with

---

[7] *Mass. Labor Report, 1866*, p. 28.
[8] *Ibid.*, pp. 25–6, 28.
[9] *Ibid.*, p. 29.
[1] *Ibid.*, p. 31.
[2] *Ibid.*, p. 44.

hindsight, seems almost clairvoyant. First, they said, legislation could and should promote the education of children, and
an act to keep the young out of the factory and in the school-
house was not only proper but absolutely necessary. Secondly,
since capital and labor beyond "the season of pupilage" should
be allowed to contract without legislative interference, the
commission "would favor . . . a policy which would discour-
age every species of monopoly, and which would impose on
excessive wealth such burdens for the support of the government, as its natural privileges make just and equitable."[3] Let
labor reformers, in other words, attack the concentrated power
of wealth and monopoly, rather than attempt by law to
restrict labor contracts. And while workmen pursued this more
appropriate goal, they should "by temperate and industrious
habits . . . by the practice of that economy which will help
them to become their own capitalists, by co-operative labor
securing to each workman a share of the profits of his work, by
associations for mutual *good* as well as mutual gain," prove
their worth, earn community respect, and dispel "the widespread distrust of [their] proper use of leisure hours. . . ."[4]

In the series of reports to the state legislature on the hours
of labor, the work of this commission was the last to receive
the unanimous approval of its members. And the legislature
quickly responded to its foremost recommendation. Prompted
by Governor Bullock, who in January had hailed the public
schools as the foundation of the whole strength and health of
the commonwealth, the legislators, with little ado, enacted a
factory act that prohibited the industrial employment of any
child under the age of ten, or of any between the ages of ten
and fourteen who did not attend school at least six months of
the year. In passing (and, as time proved, final) tribute to the
eight-hour movement, no employee less than fourteen years
of age was to toil more than eight hours a day.[5]

Labor reformers, however, were not prepared to follow
the path charted by this commission. Their commitment was

---

[3] *Ibid.*, p. 47
[4] *Ibid.*, p. 49.
[5] Act of May 28, 1866, *Acts and Resolves of the General Court of
Massachusetts in the Year 1866* (Boston, 1866), Ch. 273. For Bullock's
speech see *Mass. Labor Report, 1866*, p. 17.

to the eight-hour day, and their hope was still to convert the Republican party unreservedly to legislation for that end. The previous year the Eight Hour Leagues had challenged the backers of Nathaniel Banks in the caucuses of the Sixth Congressional District, and though failing to defeat his nomination, they did convert Banks to supporting their program.[6] Now, in 1866, an opportunity arose to influence a crucial nomination in the Third District, a stronghold of the leagues and of *Voice* subscribers that embraced parts of South Boston, Roxbury, and Brookline. Here a large, enthusiastic rally of the workingmen's caucus in September proposed the name of Wendell Phillips as its candidate for Congress.

Circumstances could not have been more favorable for this project. The Republican incumbent, Alexander H. Rice, whom the leagues considered an "exponent of the views of the moneyed class," formally announced his intention to retire from Congress. Taking advantage of this opening, the workingmen were proposing to the Republican party, in a year of Radical upsurge, the nomination of the most prominent Radical not already in Washington. Here, declared the *Voice*, was a chance for the Republicans of Massachusetts to show whether they were "truly radical" or "radical only for Louisiana." Their candidate, said labor's journal, would not only enjoy the solid support of Republican voters, but would lure the franchises of Democratic workers as well.[7] The labor reformers obviously deluded themselves if they really believed that all Republicans who would vote for Rice could be counted upon to cast their ballots for Phillips, who, after all, had first become openly active in Republican affairs when he enlisted in the 1864 effort to replace Lincoln with Frémont as Presidential nominee, and who now regularly chastised the party as timorous and unprincipled.[8] On the other hand, Phillips could certainly attract widespread Radical support running either as a Republican or as an Independent, and if elected on the Republican ticket, could form with Butler, Wilson, and the newly converted Banks a formidable phalanx

---

[6] *Daily Evening Voice*, Oct. 25, 1865.

[7] *Ibid.*, Oct. 25, 1865, Sept. 18, 19, 21, 1866.

[8] Bartlett, pp. 268–73; Austin, 247–9.

in the state's congressional delegation working for labor's interests.

Only one factor remained in doubt: the attitude of Phillips himself. A committee headed by George McNeill notified the famous abolitionist of the caucus' decision and spent five days in suspense awaiting an answer. On September 24, Phillips dropped his bombshell. "I feel that in accepting office I should, paradoxical as it may sound, incur responsibility to a far greater extent than I should gain power," he wrote McNeill. "It seems to me that I can in present circumstances serve our cause better out of Congress than in it."[9]

The *Voice* was dumfounded. On the day it printed the letter the paper commented only that it could not reconcile itself to this decision. The next day the editors voiced their bitter frustration: "Power! He would be a million-armed Briareus." Noting that neither Mill nor Wilberforce had declined to do battle in Parliament, the editors lamented: "How Jeff Davis in his cell, the party tricksters, and the plunderers must have rejoiced at that letter!"[1]

With the *Voice* forlornly appearing again without the proud banner "Wendell Phillips for Congress in the Third District," Republican leaders in the district lost no time consolidating their control. From many wards came reports that "Rice men" were excluding army veterans (often the backbone of labor strength) from party caucuses on the grounds that their names were not on regularly printed lists of voters, and were plotting to oust from the city committee all workingmen's leaders that they could not bind to whatever candidate the party might select. Republican spokesmen angrily denied these charges, but by the time the district nominating convention was held at the beginning of October, the influence of labor reformers had clearly been minimized.[2]

Meantime, the workingmen's caucus reassembled to select a new candidate only four days before the Republican district convention. The unanimity easily evoked by the name of Phillips now yielded to dispute over several possible cham-

9 *Daily Evening Voice*, Sept. 19, 24, 1866. *Cf.* Austin, p. 249; Bartlett, p. 303.
1 *Daily Evening Voice*, Sept. 24, 25, 1866.
2 *Ibid.*, Oct. 1, 2, 4, 5, 6, 1866.

pions. Prominent among those discussed were Rufus Wyman, now elderly but still fiery, a businessman and abolitionist who unequivocally supported the shorter working day; and Captain John W. LeBarnes, a close friend of Phillips who was active in the Industrial Order of the People and who had once plotted with Richard J. Hinton and Thomas Wentworth Higginson to spring John Brown's associates from prison by a daring raid.[3] By the narrow plurality of 49 out of the 91 votes cast, the meeting finally selected General Patrick R. Guiney as labor's choice for the Republican nomination.[4]

Despite the close caucus vote, the choice was excellent— in some ways better than Phillips, as Guiney had personal appeal for every group labor reformers might want to attract. Born into a Catholic family in Ireland's County Tipperary in 1835, Guiney moved to New Brunswick at the age of five, then made his way to Massachusetts and worked as a machinist in Lawrence. His social ambitions took him to Worcester College (the College of the Holy Cross), but lack of funds forced him to drop out and take up the study of law privately while he worked as assistant editor of the *Democratic Advocate* in Lewiston, Maine. At the age of twenty-one he was admitted to the bar, married Jennie Doyle, and moved to Boston to open his own law practice. The following four years provided opportunities for the young Irish lawyer to reach for the top. As a Democrat he was elected to the Roxbury Common Council in 1859, and the next year made himself well known by his speeches for Stephen A. Douglas. Simultaneously, he gained valuable social contacts by joining the Ancient Charitable Society of the Irish of Boston, an order founded in 1739—by Protestants! When war struck, Guiney enlisted as a captain in the Meagher Guard of the all-Irish Ninth Massachusetts, moved quickly to the rank of colonel as his superiors fell in battle, then was himself dreadfully wounded in the Wilderness—his left eye was shot out.

Guiney returned to Boston not only a brevet brigadier general and a war hero, but a convinced Republican who

[3] On LeBarnes, see Higginson, *Cheerful Yesterdays*, pp. 215, 231–4; *N.L.U. Proceedings, 1868*, p. 4; Wendell Phillips to B. F. Butler, May 20, 1868, Butler Papers, Box II-22-P 1.

[4] *Daily Evening Voice*, Oct. 1, 2, 1866.

leaned toward the Radicals and was friendly with the Fenians. Fully aware of the value of such a figure to his party, Governor Andrew secured for the Irishman an appointment as an assistant district attorney, an office he continued to hold until the end of Governor Bullock's administration in 1869. By that time, despite his firm support for Grant in 1868, Guiney had clearly fallen from the good graces of the party leadership—first, because he had accepted a labor nomination in 1866; and secondly, because the party's nativists who had always opposed him regained the upper hand with the advent of the Claflin administration. Hence he was elected, with Democratic support, to the office of Registrar of Probates and Insolvency, and held that post from 1871 to 1877, during which time he became ever more hostile toward the Republicans. In 1876 he announced himself "an independent with democratic proclivities," and came out for Tilden. He died the next year, survived by his devout and devoted daughter, poetess Louise I. Guiney.[5]

The Republican Convention of the Third Congressional District passed Guiney quickly by, giving him only four votes on the first formal ballot. Its nominee was Ginery Twitchell, president of the Worcester Railroad and a member of the American Emigrant Company. In every respect, Twitchell walked in Rice's footsteps and was the very archetype of the candidate "radical only for Louisiana."[6] The labor caucus angrily reassembled to designate Guiney candidate of the Workingmen's party. An enthusiastic "ratification meeting" presided over by Allen Coffin, a Republican who was soon to become a prominent spokesman for the federal government's printers, put the campaign off to a grand start. While the platform seats were shared by such notables of the trades assembly and the Voice staff as Henry L. Saxton and Ira Steward, Radicals like LeBarnes and Ezra Heywood, of future anarchist fame, German Turners, and Irish war veterans (who

---

[5] Biographical data on Guiney is compiled from Lucey, pp. 23–5, 66–9, 281–5; P. R. Guiney to Louise I. Guiney, Sept. 29, Nov. 7, 1876; P. R. Guiney to Mrs. Sarah Shaw, June 2, 1864; obituaries in Emerald, n.d., Boston Pilot, March 31, 1877; Catholic News, Aug. 2, 1930; and other unidentified clippings, all in Guiney Papers.
[6] Barnes, II, p. 539.

also supplied the brass band of the Ninth Regiment), the program of the National Labor Union was reviewed by its vice-president for Massachusetts, Alexander Troup. Guiney rose to thunderous applause and called for the election of a Fortieth Congress which would both enact labor reform—starting with an eight-hour day for public employees—and institute "instantaneous and impartial suffrage" as "the true national *panacea*." While castigating Congress for being "timid as a fawn" in its approach to Negro suffrage, Guiney advised workingmen to "insist that the negroes in the South should have a right to vote, for that will be an inducement to them *to stay where they are.*"[7]

Rally followed enthusiastic rally as Guiney warned the Republican party not to lose its "friendship to the toiling millions of the land," which had been the "secret of its success" and without which it would go into eclipse with the Whigs and the Democrats, and condemned those "incorporated aggregations" of capital "which are as soulless as an icesicle." In Roxbury he made a special appeal to the Irish voters, on the one hand advising against impeachment of President Johnson, and on the other praising Democratic workers for having spurned the Copperheads and predicting inevitable fusion between War Democrats and Republicans. His campaign won even the commendation of the clerical-minded Boston *Pilot,* despite that journal's disapproval of many of his political positions.[8] But even the best of Guiney's efforts failed to convince either Democratic or Republican workers that a vote for him would do more than simply help put in office the candidate of the party they traditionally opposed.

The tactical problems faced by labor in the Third District were soon overshadowed by those that loomed up in the Fourth District (North and East Boston and Chelsea). Here the unusual vigor of the state's Conservatives became the crucial factor shaping the course of events. The crux of the matter was that Conservatives who participated in the President's National Union movement—unlike their counterparts

---

[7] Unidentified press clippings, P. R. Guiney Scrapbook, Guiney Papers.
[8] *Daily Evening Voice,* Oct. 12, 19, Nov. 3, 7, 1866; Lucey, p. 285; clippings in P. R. Guiney Scrapbook.

elsewhere, who simply provided a tail for the Democratic kite—created in Massachusetts both an independent force to be reckoned with and a formidable influence within both major parties. Symbolic was the stance of the family of Charles Francis Adams, a National Unionist, whose son Charles Francis, Jr., worked with the Republicans, while son John Quincy Adams II was a perennial candidate for the Democrats—yet all three had roughly the same political views.[9] There were, furthermore, prominent Republicans who publicly supported their party's ticket in 1866, while their private views contained much sympathy for the President. "You and I, you know, even, had a little taint of Johnsonism," Samuel Bowles later reminded Congressman Henry L. Dawes, "and if we had held executive office, we should probably have had a little more. . . ."[1]

The National Unionists made a bid for labor support by declaring in favor of a legal limit of eight hours to the working day. When a workingmen's caucus assembled in the Fourth Congressional District one week later, the meeting hall was packed with vociferous supporters of National Unionist Judge Josiah Abbott. Veteran labor reformers, headed by William Falls, stormed angrily out of the hall when the nomination went to Abbott by a vote of 45 to 43. Judge Abbott, in turn, kept discreetly silent concerning the proffered nomination until the Republicans renominated Samuel Hooper, and the Democratic district convention was about to meet. Then the judge wrote to both the Democrats and the workingmen declining all nominations.[2] This astute maneuver left the labor reformers not only without a candidate of their own, but also facing a Republican they could not possibly endorse because he was openly hostile to the agitation for a shorter workday.

---

9 See C. F. Adams, Jr., to C. F. Adams, April 4–7, 1868, April 21, 1868; C. F. Adams to C. F. Adams, Jr., April 8, 1868; and other letters of the period, Adams Papers (microfilm, Massachusetts Historical Society) Reel 586.

1 Samuel Bowles to Henry L. Dawes, April 20, 1869, Dawes Papers, Box 19. See also Thomas J. Florence to H. L. Dawes, Nov. 21, 1865; John Hogan to H. L. Dawes, Nov. 21, 1865; C. Chapin to H. L. Dawes, Oct. 24, 1866, *ibid.*

2 *Daily Evening Voice*, Oct. 1, 4, 11, 19, 20, 1866, Sept. 12, 1867; Philadelphia *Public Ledger*, Aug. 9, 1866. On Hooper, see Barnes, II, 381–6.

The crowning blow came when the Democratic Convention nominated Joseph M. Wightman, who as mayor of Boston in 1861 had banned an abolitionist convention through police action. His platform endorsed President Johnson, called for a white man's government, and approved eight-hour legislation.[3]

Anticipating this development, the editors of the *Voice* had inquired "whether it is policy for [workingmen] to accept a platform which, side by side with its eight hour plank, will contain another opposed to the elevation of Southern labor," and concluded that "an affiliation by workingmen with the Democratic party, with its anti-suffrage plank, would be suicidal on our part." When the labor caucus, after a fierce wrangle, gave Wightman its endorsement, several prominent labor spokesmen, including William Falls, the Fourth District leader, chose simply to ignore the Wightman campaign and concentrate their efforts on the election of Guiney. The *Voice*, however, placed his name on its masthead beside that of Guiney, with the forlorn hope "that he will yet avow himself the friend of the workingmen throughout the land—whether they be white or black."[4]

On Election Day it was evident that the conflict between Johnson and the Republicans had driven the labor question into oblivion. The Republicans swept the state, Governor Bullock receiving more than twice the votes of his opponent. In the Third District Twitchell, the Republican, garnered more than 6,000 votes, while his Democratic opponent, William Aspinwall, with some 2,500 votes, carried only two wards. General Guiney's vote was hardly to be found: only a loyal 436 workingmen had placed the cause of labor above the Reconstruction contest. Even more significantly, in the Fourth District Hooper defeated Wightman by more than two to one. So small a role did the eight-hour issue play in the face of the battle over the South that the Republican plurality in the district, where Democratic and labor-reform strength had supposedly been merged, was *larger* than the Republican

---

[3] *Daily Evening Voice*, Oct. 19, 1866; Philadelphia *Public Ledger*, Oct. 24, 1866. See also Higginson, *Cheerful Yesterdays*, p. 244; Robinson, *Pen-Portraits*, pp. 247–51, 336.
[4] *Daily Evening Voice*, Oct. 4, 19, 23, 1866. On labor reformers opposed to Wightman, see *ibid.*, Oct. 23, 25, Nov. 1, 3, 5, 8, 1866.

plurality in the third, and Hooper's majority was as great as that of Governor Bullock. In other words, the eight-hour issue had not drawn a single vote out of the Republican column, when it had been tied to the platform of the Democrats.[5]

The outcome of the voting placed labor on the horns of a dilemma. On one hand, the state Republicans had demonstrated no willingness to make spokesmen of the workers major partners in their political concern, or even to embrace labor-reform issues as a vital part of their program. Events had shown, furthermore, that the Republicans had no need to do so, for the nation's attention was riveted on the South, and that area was precisely where the Radical appeal was strongest. Taunted about their electoral fiasco by the conservative Boston *Advertiser*, the *Voice* editors responded that the Republicans had been corrupted by the presence in their midst of "the Whig element," which "represents the monied interests . . . and that sort of respectability which is based on 'ownership of a gig' and the occupation of a first-class pew on Sunday." The time had arrived, concluded the *Voice*, for true "Jackson Democrats" to quit the Republican ranks in which they had enlisted to battle slavery and return to their former political home, "the natural ally of the negro slave and the oppressed workingmen. . . ."[6]

On the other hand, the Wightman campaign made it clear to the *Voice* that the workingmen could never obtain their goals by ranging themselves against Radical equalitarianism or placing themselves "even by implication, into antagonism with this great popular movement, the ultimate object of which is to eradicate slavery in America, root and branch."[7] The necessary precondition of any effective alliance of labor reform with the Democrats was that that party recognize the equality of man. Already, within a month of the November elections, the behavior of Boston Democrats suggested that they had reached the same conclusion. In December, Nathaniel Shurtleff campaigned for mayor of the city, identifying himself unequivocally with labor's demands. Not only did this Demo-

[5] *Ibid.*, Nov. 7, 1866.
[6] Editorial, *ibid.*, Nov. 10, 1866.
[7] Editorial, *ibid.*, Nov. 8, 1866.

crat and his running mates mute their traditional hostility toward Negro rights, they even placed a Negro (Richard Brown) on their slate for the Common Council. In a city which had shut them out one month earlier, the Democrats came within some nine hundred votes of winning the mayoralty and paved their way to conquest of that office two years later.[8]

MASSACHUSETTS: FAILURE IN THE MILLS

At the very time the leaders of Boston's Trades Assembly were vainly attempting to manipulate party machinery on behalf of the Baltimore Program, a spontaneous and unexpected uprising of mill hands from Connecticut to New Hampshire abruptly converted the labor-reform movement into a mass crusade. The organized leadership of the region's labor movement played no part in the upsurge of the mill operatives during its early months. Its starting point was Fall River, a cotton textiles center on the Massachusetts–Rhode Island border that was to be notorious throughout the century for its raw labor struggles. The spinners and weavers of this town stemmed largely from Yorkshire and Lancashire and naturally adopted the techniques of dealing with employers that were familiar to them from England. Smarting under the gradual decline of employment and earning during the summer, some operatives formed a Fall River Amalgamated Short Time Committee to petition the masters for a ten-hour day. When their employers refused to reduce hours unless the mills of Lowell and Lawrence followed suit, the workmen closed most of the town's mills with a two weeks' strike. Spurred to action by a strikers' meeting that selected workingmen's nominees for the state legislature, Republican state Senator Samuel A. Chase entered the dispute as a mediator and helped extract from the employers an agreement to convert all operations to a ten-hour basis on January 1, 1867.[9]

---

[8] *Ibid.*, Dec. 11, 1866; Moses Kimball to Henry L. Dawes, Dec. 16, 1868, Dawes Papers, Box 19.

[9] *Daily Evening Voice*, Oct. 31, Nov. 5, 8, Dec. 3, 1866; *Mass. BLS, 1871*, pp. 48, 500; Persons, p. 110. Persons says that the mills "yielded to pressure" to avoid a strike, but testimony before the state B.L.S. makes it evident a strike occurred, as does the account by William

After New Year's the Fall River mills abided by their
agreement and entered upon twenty-one months of short
hours and industrial peace, broken only by a single brief strike
which compelled them to rescind reductions of spinners' and
weavers' rates. Beyond this, the settlement initiated a half
decade of cooperation between the Short Time Committee and
the mill owners, climaxed by the appearance of the latter
before the state legislature in 1871 to testify *in favor of* legislation to limit the daily hours of labor to ten. The violent strike
of 1871, which marked the close of that cooperation and paved
the way for the "Long Vacation" of 1875, broke out only
because the legislature failed to enact such a law, and the
capitalists felt compelled to return to the working hours of
their competitors. In 1866, however, the shoe was on the other
foot. The Short Time Committee agreed to help the competitive position of its employers by stirring up agitation throughout the state (apparently sometimes with time off paid by the
companies) to force other textile manufacturers to accept the
ten-hour standard.[1]

The actions of Fall River roused the state's mill hands,
not only without help from the Eight Hour League–Boston
Trades Assembly–*Daily Evening Voice* clique of labor reformers but also on a scale which surpassed the wildest
dreams of that group. So utopian did the eight-hour demand
appear to textile workers that even among workmen as active
as the members of the Lowell Workingmen's City Committee,
less than a third declared themselves "eight hour men." But
the demand for shorter hours was unanimous, and the notion
of a ten-hour day and something like a fifty-six-hour week
impressed these laborers as both desirable and possible.[2]
Under the impact of the recession, furthermore, many mill
owners were already reducing hours on their own initiative,

McCauley reported in New Bedford *Daily Mercury*, March 1, 1867.
On British practices, see Henry Pelling, *History of British Trade Unionism* (Harmondsworth, 1963), p. 47.
[1] *Daily Evening Voice*, Dec. 3, 1866; Annawan Mill Journal, Labor E,
Fall River Iron Works Papers. On the "Long Vacation," see Sorge,
"1866–1876," p. 213. On the 1871 strike, see *Mass. BLS, 1871*, pp.
47–93, 459–66, 500–2.
[2] Letter from Lowell, *Daily Evening Voice*, Oct. 2, 1866.

thus encouraging their employees to regard a standardized reduction as a way both to turn bad times to good advantage and to minimize the coexistence of overwork and underemployment.

As the textile workers resorted to their traditional methods, they found veteran warriors of earlier efforts prepared to enter the fray once more. Lowell formed a new Short Time Committee at the beginning of 1867; its leadership was shared by a young machinist named Flint and T. C. Constantine, who had often taken the stump for the same cause in the 1840's and 1850's. James M. Stone left the Speaker's chair at the state House to address ten-hour rallies in Lawrence, as he had done more than a decade and a half before. Old Rufus Wyman appeared on the hustings, and a petition to the legislature inevitably carried at the head of the signatures the bold scrawl of Ben Butler.[3]

Two tactics were employed simultaneously by the committees that quickly appeared in most textile towns. One was to present petitions for ten hours directly to the treasurers of the companies and support these pleas with grand rallies, parades, and speeches by local notables (usually clergy and politicians). Thus Mayor Peabody of Lowell chaired the first meeting called by Constantine's group, and Major Charles A. Scott, state representative from the area, the next.[4] On rare occasions, as in the New Britain Knitting Mills in Connecticut, this device brought immediate success. More generally, both the suddenness of the campaign and the fact that ten hours were so widely believed to constitute a "natural" working day served to throw employers on the defensive—and into confusion: while some overseers prohibited the solicitation of signatures in their rooms, others in the same mills encouraged it.[5]

The second tactic was submission to the state legislature of petitions for a ten-hour legal limit to the working day, bearing between 7,000 and 8,000 signatures. The mill hands viewed this effort as a supplement to the direct appeal to employers, rather than as an alternative method. To Ira Stew-

---

[3] *Ibid.*, Dec. 21, 26, 1866, Jan. 25, 28, Feb. 7, 1867; Persons, p. 65. *Cf.* Persons, p. 103.
[4] *Daily Evening Voice*, Jan. 12, 28, 1867.
[5] *Ibid.*, Dec. 6, 1866, Jan. 9, 12, 15, 28, Feb. 7, 1867.

ard, on the other hand, the possibility that corporations might concede a ten-hour day to their own employees at the last moment, in order to parry legislative regulation, loomed as a major threat to the movement. He believed that "a *real* Ten Hour Law upon the statutes of Massachusetts will simplify the contest" between the corporations and the people, because it would reveal to every workman just what legislation could accomplish. Having learned this lesson, he hoped, workers in the future could simply compel the legislature to change the word "ten" in the statute to "eight."[6]

Events soon proved, however, that although the mill owners (aside from those of Fall River) were indeed especially vociferous in their opposition to reduction of hours by legislation and pleaded the advantages of being allowed to reduce hours by private action, they had no intention of granting the last-minute concession Steward feared. Nor did they heed the admonitions of James M. Stone, who, in pure Radical fashion, argued that reduced hours would benefit the workers without injuring their employers. If production fell, Stone argued, the companies could simply raise their prices, placing the burden "upon the great mass of the community, the laboring men themselves bearing their share," and surely the community would gladly bear such a small sacrifice for the sake of a higher moral and intellectual level for the whole society. The issue, he insisted, was the strengthening of "republican government."[7]

To officials of the textile mills, alas, the issue was not "republican government." They were as alert as Stone was oblivious to the fact that no relief through higher prices was available to them. No, prices were falling. Hence labor costs had to fall. True, a few agents, such as those of both the Atlantic and Pacific mills of Lawrence, discovered through experiment that increasing the pace of their machinery allowed them to maintain production levels despite the reduction of working hours.[8] Similarly, many weavers and spinners

---

[6] Letter of Ira Steward, *ibid.*, Jan. 17, 1867.

[7] Quoted in Persons, pp. 105–6.

[8] Persons, pp. 112, 120; *Daily Evening Voice,* May 31, 1867; McNeill, *Argument on the Hours of Labor,* p. 5.

on piecework, especially those in Fall River, found that they earned as much in ten hours as formerly they had in eleven and a half, because they put out as much work. But only the most efficient mills and the most efficient workmen could easily adapt themselves to shorter schedules. Marginal firms and marginal pieceworkers alike felt the pinch. Moreover, in all cases the indirect laborers who supplied materials to machine operators or performed other nonpiece-rated tasks found the effort to keep up with the piecework operatives on the new schedule intolerable. Since they were paid by the day, they had to toil more intensely for the same earnings as before, or for even less.[9] The resistance of such day hands to either wage reductions or a quickened tempo of work that would benefit only the pieceworkers provided, from the employers' point of view, an insuperable obstacle in the path of shorter hours. For company officials, therefore, as for E. L. Godkin, the question was not moral but economic.[1]

Understandably, then, toward the end of January the defensive posture of the businessmen became aggressive. A correspondent informed the *Voice* editors that word had gone out from company offices in Lowell to put a stop to ten-hour agitation in the shops. As if in confirmation of the report, Chairman Flint of the Short Time Committee was discharged by the Lowell machine shop, and overseers received instructions to "turn off all the help they can possibly spare," in order to dampen the workers' spirits.[2] William Isherwood, a mule spinner in the same town, was not only dismissed but blacklisted so effectively that he found work only by changing his name and moving to Fall River (where four years later he was to be blacklisted again).[3] At the Middlesex Mills employees were confronted with notices announcing a 10 per cent wage cut and promising that wages would be slashed further still if hours were reduced. Neither a strike by the firm's spinners and dressers nor angry speeches by J. T. Lee of the city council

---

[9] See *Mass. BLS, 1870*, 328, and the case of the Wamsutta Mills hands, below, pp. 284–5.

[1] For Godkin's argument, see above, pp. 247–8.

[2] *Daily Evening Voice*, Feb. 7, 1867.

[3] *Mass. BLS, 1871*, pp. 80–2.

and A. F. Jewett of the state legislature changed the corporation's mind.[4]

Such company reprisals were not confined to Lowell. In February five shop leaders at the Wamsutta Mills in New Bedford were discharged. Later in the month Robert Bower (the future editor and legislator) and his colleague James Holdsworth informed the legislative committee to which they gave a petition from 3,000 workers that both of them had been discharged by the Pacific Mills (employers known for their "liberal" policies). Emma Whitcher returned from the same legislative hearings to learn her overseer at Southbridge's Hamilton Manufacturing Company had fired her. Carrying her case to the company agent, she won reinstatement. But hardly had the *Voice*'s rejoicing over this victory subsided when she, her sister, and all the other seventy-three women who worked in Weaving Room E were laid off through a general policy of retrenchment.[5]

It was the New Bedford case which brought to a climax the agitation begun in Fall River. Had the gods conspired to torment middle-class reformers with the labor question, they could not have selected a more appropriate locale than this quiet old whaling town. Located hardly a stone's throw from Fall River, New Bedford was as different from that turbulent domicile of class-conscious Englishmen as whaling was from weaving. The sperm-oil trade had built the fortunes of George Howland and his cousin Joseph Grinnell, who decided in 1846 to venture their capital in cotton textiles. The move was timely, for over the next twenty years their concern grew from one factory building to three, attained a capital value of two million dollars and a labor force, at capacity, of almost 1,600 men, women, and children. Through the Bedford Commercial Bank, which they subsequently established, Howland and Grinnell spurred efforts to supply the city with abundant fresh water for manufacturing use and otherwise to attract indus-

---

[4] *Daily Evening Voice*, Feb. 1, 2, 7, 1867; Philadelphia *Public Ledger*, Feb. 4, 1867.
[5] Letter "On Behalf of the Committee," New Bedford *Daily Mercury*, Feb. 20, 1867; *Daily Evening Voice*, Feb. 25, March 5, 1867; Hamilton Manufacturing Company payrolls, Mills C and D, for Feb. 23, March 20, April 27, and May 25, Hamilton Manufacturing Company Papers.

tries to the town. In 1867, however, New Bedford boasted only one other factory of major importance, the Potumska Mill, and remained under the hegemony of the Howland family. Until he retired from office in 1851, Grinnell had been the town's Whig representative in Washington. The Wamsutta company itself, though a corporation, was largely controlled by George Howland's descendants after his death in 1852.[6]

The Howlands were devout Quakers, ardently committed to the causes of temperance, abolition, education for the poor, and charity for the castoffs of society, as were two nonfamily directors of the corporation, Thomas Mandell and David R. Greene. In Christian endeavors none surpassed Rachel Howland (wife of the founder's son Abraham), who personally founded a school in a neighboring village when she found its inhabitants unlettered, and who was appointed in 1868 to the Advisory Board of Trustees of the state's Industrial School for Girls.[7] Mrs. Howland boasted that Wamsutta employed "as fine a set of operatives as could be found in New England" and gloried in exhibiting its factory buildings and twenty-five trim company houses to visitors.[8] The workers in turn publicly praised the charitable spirit, not only of the directors, but also of the company's energetic young agent, Thomas Bennett.[9]

Small wonder, then, that the ten-hour enthusiasm captivated New Bedford. The town's representative in the state legislature, Isaac Coe (appropriately a reverend), sat on the committee on the hours of labor and goaded it to produce a bill restricting minors to ten hours' labor a day.[1] The two local newspapers were both advocates of limiting child labor for the sake of education. Both were naturally Republican in politics, but the *Evening Standard* leaned in editorial policy toward a

---

[6] Daniel Ricketson, *History of New Bedford* (New Bedford, 1858), pp. 86–7, 234–5; Elias Nason, *Gazeteer of Massachusetts* (Boston, 1874), pp. 312, 360–4; *D.A.B.*, VIII, 3–4; unsigned letter, *Daily Mercury*, March 5, 1867.

[7] *Daily Mercury*, March 1, 1867; letter of "S.M.," *ibid.*, March 4, 1867; *Revolution*, Vol. II (July 2, 1868), p. 404.

[8] *Daily Mercury*, March 6, 1867. On company houses, see unsigned letter, *ibid.*, March 5, 1867.

[9] *Ibid.*, Jan. 29, 1867.

[1] *Ibid.*, Feb. 22, March 7, 1867; *Daily Evening Voice*, March 9, 1867.

free trade-conservative position, and was dubious of labor-reform legislation beyond the minimum needed to strengthen public education.[2] Its morning counterpart, the *Daily Mercury*, on the other hand, was not only proudly Radical but warmly endorsed a statutory maximum of ten hours to a working day and hailed Speaker James M. Stone's speech on the subject.[3] But this is not all: on January 1, 1867, agent Thomas Bennett, on his own initiative, followed the example of neighboring Fall River and placed the Wamsutta Mills on a ten-hour day.[4]

Alas, none of Wamsutta's competitors followed suit. After almost three weeks of waiting, Bennett unhappily notified his workers that on February 1 the plant would return to a schedule of eleven hours.[5] In response, a group of spinners and weavers, some of them evidently members of the Eight Hour League, called a public meeting at North Mission Chapel to discuss the problem. On the evening of January 28 the chapel was filled to overflowing with operatives and other interested townspeople. Although John Hanover, a weaver, chaired the gathering, its conduct was dominated by the Reverend Isaac Knowlton and the Reverend Isaac Coe, at whose behest the assembly voted unanimously to accept a reduction of wages, if that was the necessary price of continuing the ten-hour schedule, and selected a committee of seven workmen to plead its case with Thomas Bennett. Reverend Knowlton expressed the hope that "this city, which is noted for its charity, and which has done so much for the heathen, will prove to the laborers here, its goodness, and its citizens their claim to the name of good christians."[6]

To the delight of the *Mercury*'s editor, Bennett consented. The factory was scheduled to run ten hours daily from February 1 to March 1, and to continue thereafter if other mills cut hours, and all day hands were to have their pay reduced by one eleventh. The committee, composed of spinners and weavers who were paid by the piece, was proud of its achieve-

[2] Editorial, New Bedford *Evening Standard*, March 11, 1867.
[3] Editorials, *Daily Mercury*, Jan. 30, 31, Feb. 6, March 1, 5, 6, 7, 1867.
[4] Letter of "Day Hand," *ibid.*, Feb. 19, 1867.
[5] *Ibid.*
[6] *Daily Mercury*, Jan. 29, 1867.

ment. But the day hands were not so happy. Many quit at once; others grumbled loudly about their fate. In fact, for the next two weeks the factory seems to have been converted into a debating society—on company time. This Bennett could not stand. On Saturday morning, February 16, an overseer fired a committeeman for being away from his place of work. Two of his fellow committeemen instantly packed their tools. When Chairman John Hanover went about the plant to discover what was happening, he was discharged. Storming into Bennett's office, Hanover found the agent equally irate. "Go to Fall River," said Bennett, "you are a ten-hour man." A fifth committeeman was meanwhile dismissed for being away from his machine. In response, 250 weavers and spinners walked out the west door, while others of the 857 operatives then engaged milled about the other exits, which by custom were locked. At noon, Bennett brought the chaos to an end by closing the plant for the day.[7]

Monday morning saw five hundred men and one hundred women assemble in the Eight Hour League Hall to organize their strike. Though nonworkers were present and took part, this meeting was in the hands of the skilled workers and the committee. Despite Hanover's expressed wish never to return to Wamsutta, the meeting voted to strike until the five committeemen were reinstated, the ten-hour day continued *without* any reduction in pay for the day hands, and two operatives who were outspokenly hostile to the movement dismissed by the company. The meeting established a relief committee to raise funds for the strikers and called a mass rally for Wednesday evening at City Hall.[8]

The affair at City Hall initiated a series of gatherings of operatives and their neighbors which averaged a meeting every other day for the next two weeks. Leadership clearly lay in the hands of the weavers and spinners, most prominent among whom were Hanover and Robert Slattery, a veteran of nineteen years of weaving who assumed the role of angry elder statesman among the workers. Religion was good,

[7] Letters of "Day Hand," *ibid.*, Feb. 19, 21, 1867; letter "On Behalf of the Committee," *ibid.*, Feb. 20, 1867; *ibid.*, Feb. 18, 19, 21, 1867.
[8] *Ibid.*, Feb. 18, 19, 1867.

Slattery thundered, but "it would not feed the hungry." Workers, therefore, should supplement the power of religion by struggling for their own rights.[9] To advance those rights, the committee solicited relief funds from the community, raising some $112 and receiving warm pledges of aid from Short Time committees in Fall River and Lowell. In this work women operatives assumed an especially prominent role. After six of them had enlisted in a fund-raising group, the women became vocal participants in the meetings. Their counterparts in Lowell even established a Ladies' Short Time Committee, reversed the traditional pattern of seating at meetings (the men were sent to the balcony), and inspired local politicians to advocate women's suffrage. True, the ire of the Lowell ladies had been roused by their own employers, who restored the wage cuts they had levied on their male employees while retaining those for the women. But the women did not strike; they raised funds for New Bedford instead.[1]

Wamsutta had become the decisive battle of the ten-hour campaign, and its operatives, those elsewhere, and even the editors of the Boston *Voice* were well aware of the fact. So were the middle-class friends of the reform, for the strike tore the New Bedford community asunder. Though Reverend Knowlton slipped off the stage soon after the strike had begun, and Coe found himself (truthfully) very busy with his ten-hour bill at the state legislature, other gentlemen of the town, usually claiming personal friendship with the directors, became platform orators at the strike meetings. Among them were John B. Sweet, John Cornell, and the ubiquitous Isaiah C. Ray, whose use of the label "Napoleon" for agent Bennett gave the strikers a rallying cry. Twice these speakers shared the platform with the prominent Negro Republican from Albany, New York, William Henry Johnson, whose support was enthusiastically hailed by the strikers.[2]

---

[9] *Ibid.*, Feb. 21, 1867.

[1] *Ibid.*, March 1, 4, 1867; *Daily Evening Voice,* Feb. 19, 20, 27, March 1, 5, 1867.

[2] *Ibid.*, Feb. 28, March 14, 1867; *Daily Mercury,* Jan. 28, Feb. 21, 25, March 4, 1867. On W. H. Johnson, see *Autobiography of Dr. William Henry Johnson* (Albany, N.Y., 1900).

The morning after the City Hall rally, the operatives conducted a strategy session at Eight Hour Hall. Two committees were mandated there, one the original shop committee, which was given full authority to "adjust the difficulty"; the other, proposed by Coe, was composed of Reverend Knowlton and two other townspeople, who were to sound out Bennett on his terms for settlement. After establishing this odd division of labor (perhaps because five of the seven-committeemen were no longer recognized by Bennett as his employees), the operatives called a full-dress meeting for Friday evening in the confident expectation that the matter would be settled by then.[3]

The three townsmen did confer with Bennett, but the agent's response was hardly what they had expected. He posted notice in the papers that all workers in the employ of the Wamsutta Mills as of February 16 were fired; that the company would reopen March 1 on an eleven-hour schedule at 1866 pay rates and continue to operate in that fashion until either Lowell and Lawrence changed to ten hours or a state law compelled all factories to do so; and finally, that applications for employment on these terms would now be considered.[4] In response, the Friday rally voted unanimously not to return to work until they had ten hours at no reduction in pay.[5]

Tension mounted during the idle week preceding the March 1 deadline. In a tactical master stroke the committee filled the North Mission Chapel to capacity on the afternoon of February 28. This boisterous affair was intentionally not a debate but a rally to generate maximum enthusiasm for the strike. Local speakers were joined by a Fall River weaver, who described the victory there and pledged money from his fellow workers, and by a mule spinner who had been lured from Rhode Island to scab but now refused to go to work. The rally accomplished its purpose. On opening day the company alleged that one hundred and fifty operatives reported; the

---

[3] *Daily Mercury*, Feb. 22, 1867.
[4] Notice of Wamsutta Mills dated Feb. 22 in *Daily Mercury*, Feb. 25, 1867.
[5] *Ibid.*, Feb. 25, 1867.

committee counted only sixty. At all events, the mill remained crippled.[6]

From Rhode Island, Bennett obtained twenty-two mule spinners in all. Isaiah Ray charged that they were promised $2.25 a day plus $10.00 for a spree at the end of the first day's work, and he commented: "Ain't that great for the morals of New Bedford?"[7] But the strikers saved their town's virtue by persuading all but two of the newcomers to leave and paying their fare home. The morals of one scab from Fall River, unfortunately, were not saved. Instead of returning to hearth and home, he visited a bawdy house in Taunton, where he was turned over to the police for stealing a watch and sentenced to eight months in the workhouse. Subsequently, potential strike-breakers were turned away by patrols of women who watched every rail and highway entrance into town.[8]

Two events quickly undermined the strong position the strikers had created for themselves. The first was a tactical blunder by the committee. The day after the mill opened, the committeemen met with Bennett and offered to return to work provided Wamsutta would schedule ten-hour days from April 1 until July 1. If no other mills had reduced hours by that time, they pledged to raise no objections to the company's returning to eleven hours.[9] A grave mistake! The committee's rally two days earlier had generated splendid enthusiasm among the operatives to fight for ten hours, regardless of the company's claim that it had to meet competition. Perhaps the strike leaders lost their confidence because some operatives had broken ranks; perhaps they simply found their position as vanguard of the state-wide movement unnerving and longed to be in the rear. Whatever the explanation for their proposal, it conceded the company's main line of argument—that it could not run shorter hours than its competitors. In its search for a compromise the committee had inadvertently surrendered the heart of its cause. Bennett refused to accept the proposal, but the discussion was now on his grounds.

The second fateful development was the intervention of

[6] *Ibid.*, March 1, 4, 1867; *Daily Evening Voice*, March 2, 1867.
[7] *Daily Mercury*, March 4, 1867.
[8] *Ibid.*
[9] *Ibid.*

Mrs. Rachel Howland. The vituperative Isaiah Ray publicly challenged that lady to expend as much charity on the children of her mills as she did on those of other towns.[1] On Monday she met in the mill's offices with several directors and Bennett. Later in the day she informed the committee that she had persuaded the agent to agree to their compromise proposal of Saturday, but that Bennett would not commit himself by signature to such terms until the operatives had ratified them. Presumably, all that was needed to settle the strike was a favorable vote at the meeting already scheduled for that evening in the chapel.

At that meeting, though Mrs. Howland was proffered the thanks of the workmen, her settlement was greeted with suspicion. That very afternoon committeeman John Fanning, while marching about town beating on a drum to notify the people of the evening's meeting, had fallen into bitter argument with an operative who had returned to work. A crowd assembled and roundly beat the scab, his wife, his brother, and his father. This melee set the mood for the reception of Mrs. Howland's mediation effort. The committeemen refused even to read the proposal to the strikers until the agent had signed it, Rutter calling it "a dangerous document, and calculated to produce division in their ranks."[2]

The company itself then promulgated the new terms, and Rachel Howland came in person to the North Mission Chapel meeting of Tuesday evening to urge the workers to accept them. She was there, she declared, because of her feelings for the women and children involved. Ten hours were enough for them, she said, and she begged the operatives not to send their children to the mills at too young an age. The meeting soon became a tumult, the doubts and suspicions of the operatives focusing especially on the lack of any guarantee in the Howland proposal that the committee (or anyone else) would be rehired. Mrs. Howland parried insults by Ray and restrained the temper of the affair somewhat by threatening to leave. Shouts were heard urging return to work. The tide was abruptly reversed when Joanna Maher challenged Rachel

1 *Ibid.*, March 1, 1867.
2 *Ibid.*, March 5, 1867; *Evening Standard*, March 5, 1867.

Howland, woman to woman—and worker to proprietor—with an appeal to the operatives to stand by their leaders. With a voice that was almost unanimous, the workers voted to continue the strike until they gained their "original demands."[3]

Despite the angry determination of the final vote, the corporation had won, for the next morning 300 operatives put Wamsutta's machinery in motion, and after lunch 370 were on hand. At the poorly attended evening strike meeting, a drunken workman bellowed to Chairman Thomas Rutter that he "could not live on wind," and Rutter stammered: "I hardly know what to say." His fellow operatives had voted to strike, then gone to work. The vote had obviously been misleading, for to most of the workers the company had granted what the committee asked. The only visible stumbling block was the rehiring of the discharged leaders, and at the Tuesday rally those leaders themselves had urged the strikers not to let their fates stand in the way of a settlement. Understandably, the average operative found it hard to see why he should continue to strike against employers who had conceded every explicit request of the strike leaders. Now even the stalwarts drifted steadily back to work. By March 12 the company had 700 operatives on hand, and three days later, 800, while many others applied for employment which, reported the *Mercury,* "the agent is obliged to refuse."[4]

With the collapse of the Wamsutta strike both the harmonious life of New Bedford and the hopes of the Massachusetts ten-hour movement were buried. The strike committee, together with Messrs. Ray, Cornell, and Sweet, continued to hurl anathemas at the corporation and Rachel Howland alike,[5] and "Cynic" wrote to a local paper that the pious should now add to their prayers: "Lord, bless with resignation the poor women and children whom our eleven hour rule is murdering."[6] But another letter to the same journal charged that "English bullies" encouraged by "some sentimentalists" were erecting "a power . . . that pretends to

---

[3] *Daily Mercury,* March 6, 1867.
[4] *Ibid.,* March 7, 12, 15, 1867.
[5] *Ibid.,* March 7, 1867; *Daily Evening Voice,* March 14, 1867.
[6] Letter of "Cynic," *Evening Standard,* March 5, 1867.

put a VETO upon the government of the mill," and urged Wamsutta to hold out against this "dictatorship."[7] It is up to the worker, added another correspondent, to be less "indolent," to "make himself respectable," so he will not need to strike. Surely "much of the operatives' [*sic*] time could be spent in study even while tending his loom."[8] It was only from the workers that the writer expected such high standards of behavior, for he urged everyone to understand that while "the stockholders are not lacking in heart" and "add to their taxes a large amount of charity," one could hardly expect them to "be satisfied with the excuse of an agent who told them he had been guided by his humanity and his mill had ceased to earn a profit."[9]

The strike's outcome, furthermore, disrupted the ranks of the workers as seriously as it did the life of middle-class New Bedford. The major line of discord among the operatives lay between the skilled weavers and mule spinners on piecework on one side, and the generally unskilled day hands on the other. Some unity was attained when the committee reversed its earlier stand and insisted on no wage cut for the day workers, but when the contest with the corporation was reduced to the matter of reinstatement of the committee, few day hands were inclined to persevere. More impressive yet is the fact that on the day the back-to-work movement really became serious (the day after Rachel Howland's appearance before the workers), the mule spinners held a gathering of their own and resolved to continue the struggle alone.[1] In other words, with the defeat of the strike the spinners retreated to a purely craft-oriented position. Although their private strike soon collapsed, it served as a prelude to an attempt by the newly formed national union of mule spinners to establish a ten-hour rule throughout the region. During the first week of April, spinners in Lawrence, Lowell, and Manchester either walked out or were locked out by their employers over this issue. But the mass of day hands had lapsed into despair and reported regularly for work, while the crafts-

---

[7] Letter of "V.X.," *ibid.*, March 6, 1867.
[8] Letter of "S.M.," *Daily Mercury,* March 4, 1867.
[9] Letter of "S.M.," *ibid.*, Feb. 28, 1867.
[1] *Ibid.*, March 7, 1867.

men were crushed.[2] Throughout the state mill hands faced
what Robert Howard was to call "the winter of their discontent,"[3] as those few companies which had experimented
with the ten-hour day returned to longer hours. The sixty-six-
hour week agreed upon by all the corporations of Lowell late
in 1868 became in practice the standard for the state.[4]

The failure of the strikes, furthermore, doomed all hope
of reform through legislation. After the damper thrown on
proposals for maximum-hour legislation by the Sanborn Committee in 1866, no measure could be enacted unless the effort
was given a major impetus from some new source. When he
addressed the general court in January, however, Governor
Bullock made no mention of the subject.[5] His paid commission's report to the legislature later in the month on the hours
of labor took a stand similar to that of the Sanborn Committee.
Education was the goal stressed by Amasa Walker and
William Hyde, authors of the new report. While they urged
the legislature to empower a constable to enforce the child-
labor provisions, they insisted that law "may not interfere with
the personal liberty of those who are of an adult age," other
than to keep them out of "the lager beer saloon or some
similar beneficient institution (!)."[6]

Commissioner Edward H. Rogers registered a feeble dissent. Although he filled many a page with florid quotations
about the "rights of man" and appeals to "our noble Northern
sentiments of honor to labor," he failed to rebut the economic
arguments of the majority report and even hedged on the
basic goal of the eight-hour day. His only specific recommendation was the enactment of a legal standard, in the absence
of a contract to the contrary, of ten hours for factory and farm
work and eight hours for mechanical trades. In effect, he was
saying that women should be permitted to work longer hours
than men.[7]

---

2 *Daily Evening Voice*, March 7, April 1, 3, 5, 6, 9, 13, 16, 1867;
Persons, pp. 111–12; *Strikes and Lockouts*, p. 1050.
3 McNeill, *Labor Movement*, p. 218.
4 Persons, p. 112; Philadelphia *Public Ledger*, Dec. 3, 1868.
5 *Daily Evening Voice*, Jan. 23, 1867.
6 *Mass. Labor Report, 1867*, pp. 21, 28, and *passim*.
7 E. H. Rogers, Minority Report, *ibid.*, pp. 41–141; Rogers, "Auto-
Biography," 16:1–4, 5–6. On the copy of his pamphlet *Reasons for*

Rogers's report provided little aid to the efforts of Roxbury's John Carruthers to commit the legislature first to a legal maximum of eight hours, or, failing that, of ten. The force which spurred the lawmakers into action was evidently the petition and strike movement in the factory towns. Surely the demands of the operatives alone were inadequate to win over the legislature. However, when workers anywhere succeeded in inducing their employers to shorten hours, they gave those employers a vital interest in reducing the hours of their competitors. Hence agents from Fall River and from the Atlantic and Pacific mills appeared to testify *in favor of* legislative restriction, and Representative Coe from New Bedford supported the proposal without qualms.[8] With the failure of the New Bedford strike the pressure was removed from these companies, leaving no one interested in the measure but the operatives. And their zeal was fading fast.

It is not surprising, therefore, that the bill which became law in May was essentially what Walker and Hyde had proposed. Even its central innovation, the empowering of a constable to enforce school attendance, almost met defeat in the Senate late in March when Senator Chance of Bristol County (containing both Fall River and New Bedford) attacked it as "insulting" to the honor of the community's most respected men and threatening to deprive poor parents of the earnings of their children.[9] The statute provided that no child under ten years of age could be employed in any manufacturing establishment, that no child under fifteen could be employed unless he went to school for three months of the year or three hours a day for six months, and that no child under fifteen could work more than sixty hours a week. To supervise its schooling provisions, the law created an office of special deputy constable.[1]

Believing that the People Will Use Leisure Wisely in W.S.H.S., Rogers inscribed the note: "This was my first tract; it was printed while I was writing my Minority Report on the Commission. Ira Steward was insisting on a square 8 hour Report for the whole State. E.H.R."

[8] Persons, pp. 112, 120; *Daily Evening Voice*, March 9, May 31, 1867.
[9] *Ibid.*, March 29, 1867. For legislative history of the act of 1867, see Montgomery, "Labor and the Radical Republicans," pp. 331–4.
[1] Act of May 29, 1867, *Acts and Resolves of the General Court of Massachusetts in the Year 1867* (Boston, 1867), Ch. 285.

Here was a law consistent with what the Republicans had concluded was the path of least peril for themselves. Its focus was not on the hours of labor, but on the education of children. Even in this respect, the terms of the new act represented a step backward from the law of ᵻ866. The older measure had specified that children ten to fourteen years old should attend school for six months of the year, not three, and that children under fourteen might not work more than eight hours a day, not sixty hours a week. The only positive result for labor of the whole year's struggle was the appointment of Henry Kemble Oliver to the office of deputy constable. A former manager of the Atlantic Mills, Oliver thought in much the fashion of John Stuart Mill in his later days: a more equitable distribution of income and universal education of quality should be primary objectives of state policy. But despite all his diligence, Oliver found himself unable to win a single court conviction for violation of the schooling provisions.[2]

For nine months following the Baltimore Congress, labor reformers in Massachusetts had worked for the N.L.U. program on every front from the party caucus to the picket line, and on every level from manifestoes to massive strikes. With what results? The dominant Republican party had unmistakably dampened its ardor for labor reform, or, more precisely, had become much more specific as to what reforms were acceptable to it and what were not. Two years of legislative activity had yielded only an ineffective measure to keep the children of factory operatives in school. The "free contract" stance of the Sanborn and Walker reports were becoming the standard reply of party leaders to demands for legislative ceilings on the hours of adults' labor. Simultaneously, the textile corporations had successfully refused to alter the terms of contract for their own employees. The shorter day

---

[2] Persons called the 1867 act an improvement over that of 1866 because it took community prejudices into account. Sorge denounced the later measure as an unqualified retreat, and McNeill called the 1866 law the best the state ever had. Persons, p. 96; Sorge, "1860–1866," p. 405; McNeill, *Argument on Hours of Labor*, p. 18. For Oliver's view of the law, see *Mass. BLS, 1870*, pp. 134–58. For his social philosophy, see Oliver, "Landmarks in the History of Labor," MSS in Labadie Collection, Biography and Papers, A–Z.

was not brought to pass either by "workingmen outside the State House" or by "legislators inside."

Defeat in the Bay State bore even broader significance for labor itself. Free agency and good will had been the beacons toward which workingmen oriented their hopes. All concurred in T. C. Constantine's hope that the reduction of working hours would be achieved in a way that was "gradually progressive," rather than through conflict.[3] This dream was shattered at New Bedford. Good will proved a frail shelter against the hurricane of competitive pressure and a tight market. Charitable employers could be as hard-nosed as Scrooge when dividends were at stake. What an ironic lesson lay in the contrast with Fall River! There class-conscious English immigrants made use of their bargaining strength to effect a cash-and-carry deal with their employers, and they alone not only enjoyed two years of shorter hours, but lived in harmony with their bosses.

But Massachusetts's labor reformers drew no such conclusions from their fate. It never occurred to them that any fault lay in their own ideology, in the reform syndrome which was so fundamental a part of their own characters. Rather, they sought to continue their pursuit of the Baltimore Program through better tactics. Two new ideas of this order were broached at a large rally in May. First, Ezra Heywood called on the workers to desert the Republican party, which he said "has turned its back upon our movement," and follow the example of political independence recently displayed so capably by the workingmen of Connecticut. Wendell Phillips introduced the second new theme: he summoned the workers of Massachusetts to look to the West, where a decisive struggle over the eight-hour day was then taking place.[4] As the labor reformers of Connecticut were blazing new paths of political action, so those of Illinois were adding a new dimension to trade unionism during the very months that the pioneering labor movement of Massachusetts was being forced to a halt.

---

[3] Persons, p. 104.
[4] *Daily Evening Voice,* May 16, 1867.

_____

CHAPTER 8

A "Legal Day's Work"

The turmoil in Massachusetts heralded a series of challenges to the Republicans and to the business community by labor reformers across the country. Whether the confrontations resulted in victory or defeat for the workingmen, radicalism was the loser. The ranging of labor against capital in industrial communities sapped its ideological foundations. And these bitter conflicts nourished among both workingmen and manufacturers an attitude of contempt or hostility toward the state itself.

On April 1, 1867, the voters of Connecticut scurried through the rain to elect Democrat James E. English as their governor. For the first time since 1855, the Republican gubernatorial candidate failed to carry the state. The upset was hailed by N.L.U. Vice-President William Gibson as "a Labor Reform triumph, and that alone."[1] Organized labor in Con-

_____

[1] *Daily Evening Voice*, April 18, 1867.

necticut had, in fact, made artful use of opportunities which were but partially of its own making. The Republican margin of victory had already fallen from a glorious 11,035 votes in April 1865 to a mere 541 votes a year later. In part, the Democratic revival stemmed from the popularity of that party's ardent and successful campaign to block extension of the suffrage to Negroes in the fall of 1865.[2] It was aided by the serious defection of Johnson Conservatives to the Democratic side in the spring of 1866, led by Senator James Dixon and other party notables.[3]

The Democratic standard-bearer of both 1866 and 1867 was ideally suited to attract Conservative votes, for he did not adhere to the old guard of his party. Proprietor of the New Haven Clock Company, as well as a lumberman and banker, James English had served in Congress during the war and contributed unstinting aid to the war effort. He had, moreover, been one of the sixteen non-Republicans in the House who cast ballots in favor of the Thirteenth Amendment.[4] So fearful had the Republicans been in 1866 of a surge of Conservative voters to English that they jettisoned their previous year's militancy on behalf of Negro suffrage and sought to outdo the Democrats in identifying themselves with President Johnson (who remained deliberately aloof from the contest).[5]

By the early months of 1867 the ten-hour movement sweeping New England added another variable for party leaders to consider. Incumbent Governor Joseph R. Hawley had written the state's Eight Hour League during the 1866 campaign that he would never veto an eight-hour law if one were submitted to him by the legislature. The pledge meant little—first, because a simple legislative majority in Connecticut was sufficient to override any gubernatorial veto; and secondly, because the proposed bill lay on the table until the

---

[2] New York *Tribune*, March 15, 1867; McPherson, *Reconstruction,* p. 120; *American Annual Cyclopaedia,* VII (1867), 256.

[3] *Nation,* Vol. IV (March 28, 1867), pp. 255–6; *Daily Evening Voice,* April 12, 1867.

[4] *American Annual Cyclopaedia,* VII (1867), p. 256; *Biographical Directory of the American Congress,* p. 1133; *D.A.B.,* VI, 165–6; Rollin O. Osterweis, *Three Centuries of New Haven, 1638–1938* (New Haven, 1953), pp. 252, 325; Cox, *Politics,* pp. 3, 144.

[5] *Ibid.,* 143–50.

very end of the legislative session, when it was defeated, charged a labor reformer, "by a dodge engineered by P. T. Barnum (the humbug). . . ."[6] The indignation of the eight-hour men (whose main base of strength was the New Haven Trades Assembly) blended with the subsequent outcry of the factory hands. A huge rally at Rockville in mid-February, addressed by Edward Senior, president of the state Ten Hour League, and a half dozen local clergymen, revealed an angry mood among the textile workers, a mood which could mean votes for the candidate who made proper use of it.[7]

Neither party had recognized this possibility in January. The Democrats, covening as usual on the anniversary of Jackson's victory at New Orleans, had made no mention of the hours of labor—or of anything at all other than the sins of congressional Reconstruction. But they shrewdly recessed their convention, deferring action on both nominations and platform until after the Republicans had made their moves.[8] The latter, gathering toward the end of the month, renominated Governor Hawley, applauded Congress, charged the Democrats with threatening to "renew the horrors of civil war," and resolved their sympathy for oppressed Negroes, Greeks, Irish, Mexicans, and "the toiling masses of society," to whom they pledged "every needed legislative remedy" for their troubles. The hours of labor, however, passed unmentioned.[9]

The way was thus left open for the Democrats to appeal to both the Conservatives and the labor reformers of the state; and they proved themselves equal to the task. Reassembling in February, the party leaders chose James English to oppose Hawley a second time. They reasserted their resolves of January but shifted the emphasis of their appeal from "white man's government" to "constitutional government." Last, but hardly least, they drafted a new platform pledging themselves to enact laws making eight hours a legal day's work and

[6] Letter of Joseph R. Hawley, quoted in New York *Tribune*, March 18, 1867; letter of C. W. Gibson, *Daily Evening Voice*, March 28, 1867; Osterweis, pp. 359–60.
[7] *Daily Evening Voice*, Feb. 15, 1867.
[8] *Ibid.*, Jan. 9, 1867; McPherson, *Reconstruction*, pp. 244–5.
[9] *Ibid.*, pp. 243–4; *American Annual Cyclopaedia*, VII (1867), 256.

prohibiting the employment of children more than ten hours daily, and declaring that "all attempts on the part of employers to reduce their workingmen to a condition of political slavery by coercing their votes, should be held up to the execration of freemen, and, if possible, frustrated by legislative action."[1]

The Democratic actions confronted the labor movement with both opportunities and dangers. The dangers lay in the efforts Democrats immediately made to infiltrate labor organizations and convert them into engines of the English campaign. The State Convention of Connecticut Workingmen at Hartford, attended by some three hundred delegates of sixty unions two weeks after the Democratic Convention, was turned into a bedlam by the efforts of Democrats to seize control. Veteran New Haven leaders like Gibson and Phelps used the voting power of predominantly Republican out-of-town delegates to exclude everyone but known trade unionists from the hall. As workingmen hooted "See the soft hands. There's your lawyer's hands. Put on your kids," the outvoted Democrats started such a brawl that police had to clear the hall. "Taken, all in all," remarked the correspondent of the New York *Tribune*, "it is the most exciting Convention ever held in this State."[2]

The *Tribune*'s belief that the outcome was "a complete triumph for the Republicans,"[3] however, could not have been further from the truth. The workingmen had adopted a platform of their own, calling for repeal of the poll tax and reapportionment of the state legislature. On the hours of labor their program was identical to that to which the Democrats had committed themselves, and the workers offered support to whichever candidate would endorse their demands. While Hawley's subsequent letter to the labor reformers added nothing to his stand of the previous year, English only needed to pledge loyalty to the platform of his own party in order to have organized labor enter the campaign on his behalf.[4] Even

---

[1] *Ibid.; Daily Evening Voice*, Feb. 7, 1867.
[2] *Daily Evening Voice*, Feb. 23, 26, 1867; *American Annual Cyclopaedia*, VII (1867), 256–7; New York *Tribune*, Feb. 23, 1867.
[3] *Ibid.*, Feb. 23, 1867.
[4] *Daily Evening Voice*, Feb. 23, 26, March 7, 1867.

Jonathan Fincher, who had come from Philadelphia to address the Hartford convention, remained to stump for English. Skeptical as ever of political action, still convinced that both parties were "rotten," Fincher was impressed by the skill with which Connecticut's workers had put their votes "up for sale," and he saw the Democrats as "the highest bidder."[5]

From Boston the editors of the *Voice* welcomed the use their neighbors were making of this "golden moment." Noting with pleasure Congress's passage of the Reconstruction Act at the beginning of March, the Bostonians were certain labor's hour had arrived. "The old issues are dying out," they argued, for "the reconstruction problem which has been the much mooted topic during the past year or two is practically solved."[6] The time had thus arrived "for workingmen to sunder old party ties, to conquer old political prejudices," and to realize that the "party in power is, as it always has been, in the interest of capital. . . ." By making common cause with the Democrats, workers could "reach all the ends of their reform . . . much sooner and with more certainty than if they waited for the slow growth of a labor party. . . ."[7]

To orient an electoral conflict between two major parties around an issue raised by a group extrinsic to both of them is no easy task. Despite the agility with which Connecticut's labor reformers had kept their organization independent of the Democrats and thus avoided the fate of the workingmen of Boston's Fourth Congressional District, despite the speakers from other states, like Fincher and Ezra Heywood, who lectured just on the labor question, and despite the tireless efforts of Gibson, Phelps, and Senior to identify themselves on the rostrum as labor reformers favoring English, the labor message usually reached the public through the Democratic press and at Democratic rallies.[8] The New York *Tribune*, which soon made the Connecticut campaign its favorite editorial topic, argued that the real question at stake was "the old issue between the Copperheads and the Union men," which English

---

[5] *Ibid.*, March 16, 1867.
[6] Editorial, *ibid.*, March 12, 1867.
[7] Editorial, *ibid.*, March 5, 1867.
[8] *Ibid.*, editorial March 26, 28, April 6, 1867.

was trying to disguise with the labor question.[9] But a week and a half before Election Day the Republicans concocted a "workingmen's State Central Committee" that queried both candidates on the hours of labor. The reply of Hawley it found "frank and favorable," while English, it announced, gave "practical denial by working men in his employ 12 hours a day."[1] Both parties distributed "workingmen's tickets" on Election Day.[2]

English triumphed over Hawley by a vote of 47,565 to 46,578. Over 6,700 more votes were cast than in 1866, and 61.4 per cent of the increase went to the Democrats. In New Haven—usually a Democratic town, but the center of labor organization—67 per cent of the increased vote favored the Democrats. Hawley, furthermore, ran 140 to 275 votes behind the other state-wide candidates on the Republican ticket, while English held comparable margins ahead of his running mates. To complete the satisfaction of the workingmen, P. T. Barnum had lost out to iron manufacturer William H. Barnum in his race for Congress. Only Connecticut's historic gerrymandering kept the lower house of the legislature in the Republican grasp.[3]

New England labor reformers were ecstatic over the outcome of the voting. By no means had Connecticut shifted its allegiance firmly to the Democratic ticket. Although English was returned to office in 1868 by a handsome majority, Republican Presidential nominees carried the state that year and in 1872, just as they had since 1856; and in 1869, English was narrowly defeated for the governorship by Marshall Jewell.[4] So clearly had the labor question tipped the party balance in 1867 that Horace Greeley's *Tribune* editorials had to grapple with the issue he had previously termed a sham.

---

[9] New York *Tribune*, editorial Feb. 28, 1867. See also editorials, *ibid.*, March 2, 6, 30, 1867.

[1] *Ibid.*, March 26, 1867.

[2] *Daily Evening Voice*, April 1, 1867.

[3] *Connecticut Register: Being a State Calendar of Public Officers and Institutions for 1868* (Hartford, Conn., 1868), p. 18; New York *Tribune*, April 20, 1867; *American Annual Cyclopaedia*, VII (1867), 256–7.

[4] Editorials, *Daily Evening Voice*, April 2, 6, 1867; Burnham, *Ballots*, 318–19; McPherson, *Reconstruction*, pp. 372, 506.

Although he favored legislation to limit minors to eight hours of factory labor daily, Greeley denounced all schemes to oblige adults to quit work after eight hours or to exact a full day's pay for reduced hours. If Republicans lost votes by adhering to the "Divine law" that he who works less is paid less, Greeley concluded, so be it—for they "cannot run a race in demagogism with those who make a trade of it."[5]

Connecticut's legislature assembled in May to discuss labor legislation in an atmosphere very different from that which prevailed at the same time in Massachusetts. Eighteen members of the lower house, which heard Governor English appeal for an eight-hour law, listed their occupation as "mechanic," and among them was Alfred Phelps, state vice-president of the N.L.U. Phelps sat on the Joint Select Committee on Labor Reform, along with two carpenters, a printer, and an unspecified mechanic.[6] The Republican majority in the lower house supported the eight-hour bill and even made a pretentious motion to strike out its free-contract proviso. Had such an amendment been adopted, it might have guaranteed the defeat of the bill in the upper house, where the measure passed by a vote of 11 to 9. Toward the end of the session, the legislature supplemented the eight-hour act with a measure prohibiting the employment of anyone under fifteen years of age for longer than ten hours a day or fifty-eight hours a week. This statute was clearly drafted, a remarkable contrast to the easily evaded law of Massachusetts.[7]

THE FUTILITY OF VICTORY

Wisconsin, Missouri, Illinois, California, and New York all joined Connecticut in making eight hours a legal day's work during the spring of 1867, and Pennsylvania followed suit the next year. The standard length for the working day proposed by the Baltimore Congress had gained official recognition

---

[5] Editorial, New York *Tribune,* April 5, 1867.
[6] *Daily Evening Voice,* May 2, 1867; *Connecticut Register, 1868,* pp. 18–26.
[7] *Daily Evening Voice,* May 2, 25, June 13, 21, 1867; Act of June 28, 1867, *Public Acts Passed by the General Assembly of the State of Connecticut, 1866, 1867, and 1868* (Hartford, Conn., 1868), p. 77; Act of July 27, 1867, *ibid.,* pp. 119–20.

within ten months after that body's adjournment. The resolutions of that congress, furthermore, were published in the proceedings of the first congress of the International Workingmen's Association in Geneva, and that gathering urged the workingmen of the world to rally to the eight-hour banner raised by the Americans. "*Nous proposons huit heures de travail comme limite légale du jour de travail*," reported the General Council to the Geneva Congress. "*Cette limite étant généralement demandée par les ouvriers des Etats-Unis d'Amérique; le vote du Congrès en fera l'étandard commun de toutes les réclamations des classes ouvrières de l'univers.*"[8]

The instant discussion of this "universal" demand moved from the conferences of labor agitators to the chambers of lawmakers, however, the problem of formulating an effective statute appeared. It is tempting but misleading to describe the state laws as a "harmless gesture"[9] to labor leaders who were "easily befuddled by skillful politicians."[1] To be sure, the effective scope of such statutes was seriously limited, and without such limitations they would never have passed a single legislature. First, farm labor was exempted. In both New York and Wisconsin rural representatives constituted an insurmountable opposition until that exclusion was made.[2] Secondly, few legislators of any party or any constituency were prepared to defile the sanctum sanctorum of "free contract." The pattern of tolerating full freedom of contract, while prescribing a legislative declaration of community goals and sentiments, had already been set in the ten-hour laws of New Hampshire, Pennsylvania, and other states in the late forties and early fifties.[3] The new measure simply followed suit.

The juxtaposition of freedom of contract with a legal standard for the working day in the legislative proposals of Governor English was ridiculed by *Harper's Weekly* as meaning "in substance, that when the employer and the working-

---

[8] *Prem. Int.*, I, 13. For the debate on this proposal, stressing the theme of standing by the Americans, see *ibid.*, I, 47–9. Resolutions of the Baltimore Congress are printed in *ibid.*, I, 58–60.

[9] Ozanne, p. 135.

[1] Commons, *Labour*, II, 169–70.

[2] On New York, see Philadelphia *Public Ledger*, March 12, 17, 1866. On Wisconsin, see Merk, pp. 185–8.

[3] See Commons, *Labour*, I, 541–4.

man agree that only eight hours shall be a working-day, he shall be perfectly satisfied." Surely, the Republican journal concluded, no "law of a Legislature can outwit . . . the law of supply and demand."[4] Indeed, the Connecticut supreme court gave that "law of nature" precedence over the handiwork of obviously mortal legislators when it denied the first appeal to reach it under the new law. The decision was handed down in reply to a suit by Thomas Luske, who labored not eight but sixteen hours daily in a gas works for $10.50 a week, and now sought double pay (for the two legal days he toiled during every calendar day). The only legal claim the statute gave a workingman, ruled the court, was the right to go home at the end of eight hours, provided he had not agreed to remain longer and his employer did not ask him to stay. And if he worked more than eight hours, the justices continued, the extra labor would be legally regarded as voluntary and entitle him to no extra compensation.[5]

Some labor reformers reacted swiftly to plug the obvious hole in the newly erected legal dike. The Workingmen's Union of New York City lobbyed unsuccessfully in Albany during the spring of 1868 to have the free-contract proviso stricken from the state's eight-hour law. By late July of that year the striking Workingmen's Benevolent Association of the anthracite fields called for revision of the Pennsylvania statute to provide that all work after eight hours be paid at "time and one-half time." A miners' circular explained the novel phrase as meaning "that forty minutes shall constitute one hour."[6] The Pennsylvania law itself was denounced by Editor C. Ben Johnson of the *Coachmaker's International Journal* as a "glaring fraud."[7]

Such views were expressed only by a minority of labor reformers. The editors of the Boston *Voice*, aware that even the unequivocal limitations of hours found in their state's child-labor laws were violated regularly with impunity, argued that it would be fruitless "to have on the statute book of any State an eight hour law of such rigid features that the people would

---

[4] *Harper's Weekly*, Vol. XI (May 25, 1867), p. 323.

[5] *Luske* v. *Hotchkiss*, 37 Conn. 219.

[6] *Workingman's Advocate*, April 11, 1868; Philadelphia *Public Ledger*, Aug. 4, 1868.

[7] Letter of C. Ben Johnson, *Workingman's Advocate*, May 30, 1868.

not approve of it." The Connecticut law, therefore, met with their complete approval, and the responsibility to "enforce" such laws the editors now placed on the labor reformers themselves.[8] Ezra Heywood echoed this view, for to him the eight-hour law was valuable not "as an arbitrary standard, but as a rule expressing the public sense of right, to be observed in the public service; as an enabling act *to assist labor to make fair terms*."[9]

William Sylvis, advocate of an active state, came close to the position of Heywood the anarchist. He told the Molders' Union Convention in 1867 that "when we estabish eight hours as a legal day's work, those now forced to work ten or twelve will be allowed to reduce theirs to ten." Shifting his grounds, Sylvis demanded in the next sentence that the "law must mean what it says—eight hours and no more," and must leave the capitalists no "quirks and quibbles" through which to "render it nugatory."[1] As if his stand were not already confused (and confusing) enough, he informed the union's next convention that he had advised the locals *not* to strike for shorter hours during 1867 because "what we want is agitation, education, and legislation."[2]

In short, while virtually all labor reformers believed the eight-hour day should be achieved through legislation, their conception of what the laws should provide was painfully ambiguous. The source of this ambiguity was not the trickery of politicians, but the workers' conception of government, which permitted the coexistence of a "legal working day" and "free contract" in the same statute. Labor reformers thought of the state as lawmaker rather than administrative agency. From the government, workingmen demanded "just laws." They never requested, or even dreamed of, the establishment of bureaucratic agencies to administer such laws. Only in Massachusetts was a constable empowered to see to the enforcement of labor laws, and his jurisdiction was limited to the truancy of

---

[8] *Daily Evening Voice*, June 21, 1867.
[9] E. H. Heywood, *The Labor Party: A Speech Delivered before the Labor Reform League of Worcester, Mass.* (New York, 1868), p. 13. My italics.
[1] Sylvis, p. 208.
[2] *Ibid.*, p. 276.

working children of school age. Labor reformers demanded bureaus of labor statistics to reveal to the public the need for eight-hour statutes. They did not demand departments of labor to supervise their enforcement. Even the Eight Hour Leagues, the vanguard of the movement, failed to see the need for administrative machinery to coerce private entrepreneurs. Their major demands were three: that all units of government set a good example by instituting the eight-hour day for their own employees, that incorporated enterprises be limited to eight hours' work daily by the terms of their charters, and that eight hours be made a legal day's work for private (unincorporated) enterprises, "in the absence of a written agreement."[3]

The problem of persuading recalcitrant employers to conform to the newly expressed "public sense of right" became brutally clear in Chicago. As early as April 1866, that city's trades assembly had exerted enough influence on the municipal elections to assure favorable consideration by the aldermen of an eight-hour day for city employees.[4] Using the Grand Eight Hour League of the State of Illinois as their instrument, the labor reformers then undertook a fumbling but ultimately successful effort to commit both parties to a state law. Despite the facts that the partisan issues of Reconstruction were fought with such bitterness in Illinois that all other questions faded from view, and that the Eight Hour League itself was rendered ineffective by falling into the hands of ardent Republicans, organized labor did exact pledges from many candidates without committing itself to either party. During February and March of 1867, therefore, an eight-hour bill glided through both houses of the legislature almost unopposed. This was, in fact, the nation's first eight-hour law, signed into law by Governor Richard B. Oglesby on March 5, the very day Rachel Howland urged the Wamsutta Mills strikers to return to work.[5]

---

[3] McNeill, *Labor Movement,* p. 144. See also platform of Eight Hour League of Illinois, *Workingman's Advocate,* May 5, 1866.

[4] *Workingman's Advocate,* April 21, Sept. 1, 1866.

[5] *Ibid.,* April 28, May 5, June 16, 23, July 7, 21, August 4, 18, Sept. 1, 8, 10, 1866, Aug. 17, 1867; *New-York Times,* May 7, 1867; Moses, II, 764–5, 1208; Cole, *Era of the Civil War,* pp. 370, 400–3; Pierce, II, 175;

Labor's hopes ran high in Chicago, for to all appearances local workers and Radicals were striding vigorously toward the same goal. Two other Republican-controlled legislatures in the region, Missouri and Wisconsin, passed similar bills within a month after Illinois.[6] On March 30, Governor Oglesby addressed a mass rally of Chicago workmen held to "ratify" the new law and declared that eight hours of leisure daily "is none too long for study and recreation." Not to be outdone, Attorney General Robert Ingersoll argued that the working day should be even further reduced and that workers should "educate themselves until they become the equals in all respects of any class." A local labor reformer waxed ecstatic describing the occasion to the *Voice:*

> In this great western emporium, to all outside appearances devoted to the interests of commerce and middlemen, it was a sublime spectacle; this clasping of fraternal hands, between the laborer and the highest officers of the State, over the heads of the defiant capitalists. . . . Our State is full of rail-splitters turned statesmen, and they have proved and are proving to be the strongest and toughest timber ever used in the construction of national councils.[7]

In the very midst of these jubilant celebrations, however, both the laborers and the "defiant capitalists" were girding themselves for war. By the terms of the act, eight hours was to become a legal day's work for all nonagricultural labor hired by the day on and after May 1, 1867. Weeks before that deadline more than seventy Chicago manufacturers had instituted the practice of paying their workers by the hour.

Act of March 5, 1867, *Public Laws of the State of Illinois, 1867* (Springfield, 1867), p. 101.

[6] Act of March 13, 1867, *Laws of the State of Missouri, 1867* (Jefferson City, 1867), p. 132; Act of April 6, 1867, *General Laws Passed by the Legislature of Wisconsin in the Year 1867* (Madison, 1867), Ch. 83. Commons mistakenly says the Wisconsin law applied only to women and children. *Doc. Hist.,* IX, 278. It did provide that an employer could not "compel" women, or children under eighteen, to work more than eight hours, or "permit" children under fourteen to work more than ten hours, but it also contained the general provision of eight hours as a legal day's work.

[7] Letter of H. H. Marsh, *Daily Evening Voice,* April 6, 1867.

Especially adamant were the railroads, whose officials declared with one voice that they intended to employ workmen only on an hourly basis, and at the same wages and hours after May 1 as before.[8] By the end of April, Mayor John Rice, an outspoken opponent of the shorter day, had special police and light artillery mobilized in anticipation of trouble.[9]

Trade unions also made careful preparations. The machinists and blacksmiths resolved at a large conference to adhere to the new legal standard, regardless of the effect on wages. One craft after another followed this example, passing rules to cut daily wage scales and hours simultaneously on May 1, and finally the trades assembly sanctioned these rules for all labor in the city. William Sylvis appealed to molders throughout the nation to stay clear of Illinois until the issue had been settled, and the Boston *Voice,* sensing that "capital has its back up" in Chicago, concluded that the fate of the "eight hour system" for many years to come was about to be settled there.[1]

On Wednesday, the first of May, the workshops of Chicago lay idle as forty-four trade unions staged a spectacular parade from Back of the Yards to the shores of Lake Michigan. When the marchers, who numbered between 5,000 and 6,000, arrived with their floats, trade emblems, and brass bands, they were welcomed with messages from their leaders and prominent government officials. Presiding was Mayor Rice himself, the outspoken foe of the eight-hour movement, who now urged "reason, calmness, and conciliation" upon the workers. Efforts of local labor officials, speaking in both English and German, to rally the audience to firm "enforcement" of the new law were reinforced by guest orators Richard Trevellick and ex-Congressman Andrew J. Kuykendall of the Cairo district. The voice of Radical office-holders, however, was heard only in the form of letters which were read to the assembled workingmen. A *Voice* correspondent

---

[8] Pierce, II, 176–7.

[9] *Daily Evening Voice,* May 4, 1867.

[1] *Ibid.,* March 19, 25, April 1, 20, 25, May 3, 1867. The unavailability of almost any Chicago newspapers from these months today forces this account to rely heavily on reports sent to out-of-town papers.

suggestively described these communications as a "gushing" letter from Governor Thomas C. Fletcher of Missouri, a "guarded" one from Governor Oglesby—who now cautioned labor not to press its cause so strongly as to make business suffer—and a "brief dispatch" from Indiana's Oliver P. Morton. A "diplomatic note" also arrived from the office of Andrew Johnson.[2]

The next day it became clear why Oglesby and his fellow Radicals were no longer "clasping fraternal hands" with the workingmen: the "defiant capitalists" had not acquiesced in the new legal working day. Typical was the situation at the McCormick reaper works, where the company reopened on Thursday overtly prepared to work a full ten hours, only to have its workingmen go home on their own initiative at the end of eight. While ship carpenters and many lumber yard employees were enjoying the new eight-hour day, most boot and shoe manufacturers, bookbinders, brewers, harness makers, and furniture plants continued to operate on ten-hour schedules. The unions of machinists and iron molders quickly responded to the recalcitrance of proprietors in their trades by closing down almost all operations under their jurisdiction. The strike, however, was not general. Only in the largely Irish community of Bridgeport were the packinghouses, rolling mills, and other works all closed.[3]

Both legislation and trade-union action having failed to bring all the city's manufacturers to heel, a third level of pressure appeared on Saturday. The "riot element has been aroused," cabled a correspondent of the *New-York Times*. Out of Bridgeport it came, a crowd which soon swelled to 5,000 or more, picking up workers, boys, and vagrants as it moved along Archer Avenue chasing operatives out of factories, cutting belts on the machinery, and blowing off the steam from boilers. At Halsted Street the marchers battled a special company of police in a brickyard. Everywhere workers armed themselves, many recalling their recent military experi-

---

[2] *Ibid.*, May 2, 4, 1867; *New-York Times*, May 7, 1867; Cole, *Era of the Civil War*, pp. 417–18; Hicks, p. 45; Pierce, II, 177–8.
[3] Ozanne, pp. 135–7; Hutchinson, II, 485; *Daily Evening Voice*, May 6, 8, 1867; Pierce, II, 178–9.

ence in the nation's service, and others certain that, if they were imprisoned, Governor Oglesby would pardon them.[4]

"The rioters have produced a reaction of public sentiment," noted the astute observer of the *New-York Times*.[5] Indeed, a call of the Radical *Tribune* for liberation of the city from "fear of the mob" and the adamant hostility to the strike expressed by every nonlabor newspaper in the city save the small Chicago *Republican* were unmistakable evidence that the propertied and professional classes of Chicago hungered for a champion of law and order. It was Mayor Rice who assumed the heroic posture. While Governor Oglesby rejected all appeals for state troops (expressing his "perfect confidence" in the peaceful intentions of labor), Rice used the Dearborn Light Artillery to police the city and issued a proclamation based on the LaSalle Black Laws of 1863, prohibiting anyone from interfering with another man's pursuit of his daily occupation.[6]

Within a week of May 1, the day labor and the Radicals had ushered in the eight-hour regime in happy harmony, the Radical leaders of the state had abdicated all responsibility; the business community, with strong public sympathy, had rallied to Conservative Mayor Rice; and the labor reformers were facing the task of sustaining an almost general strike in a setting that approached martial law. For the rest of May and into June, strikes limped on, firm among molders, machinists, and carpenters, but weak to nonexistent in other occupations. A hastily established Executive Committee of the Workingmen's State Convention held daily meetings as the general staff of the work stoppage. Denouncing both the Democrats and the Republicans for "deserting" labor once they had enacted the eight-hour statute, the committee appealed to workers' organizations throughout the country for help. Little came. Despite their pleas that victory "in Illinois means success in New York . . . in Wisconsin . . . in every State in the American Union," only $200 actually arrived in the head-

---

[4] *New-York Times*, May 7, 1867; *Daily Evening Voice*, May 6, 8, 1867.
[5] *New-York Times*, May 7, 1867.
[6] *Daily Evening Voice*, May 6, 8, 17, 1867; *New-York Times*, May 7, 1867; Pierce, II, 178–9; Cole, *Era of the Civil War*, p. 371.

quarters before June 21.[7] By mid-June the rolls of Chicago trade unions were drastically reduced, their funds exhausted, and their stalwart members left without work. True, several trades did work only eight-hour days in June, but the failure of the strike meant that all ultimately returned to longer hours.[8] Even the Ship Carpenters' and Caulkers' Union, first beneficiary of the new order, resolved in August to repeal its eight-hour rules because "at present the pressure is too strong against them."[9]

Labor's defeat in Chicago sealed the fate of the eight-hour movement in the Middle West. Although the trades assembly of St. Louis attempted to emulate the Chicagoans by "enforcing" the Missouri statute, which also took effect May 1, there was little similarity between the union efforts in the two cities. Poorly conceived and wretchedly executed, the St. Louis strike call roused no enthusiasm among the workmen of the great river port and was most notably spurned by the numerous German immigrants. To cap the climax, the treasurer of the local bricklayers' union, the only organization well prepared for a work stoppage, absconded with the strike funds.[1] With both this experience and that of Chicago to dishearten them, the trade unionists of Milwaukee understandably welcomed the July Fourth inauguration of Wisconsin's eight-hour era by staging a little parade, then discreetly returning to their jobs at ten hours a day.[2]

THE AMBIGUOUS FEDERAL EXAMPLE

Although the Chicago strike was "attended by a temporary defeat," editorialized Andrew Cameron, the public notice it gave the world of labor's insistence on the eight-hour day

---

[7] *Illinois State Workingmen's Convention—Record Book 1867* (in W.S.H.S.); Ozanne, pp. 136–7; *Daily Evening Voice*, May 28, 31, June 7, 21, 1867. The strikers' appeal is in *ibid.*, May 28, 1867.

[8] *Ibid.*, June 11, July 6, Aug. 10, 1867; Pierce, II, 179.

[9] *Daily Evening Voice*, Aug. 10, 1867.

[1] *Daily Evening Voice*, March 30, May 2, 3, 6, 9, 1867; letter from St. Louis Workingmen's Union to William Jessup in *ibid.*, June 6, 1867; Bates, pp. 26–7.

[2] Merk, pp. 185–8; Thomas C. Tinker to Frederick Merk, March 31, 1914, Tinker Letters; *Daily Evening Voice*, June 13, 1867; *Welcome Workman*, Aug. 24, 1867.

was a "signal triumph." Its outcome demonstrated, however, that the indispensable "stepping stone to further success" was to secure "the sanction of our national legislature. . . ."[3] Jonathan Fincher concurred. Illinois employers, he argued, had been compelled to resist their own workmen lest they be undersold by competitors from other states. Subsequent efforts by the workingmen, therefore, had to be focused on the federal government.[4]

What these labor reformers demanded of Congress, however, was not that it enact a legal working day of eight hours for the entire nation, but only that it make the federal government an experimental model. By employing its own mechanics on an eight-hour basis, the national government was to demonstrate the economic and social benefits of the shorter day and provide an example for private concerns to emulate. Ira Steward made the establishment of such exemplary hours for public employees the first item in the "programme for a Century" which he elaborated in 1868.[5] The proposal received universal endorsement in the labor movement, from the aggressive National Typographical Union, whose delegates faithfully took part in every National Labor Congress, to the isolationist Brotherhood of Locomotive Engineers, who spurned both militant action and the N.L.U.[6] Only once during the decade's incessant debate over shorter hours did any labor reformer of note suggest federal action going beyond the model-employer role. In 1864, Fincher had observed: "Under the Constitutional grant to regulate commerce, Congress has the right and power to regulate the number of hours that shall be considered a 'day's work.' "[7] The uniqueness of the comment underscores the point that labor reformers relegated the authority to determine the legal hours of labor to the police powers of the states as if by a Pavlovian response. Not even

---

[3] Editorial, *Workingman's Advocate*, Aug. 17, 1867.
[4] Editorial, *Welcome Workman*, Aug. 24, 1867.
[5] Steward, *Meaning of the Eight Hour Movement*, p. 11.
[6] National Typographical Union petition in U.S., Congress, 40th Cong. 2d Sess., Senate Committee on Finance, National Archives, file S 40A-J1 (hereafter this and similar files will be cited in this fashion: Natl. Archives, S 40A-J1); *Locomotive Engineers' Monthly Journal*, Vol. I (Feb. 1867), pp. 6–7.
[7] Editorial, *Fincher's Trades Review*, Sept. 17, 1864.

Fincher ever broached the possibility of federal control again; his 1867 demand for congressional action specifically referred to public employees.[8]

As early as the congressional session that began in December 1865, proposals to undertake the experiment were introduced by B. Gratz Brown, George W. Julian, and Ebon Ingersoll on the Radical side, and by Democrats Andrew Rogers and William Niblack.[9] Serious consideration of the subject began when the House Judiciary Committee unanimously endorsed the bill George Julian submitted in March 1867 to provide an eight-hour day for all mechanics and laborers employed by or on behalf of the federal government. Nathaniel P. Banks called up the bill, which was adopted without debate or roll-call vote. This hasty action by the Radical camp was interrupted only by the protest of New York's ardent Mozart Hall Copperhead William S. Chanler that the bill did not specify whether or not the pay of workmen was to be reduced, as well as their hours. This question, which was to vex the history of the law for the rest of the nineteenth century, was simply ruled out of order by the Speaker.[1]

Julian's bill was received and debated in the Senate on the day it passed the House. While Democrats and Johnson Conservatives watched in silence, Republican senators debated each other. John Conness of California and Massachusetts's Wilson spoke eloquently in favor of the plan, only to be answered with denunciations of both the bill and labor unions in general from Simon Cameron, William P. Fessenden, and William Sprague. A motion of Vermont's George F. Edmunds to send the measure to the Committee on Finance carried 18 to 17, and in that committee the bill died. All the opponents of the referral motion were Republican save one, Connecticut's James Dixon, who was at that moment associated with the gubernatorial campaign of James English. On

---

8 Editorial, *Welcome Workman*, Aug. 24, 1867.
9 *Congressional Globe,* 39th Cong., 1st Sess., 918 (Feb. 19, 1866), 1969 (April 16, 1866); Philadelphia *Public Ledger,* Dec. 1, 15, 1865, April 11, 1866.
1 *Congressional Globe,* 40th Cong., 1st Sess., 105 (March 14, 1867), 425 (March 28, 1867).

the other hand, only two supporters of the motion were not Republicans, and both of them (Reverdy Johnson and Charles R. Buckalew) were to cast their ballots in favor of the bill a year later.[2]

Angered by the Senate's action, the Chicago Labor Congress authorized President Whaley to launch a national petition campaign in support of the bill. In October 1867, Whaley sent copies of a standard form to all officers, but it was not until the following spring that the appeals reached the Senate, through the hands of Republicans Oliver P. Morton, Benjamin F. Wade, and Cornelius Cole and Democrats Thomas Hendricks and Thomas McCreery. Largest of the 19 collections of signatures appearing under the heading, "Petition of the Mechanics and Other Laboring Men of——," was the New York appeal, with 2,713 names. The sequence of addresses indicates that most of them were collected by door-to-door canvassing. Others were evidently gathered at meetings, like the 70 signatures on the plea from Spuyten Duyvil Iron Molders' Union No. 11. Jessup's strenuous efforts made New York lead the nation on the drive, but it did not stand alone. Pittsburgh's Allegheny Arsenal sent 348 names; while other tabulations included Cincinnati, 213; McGregor, Iowa, 242; Hartford, Connecticut, 265; Nashville, Tennessee, 225; and so on around the nation.[3] Without doubt, this campaign was the most extensive organizational effort ever undertaken by the N.L.U.

The largest petition of all contained some 4,880 signatures on sheets beautifully bound between hard covers. Introduced by Senator Cornelius Cole of California, this appeal was not the work of the N.L.U. but came from the Mechanics' State Council of California and the House Carpenters' Eight Hour League of San Francisco.[4] Skilled workmen in California had

---

[2] *Ibid.*, 413–14 (March 28, 1867).

[3] *Workingman's Advocate*, Jan. 25, 1868; *N.L.U. Proceedings, 1868*, pp. 8–9; *Congressional Globe*, 40th Cong., 2d Sess., 453, 950, 980, 1863, 2067, 2236, 2434, 2653, 2856, 3347 (Jan. 11, Feb. 4, 5, March 13, 23, April 4, May 13, 29, June 5, 22, 1868); Natl. Archives, S 40A-J1, S 40A-H7, S 40A-E5. The files of the Committee on Naval Affairs in Natl. Archives also contain seven petitions.

[4] Natl. Archives, S 40A-H7.

been able to establish the eight-hour day in fact as well as law by this time, because their employers faced no serious competition from the rest of the nation. Their sheltered domain was threatened, however, by competition from some relatively low-cost producers in the East and from others in California itself who used Chinese labor. The state's labor movement consequently advanced two major demands: Chinese exclusion and a federal eight-hour law. By 1868 control of the Mechanics' State Council had been captured by a Democratic politican, "General" Albert M. Winn, who had capitalized astutely on these two demands to advance the aspirations of Eugene Casserly to the United States Senate. The Republicans, unable to embrace Chinese exclusion with a fervor matching that of their opponents for fear of undermining their own equal rights position regarding Negroes, had responded by pushing the eight-hour cause with great fanfare.[5] So far had the rivalry progressed that in 1869 the state Democratic platform pointed "with pride to the fact that . . . it was the Democratic element in the legislature that passed and a Democratic governor that approved the eight hour law," while their opponents claimed "to have originated in this State . . . the 'eight-hour law,' the sound policy of which has been proclaimed by a Republican Congress, and by a proclamation of a Republican President made applicable to the public works of the United States."[6]

California's John Conness, whose term in the Senate was to expire in 1869, was the leader of the erstwhile Anti-Lecompton Democrats, who had affiliated with the Union (Republican) party only in 1864, and were presently recognized in the state as the "short hairs," or the working-class wing of the party. Faced with challenges to his position from both the "long hairs" (professional and mercantile elements) in his own party and the Democrats, whose contender Eugene Casserly was in fact to wrest the seat from him, Conness

---

[5] See Montgomery, "Labor and the Radical Republicans," pp. 372–81; Ping Chiu, pp. 52–66, and *passim;* A. M. Winn, *Address of Gen. A. M. Winn, President of the Mechanics' State Council of California, Delivered before the Council, the Eight Hour Associations and United Mechanics* . . . (San Francisco, 1870).

[6] McPherson, *Reconstruction,* pp. 478–9.

understandably made himself the prime mover in reviving the Senate bill.[7] His counterpart in the House was Banks, whom the power in the Eight Hour Leagues in his own bailiwick had converted to the cause in 1865.[8] To evade parliamentary obstacles, Banks had reintroduced the moribund Julian bill in the House as his own in January 1868. After a brief debate in which Banks, Leonard Myers, and Norman Judd clashed with their more moderate fellow Republicans Frederick A. Pike and Elihu B. Washburne, the bill passed without a recorded vote. As usual, the discussion was confined primarily to Republican participants on both sides, but this time Cincinnati's newly elected Labor Reform congressman, Samuel F. Cary, lent his support to the bill, as did Mozart Hall's Chanler.[9] Once the measure had cleared the House, Conness took command to guarantee the plan did not die again in committee.

Having evaded the hostile Committee on Finance by tabling the bill the day it arrived in the Senate, Conness faced a second hazard, an effort by Democratic senators to identify the bill with their party. Thomas Hendricks of Indiana, then aspiring for the Democratic Presidential nomination, interrupted the debate over a Republican proposal to admit the reconstructed government of North Carolina with a motion to take up the tabled eight-hour bill. When several Republicans protested that the future of North Carolina was the business before the Senate, Hendricks capitalized upon the opportunity to charge his foes with being more concerned with Negroes than with white workingmen. Realizing that this line of argument spelled certain defeat for the eight-hour bill in a chamber that was overwhelmingly Republican, Conness and Wilson leapt to their feet to identify themselves with the bill. At this point adjournment abruptly ended the debate.[1]

The final hurdle confronted the measure when Conness called it up on June 24. John Sherman, in whose Finance Committee the 1867 measure had died, focused the discussion on the question House Republicans had always evaded, by

---

[7] Davis, pp. 23, 101, 108, 120, 178–9, 207, 213–40.

[8] Harrington, pp. 169–70, 199–200.

[9] *Congressional Globe*, 40th Cong., 2d Sess., 334–36 (Jan. 6, 1868).

[1] *Ibid.*, 358 (Jan. 8, 1868), 2082–4 (June 3, 1868).

moving an amendment that "the rate of wages paid by the United States shall be the current rate for the same labor *for the same time* at the place of employment." In other words, federal mechanical employees should have their pay reduced by one fifth when their hours were cut, since an act of 1862 had fixed their wages at the prevailing standards of the communities in which they worked. Both Californians, Conness and Cole, hotly opposed the Sherman amendment, and their efforts were supported by their neighbor William H. Stewart of Nevada, as well as by Wilson, and by Hendricks and Buckalew from the Democratic side. William P. Fessenden, Roscoe Conkling, Lot M. Morrill, and Orris S. Ferry of Connecticut defended the amendment. "In this country," charged Ferry, "the agitation for an eight-hour law did not begin with the industrious laborer, it began with clamorous demagogues seeking votes." Fessenden warned that the bill would set "an evil example" and stir up "excitement throughout the country upon the same subject between employer and employed." But Sherman's amendment was voted down, 16 to 21, and the bill passed by a margin of 26 to 11.[2]

The Senate vote revealed rather clearly the political alignments that had developed around the eight-hour question. Treating as Republicans those who voted to override President Johnson's veto of the Tenure of Office Act (with the obvious exception of Reverdy Johnson, whose vote to override must be relegated to the maverick category), plus senators who were absent when that veto was overridden but who later voted "Guilty" at the trial of the President, leads to the conclusion that the final bill was supported by 20 Republicans, three Democrats, and three Johnson Conservatives (Patterson, Dixon, and Doolittle), while it was opposed by ten Republicans and one Democrat. Quite a different alignment emerged, however, on the crucial Sherman amendment. Only 14 Republicans joined the four Democrats and three Johnson Conservatives in opposition to the wage-cutting proposal, in contrast to the 15 Republicans and one Democrat who favored it. Among the 14 Republicans who might thus be classed as unequivocal friends of the bill were Samuel Pomeroy, who subsequently

2 *Ibid.*, 3424–9 (June 24, 1868).

voted against the measure, and Roscoe Conkling, who was absent at the final vote but who had twice spoken in opposition to the bill. Removing them from the list of "friends" leaves an ardent minority of 12 Republican senators who not only provided the decisive force in the enactment of the law, but who were also determined that the federal example should not be sullied by any reduction of wages. All of them were Radicals: Cole, Conness, Cragin, Harlan, McDonald, Morton, Nye, Ramsey, Steward, Tipton, Wade, and Wilson. Charles Sumner voted with the bill's foes, but four years later he declared himself a friend of the "experiment."[3]

Eight hours now constituted "a day's work for all laborers, workmen, and mechanics . . . employed by or on behalf of the government of the United States."[4] No sooner was this the case than the dispute over the Sherman amendment was transferred from parliamentary debate to administrative practice. Defeated in the Senate despite its support by the Republican majority, the wage-reduction plan was put into practice by many executive officials before 1873 and was used almost universally after the great depression broke.

Although most of the 54,000 federal employees were in clerical occupations not covered by the bill (and already often working less than eight hours), and the largest group affected consisted of the 6,339 men then employed in navy yards, the question of pay scales first came to a head in the War Department. At the Springfield Arsenal in Massachusetts, after a month of working the new hours at the old pay, several classes of workers were subjected to a 20 per cent wage cut and immediately appealed to Washington. Meantime, the wages of workmen at the Rock Island arsenal had been cut, but the commandant offered his men a 25 per cent raise if they would volunteer to work ten hours daily. When Secretary of War John M. Schofield upheld the commandant, 400 arsenal workmen struck. Their grievance was twice presented to Presi-

---

[3] The data on senators used in this analysis is taken from McPherson, *Reconstruction*, p. 173; Barnes; *Biographical Directory of the American Congress*; Ben: Perley Poore, *Congressional Directory for the Second Session of the Fortieth Congress of the United States* (Washington, 1868). For Sumner's 1872 position, see Sumner to Massachusetts Labor Union, May 25, 1872, in Sumner, *Works*, XX, 79.

[4] Act of June 25, 1868, *U.S. Statutes at Large*, XV, 77.

dent Johnson, first by a delegation from the Workingmen's Assembly of Washington, D.C., and later by Whaley and A. T. Cavis for the N.L.U.[5]

Johnson referred the problem to Attorney General William M. Evarts, who handed down a ruling on November 25, 1868, stating first that since a War Department order was involved, the problem was no concern of printers (meaning Whaley and Cavis). Although nothing in the act required wages to be reduced together with hours, he continued, neither did the law assert that government employees "must receive as high wages for their day's labor of eight hours as similar industry in private employments receives for a day's labor of ten or twelve hours." The equality specified in the act of 1862, concluded the Attorney General, "requires that the same *worth* of labor should be compensated in the public employment at the same rate of wages that it receives in private employment." In other words, not only was the government within its legal rights to reduce wages, but not to do so would allow workers in private industry to demand an increase of wages, "and thus in turn each system would be encouraged to rise upon the demands of the other."[6]

Evarts's ruling nullified labor's basic objective in the federal eight-hour law: that the government's example would do just what he feared—encourage rising demands in the private sector. President Johnson stood by his Attorney General, and Evarts's successor, E. R. Hoar, explicitly reiterated the ruling. As if to rub salt in labor's wounds, the new Grant administration transferred General Schofield from the War Department to the command of the Department of the Missouri where he promptly ordered all workmen under his jurisdiction to work ten hours for the old pay.[7] President Sylvis

---

5 *Hist. Stat. 1945,* 294; U.S., Congress, Senate, *Letter of the Secretary of the Navy, July 17, 1868,* 40th Cong., 2d Sess., Sen. Exec. Doc. 76; Philadelphia *Public Ledger,* Aug. 8, 10, 19, 25, Dec. 11, 24, 1868; *N.L.U. Proceedings, 1868,* 6; Order of J. G. Benton, Bv't Col. commanding the U.S. Armory at Springfield, July 30, 1868, Dawes Papers Box 19.
6 U.S. Department of Justice, *Official Opinions of the Attorneys General of the United States,* ed. J. Hubley Ashton (Washington, 1870), XII, 530–6.
7 *Ibid.,* XIII, 29–31; U.S. Congress, House, 44th Cong., 2d Sess., Report No. 11.

of the N.L.U. dispatched a series of angry letters to Attorney General Hoar, and assigned his organization's Washington lobby the task of reversing the War Department's actions. "General" Winn came from California to head a National Executive Eight Hour Committee in the capital, while in the House both friends of the administration (like Henry Dawes and Aaron Stevens) and foes (like William Niblack) introduced measures to restore the cut wages. When such a resolution passed the House, only to be buried in a Senate committee, President Grant brought the question before his cabinet. Over the objections of Secretaries Rawlins (War) and Borie (Navy) and Attorney General Hoar, the President issued an executive order "that from and after this date [May 19, 1869] no reduction shall be made in the wages paid by the Government by the day to such laborers, workmen, and mechanics, on account of such reduction in the hours of labor."[8]

For the first and only time in his life William Sylvis found reason to praise Ulysses S. Grant. Despite "the attorney-general's very learned opinion," the leader of the N.L.U. wrote Grant, "your order came, and coming unexpectedly, is doubly welcome. . . ." By his actions the nation's chief executive had strengthened the workers' faith in their government, Sylvis wrote, because "the learned decision of a self-puffed lawyer [was] compelled to give way to the unvarnished rendering of a practical citizen."[9]

Just how effective the President's "unvarnished rendering" of the law turned out to be is graphically revealed by the fact that three years later he issued the same proclamation a second time, prefaced by the words: "And whereas it is now represented to me that the Act of Congress and the proclamation [of 1869] have not been strictly observed by all officers of the government having charge of such laborers, workmen, and mechanics. . . ."[1] Simultaneously, Henry Dawes introduced

---

[8] Sylvis, pp. 320–6; *Workingman's Advocate*, Jan. 3, 1870; *Congressional Globe*, 40th Cong., 3d Sess., 9 (Dec. 7, 1868); *ibid.*, 41st Cong., 1st Sess., 506, 556, 637, 653, 679 (April 5, 6, 8, 9, 1869); Cleveland *Leader*, April 29, 1869, May 20, 1869 (in *Annals of Cleveland*, Vol. 52, pp. 1300, 1301); Richardson, VII, 15.
[9] W. H. Sylvis to U. S. Grant, May 27, 1869, in Sylvis, pp. 326–8.
[1] Richardson, VII, 175–6. See below, pp. 328–9, for immediate circumstances of this decree.

in the House an appropriation bill for restoration of all pay lost by federal employees on account of pay reduction between passage of the bill and Grant's first proclamation. The measure carried the House with the support of 67 Republicans and 50 Democrats, and against the votes of 28 Republicans and 14 Democrats, then cleared the Senate by voice vote.[2]

Rather than settling the administrative fate of the federal example, the 1872 appropriation move exposed it to assault from two directions. First, during the Senate debate on the measure, Vermont's Justin Morrill moved an amendment providing that "all laws regulating the hours of labor are hereby repealed." Nineteen Republican senators joined a lone Democrat in opposition to the tabling motion with which Alabama Republican George Spencer killed Morrill's amendment, while only fifteen Republicans voted to table. Only the votes of nine Democrats provided the margin of safety for the eight-hour bill.[3] The counteroffensive begun in 1872 became more public two years later, when Arthur B. Mullett, supervising architect of the Treasury Department, climaxed more than six years of feuding with the Washington bricklayers' union by openly calling for the repeal of the eight-hour law. Forty-two Baltimore manufacturers quickly sent the House of Representatives a petition endorsing Mullett's view. "The demoralizing effect on the labor which the Government has temporarily employed," protested the manufacturers, "has unfitted mechanics and laborers for a regular day's work."[4]

The law was never repealed. Instead its subversion continued through a second route opened by the 1872 appropriation bill. While claims for retroactive pay totaling some $149,584 were ultimately ceded by the Quartermaster General,[5] many workmen took disputed claims to the courts.

---

[2] Edward McPherson, *Hand-Book of Politics for 1872* (Washington, D.C., 1872), pp. 70–1 (hereafter cited as McPherson, *1872*); *U.S. Statutes at Large*, XVII, 134.

[3] McPherson, *1872*, pp. 80–1.

[4] U.S. Congress, House, *Letters from the Secretary of the Treasury in Reference to the Operation of the Eight Hour Law, Feb. 6, 1874,* 43d Cong., 1st Sess., House Exec. Doc. 117. For Mullett's disputes with bricklayers, see Bates, p. 26; Philadelphia *Public Ledger,* June 18, 24, 1867.

[5] U.S. Congress, House, *Letter from the Secretary of the Treasury in Answer to a Resolution of the House in Relation to the Decisions of the*

Through the cases arising in this fashion, the Supreme Court of the United States performed a disappearing act on the eight-hour law that would have put Houdini to shame.

Case one arose when quarrymen employed by Ralph Ordway near Richmond, Virginia, appealed to Congressman Banks to intervene with the administration on behalf of their claims for overtime pay. Ordway's firm was supplying granite to the federal government under contract. Arguing that they were employed "on behalf of" the government, the stone-cutters asked overtime pay for their ten-hour schedule, on the basis of the eight-hour law. When Attorney General Benjamin H. Bristow ruled against Banks's plea on the grounds that the law did not cover workmen of firms under government contracts, the workers went to court. Five years later, Justice Noah H. Swayne wrote the unanimous opinion of the Supreme Court: the government's contract being with Ordway, not his workers, the law could not affect the relations between Ordway and his workers.[6] In a word, employment "on behalf of" the government was deemed not to mean employment by government contractors.

The seriousness of this decision can best be understood in the light of another ruling the court had made the previous year. A workman in the boiler room of the Naval Academy who toiled twelve hours daily during the winter months sued his employer, the Navy Department, for retroactive overtime pay under the acts of 1868 and 1872. In 1876 the Supreme Court threw out his suit. The act of 1868, reasoned Justice Ward Hunt for the Court, was not a contract between the government and its employees, but "a direction by Congress to the officers and agents of the United States, establishing the . . . length of time which should amount to a day's work, when no special agreement was made upon the subject." Since the workman had not refused to work twelve hours over the course of several years, he must be understood as having consented to the contract. At one time, the Court continued, laws did establish the price for a day's work. But since the

Second Comptroller of the Treasury, 43d Cong., 1st Sess., House Exec. Doc. 72, 1–5; U.S. Congress, House, 46th Cong., 2d Sess., Rept. 1267. [6] Opinions of the Attorneys General, XIV, 45–8; United States v. Driscoll, 96 U.S. Rep. 421 (1877).

days of Adam Smith, a "very different principle is now almost universally adopted . . . [namely,] the hours of labor and the prices to be paid are left to the determination of the parties interested." The eight-hour law, Justice Hunt concluded, "does not conflict with this principle."[7]

Deducing from the Court's position that any workman "willing to contract to labor more than eight hours a day" might properly be employed at terms different than those prescribed by the law, Secretary of the Navy R. W. Thompson fixed all wages and hours under his jurisdiction on a ten-hour basis and announced he encountered "no difficulty in finding laborers ready and willing to occupy all the positions in the navy-yards upon these conditions."[8] By 1880 the chairman of the House Committee on Education and Labor concluded that the "law is practically now a dead letter."[9] Without questioning the constitutionality of the act of 1868, the Supreme Court had first inferred into it a free-contract clause, then held that government officials need not obey its provisions if they found them undesirable. A statute which the high court deemed valid but not obligatory was surely an unusual law. But, as a claims court soon declared, the eight-hour law was simply "passed in deference to a sentiment of philanthropy," while wages and hours must be "determined by the inexorable laws of business."[1]

THE POWER OF ORGANIZATION

The shift of labor reformers' concern from the problem of enacting a legal working day of eight hours to the more vexing task of "enforcing" the new laws elevated the trade unionists of New York City to the forefront of the movement for shorter hours. By the fall of 1872, William J. Jessup could estimate

---

[7] *United States* v. *Martin,* 94 U.S. Rep. 400 (1876).

[8] U.S. Congress, House, *Letter of Secretary of the Navy R. W. Thompson to the Committee on Naval Affairs, Oct. 31, 1877,* 45th Cong., 1st Sess., House Exec. Doc. 9.

[9] U.S. Congress, House, 46th Cong., 2d Sess., Rept. 520. For confirmation of this view see Senate, *Labor and Capital,* I, 296–301, 328–31, 403–4, II, 40–1, 437; U.S. Congress, House, 52d Cong., 1st Sess., Rept. 1267.

[1] *James Averill* v. *United States,* in *Washington Law Reporter,* VII (1879), 169–71. *Cf. Isaac Miller* v. *United States,* in *ibid.,* p. 171.

reliably that some 15,000 workmen enjoyed the eight-hour day in his city, while adding that he had "no knowledge of any trades outside of New York State, except those in Government employ, working eight hours."[2] Five years had then elapsed since the enactment of the state's eight-hour day, and the experience of those years had carried New York's labor reformers far afield from the Baltimore Program's conception of how the shorter working day was to be established.

Although the text of the New York statute presented May 1, 1867, as its effective date, the bill was not actually signed into law by Governor Fenton until May 9. The strikes and riots which rocked Chicago during the intervening week prompted the Workingmen's Union of New York, while welcoming the new law, to "recommend local unions to move with caution and avoid premature action," and to seek through conferences with the employers "the ultimate adoption of the Eight Hour rule." It was, declared this powerful city assembly, the responsibility of the working classes to make the transition to the shorter day "with as little jar as possible to the industries of the state."[3]

This resolution implied both that the trade unions were consciously taking unto themselves the task of administering the law, and that they approached this task with deliberate caution. Many a labor leader, including William Sylvis, considered prevailing economic conditions inauspicious for unilateral efforts to shorten hours by union rules. Such prudence prevailed over the enthusiasm of delegates from the Mohawk Valley cities when the State Workingmen's Assembly met in June. That body warned the workingmen against taking "extreme measures," and urged them to establish eight-hour rules only after November 1, and then "at such reduction of wages as the different localities may determine upon."[4] Because the November date fell after the close of the construc-

[2] *Mass. BLS, 1873*, p. 258.

[3] Act of May 9, 1867, *Laws of the State of New York passed at the Nineteenth Session of the Legislature* (Albany, 1867), Ch. 856; *Daily Evening Voice*, May 21, 1867.

[4] *Ibid.*, May 21, June 1, 1867; letter of "a molders' leader" to *ibid.*, June 6, 1867; Philadelphia *Public Ledger*, May 31, June 6, 7, 8, 10, 23, 28, 29, 1867.

tion season, the trade unions in effect had postponed "enforcement" until 1868.

In one respect, however, the Workingmen's Assembly did amend the stand initially taken by the New York City unions. At its June session the assembly demanded that the current convention to revise the state constitution provide for an eight-hour day in all public works and "for all Union operatives" of corporations chartered by the state, and that the United States Senate pass the eight-hour bill then before it. In other words, labor tried to buttress the new law with more legislation of the same stripe. Simultaneously, the assembly echoed Chicago labor's denunciation of the Democratic and Republican parties and summoned the N.L.U. to launch a National Labor party at its forthcoming convention.[5]

Less than a month before the November 1 "enforcement" date the workingmen appear to have realized that the issue confronting them was one not of legislation but of execution; that no piling of statute upon statute could change anything unless some administrative agency compelled citizens to comply with the laws' provisions. They dispatched a committee to Governor Fenton to advise him that his appointees in administrative positions were not making employers adhere to the new law, and to urge him to issue a special proclamation drawing the attention of officials and citizens alike to the terms of the eight-hour statute. The naïveté of the labor reformers' conception of public administration was matched by the disingenuousness of Fenton's reply. To issue the pronouncement requested of him, Fenton declared, "would be an unwarranted assumption on my part," because every general law "is obligatory in its own nature, and derives no additional force from a proclamation by the Executive Department." Refusing "to assume that public officers . . . are acting in disobedience to the laws," the governor concluded that it would be improper for him to "designate particular statutes as those which they are specially bound to obey, where they do not directly involve the preservation of the public peace, and the repression of disorder and violence."[6]

---

[5] *Ibid.*, June 28, 29, 1867.
[6] *Workingman's Advocate*, Oct. 12, 1867.

Fenton's restriction of executive functions to the "repression of disorder and violence" made the administrative task of translating statutory prescription into public practice revert to the trade unions. True, the Workingmen's Assembly continued to lobby for improvement of the statute, and in 1870 the legislature rewarded these efforts by requiring employers to grant some unspecified "extra compensation" for "overwork" after eight hours, and by prescribing the eight-hour standard for all workers employed by the state or by employers fulfilling contracts with the state. State officials who violated these terms were to be suspended.[7] More than a year later, however, at a massive labor rally in New York City, Jessup and other speakers called angrily for the election of a governor who would "enforce" the eight-hour law and the imprisonment of state officials who continued to "violate" the statute.[8] The only workmen then enjoying the eight-hour day in fact were the bricklayers, and it was not the state but their well-fought strike of 1868 that had won that gain. In other words, even after political action had earned the desired law, the trade union remained the agency for administering the reform.[9]

The futility of appeals to the state for enforcement led in the spring of 1872 to direct confrontation over the issue between the organized power of labor and the organized power of capital. The intransigent mood of both parties was reflected in their resolutions. A strike rally staged by the Workingmen's Union, concluding that the "laws of different States, fixing eight hours as the legal working day, have been entirely disregarded by the employer," resolved: "That we are entirely within the law in asking for eight hours, and that those who oppose us are guilty of a flagrant violation of the law."[1] In response, a meeting of some four hundred businessmen denounced the workingmen for having construed the statute "as a mandatory law compelling manufacturers to run their establishments only eight hours," and vowed to hire labor only by the hour, to continue in operation ten hours daily at

---

[7] Act of April 26, 1870, *Laws of the State of New York . . . Twenty-Second Session . . .* (New York, 1870), Ch. 385.

[8] *New-York Times*, Sept. 14, 1871.

[9] See argument of Peter J. McGuire in *Chicago Socialist*, Aug. 16, 1879.

[1] *Workingman's Advocate*, June 1, 1872.

the old wage scales, and to refuse employment to "any work-man guilty of an act looking to the arbitrary establishment of relations between employer and employed."[2]

New York's workingmen seemed well prepared for just such a test of strength. Already in September 1871 an impressive demonstration of solidarity with stonecutters striking for the eight-hour day had been organized by Jessup of the Workingmen's Union, Troup of the N.L.U., and Ira Steward of the Eight Hour Leagues. More than 8,000 workers, representing primarily the building trades and the International Workingmen's Association, participated in the affair.[3] The diversity of leadership that appeared at the numerous rallies for the eight-hour day staged during the spring of 1872 revealed both an extraordinarily high degree of organization among the city's workers and the sharp focus of efforts of all their societies on the single objective of realizing the promise of the eight-hour law. James Connolly of the painters, John Ennis of the plasterers, and Michael Daly of the bricklayers appeared time and again in the company of Robert Blissert and Theodore Banks of the International, as well as Jessup and Troup. Their appeals were seconded in German by Fred Homrighausen and Karl Speyer of the furniture workers, Jacob Morstadt of the cigar makers, Siegfried Meyer from the I.W.A., and the influential Socialist Conrad Kuhn, who headed both the *Arbeiter-Union* and the German cigar makers.[4]

The prominence of Internationalists and adherents of Steward's Eight Hour Leagues indicates that the leaders of this movement were prepared ideologically, as well as organizationally, for overt class conflict on a massive scale. The I.W.A. had expanded from three sections to twenty in New York and vicinity during its four years of existence on this side of the Atlantic, and, more significantly, had become an accepted part of the labor-reform movement. Both the N.L.U. and the New York Workingmen's Assembly had endorsed its principles, and in 1869 the former had even declared its inten-

---

2 Quoted in A[dam] S. Cameron, *The Eight Hour Question* (n.p., n.d.), p. 8.
3 *New-York Times*, Sept. 14, 1871; Commons, *Doc. Hist.*, IX, 367–8.
4 *Workingman's Advocate*, June 1, 1872; New York *Tribune*, June 20, 1872; *New-York Times*, June 22, 1872.

tion to affiliate with the General Council in London at some unspecified future date. Despite the schism which had occurred in its Central Committee at the end of 1871, both warring factions of the I.W.A. participated in the leadership of the strike movement and lent it a class-conscious flavor.[5]

The tone imparted to the workers' efforts by the I.W.A. was echoed and magnified by Ira Steward's followers in the North American Eight Hour League, which formed the organizational center of the movement. From Teutonia Hall, where executive sessions of the League met almost daily during May, June, and July, a network of subordinate bodies fanned out, the most significant of which were the Building Trades League, the Furniture Workers' Eight Hour League, and the Iron and Metal Workers' Eight Hour League. The first of these groups was primarily English-speaking, the second totally German, and the third mixed. While close to 100,000 workers struck at one time or another during this period, their actions did not constitute a general strike because much of the action was totally spontaneous and uncoordinated, and many workers were simply taking advantage of the general turmoil to seek higher wages. The deliberate pattern of activity which gave meaning to the upheaval, however, was provided by the 21,400 members of these three Leagues.[6]

The housepainters of Brooklyn actually opened the battle when they halted work in April. As other building tradesmen prepared to join the fray, their cause was suddenly given both publicity and encouragement by President Grant. The nation's chief executive entered the picture when he was visited late in the month by a delegation of New York bricklayers who protested that the contractors employing them to erect a new post office building were violating the federal eight-hour law. Ignoring the fact that Secretary of the Treasury Boutwell had spurned a plea from workmen at the same site in 1869, Grant kept a weather eye out for the pending elections and assured

[5] J. T. Elliott to the Officers & Members of Section 26, I.W.A. (n.p., May or June, 1872), I.W.A. Papers, Box 1; Commons, *Doc. Hist.*, IX, 358–9; *Workingman's Advocate*, Aug. 27, 1870. On the split in the I.W.A., see Bernstein, pp. 109–61.
[6] New York *Tribune*, May 31, June 8, 1872; Schlüter, *Internationale*, pp. 470–80.

the bricklayers that they were entitled to an eight-hour day, and to overtime pay if they stayed longer on the job. Less than two weeks later he issued an executive proclamation reminding federal officials that the act of 1868 authorized no reduction of wages as a consequence of shortening hours of labor for workmen under their jurisdiction.[7]

Heartened by this success, the Building Trades League rallied every major union in its field to proclaim eight-hour rules early in May. So widely was work interrupted, according to the city's Department of Buildings, that the total value of structures erected in the five weeks prior to July 1 fell from $5,617,600 the previous year to $2,327,600 in 1872, and by early June most of the workers involved had won their demand.[8] As the building trades strike approached its climax, the Furniture Workers' League summoned thousands of Germans to quit the woodworking shops. Realizing that most of these immigrants had never before been enlisted in trade-union efforts, the League decided to stage a great parade on June 10 to dramatize its cause. It urged all labor organizations to participate in the march and demanded that on that day all storekeepers display signs friendly to the eight-hour cause on pain of boycott by the workingmen.[9]

Five days before the scheduled parade, Theodore Banks, a painter of prominence in both the Workingmen's Union and the anti-Marxist sections of the International, issued a public circular calling for the use of arson by the workers if the capitalists refused to accede to their demands. As if the sensation created by Banks's letter was not great enough, the very next day one striker was arrested for attempting to murder a scab and another was incarcerated for loudly threatening to burn down a factory where the workmen had failed to strike.[1] Whether the alleged incendiary (one Valentine Weinberg) was in any way connected with Banks, a police

[7] Ibid., pp. 470–5; New-York Times, Nov. 12, 1868, April 30, 1872; Richardson, VII, 175–6.
[8] Workingman's Advocate, May 25, 1872; New York Tribune, July 1, 1872.
[9] Ibid., June 3, 8, 1872; New-York Times, June 6, 9, 1872; Workingman's Advocate, June 15, 1872.
[1] New York Tribune, June 7, 1872; New-York Times, June 7, 1872; Schlüter, Internationale, pp. 475–80.

agent, or an overexcited striker, or whether he was simply demented went not only unknown, but unasked by the press. Several sections of the International quickly condemned Banks's letter and declared that he could not be considered a member since his section did not recognize the authority of the General Council in London. The Eight Hour League also repudiated Banks and Weinberg and soon established a special committee to screen all press releases and public statements. When Banks and his comrade John T. Elliott arrived at the assembly point for the June 10 parade, they were brusquely shunted to the rear. But all these efforts to disassociate the movement from the Banks letter were in vain. Only German woodworking unions appeared in force for the march. Since even the building trades shunned the demonstration, hardly one tenth of the expected turnout of forty thousand materialized.[2]

Strikes in progress on June 10 or beginning after that date were doomed to failure. Employer resistance stiffened remarkably when larger firms such as the Singer Sewing Machine Company and J. B. Brewster and Co. made themselves the bulwarks of the ten-hour day. The *Times* and *Tribune,* which up to this point had been remarkably dispassionate in reporting the strikes, began to see Communists "inciting trouble" in a strike which each day was "losing its vigor." Most serious of all for the strikers was the new attitude of the police, who directed their clubs at workingmen's heads with utter abandon as the strength of the eight-hour movement ebbed. Not a day passed without more "clubbing" for the leagues to denounce. But while labor reformers appealed to a police review board against the "brutality" of the bluecoats, the *Times* editorially asked the governor to send the National Guard to buttress the forces of law and order.[3]

In this setting the last round of the strike commenced: the Iron and Metal Workers' League called out its followers, who were the most poorly organized of all the major groups

---

[2] *New-York Times,* June 9, 11, 1872; New York *Tribune,* June 8, 11, 19, 1872. *Cf.* Gompers, I, 60.
[3] *New-York Times,* June 9, 15, 16, 17, 19, 20, 21, 22, 1872; New York *Tribune,* June 14, 17, 1872; *Workingman's Advocate,* editorial, June 22 and 29, 1872 (single issue).

participating in the movement. President John Fehrenbatch of the Machinists' and Blacksmiths' International Union rushed to New York to patch together what organization he could, but the first and only German local of his union in the city was scarcely a year old. A rally at Cooper Institute on June 20 addressed by a stellar cast of leaders helped fire the iron and metal tradesmen with enthusiasm, but it could not compensate for their lack of funds and experience and their secondary leadership. Facing them was a tightly organized employers' association, determined to yield nothing, which provided police protection to "loyal" workmen and financed the prosecution of pickets.[4] The secretary of the association, A. S. Cameron, ridiculed labor's complaints against the police as comparable to the 1861 plea of the Confederacy that it wished to be "left alone."[5] His June 18 speech, issued in pamphlet form, captured the mood of the embattled manufacturers. Arguing that a shorter working day would ruin business in the city, Cameron denounced the strike as embodying "a spirit . . . entirely foreign to the disposition of our industrial population," and continued:

> It is impudent, aggressive and unreasonable. It opens with a demand for eight hours per day, and says it will follow it up by a demand for six hours instead of eight; in its low mutterings we hear demands for an equal division of property, and other kindred absurdities. I can see the outline of the spirit of communism behind this movement, and I recognize the bold attempt that is being made, at this time, to engraft it on our social system.
>
> And what is communism but another form of trade union?[6]

Faced with such resistance, the strikes of furniture, iron, and metal workers crumbled. In fact, a reverse momentum developed that even cost many workers the gains they had won in May. Although the Furniture Workers' League did not discontinue its daily strike meetings until July 17, and inter-

---

[4] *Machinists and Blacksmiths' International Journal*, Vol. VIII (Feb. 1871), pp. 103–4, 119–20; New York *Tribune*, June 19, 20, 21, 26, 1872.
[5] Cameron, *Eight Hour Question*, pp. 6–7.
[6] *Ibid.*, pp. 2–3. See also J. W. Orr Engraving Co. to McCormick Bros. and Co., June 19, 1872, in Hutchinson, II, 485–6, n. 117.

ruptions of work remained common after that date, the great strikes had come to a close with the shorter day being enjoyed only by some 15,000 workers, mostly in the building trades. Before the season had closed even the carpenters and plasterers had surrendered their eight-hour day for a nine-hour schedule.[7] In his post-mortem assessment, John Fehrenbatch noted that the iron and metal workmen, infected by the success of the building tradesmen, had risen as "a multitude gathered together upon the impulse of the moment, with but little training and no stability, to engage in a gigantic struggle in which even the most thorough and perfect organization should have hesitated to embark." Faced with fierce resistance from their employers, the "raw recruits began to waver, and finally desertion became the order of the day."[8]

The ebb tide did more, however, than just undermine trade-union "enforcement" of the eight-hour law. It also prompted labor reformers to dissociate themselves loudly from the International. Although Banks still appeared as an orator for the Workingmen's Union in July and his comrade Elliott was dispatched by the Painters' Union to organize in St. Louis in September,[9] the notoriety of the "incendiary letter" cast a pall over relations between many trade unions and the I.W.A. In 1871 the *Workingman's Advocate* had printed Karl Marx's defense of the Paris Commune and argued that "the International don't mean murder, arson or treason," but only that "our Tom Scotts, with their $400,000,000 and their subsidized legislatures, shall lose their power—peaceably if they will; FORCIBLY, IF THEY MUST!"[1] By October 1872, however, when editor Cameron heard of the International's intention to move its General Council from London to New York, he cried out against "the *importation* of a class of intellectual dyspeptics,

---

[7] New York *Tribune*, June 18, 28, 29, July 1, 6, 18, 1872; *Eighth Annual Report of the Bureau of Statistics of Labor of the State of New York, for the Year 1890* (Albany, 1891), I, 155, 397.

[8] *Workingman's Advocate*, Aug. 31, 1872. The author of this article was identified as Fehrenbatch in *ibid.*, Sept. 14, 1872.

[9] New York *Tribune*, July 1, 1872; *Workingman's Advocate*, Sept. 14, 1872.

[1] Editorial, *ibid.*, July 8, 1871. Marx, *Civil War in France* was serialized in *ibid.* starting Aug. 1, 1871.

who refuse and who intend to refuse, allegiance to our institutions. . . ."[2]

The prospect of such an invasion gave new urgency to Cameron's familiar plea for a reorganized Industrial Congress. Now he saw that institution as the embodiment of "the sentiments of the American mechanic" and the only alternative to permitting "a purely foreign organization to sow the seeds of distrust and discord . . . confusion and anarchy. . . ."[3] Though Cameron had himself proudly traveled to Basle in 1869 to attend the I.W.A.'s congress as the delegate of a National Labor Union which had declared its intention to affiliate with the world body, he now urged the congress to spurn the "Anti-American element."[4] His sentiments were shared by many New York trade unionists who publicly avoided connections with "Communists, Internationalists, and other social disturbers" even before the famous Tompkins Square incident of 1874.[5] That affair simply reinforced the desire among labor reformers to disavow the International that had arisen from the 1872 strikes. The Iron Molders' International Union adopted a standing rule that "no Union of this organization shall participate in any demonstration of the association known as the 'International' or 'Commune,' either by association or contribution."[6] And the Industrial Congress declared itself in 1874 "a purely American institution . . . neither having nor seeking an entangling alliance with foreign organizations or institutions," which had only "a friendly feeling" for workingmen of other nations.[7]

The major dissent to this trend came from the Eight Hour Leagues. Steward and McNeill moved steadily closer to the

---

2 Editorial, *ibid.*, Oct. 26, 1872.

3 *Ibid.*

4 *Prem. Int.*, II, 115–17; editorial, *Workingman's Advocate*, Nov. 2, 1872.

5 Herbert H. Gutman, "The Tompkins Square 'Riot' in New York City on January 13, 1874," *Labor History*, Vol. VI (Winter 1965), pp. 50–2. Gompers, in order to sustain his argument that Tompkins Square served as the decisive warning of his career against revolutionaries, ignores this earlier development of animosity toward the I.W.A. *Cf.* Gompers, I, 59–61, 93–8.

6 *Constitution and Rules of Order of the Iron Molders' Union of North America* (Cincinnati, 1876), p. 41.

7 *Workingman's Advocate*, April 25, 1874.

Internationalists and, specifically, to the Marxists in the
I.W.A., from 1872 on until their forces actually merged in the
International Labor Union of 1878.[8] This exception only
underscores the paradoxical outcome of the eight-hour conflict
of the sixties and early seventies. The legislation through
which labor reformers had dreamed of ushering in a new era
had proven worthless. Only the development of a governmental bureaucracy to administer such laws could have made
them effective, and the workers were no more prepared
ideologically to ask for the expansion of state activities that
would have entailed than their employers were ready to
accept it. "Enforcement," therefore, became a trade-union
function. The conflicts that emerged from trade-union efforts
to administer the laws certainly helped perfect the organizational machinery and striking power of the unions themselves.
But they did not impart a revolutionary class-consciousness to
these unions.

Quite the contrary, at the very climax of the movement,
American labor reformers overwhelmingly disavowed the
revolutionaries. It was not a socialist ideology but a greenback
ideology that emerged as the main intellectual current among
the leaders of the formidable trade-union movement at the
beginning of the 1870's. Class conflict failed to make American
labor reformers more class conscious. Rather, they found a
formula which allowed them to explain such conflict in traditional, classless, democratic terms. That formula they inherited
from the disintegration of radicalism.

---

[8] Sorge, "1866–1876," pp. 174–9; Commons, *Labour*, II, 301–6.

CHAPTER 9

The Eclipse of Radicalism

"Many persons who have been Radicals all their lives are in doubt whether to be Radical any longer," noted E. L. Godkin in 1871, "but at the same time have such a traditional horror of standing still, that they shudder at the thought of bringing on themselves the name of 'Conservatives.' "[1] The root of the dilemma, he explained, was that the once-honored "Radical" label had become associated with causes which were not only dubious, but dangerous to society. The Radical vision of a harmonious community of equal men aided by an active state in their pursuit of the common good now found itself confronted by the brutally real "politics of class feeling."[2] Though he welcomed with Wendell Phillips "the accomplishment of all that the friends of freedom have ever asked of the nation . . .

---

[1] [E. L. Godkin], " 'Radicals' and 'Conservatives'," *Nation*, Vol. XIII (July 13, 1871), p. 21.
[2] [E. L. Godkin], "Classes in Politics," *ibid.*, Vol. IV (June 27, 1867), pp. 519–20.

that is, the absolute civil and political equality of the colored man under our institutions and government,"[3] Godkin was haunted by the specter of a workingmen's party demanding interference with freedom of contract, an Irish party calling for American aid to the Fenians, and a Negro party, "whose mission it will be to remind the nation incessantly that the blacks are a class apart, with separate interests and aims." All these groups, he warned, are "bent on the promotion of their own interests at whatever cost . . . and leading ambitious politicians into follies of which the worst exploits of the great political deceivers of the present day afford but a very imperfect idea."[4]

Like the proponents of the legal eight-hour day, Godkin was tormented not by defeat but by success, which turned out to have an unexpectedly bitter taste. War had been fought and the subsequent battles of Reconstruction won in the name of the sovereign people, to whom all power rightly belonged. Now the people were behaving in a manner no Radical had anticipated. They were using their power to pursue class interests.

Samuel Johnson was so vexed by this development that in 1871 he wrote a series of articles for *The Radical,* which were soon reprinted in pamphlet form under the title *Labor Parties and Labor Reform.* Johnson had been prominent in Massachusetts reform circles since he had left Harvard Divinity School in the early 1840's to preach in a highly unorthodox Unitarian chapel in Lynn. After years of antislavery activity and propagation of transcendentalism and "natural religion," he had watched with mounting anxiety the growing power of the Knights of St. Crispin, sensing in their behavior a spirit of materialism and monopoly that threatened to revive autocracy.

America has no Vendôme Column to overturn, no palaces to fire, no priesthood to spoil and slay. But it is none the less true that there lies a perilous fascination for intensely democratic instincts in the theory that property has no

---

[3] Phillips, quoted in James M. McPherson, *Struggle for Equality: Abolitionists and the Negro in the Civil War and Reconstruction* (Princeton, 1964), p. 376.
[4] Godkin, "Classes in Politics," pp. 519–20. *Cf.* [Godkin], "The Working-Men and Politicians," *Nation,* Vol. V (July 4, 1867), pp.11–12.

rights which the majority may not abrogate at will. The authority of numbers, the worship of popular desire, is pushed to its extreme in the phase of republicanism through which we are passing. The true industrial problem for our politics is not, how shall majorities prove the extent of their power, but how shall they learn to respect the principle that the rights of labor and the rights of property are mutual guarantees.[5]

Labor's protests against monopoly, against railroad land grants, speculation, dishonest tariffs and trading were all well taken, Johnson allowed. Its proposed cures, however, were worse than the ills they sought to correct, for trade unions opposed monopoly with monopoly, and legislative remedies engendered an authoritarian state. Conceding that workingmen in America rarely assailed private property itself, he charged that their organizations did attack the accumulation and enjoyment of the fruits of property: profits, interest, and rent. Hazardous was their plan to solve social ills through manipulation of the currency, worse was their call to cure poverty through eight-hour laws, and most ominous of all was the ease with which labor movements were manipulated by designing politicians. The nation's only hope, he concluded, lay in spiritual regeneration (following "the great soul of Mazzini"), to elevate moral values above material. America needed not "vox populi, vox Dei," but "self-control."[6]

True, European observers like Laurence Oliphant and Georges Clemenceau had long cautioned American Radicals, with whom they were sympathetic, that a democracy could be as authoritarian as a monarchy.[7] Conservatives and old-line Democrats had warned since the war years that "Black Republicanism" in America, like "Red Republicanism" in the Europe of 1848, led "through anarchy, to military despotism, to corrupt class legislation. . . ."[8] Appealing to Jay Cooke to rouse executives of national banks to defend themselves, William E.

---

[5] Johnson, *Labor Parties,* p. 14. On Johnson, see Samuel A. Eliot (ed.), *Heralds of a Liberal Faith* (Boston, 1910), III, 185–90.

[6] Johnson, *Labor Parties,* pp. 1–29.

[7] Oliphant, pp. 26–8; Clemenceau, pp. 97–99, and *passim.*

[8] [B. E. Green], "William Sylvis," reprinted in *Revolution,* Vol. I (July 2, 1868) p. 405.

Chandler argued: "This universal suffrage country will never see the end of attempts of demagogues to excite the poor against the rich, labor against capital, and all who haven't money against the banks who have it."[9] But Radicals had rebuffed such admonitions with sanguine faith in the righteousness of the people, who, after all, had proven their trustworthiness during the great rebellion. Even Godkin, who found it impossible to read the N.L.U.'s program "without pain," assured his readers in 1867 that the weakness of organized labor "enables us to read it without anxiety."[1]

Five years later, he was anxious. The business community, almost as a whole, was recoiling from the hazardous path down which the Republican party had led it. As early as the state elections of 1867 the editors of *Harper's Weekly* interpreted Republican losses not as an indication that "the sober, thoughtful, influential body of people" had "tired of the sublime American doctrine of equal rights," but as evidence that they had lost confidence in the leadership of Stevens, Butler, Ashley, and company.[2] Both Radical eagerness for a "thorough" policy in the South and Radical complicity in the turmoil over labor in the North contributed to this reaction. "What this country wants most," editorialized the influential Philadelphia *Public Ledger*, "is a steady period of rest from agitation. . . ."[3] To Henry Cooke the only solution was a purge of "the ultra infidelic radicals like Wade, Sumner, Stevens, *et id omne genus*," who were "dragging the Republican party into all sorts of isms and extremes." With Wade trying to array labor against capital, Butler urging "wholesale repudiation" of the debt, Stevens "advocating the idea of a flood of irredeemable paper money," and "Pomeroy and Wade and Sprague and a host of others clamoring for the unsexing of women and the putting of the ballot into her hand," Cooke was not at all amazed that the party broke down under the "accumulated load."[4]

---

[9] W. E. Chandler to Jay Cooke, Dec. 2, 1867, in Oberholtzer, II, 56.
[1] *Nation*, Vol. V (Aug. 29, 1867), p. 162.
[2] Editorial, *Harper's Weekly*, Oct. 26, 1867. *Cf. Nation*, Vol. V (Nov. 14, 1867), p. 385.
[3] Philadelphia *Public Ledger*, Jan. 21, 1868.
[4] Henry Cooke to Jay Cooke, Oct. 12, 1867, in Oberholtzer, II, 28–9.

Godkin's concern, however, went beyond that of a politician who feared his party's course was jeopardizing business support it could ill afford to lose. The deeper danger, he believed, was that by the end of the decade the workers had taken the place once occupied by the soldiers as the group inevitably courted by every party platform. Granted the legislation enacted at labor's behest lacked enforcement, and granted the "labor plank" found in each party's platform was a jungle of ambiguities and evasions, the fact remained, argued Godkin, that such partisan antics had an inflammatory effect on ignorant voters. Shocked by the sweeping promises made to labor by the Massachusetts Republicans in 1872, he wrote:

> There are plenty of men, and sober and sensible men too, who believe that [the labor question] contains the disease of which this Christian civilization of ours is to perish; that the passionate pursuit of equality of conditions on which the multitude seems now entering, and the elevation of equality of conditions into the rank of the highest political good, will eventually prove fatal to art, to science, to literature, and to law; and that, after having gone down into barbarism, and witnessed the decay and destruction of all the great monuments of our epoch, we shall have to begin again the old and toilsome ascent made by our forefathers under the lash of hunger and the brute rule of force.[5]

The advance of democracy, Godkin concluded, does not necessarily entail either the improvement of government or more security for life and property. He was sufficiently systematic in his thinking to realize that this conclusion shattered the underlying assumptions of the optimistic utilitarianism which had made him a Radical at the war's end. In 1867 he was already searching for a formulation of "True Radicalism" which could somehow restrict the legitimate area of governmental activity to the guarantee of "fair and equal opportunity."[6]

---

[5] [E. L. Godkin], "The Danger of Playing Tricks with the Labor Question," *Nation*, Vol. XV (Sept. 5, 1872), p. 148. *Cf.* "Labor and Politics," *ibid.*, Vol. XV (June 13, 1872), pp. 386–7.
[6] E. L. Godkin, "Legislation and Social Science," *Journal of Social Science*, III (1871), 116; [Godkin], "True Radicalism," *Nation*, Vol. V (July 18, 1867), pp. 50–1.

Godkin's groping for a new political philosophy typified the doubts the labor question had generated in the minds of Radical intellectuals. Once men like Godkin and Samuel Johnson had concurred in Sinclair Tousey's judgment that a government "of and from the people . . . cannot destroy its (or their) liberties."[7] Now they looked upon the hybrid of their own creation—the mixture of the democratic state and the active state—as Frankenstein's monster. "It became only too apparent," recalled Washington Gladden, "that a whole people, swept by a flood of excitement, may go hopelessly wrong." Salvation for the republic, he believed, lay only "in the rise of a class of leaders who have the courage to resist the mob."[8] These men had not repudiated universal suffrage or popular rule. They sought, rather, a way to limit the sphere of operation of democratic government. In this respect they were part of that "great 'middle class,' which now governs the world," described by the New-York Times as "terrified" at the "great social storm" shaking industrial nations, and endeavoring to "hold a stronger rein on the lower."[9]

THE GREENBACK IMBROGLIO

The cruel quandary which the effort to rein in the lower classes created for radicalism became enmeshed in the debate over the greenback currency. Despite all its complexities, the currency question typified the fate of Radical doctrines, for here the Republican party repudiated its own radical handiwork. So thoroughly have the political aspects of the paper-money question been discussed—by Elbridge Spaulding in the 1860's, and a century later by Robert P. Sharkey and Irwin Unger—that there is no need to dwell on them here.[1] Very relevant, however, is their significance for the Radicals.

---

[7] See above, pp. 79–80.

[8] Washington Gladden, Recollections (Boston and New York, 1909), p. 156.

[9] Editorial, New-York Times, April 17, 1871. Cf. editorial, ibid., July 29, 1869.

[1] E. G. Spaulding, History of the Legal Tender Paper Money Issued during the Great Rebellion (Buffalo, N.Y., 1869); Robert P. Sharkey, Money, Class, and Party: An Economic Study of Civil War and Reconstruction (Baltimore, Md., 1959); Irwin Unger, The Greenback Era, A Social and Political History of American Finance, 1865–1879 (Princeton, N.J., 1964).

Both the plan for a managed fiat currency and the rhetoric subsequently used in its defense were the offspring of the Radical wing of the Republican party. The legal tender bill was taken up by Congress at the end of 1861 because gold loans floated by the Treasury had exhausted the coin supply of the banks and forced them to suspend specie payments. The Union was confronted by the prospect of runaway bank-note inflation and the sale of its bonds below par value, either of which would have raised the cost of prosecuting the war toward a prohibitive level. At this juncture, Elbridge Spaulding, a Buffalo banker and Republican congressman, proposed a solution in defiance of the national traditions of states' rights, hard money, and bank control of currency: that the federal government should issue its own interest-free notes receivable for all public dues and legal tender for all private transactions. The value of these notes was to be stabilized by permitting their conversion into government bonds bearing 6 per cent interest, which were payable in five years and redeemable in twenty, commonly known as 5-20's.

This majestically simple scheme met with furious opposition from the Democrats and many bankers. Pendleton, Vallandigham, Conkling, and Justin Morrill stood shoulder to shoulder against the bill; but its Radical supporters, led by Thaddeus Stevens, enlisted enough Conservative (and even banker) support for the scheme as a temporary war measure for it to pass the House 93 to 59. Senate opponents were strong enough to graft on an amendment providing for payment of interest on the 5-20 bonds in coin. This action created the problem of how to raise the promised gold. Because the House had rejected the Senate's solution of selling bonds for gold below par, a conference committee adopted the alternative of requiring that tariff duties be paid in specie. Thus, over the furious objections of Stevens and Spaulding, their plan was transformed into a dual currency system: gold for the importer and bond-holder, greenbacks for everyday domestic purposes.[2]

---

[2] Spaulding, pp. 5–12; Bray Hammond, "The North's Empty Purse, 1861–1862," *American Historical Review*, Vol. LXVII (October 1961), pp. 1–18; Sharkey, pp. 27–8; Woodley, pp. 240–4.

As the war continued and governmental needs for borrowed funds soared, both the currency supply and the debt structure grew ever more complex. Short-term interest-bearing notes, new bonds payable in ten years and due in forty (the 10-40's), and then the notes of the new national banks all came into circulation. By the war's end the country was faced with rampant inflation, constant manipulation of gold prices by speculators, a morass of different bond issues, and four major forms of currency—greenbacks, specie, national bank notes, and state bank notes. The task of unraveling the mess fell on Secretary of the Treasury Hugh McCulloch, who, with the aid of Revenue Commissioner David A. Wells, sought to guide the nation as quickly as possible toward a resumption of specie payments, reduction of tariff levels, and scaling-down of wartime internal taxes. With authority granted by Congress in March 1866, McCulloch initiated a steady withdrawal of greenbacks from circulation, and redemption of short-term notes.[3] The need of the country, he wrote, was to "check extravagance" and "restore former habits of economy."[4]

Both President Johnson and congressional Conservatives hailed McCulloch's policy, as did even some New Englanders of free trade inclinations who otherwise aligned themselves with the Radicals, like Edward A. Atkinson and Charles Sumner. Such a howl of protest arose from manufacturers, however, who blamed the postwar economic decline on the Treasury's contraction policy, that McCulloch cautiously eased the pace.[5] Meanwhile, Republican governors, congressmen, and journals warned with increasing frequency against "too hasty" a return to specie payments. By early 1868, Ohio's James A. Garfield found himself "almost alone in my own state and in the West generally" in his support for McCulloch.[6]

---

[3] Spaulding, pp. 167–88, Appendix pp. 14–17; Woodley, p. 245; Oberholtzer, I, 329–94; *American Annual Cyclopaedia,* VII (1867), 304.

[4] Hugh McCulloch to Edward A. Atkinson, May 11, 1867, Atkinson Papers, Box 2.

[5] William Gray and others to Hugh McCulloch, April 30, 1867, Atkinson Papers, Box 2; Charles Sumner to Edward A. Atkinson, Jan. 3, 1868; Sumner to Atkinson, Feb. 21, 1868, *ibid.,* Box 2; Unger, *Greenback Era,* pp. 120–62. For President Johnson's position, see above, pp. 65–6.

[6] James A. Garfield to Edward A. Atkinson, May 17, 1868. See also Garfield to Atkinson, May 21, 1868; Hugh McCulloch to Atkinson, May

When Samuel Bowles toured western Pennsylvania in the company of Fessenden, Henry Raymond, and others to propagate the views of McCulloch and Wells, he reported that his discussion of "tariff and currency and turkey and champaign with the Pittsburgh iron and steel lords" revealed "enthusiastic agreement on the two latter themes," which "augured well for the property and perpetuity of the Republic," while at best it "mitigated the shocks of difference as to the other topics."[7]

No part of the grand design of McCulloch and Wells won substantial support among the manufacturers except the proposal to reduce internal taxes. Wells's tariff reduction bill, which had come within a hair of enactment in 1866, was soundly defeated in 1867, and Congress passed in its place the protectionist Wool and Woolens Act.[8] In May 1867, Peter Cooper, Henry C. Carey, John A. Griswold, and others founded the American Industrial League to combat free-trade sentiment and demonstrate to the electorate "the identity of interest of all classes of the people . . . in promoting American production."[9] The extent of their success in Pennsylvania was revealed the next year when petitions calling for increased tariff protection were circulated by manufacturers and signed by their workers and fellow townsmen in such numbers that four full pages of the *Congressional Globe* were needed just to list the petitions received.[1] Simultaneously, a bill introduced by Robert Schenck to force a halt to the Treasury's contraction policy enlisted the support not only of Stevens, Butler, and Logan, but also of Senator Sherman and Jay Cooke, and of numerous Democrats. The measure swept the House by a vote

---

11, 1867; McCulloch to Atkinson, Aug. 3, 1867; S. Lester Taylor to Atkinson, April 25, 1868, Atkinson Papers, Box 2.

[7] Merriam, II, 53; David A. Wells to Henry L. Dawes, Sept. 21, 1866, Dawes Papers, Box 19. See Sharkey, pp. 153–73, and Unger, *Greenback Era*, pp. 44–67, on anticontraction sentiment among businessmen.

[8] Ida M. Tarbell, *The Tariff in Our Times* (New York, 1911), pp. 34–43. For attitudes of manufacturers toward internal taxes, see report on the Cleveland Manufacturers' Convention, Boston *Daily Advertiser*, Jan. 23, 1868.

[9] *New-York Times*, May 9, 1867; Butler, *Correspondence*, V, 718; Cooper, pp. 339–45.

[1] *Congressional Globe*, 40th Cong., 2d Sess., 2582–3 (May 25, 1868), 2592–3 (May 26, 1868).

of 127 to 14, and in the Senate only four Conservative Republicans voted against it. President Johnson deserted McCulloch for the first time; he allowed the bill to become law without his signature.[2] The Conservative economic program had been thoroughly defeated.

A rhetoric highly charged with emotional value had been infused into the currency controversy from the outset. Hard-money advocates characterized their own position as scientifically sound and moral, and that of their foes as demagogic and dishonest. These epithets were employed with equal facility by Conservative Republicans advocating contraction after the war and by old-line Democrats denouncing the passage of the legal tender act in Congress or resisting the efforts of Republicans in the New York legislature to pay the interest on state bonds in greenbacks.[3] Friends of greenbacks in turn labeled them "the people's money." Speaking for Spaulding's bill in 1862, Henry Wilson had described the debate as "a contest between brokers, and jobbers, and money-changers on the one side, and the people of the United States on the other."[4] Not to be outdone, John Bingham charged the bill's foes with misconstruing the Constitution for "the purpose of denationalizing the people: for the purpose of stripping the American people of the attributes of sovereignty; for the purpose of laying . . . at the feet . . . of brokers and hawkers on 'Change [the exchange] the power of the people over their monetary interests in this hour of national exigency."[5]

Here was Radical ideology in its purest form, printed, as it were, on bills of "Lincoln green." Understandably, Henry Carey attributed both the economic vigor and the patriotic spirit of the nation to protection and greenbacks, "Pig Iron" Kelley persisted in championing both down through the 1870's, and Thaddeus Stevens, who judged the whole national banking system "a mistake," declared: "Every dollar of paper in circulation ought to be issued by the Government of the

---

[2] Sharkey, pp. 110–15.

[3] Spaulding, pp. 43–4, 52–4, 64–6; Brummer, pp. 366–76.

[4] Spaulding, p. 111.

[5] *Ibid.*, p. 67. See also *ibid.*, pp. 128, 147 for more examples of such rhetoric. *Cf.* Unger's dichotomy of the Calvinist heritage versus the Agrarian Myth, *Greenback Era*, pp. 24–40.

United States."[6] Benjamin Bannan, who belabored the Democrats for more than three decades from the editorial office of the Pottsville *Miners' Journal*, devised a scheme for the circulation of greenbacks as the exclusive currency of the nation, with national banks serving as distribution centers only. The combined impact of this plan, higher tariff protection, and funding the national debt at lower interest rates, he believed, would mean prosperity for the nation. "Every producer and laborer who works in a factory, mine, or on a farm, or in any branch of business that creates wealth are [*sic*] in the same boat," he wrote in the best Radical fashion, "their interests are identical. . . ." Against them stood only capital, "which is nonproductive and is worked as money in speculating, discounting paper at high rates of interest, and shaving." From the tariff of 1846 until the Republican legislative triumphs of 1862, Bannan argued, nonproductive capital had ruled the land, and now it was again "striving to gain the ascendency."[7]

By 1868, however, this rhetoric was no longer the exclusive property of its Radical progenitors. In fact, it was being hurled against the Republicans by both Democrats and labor reformers. Few Republicans, furthermore, allied themselves with Stevens, Kelley, and Bannan in their desire to make greenbacks the *exclusive* currency of the nation. Party cohesion extended only to halting McCulloch's contraction, no further, and even on that point important Conservative Republicans dissented.

The explanation of this paradox lies in the inseparable relationship between the currency on one hand, and the national debt and national banks on the other. The debt, which stood at the end of June 1867 at $2.7 billion, was drawn into the fray because almost half of it was in the form of 5-20 bonds, more than $500 million of which became payable April

---

[6] Henry Carey, *The Way to Outdo England. The Currency Question*, in Carey, *Works*, I, 33; William D. Kelley to Edward Daniels, Nov. 8, 1875, Daniels Papers, Box 1; Stevens quoted in W. R. Brock, *An American Crisis, Congress and Reconstruction, 1865–1867* (London, 1963), p. 217.
[7] *Pa. BLS, 1872–1873*, pp. 523–31. (Quotations are on pp. 523–4.) For biographical sketch of Bannan see Henry W. Ruoff and Samuel T. Wiley, *Biographical and Portrait Encyclopedia of Schuylkill County Pennsylvania* . . . (Philadelphia, 1893), 213–15.

30, 1867. The act authorizing their issue, although it specified that the interest was to be paid in gold, made no such provision concerning redemption of the principal. Indeed, the two congressmen most intimately associated with the passage of the loan disagreed on how they had intended the bonds be repaid: Spaulding said in gold, and Stevens said in greenbacks.[8] Because the bonds had been purchased in inflated legal tender currency, Stevens argued that to repay them in specie would offer the bond-holders a windfall profit at the expense of the taxpayers. He proposed, therefore, to solve the problem of the currency and the bonds at one blow by simply issuing additional greenbacks to redeem the 5-20's as they fell due.[9] Although this proposition was endorsed by Benjamin Butler and such Radical organs as the Cincinnati *Daily Gazette*, other Republicans, among them Godkin and Greeley, denounced it as "repudiation" of the debt.[1]

To complicate the picture further, these bonds provided the foundation upon which the whole structure of the national banks rested, for they were a reserve against which those banks issued their own notes. In less than half a decade of existence these banks had been inextricably integrated into the nation's economy. Politicians ranging in outlook from Oliver P. Morton and Daniel Morrell through William H. English to Thomas A. Hendricks sat on boards of directors of such banks.[2] More important, even in regions where hostility to McCulloch's contraction policy was most widespread, national banks were firmly entrenched. Ohio, for example, had 37 per cent of the national banks formed in the first year of operation of the new system, and 137 such banks by 1867. Banks in Illinois took national charters so quickly that in 1865 the state simply abolished its office of state banking commissioner. The editors of *Iron Age* and the delegates to the National Manu-

---

[8] *American Annual Cyclopaedia*, VII (1867), 303; Spaulding, Appendix pp. 22–7; Woodburn, pp. 577–8.
[9] Woodburn, p. 578.
[1] [E. L. Godkin], "General Butler's Ethics," *Nation*, Vol. V (Sept. 12, 1867), pp. 210–11; New York *Daily Tribune*, July 1, 1868.
[2] Barnes, I, 251–4; *Revolution*, Vol. II (Dec. 3, 1868), p. 342; John W. Forney, *Life and Military Career of Winfield Scott Hancock* (Philadelphia, 1880), pp. 492–3.

facturers' Association Convention in 1868 called, not for the elimination of national banks, but for the removal of all restrictions on their issue: for *both* continued greenbacks and more banknotes.[3] Consequently, any plan for a greenback currency which entailed disruption or dissolution of the national banks could not possibly enlist more than marginal support among Republicans.

Finally, the 5-20 bonds enjoyed a symbolic status which guaranteed them Republican support. Their sale had been managed by Jay Cooke, who circumvented the reluctance of major banks to buy federal securities before the Union victory at Gettysburg by launching a nation-wide appeal to the patriotism of "the little people."[4] Three important consequences flowed from Cooke's role. First, in the minds of many Americans these bonds bore all the nationalistic trappings of the war itself. An attack on them was easily identified with an attack on the Union. Second, although much of the 5-20 sale ultimately went to sizable banks, there is no doubt that farmers and mechanics who held small quantities of 5-20's did number in the millions, as Cooke's propaganda constantly stressed.[5]

Third, Cooke was a master publicist, with a formidable personal stake in the redemption of these bonds. During his sales campaign, he had subsidized editors and columnists of most of the important papers of the nation. These journals were still in his pay when he undertook to guarantee that the bonds would be redeemed in gold, as he had personally promised they would be.[6] Hardly had the Confederate armies surrendered when Cooke undertook to convince the masses, "with whom I, perhaps more than any other man in the country—come in contact—that this debt is *not* what croakers & demagogues are seeking to portray it—*viz* an unmitigated

---

[3] Roseboom, p. 143; Cole, *Era of Civil War*, p. 362; letter of Salmon P. Chase in *Revolution*, Vol. II (Dec. 3, 1868), p. 342; *Nation*, Vol. V (Nov. 14, 1867), pp. 394–5; *ibid.*, Vol. V (Sept. 19, 1867), pp. 234–5; Sharkey, p. 169; Dorfman, III, 7; Irwin Unger, "Business Men and Specie Resumption," *Political Science Quarterly*, Vol. LXXIV (March 1959), pp. 54–7.

[4] Oberholtzer, I, 249–54.

[5] *Ibid.*, I, 317, 586.

[6] *Ibid.*, I, 232–9, 579–84, 637–46.

evil burden," but "a cement which shall bind our people to the *Union*."[7] His efforts were supplemented by the Loyal Publications League, which was resuscitated in 1868 in order "to spread throughout the country correct views upon the subject of taxation and currency."[8]

In a word, the congressman who wished to redeem the 5-20's in greenbacks, legal though his proposition was, encountered the opposition of Cooke's organization, with a publicity machine of unequaled effectiveness and a mass following numbering in the millions, and he courted the charge of disloyalty to his country. Small wonder McCulloch welcomed the controversy over the redemption of the 5-20's as "well calculated" to open the eyes of his opponents "to the danger to which their teachings lead."[9]

On his proposal to redeem the 5-20's with new issues of greenbacks, therefore, Stevens and the handful of Radical colleagues who supported him did not stand the slightest chance of winning over their party. Ironically, support did appear from the other extreme of the political spectrum. Old-line Democrats of the type of "Brick" Pomeroy and Henry Clay Dean saw no sanctity in the national debt and no virtue in the national banks. For them, both the bonds and the banks represented a Hamiltonian conspiracy to centralize power in the federal government and create a privileged "bondocracy" allied to the state. Accusations of being unpatriotic held no terrors for these old Copperheads, who had been so indicted by every Republican orator for half a decade. Their faithful followers, the farmers of the "butternut" regions, had greeted Cooke's bond salesmen with a scorn matched only by the ridicule heaped on Cooke's appeals by the local Democratic press.[1] True, their Jacksonian bullionist inclinations had made

---

[7] Jay Cooke to Edward A. Atkinson, June 27, 1865, Atkinson Papers, Box 1.

[8] Hugh McCulloch to Edward A. Atkinson, Jan. 3, 1868; C. E. Norton to Atkinson, April 7, 1868, Atkinson Papers, Box 2.

[9] Hugh McCulloch to Edward A. Atkinson, Oct. 9, 1867, Atkinson Papers, Box 2.

[1] Oberholtzer, I, 605. McCulloch correlated the strength of animosity toward the bonds conversely with the extent of bond-holding in his 1868 report. *Congressional Globe*, 40th Cong., 3d Sess., Appendix p. 13 (Dec. 1, 1868).

Dean and Pomeroy denounce the introduction of the green-backs in the war years; but the issues of bonds and banks which restrained most Radicals from following the greenback path provided the very route through which these old-line Democrats entered it. Tax the bonds! End the privileged status of the bloated Eastern bond-holders! These were the battle cries with which the "butternuts" charged into the fray.[2]

Several Democratic strategists, such as Wilbur Storey of the Chicago *Times* and the editors of the Richmond *Daily Dispatch* were quick to see the tactical advantages for their party in championing an issue which could not harm them, but could thoroughly confuse and divide their opponents.[3] Among them was Washington McLean, editor of the Cincinnati *Enquirer,* who took up the Stevens plan for redemption of the national debt as a platform from which to increase his own influence within Ohio's Democratic party during the 1867 gubernatorial campaign. To counteract McLean's efforts, Senator George H. Pendleton evolved and publicized a moderate scheme of his own. In substance, Pendleton asserted that greenbacks should be substituted for national bank notes but stabilized at their existing gold value, that the 5-20's should be redeemed in greenbacks (and the other bonds in gold, as the law required), that all bonds should be retired by means of a sinking fund, and that the country should return to the gold standard by 1881, when the last of the 5-20's would have been paid off.[4]

Pendleton's "Ohio Idea" was the soul of moderation: it involved no emission of additional currency, no repudiation of legal obligations, no abandonment of the gold standard. The proposal roused widespread enthusiasm in the West, where its partisans were able to make it promise all things to all men, and it struck the Republicans at just those points where their commitment to the national debt and the war bonds made it

---

[2] Pomeroy, *Soliloquies;* H. C. Dean speech reported in Richmond *Daily Dispatch,* Aug. 22, 1867.

[3] Unger, *Greenback Era,* pp. 78–9; editorial, Richmond *Daily Dispatch,* Aug. 28, 1867.

[4] This account of the origin of the Pendleton Plan follows Chester M. Destler, *American Radicalism, 1865–1901, Essays and Documents* (New London, Conn., 1946), pp. 32–43.

impossible for them to maneuver. Hence by 1868 Democratic conventions in twelve states had pledged themselves to the plan and to Pendleton as their candidate for the Presidency. With great gusto, delegates from these states paraded in and around the New York Democratic Convention of 1868 and cheered when they heard the platform committee demand that the 5-20's be redeemed in greenbacks and that bonds be taxed on the same basis as every other species of property. When the chairman of the Resolutions Committee read the words "One currency for the government and the people, the laborer and the office-holder, the pensioner and the soldier, the producer and the bond-holder," the Pendleton men went wild with joy and insisted that the passage be read again and again.[5]

Formidable opponents arrayed themselves against Pendleton's move for the Presidential nomination. Tilden, Seymour, Hancock, and other spokesmen of commercial and financial interests within the Democratic party were determined to check Pendleton and hold the party to its traditional course. On their behalf National Chairman August Belmont, in his keynote address, denounced the *Republicans* as authors of "a vicious, irredeemable, and depreciated currency."[6] The New York Democrats headed off Pendleton's early lead in the balloting by nurturing a boom for Thomas A. Hendricks, then cultivated votes for Winfield Scott Hancock to stem the Hendricks drive, and finally brought Horatio Seymour to the forefront as the only means to break the Hancock-Hendricks deadlock they had created. Thus control of the party remained in the hands of adamant foes of the Pendleton Plan, and one of their number was the standard-bearer.[7]

Seymour reconciled his own views with the expressions of the party platform by pledging himself to restore greenbacks to par value in terms of gold before redeeming the 5-20's. But this stand implied resumption of the policy of contracting the

---

[5] *Official Proceedings of the National Democratic Convention, Held at New York, July 4–9, 1868* (Boston, 1868), p. 58; Philadelphia *Public Ledger*, July 8, 1868. On support for the Pendleton Plan, see Coleman, *Election of 1868*, pp. 102–16, 128–49, and *passim*.

[6] *Proceedings . . . Democratic Convention*, p. 4.

[7] *Ibid.*, pp. 152–61; Coleman, *Election of 1868*, pp. 235–52; Clemenceau, pp. 208–13; George D. Woods, "The New York Convention," *North American Review*, Vol. CXIII (Oct. 1868), pp. 445–65.

legal tenders. Small wonder McCulloch was among the few members of Johnson's cabinet who backed Seymour.[8] The candidate himself made no effort to enlist farmer or labor support through his party's platform. "My theory is that this election is in the hands of business men," he wrote to Cyrus McCormick. "It will go as their judgement shall dictate."[9]

When William D. Kelley addressed the House of Representatives in favor of greenback redemption of bonds, his Democratic colleague from Pennsylvania, George W. Woodward, took the floor to urge national bankers to withdraw their support from the party of radicalism and seek safety under the Democratic wing.[1] A significant movement had, in fact, materialized to convert the Democratic party into a truly Conservative institution through the nomination of Salmon P. Chase as its Presidential candidate. This scheme bore less fruit even than Pendleton's efforts, for the Tilden-Seymour-Belmont group that had blocked the Ohio Idea's proponents was equally dead set against the introduction of any other new principles, or new leaders, into their party. Tilden expressed complete accord with the views of Pennsylvania's erstwhile governor, William Bigler, when he classed the "restoration of the ten absent states . . . with their local government in the hands of the white population" as "the absorbing question" to which all "else must be subordinate and secondary."[2] Frank P. Blair, Jr., accepting his nomination for vice-president, called it "idle to talk of bonds, greenbacks, gold, the public faith, and the public credit" before the country accomplished its first need: to "disperse the carpet bag state governments."[3]

This attitude toward the Southern question alienated the

---

[8] Philadelphia *Public Ledger*, Sept. 8, 1868; *New-York Times*, Aug. 7, 1868.

[9] Horatio Seymour to C. H. McCormick, Sept. 15, 1868, in Hutchinson, II, 312.

[1] Philadelphia *Public Ledger*, Jan. 21, 1868.

[2] William Bigler to Samuel J. Tilden, Feb. 3, 1868, in *Letters and Literary Memorial of Samuel J. Tilden*, ed. John Bigelow (New York, 1908), I, 216–17. See also Horatio Seymour to Tilden, Dec. 13, 1867, *ibid.*, I, 214–15; S. J. Tilden to R. C. Root (probably), Feb. 28, 1868, *ibid.*, I, 219–21. The last letter was mislabeled by Editor Bigelow. Internal evidence indicates clearly that it was from Tilden to Bigler.

[3] Francis P. Blair, Jr., to Col. James G. Broadhead, June 30, 1868, in McPherson, *Reconstruction*, pp. 380–1.

Democrats once again from Conservatives. A correspondent on Wall Street reported that the Democratic platform's partial espousal of the Pendleton Plan caused little concern on the Street, but the plank calling the Reconstruction Acts null and void roused grave anxiety.[4] Long before the convention an editorial in the Philadelphia *Public Ledger* called "a steady period of rest from agitation" the land's foremost need, and one in the Boston *Daily Advertiser* dreaded the resumption of the whole Reconstruction controversy and advocated the election of a Republican President as "the indispensable condition of the permanence of the newly established governments at the South. . . ."[5] Although Senate Conservatives, led by William P. Fessenden, had fought to delete Negro suffrage from the Reconstruction Act of March 1867, then yielded only to prevent the future of the South from falling into the hands of the incoming Fortieth Congress (far more radical than the Thirty-ninth), and though enough of them openly broke with the Radicals to acquit Andrew Johnson in the spring of 1868, they now regarded the Radical accomplishment of Negro suffrage and new governments for the Southern states as irreversible.[6]

Even some noteworthy Conservatives who had backed Johnson in 1866 agreed with this view. Manton Marble editorialized in the New York *World* that any attempt to undo Negro suffrage in the South would be disastrous.[7] Charles Francis Adams, who saw in the impeachment of Johnson a sentiment which would have effected the impeachment of his father in 1828 and his grandfather in 1799, came out for Grant and "peace."[8] Secretary of State Seward warned that a Democratic victory would "increase the lamentable political excite-

[4] Philadelphia *Public Ledger*, Aug. 6, 1868. For the Democratic platform stand on the Reconstruction Acts, see *Proceedings . . . Democratic Convention*, p. 60.
[5] Philadelphia *Public Ledger*, Jan. 21, 1868; Boston *Daily Advertiser*, Jan. 6, 1868.
[6] See Jellison, pp. 216–31; Rhodes, VI, 13–21, 29–30, 113, 144–52; Fessenden, II, 228–39; Adams Sherman Hill, "The Chicago Convention," *North American Review*, Vol. CVII (July 1868), pp. 167–86.
[7] Clemenceau, pp. 201–2.
[8] Charles Francis Adams Diary, Nov. 3, 6, 1868, Adams Papers, Reel 81; Charles Francis Adams, Jr., to Charles Francis Adams, April 4, 1868; C. F. Adams to C. F. Adams, Jr., April 8, 1868, *ibid.*, Reel 586.

ment which alone has delayed the restoration of the Union up to the present time."[9] And Judge Edwards Pierrepont, then a Grand Sachem of Tammany Hall, wrote: "I cannot conceive how any intelligent man, who does not wish the Rebels returned to power, the Nation's faith violated, its debt repudiated, its name dishonored, its prosperity destroyed, its patriots insulted, and the '*Lost Cause*' restored, can vote against Grant."[1]

Grant, then, became the embodiment of Conservative aspirations. His nomination promised the popular triumph of a Republican party committed to stabilizing the status quo, silencing agitation for further reforms, and returning to specie payments. Jay Cooke openly refused to make any contributions to the Republican campaign funds until he was certain that party Chairman William Claflin and Secretary W. E. Chandler were in accord with his views, then he contributed heavy subsidies to the friendly press. Hamilton Fish, A. T. Stewart, Edwards Pierrepont, Cornelius Vanderbilt, and William B. Astor opened a public campaign to advance Grant to the nomination late in 1867. Further, they advised the Republicans to restore the reconstructed states of the South before Election Day, thus presenting the Democrats with an accomplished fact and depriving them of the charge that the South was under military rule. These actions were capped by the simple, effective slogan which echoed the cry heard in commercial circles for two years: "Let us have peace."[2]

At the party convention held in the wake of Johnson's acquittal, Radicals were relegated to obscurity. Wade was deprived of even the vice-presidential nomination, which went to the innocuous Schuyler Colfax. The convention rejected a Union League appeal for Negro suffrage in all states and resolved instead to support only "equal suffrage to all loyal men of the South," while leaving the question of suffrage in the loyal states to "the people of those states." In ringing tones

---

9 Philadelphia *Public Ledger*, Nov. 2, 1868, financial page.
1 Edwards Pierrepont to Alex T. Stewart, Oct. 10, 1868, unidentified press clipping in A. A. Lawrence Papers, 1868.
2 Oberholtzer, II, 70–6; *Workingman's Advocate*, Feb. 1, 1868; William B. Hesseltine, *Ulysses S. Grant, Politician* (New York, 1935), pp. 99–103; Nevins, *Fish*, I, 100–2; Coleman, *Election of 1868*, pp. 16–17.

the platform denounced "repudiation" and called for payment of the national debt "not only according to the letter, but the spirit of the laws under which it was contracted." Greeley's *Tribune* rejoiced that the convention "was not impregnated with the financial theories of Pendleton," and the *New-York Times* described the proceedings as "the triumph of other purposes" than those of Thaddeus Stevens and as foreshadowing "a more generous and more judicious policy than that which he had favored."[3]

The election results, rejoiced *Hunt's Merchants' Magazine,* were "a triumph of the conservatism and honesty of our people."[4] In truth, they had marked the close of the brief but decisive dominance of radicalism in national political life. This was the case primarily because the victorious Republican party conceded the cardinal Radical principle: equality of all men before the law. Even the cringing formulations of the party platform on the question of Negro suffrage could not disguise the success of the Reconstruction Acts in carrying the nation across this Rubicon. Immediately after Election Day the Republicans drafted, passed, then ratified the Fifteenth Amendment with whirlwind speed. Although the Democrats mounted their customary ardent but futile opposition to this new amendment, they too soon granted formal recognition to the revolutionary changes the previous decade had wrought in the Negro's status. In the spring of 1871, Ohio's Democrats, guided by Vallandigham himself, announced their "New Departure," accepting the Thirteenth, Fourteenth, and Fifteenth amendments to the Constitution, and a year later this policy was enshrined as the official national line of the Democratic party. Nowhere was the reversal more abrupt than in New York. There, Democrats who had revoked the state's ratification of the Fifteenth Amendment in 1870, solemnly declared two years later "that equality of all citizens of whatever creed or race is one of the cardinal principles of Democ-

---

[3] *Proceedings of the National Union Republican Convention, Held at Chicago, May 20 and 21, 1868* (Chicago, 1868), pp. 65–9, 84, 118–31; New York *Daily Tribune,* May 21, 1868; obituary editorial on Stevens, *New-York Times,* Aug. 31, 1868.
[4] *Hunt's Merchants' Magazine and Commercial Review,* Vol. LII (Nov. 1868), p. 270.

racy."[5] Equality before the law and full voting rights for Negroes, North and South, were no longer matters of controversy in the mainstream of American political life. They were not (at least for the next three decades) the objectives of crusades to be fought, but institutions to be safeguarded.

On the other hand, the Conservatives had successfully placed the label "repudiation" on all efforts to redeem the bonds in greenbacks. The same lame-duck session of the Fortieth Congress that sent the Fifteenth Amendment to the states also passed by overwhelming vote a bill pledging the redemption of the 5-20's in coin and the gold redemption of legal tender notes "at the earliest practicable period." Although President Johnson pocket vetoed the bill, another measure containing these provisions was enacted and signed into law by President Grant as the Public Credit Act of March 1869.[6] The passage of the original bill by the very congressmen who had frustrated McCulloch's contraction policies revealed that the Conservative defense of the bonds and banks had acquired the sanction of party discipline, and that the views of their opponents were now generally regarded in Republican circles as not simply unsound, but immoral and unpatriotic.

John Lothrop Motley, the famed historian of the Dutch Republic, wove the various strands of the emerging official Republican ideology into a dazzling rhetorical fabric. He thunderously affirmed: "We are a nation. We are not a confederacy," for the central government "deals with every individual of us directly within its carefully limited sphere." This government, expressing the "will of the American people," may not only crush insurrection, but suppress "the re-establishment of something much resembling slavery by means of vagrant laws and the denial to freedmen of civil rights, and the repudiation of the national debt by the assistance of those by whose rebellion it has been created." Having placed equal

---

[5] James K. McGuire, ed., *Democratic Party of the State of New York* (New York, 1905), I, 401–4, 416. On Ohio origins of New Departure, see Roseboom, pp. 469–76.

[6] McPherson, *Reconstruction*, pp. 395–7, 412–13. See Sharkey, pp. 124–9, and Unger, *Greenback Era*, pp. 93–4, 409, for analyses of the vote on the Public Credit Act.

rights and gold redemption of the 5-20's on the same moral plane, Motley proceeded to make popular honesty the moral foundation of the Republic and denunciation of greenbackism the criterion of popular honesty. The bond-holders, he charged, were not a "bloated aristocracy," but even if they were, that fact would not justify despoiling them. "Let us," Motley concluded, "get rid of this irredeemable paper currency, which converts us all, whether we like it or not, into a nest of gamblers. . . ."[7]

THE STALWARTS

In 1866 the Radicals had leapt into the saddle of the Republican party because they alone had a clear and effective program which could unify their party and secure the "fruits of victory" for the triumphant Union. Two years later they slid down again because they had no coherent program at all to deal with the problems then beginning to dominate public discussion. Nationally, their hegemony dated from the passage of the Civil Rights Act over the veto of President Johnson in April 1866 to the acquittal of Johnson in May 1868. The *New-York Times* had been correct in its judgment that the convention which nominated Grant represented "the triumph of other purposes" than those of Stevens.[8]

On the other hand, any Conservative who believed the Republican party had been safely piloted into his port was in for cruel disillusionment. Congress kept him in suspense down to the last day of its July 1868 session. Not only did the eight-hour law pass, but it seemed to James A. Garfield "as if the wild devil of repudiation, & crazy financiering had broken loose—Butler came within an ace of carrying the whole gang of carpet baggers at his heels today, into a new impeachment movement—Thank the Lord, we adjourn on Monday."[9]

The focal point of Garfield's concern was a funding bill introduced by Senator John Sherman essentially as a means of

---

[7] John Lothrop Motley, *Four Questions for the People, At the Presidential Election* (Boston, 1868). (Quotations are on pp. 9–10, 24, 30, 53, 66.)

[8] See above, p. 354.

[9] James A. Garfield to Edward A. Atkinson, July 24, 1868, Atkinson Papers, Box 2.

spelling out in practice the meaning of his party's pledges to redeem the debt in gold, while funding it at lower rates of interest. Sherman set out to satisfy manufacturers who opposed further contraction and longed for lower interest rates, while in the same gesture he buried the ghost of "repudiation." Aided by Robert Schenck in the House, he executed a brilliant bit of legislative legerdemain, by which the government was authorized to issue new thirty-year bonds at 4.5 per cent interest and forty-year bonds at 4 per cent, with interest and principal payable in gold and exempt from all taxes but the income tax. Holders of 5-20's were offered the options of exchanging their bonds for the new issues or redeeming them immediately in greenbacks, and a sinking fund was established for payment of interest and the gradual redemption of the national debt as a whole.[1] "The drift of opinion," Sherman later explained, "was in favor of resumption without contraction, and funding at low rates of interest on a coin basis." He regarded as "settled" both the proposition "that no further contraction of the currency should occur," and that "no question would be made as to the payment of the bonds in coin."[2]

Because President Johnson subjected the bill to a pocket veto, Sherman's funding bill has largely escaped the attention of historians. Its significance was twofold. First, the plan it represented became the monetary policy of the Grant administration down to the depression, or more precisely, until the veto of the Inflation Act of 1874. In 1870, virtually the same bill, again sponsored by Sherman, became law.[3] In the meantime, Secretary of the Treasury George Boutwell failed to resume McCulloch's contraction policy, but persisted in reissuing greenbacks, which came into the Treasury in exchange for bonds. Both the administration and leading congressional Republicans, furthermore, expanded the circulation of national banknotes permitted in the West, thus adding further to the nation's bouyant currency supply. On the very eve of the election of 1872, the Treasury Department responded to a plea

---

[1] *Congressional Globe,* 40th Cong., 2d Sess., 4466, 4497–9 (July 25, 1868).

[2] John Sherman, *Recollections of Forty Years in the House, Senate, and Cabinet* (New York, 1895), I, 440–1.

[3] Richardson, X, 380.

from Western manufacturers by reissuing $4 million worth of legal tender notes which had accumulated in its reserves.[4] The Republican party, in other words, had dubbed greenbacks dishonest, then kept them in circulation.

Boutwell's action was denounced by Godkin as "an act of the most monstrous recklessness and abuse of authority," while labor reformers like Cameron and Sylvis persistently labeled both the administration's funding policy and its consistent support to national banks as proof of its domination by capitalists and bond-holders.[5] Manufacturers and farmers throughout the land, on the other hand, were generally satisfied with this very pragmatic approach to the currency, and the booming prosperity muted even the grumblings of the merchant community.[6] The dimensions of this achievement were recognized by both Henry Raymond and Thaddeus Stevens at the time Sherman's bill passed Congress in 1868. Raymond's New-York Times praised the measure for lowering the interest rate with the consent of the bond-holders and offering them "a way of escape from the controversies which affect the value of the five-twenties. . . ."[7] Stevens concurred that the bill had put controversies regarding the bonds at an end, especially since it lent verbal substantiation to his position that the 5-20's were redeemable in greenbacks.[8]

The second noteworthy point about Sheman's bill is that it was the handiwork of a new grouping of party leaders. Sherman's policy gave both the Radicals and the Conservatives only *verbal* concessions. Stevens had been satisfied with the inference that his judgment (and his memory) had been correct, but holders of the bonds were invited to escape the implications of that judgment by trading them in at par for new bonds redeemable in gold. Similarly, the famed Public Credit Act of 1869 gave the Conservatives the *promise* of

---

[4] Unger, *Greenback Era*, pp. 169–72; *Nation*, Vol. XV (Oct. 24, 1872), p. 258; *ibid.*, Vol. XV (Nov. 7, 1872), pp. 290–1.

[5] *Nation*, Vol. XV (Nov. 14, 1872), pp. 308–10; *Workingman's Advocate*, Dec. 7, 1867; Sylvis, pp. 237–8.

[6] Unger, *Greenback Era*, pp. 169–72; J. Edgar Thompson to John Covode, Jan. 30, 1868, Covode Papers, Box 1.

[7] Editorial, *New-York Times*, July 30, 1868.

[8] Letter of Thaddeus Stevens in Philadelphia *Public Ledger*, July 31, 1868.

resumption of specie payments for legal tender notes. But fulfillment of that promise was withheld for almost another decade.

In other words, the dissipation of the Radical crusade had not meant the triumph of the Conservatives, but the emergence of a new leadership bloc capable of dealing with the social and political realities of the day, rather than with outmoded ideologies. These Stalwarts (as they soon became known) had but one central concern, the perpetuation of their party in office. To that end they offered concessions to any social group that represented a significant body of votes. The label "Radical" was often applied to them, especially by Democrats, but the term was clearly anachronistic. True, their party had committed itself irrevocably to many of the works of radicalism—among them Negro rights, the new Southern regimes, the tariff, the plentiful currency, but these were now institutions to be defended, not causes to be won. The now-traditional slogans they represented were easily blended with the new demands of the business community, of the party's financial backers, and at times, of labor, by men who hankered after no new world but were simply hanging on. In this sense American politics were resuming a normal condition.

Some Stalwarts had once been ardent Radicals, like Butler, Morton, and Schenck, but no common dream linked them any longer to other former Radicals, such as Godkin and practically the whole Bird Club, who daily drifted further away from them. Some, like Sherman and Blaine, rose from the old Republican center—Jay Cooke's wing of the party. A third type embraced former Democratic leaders such as Cameron and Logan who were adept at party management and swimming with any tide. A fourth type, typified by Roscoe Conkling, represented young strivers who had played virtually no part in the formative struggles of their party. Impressively, onetime Democrats tended to eclipse former Whigs among the party notables, and even to drive many of the latter into the opposition.[9]

Radical intellectuals were readily alienated from the Stalwarts on two counts. First, they embodied the total eclipse of

[9] Evarts B. Greene, "Some Aspects of Politics in the Middle West, 1860–1872," pp. 60–76.

political principles (Radical, Conservative, old-line Democrat, or any other) by pure careerism. The danger of the hour, wrote "Warrington" Robinson time and again, was the ascendancy of "personalism." Since the great issues were settled and the government was no longer challenged by tasks of saving or destroying social institutions, it had degenerated into a theater for individual advancement. Politics, Robinson grieved, was no longer the art of saving the Union or abolishing slavery or establishing equality, or even of dissolving the Union and saving slavery, but solely the art of manipulating power for the sake of the politician and his retainers. This "worst—I might almost say the only vicious—principle of our present affairs,—the tendency toward personal government, instead of a government of politics," found for Robinson its supreme manifestation in Benjamin F. Butler.[1] But Butler was by no means its only representative. "Tammanyism," as manifested in the Tweed Ring, was but the same phenomenon under the Democratic banner, and President Grant had "not the slightest comprehension of political government. His administration is a personal one."[2]

Secondly, in contrast to Godkin, who was shocked by the "politics of class feeling" that was undermining the Radical vision of America, the new "personalists" reveled in such politics and were its expert manipulators. The astute maneuvers by which they had extricated themselves from the rhetorical conflict between the "people's money" and "honest money" exemplified this talent. The same approach was taken by the Stalwarts toward the labor question as a whole. Where the labor reform cause represented votes, the Stalwarts attached themselves to it with gusto. Where such a course promised to alienate more votes than it attracted, labor reform was spurned.

THE GENERAL AND THE GENTLEMAN

Ben Butler, called by Robinson the "most complete representative" of the corruption and degeneration of the Republi-

---

[1] Robinson, Pen-Portraits, p. 439; "Warrington," "General Butler's Campaign in Massachusetts," Atlantic Monthly, Vol. XXVIII (Dec. 1871), pp. 742–50.
[2] Robinson, Pen-Portraits, pp. 480–1.

can party,[3] practiced the arts of personalism and class politics with such finesse that he consistently routed efforts to dislodge him. Easily elected in 1866 to the congressional seat formerly occupied by the Radical shoe manufacturer John B. Alley, Butler quickly won the hearts of the numerous shoe, textile, and other workers of the Fifth Congressional District (Essex County) through his persistent championing of legislative reduction of the hours of labor, those of local manufacturers by his solicitude for their needs, and those of Radicals throughout the state because of his vigorous insistence on Negro rights. By 1868 the infirmities of age forced Thaddeus Stevens to surrender much of the leadership of his party in Congress to younger and more vigorous colleagues, and as the trial of Andrew Johnson especially revealed, none was more vigorous than Butler. By the summer of 1868 he was the recipient of daily correspondence from every corner of the nation, asking his intercession for everything from pensions through civil service employment to general legislation. Pleas even came to him for jobs on the Union Pacific Railroad and for his personal investment in diverse mining and manufacturing ventures.[4]

The Grant nomination and the national party platform of 1868, however, proved embarrassing to Butler, first because he had aspired to the Presidency, and secondly because he had prominently identified himself with Stevens's proposal to issue greenbacks to pay off the national debt. Despite warnings from admirers to let the currency question "rest awhile," Butler opened his own campaign for re-election with a vigorous speech at Gloucester identifying his plan for greenback redemption of the bonds as the decisive issue of his program.[5] The discrepancy between his position and the national platform of his party provided local Conservatives a splendid opportunity to try to dislodge the general. The move was

---

[3] *Ibid.*, p. 447.
[4] Benjamin F. Butler, *Butler's Book* (Boston, 1892), pp. 919–21; Butler Papers, *passim,* esp. Box 56.
[5] George Wilkes to Benjamin F. Butler, Aug. 11, 1868; William B. Pike to Butler, Aug. 10, 1868; D. D. Cone to Butler, Aug. 8, 1868; Charles Winslow to Butler, Sept. 17, 1868; Gilman H. Tucker to Butler, Sept. 25, 1868, Butler Papers, Box 56; Louis T. Merrill, *General Benjamin F. Butler and the Campaign of 1868* (Chicago, 1939), pp. 208–14.

initiated by Johnson supporters, among whom the key figure was Attorney General William Evarts, who had defended the President during his Senate trial and there developed a dread of Butler's rising unrestrained to prominence in the Republican party, surrounded by fawning "pseudo representatives from the South."[6] Their overtures struck a responsive chord among those merchants and textile mill directors of Essex County who (Charles Francis Adams noted) "utterly disapproved" of the "extravagant course of Congress" but could think of "no mode of meeting it with any adequate check."[7]

Johnson Conservatives, of course, could not dream of carrying Essex County. They needed a champion from outside their own ranks, and they found him in Richard H. Dana, Jr., who had been associated with Evarts since February in preparing the government's case against Jefferson Davis for presentation to a Richmond grand jury. This former Free Soiler, famed for his novel *Two Years Before the Mast*, had publicly opposed Johnson's policy toward the South. On the other hand, he had never associated himself with the Radicals or with the Democracy, which, wrote Robinson, "to his mind is synonymous with insubordination and license."[8] A doctrinaire free-trader, Dana had opposed all legislation to reduce hours of labor when he served in the state House.[9] Good family, good credentials, outspoken hostility toward the impeachment of the President—all these assets made Dana attractive to the Conservatives of Essex County. And with the Republican financial plank he was to impale Butler.

The state Republican Convention at Worcester early in September dealt Butler a heavy blow. His candidate for the gubernatorial nomination, Dr. George B. Loring, was handily defeated by William Claflin. Worse yet for Butler, Edward Atkinson, who had long since agreed with James A. Garfield to utilize the Presidential campaign to educate the public in

6 Charles Francis Adams Diary, Sept. 11, 1868, Adams Papers, Reel 81; F. J. Child to C. F. Adams, July 19, 1868, *ibid.*, Reel 586.
7 C. F. Adams Diary, July 17, 1868, Adams Papers, Reel 81.
8 William M. Evarts and Richard H. Dana, Jr., to Henry Stanberry, Feb. 26, 1868, Dana Papers; Robinson, *Pen-Portraits*, p. 465.
9 *Ibid.*, pp. 464–6; Samuel Shapiro, "'Aristocracy, Mud, and Vituperation': The Butler-Dana Campaign in Essex County in 1868," *New England Quarterly*, Vol. XXXI (Sept. 1958), p. 347.

"sound finances," delivered a learned address on the subject of currency and the bonds. Not only did Atkinson sweep the convention off its feet, he received an enthusiastic response from businessmen and economists throughout the land, and the Republican National Committee hastened to publish the speech as a campaign pamphlet.[1] Butler saved himself from total rout only by entering the hall in the midst of an oration by Dana, ascending the rostrum to the applause of his claque, and forcing Dana to yield the platform to him. There Butler pledged his allegiance to the party's financial platform, called himself a bond-holder, and appealed for party unity to defeat the traitorous Democrats. As the convention roared its approval, he stepped down to permit Dana pathetically to finish his interrupted speech.[2]

In his own bailiwick at the end of the month, Butler's machine rolled up a vote of 175 to 4 for his renomination. From one side of his mouth the congressman denounced swindling bond-holders for instigating an opposition against him, and from the other he vowed that no conflict existed between his own financial views and those of the national party platform. Already, however, Dana's backers had issued a call for a rival "Republican" district convention, free of the tyranny of Butler's cohorts. Meeting in Salem on October 5, they tendered Dana their nomination.[3]

Pledges of support flowed to Dana from the National City Bank of Lynn and the Third National Bank of Springfield, from Francis Peabody and Amos A. Lawrence. Former Governor Hawley of Connecticut lent aid through his Hartford *Courant*, William Schouler through the Lowell *Courier*, and Samuel Bowles through the Springfield *Republican*.[4] From

[1] James A. Garfield to Edward A. Atkinson, May 25, 1868; Garfield to Atkinson, Aug. 4, 1868; C. Curry to Atkinson, Sept. 11, 1868; William Whiting to Atkinson, Sept. 10, 1868; Francis Lieber to Atkinson, Sept. 10, 1868; Amasa Walker to Atkinson, Sept. 11, 1868, Atkinson Papers, Box 2.

[2] Shapiro, p. 342; Merrill, *Butler and 1868*, pp. 217–18.

[3] Shapiro, p. 343; Merrill, *Butler and 1868*, pp. 218–19.

[4] B. H. Franch to Richard H. Dana, Jr., Oct. 6, 1868; George Walker to Dana, Oct. 6, 1868; Francis Peabody to Dana, Oct. 6, 1868; Amos A. Lawrence to Dana, Oct. 7, 1868; William Schouler to Dana, Oct. 13, 1868; J. R. Hawley to Dana, Sept. 28, 1868; George Derby to Dana, Oct. 9, 1868, Dana Papers; Merriam, II, 91–7.

many parts of the nation, and even from Paris, came messages of praise, all concurring in the judgment of a correspondent from Iowa that Butler's "financial policy will never do in this Country so long as we pretend to observe the old statute, 'Thou Shalt Not Steal.' "[5]

But Dana did not rely on expressions of sympathy to win his struggle. He used Edward Atkinson as his confidant on financial and organizational questions, and from Washington he obtained the assistance of Evarts and Samuel Ward, the famous King of the Lobby.[6] In the interests of the campaign to restore "sober & respectable politics," Evarts suppressed until after the elections the news that he and Dana had concluded to drop the prosecution of Jefferson Davis.[7] To sully Butler's war hero image the Dana men brought Generals George H. Gordon and Hugh J. Kilpatrick to Essex County, where they charged Butler with having traded with the enemy.[8] Information was lifted from classified documents in War Department files by Evarts himself (among others) and telegraphed customarily from Ward to Atkinson for publication in the Fifth District.[9] It is probable, in fact, that Grant was cooperating in this effort.[1]

Butler used three formidable weapons to frustrate his foes. The first was his mastery of local party machinery. Publicly, he offered a reward of $500 for information leading to the detection of any patronage employee acting against him.

---

[5] Dawes Putnam to Edward A. Atkinson, Oct. 3, 1868, Atkinson Papers, Box 2. See also James Connor (?) to Dana, Oct. 7, 1868; Dr. James C. Ayer to Dana, Oct. 7, 1868; William Endicott to Dana, Oct. 21, 1868, Dana Papers.

[6] Edward A. Atkinson to Dana, Oct. 7, 1868, Dana Papers; Samuel Ward to Atkinson, Oct. 6, 1868, Atkinson Papers, Box 2; Geo. B. Cowlam to Benjamin F. Butler, Oct. 10, 1868, Butler Papers, Box 56.

[7] William M. Evarts to Andrew Johnson, Oct. 9, 1868 (copy in Dana Papers); Evarts to Dana, Sept. 30, 1868; Evarts to Dana, Oct. 17, 1868, Dana Papers.

[8] James A. Garfield to Edward A. Atkinson, Oct. 17, 1868; George H. Gordon to Atkinson, Oct. 6, 1868, Atkinson Papers, Box 2; "Anti-Grant Radical" to Benjamin F. Butler, Oct. 6, 1868, Butler Papers, Box 56; Merrill, *Butler and 1868*, p. 223.

[9] H. P. Curtis to Edward A. Atkinson, Oct. 12, 1868; T. S. Lang to Atkinson, Oct. 14, 1868; William Evarts to Atkinson, Oct. 17, 1868, Atkinson Papers, Box 2; George B. Cowlam to Benjamin F. Butler, Oct. 19, 1868, Butler Papers, Box 56.

[1] Merrill, *Butler and 1868*, pp. 223–6.

From the start he was privy to the transmission of War Department data from Ward to Atkinson, for the telegraph operator who dispatched the messages was Butler's spy—at least until the company became suspicious and dismissed the man in mid-October.[2]

A second and greater weapon was the fact that Butler was the regular nominee of the Republican party. The prestige accorded him by public invitations from the Republicans of New York and Pennsylvania to speak in their behalf drew to him Republican voters who thoroughly disagreed with his greenbackism—that is, with his currency stand before he muddied it so thoroughly no man could say with certainty what it was. Efforts of Bowles, Atkinson, and other Dana supporters to lure Sumner, Wilson, Dawes, and Claflin into statements hostile to Butler were consistently met with silence. Claflin evaded Dana's angry charge that he had opposed General Kilpatrick's tour of the district.[3] The National Committee of the party ultimately offered Butler outside speakers to aid his campaign (though too late to make any difference) and Chairman Chandler wrote the congressman: "I differ from you financially, but you have always been my personal friend, and I heartily wish you that success which you are about to achieve, the failure of which would cause a howl of delight among the Rebels of the South, which gratification we cannot afford to give them."[4]

Nor was the Republican intelligentsia unanimous in support of Dana. Horace Greeley pursued his usual policy of wavering. Early in October he asked David A. Wells to use his influence with Atkinson "to let Butler alone—on the ground that Sherman & Morton stood on the same platform, & we

[2] Richard H. Dana, Jr., to Amos A. Lawrence, Oct. 9, 1868, Dana Papers; Geo. B. Cowlam to Benjamin F. Butler, Oct. 10, 1868; Cowlam to Butler, Oct. 19, 1868, Butler Papers, Box 56.
[3] Galusha Grow to Benjamin F. Butler, Aug. 6, 1868; James Terwilliger to Butler, Sept. 4, 1868; Henry C. Bowen to Butler, Oct. 14, 1868, Butler Papers, Box 56; Merriam, II, 93; John L. King to Edward A. Atkinson, Oct. 26, 1868, Atkinson Papers, Box 2: telegrams: Dana to William Claflin, and Claflin to Dana, Nov. 2, 1868, Dana Papers.
[4] W. E. Chandler to Benjamin F. Butler, Oct. 21, 1868; J. K. Herbert to Butler, Oct. 22, 1868, Butler Papers, Box 56.

could not afford to make war on them also."[5] Then, at the urging of his paper's largest stockholder, Dr. James C. Ayer, a millionaire manufacturer of patent medicines from Lowell, Greeley privately encouraged Dana's efforts, while his paper maintained editorial silence.[6] William S. Robinson and George William Curtis, who within three years were to stand at the very forefront of anti-Butler drives, both declined to enter the lists on Dana's behalf.[7]

The third and greatest of Butler's weapons was the solid support of the working classes on Election Day. Dana's desperate efforts to woo the toilers of Lynn by assuring them that when he was a young man before the mast scrubbing filthy hides, he was, "fellow-citizens . . . as dirty as any of you," only lent themselves to Butler's savage ridicule.[8] When the votes were counted, Butler was found to have carried 66 per cent, while Otis P. Lord, a die-hard Democrat of the proslavery stripe, drew a loyal 25 per cent. Poor Dana had garnered only 9 per cent of the ballots cast for the office. Samuel Shapiro's study of this campaign revealed that Dana's vote did go as high as 27 per cent in the little farming community of Lynnfield, but in Lynn he scarcely obtained 6 per cent of the votes. The six wards of Salem showed a steady decline in the proportion of votes cast for Dana, together with their per capita valuations, so that in the two wealthiest wards he won 16 per cent of the votes, while the two poorest gave him 9 and 5 per cent.[9]

Despite Butler's evasiveness on the currency question during the campaign, he was hailed as a conquering hero by doctrinaire Greenbackers of the National Labor Union. Moses Field and Alexander Campbell wrote congratulatory letters calling him the man of the future. Horace H. Day, who was

---

[5] David A. Wells to Edward A. Atkinson, Oct. 4, 1868, Atkinson Papers, Box 2.

[6] James C. Ayer to Richard H. Dana, Oct. 7, 1868; Ayer to Dana, Oct. 22, 1868, Dana Papers. On Ayer see *Appleton's Cyclopaedia of American Biography* (New York, 1900), I, 123. (Hereafter cited as *App. Cyc. Bio.*)

[7] Robinson, *Pen-Portraits*, p. 441; George W. Curtis to Richard H. Dana, Jr., Oct. 24, 1868, Dana Papers.

[8] *Butler's Book*, p. 922.

[9] Shapiro, pp. 353, 358–9.

then aspiring to the leadership of the N.L.U., stopped by Butler's home to help the congressman prepare an article on the money question for publication in the New York *Herald*, and proposed that he utilize the N.L.U. and the Fenians to secure "the position of Leader of House Reps. on the coming in of Congress."[1]

The point should be noted with great care, however, that the relationship of the working classes and labor reformers to Butler at this time was solely one of voting support. Butler's managers were professionals and career politicians. "He is not, like one of the *sans-culottes* of Paris, ready to lead a mob of prostitutes and ruffians to the sacking of rich men's houses," "Warrington" accurately warned the workers, "but (as he says) the owner of a major part of the stock in one corporation and of part of another, and an enemy of strikes. . . ."[2] Neither Butler nor his entourage were labor reformers. The fact becomes crystal clear when his campaign is contrasted with the futile efforts of Samuel F. Cary in Cincinnati and Andrew Burtt in Pittsburgh to win congressional seats in 1868. While neither Cary nor Burtt was a worker, their platforms were taken straight from the N.L.U. and their electoral efforts were managed by the trades assemblies of their respective cities.[3] They were labor candidates. Butler was not.

In the minds of Massachusetts's propertied classes, therefore, Butler conjured up the image of the Caesar—the wealthy demagogue who seized power by catering to the ignorance and vice of the rabble. The condolences which flooded Dana's desk echoed and reechoed the lament of one Boston gentleman that a few more such struggles would lead to "the result in all previous despotisms—that cultivated and honest men would consider themselves as having no part nor lot in the Country, in fact, as being in the position of exiles."[4] Joseph R. Hawley, who had volunteered consistent aid to Dana's cam-

---

1 Moses Field to Benjamin F. Butler, Nov. 19, 1868; Alexander Campbell to Butler, Nov. 25, 1868; Campbell to Butler, Nov. 28, 1868; Horace H. Day to Butler, Nov. 10, 1868, Butler Papers, Box 56.
2 Robinson, *Pen-Portraits*, p. 443.
3 See below, pp. 389–94.
4 Francis E. Parker to Richard H. Dana, Jr., Nov. 9, 1868. See also James Lawrence to Dana, Nov. 5, 1868; J. R. Hawley to Dana, Nov. 13, 1868; William M. Evarts to Dana, Nov. 9, 1868, Dana Papers.

paign while he was touring the East for Grant and Colfax, charged the Radicals with having demoralized Massachusetts politics, since "F. W. Bird, W. S. Robinson, Geo. H. Monroe—many staunch radicals are more than half poisoned by Butler." He concluded sorrowfully: "Eastern Massachusetts is more thoroughly debauched on the great financial—which is the great *moral*—question of the day than any other Republican region."[5]

THE ROAD TO REFORM

Radicalism had been tried and found wanting: by labor reformers because the support it provided working-class needs was at best ambivalent, by manufacturers because it failed to provide an adequate barrier to working-class pretensions, and by professionals and intellectuals because its practical fruits had turned out to be not a harmonious republic of virtue, but a regime of self-perpetuating careerists who pandered public vice to the point of jeopardizing the foundation of social order—property. In this context the greenback legacy of radicalism assumed for its opponents the moralistic coloring which made it symbolic of all their fears. Popular ignorance of the intricacies of finance, they believed, made it easy for scheming office-seekers to harvest votes with promises of monetary measures that would "repudiate" the debt, "dishonor" the public credit, and undermine the value of property, the bonds themselves. Aware that the security of property rights lies ultimately in the respect accorded them by community sentiment, the propertied and professional classes easily equated "honor" or "public virtue" with unequivocal deference to property. But where could "honest men" be found, and how could they be rallied against the Caesaristic threat?

In Massachusetts they were mobilized when Butler stepped outside his congressional district to strike for the governor's chair. The cohesive leadership of the Bird Club having disintegrated, the state's Republicans found themselves by 1869 divided between two conflicting political machines, one led by Butler, and the other by Henry L. Dawes and George F. Hoar; while Senator Wilson tried to play the honest

---

[5] J. R. Hawley to Richard H. Dana, Jr., Nov. 13, 1868, Dana Papers.

broker between them, and Sumner found himself each day more isolated from the practical manipulations of party power. Ugly disputes over liquor control sundered the party's ranks, while the waxing might of the labor movement drew consistently more of its attention. A petition by the Knights of St. Crispin asking the legislature for incorporation roused an anguished protest from shoe manufacturers, who feared both the competition of proposed Crispin-operated cooperative shoe factories and the augmented power to enforce trade rules which incorporation suggested. The Senate defeated the proposal 5 to 22, and thereby provoked the fury of the Crispins, who quickly made use of the machinery of the N.L.U. to launch an Independent party, with a large slate of legislative candidates. Edwin M. Chamberlain, the prosperous steward of an elite club and a post commander of the Grand Army of the Republic, was named its candidate for governor. Anxious Republicans in the legislature exhumed and hastily enacted a bill to establish a bureau of statistics of labor, which had been proposed by Ira Steward's Eight Hour League; Governor Claflin staffed the bureau with men of the league's choice, and the party commissioned Steward's colleague Edward Rogers to polemicize against the Independents.[6]

"Verily, these high officials, or would be officials, are showing an unwonted aptness in applying themselves to the labor question," quipped the *American Workman,* but its editors were unsure whether the cause of labor would "reap some substantial gain or gilded and delusive pledges."[7] The 13,500 votes cast for Chamberlain brought the Republican margin of victory down to 8,000 votes out of some 138,000 cast, while 12 Labor Reform nominees won seats in the lower house. This show of strength inspired Wendell Phillips to merge the forces of labor reform, the new Prohibitory party,

---

[6] Robinson, *Pen-Portraits,* pp. 339–41; Hoar, I, 192–253; Samuel Bowles to Henry L. Dawes, April 30, 1869, Dawes Papers, Box 19; Emory Washburn to A. H. Bullock, Aug. 15, 1869, Bullock Papers; Hall, "Gentle Craft," pp. 336–8; biographical sketch of E. M. Chamberlain, *Workingman's Advocate,* March 7, 1874; *Mass. BLS, 1873,* pp. 5–9; Rogers, "Auto-Biography," 16:10–11; Rogers, *Is It Expedient to Form a Political Party in the Interest of Labor?* (Chelsea, Mass., 1869).

[7] *American Workman,* Oct. 2, 1869.

and the women's suffrage movement behind himself as candidate for governor. Although Phillips polled 21,900 votes (14.5 per cent as compared to Chamberlain's 10 per cent), it became evident to some observers that he was engaged in something more than a campaign for the governor's chair. The cutting edge of his oratory was always directed against Claflin, Bird, Wilson, and other Republican leaders. Time and again he implied broadly that he was paving the way for someone else who was to be "judge and executioner" of the Republican party.[8]

The state needed to wait but a year to discover for whom Phillips had played John the Baptist. In the months preceding the 1871 Republican Nominating Convention at Worcester, Phillips rallied his labor reformers, prohibitionists, and suffragettes to enter Republican ward caucuses and there support delegates pledged to Butler for governor. Through their efforts, Milford, Haverhill, Marlborough, and other industrial towns augmented the secure power of Butler's Essex County machine. This threat revitalized the Bird Club and brought Wilson, Claflin, Sumner, and Dawes all into public opposition to the general. They installed George F. Hoar as chairman of the convention and the general's arch-foe, Judge E. Rockwood Hoar, as head of the vital Credentials Committee. When that committee threw out the claim of pro-Butler delegates from Boston, all other candidates but William B. Washburn withdrew from the scene in advance of the balloting, and Chairman Hoar used a hundred policemen to control the proceedings. Butler's fate was sealed. Washburn was nominated by a vote of 643 to 464.[9]

Godkin drew a deep sigh of relief. "No reflecting man," he wrote, will deny that Butler's effort represented "the organization, prematurely and under false colors, but still the organization of such a *commune* as America would now supply," and

---

[8] *Tribune Almanac and Political Register, 1871*, p. 49; Austin, pp. 252–63; Sherwin, p. 579; Robinson, *Pen-Portraits*, pp. 130–1, 441–5; [E. L. Godkin], "Lessons of the Butler Canvass," *Nation*, Vol. XIII (Oct. 5, 1871), p. 221.

[9] Robinson, "Butler's Campaign," 742–50; Robinson, *Pen-Portraits*, pp. 131–4; *Nation*, Vol. XIII (Oct. 5, 1871), p. 217; *ibid.*, Vol. XIII (September 28, 1871), p. 202; Hoar, I, 347–9.

few "will not allow that it came dangerously near to success." He suggested that this narrow escape was but the prelude of still worse threats to come if politics were not thoroughly reformed. Voting at the Worcester convention revealed "a clean-drawn struggle between the manufacturing and other operatives of the State, in combination with the Sentimental reformers of the Phillips school, on the one side, and the more well-to-do and observing classes, aided by the old New England yeomanry, which, up to this time, has constituted the moral backbone of Massachusetts politics, upon the other."[1]

This judgment was seconded by Charles Francis Adams, Jr., a few months later. But Adams stressed the point that the rapid industrial development of the state, which he attributed to tariff protection, and the steady exodus of farming population to more promising Western regions, were converting Massachusetts from a society of town-meeting democracy, well exercised in moral self-restraint, into one dominated by factory cities teeming with "inarticulate discontent." Though great reformers had always arisen from classes with a propertied status, whose education and reflection permitted them to discern the obstacles to human progress, power in the state was shifting into the hands of those who had no such stake in society. In fact, Adams continued, 42 per cent of the state's voters paid no tax but the poll tax. Such an electorate was easily deluded by labor reformers into calling for reform legislation, which politicians happily enacted while permitting those opposed to such acts to violate them with impunity. Such behavior might, for the nonce, give everyone "all that he desires," but it eroded popular respect for the rule of law. Hence the attempt to promote the interests of labor through political agitation had to be denounced as "a dangerous error," while efforts were made through the promotion of profit-sharing and savings banks for the poor to convert Massachusetts into "one great voluntary industrial co-partnership."[2]

The Stalwarts drew a different moral from the Butler canvass, for it provided them further evidence of the strength of the labor vote. Bureaus of labor statistics were hastened

[1] Godkin, "Lessons of the Butler Canvass," pp. 221–2.
[2] [Charles F. Adams, Jr.], "The Butler Canvass," *North American Review,* Vol. CXIV (Jan. 1872), pp. 147–70.

into existence by the legislatures of Connecticut and Pennsylvania, and though the former soon expired from neglect, that of Pennsylvania was placed under the direction of Thomas C. MacDowell, who quickly became Governor John W. Geary's spokesman within the Labor Reform party of that state.[3] The success of this formula inspired Congress to consider a bill creating a federal commission to study the wages and hours of labor and the division of profits between labor and capital. It was introduced by none other than George F. Hoar. Warm support was provided by Dawes, by W. D. Kelley, and by new Republican Representatives such as John P. C. Shanks of Indiana and Legrand W. Perce of Mississippi. Passed in the House by the margin of 135 to 36, the bill was managed unenthusiastically in the Senate by Frederick A. Sawyer of South Carolina, became bogged down in partisan debates over tariffs and taxation, and was finally defeated 17 to 37.[4]

The most impressive aspect of the career of Hoar's bill was the nature of the debate in the House. Gone were the old ideological lines, with scarcely a shadow remaining save an occasional Democratic warning against government bureaus. Advocates of the measure considered it just because the working people desired it and timely because the rapid urbanization of the nation made the subject of the proposed commission's investigation the great question of the future. Hoar explicitly repudiated the doctrine that legislation cannot improve working conditions, and used the experience of his own state to prove his point. Most striking—should one say astonishing?—was the fact that Hoar, Kelley, and New York's S. S. Cox identified their positions with that of the International. Hoar had the clerk read the House a resolution of the I.W.A. calling for the collection of labor statistics to *support* his argument for passage of the bill. More than that: he praised the valor of the Paris Communards, told Congress it had "not heard their side of the story," and called theirs a cause "entitled to the respect of Americans everywhere." These words

---

[3] *Ohio BLS, 1878*, pp. 35–7; *Pa. BLS, 1872/1873*, xiv, 332.
[4] *Congressional Globe*, 42d Cong., 1st Sess., 561 (April 10, 1871); *ibid.*, 42d Cong., 2d Sess., 102–5, 217–28, 251–8, 3813, 3868 (Dec. 13, 19, 20, 1871, May 24, 25, 1872); McPherson, *1872*, pp. 71–2.

were not from Wendell Phillips's famous speech to the 1871 Massachusetts Labor Reform Convention, but from George Frisbee Hoar on the floor of Congress.[5]

With a Presidential election pending, the Republicans in Congress acted as if they could not be too generous to labor. Through the efforts of Senator Cole a comprehensive statute designed to protect merchant seamen against swindling keepers of boardinghouses, abusive captains, poor food rations, and abandonment in foreign ports became law.[6] A bill fathered by Dawes to reimburse federal employees for pay lost through misapplication of the 1868 Eight Hour Law readily passed both houses and served to supplement President Grant's enforcement proclamation.[7] These actions caused the *Nation* to protest that the government had thrown "its weight into the scale against private employers" during the great New York strikes of that year.[8] New York journals friendly to the Grant cause, like *Harper's Weekly* and the *New-York Times*, reported those strikes with remarkable restraint and impartiality, as though determined to alienate no one involved.

When their national convention met, the Republicans jettisoned loyal Schuyler Colfax in favor of the newly dubbed "father of the eight-hour law," Henry Wilson, and placed the drafting of the "labor plank" in the hands of Wendell Phillips and S. P. Cummings of the Crispins. Their handiwork pledged that "the Republican party recognized the duty of so shaping legislation as to secure full protection and the amplest field for capital, and for labor, the creator of capital, the largest opportunities and a just share of the mutual profits of these two great servants of civilization." Butler returned to the hustings for Grant with full party honors, and a large, patently fraudulent National Workingmen's Convention was staged in New York to nominate Grant and Wilson.[9] Sorge of the I.W.A. even

---

[5] *Congressional Globe*, 42d Cong., 2d Sess., 102, 220 (Dec. 13, 19, 1871).

[6] J. Grey Jewell, *Among Our Sailors* (New York, 1874), pp. 155, 39–69, 267–8.

[7] McPherson, *1872*, pp. 70–1.

[8] *Nation*, Vol. XIV (May 23, 1872), p. 333.

[9] Francis Curtis, *The Republican Party . . . 1854–1904* (New York, 1904), II, 26; Godkin, "Labor and Politics," pp. 386–7; *Nation*, Vol.

complained that the Republicans were "trying hard to gain a foothold . . . in our Sections" as a means of securing votes.[1]

The contacts established between Grant's partisans and the International were incidental to a much larger effort to woo Irish votes, but the whole story reveals much about the Stalwart style of politics. Irish Republicans were few, but richly rewarded. During his first administration, Grant appointed Irishmen to the best offices at his disposal in New York City: postmaster, collector of internal revenue, and collector of the port. The last-named position went to Tom Murphy, the key figure in Republican efforts to penetrate the bedrock of Tammany strength. Through the stanchly Republican United Irishmen, Murphy had contacts with the Fenians, and William J. Nicholson, secretary of the United Irishmen, was also secretary of the Fenian offshoot, Clan na Gael.[2] Since the fiasco of 1866, however, the Fenians had provided little glamor for Irish Republicans. Murphy's hopes revived at the beginning of 1871 when the British government responded to a world-wide protest campaign by releasing a dozen imprisoned Fenians and sending them into exile. The arrival of the first group of these heroes of Irish nationalism in New York, where they were named the "Cuba Five" for the ship on which they traveled, created a public sensation and a golden opportunity for politicians.

As the *Cuba* sailed into New York harbor, she was met by a government revenue cutter with Tom Murphy aboard, ready to escort the exiles to a federal (i.e., Republican) reception. The City of New York (Tammany) also had a parade waiting, as, on a far smaller scale, did the International; and guiding the Cuba Five toward their reception, away from the more prestigious federal fanfare, was a formidable challenge to the Tweed forces. They rose to the occasion: on board the *Cuba* climbed a city health inspector, who quarantined the ship. As soon as the *Cuba* was moored at the pier where Tammany's

---

XIV (June 13, 1872), p. 381; *ibid.*, Vol. XV (Sept. 26, 1872), p. 194; *New-York Times,* May 24, 1872; Meyers, *The Republican Party the Workingman's Friend.*

[1] Quoted in Bernstein, p. 131.

[2] Devoy, *Recollections,* pp. 361-2; *Devoy's Post-Bag,* I, 24, 55, 74.

reception was waiting, all aboard were ruled in good health and dispatched ashore.[3]

The rivalry was not to end here. When city officials offered the most famous of the Cuba Five, Jeremiah O'Donovan Rossa, the office of deputy comptroller, federal authorities countered with a promise of Washington jobs to all five. At the suggestion of a delegation from the United Irishmen, Butler proposed that Congress provide the exiles with a reception in the manner of that given Louis Kossuth two decades earlier. Official welcomes from a series of Eastern city councils were climaxed by the one in Washington, where President Grant greeted them on the steps of the White House.[4] All this wining and dining, however, simply left the Fenian leaders disgusted with American politics, and especially with the "accursed Yankee Irish politicians," who, in the words of one of the Cuba Five, used Ireland as "a mere catchword for American political parties."[5] On the other hand, the persistence with which the I.W.A. had campaigned for their release and for Irish independence impressed some of the exiles so favorably that once here they joined it. Soon John Devoy was secretary of Section 7 in New York City, and Nicholson had become secretary of Section 24 in Jersey City, both small Irish sections. O'Donovan Rossa, who at first hesitated to join the International, aligned himself with it when it demonstrated against the execution of Parisian Communards late in 1871.[6]

These developments inspired Tom Murphy's attempt at a political coup. When O'Donovan Rossa complained to him of the corruption of American politics, Murphy suggested that the Fenian run for the New York Senate, against Tweed himself. To help this effort, Murphy quickly rounded up

---

[3] Jeremiah O'Donovan Rossa, *O'Donovan Rossa's Prison Life* (New York, 1874), pp. 424–7; *Devoy's Post-Bag*, I, 4–6, 20–1; Devoy, *Recollections*, pp. 361–2.

[4] O'Donovan Rossa, *Prison Life*, 428–9; Devoy, *Recollections*, 297, 362; *Devoy's Post-Bag*, I, 24.

[5] E. P. St. Clair to John Devoy, June 28, 1871, in *Devoy's Post-Bag*, I, 42–43. Cf. O'Donovan Rossa, *Prison Life*, pp. 430–1.

[6] F. A. Sorge to John Devoy, June 23, 1871, in *Devoy's Post-Bag*, I, 42; J. F. Elliott to Isaac Rehn, [*c.* Jan. 1872] IWA Papers, Box 1; O'Donovan Rossa, *Prison Life*, pp. 438–40.

citizenship papers, the nomination, and $1,000 for campaign funds. Again the Republicans underestimated Tweed's talents. Although this was the year of the Ring's defeat, and anti-Tammany candidates carried most of the city's legislative seats, Tweed trounced O'Donovan Rossa 18,706 to 6,927. The returns were truly marvelous. In one ward 287 votes were cast, and 490 counted. In five other precincts the aggregate male population over the age of twenty-one, including aliens, was 1,407, yet those precincts polled 1,813 votes. Republican poll-watchers were usually docile because they were city employees, but a few who did protest roving bands of repeaters were arrested by the police for interfering with the voting.[7]

Paradoxically, such political behavior convinced many middle-class reformers that the rabble had already become the decisive force in urban, if not national, government, at the very time labor reformers were crying that government was hopelessly in the grip of capitalists and bond-holders. In New York and Chicago, protested Godkin, the upper classes stood "helpless as the oligarchy stood before the Roman mob in the last days of the Republic." Shifting the image, he argued that industrial society had created "barbarians . . . within its own borders," whose "rush into the forums and into the temples and palaces and libraries" portended a "period of much ignorant fermentation."[8] He was perceptive enough to realize, however, that "in a commercial and manufacturing community, it is not possible to prevent the union of wealth and political power." What the democratization of politics had done was to admit poor men to political office, and hence allow them to use the powers of office to accumulate wealth and property for themselves. All members of the Tweed Ring had begun their careers in poverty, he argued with considerable exaggeration, but their exploits demonstrated that where the wealthy did not dominate the offices of state, the office-

---

[7] O'Donovan Rossa, *Prison Life,* pp. 431–3; *Devoy's Post-Bag,* I, 219; Devoy, *Recollections,* pp. 327–9; O'Donovan Rossa, *In Senate, before Committee on Privileges and Elections, in the Matter of Petition of Jeremiah O'Donovan Rossa, for Seat as Senator from Fourth Senate District, State of New York* (New York, 1872), pp. 8, 13, 20, 27, and *passim.*

[8] Godkin, "Legislation and Social Science," pp. 118, 132.

holders would plunder wealth. Hence the practical question of government was "whether the property which weighs heavily in politics, shall be property honestly earned in commerce and manufactures and lawful speculation, or property accumulated in cheating, stealing, and corruption; whether, in short, it shall be the property of men whom our churches, and schools, and literature are encouraging boys to imitate, or the property of men for whose restraint and correction we build our jails."[9]

The tendency of New York's electorate to offer its suffrages to candidates who promised to tax the wealthy and dispense the largess thus acquired liberally to the poor and to municipal improvements, while pocketing their own handsome, if informal, fee, estranged the upper classes of the city from its government as thoroughly as Butler's regime had their counterparts in Essex County. The fact that Tweed's forces actually reduced the city tax rate, while pursuing their objectives through deficit financing, mollified their propertied opponents until two events in July of 1871 roused them to action. The first was the open refusal of bankers—most significantly, those of London, Frankfurt, and Paris, who carried much of the city's $90,000,000 debt—to extend further credit. Inside revelations of corruption and waste in the improvement of municipal buildings triggered this reaction among creditors, who had long been uneasy about the city's financial position, and, as Seymour Mandelbaum has pointed out, "made it imperative to break the Ring" lest the city default its current obligations.[1]

The second development was a riot which erupted when the city's Orangemen paraded on the anniversary of the Battle of the Boyne. The request of the Loyal Order of Orange for a police permit to commemorate the historic defeat of the Catholics by "William of Glorious Memory" evoked a chorus of indignation from organizations of Catholic Irish. When the superintendent of police deferred to the Catholics and denied the Orangemen their permit, the *New-York Times* voiced the

---

[9] [E. L. Godkin], "Rich Men in Politics," *Nation*, Vol. XIII (Nov. 16, 1871), pp. 316–17.
[1] Seymour J. Mandelbaum, *Boss Tweed's New York* (New York, 1965), pp. 76–86. (The quotation is on p. 80.) See also John W. Pratt, "Boss Tweed's Public Welfare Program."

general outrage of the Better Classes and Protestants against this trampling of civil liberties by municipal officials, who "dare not disobey the commands of the Irish Catholics." Shaken by the vehemence of this reaction, Democratic Governor John Hoffman overruled the city authorities and dispatched 2,200 soldiers to escort the 160 Orangemen on their way up Broadway. Pelted by stones from Catholic spectators, the troops fired point-blank into the crowd, leaving 37 dead or mortally wounded and another 67 bleeding.[2]

The *Times* and the *Tribune* were quick to blame the deaths on the original police capitulation to the "guttersnipes," hail the employment of massive force to defend American liberties as "sublime," and remind their readers that the city would know no peace until "that corrupt party which depends for its existence upon the votes of the ignorant and vicious loses its tyrannical control of our public life."[3] The next month saw the formation of the Executive Committee of Citizens and Taxpayers for Financial Reform of the City (often called the Committee of Seventy). Headed by Henry C. Stebbins, this group of notables spearheaded the concerted refusal of 1,000 property owners to pay municipal taxes until the books of the city were exposed to proper audit. Triumphantly, the committee welcomed the adhesion of the German Democratic Committee and its influential *Staats-Zeitung* to the cause. All these developments were vividly publicized in a pamphlet issued anonymously (but the contents suggest it was done jointly by the *Times* and *Tribune*) under the all-embracing title: *Civil Rights. The Hibernian Riot and the "Insurrection of the Capitalists."* Its cover displayed the feminine figure of "Reform" beckoning New York away from a hideous mob of murderers and pillagers, waving flags emblazoned "Commune," "Hibernia," and "Socialism, Robbery, Arson."[4]

---

2 [Anon.], *Civil Rights. The Hibernian Riot and the "Insurrection of the Capitalists." A History of Important Events in New York, in the Midsummer of 1871* (New York, 1871). (*New-York Times* quotation is on p. 14.) *Cf.* Headley, pp. 289–306; Devoy, *Recollections*, p. 379. The incident is not mentioned in Mandelbaum.

3 *Civil Rights*, pp. 27, 29.

4 *Ibid.; Nation*, Vol. XIII (Aug. 31, 1871), p. 137; *ibid.*, Vol. XIII (Sept. 7, 1871), p. 153.

This joint effort of European bond-holders, the chamber of commerce, and the intelligentsia shattered the Tweed Ring's grip on the city at the November elections. It demonstrated, as had the frustration of Butler's campaign for governor in Massachusetts, that by 1871 a formidable force was at work in American politics, vaguely styling itself "Reform." This movement differed remarkably from both radicalism and labor reform in its orientation toward the constituent parts of society. It did not sanctify "the nation," glorify the working classes, or view financiers and merchants ("the capitalists") as inherent foes of reform. On the contrary, this new reform current regarded the lower orders of society with scorn and anxiety and sought its support from the top of the social ladder. It was, in a word, elitist.

LIBERALISM

By 1872 the new elitist reform movement had evolved an impressive and rather systematic body of doctrine and provided itself with a name. Early that year William Dean Howells remarked on the tendency toward convergence evident in current activities to reform the civil service, abolish tariff protection, return to specie payments, introduce minority representation in government, abolish the elective judiciary, "and to prevent, at least for the present, any extension of the elective franchise to women." These diverse efforts shared a common aspiration "to evolve order out of chaos, government out of anarchy" and an agreement that the "political ideal of the Anglo-Saxon is liberty." From these premises emerged the fundamental conclusion that "the most perfect state is that in which moral self-control is substituted for the sanctions of government."[5]

Initially, many advocates of these reforms styled themselves Conservative Republicans, to distinguish themselves from the Radicals.[6] The label was clearly a misnomer, for the new movement accepted unequivocally the principles of uni-

---

[5] Editorial, *Atlantic Monthly*, Vol. XXIX (Jan. 1872), pp. 124–8. (Quotations are on p. 126.)
[6] *Eg.*, O. P. Fitzgerald to Lyman Trumbull, Jan. 4, 1871 [*sic*]; L. G. Fisher to David Davis, Jan. 3, 1872, Davis Papers.

versal manhood suffrage and equal rights for all citizens on which Radicals had insisted. Its commitment to popular government was as complete, if not as enthusiastic, as that of the Radicals. Godkin, who was emerging as the most systematic theorist of the new movement, believed that "the steady and rapid descent of political power into the hands of [the working] class," was not only irreversible but desirable. What society needed was to teach its new masters by "the steady and persistent preaching and *practice*, by all classes," that "there is nothing so good either for the individual or the nation as liberty."[7] From this supreme value, liberty, the movement took its name—Liberal.

The heart of Liberal theory was a doctrine of limits to the proper functions of democratic government. It was concerned, in other words, not with the Radical ideological problem of the source of the state's authority but with the proper sphere of state action. "The government," argued Godkin, "must get out of the 'protective' business and the 'subsidy' business and the 'improvement' and the 'development' business. It must let trade, and commerce, and manufactures, and steamboats, and railroads, and telegraphs alone. *It cannot touch them without breeding corruption*."[8]

In time, the high priest of liberalism was to be Herbert Spencer, whose work *Social Statics* appeared in its first American edition in 1865.[9] At that time, however, few American intellectuals were prepared for Spencer's icy materialism, let alone the disdain his logical mind held for hallowed social conventions. Given the American penchant for thinking in legal terms, further more, it is not surprising that the first systematic exposition of the new liberalism was an essay on the Constitution. In 1868, Thomas McIntyre Cooley, then chief justice of the supreme court of Michigan, published *A Treatise on the Constitutional Limitations which Rest upon the Legislative Power of the States of the American Union*. Cooley

---

[7] [E. L. Godkin], "How Protection Affects Labor," *Nation*, Vol. XII (May 25, 1871), pp. 352–3.

[8] Quoted in Grimes, p. 26. My italics.

[9] Sidney Fine, *Laissez Faire and the General-Welfare State, A Study of Conflict in American Thought, 1865–1901* (Ann Arbor, Mich., 1956), pp. 33–41.

confessed that he had "written in full sympathy with all those restraints which the caution of the fathers had imposed upon the exercise of the powers of government," and with a "greater faith" in "checks and balances . . . than in a judicious, prudent, and just exercise of unbridled authority by any one man or body of men, whether sitting as a legislature or as a court."[1]

There is, Cooley argued, a law greater than the sovereignty of the people, an unwritten law which stands behind the Constitution and in the light of which the organic law must be interpreted. Through that higher moral law the sphere of exercise of popular sovereignty is limited. Its limits, furthermore, exceed those of the traditional but inadequate American belief that laws must be general (must apply universally rather than to individuals), for "general rules may sometimes be as obnoxious as special, when in their results they deprive parties of their vested rights." Hence legislatures may not under any formula transfer property from one man to another or otherwise interfere with property for any purpose other than the needs of government.[2] What Cooley did in this passage was to convert "due process of law" from a procedural to a substantive right, and thus to shield any prerogatives classed as "property rights" from governmental interference, regardless of how scrupulously that interference conformed with the written requirements of the Constitution. This view soon became authoritative among lawyers and grew from Justice Stephen J. Field's famous dissent in the *Slaughterhouse* cases of 1873 to become the official doctrine of the Supreme Court.[3]

Both trade-union practices and the legislative demands of the labor movement could be resisted much more effectively in terms of this doctrine than they could be by utilitarianism. The fate of the federal eight-hour law at the hands of the Supreme Court in the late 1870's made that point quite clear.[4] But the

[1] Thomas McIntyre Cooley, *A Treatise on the Constitutional Limitations which Rest upon the Legislative Power of the States of the American Union* (Boston, 1868), p. iv.

[2] *Ibid.*, pp. 356–7.

[3] See John P. Roche, "Entrepreneurial Liberty and the Fourteenth Amendment," *Labor History*, Vol. IV (Winter 1963), pp. 3–31; Fine, pp. 128–49.

[4] See above, pp. 321–3.

whole spirit of liberalism is missed if one fails to recognize it as a reform crusade. It was a body of thought rationalizing an attack on the status quo, an attempt to exclude government from spheres in which it was very active in the early 1870's. Yet this attack spared (indeed protected) the fundamental institutions of society, because it found them good. Godkin spelled out the role of "the reformer of to-day":

> His one duty is to find out things. His father was occupied in assailing monstrous and palpable evils, and getting the government into the hands of the many; the son has no such duty. He has no abuse of any magnitude to attack which is maintained by the few for their own comfort. His work is to adjust the relations of the individuals of the great crowd to each other, so that they may be enabled to lead a quiet, and comfortable, and free life.[5]

Liberalism worshipped at the shrine of Spencer's god, science. But the world of industrial technology which science had created was a delicate mechanism easily fouled by mismanagement. Ignorance, custom, and habit rendered the mass of mankind unfit to be at the controls of industrial society. To allow legislative intervention in economic affairs was, therefore, to place reactionary barbarians at the controls of the highest developments of modern science and technology.

Furthermore, liberalism sought to bring under the sway of science the management of the social order itself. The focal point of the intellectual activity that perfected Liberal doctrine, therefore, was the American Association for the Promotion of Social Science, which was founded in 1865 and began holding annual conferences in 1869. Its officers were from the cream of the Northeastern intellectual community, among them Edward Atkinson, Dr. Samuel G. Howe, Caroline H. Dall, Francis Lieber, and Theodore W. Dwight, but its moving spirit was Franklin B. Sanborn, who in 1866 had played so prominent a role in redefining the attitude of Massachusetts Republicans toward labor legislation.[6] At its conferences in 1870 and 1871, papers were read urging close attention to the education of "our working classes," who had shown by their

---

[5] Godkin, " 'Radicals' and 'Conservatives'," pp. 21–2.
[6] F. B. Sanborn to E. A. Atkinson, Oct. 6, 1865, Atkinson Papers, Box 1.

wild proposals that they "are not a whit more advanced than those of the Old World," and the activizing of chambers of commerce to guide men with business experience into government service to replace the lawyer-politicians.[7] The Reverend T. D. Woolsey pointed out the tendency of "our system of party and government" to ignore vice and crime, in order to show that "the better classes of society need that the ultimate control of the police should be out of the reach of municipal politics, as much if not more than they need that the city budget should be safe from the same influences."[8] And Godkin argued the desirability of replacing parliamentary government itself with some means "of giving prompt, but also scientific expression to the popular will, or, in other words, [to] place men's relations in society . . . under the control of trained human reason."[9]

When Liberals turned to the labor question, the science of production and the science of human relations converged. Their road to social progress scrupulously avoided both legislation and trade-union coercion; it moved instead through cooperation and rising productivity. Every effort to promote profit-sharing or other relationships which might somehow be classed as "cooperation" (including even Southern sharecropping) was praised by the editors of the *New-York Times*, *Hunt's Merchants' Magazine*, and other such journals as the effective alternative to industrial strife.[1] Godkin urged employers to take their workmen into their confidence, show them the company books, and develop "the association of the men with the masters as partners, receiving in lieu of wages, or in addition to wages, a share in the profits."[2] He even wove this aspiration into an intriguing theory of the historical evolu-

---

[7] *Journal of Social Science*, II (1870), 208; Hamilton A. Hill, "Relations of the Business Men of the United States to the National Legislation," *ibid.*, III (1871), 148–68.

[8] T. D. Woolsey, "Nature and Sphere of Police Power," *ibid.*, III (1871), 97–114. (Quotation is on p. 113.)

[9] E. L. Godkin, "Legislation and Social Science," *ibid.*, III (1871), 130.

[1] Editorials, *New-York Times*, June 27, 28, 1869, Jan. 30, 1870, Jan. 8, 1871; *Hunt's Merchants' Magazine and Commercial Review*, Vol. LIX (Oct. 1868), pp. 292–5; Merchants, Farmers & Mechanics' Savings Bank, Chicago, *The Labor Question* (Chicago, 1867), pp. 93–8, 132–6; Philadelphia *Public Ledger*, Oct. 1, 1868.

[2] Godkin, "The Labor Crisis," p. 197.

tion of labor movements. Initially, Godkin reasoned, workers made reckless calls for governmental interference in the economy, as had the Chartists in England and the eight-hour movement in America. The futility of such efforts led the operatives to form their own coercive associations, trade unions. But union action only reduced production, thereby diminishing labor's income. Consequently, both manufacturers and employees came to recognize the uselessness of conflict and to form "industrial partnerships." Such undertakings, he believed, were as consistent with free trade and competition as was "any joint-stock company."[3]

The gospel of "human engineering" that these Liberals anticipated influenced industrial practices significantly only in the twentieth century. The latter-day consultant in this field, however, could discern in the papers of the American Association for the Promotion of Social Science an elitist bias and a set of premises about industrial relations recognizably similar to his own. Some Liberals, in particular Atkinson and the remarkable Philadelphia physicist and statistician Lorin Blodgett, explicitly argued that "better paid, more intelligent and effective labor" was a necessary condition for increased productivity, and that symmetrical economic growth could be assured only when society treated its workers as customers as well as producers.[4] From these propositions Atkinson developed by 1878 the central idea on which writers of the next century were to rest the doctrine of "people's capitalism":

> [The] absence of communism—that is to say, inequality in respect to possession or property—leads, as time goes on, to practical communism in consumption; that is, to a more and more equal distribution of the products or means of subsistence that are necessary to comfort.[5]

By 1872, in short, a new cycle of American politics had replaced the triangular tussle of old-line Democrats, Conservatives, and Radicals generated by the war itself, and the labor

---

[3] E. L. Godkin, "Co-operation," *North American Review*, Vol. CVI (Jan. 1868), pp. 150–75.
[4] *Pa. BLS, 1872/1873*, pp. 417–45. On Blodgett, see *App. Cyc. Bio.*, I, 295.
[5] Atkinson, *Labor and Capital Allies*, p. 45.

question had played a central role in this realignment. The major categories of political behavior had become Stalwart and Liberal, groupings which crossed party lines just as those of 1866 had. The "New Departure" by which the Democrats in 1871 and 1872 pledged their acceptance of Negro equality in civil rights and suffrage was symbolic of the fact that a political epoch had closed, or, in Georges Clemenceau's words, "the American revolution is over."[6]

The very set of experiences in their own communities which bred the Liberal reform movement, furthermore, induced many Northern intellectuals to cast a more kindly eye than they had done hitherto toward the white foes of the Republican regimes in the South. To their endorsement of universal male suffrage, Liberals coupled a demand for universal amnesty. Interspersed with Godkin's 1871 editorials assaulting the Tweed Ring were others manifesting sympathy toward the taxpayers' conventions staged by "conservatives" in the Southern states, and even toward the Ku Klux Klan. Having lost his proselytizing zeal for unlimited democracy, Godkin had come to regard Southern men of property and culture as allies of their Northern counterparts in a common struggle against corrupt mass politics. From that vantage point the violence of the Klan was justifiable: the reaction of society's legitimate leaders against usurpers of political power. The same logic applied to New York, where Godkin advocated a violent end for Tweed and his associates, which would "be no more lynching than the execution of Robespierre and Rigault was lynching."[7]

A word of caution. The Liberal Republican party of 1872 has passed unmentioned in this discussion because it was *not* the political embodiment of the Liberal reform impulse. To a large degree, the movement which culminated in the Cincinnati Convention was genuinely Liberal, but the mere fact that the convention gathered all political out-groups to form a party and nominate a Presidential candidate made its fate inevitable. Its control was assumed by men prepared to do

---

[6] Clemenceau, p. 299.

[7] *Nation*, Vol. XIII (Sept. 7, 1871), p. 153. For *Nation* views of taxpayers' conventions and the Ku Klux Klan, see *ibid.*, Vol. XIII (July 6, 1871), pp. 4–5; *ibid.*, Vol. XIII (Dec. 7, 1871), pp. 364–5.

"anything to beat Grant," that is to say, by men whose political behavior was in the best Stalwart style. Samuel Bowles expressed this outcome better than he realized when, stunned by the defeat of Charles Francis Adams, he tried to describe the bright side of the nomination made at Cincinnati: that the Irish and the workers and the Western farmers would be attracted by Greeley's record of friendship to their particular interests. Hence, though he did not stand for all Liberal reforms, Bowles reasoned, Greeley would get votes. "Mr. Adams' strength would have worked from the rich and cultivated and business classes down," Bowles concluded. "Mr. Greeley's will develop from the laborer, the poor and discontented, up."[8] This line of argument makes crystal clear the truth of "Warrington's" sad judgment that in the Grant-Greeley race there was no Liberal candidate.[9]

But liberalism as a political trend was as real as the Stalwart style of political behavior. These were the constituent parts of the dynamic equilibrium into which the mainstream of American politics had settled by 1872. Stalwarts ran the machinery of state, while Liberals attacked them, and their attack provided a lightning rod which permitted irate Americans to "reform" furiously without jeopardizing any of the basic social or political institutions of the nation. In contrast to the Radical aspiration to tear out the roots of social maladies, Liberals were convinced the roots were sound. Such an equilibrium cannot be static, but it was surely stable.

---

8 Quoted in Merriam, II, 188.
9 Robinson, *Pen-Portraits*, pp. 475–9.

CHAPTER 10

Sentimental Reformers
and the Lure of Labor

"The great, the all-embracing Reform of our age is . . . the SOCIAL Reform,—that which seeks to lift the Laboring Class, as such,—not out of labor, by any means,—but out of ignorance, inefficiency, dependence, and want, and place them in a position of partnership and recognized mutual helpfulness with the suppliers of the Capital which they render fruitful and efficient."[1] So wrote Horace Greeley in the mid-1850's, defending the proposition that "not the Worker only—the robust, earnest Thinker also—is of necessity a Radical."[2] Despite his vacillating cowardice in the face of actual political conflicts which persistently threw him in practice into the Conservative camp, Greeley had no equal as the exponent of the social and moral significance of mid-nineteenth-century

---

[1] Horace Greeley, *Recollections of a Busy Life* (New York, 1868), p. 508.
[2] *Ibid.*, p. 500.

American radicalism. A decade before Radicals obtained the political power to implement any part of their dream, Greeley had spelled out their two essential goals. First stood "the equality of Human Rights, regardless of all disparities of strength, or knowledge, or caste, or creed, or color"; and second stood the reorganization of society around the principle that it is better for men "to earn their subsistence by fair, honest service to their kind, than to have it supplied them for nothing."[3] The two were held inseparable because slavery was but "a logical deduction" from the principle "that I have a right to consume in idleness the products or earnings of half a dozen workers, if my income will justify the outlay."[4]

By 1872 the first of those objectives had been enshrined in the national Constitution and accepted by both parties in the mainstream of national politics. Controversies over the second had torn asunder the apostles of reform themselves. Anxiety over the rude efforts of workingmen to reform their conditions by their own efforts, and still greater concern over the specter of Caesaristic politicians grasping for personal power in the guise of champions of the downtrodden, had driven most Radical intellectuals toward the new Liberal crusade to limit the sphere of future state action. They agreed with Godkin that the only improvements still needed by American society were matters of adjusting "the relations of the individuals of the great crowd to each other," and that such tasks were best performed by private initiative.[5]

Not all Radicals followed Godkin into the Liberal camp. Some remained convinced that individual relations were molded by the patterns of distribution of power and wealth in society. As Greeley had said (in his younger days), the possibilities of extracting "sustenance and comfort from the elements" surrounding men were "appropriated,—monopolized,—*tabooed*,—the private, exclusive possessions of a minority."[6] While such thinkers continued to believe that only men of education and independent means could properly lead efforts to remedy maldistribution of society's benefits, events

---

[3] *Ibid.*, pp. 504, 514.
[4] *Ibid.*, pp. 503–4.
[5] See above, p. 382.
[6] Greeley, *Recollections*, p. 497

of the 1860's made it painfully evident that other (indeed most) men of similar social status posed the most formidable obstacles to their efforts. Just as Messrs. Ray, Cornell, and Sweet had repudiated their faith in "Christian employers" at the climax of New Bedford's 1867 strike and attached their hopes for the town's future to the strikers themselves, so all over the nation a significant minority of middle-class reformers lifted from the dirt the Radical banner so rudely jettisoned by their own colleagues and offered it to the safekeeping of the working classes. Since American culture has traditionally associated property rights and "immutable economic laws" with the head and social justice with the heart, it was quite appropriate that Godkin dubbed such men "Sentimental reformers of the Phillips school."[7]

Andrew Burtt of Pittsburgh was more nearly typical of this group than the famous Wendell Phillips. Burtt was an educator, for twenty-one years the principal of a public school located amidst the iron mills, railroad depots, and tenement houses of his city's fifth ward. Not only was his school district the scene of bloody fighting during the strike of 1877, it ranked second among all wards of the city in number of school-age children. Since many boys and girls attended school only when the cotton mills across the Allegheny River laid them off, his district boasted the city's highest absentee rate. For his young charges Burtt wrote an English grammar that was adopted as the standard text for the city, and around their needs he developed a number of unique pedagogical practices, which he imposed on a reluctant board of principals by sheer force of personality. For the parents of his pupils he conducted two lyceums, one in the fifth ward and the other for the iron and glass workers of Birmingham, on the south side of the Monongahela, where he resided.[8]

The workers around whom Burtt's life centered were as

---

[7] See above, p. 371.

[8] "Professor Burtt," *Pittsburgh Commercial Gazette,* July 6, 1881; *First Annual Report of the Superintendent of Public Schools for the School Year Ending June 1, 1869* (Pittsburgh, 1869), pp. 90, 477; *Directory of Pittsburgh and Allegheny Cities . . . for 1866–1867* (Pittsburgh, 1867), p. 73; P. W. Siebert, "Old Bayardstown," *Western Pennsylvania Historical Magazine,* IX (1926), 90–103; James A. Beck, "The Old Fifth Ward of Pittsburgh," *ibid.,* XXVIII (1945), 111–26.

proud as they were industrious. In this city where James Parton saw "men performing labors so severe that they have to stop, now and then, in summer, take off their boots, and *pour the perspiration out of them,*"[9] puddlers, catchers, rollers, molders, and glass blowers were highly organized, ably led, and paid substantially better than their counterparts to the East. Strong Republican allegiances among the native Americans and Protestant Britons served to keep most constituencies of wage earners safely out of Democratic hands, but also infused into the city's political life a powerful strain of working-class republicanism. When the dominant party experimented with nominations by primary elections in 1865, it found the incumbent mayor (and subsequently, the Democratic challenger as well) routed at the polls by a printing pressman, William C. McCarthy, toward whom the tide of votes shifted late in the afternoon when the mills let out. McCarthy identified himself so thoroughly with the Radicals that he refused even to tolerate an official reception for Andrew Johnson when the President barnstormed into the city in 1866.[1]

Because Burtt's father had been a coal miner, and he himself had toiled sixteen years as a glass blower by the banks of the Monongahela, he readily understood such workmen. His youthful religious fervor made it easy for Burtt to cast his ballots with loyal regularity first for the Whigs and then for the Republicans, and McCarthy was his kind of Republican. At the age of forty-one Burtt crowned years of spare-time study with a Master's degree from Jefferson College (awarded to him in 1858) and settled into life as a school principal among workers who affectionately bestowed on him the title "Professor."[2]

It was to Professor Burtt that labor reformers turned in 1867 when they founded a party of their own. A protracted series of strikes among both iron puddlers and iron molders had kept Pittsburgh strangely idle from January to November.

---

[9] James Parton, "Pittsburgh," *Atlantic Monthly,* Vol. XXI (Jan. 1868), p. 33.
[1] Kerr, pp. 127–36.
[2] "Sketch of Andrew Burtt," Pittsburgh *Daily Post,* Sept. 3, 1868; obituary of Burtt, *National Labor Tribune,* July 9, 1881.

In May the embattled manufacturers solicited the American Emigrant Company and United States consuls to import some two hundred Belgian and eight hundred Prussian iron workers to replace the strikers. As if this "invasion from Westphalia" were not enough to inflame the workmen, cotton mills in the area imposed a wage reduction on their hands (customarily the wives and children of iron workers) by threatening to replace them with the families of the Prussian strikebreakers.[3] Local trade unionists furiously denounced both the Democrats and the Republicans for failing to safeguard workers' interests and hailed the appeal of the N.L.U. for the founding of labor parties. When the Republican organization abandoned the primary scheme, which had been the source of McCarthy's influence, and thus blocked his hopes of re-election, the impetus toward a new party was accelerated.[4]

The large, orderly body of workingmen elected from ward caucuses that assembled in September to form the Labor Reform party of Allegheny County chose Burtt to head its ticket as nominee for state senator. The new party's vehement denunciation of "organized *purchased* importations" of labor, and its appeals for equalization of the tax burden, for legislative regulation of mine safety, and for tariff protection for American industry were warmly supported by the professor, as was its contention that employer flouting of legal limitations of the hours of labor stemmed from a heartless philosophy which "places labor in the market only to regulate it by the rule of 'supply and demand'."[5] Although Burtt lost badly to his Republican opponent, he carried eight wards and slashed heavily into Republican tallies in working-class neighborhoods like the eight and ninth wards and the south side of the Monongahela River.[6] His was "the most flattering vote ever given an opposition candidate in this county," declared a labor paper fourteen years later.[7]

Though Burtt ran for Congress the next year, stood as an

---

[3] *Pa. BLS, 1880–1881*, pp. 281–4; Grossman, *Sylvis*, pp. 173–7; *I.M.I.U., 1868*, pp. 6–13: Sylvis, pp. 251–63; Erickson, pp. 53–4.
[4] Pittsburgh *Advocate*, quoted in *Workingman's Advocate*, Aug. 10, 1867; Kerr, pp. 138–41.
[5] Pittsburgh *Daily Gazette*, Sept. 12, 1867.
[6] Election data may be found in *ibid.*, Oct. 12, 1867, Oct. 13, 1866.
[7] *National Labor Tribune*, July 9, 1881.

elector for the Peter Cooper–Samuel F. Cary ticket in 1876, and frequently spoke at political meetings of the greenback-labor stripe until his death in 1881, it was primarily as a friend and educator of the workers, not as their political tribune, that he challenged both Liberal elitism and Stalwart personalism through the years. His passing was marked by a grand funeral staged jointly by the Masonic Order and the school principals of the city. His former pupils gave orations and recited William Cullen Bryant's *Thanatopsis;* and the *National Labor Tribune* eulogized: "His sympathies were always with work-ingmen."[8]

Clearly, Burtt's whole life had prepared him to move toward labor reform and to shun the Liberals when the crisis of radicalism brought him to the point of choice. So was it with Samuel Fenton Cary, who abandoned the Republicans to become "labor's Congressman" in 1867. The temperance move-ment had elevated this Cincinnati lawyer to prominence in the 1850's, when he had stumped his state for prohibition. Leaving the Whig for the Republican party in 1855, the thirty-one-year-old Cary sought the new party's gubernatorial nomination without success. He was later appointed collector of internal revenue in his native city, but his hostility toward the Johnson administration led him to resign that post. When his bid for a congressional nomination in 1864 was frustrated by supporters of the personable young Rutherford B. Hayes, party leaders placated Cary with a promise of "the next opening." But by the time Hayes's campaign for the governor's chair in 1867 created such an opening, Cary's public identification with Negro suffrage, temperance, and greenbacks inspired local Republican leaders to mobilize their caucuses against him. Rejected by a convention which lasted only fourteen minutes, Cary stormed out of the meeting hall.[9]

Spurned by the Republicans, Cary was embraced by the Cincinnati Trades Assembly, which invited him to run for

---

[8] Pittsburgh *Daily Post*, July 23, 1868; Pittsburgh *Daily Gazette*, Oct. 17, 1868; *National Labor Tribune*, Sept. 30, 1876, Oct. 21, 1876; letter of C.C.C., *ibid.*, July 16, 1881; obituary of Burtt in *ibid.*, July 9, 1881.
[9] *Bio. Dir. Amer. Congress*, pp. 955–6; Barnes, II, 415–18; Roseboom, pp. 224, 237, 304, 375; Cincinnati *Commercial*, Aug. 28, Sept. 13, 19, Oct. 12, 1867; Chicago *Daily Tribune*, Aug. 9, 1867.

Congress as its candidate on the platform adopted by the Chicago Labor Congress. Warily, Cary addressed a rally of 1,500 workingmen, endorsing their program but agreeing to be their candidate only on the condition that the Democrats nominated no opponent. Should a Democrat enter the lists, he warned, he would return to the Republican fold. Despite the rump action of a group of old-line Democrats who advanced their own champion (Charles Reemelin) to "spike the Abolition guns," the Hamilton County Democratic Executive Committee, which was then interested in raising the greenback banner against the Republicans, issued a communique stating that it was "inexpedient" for the party to nominate any congressional candidate.[1] On Election Day, Cary emerged victorious, with 10,390 votes as against 9,431 for Richard Smith, the Republican, and 120 for Reemelin. More votes were cast in his congressional district in the Cary-Smith race than in the Hayes-Thurman gubernatorial contest, and Cary almost matched Hayes's vote in the district, garnering 1,233 more votes than Thurman received.[2]

Despite the fact that he could never have been elected had the Democrats opposed him, Cary consistently spoke of himself as labor's candidate and explicitly dissociated himself from the democracy. In his 1867 acceptance speech he endorsed Negro suffrage and thundered: "I would see Andy Johnson in hell before I would say one word in defense of his administration or his policy."[3] Even when the Democrats gave Cary open support in his unsuccessful 1868 campaign for reelection, the congressman repudiated them and declared himself neutral in the Grant-Seymour race.[4] He had, however carefully voted against the impeachment of President Johnson, arguing that Congress "cannot afford to spend these precious days . . . in deranging still more every industrial interest of the country in settling a difficulty between the President and his Cabinet minister which can be more satisfactorily settled by a judicial tribunal. . . ."[5] After losing his seat in the

[1] Cincinnati *Commercial*, Aug. 16, Sept. 8, 10, 13, 18, 22, 1867.
[2] *Ibid.*, Oct. 13, 1867.
[3] *Ibid.*, Sept. 13, 1867.
[4] Pittsburgh *Daily Post*, Sept. 1, 19, 1868.
[5] *Congressional Globe*, 40th Cong., 2d Sess., 1398 (Feb. 24, 1868). For Cary's votes, see *ibid.*, 1616, 1617, 1618, 1642, 1643 (March 2, 3, 1868).

House, Cary allied himself ever more closely to the greenback bloc built by Thomas Ewing, Jr., in Ohio's Democratic party, until in 1875 he ran for lieutenant governor as William Allen's running mate. That unsuccessful campaign set the stage for his nomination by the Independent party to run for vice-president on the ticket with Peter Cooper.[6]

While in Congress, Cary devoted himself unsparingly to three objectives: reservation of the public domain for actual homesteaders, the emission of fiat paper money as the exclusive currency of the nation, and the establishment of an eight-hour day for federal employees. These plans he presented as the fruition of Lincoln's doctrine that labor is "superior to capital." Through them, said Cary, the country could approach the day "when our 'white slaves' will reconstruct society."[7]

Cary's election, supplemented by labor's electoral activity in Boston, Pittsburgh, Chicago, and a host of lesser towns, inspired the leadership of the N.L.U. to attempt to influence the 1868 Presidential elections, and that effort, in turn, led the N.L.U. to solicit the help of Sentimentalists from all parts of the nation. In so doing, the N.L.U. followed the advice of the Boston *Voice* to broaden its program so as to attract "the intelligent 'middle classes'—speaking, to be understood, after the fashion of the day—who are not capitalists or otherwise selfishly involved in the present order of things."[8] Although a few businessmen interested in currency reform—notably, William A. Berkey of Grand Rapids, Michigan, and Alexander Campbell and three associates from LaSalle, Illinois—had participated in the 1867 Chicago Labor Congress,[9] the first large-scale participation of "the intelligent 'middle classes'" was at a Special Council held by the N.L.U. in New York City on the eve of the Democratic National Convention.

After the Republican National Convention had convinced most of the N.L.U. leadership that the party of Grant was in the hands of "the monied aristocracy," Trevellick, Cameron,

---

[6] Unger, *Greenback Era*, pp. 183–6, 269–79; *Bio. Dir. Amer. Congress*, pp. 955–6.

[7] *Congressional Globe*, 40th Cong., 3d Sess., 195–200 (Jan. 5, 1869). (Quotation is on p. 196.) See also Cary's speech in Birmingham, Pa., Pittsburgh *Daily Post*, Sept. 19, 1868.

[8] *Daily Evening Voice*, July 26, 1867.

[9] *Workingman's Advocate*, Aug. 24, 1867.

Lucker, and others pressed President Whaley to summon a special labor congress for the purpose of nominating a national labor-reform ticket.[1] Whaley responded in June by inviting "a few friends of labor reform" to assemble in New York and advise the workingmen as to their best course of action "in this crisis in our national affairs."[2] Because the gathering was not an official labor congress, it was unnecessary for delegates to bear credentials from recognized labor-reform organizations. As a result, among the thirty-nine people taking part were not only such tested trade unionists as Lucker, Troup, Fincher, Jessup, and Whaley—and some already familiar middle-class allies like Ezra Heywood and Alexander Campbell—but also some faces totally new to the N.L.U., among them Horace H. Day, R. W. Hume, John Magwire, Austin M. Puett, Daymon Y. Kilgore, Mary Kellogg Putnam, Susan B. Anthony, and Elizabeth Cady Stanton. The meeting made no nominations, but passed instead a series of resolutions calling for a green-back currency, reservation of the public domain to actual settlers, and enforcement of the eight-hour laws. "Unless these principles are adopted by one of the two great parties—we care not which," concluded the council, "we advise the National Labor Union, at its annual convention . . . to put in nomination an independent labor candidate for the Presidency, and rally the masses to his support."[3]

The most intriguing aspect of the Special Council was hidden from public view. Some delegates obviously wished to present the resolutions formally to the Democratic Convention then assembling in the same city, but the majority feared becoming directly entangled with a major party.[4] Among the minority were Susan B. Anthony and her colleagues, who at

[1] Editorials, *ibid.*, Feb. 1, June 6, 1868. Letters of Trevellick and Lucker, *ibid.*, May 30, 1868. See also *Revolution*, Vol. I (June 4, 1868), p. 339.
[2] *N.L.U. Proceedings, 1868*, p. 6; *Workingman's Advocate*, Aug. 22, 1868.
[3] *Ibid.*, Aug. 22, 1868; *ibid.*, July 11, 1868 (article on New York rally and letter of "a mechanic"); New York *Tribune*, July 4, 1868; *Revolution*, Vol. II (July 23, 1868), p. 42.
[4] The report of the Special Council in the *Workingman's Advocate*, July 11, 1868, conflicted with that in *ibid.*, Aug. 22, 1868. For an argument that the former was deliberately falsified, see Montgomery, "Labor and the Radical Republicans," pp. 577–8.

the beginning of June had already challenged the Democrats to embrace reforms on which the Republicans had failed, by making their platform: "Universal Suffrage and universal amnesty, free trade and greenbacks, and a financial policy that shall protect labor against capital."[5]

The Women's Suffrage Association, headed by Miss Anthony, was scarcely a month old at the time of the Special Council. It had sprung from the weekly magazine *The Revolution*, which was financed by George Francis Train (the spiritual father of the Crédit Mobilier), managed by Miss Anthony, and edited by Elizabeth Cady Stanton and Parker Pillsbury. Soon after the magazine was founded, Train left for Ireland in hopes of participating in a Fenian uprising and was jailed by the British authorities. In his absence the staff was joined by David M. Melliss, a financial columnist for the New York *World* who used *The Revolution* both to express views which would have cost him his job if printed in the *World* and to write a spicy Wall Street gossip column which brokers read eagerly.[6] Calling itself the "Organ of the National Party of New America," *The Revolution* endorsed the "principles of the National Labor Union," and offered its own elaborate platform, which included the following demands:

1. IN POLITICS——Educated suffrage, irrespective of sex or color; Equal Pay to Women for Equal Work; Eight Hours Labor; abolition of Standing Armies and Party Despotisms. . . .

2. IN RELIGION——Deeper Thought; Broader Idea; Science not Superstition; Personal Purity; Love to Man as well as God. . . .

3. IN SOCIAL LIFE——Morality and Reform; Practical Education, not Theoretical; . . . Cold Water not Alcohol Drinks or Medicines. . . .

4. THE REVOLUTION proposes a new Commercial and Financial Policy. . . . Greenbacks for money. An American System of Finance. American Products and Labor

---

[5] *Revolution*, Vol. I (June 4, 1868), p. 344.

[6] Katherine Anthony, *Susan B. Anthony: Her Personal History and Her Era* (Garden City, N.Y., 1954), p. 215; Alma Lutz, *Susan B. Anthony, Rebel, Crusader, Humanitarian* (Boston, 1959), pp. 138–9; Israel Kugler, "The Trade Union Career of Susan B. Anthony," *Labor History*, Vol. II (Winter 1961), pp. 91–2.

Free. Foreign Manufactures Prohibited. . . . New York the Financial Centre of the World. Wall Street emancipated from Bank of England. . . . The Credit Foncier and Credit Mobilier system, or Capital Mobilized to Resuscitate the South and our Mining Interest, and to People the Country from Ocean to Ocean. . . . Ten millions of Naturalized Citizens DEMAND A PENNY OCEAN POSTAGE, to Strengthen the Brotherhood of Labor. . . .[7]

On the Sunday following the close of the Special Council, David Melliss invited Miss Anthony, Mrs. Stanton, some Wall Street colleagues, and President Whaley to breakfast at his home to discuss the prospects for urging the demands of *The Revolution* and the N.L.U. on the Democratic Convention, which had opened the previous day.[8] Whaley's participation in this affair had no authorization from the council, though it was subsequently approved by the labor congress in September.[9] It is plausible to infer that his actions were at least spurred on by the fact that scarcely a week earlier Whaley had been forced to resign from his job in the Government Printing Office because some Republican congressmen feared his Special Council had been convened to aid the Democrats.[1] As a consequence of the breakfast conference, Representative James Brooks of New York introduced the Special Council resolutions to the Democratic Convention Monday morning, and Chairman Horatio Seymour read Miss Anthony's appeal for women's suffrage. The Democrats took no action on the labor platform, but they ridiculed the Anthony resolution by referring it to the Committee on Credentials.[2]

Although the power play of the breakfast table came to naught, it did reveal the propensity of Sentimental Reformers to utilize the N.L.U. as the springboard for rhapsodic and visionary political ventures. In this respect it was but a foretaste of the grandiose schemes of 1872. Furthermore, Miss

---

[7] *Revolution*, Vol. I (Jan. 8, 1868), p. 1. For the endorsement of the N.L.U., see *ibid.*, Vol. I (April 9, 1868), p. 213.
[8] Ida H. Harper, *Life and Work of Susan B. Anthony* (Indianapolis and Kansas City, 1899–1908), I, 305.
[9] *N.L.U. Proceedings, 1868*, pp. 22–3.
[1] Pittsburgh *Daily Post*, July 1, 1868. The exchange of letters between Whaley and the congressional printer is reprinted in *ibid.*, July 6, 1868.
[2] *Proceedings . . . Democratic Convention*, pp. 27–30.

Anthony and her cohorts, having entered into not only the public sessions but the backstage maneuvers of the N.L.U., felt very much at home and settled down to stay. On the eve of the September New York Labor Congress she qualified herself for credentials to the N.L.U. by gathering nearly a hundred working girls into a Wokingwomen's Protective Association. Mrs. Stanton, appearing as a delegate from the Women's Suffrage Association, was challenged by some delegates, but by a vote of 45 to 18 the congress allowed her a seat, though it explicitly repudiated the main demand of her organization.[3]

No single organization more graphically illustrated the tensions Sentimentalists could arouse within the labor-reform movement than the Workingwomen's Protective Association. The bulk of its members were schooled by Miss Anthony in the art of printing. Finding few jobs open to them, she sent her protégés to work in shops on the typographical union's rat list, at times as actual strikebreakers.[4] Consequently, at the 1869 Labor Congress Miss Anthony's credentials were challenged by delegate Walsh of New York's Typographical Union No. 6, who charged her organization with training rat printers. His challenge provoked a classic confrontation between middle-class and working-class prejudices. Austin Puett, an Indiana attorney, entered the lists as Miss Anthony's champion. Proclaiming his faith in universal equality of rights, Puett said he wished everyone to "enter upon the grand platform of competition, and I do not care whether he is a 'rat' or a mouse." The N.L.U. existed, he admonished the typographers, "to liberate the labor of the United States from intolerable taxation," and should not concern itself with "trifling petty matters." He then justified his own presence at the labor congress with the argument that a man who "labors at anything is a workingman," and drew hisses from wage-earner delegates when he added that mental toil can be "a great deal harder on the constitution" than physical.

---

[3] *N.L.U. Proceedings, 1868,* pp. 19–20, 23; *Revolution,* Vol. II (Oct. 1, 1868), pp. 204–5; Philadelphia *Public Ledger,* Sept. 18, 1868; speech of Augusta Lewis, *Workingman's Advocate,* Sept. 4, 1869.
[4] *Revolution,* Vol. II (Sept. 24, 1868), pp. 181–2; *ibid.,* Vol. II (Oct. 15, 1868), p. 231; *ibid.,* Vol. II (Nov. 5, 1868), p. 280; Kugler, p. 99.

Astounded by Puett's ignorance of trade-union principles and unimpressed by the glories of competition, Walsh replied: "The gentleman who has just taken his seat has convinced me that he is not a workingman or he would know what a 'rat' is." Turning to the union men, he declared: "I agree with the last speaker—'Equal rights for all'—but if I am a rat or a renegade, I do not expect anything from fair men, and I do not expect to give them anything." Not knowing when to stop talking, Walsh let his arguments slip from the level of trade-union fundamentals to simple male hegemony. "The lady goes in for taking women away from the wash tub," he cried, "and in the name of heaven who is going there if they don't?"[5]

The issue of restricting N.L.U. participation to genuine spokesmen of labor reform was thus so thoroughly confused with that of keeping women at the washtub that no clear pattern emerged in the 55-to-52 vote which seated Miss Anthony. When the next day the Typographical Union delegates threatened to bolt the N.L.U. if she were not expelled, a much sharper delineation appeared. Forced to choose between middle-class reformers and one of the country's most important trade unions, some twenty-five trade-union delegates and even a few Sentimentalists either reversed their votes or abstained. Miss Anthony was ejected by a vote of 63 to 28.[6]

Despite the inevitable antagonisms between Sentimentalists, who wished the N.L.U. to be "higher and holier than all the Trades Unions,"[7] and trade-union executives, who looked askance at delegates "in no wise connected with labor,"[8] using the N.L.U. to ride a favorite "hobby,"[9] both groups concurred on the matter of political program. And that program, it will be remembered, was the *raison d'être* of the N.L.U. For this

---

[5] *Workingman's Advocate*, Sept. 4, 1869.

[6] *Ibid.* A roll call of the votes on seating Anthony may be found in *Report of Proceedings of the Eighteenth Annual Session of the International Typographical Union, Held in Cincinnati, Ohio, June 6, 7, 8, 9 and 10, 1870* (Philadelphia, 1870), pp. 52–3. (Hereafter proceedings of this union will be cited: *N.T.U. Proceedings.*)

[7] Charles McLean at the 1869 National Labor Congress, *Workingman's Advocate*, Sept. 4, 1869.

[8] William Jessup, quoted in Excerpt from *Proceedings*, Workingmen's Assembly, State of N.Y. 1870, in Labor Collection, Misc. General Labor Organizations & Conventions, Box 2, W.S.H.S.

[9] Letter of J. W. Browning, *Workingman's Advocate*, Oct. 19, 1872.

reason the role of middle-class reformers in the organization grew steadily after the 1868 Congress, until by 1872 they were in complete command of its machinery. Shortly after the New York Congress, newly elected President Sylvis appointed five men to work with congressman Cary as a permanent Washington lobby for the N.L.U. At first glance this group resembled the legislative committee of the British Trades Union Congress or of America's later Federation of Organized Trades and Labor Unions. There was, however, one formidable difference. Only two of the five members of Sylvis's lobby were trade unionists, Whaley and Cavis. Two of the others were manufacturers (Horace H. Day and John Magwire) and one (Austin Puett) was a professional politician.[1]

There was a good practical reason for appointing such members. Operating on a budget of less than $2,000 a year, the N.L.U. could not compensate its lobbyists. Aside from Whaley and Cavis, who were residents of the national capital, it needed spokesmen of independent means. New York's Workingmen's Assembly, furthermore, provided something of a precedent for the N.L.U.'s action in its regular Albany lobby, made up of trade unionists who lived in the vicinity of the capital and legislators friendly to labor's program.[2]

But just as the legislative committees of the T.U.C. and the F.O.O.T. and L.U. were to become the main administrative bodies of the organizations they represented, so Sylvis's lobby quickly evolved into the Executive Committee of the N.L.U. When the 1869 Labor Congress authorized President Trevellick to appoint members to such a standing administrative body, the appointees included one trade unionist (Crispin Grand Sir Knight McLaughlin) and four middle-class reformers (Puett, Magwire, Alexander Campbell, and Absalom M. West). These were the men who actually brought the long-promised National Labor Reform party into existence in January 1871, and who determined its political tactics. From 1869 on, the locus of operative power in the N.L.U. shifted decisively from the elected officers, who were always wage

---

[1] Sylvis, p. 371.
[2] See 1870 proceedings of New York Workingmen's Assembly, *Workingman's Advocate*, Feb. 5, 12, 1870.

earners, to the Executive Committee, which contained but one wage earner. The latter was always a leader of the Crispins, for S. P. Cummings succeeded to McLaughlin's post.[3]

The wealthiest of the N.L.U.'s new leaders was also the stormy petrel of the group, Horace H. Day. Born in Great Barrington, Massachusetts, in 1813, Day came from a well-established Yankee family. His experiments with rubber led to patent disputes with Charles Goodyear so fierce that one year he spent the entire $50,000 profit of his New Jersey factory on litigation, but ultimately a lawyers' agreement awarded Day exclusive rights to manufacture shirred rubber for use in shoes. Twice in his career Day was worth a million dollars, but time and again he lost his fortune in unsuccessful ventures, such as an attempt to transmit compressed air directly from Niagara Falls to Buffalo. An avowed spiritualist, Day rented a three-story house in New York for the use of mediums and the publication of the *Christian Spiritualist*.[4]

As was so often the case among Sentimentalists, Day was interminably engaged in Machiavellian plots to manipulate the course of national politics from behind the scenes. Already in 1856 he had provided the funds to maintain delegates at the American Party Convention pledged to nominating Nathaniel Banks for President with the understanding that Banks would withdraw in favor of Frémont. Twelve years later the disintegration of wartime political alignments directed Day's attention toward the N.L.U. Having appeared at the 1868 Special Council and failed in an effort to impose upon it a platform entirely of his own making, Day unilaterally invited Andrew Johnson to run for re-election in the name of labor, then offered the N.L.U. to Ben Butler's use when the congressman defeated Dana.[5] Quickly making the N.L.U. indebted to him for such financial assistance as paying the fare of Andrew Cameron to attend the Basle Congress of the International and the rent for the N.L.U.'s meeting hall, Day emerged in 1871 as

---

[3] *Ibid.*, Sept. 4, 1869, Aug. 27, 1870, Aug. 19, 1871.

[4] *D.A.B.*, V, 159; obituary in New York *Tribune*, Aug. 27, 1878.

[5] Harrington, pp. 36–7; *Workingman's Advocate*, Aug. 22, 1868; Destler, pp. 57–8; Horace H. Day to Benjamin F. Butler, Nov. 10, 1868, Butler Papers, Box 56.

its first vice-president. By this time Alexander Troup, the vice-president for New York, was his most eminent ally.[6] Defeated in his own bid for the 1872 Presidential nomination of the labor reformers, and irate over the offer to Justice David Davis, Day, with the aid of Troup, turned first to the women's suffrage movement, then to the Straight-Out Democrats in search of a nominee more to his liking. The last move was the most anomalous of all. In the name of a union of all antispoilsmen "regardless of sex, nationality, color or condition," Day placed himself in league with Blanton Duncan of Kentucky, organizer of the convention of Democrats who could not stomach Greeley or the New Departure.[7] Yet the cooperation begun there continued through the 1870's, as both men participated in the greenback party movement, until Day's death in 1878.[8]

Like Day, John Magwire was a manufacturer with Republican antecedents, and (also like Day) he was attracted to the N.L.U. by its financial program. Born in 1805, Magwire was a success in the business of blooming pig iron by the age of twenty-three. Moving to St. Louis, initially as the agent of a Pittsburgh iron company, he soon opened his own iron mines, foundries, and docks to build steamboat hulls. Further resemblance to Day lies in the fact that Magwire was involved in a ruinous court battle lasting twenty-six years. Having been an ardent admirer of Andrew Jackson, Magwire helped mobilize a Union Club in St. Louis during the secession crisis, then was appointed an inspector of steam vessels by the Lincoln administration, a position he still held in 1868.[9] By that year, when he appeared at the Special Council, he believed the distribution of public lands to be the burning issue of the day. "The person having no interest in the soil," he wrote, "has nothing at stake, and is not, therefore, a citizen in the full

---

[6] Foner, *Labor*, I, 412; *Workingman's Advocate*, Aug. 19, 1871, May 11, 25, 1872.
[7] *Ibid.*, April 27, May 11, 1872. Blanton Duncan to Horace H. Day, July 10, 1872, and Day to Duncan, July 13, 1872, *ibid.*, July 20, 1872; New York *Tribune*, Aug. 31, 1872.
[8] Commons, *Labour*, II, 168–70; Unger, *Greenback Era*, pp. 377, 399.
[9] *Workingman's Advocate*, Sept. 5 and 12, 1874; *St. Louis Directory, 1868*, 578.

meaning of the term citizen."[1] Second only to the safeguarding of homestead rights was the emission of a government-managed paper currency, a notion to which he had been converted by the works of Edward Kellogg. To promote these ideas Magwire invited his old friends Francis P. Blair, Jr., and Thomas Ewing, Jr., to participate with him in the N.L.U.[2]

The readiness with which both Day and Magwire drew into the labor movement with them men who had been their partisan opponents in the very immediate past bears witness to the disintegration of the political spectrum of 1866 and indicates that not all the middle-class participants in the N.L.U. were former Radicals. Quite the contrary, Absalom M. West had been a Confederate general. Unlike his colleagues on the Executive Committee, West found reform politics of any type a novel experience. The key to his strange career appears to lie in the fact that he had been a reluctant secessionist. A prominent Mississippi Whig before the war, West had been a political spokesman for great planters and cotton merchants of the Delta. But though he served as his state's quartermaster general, he had been a conditional unionist in 1861, and two years later he campaigned for governor in opposition to the fire-eating seccessionists of Governor Pettus's organization. Discovering that most of his votes at that time came from the Piney Woods region, West reoriented his political career toward the needs of the poor whites. Having been elected to Congress from northeastern Mississippi in both 1865 and 1868, only to be barred from his seat both times, West associated himself with projects to import white labor into his state, to organize a state grange, and to promote an agricultural college. While West was engaged in these activities Sylvis passed through Mississippi and established the first Labor Unions there. From such a group in Water Valley, location of some foundries and railroad shops, West came to the 1869 Labor Congress. He was quickly placed on the executive body as the representative of the South. So thor-

---

[1] John Magwire, *Response of the Hon. John Magwire, to a Resolution of the National Labor Council . . .* (St. Louis, 1874), p. 16.
[2] *Ibid.*, pp. 17–36; *Workingman's Advocate*, Sept. 5 and 12, 1874; J. Magwire to F. P. Blair, Jr., Aug. 7, 1869, in *ibid.*, Sept. 11, 1869; Blair to John Maguire [*sic*], Aug. 14, 1869, in *ibid.*

oughly was the general associated with labor-reform politics thereafter that in 1884 he was Butler's running mate on the national Greenback-Labor ticket.[3]

Austin Montana Puett had been a Peace Democrat. Stemming from a North Carolina family which moved to Parke County, Indiana, in the 1820's, he found himself constantly on the minority side among neighbors who also came from the Carolinas, but who were largely antislavery Quakers. The best Puett could ever do in years of campaigning was to secure brief posts as county sheriff and state canal commissioner. As his county swung into the Republican column, Puett became a staunch supporter of Stephen A. Douglas, hating Buchanan as the wrecker of his party even more, if possible, than he did the Republican foes. As wartime tensions erupted into armed clashes between local Union Leagues and local Knights of the Golden Circle, he became so thoroughly tainted with the odium of treason that by 1865 his political aspirations seemed futile. Democrats offered him no prospects of success, and Republicans he despised. Appearing at the Labor Congress of 1868, therefore, Puett opened a new career in labor-reform politics.[4]

Kingpin of the new executive board was Alexander Campbell, a lawyer and currency-reform theorist from La-Salle, Illinois. Born on a Pennsylvania farm in 1814, Campbell had successfully established himself in the iron business first in Pennsylvania, then in Virginia and Missouri. Sensing a prosperous future in the coal lands around LaSalle, he moved to that region as a promoter of mines in 1850. Entering politics

[3] John K. Bettersworth, *Confederate Mississippi* (Baton Rouge, La., 1943), pp. 52–4; J. F. Power, "The Black and Tan Convention," *Publications of the Mississippi Historical Society*, III (Oxford, Miss., 1900), 77; J. M. White, "Origin and Location of the Mississippi A & M College," *ibid.*, III, 347–8; J. S. McNeeley, "From Organization to Overthrow of Mississippi's Provisional Government," *ibid.* (Centenary Series, 1916), p. 12; *O.R.*, Series i, XVII, 10; *O.R.*, Series i, LIII, 701–2; *O.R.*, Series iv, II, 697, 922–4; Wharton, pp. 100, 127; Sylvis, p. 348; B. W. Terlinde to Edward Daniels, Oct. 9, 1884, Daniels Papers, Box 1.
[4] Maurice Murphy, "Some Features of the History of Parke County," *Indiana Magazine of History*, XII (1916), pp. 144–57; A. M. Puett to John G. Davis, Jan. 3, 1860, Puett to Davis, Jan. 15, 1860, in "Some Letters to John G. Davis, 1857–1860," *ibid.*, XXIV (1919), 207–10; Logan Esary, "Internal Improvements in Early Indiana," *Indiana Historical Publications*, V (1912), 146.

through the Whig party, Campbell was elected the town's first mayor in 1852, a year when Democrats enjoyed a narrow lead in the county over the combined Whig and Free Soil tallies. By 1856 the Republican party had established the commanding local majority that it was to enjoy for the next two decades, and Campbell had joined it. By 1858 he was a state representative, and four years later he was elected a delegate to the state's Constitutional Convention. He was familiar with the national "Safety Fund" scheme Edward Kellogg had developed in the 1840's for ensuring orderly economic growth, and this he blended with a promotional spirit worthy of Henry Carey to produce his own plan for a government-managed currency, a plan destined to become gospel with the N.L.U.[5]

The 1870 decision to separate the industrial and political arms of the N.L.U. placed these men in a decisive position to shape the organization's immediate future. So thoroughly had the N.L.U.'s activity already become focused on its political program that the industrial congress quickly passed into oblivion.[6] Establishment of the long-promised party, on the other hand, was entrusted to a Committee on National Political Organization, dominated by Campbell and Puett. Among their eleven colleagues on this body were only three workers of prominence (Siney, Cummings, and Phelps), while the ranks of middle-class reformers included Moses Field, a Detroit businessman and longtime Republican, and Clinton Briggs, an old abolitionist and railroad promoter from Omaha, in addition to Magwire and West.[7]

On behalf of this committee Campbell and Puett issued an appeal for a nominating convention to assemble in Columbus, Ohio. Their obvious aim was to utilize the Labor Reform party as a rallying center for all foes of Stalwart politics, whether Liberal, Sentimentalist, Democrat, or labor. To this

---

[5] *Workingman's Advocate*, Aug. 8 and 15, 1874; *Bio. Dir. Amer. Congress*, p. 940; Moses, *Illinois*, II, 622, 656. For Kellogg's plan, see his *Labor and Other Capital: The Rights of Each Secured and the Wrongs of Both Eradicated* . . . (New York, 1849). For elaboration of Campbell's plan, see below, Chapter 11.

[6] See above, pp. 191–4.

[7] *Workingman's Advocate*, Aug. 27, 1870. On Field, see *Bio. Dir. Amer. Congress*, p. 885; *Workingman's Advocate*, Aug. 17, 1872. On Briggs, see Roney, pp. 203, 241–2.

end they announced an all-inclusive program of reforms, ranging from greenback currency and reservation of the public domain to actual settlers through a "tariff for revenue only," a just Indian policy, and the prohibition of coolie importation, to a policy of general amnesty and the creation of a board of "intelligent businessmen" to manage the currency and reform the civil service.[8] Joyously, the new party welcomed the New Departure of Ohio's Democrats as burying "all dead issues" and leaving "no difference in principle between them and the Labor Reformers."[9] Although they were distressed that these Democrats also embraced resumption of specie payments, Campbell and his associates blandly operated on the assumption that through a combination of rational discussion and astute electoral maneuvers the tide of Liberal reform could actually be swept into the Labor Reform camp. Aware only of ideas and individuals, the Sentimentalists at the party's helm were oblivious of social forces.

Hence Campbell was easily enticed by the campaign managers of Justice David Davis into using the power of his office to impose Davis on the labor party, despite the Justice's consistent refusal to endorse the greenback plan, and despite the utter contempt of Davis's aides for both greenbacks and Campbell personally.[1] His strategy was to nominate a "People's Ticket," with candidates so attractive to Liberals and New Departure Democrats that, as he prophesied to Davis, "but little interest will be felt in the Cincinnati [Liberal Republican] Convention and if it shall meet at all it will be compelled to accept the people's Candidates." The same course, he continued, "will also bring the Democracy into our ranks."[2] So thoroughly was Campbell persuaded of the brilliance of this maneuver that he, the author of the N.L.U.'s

---

[8] *Workingman's Advocate*, Feb. 4, 1871. The N.L.R.P. Convention reversed the revenue tariff position posed here. *Ibid.*, March 2, 1872.

[9] Editorial, *ibid.*, May 21, 1871.

[1] See Jesse W. Fell to Alexander Campbell, Jan. 8, 1872, enclosed in Fell to David Davis, Jan. 15, 1872; Fell to Davis, Feb. 24, 1872; C. H. Moore to Davis, Feb. 28, 1872; Samuel C. Parks to Davis, Feb. 26, 1872; Thomas Ewing, Jr., to Davis, Feb. 22, 1872, all in David Davis Papers.

[2] Alexander Campbell to David Davis, Feb. 29, 1872, Davis Papers. *Cf.* Thomas Ewing, Jr., to Davis, Feb. 22, 1872, *ibid.*

greenback plan, conspired to prevent any labor reformers from embarrassing Davis by quizzing him on the currency question.[3]

In his scheme Campbell easily acquired the assistance of Puett and the Ohio Greenbacker Thomas Ewing, Jr., who operated simultaneously within the Labor Reform and Democratic parties. To control the nominating convention of the Labor Reform party, however, involved influencing the delegations from Pennsylvania and New York, in addition to Illinois and Ohio, for the electoral votes of those four states controlled 98 of the 201 ballots cast at the convention. The Workingmen's Benevolent Association provided the gravitational center of Pennsylvania's Labor Reform party, while around it clustered three satellite blocs: the labor-oriented wing of Schuylkill County's Democratic Party, led by former congressman Hendrick B. Wright; the followers of incumbent Republican Governor John W. Geary, who was extremely popular with the miners and was represented in the labor party by his new commissioner of industrial statistics, Thomas C. MacDowell; and Philadelphia Section 26 of the International, led by attorney Daymon Y. Kilgore. This group came to Columbus eager to nominate Geary, but it was amenable to manipulation by Campbell and Puett because it shared their dearest wish, to influence the forthcoming Liberal Republican gathering. Since this common motive led them to want a nominee with "availability," when Geary's boom failed to secure its needed majority, his followers readily shifted to Davis.[4] More formidable was the opposition from New York. An intriguing array of trade-union leaders and anti-Marxists from the I.W.A. had come in the company of Wallace P. Groom and Pliney Freeman from the small soft-money wing of the New York Chamber of Commerce determined to nominate Horace Day. In cooperation with Troup and his Connecticut delegation, Day mobilized an impenetrable bloc of fifty-nine votes.[5]

By the third ballot the Davis forces had gathered Penn-

[3] C. H. Moore to David Davis, Feb. 28, 1872, Davis Papers. *Cf.* Unger, *Greenback Era*, pp. 186–90.

[4] *Workingman's Advocate*, March 2, 1872.

[5] *Ibid.* On Groom and Freeman, see Unger, *Greenback Era*, pp. 114–19.

sylvania and enough assorted delegations into their camp to rout the New Yorkers. Informed of his nomination by the chairman of the convention, Justice Davis telegraphed an evasive reply thanking the Labor Reformers for the honor and adding: "The Chief Magistracy of the Republic should neither be sought nor declined by an American citizen."[6] When the convention appointed a committee to interview Davis in hopes of discovering whether his reply meant yes or no, the committee itself became the theater of wild maneuvers, among them feeding misinformation to Andrew Cameron so that he would not be present with any possibly untoward questions when the group finally did meet the judge.[7] Campbell eagerly advised Davis on campaign strategy, calling the land and currency questions "paramount," with civilian government, general amnesty, and civil-service reform following in that order. So involved was he in his design to weld together the nation's diverse reformers under his leadership, that Campbell lost sight completely of the working-class origins of his own party. "Very little general interest is felt in the questions of legalizing the hours of work or the management of convict labor and other kindred subjects," Davis was assured by this executive of the Labor Reform party.[8]

All Campbell's efforts were in vain, because he failed to realize that Liberals and Sentimentalists represented antagonistic, not complementary, reform currents. Liberals at the Cincinnati Convention in June shunned the labor reformers, their candidate, and their financial ideas. David Davis, having made what use he wished of the Labor Reform party, then explicitly declined its nomination.[9] Amid all the regrets and mutual recriminations that subsequently ran through the party's ranks, it was a leader of the coal miners of Braidwood, Illinois, who saw most clearly what had happened. The Liberals had failed to make common cause with the Labor

[6] Telegrams, E. M. Chamberlain to David Davis, and Davis to Chamberlain, Feb. 22, 1872, Davis Papers.
[7] Wallace P. Groom to David Davis, Feb. 27, 1872; J. S. Black to Davis, Feb. 28, 1872; Horace H. Day to Davis, March 5, 1872, Davis Papers; editorial, *Workingman's Advocate*, May 10, 1873.
[8] Alexander Campbell to David Davis, Feb. 29, 1872, Davis Papers.
[9] David Davis to E. M. Chamberlain, June 24, 1872, in *Workingman's Advocate*, July 6, 1872.

Reform party, wrote John James, because they "could not reach over the gulf that divides capital and labor."[1]

From this point on the complexity of the Labor Reform party's history rises in direct proportion to its insignificance. With labor-reform journals announcing themselves almost at random for Greeley or for Grant, the disheartened Executive Committee summoned the party convention into resumed session in New York. Here genuine working-class delegates predominated, in marked contrast to Columbus. Consequently, Day and Troup, having presented themselves to the Columbus Convention as the champions of "true labor reformers" against middle-class manipulators, were in a good position to seize the helm, and they did so.[2] But where did they steer the party? Toward yet another convention in Philadelphia, which turned out to be a rallying point, not for labor, but for the flotsam and jetsam of the democracy which had been set adrift by the New Departure. Remnants of the Executive Committee met one last time to denounce "the Philadelphia fraud," while Day scurried about luring Straight-Out Democrats to the banner of Charles O'Connor, an anti-Tweed Democrat and one-time apostle of slavery whom the *Workingman's Advocate* characterized as "cold, calculating and unscrupulous."[3] Understandably, editor Cameron concluded: "The labor reformers have little if any interest in the result" of the Presidential campaign.[4] So discouraging was the whole imbroglio that a generation of American labor leaders looked back upon the experience of 1872 as evidence of the perils that lay in wait down the path of party politics.

THE OLD ORDER AND THE NEW

The typical abolitionist, David Donald has written, was born very early in the nineteenth century in rural New England of a respected "old family" which was "neither rich nor

---

[1] Letter of John James, *ibid.*, May 25, 1872. *Cf.* editorial, *ibid.*, Nov. 16, 1872.
[2] *Ibid.*, July 18, Aug. 17, 1872; New York *Tribune*, July 31, Aug. 1, 1872.
[3] *Workingman's Advocate*, Aug. 17, 24, 31, 1872; New York *Tribune*, Aug. 23, 26, 27, 31, 1872.
[4] Editorial, *Workingman's Advocate*, Oct. 12, 1872.

poor," and was reared "in a faith of aggressive piety and moral endeavor." Men and women of such origins, shocked by the crass lust for wealth which they feared was replacing yester-year's moral order of status and stability, turned readily to the pursuit of social reforms.[5]

There is merit in Donald's analysis, and with minor amendments its description fits many of those Sentimental Reformers who enlisted in the New England Labor Reform League and the American sections of the International as well as it does Donald's abolitionists. The amendments are, first, that the typical Sentimentalist was ten to twenty years younger than the typical abolitionist, coming to political maturity in the 1840's rather than the 1830's; and second, that he was most commonly of small-town, rather than strictly rural, origin—a man of Worcester, Braintree, or Fall River. Many of them, however, resided in Boston or its suburbs by the 1860's.

Unfortunately, this characterization seems to fit the Liberals as appropriately as it does the Sentimentalists. True, most members of the American Association for the Promotion of Social Science in the 1860's were just entering into the professional eminence they were to enjoy for at least another two decades, while the roster of the New England Labor Reform League resembled a final gathering of lesser notables from the ante-bellum era. Yet if Stephen S. Foster, William B. Greene, William Henry Channing, Josiah Warren, and John Orvis were unmistakably the elders of, say, Dana, Godkin, and Sanborn (and old enough to be fathers of most working-class labor reformers), there were prominent Liberals like Frank Bird, Amasa Walker, and Dr. Samuel G. Howe who were the Sentimentalists' contemporaries. In two respects, however, the two types of middle-class reformers do tend to cluster around opposite poles.

First, the Liberals on the whole were both more wealthy and far closer to the operative centers of political and economic power than were the Sentimental Reformers. The "alienation of the Mugwumps" has been overdone by recent historians. Liberal reformers were both highly respected and

---

[5] Donald, *Lincoln Reconsidered*, pp. 25-33. *Cf.* Richard Hofstadter on the "Mugwump personality," *Age of Reform, From Bryan to F.D.R.* (New York, 1955), pp. 135-42.

influential among the industrialists, to whom they were allegedly diametrically opposed.[6] Secondly, even before the Civil
War and during the days when both groups tended to be
found in the Radical camp, future Liberals were more suspicious of governmental action in general than were future
Sentimentalists, to whom labor reform, land reform, associa-
tionism, and other critiques of the emerging industrial capitalism were familiar fare. In this sense, after the rupture of
radicalism they simply reverted to their ante-bellum beliefs
and allegiances. This generalization is especially true of participants in the New England Labor Reform League, though it
does not hold for business promoters like Campbell and
Ewing who were attracted to the N.L.U. primarily for the help
it could offer their currency reform ideas. The greenback
movement, after all, was an offspring of the war itself.

Two ideas, both well rooted in prewar humanitarian
crusades, provided the core of the Sentimentalist credo. The
first was that any exercise of power by one human being over
another was "a usurpation." Republican simplicity they identified not simply with equality of opportunity but with the
absence of any subordination of one man or woman to another. For people of such beliefs the labor-reform movement
and the struggle for women's rights were but logical extensions
of the assault on chattel slavery.[7] Secondly, both excessive
accumulation of personal wealth and the cute business practices needed to accumulate it they deemed immoral, as they
associated virtue with moderation and "honest industry." Both
principles led the Labor Reform League to denounce "the
vassalage of the producing to the speculating classes."[8] Society
now denied him Emersonian self-reliance, protested Ezra
Heywood—"I must be a serf, bound to the soil, an itinerant
chattel forced to sell myself, by the day, to the highest bidder,
or, what is worse, by the chicanery of business, to subsist on
others' earnings. . . ."[9] The only element of society the Senti-

---

[6] See Kirkland, *Dream and Thought*, pp. 12–28. *Cf.* Hofstadter, *Age of Reform*, pp. 135–42.

[7] *Eg.*, Frederic A. Hinckley, *The Just Demand of Labor, A More Equal Distribution of Wealth* (Boston, 1871); Hinckley, *Philosophy of the Labor Movement* (Boston, 1874).

[8] *Revolution*, Vol. III (Feb. 11, 1869), p. 84.

[9] E. H. Heywood, *The Labor Party*, p. 10.

mentalists believed willing to help them reform such thorough corruption was "the laboring poor," who "know nothing of the luxury of wealth or of its debasements." Aghast at the gluttony of the rich, they conjured up an idyllic image of the workers: "They rise with the lark. Their humble morning meal, sweetened with the kiss of her who spreads it, sends them to the toil which makes the earth inhabitable; and they return at night to clasp the blossoms of their love upon their breasts, with an honest joy which is in itself the purest praise to Heaven."[1]

Ezra H. Heywood was the moving spirit of the New England group. Younger than most of his associates, this Worcester farm boy had graduated from Brown University in 1856 at the age of twenty-seven and plunged into the antislavery movement. During the war he made himself the center of endless controversy by coupling extreme abolitionist views with pacifism and a willingness to condone secession. At the close of the war he made numerous speeches among the mill hands in defense of the ten-hour movement and formed a small circle of friends of labor reform in Worcester. Believing as earnestly as Godkin and Atkinson that the law of supply and demand was "one with the movements of the sea, the air and the sunlight," and that the "dangerous classes" of the cities threatened to engulf civilization's greatest monuments in "a fiery tide of barbarism," Heywood found the remedy in the abolition of every monopoly of social power and of monopoly's iniquitous spoils, rent and interest.[2] This doctrine led him to found the anarchist journal *The Word* in 1872 and to pursue a relentless polemic against the institution of marriage. His book *Cupid's Yokes* earned him eighteen-months imprisonment late in the seventies, and as late as 1892 he was jailed again on obscenity charges for such writings. The next year he became ill at a Boston labor convention and died.[3]

After attending both the Special Council and the regular 1868 Labor Congress, Heywood enlisted the aid of Ira Steward and George McNeill, Edward D. Linton, who was soon

---

[1] George Wilkes, *The Internationale: Its Principles and Purposes* . . . (New York, 1871), p. 8.
[2] Heywood, *Labor Party*, pp. 5, 12, and *passim*.
[3] Obituary, Boston *Globe*, May 23, 1893, and assorted clippings in Heywood Papers. See also Dorfman, III, 37.

secretary of Boston's Section 20 of the I.W.A., and Mrs. Elizabeth La Pierre Daniels of the women's rights movement for the purpose of staging a meeting "to explain and enforce the principles of the National Labor Union."[4] Crispins, eight-hour men, legislators, and veterans of the industrial congresses of the 1840's all participated in a gathering so harmonious that everyone's ideas found a place in the final program of the New England Labor Reform League they established. To prove the universal merit of its claims the League confidently urged "the manager whose genius and energy make him the natural head of the concern, the honest merchant . . . the philosopher in his closet, preachers of truth, poets, painters, sculptors, counsellors in equity, statesmen exacting justice, women adorning industry, the whole fraternity of workers to aid in this great struggle for human redemption."[5]

The League's internal concord was quickly shattered by the turbulent currents of the Bay State's labor politics. This was the spring when the Republican legislators rejected the Crispins's plea for incorporation, then tried to soothe the workingmen by enacting the Eight Hour League's proposal for a bureau of labor statistics.[6] The shoemakers spurned the bureau, while Eight Hour men staffed it, and the resulting antagonisms spilled over into the Labor Reform League. At its meeting in July, 1869, Heywood, supported by the Crispins, carefully planned the agenda so as to emphasize currency reform and relegate the whole eight-hour movement to a single speech by McNeill.[7] Here began the close cooperation between the League and the Crispins that bore fruit in the state's Labor Reform party and in the continuous representation of the shoemakers' union on the otherwise middle-class executive board of the N.L.U. In the early years of the 1870's Wendell Phillips became the Labor Reform League's most forceful leader and directed its merciless and unabating dis-

---

[4] *Revolution,* Vol. III (Jan. 7, 1869), p. 10.
[5] *Ibid.,* Vol. III (Jan. 21, 1869), p. 33; *ibid.,* Vol. III (Feb. 11, 1869), p. 85.
[6] See above, p. 369.
[7] *American Workman,* June 5, July 3, 1869; *Declaration of Sentiments and Constitution of the New-England Labor-Reform League* (Boston, 1869).

paragement of both the bureau and the Eight Hour League.[8]
Steward and McNeill, however, angrily left the league, reconstituted their Eight Hour League, and set off on their quest for
a genuinely working-class movement that led them into co-
operation with the I.W.A.'s Marxists.

With the subsequent decline of the K.O.S.C., however,
the wage-earner base of the Labor Reform League shriveled
up, and the group yielded its focal role among Sentimental
Reformers to newer societies like the Sovereigns of Industry
and the Christian Labor Union. John Orvis, elected the
league's president in 1873, exemplified this trend. Born on a
Vermont farm in 1816, Orvis was schooled at Oberlin College
and Brook Farm. From the 1840's to his death in 1897 he
castigated the "wages system" with Garrisonian fervor.
Through cooperative societies of producers he wished to abolish subordination of man to man, and through spiritualism he
aspired to end subjugation of man to an omnipotent God. To
promote cooperatives he helped found the Sovereigns of Industry in 1874, then entered the Knights of Labor, where the
1880's found him an officer of District Assembly 30. His late
years were passed among the followers of Edward Bellamy in
Boston's Nationalist Club.[9]

Class conflict was the corollary of industrialism that most
distressed Orvis, and in this respect his outlook resembled that
of the Liberals. His penchant for cooperative production as a
solution to social antagonisms was also shared by Godkin,
Atkinson, Sanborn, and Blodgett. To those Liberals, however,
"cooperation" meant the spawning by businessmen of profit-
sharing schemes and savings banks to make wage earners feel
an identification with the existing social order. Orvis, on the
other hand, wished to restructure that order entirely on the
basis of common ownership of productive facilities. This aspiration attracted him to the International Workingmen's Association, which early in the 1870's was being deluged with

---

[8] *Weekly American Workman,* June 19, 1869; *Mass. BLS, 1873,* pp.
5–16; Boston *Commonwealth,* June 1, 1872; letter of E. M. F. Denton,
ibid., June 8, 1872; letter of Ira Steward, *ibid.,* June 22, 1872; letter of
Steward, *ibid.,* June 29, 1872; McNeill, *Labor Movement,* pp. 139–40.
[9] *Labor Leader,* Jan. 15, 1887; obituary in *ibid.,* May 8, 1897; T. D. Seymour Basset to Ernest C. Miller, Dec. 19, 1947, Thaddeus L. Sheldon
Papers; letters of John Orvis, *American Workman,* June 26, July 3, 1869.

Sentimental Reformers to a degree surpassing even the N.L.U. at the same time.

Society organized as a single joint-stock company conducting all its productive and distributive functions—that was the vision described by Cyrenus Osborne Ward in 1871. Brother of the more famous Lester Ward, Cyrenus was a master machinist at the Brooklyn Navy Yard and in his midthirties when he turned his attention to the labor question. Traveling to the Basle Congress of the I.W.A. with Andrew Cameron in 1869, Ward sought to convince the International's General Council to finance large cooperative enterprises in America and simultaneously to enter American politics. When at some future date their spokesmen had won control of Congress, they could simply decree the cooperatives government property. The friendly response offered Ward's scheme by Belgian and French leaders of the I.W.A. and the enthusiasm he encountered among Spanish maritime workers contrasted sharply with the scorn of the Marxists, and previewed the coming rift in the International's ranks in America. Though Ward declined the position on the General Council to which the Hague Congress elected him in 1872, he subsequently became an organizer for the Socialist Labor party, then while a librarian for the federal Bureau of Labor he wrote his classic work, *The Ancient Lowly*.[1]

Ward's views drew support from Richard J. Hinton, surely the most influential member of the I.W.A. on this side of the Atlantic. The secretary of Section 23 in Washington, D.C., which was constituted primarily of civil servants, Hinton bore a commission from Marx to organize for the International and consistently corresponded directly with the General Council in London, to the distress of the Central Committee in New York. He was an English-born free-lance newspaperman who had come to the United States in 1851. With a new degree as a topographical engineer, Hinton went to Kansas, associated himself with John Brown, T. W. Higginson, and Franklin B. Sanborn, and emerged as secretary of the 1857

---

[1] C. Osborne Ward, *The New Idea. Universal Co-operation and Theories of Future Government* (New York, n.d.); Ward, *Ancient Lowly* (Washington, D.C., 1889–1900); Bernstein, pp. 46, 163; *Prem. Int.*, II, 362; Agnes Inglis notes, C. O. Ward, JAL.

Free State Convention in Topeka. When the first regiment of Negro troops was mustered in Kansas, Hinton became one of its officers. A prolific writer, he was a chronicler of the Western armies, regular correspondent for the New York *Tribune* and the *Anti-Slavery Standard*, and author of articles for the *Atlantic Monthly*, *Galaxy*, and other leading periodicals on everything from the International through Western land frauds to the impending struggle among the great powers for control of the China market. Drawn to the I.W.A. by his devotion to cooperatives, Hinton went on to become a journalist for the Socialist Labor party and, in the late 1890's, chief of the colonization commission for Eugene V. Debs's Social Democracy of America. An indication of the astuteness of the Republican party's 1872 appeal for the labor vote lies in its selection of this man to serve as secretary of its National Executive Committee.[2]

But an administrator of Grant's campaign for re-election is hardly typical of the middle-class members of the International. Most of them were elderly land reformers residing in New York City. These disciples of George Henry Evans provided the only living bridge between the new labor-reform movement and the age of the Locofocos. Among them were John Commerford, who as a leader of New York's chair makers had been elected the last president of the National Trades Union in 1835; Lewis Masquerier, who had helped Evans found his National Reform Association in 1844; Joshua K. Ingalls, a prominent figure in the Industrial Congresses of 1847 and 1848; and William West, who had participated in New York's trade unions and its Kansas League in the early 1850's.[3] Ardent foes of any form of monopoly, these men

---

[2] Bernstein, pp. 31, 64; Bliss, p. 689; Yearley, *Britons*, pp. 220–1; Higginson, *Cheerful Yesterdays*, pp. 215, 231–4; Wilder, *Annals of Kansas*, pp. 164, 208, 237, 316, 340, 426, 483, 563; Aveling, pp. 196–8; Independent Order Knights of Labor, *Official Historical Hand-Book* (Jersey City, 1898), no pagination, in W.S.H.S.; Richard J. Hinton, "Organization of Labor"; Hinton, "John Bright at Home"; Hinton, "The Race for Commercial Supremacy in Asia," *Galaxy*, Vol. VIII (Aug. 1869), pp. 180–94; letterhead of Union Republican Executive Committee, Washington, D.C., in Republican party (Union Republican) 1872, JAL.
[3] Walter A. Hugins, *Jacksonian Democracy and the Working Class: A Study of the New York Workingmen's Movement, 1829–1837* (Stanford,

attacked with equal fervor "landlordry," which pre-empts the soil, "elective officery," which engenders self-perpetuating clique control of governmental machinery, and "Godology," through which clergymen corner the supply of "saving grace."[4]

The epithet "anti-industrial" has today become a commonplace in historical analysis of any and all critics of nineteenth-century American capitalism. For the land reformers (and for them alone) it is thoroughly appropriate. Wage labor, the state, bureaucratization of power—the whole fabric of industrial life roused their ire. "Instead of railroads and all the great thoroughfares of travel being thronged with people trying to swell the already over-populated cities, and loaded with withered, adulterated, half-decayed provisions at starvation prices," wrote Lewis Masquerier of the proposed republican townships, "each owner of a share in the soil could sit down under his 'own vine and fig tree,' and partake of the fresh fruits of his own labor."[5] Other Sentimentalists longed to enjoy the productive benefits of the machine age while avoiding the exploitation, social antagonisms, and concentration of power which accompanied them. They sought formulas to improve the emerging society. Land reformers, despairing of any such improvements, beckoned toward a static utopia on the farm.

While the N.L.U.'s fixation on currency reform repelled these thorough anarchists, the universal pretensions of the I.W.A. made it appear to them an ideal institution through which to institute their republican townships with equal and inalienable homesteads. Easily exchanging ideas and information with several New York reform societies, among them an offshoot of the New England Labor Reform League, the land reformers constituted by 1871 the backbone of Sections 9 and 12 of the International.[6] It was through these groups, in turn,

---

Cal., 1960), pp. 72–4; Lewis Masquerier, *Sociology: Or, The Reconstruction of Society* . . . (New York, 1877), pp. 126, 132–6; Degler, pp. 157–63, 206; Joshua King Ingalls, *Reminiscences of an Octogenarian* . . . (Elmira, N.Y., 1897); Helene S. Zahler, *Eastern Workingmen and National Land Policy, 1829–1862* (New York, 1941).

[4] See Masquerier for an excellent presentation of the land-reform doctrine.

[5] Masquerier, p. 18.

[6] Bernstein, pp. 104–8.

that the mercurial Victoria Woodhull and her sister Tennessee Claflin rose to fame and glory.

Victoria and Tennie were dazzling beauties in their early thirties when they kicked up such a storm in the International as to draw its attention away even from Europe's Bakunin anarchists and League of the Three Emperors. During the decade and a half since they had left the Ohio farm community of their birth, they had staged spiritualist seances, peddled wondrous cures for cancer, been run out of an Illinois town when their patients began dying, and attracted a host of ardent, devoted lovers. Their great opportunity came in 1868, when Tennie administered such memorable treatments to Cornelius Vanderbilt that he set her and her sister up as stockbrokers on Wall Street. While public knowledge of their link to the railroad magnate made the brokerage firm an overnight success, the sisters also persuaded Vanderbilt to finance a newspaper, *Woodhull and Claflin's Weekly*, through which Victoria opened a campaign to become President of the United States. By a dramatic appearance before a congressional committee to appeal for women's suffrage, Victoria forced Stanton, Anthony, and other established leaders of that cause to accept her into their ranks. And by presenting a paper on labor and capital (written by the former Brook Farm Fourierist Stephen Pearl Andrews) to a convention organized in New York by the New England Labor Reform League, she gained entrance into Section 12 of the I.W.A.[7]

Because *Woodhull and Claflin's Weekly* was the only journal attached to the International on this side of the Atlantic, and because Victoria planned and led a spectacular memorial procession for executed French Communards through the streets of New York, she quickly came to symbolize the International for much of the American public.[8] Scandalized by her behavior and fearful lest the I.W.A. become "merely the seat of long forgotten and small Reformers and

---

[7] Emanie Sachs, *"The Terrible Siren"*: *Victoria Woodhull* (*1838–1927*) (New York, 1928), pp. 1–96; *Religio-Philosophical Journal*, Dec. 7, 1872, p. 4; Harper, I, 375–9; M. F. Darwen, *One Moral Standard for All. Extracts from the Lives of Victoria Claflin Woodhull, Now Mrs. John Biddulph Martin, and Tennessee Claflin, Now Lady Cook* (New York, n.d.).

[8] Sachs, p. 146.

other benefactors of mankind," Sorge, Bolte, and other Marxist leaders assembled a rump meeting of the Central Committee, with representatives of only eight sections invited, passed a statute requiring two thirds of all members of any section of the I.W.A. to be wage earners, and used this regulation to expel Section 12.[9]

Both sides in the dispute appealed to the Hague Congress of the I.W.A. for support, and when that congress threw its weight behind Sorge's group (in fact, it moved the General Council itself to New York and Sorge's tutelage), the middle-class reformers held their own congress in Philadelphia and established a rival International Workingmen's Association.[1] By this time, however, Woodhull and Claflin had faded out of the picture. Two months prior to the Philadelphia meeting, they had held a convention of their own to make Victoria the Presidential nominee of the Equal Rights party. By Election Day she had lost interest in even that cause, for Victoria was then hatching the most sensational exposé of the nineteenth century. At a spiritualist meeting in December 1872, she charged the Reverend Henry Ward Beecher with cuckolding Theodore Tilton. Having been jailed several times on flimsy slander and obscenity charges for the storm she had thus created, Victoria abruptly came out for God and Motherhood, sailed to England with her sister on a munificent expense account just as the Vanderbilt will was about to be contested, married a titled British banker (and found a baron for Tennie), and passed stately years as lady of an English manor.[2]

Woodhull and Claflin were catalysts of the split in the International, not its cause. Though Marxist historiography has posed the issue as Victoria and Tennie versus the working

---

[9] MSS circular signed F. Bolte, to all sections of the Intl. Workingmen's Assn. in America, dated Dec., 1871, I.W.A. Papers, Box 1; Provisional Federal Council of the I.W.A. in North America, *Appeal to the Workingmen of America* (pamphlet dated May 19, 1872), *ibid.*; J. F. Elliott to Citizen Rehn, Dec. 5, 1871, *ibid.*

[1] *Prem. Int.*, II, 376, 379; *Proceedings of the First Congress of the American International Workingmen's Association, Held in Philadelphia, Pa., July 9 and 10, 1872* (New York, 1872). (Hereafter cited as *Proceedings, Phila. I.W.A.*)

[2] Sachs, *passim;* Darwen, *passim;* clippings in "Anarchism—Woodhull, Victoria C.," JAL Collection.

class,[3] the fact remains that there were fifty sections of the International in America at the end of 1871, of which only eight supported the expulsion of Section 12. Six of those eight were German, the other two were tiny Irish groups. While one French, one Irish, and one American section (Hinton's in Washington) stood neutral, and one French section disbanded, the other thirty-eight sections went over to the new International, which defied Sorge and the Hague Congress. Seventeen of these sections were "American" (conducted in the English language), while four were German (Lassallean), fifteen were French, one Spanish, and one Italian.[4] Since the core of the group was made up of French refugees from Napoleon III and anarchistically inclined American natives, it is not surprising that the French, Spanish, and Italian followers of Bakunin whom the Hague Congress also expelled made common cause with these groups in America. Through men such as Elliott and Banks in New York and Thomas Phillips in Philadelphia, the anti-Marxists had significant ties with organized workers, despite the fact that they were preponderantly middle class. It was, in fact, their group, not Sorge's, with which the New York Workingmen's Assembly dealt during 1872 and 1873 as the "genuine" International.[5]

The crucial point is that the International split not simply over the antics of two remarkable ladies, but over the deeper issue of the relationship of middle-class reformers to a labor movement. The French sections held no special love for Woodhull and Claflin. Indeed, when Victoria briefly revived her interest in the I.W.A. and tried to install herself on the council of the anti-Marxist International, the most important French sections seceded, as did Banks.[6] But the French and all the American participants concurred in C. O. Ward's

---

[3] Sorge, "1866–1876," pp. 394–5; Foner, *Labor*, I, 414–15. This view is reflected in Commons, *Labour*, II, 211–13. Bernstein, pp. 112–19, offers a balanced presentation of the dispute.

[4] J. F. Elliott to Citizen Rehn, n.d., I.W.A. Papers, Box 1.

[5] For background of the French sections, see their original journal, *Bulletin de l'union républicaine de la langue française*, 1869–71, and its short-lived successor, *Le Socialiste*. For relations of the Philadelphia (or Spring Street) I.W.A. with the New York Workingmen's Assembly, see Bernstein, pp. 179–88.

[6] Bernstein, p. 185.

judgment that Sorge's effort to restrict the International to sections two thirds of whose members were wage earners was an act of "bigotry."[7] And the program they adopted in the absence of the Marxists was as all-embracing as the N.L.U.'s ever was.[8] While Sorge denounced the reformers as "carpet-baggers" in the North, dispatched by the *bourgeoisie* to confuse the workers, William West declared: "The bourgeoisie possess and acquire the experience and the intelligence which the movement needs."[9]

The relationship between labor reformers and the Senti-mentalists, therefore, played a crucial part in fitting the workers' movement into the new balance of social forces that was emerging in the Reconstruction era. The Sentimental Reformers, as true bearers of the Radical legacy, entertained no fears of popular government and looked to the "laboring poor" as the most likely supporters for their schemes of social redemption, but they still believed that the natural and deserving leaders of society were to be found in the middle class. They retained the Lincolnian faith that exertion and virtue carried "the prudent, penniless beginner in the world" up the ladder of success whereby he proved himself "more worthy to be trusted" than any other member of society.[1] Ezra Heywood reflected this set of beliefs when he wrote of "the capitalist whose genius and energy make him the natural head of the concern."[2]

The indispensable obverse of this value system is that the working-class leaders accepted it. The mentality of labor leaders (the reform syndrome) and the labor-reform commu-nity within which they operated exposed them consistently and effectively to the preachings of the Sentimentalists. Hence the active labor reformer functioned as a transmission belt,

---

[7] Ward, *New Idea*, p. 22.

[8] See *Proceedings, Phila. I.W.A.*; "The International Workingmen's Association," printed handbill signed by J. F. Elliott, I.W.A. Papers, Box 1.

[9] Sorge, "1866–1876," p. 173; West speech at the Hague Congress, *Prem. Int.*, II, 343. My translation from the French transcript: "*Les bourgeois possèdent et acquièrent l'expérience et l'intelligence dont le mouvement a besoin.*"

[1] Lincoln, *Works*, V, 52–3.

[2] Heywood, *Labor Party*, p. 12.

carrying middle-class ideas and values to the workers, and the farther the belt was removed from leadership councils, the less effectively it operated. "If we ask our friends to attend a meeting for the purpose of discussing the effect of giving away land, or the issuing of National Banks, or the importation of cheap labor," wrote the bricklayers' leader, John W. Browning, "they look at you with blank amazement and wonder. What business have they with such weighty subjects!" Through trade unions like his own, Browning believed, workers could learn to "think, to sacrifice, and to lose our prejudices," and thus become mentally prepared to enter the "higher field" of politics.[3] He understood that it was at the top echelons of the labor-reform movement that the doctrines of Alexander Campbell or Horace Day or Wendell Phillips were most likely to generate enthusiasm.

Following its 1870 Cincinnati Congress, the N.L.U. issued a new *Address to the People of the United States,* which stands in remarkable contrast to the 1867 *Address to the Workingmen.* Currency reform occupied twelve of the fifteen pages in the new document, and its learned rhetoric gave unmistakable evidence of Sentimentalist authorship (probably Campbell's). The demand for the eight-hour day appeared only on the next-to-the-last page, and then with the following argument to support it: "The power of men and animals is properly expressed by three quantities: force, velocity, and time. In every organization there is a fixed value of these quantities subject to use, beyond which we cannot go without injury. The best formula for the highest results from these quantities is" eight hours for work, eight for culture, eight for sleep. "This division is in harmony with the Encyclopaedia Britannica . . . is based in scientific and natural laws . . ." and so on and so forth.[4] But all this sound and fury bore the signatures not only of Campbell and Puett, but also of Richard Trevellick, Conrad Kuhn, A. T. Cavis, and Henry J. Walls.

Labor reformers not only accepted ideas and leadership from middle-class friends, but mimicked their behavior as

---

[3] Letter of John W. Browning, *Workingman's Advocate,* Oct. 19, 1872.
[4] *Address of the National Labor Union to the People of the United States, on Money, Land and other Subjects of National Importance* (Chicago, 1870), p. 14.

well. Both the nature of the affair and the tone of the narrative made this clear when the *Workingman's Advocate* reported the First Grand Annual Ball of Carpenters' and Joiners' Union No. 1:

> The grand saloon of the hall was handsomely lighted by gas jets, aided by a circle of jets shedding their lights from the centre of the ceiling. At 9 o'clock precisely, the Great Western Light Guard Band having taken position on the stand, the ball was opened with a grand promenade. The company having made the circuit of the saloon several times, at a given signal formed the "Sicilian Circle," and the real amusement of the evening commenced.

> The Floor Director, Mr. James F. Killilea, displayed much skill, taste and good judgement in the make-up of the programme, and selection of the dances, many of which were new and novel, especially the "Contra": C. and J. Victory which was an entirely new piece. Mr. Killilea, in his arduous duties as Floor Manager, was ably assisted by Mr. G. W. Eakle, who paid particular attention to the ladies, not a few of whom complimented him upon his good looks and gallantry. (As Mr. "E." is a young man and unmarried, we have serious apprehensions for the future state of his felicity.) The President, Mr. Owens and the Vice President, Mr. Lynch, both acted in their sphere in admirable style. Deputy Schindler was on hand, looking very pale and careworn, but nevertheless he participated in the merry maze, and seemed to enjoy himself as though he was in perfect health. We also noticed Mr. O'Donohue, President of the Stone-cutters' Union in the hall, as well as the worthy Financial Secretary of the same Association and several of the members, all of whom seemed to enjoy themselves. Last, though not least by any means, are the ladies; of whom we would say, were it not from fear we would be accused of flattery, that they were the prettiest little dears we have seen in Chicago, and their sylph-like forms, flitting around the saloon were perfectly enchanting. The dancing of the ladies was par excellence; the most difficult and intricate figures being executed with perfect ease, elegance and gracefulness. To discriminate would seem unfair, and yet we cannot re-

frain from saying that "roguish eyed damsel" Miss C——, was the belle of the evening, and her dancing was admired by all who noticed her, as was also her congeniality by all who came in contact with her. Yet she was but a counterpart of many others who were present. The dancing was kept up until sometime after the hour, a friend at our elbow says we must say "rooster," well then after the hour the rooster crowed, when to the melo strains of "Home sweet Home" the "lads and lasses" retired to dream in the blissful regions of morpheus.[5]

---

[5] *Workingman's Advocate*, Nov. 16, 1872.

_____

CHAPTER II

The People's Money

The most important ideological bond between the Sentimental Reformers and the working-class movement, the greenback doctrine, was inherited directly from radicalism. Here was a scheme to guarantee that "the workers, which term includes generally employers as well as employed, will have something to amicably divide, instead of fighting as now for the profit which capital has carried off from both."[1] An analysis of that doctrine and the nature of its introduction to the labor-reform movement can, therefore, provide a splendid vantage point from which to sum up the transmission of the Radical legacy to the adolescent labor movement and through it to the coming generation of Americans.

The greenback rhetoric, which symbolized for Liberals the untrustworthiness of the masses, became for the Sentimentalists a touchstone of unswerving loyalty to popular

[1] Thomas Ewing, Jr., to Messrs. Trevellick and Campbell, Aug. 15, 1870, in _Workingman's Advocate_, Sept. 3, 1870.

government. So generally did labor's middle-class allies favor some form of fiat currency that only a few elderly land reformers among them shunned the idea. But among the many currency reform schemes they entertained, the one developed by Alexander Campbell most nearly deserves to be ranked as the official doctrine of the labor-reform movement, for it was actually enshrined in the program of the N.L.U. and its successor, the Industrial Congress. Campbell was familiar with the writings of Edward Kellogg, a New York merchant who in 1849 had published a proposal for replacing all banks with a "National Safety Fund" as a means of ensuring orderly economic growth.[2] In fact, Campbell quoted extensively from the work of the earlier author and thus promoted the fame and influence Kellogg was to enjoy down to the 1890's. But Campbell merits his own unique significance, for he cast Kellogg's ideas in quite a new theoretical framework and in the process infused the whole body of thought with a new mood: a spirit of enterprise and growth which overshadowed Kellogg's longing for security and stability.

The explanation of Campbell's *élan* lies in his own background. He was a promoter of coal mining and iron manufacture, a resident (and first mayor) of a small town typical of the ebullient economic growth of the Midwest. Having been opened for manufacturing by the canal and railroad developments of the 1840's and 1850's, LaSalle, Illinois, was by the early seventies the commercial center of a prosperous farm region. It boasted a window-glass company, four zinc works, several wagon and farm implement shops, three foundries, and two breweries. Its population, some six thousand in 1872, consisted largely of zinc and glass workers, but many employees of local mines also resided in town.[3] Abundant coal—

---

[2] Kellogg, *Labor and Other Capital.* A revision of this book edited by Mary Kellogg Putnam was entitled, *A New Monetary System: The Only Means of Securing the Respective Rights of Labor and Property, and Protecting the Public from Financial Convulsions* (4th ed., New York, 1868). Kellogg's ideas are well analyzed in Destler, pp. 50–77; Sharkey, pp. 187–91; Unger, *Greenback Era,* pp. 94–100.

[3] Elmer Baldwin, *History of LaSalle County, Illinois* (Chicago, 1877), pp. 188–90, 210, 505–8, 542–3; [Anon.], *The Past and Present of LaSalle County, Illinois* (Chicago, 1877), pp. 302–7; *LaSalle County General Directory for 1872–3* (Joliet, Ill., 1872), pp. 101–24.

four seams of it lying within the rim of the Illinois River Valley—provided the foundation of this economy. Besides several small mines that fed local enterprises, there were three large companies selling primarily in the Chicago market. One was the Illinois Valley Coal Company, which included among its owners Horace White and Joseph Medill of the Chicago *Tribune*, the state's lieutenant governor, William Bross, and the remarkable geologist Colonel Edward Daniels, all of whom were personal associates of Campbell.[4] It was from this environment that he, as the most prominent local Republican leader, learned to approach economic thought in the entrepreneurial spirit of Henry Carey.

As early as June 1861, Campbell published a plan to finance the war by means of a fiat currency, and in September 1862 he elaborated the scheme in a speech before the Mercantile Association of Chicago.[5] Two years later he published his most significant work, a slender pamphlet entitled *The True American System of Finance; The Rights of Labor and Capital, and the Common Sense Way of Doing Justice to the Soldiers and their Families. No Banks: Greenbacks the Exclusive Currency*. In it he promised his readers both an analysis of the paradoxical poverty of labor, the wealth-producing power of the world, and an effective remedy for that poverty which contemplated "no agrarian or other distribution of property, nor any interference in contracts between capitalists and laborers." Because of its "perfect adaptation to the genius of our free institutions" and the "justness of its bearings on all classes and interests," this remedy was sure to earn the admiration of "every disinterested and intelligent mind."[6]

Campbell's analysis was based on a labor theory of wealth, but it posited a utility theory of value: "Value consists

---

[4] *Past and Present of LaSalle County*, p. 307; Illinois Valley Coal Company, statement for Dec. 31, 1866, in Edward Daniels Papers, Box 1; Edward Daniels Diary, 1866, Feb. 24, March 2, April 11, June 23, July 19, *ibid.*, Box 4.
[5] *Workingman's Advocate*, Aug. 8 and 15, 1874. For a biographical sketch of Campbell, see above, pp. 404–5.
[6] Alexander Campbell, *True American System of Finance; The Rights of Labor and Capital, and the Common Sense Way of Doing Justice to the Soldiers and their Families. No Banks: Greenbacks the Exclusive Currency* (Chicago, 1864), p. 3.

in those properties that render anything useful. The value of property is estimated by its usefulness, and not by its cost of production."[7] Since every civilized society rested upon a division of labor, there had to be a standardized representation of value, and this function was performed by money. No material was money by virtue of its natural properties, he argued, for gold, silver, cows, paper, or what-have-you became money only when the government declared it so. The value of money, then, was measured not by the labor time necessary to produce it (as advocates of the labor theory of value from Adam Smith to Karl Marx would have it), but by money's utility, that is, by the rate of interest money earns.

But here lay a problem. "The right to fix the value of money," Campbell argued, "is as much reserved by the Government, as the right to fix the weight of the pound or the length of the yard." He found, in fact, that money had no uniform cost, for rates of interest varied from place to place and from time to time.[8] The state, he concluded, had clearly abrogated one of its sovereign powers and basic responsibilities. The abandonment of this function, furthermore, had had dire social consequences. The reason: the rate of interest in turn governed the distribution of income between labor and capital.[9]

Since there could be no enterprise without loan capital, Campbell explained, there had to be interest, for no investment could be expected without the promise of its reward. Campbell's problem, then, was to find a "just rate of interest," and such a rate, he believed, would equal the annual percentage increase of the national wealth. By elaborate statistical calculations he concluded that the national wealth had increased on a per capita basis at the rate of 3 per cent annually since 1790. Far from resting at this just rate, however, interest

---

[7] *Ibid.*, p. 4. Both Destler (p. 52) and Sharkey (p. 188) mistakenly attribute a labor theory of *value* to the doctrines of Kellogg and Campbell. Kellogg, like Campbell, said, "Value consists in *use*. . . . The value of all property is estimated by its usefulness." *Labor and Other Capital*, p. 37.

[8] Campbell, pp. 6–7.

[9] *Ibid.*, pp. 9–15. Campbell also stated that the product of labor goes either to labor or to rent *and* interest. But he failed to develop this point or to offer any theory of rent.

on business paper during that time had fluctuated between 6 per cent and 12 per cent. Here Campbell believed he had discovered the secret of both concentration of wealth and economic crises. Flowing at an excessive rate toward the coffers of moneylenders, wealth had been centralized more rapidly than it had been created. Consequently, the producing classes had been impoverished, the economy had periodically broken down, and "the few capitalists" now threatened to "absorb the whole national wealth."[1]

Starting from the chronic concern of the nineteenth-century entrepreneur, the rate of interest, and viewing it through the perspective offered by the Radical notion of the sovereign people, Campbell had produced an analysis that conformed splendidly to contemporary patterns of American thought. Extolling private property and free contractual relations between worker and employer, he attributed the nation's social ills exclusively to bad laws. The power of capital to accumulate wealth he found unavoidable "because it is instituted and enforced by the national laws, and is the basis upon which all market values are founded."[2] Evils created by legislation could be eliminated by legislation—it was as simple as that. The provision for solving the nation's economic woes, furthermore, Campbell found already existing in the (always perfect) Constitution, for it authorized Congress to fix and regulate the value of money. All that was needed was to scuttle the arbitrary inhibitions of the gold standard by giving the "sovereign people the right to determine the amount of money necessary to transact the business of the country."[3]

Unfortunately, once alienated from the people, this power had been surrendered to associations of private persons, who expanded and contracted the currency at will in order to maximize the interest they garnered. The principle circulating medium, Campbell lamented, was not even specie, but bank paper. Although the war crisis had given the country the best system yet devised—the greenbacks, which saved the Union in its hour of peril and created the possibility of a "strictly

---

[1] *Ibid.*, pp. 11–14.
[2] *Ibid.*, p. 10.
[3] *Ibid.*, p. 16.

national" currency—the creation of national banks had frustrated that promise.[4] The control arbitrarily wielded by banks over the supply and value of money now oppressed agriculture and industry alike. Through manipulating the market price of gold, Campbell charged, bankers could regulate both the import of foreign manufactures and the prices of agricultural exports. With farm prices under their control, he warned, bankers "will soon find the means to regulate the price of labor in our manufactories."[5]

Although he termed agriculture "the leading interest, and the foundation of the national wealth,"[6] Campbell emphasized that farmers' needs were harmonious with those of industry, even on the subject of tariffs. In classic Whig fashion he argued that industrial growth created a domestic market for farm produce far more advantageous to the farmer than world trade. Most farmers, he believed, favored tariff protection "so far as the same may be necessary for the protection of LABOR in the development of the national resources," despite their proper hostility toward such tariff schedules as simply aided "a few bankers and usurers and overgrown monopolies."[7] The decisive factor in economic growth, however, was not protection or free trade, but the rate of interest on loan capital. With "capital at the same rates that rule in England and other European countries," he later wrote, "we can manufacture iron and other articles of prime necessity without protection beyond that afforded by a strictly revenue tariff. . . ."[8] Or, as the N.L.U. put the point (in a document probably written by Campbell): "It is the *cheap capital*, rather than the *cheap labor* of Europe, that our manufacturers need protection against. . . ."[9]

Having stated the problem, Campbell presented his formula for the vigorous and harmonious growth of the national economy:

---

[4] *Ibid.*, p. 17.
[5] *Ibid.*, pp. 25–6.
[6] *Ibid.*, p. 12.
[7] *Ibid.*, p. 26.
[8] Campbell to David Davis, Feb. 29, 1872, Davis Papers.
[9] *Address of the National Labor Union to the People of the United States*, p. 12.

> *The issue of Treasury Notes, without interest, made a
> legal tender for the payment of all public and private
> debts, in denominations to meet all the wants of the
> business interests, and convertible, at the option of the
> holder, into Government Stocks bearing three per cent.
> interest per annum, payable annually in lawful money of
> the United States. These stocks to be made re-convertible
> into legal tender Treasury Notes, at the option of the
> holder.[1]*

There is remarkable similarity between Campbell's plan
and Elbridge Spaulding's original bill of 1862 authorizing the
federal government to issue legal tender notes without interest
and to stabilize the value of those notes by making them
convertible at par into government bonds (5-20's) which
could be redeemed at the end of the war.[2] Campbell's scheme
was Spaulding's with four amendments. First, the greenback
currency was to be permanent, not an emergency war measure. Second, Campbell wanted the bonds used to stabilize the
currency convertible at will, whereas the 5-20's could not be
redeemed for five years. Third, while Spaulding wished the
bonds redeemed in gold and hence used them, in effect, as the
instrument of a deferred gold standard for the currency,
Campbell contemplated no specie redemption at any time. In
fact, by the spring of 1866 he had enlarged Stevens's greenback redemption proposal into his own "People's Plan" for
paying off the debt.[3] Finally, Campbell wanted the rate of
interest on the bonds set at 3 per cent, instead of the 6 per cent
borne by the 5-20's, so that the bonds would not drive the
commercial interest rate above a "just" level.

The provision for interconvertibility of bonds and greenbacks became the trademark that distinguished Campbell
from the host of fiat currency advocates in the 1860's. This
mechanism was designed to prevent either inflation or interest
rates so high as to retard economic growth and promote
centralization of wealth. He postulated that if the quantity of
currency issued was so great in proportion to that demanded

---

[1] Campbell, p. 27.
[2] See above, p. 341.
[3] "Our National Debt: The People's Plan of Paying It and Emancipat-
ing Labor," *Workingman's Advocate*, June 9, 1866.

by current economic activities that money prices were forced up, the commercial interest rate would fall below 3 per cent. In such an eventuality, money would be attracted away from the private economy into the more remunerative government bonds, which would act as sponges to sop up potentially inflationary greenbacks. Unlike Kellogg, however, Campbell did not wish the government to operate as a bank, lending money or discounting notes. He naïvely considered routine government purchases an adequate mechanism for the emission of the currency supply needed by the economy.[4]

In short, Campbell proposed a purely nationalist formula for augmenting industrial growth and prosperity, a design for social harmony well adapted to accepted patterns of American thought, and a solution to the economic problems of the hour realizable by reason and legislation rather than through class conflict. Because the "interest of employer and employee is mutual" and could be permanently secured only "by the overthrow of the present falsely constituted money power," no "lasting good" could result from labor's efforts to coerce employers through either strikes or legislative interference with freedom of contract. Since the "rights of property can only be protected by general laws," he rejected government supervision of "individual agreements and business transactions" as "utterly impracticable." The sole function of the state was "to make such general laws for the government of property as will tend to effect its equitable distribution."[5] Such incapacity to envision the state as an administrative agency, rather than simply as a law-giver, Campbell shared with Liberals, Ira Steward, and the trade unionists of New York and Connecticut then striving for the elusive eight-hour day. This mental limitation was endemic to the national culture rather than to that of any particular social class.

The very structure of Campbell's theory left no place for disharmony between employer and employee, for neither

---

[4] Campbell, p. 32. *Cf.* Kellogg, *Labor and Other Capital,* pp. 251–5, where the National Safety Fund is to issue notes as loans against real estate collateral. Subsequent development of greenback thought tended to be closer to Kellogg than to Campbell on this point. See Destler, pp. 68–72; Sylvis, pp. 351–87.

[5] Campbell, pp. 45, 47.

wages nor profits were categories of his economics. His protest was not that of Ira Steward against the exploitation of wage earner by factory owner. In the then-traditional American fashion he included proprietor, wage earner, and farmer all under the rubric "labor," and he protested their concurrent exploitation by the moneylender. The common status of employer and employee within the "wealth-producing classes" made their natural relationship one of cooperation. By implication, therefore, the greenback doctrine pointed not only to the elimination of banks, but also to some cooperative organization of the process of production. In LaSalle this relationship became explicit and provided the ideological foundation for an influential political movement.

Campbell's doctrine was first embraced by the Anti-Monopoly Association of Illinois. Founded at a convention in Bloomington that advocated federal improvement of the St. Lawrence River and other waterways and asserted the right of the "sovereign people" to regulate the tariffs of chartered railways, this association was initially indistinguishable from the Anti-Monopoly League established under the aegis of the St. Paul, Minnesota, Board of Trade, the Anti-Monopoly Convention organized by Schuylkill County colliers, the National Anti-Monopoly Cheap Freight Railway League, or any other of a swarm of shippers' organizations founded between 1865 and 1868.[6] Among its prominent participants were Campbell, Edward Daniels, and the editor of the *Ottawa Republican,* William Perkins.[7] However, when it convened next, on June 20, 1866, the association adopted a Declaration of Principles embodying Campbell's theories. Denouncing "unscrupulous bankers and usurers" as the cause of the sufferings of labor in "legitimate enterprise," the declaration proposed legal tender notes stabilized by interconvertible bonds as the means to "destroy the carrying monopoly" by encouraging the construction of competing railroad lines, to "foster legitimate enterprise in the development of our natural resources more than all the

---

[6] See Robert C. Toole, *"Anti-Monopoly League of 1866* v. *LaCrosse Packet Company Et Al.,"* *Mid-America,* Vol. XLIII (Oct. 1961), pp. 211–25; Yearley, *Enterprise and Anthracite,* pp. 197–8; Destler, p. 4; Cole, *Era of the Civil War,* pp. 384–5.

[7] *Ottawa Republican,* Dec. 21, 1865.

tariff laws that were ever enacted," and simultaneously to reduce the hours of labor.[8]

Having invited "all classes of laboring men" to enlist in their cause, the Greenbackers expanded their proselytizing to the Republican party and the National Labor Union. Through the county Republican organization they carried the declaration to the party's state convention in Springfield, only to have the party managers smother the proposal before the convention even opened.[9] Access to the N.L.U. was first acquired through the *Workingman's Advocate*, its official organ in Illinois. Even before the Baltimore Congress had established the N.L.U., Campbell had been permitted by Editor Andrew Cameron to publish in the labor paper both a lecture on greenbacks and an editorial explaining the lecture's appearance.[1] The Bloomington Declaration of Principles was later printed verbatim in Cameron's paper.[2]

Campbell and his colleagues soon purchased a controlling interest in the *Workingman's Advocate*. This deal was probably accomplished with ease, for during the recession of 1866–7 all labor papers were in dire financial straits. The subsequent failure of the Boston *Daily Evening Voice*, *Fincher's Trades Review* in Philadelphia, and the *National Workman* of New York left the freshly dubbed *Workingman's Advocate and Anti-Monopolist* the only one of the N.L.U.'s half dozen "official organs" that enjoyed any substantial circulation. Even with its new owners, however, the *Advocate* remained the mouthpiece of the Chicago Trades' Assembly and continued to bear on its masthead the slogan "Eight Hours a Legal Day's Work."[3]

In the meantime, Anti-Monopoly Association leaders marched directly into the N.L.U. councils at the 1867 Chicago Congress. Their influence at that gathering, not to mention their admission as delegates, stemmed from the fact that they arrived arm in arm with the representatives of the American Miners' Association. That development, in turn, was the result

---

[8] *Workingman's Advocate*, June 30, 1866.
[9] *Ibid.*, Aug. 18, 1866.
[1] *Ibid.*, June 9, 1866.
[2] *Ibid.*, June 30, 1866.
[3] *Ibid.*, Dec. 13, 1866, Aug. 3, 24, 1867; *Daily Evening Voice*, Oct. 16, 1867 (last issue); Foner, *Labor*, I, 350.

of the role played by Greenbackers in the strikes that gripped the LaSalle County coal fields during the spring and summer of 1867.

Although the American Miners' Association had by this time lost the formidable influence it wielded early in 1865 throughout the Old Northwest, it remained a force to reckon with in central Illinois, the region of its origin. Having frustrated an 1866 effort by several mining companies of the LaSalle area to reduce the local miners' pay scales, often as high as $1.50 per ton, the union found itself confronted by a perilous gap between the wages of its members and those of miners in the Mahoning and Tuscarawas valleys, whose output competed with their own for the Chicago market. Hence, when a united bloc of operators notified the A.M.A. that after March 1, 1867, the rate for mining bituminous would be reduced to $1.25 a ton, the union accepted the reduction rather than risk battle under the circumstances. No sooner had the workers conceded than the companies increased their demand, saying they would pay only $1.00 a ton and would sift the coal over a one-inch screen before weighing, so that miners would get nothing for waste they had loaded and brought to the surface. At this proposition the union balked, claiming it would reduce its members' actual returns to 75 cents a ton, and some 800 to 1,000 miners and laborers walked off the job.[4]

Faced with intense competition for a declining coal market in this recession period, the operators adamantly clung to their position for four months. Late in July the Northern Illinois Coal and Iron Company, the Illinois Valley Coal Company, and the Chicago Coal Company offered to pay $1.25 per ton, but they made no change in the screening proposition, which was at the heart of the dispute. Finding no hands in the county willing to work on this basis, they advertised in the Chicago *Tribune* for three hundred miners and laborers, declaring that the price offered was 25 per cent

---

[4] Letter of "A LaSalle Miner," *Workingman's Advocate*, Aug. 3, 1867; *Chicago Daily Tribune*, Aug. 15, 1867; *Ottawa Republican*, Aug. 8, 1867. See also Wieck, pp. 135–7, 162, 172–83; McNeill, *Labor Movement*, pp. 247–8. Roy, *History of the Coal Miners*, pp. 69–70, is badly garbled on this subject.

higher than the scale in Eastern mines and 50 per cent higher than that in most Western pits, and that they had "exhausted all reasonable means to obtain the services of these LaSalle miners."[5] Following the warning of a local Republican newspaper that "the old hands threaten to prevent the new ones by physical force," the operators appealed to Governor Oglesby for troops, an appeal quickly seconded by the Democratic Chicago *Times*: But Oglesby was absent, and Lieutenant Governor Bross was known to be among the owners of one of the struck mines. Whether through principle or through fear for his reputation, Bross refused to dispatch troops, expressing instead his complete confidence in the ability of the county sheriff to keep peace.[6]

At this point the initiative was seized by Edward Daniels, who was both a co-owner of the Illinois Valley Coal Company, with Bross and Medill of the *Tribune*, and geologist for the company. This remarkable Radical, then only thirty-three years old, had served as state geologist of Wisconsin during much of the 1850's, then as a cavalry colonel during the war. He was a man of catholic interests. Tirelessly searching for an ever-elusive fortune, Daniels had invested heavily in coal lands which his own scientific knowledge did much to develop. At this stage of his career his first interest was an experimental furnace that could use inferior coal to smelt iron and other metallic ores. After a futile tour of the East to promote this furnace, he was to settle down in Virginia, where he purchased Gunston Hall, the ancestral Mason estate in Fairfax County, and used it as the terminus for steamboat excursion trips from Washington. While living there, from 1869 to 1878, Daniels published a Republican newspaper, promoted a cooperative colony, and conspired with William D. Kelley in an effort to forge Southern Republicans into a bloc of Greenbackers. The 1880's found him assembling mineral collections for museums, editing *Our Country*, a journal devoted to currency reform, and working with Albert K. Owen to build a cooperative colony at a prospective terminus for the Southern Pacific Railroad in Sinaloa, Mexico.

---

[5] *Chicago Tribune*, July 21, 1867.
[6] *Ottawa Republican*, Aug. 8, 1867; Chicago *Times*, Aug. 4, 5, 1867; *Workingman's Advocate*, Aug. 10, 1867.

Bursting with energy and ideas, Daniels saw in the bitter LaSalle strike an opportunity to demonstrate in practice the merits of his philosophy.[7]

Strikes were not new to Daniels. He had hired and armed four Pinkerton detectives and accompanied them by rail from Chicago to "put down rioters in LaSalle" during the dispute of 1866.[8] Faced with the harsh and protracted conflict of 1867, however, Daniels tried a new approach. Late in June and early in July he took time off from his new furnace to urge upon other stockholders of the Illinois Valley Coal Company the virtues of taking the employees into the firm on a cooperative basis. Perhaps to drive home his point, he took Medill and company President J. Jones with him to LaSalle to note the contrast between the silence of the company's pits and the productive bustle of the new cooperative glass works, of which Daniels was a founder.[9]

The fact that the *Tribune* advertisement for strikebreakers appeared one week after this visit indicates that dominant opinion among the company directors favored a forceful effort to terminate the strike, but the 1867 show of force was no more successful than that of the previous year. When Daniels toured the pits again ten days after the ostensible resumption of work, he found the men idle. Approaching his goal from a new direction, he "met with a large party of miners with whom I had a general talk proposing to organize on a cooperative basis." Among the miners friendly to his idea was John Bingham, president of the striking union. Delighted, Daniels arranged with the union to address its entire membership. In a carefully prepared hour-and-a-half lecture, Daniels deplored the recent months of fruitless conflict between labor and capital, whom he portrayed as natural allies. He urged the miners to seek a reorganization of the mines on a basis that would provide the workers with wages and the owners with the current rate of interest on their individual investments, with any surplus to be divided between the two groups. So

---

[7] The biographical sketch of Daniels is based on letters, diaries, and other records in Daniels Papers, Boxes 1–4.

[8] Daniels Diary, 1866, Jan. 26, March 8, 12, 14, 15, Daniels Papers, Box 4.

[9] Daniels Diary, 1867, June 20, July 12, July 13, Daniels Papers, Box 4.

impressed were the strikers that they selected a committee to discuss the proposition with the employers.[1]

Regular progress reports from Daniels appeared as news columns in the pages of the *Tribune*, while Medill's editorials praised the cooperative scheme without ever indicating its origin. When Daniels returned to Chicago to consult Horace White and other members of the firm, he confided to his diary that he "found the sentiment generally friendly to the project."[2] An accord based on Daniel's proposal quickly terminated the strike, though unfortunately his departure for a scientific conference in Massachusetts at this critical moment brought an abrupt end, not only to discussions of the settlement in the Chicago and local press, but also to the revelations in Daniels's diary. When Alexander Macdonald, president of the Miners' National Association of Great Britain, visited the area in October and spoke from the same platform with Bingham of the A.M.A., Macdonald referred critically to the "co-operation" he had observed in the Illinois coal fields. The effort of miners so employed to "out-sell all in the market" was generating a "violent competition" that was undermining both coal prices and the security of their own wages, said the visiting Scotsman. Although such behavior (called by Macdonald "sheer and utter madness") would certainly have been encouraged by the Daniels plan, there is no clear evidence he was referring to it. The only cooperative colliery Macdonald cited specifically was at DuQuion—in the coal fields of southern Illinois.[3]

Regardless of the subsequent fate of LaSalle's mining concerns, the ideology espoused by Campbell and Daniels had clearly taken root among the striking miners. At the beginning of the year workingmen in St. Johns, which lies scarcely a mile north of DuQuion, had already triumphantly elected a slate of town officers on a workingmen's ticket, and the congressman from that area, Alexander Kuykendall, had introduced in the House a national currency bill drafted by Campbell himself. Before the summer was out Editor John Hinchcliffe of the

---

[1] *Ibid.*, July 31, Aug. 1, 7, 8, 9; *Chicago Tribune*, Aug. 11, 1867.

[2] *Ibid.*, Aug. 9, 10, 11, 13, 1867; Daniels Diary, 1867, Aug. 10, 12.

[3] Daniels Diary, 1867, Aug. 13–Sept. 28; *Workingman's Advocate*, Nov. 9, 1867, Feb. 8, 1868.

union's state journal had attributed the miners' sufferings to the national banks and the "bond-holding aristocracy," and the Anti-Monopoly Association had called for the formation of a political party with a platform based on the Kuykendall Bill.[4]

From these efforts arose the nation's first political party with a greenback platform. The delegates to its founding convention, most of them LaSalle County farmers, were described by the local Republican paper as "men of all shades of political complexion, from the most Pharisaical of the Democratic sect, up to the most ultra Republicans."[5] Over the protests of two delegates who wanted the new party to confine itself to resisting currency contraction, the assembly adopted the Campbell plan, declared its adherence to the principles of the N.L.U., and styled itself the National Labor party. Traditional party loyalties among farmer participants soon disrupted the new organization. Already the venom stirred by a debate at the founding convention over Negro suffrage had cast an ominous shadow over the gathering, and the incessant hammering by the editors of the *Ottawa Republican* on the theme that the issues of Reconstruction were not yet settled helped rally rural Republicans back to the party fold. Only seventeen delegates appeared for the party's nominating convention. They selected William H. Clark, a prominent Republican farmer, for county treasurer, and D. F. Hitt, a popular Democrat and business associate of Daniels, for county surveyor.[6]

While the pattern of voting on Election Day proved most inauspicious for the new party, it clearly located the base of greenback strength. Clark ran a distant third in county votes, while Hitt, who also enjoyed Democratic endorsement, was victorious. In the town of LaSalle, residence of most of the miners and factory hands, both Labor candidates won more than twice the combined votes of the Republicans and the

4 *Daily Evening Voice*, March 21, 1867; *Congressional Globe*, 39th Cong., 2d Sess., 318 (Jan. 7, 1867), 576–83 (Jan. 18, 1867); Magwire, *Response*, p. 25; John Hinchcliffe to Jonathan Fincher, *Welcome Workman*, Sept. 10, 1867.

5 *Ottawa Republican*, Sept. 12, 1867; *Workingman's Advocate*, Aug. 3, Sept. 9, 1867.

6 *Ibid.*, Sept. 9, Oct. 5, 1867; *Ottawa Republican*, Sept. 5, 12, Oct. 10, 24, 31, 1867.

Democrats. It was the farmers who had scurried back to their established party allegiances. The greenback vote was a worker vote. The same pattern was repeated in 1868, when Labor's B. M. Hetheringten was elected supervisor of the town of LaSalle over the opposition of both Republicans and Democrats.[7]

The political movement in Illinois that carried the Campbell plan to the N.L.U. was certainly not the voice of "farmers' interests," as claimed by John B. Andrews.[8] On the other hand, farmers were not as passive in the early currency debate as Robert P. Sharkey described them.[9] A clique of manufacturers and professionals raised the issue and formulated the doctrine, which roused interest among the farmers but not enough support to divorce them from their former political loyalties. On the other hand, workingmen who had felt the impact of the long strike in the mines and participated in the debate over cooperation were prepared to support a new party and to make greenbacks its central issue.

The coalescing of the miners' union and the greenback movement was seen in the delegation sent from central Illinois to the Chicago Labor Congress. Hinchcliffe and Bingham of the union arrived with Campbell and Kuykendall. Their common intention, as described by William H. Clark, was "the institution of a principle of true co-operation between capital and labor" through the enactment of the Kuykendall Bill and the founding of "a National Co-operative Party" in which "labor unions, anti-monopoly associations and anti-usury societies, can stand and co-operate harmoniously."[1] And sweet success was theirs. When the congress adopted its routine resolution favoring a National Labor party, appended was a lengthy Declaration of Principles, obviously based on Campbell's Bloomington Declaration of 1866. It called for repeal of the National Banking Act and "the substitution of legal-tender Treasury notes as the exclusive currency of the nation," a reform which would lead to "true co-operation

---

[7] Ibid., No. 14, 1867; Workingman's Advocate, Nov. 9, 1867, April 18, 1868.
[8] Commons, Labour, II, 114–15.
[9] Sharkey, pp. 135–40.
[1] Letter of W.H.C., Workingman's Advocate, Aug. 17, 1867.

between labor and capital."[2] Although the word "exclusive" was stricken out after considerable debate, it was quietly slipped back into the proposal as it was espoused at the 1868 Congress, and the Campbell plan was permanently enshrined in the program of the National Labor Union.[3]

This account of the origins and significance of the N.L.U.'s greenback scheme should serve to dispel three interrelated misconceptions which are widely entertained among historians: that currency reform was a Midwestern dream shunned by Eastern labor, that it was opposed by trade unionists, and that it was essentially anti-industrial. Campbell's plan faced very little opposition within the N.L.U. because the furious strikes of 1867 and the concurrent national debate over the currency had between them prepared the minds of labor reformers everywhere to look favorably upon it. By the opening of the Chicago Labor Congress, Andrew Cameron's incessant denunciations of speculation, banking, and usury were being echoed even by Philadelphia's cautious Jonathan Fincher. Although he was still hostile to any talk of a new party, Fincher asked the forthcoming session of the N.L.U. to adopt a declaration of principles "in which the injustices of the present financial system are clearly set forth, and the obnoxious features of our anti-republican land system are fully exposed."[4] From New England, President J. B. Roys of the Boston Carpenters' and Joiners' Union called for an end to national banks and untaxed national bonds, while William Falls told the Workingmen's party of Lowell that poverty was caused by the control "banks and money lenders" exercised over the money supply.[5] Picking up the theme, the editors of the Boston *Voice* (over furious protests from Ira Steward) proposed that the N.L.U. turn its attention to the currency question and suggested that state governments might issue money at 1 per cent interest and thus eliminate the need for private banks. A national labor party was needed, argued this

---

[2] *Ibid.*, Aug. 31, 1867.
[3] *Ibid.; N.L.U. Proceedings, 1868*, pp. 16, 32–5.
[4] *Welcome Workman*, Aug. 24, 1867. *Cf.* Grob, *Workers and Utopia*, p. 17. For Cameron's views, see editorials, *Workingman's Advocate*, Aug. 3, 10, Nov. 30, Dec. 14, 1867.
[5] *Daily Evening Voice*, Jan. 8, Aug. 12, 1867.

organ of the Boston Trades Assembly, to advocate "a co-operative system of industry, backed by a truly Republican
currency."[6]

Secondly, trade-union executives favored currency reform
by overwhelming odds. The contrary notion, that trade unionists and currency reformers were aligned as opposing camps
within the workers' movement, is not, however, simply an
invention of recent historians. It stems from the writings of
F. A. Sorge and Terence V. Powderly, each of whom asserted
that trade unionists opposed the greenback reform scheme,
Sorge giving them credit for doing so, and Powderly denouncing them for their ignorant selfishness.[7] The source of the
misconception is to be found not in the partisan biases of
Sorge and Powderly alone, but also in the ubiquitous trade-
union regulation prohibiting discussion of political topics at
union meetings. This rule was necessary to the internal harmony of the union, but it forced union officials to express their
sentiments about banks and finance as personal opinions. The
role of the N.L.U. as the political instrument of these trade
unionists made it an appropriate theater for the discussion of
currency reform, but it also gave rise to the illusion that the
trade unions and the N.L.U. were antagonistic. In fact, they
were complementary institutions in which the same leaders
played two different roles.

Thus William Sylvis, whose devotion to currency reform
led him to declare that greenback reform won through political action could "do away with the necessity of trades-unions
entirely,"[8] remained an outstanding trade-union official until
his dying day but never breathed a word about currency
reform at a convention of his Iron Molders' International
Union. John Fehrenbatch, head of the Machinists' and Blacksmiths' International Union, wrote an editorial in his union
journal giving the national currency plan as concise and
eloquent a brief as it ever enjoyed, but he was careful to
describe his views as personal, not official.[9] The Campbell

[6] Ibid., July 17, 26, Aug. 2, 16, 1867.
[7] Sorge, "1866–1876," pp. 73–4, 173–207; Powderly, Thirty Years,
pp. 76–81.
[8] Sylvis, pp. 76–7.
[9] Machinists' and Blacksmiths' International Journal, Vol. IX (Jan.
1872), pp. 474–6.

plan of the N.L.U. enjoyed explicit endorsement from Harding of the coachmakers, McLaughlin of the Crispins, Jessup of the New York Workingmen's Assembly, Phelps and Rosemon of the carpenters and joiners, McKechnie and Cavis of the Typographical Union, McLean and Ennis of the plasterers, Daly of the machinists and blacksmiths, Junio and Lavine of the cigar makers, Siney of the W.B.A., and Owens of the A.M.A.[1] On the sole occasion the proposal for a fiat currency was put to a roll-call vote during this period, it carried by the margin of 52 to 7. That occurred at the Industrial Congress of 1873, a truly representative gathering of trade-union executives.[2] The minority was composed exclusively of delegates from the upper Ohio Valley region, whose main spokesmen were Thomas A. Armstrong, Miles Humphreys, and John O. Edwards, who vehemently opposed any new "political combinations" at that time and feared that explicit espousal of the greenback plan by the Industrial Congress would lead it down the political path so recently taken by the N.L.U. Within a year of the 1873 vote, however, their own journal editorialized *in favor of* direct government issue of a managed paper currency.[3] In fact, so thoroughly did labor leaders become imbued with currency reform ideas that as late as 1898 a resolution denouncing national banks on the grounds that "to delegate to private and selfish interests the supreme sovereign function of issuing the money of a nation is to place in their hands the weal and woe of the people" was adopted by a convention of the American Federation of Labor.[4]

Finally, it is impossible to accept Gerald Grob's judgment that labor Greenbackers "expressed their hostility to an industrial society through a plan that offered to the workers a restoration of their entrepreneurial status as well as a just share of the national income."[5] Very few labor leaders had

---

[1] *Workingman's Advocate*, Aug. 24, 1867 (Harding speech); *American Workman*, June 19, 1869 (McLaughlin speech); editorial, *Workingman's Advocate*, Feb. 8, 1873.

[2] *Ibid.*, July 26, 1873.

[3] See "The People's Plan" and "The Industrial Platform," *National Labor Tribune*, May 16, 1874.

[4] *Report of Proceedings of the Eighteenth Annual Convention of the American Federation of Labor* (n.p., 1898), pp. 63–4, 91.

[5] Grob, *Workers and Utopia*, p. 16.

ever enjoyed "entrepreneurial status." None had any "hostility to an industrial society." Those who had not been born in industrial towns had been lured there by the promise of a life richer than they had known on American or European farms.[6] They now marveled at the machine age, wishing through greenbacks to "awaken and develop every productive energy and resource of the land,"[7] and through cooperation to "carry on the great works and improvements of the age," and "fill the land with the noise of loom and spindle."[8]

Throughout labor's discussions of currency reform the money question and the proposal for producers' cooperatives were inextricably woven together. The explanation for this confluence of ideas that experience with cooperatives taught workers the high price of loan capital and thus led them to favor currency reform has attracted many historians, but it is too mechanistic to be satisfactory.[9] Very rarely was such a logical connection made explicit by labor reformers of the 1860's.[1] The significant link between them lay in the common assumption underlying both efforts: that employer and employee were natural allies, exploited alike by the financier. Hence no clear line of distinction was drawn between cooperatives and profit-sharing plans. At one point the Boston *Voice* even welcomed the emergence of sharecropping with an editorial entitled "Industrial Partnership in the South."[2]

It is in this sense also that the cry of Sylvis to "strike down the whole system of wages for labor" must be understood.[3] Only for Ira Steward and the Marxists did the goal of "abolishing the wages system" involve the elimination of private property and the price and profit mechanisms. Others saw the

---

[6] See above, pp. 205–8, 220–9.

[7] Thomas Ewing, Jr., to Messrs. Trevellick and Campbell, *Workingman's Advocate*, Sept. 3, 1870.

[8] *Address of the National Labor Congress to the Workingmen of the United States* in Commons, *Doc. Hist.*, IX, 151–2.

[9] *Eg.*, Commons, *Labour*, II, 112; Foner, *Labor*, I, 421–2. Unger's analysis is more sophisticated than these. *Greenback Era*, pp. 95–105.

[1] See editorial, *Daily Evening Voice*, July 26, 1867, for the only expression of such a connection I have found.

[2] *Ibid.*, July 31, 1867. An editorial in the *New-York Times*, June 28, 1869, took the same position.

[3] Sylvis, p. 266.

task as "defeating that cruel law of supply and demand."[4] As H. J. Walls, longtime leader of the iron molders, stated the case: "Wages are gauged, not by the value of services done, or the product of such labor, but by the present necessities of the laborer." The remedy, he concluded, lay in "a coöperation between capital and labor in which labor will be a recognized equal factor with capital, in which product and not wages will determine the reward of labor."[5] The appeal is precisely that which Samuel Gompers was to make in asking for the Clayton Act's legal declaration that "the labor of a human being is not a commodity or article of commerce." Passionately, vainly, the labor reformers were attempting to impart to the emerging industrial order some values other than purely commercial ones, to impose moral order on the market economy. True, they were pursuing a fantasy, but their will-o'-the-wisp was social harmony within the new world of the factory, not an imaginary arcadia of days gone by.

The fact that these men toiled in mines or mills for their daily bread and engaged in periodic conflicts with their employers over wages and trade rules served to rein in even these flights of fancy. Although many workers were weary of such disputes, the flirtation of Sylvis and the carpenters' Alexander Phelps with the notion that strikes might be abandoned immediately in favor of exclusive reliance upon cooperatives and political activity was both unusual and short lived.[6] The general direction of the labor movement was toward energetic improvement of trade-union practices carried on simultaneously with the pursuit of currency and land reform. Nor did the movement relax its demands for protective mine and factory legislation, despite all Campbell's devotion to freedom of contract. Thus the demarcation between Sentimentalist and wage earner was clearly drawn by spokesmen of Pittsburgh

[4] Editorial, *Workingman's Advocate*, March 25, 1865.
[5] *Ohio BLS, 1877*, pp. 12–13. Note the similarity to the view Martin Foran expressed in *The Other Side*. See above, pp. 220–1.
[6] For Sylvis' view, see *I.M.I.U. Proceedings, 1868*, pp. 22–31; Sylvis, pp. 265–78. For Phelps, see proceedings of Carpenters' and Joiners' International Union, fifth annual convention, *American Workman*, Oct. 2, 1869. Many expressions of rank and file antipathy toward strikes may be found in *Mass. BLS, 1872*, pp. 270–92.

labor when they asked at the time of the Cooper-Cary campaign: "What will our greenback people do to help lessen the hours of labor or improve the condition of the workingmen?" That "is not alone a money question," they continued, and "because the greenback issue does not go to the bottom of this question . . . we are not ready to surrender our forces. . . . We will fight for more greenbacks, but we will do it as trade unionists, as Labor reformers."[7]

To labor reformers and their Sentimentalist allies the greenback plan promised both full employment at ever-rising levels of industrial activity and peace between proprietors and their workmen. The very fact that such hopes could be entertained by men who were themselves engaged in relentless conflict with employers over everyday matters of economic interest testifies to the resiliency of the social equilibrium that was emerging from the Reconstruction era. The facts of social life were those of inescapable group conflict. But in the realm of ideas there was broad consensus. Especially were reformers —labor, Sentimental, and Liberal—committed to the illusion of harmonious society. The first two foresaw the prevalence of social peace if only the sovereign people would eliminate iniquitous laws awarding special privilege to bankers and land speculators. Liberals assumed the same result would flow from the strictest limitation of the sphere of governmental action. Both currents of reform, therefore, served to disguise class conflict and to divert popular anger from such social foundations as private property and constitutional government.

Yet class conflict did in fact exist. Its existence had been the undoing of the Radicals' utilitarian nationalism. Radicalism was admirably suited for the task of erecting the equality of all citizens before the law, but beyond equality lay the insistence of labor's spokesmen that as the propertyless, as factors of production, wage earners were effectively denied meaningful participation in the Republic. No one grasped the significance of this challenge more profoundly than Ira Steward. When labor reformers sought a remedy in legal

---

[7] Editorial, *National Labor Tribune*, Aug. 26, 1876.

reduction of the hours of labor, the Radicals found there was no common ground between the disputants, no common good to be sought, and the workers found their statutory victories totally impotent in the face of employer defiance. The Stalwart style of politics sprang from the wrecked dreams of radicalism because the office-hungry "personalists" based their political practice on the facts of conflict, leaving the ideal of consensus to the various schools of reformers. Hence in 1872 it was the triumphant machine of President Grant, rather than any of his diverse opponents, that responded most effectively to the real aspirations and the actual power of the wage earners.

Still, though their moment in power was brief and their response to the dilemmas of that moment confused, the Radicals left America a legacy both rich and various. To Negroes they bequeathed the promise of equality, enshrined in the organic law of the land. To Liberals they imparted faith that an educated and propertied elite might shepherd the nation through the morass of democratic ignorance toward an increasingly prosperous, harmonious, and rational life. Upon the Sentimental Reformers, and through them, on the working classes, they bestowed the ideal of popular use of governmental machinery to promote the common good, and a conception of that good as something nobler than a larger gross national product. Henry Carey's sense of revulsion toward the consecration of "selfishness and individualism as the prime feature of society," and Thaddeus Stevens's aspiration for a community "freed from every vestige of human oppression,"[8] jettisoned by a nation in frantic pursuit of wealth, were left in trust to its labor movement.

---

[8] Henry C. Carey, *A Memoir of Stephen Colwell* (Philadelphia, 1871), pp. 19–20; Stevens quoted in Woodley, p. 375.

Statistical Outline of American
Social Stratification, 1870

The figures offered in Chapter 1 (pp. 28–30) on the relative sizes of various occupational groups have been calculated from the data in *Comparative Occupation Statistics*, pp. 104–12. This data was obtained by the Census Bureau in 1940 by the process of reviewing and revising the materials of the *Ninth Census* (1870). Similar calculations of sizes of occupational groups can be made from the original published data of 1870. The two sets of statistics differ in two ways: first, the absolute totals based on the 1940 data are larger than those based on the original 1870 figures; and second, the relative importance of the group of agricultural wage earners is much greater when one follows the 1940 revisions. Both these divergences have their root in the facts that the census takers of 1870 failed to count 419,028 gainfully employed in the South, of whom 314,833 were in agriculture, and that they assigned 616,527 other farm laborers to the category "laborers, (not specified)."[1]

In the following table both sets of results are given.

---

[1] *Comp. Occ. Stat.*, pp. 141–56, esp. 143–4.

Under 1940 Revisions will be found the basic data used in the text. Under 1870 Data are the calculations based directly on the *Ninth Census,* Volume I, pp. 674–85. The latter are given not only for comparative purposes, but also because they provide the basis for some estimates made later in the chapter, notably, relative sizes of ethnic groups among wage earners. Such estimates must draw directly on the *Ninth Census,* because the 1940 revisions gave no information on the subject, and their categories are not commensurate in all cases with those used in 1870.

SOCIAL STRATIFICATION, 1870

	1870 Data		1940 Revisions	
EMPLOYMENT STATUS	NUMBER	PER CENT OF TOTAL	NUMBER	PER CENT OF TOTAL
Nonagricultural employers, company officials, and self-employed	1,208,840	9.6	1,108,664	8.6
Farmers and planters	3,034,358	24.3	3,127,715	24.2
TOTAL "INDEPENDENT"	4,243,198	33.9	4,236,379	32.8
Wage earners: agriculture	2,888,113	23.1	3,722,057	28.7
Wage earners: industry, transportation, and service	5,374,612	42.9	4,966,515	38.4
White-collar	316,057	2.5	387,559	3.0
Domestic	975,734	7.8	1,032,656	8.0
Industrial	4,082,821	32.6	3,546,300	27.4
TOTAL EMPLOYEES	8,262,725	66.1	8,688,572	67.1
Total, all occupations	12,505,923	100	12,949,951	100

Many problems of judgment were involved in deriving both columns of figures. Most of them stem from the fact that many census categories include both employers and employees, as well as self-employed. The classes employed in 1940 tended to segregate these groups more clearly than did those in 1870, but they did not eliminate the problem. Fifty-two groups were selected from the 1940 list as representing employees.

Seven of these groups offered serious difficulties.

(1) The 32,360 participants in the lumber industry included both owners and workers. I counted 20,000 as employees—a proportion much smaller than that of the 1910 census, where the first breakdown was offered, but appropriate to the scale of operations in 1870.

(2) In the metal industries, jewelers, watchmakers, and operatives in watch factories were all included in the census figure 1,792. I omitted all of them. Many employees were thus lost, but this loss is probably compensated by the inclusion of some self-employed elsewhere.

(3) Turpentine operatives and laborers were included, without their number being specified, under the heading "Miscellaneous manufacturing industries." These workers were classed in 1870 under the general heading of agricultural labor. I left them in manufacturing.

(4) Boatmen, canalmen, sailors, captains, deck hands, etc. were put together without distinction between owners and their crafts and employees. I included 60,000 of the 89,797 listed by the census as employees.

(5) A similar and more serious quandary arose with draymen, teamsters, and carriage drivers, most of whom were probably independent. This is especially probable because the 1940 figures removed deliverymen for stores, bakeries, and laundries from this category and placed them with the stores, bakeries, etc. I estimated approximately one third, i.e., 27,700 out of the listed 83,797, to be employees.

(6) An unknown number of agents and messengers of express and transfer companies were grouped with many proprietors in the field. Of the 12,501 listed, I assigned 5,000 to the employee side.

(7) In service occupations, launderers, laundresses, own-

ers of laundries, and operatives of laundries were all lumped together. Although the factory system had entered this field, so great was the proportion of laundering done by individual or family operations that I omitted all the 64,055 in this group from my enumeration of employees. By making all these estimates intentionally low, I hope to have compensated for any employers or self-employed who may have been found in groups I counted, such as blacksmiths.

With these qualifications in mind, the 52 categories counted were: fishermen and oysterman; lumberman, etc.; coal-mine operatives; blacksmiths; boilermakers; brick and stone masons; cabinetmakers; carpenters; coopers; electricians; stationary engineers; engravers; machinists; painters; paper hangers; pattern makers; plasterers; plumbers; roofers; building laborers; chemical workers; those in cigar and tobacco factories; clay and glass; clothing industries; food industries; iron and steel; metal industries (omitting jewelers, etc.); leather industries; liquor and beverage; lumber and furniture; paper and printing; textiles; miscellaneous manufacturing; boatmen, etc.; draymen, etc.; garage laborers; street and transportation laborers; express and cab companies; street railway; steam railroad; telegraph operators; "all other occupations" under transportation and communication; deliverymen; newsboys; salesmen; "all other occupations" under trade; public service; janitors; laborers in domestic and personal service; housekeepers and other domestic servants; "all other occupations" under domestic and personal service; and clerical occupations. All other nonagricultural groups were allotted to the "independent" category—employers, professionals, company officials, and self-employed.

A similar procedure was used to derive the statistics from the original 1870 data. In that case (column one) three subtotals were assembled to reach the figure of 5,374,612 nonagricultural wage earners. The first was 2,071,445 from professional and personal service. Nine of the 72 groups in this census class were used: apprentices to barbers, clerks and copyists, clerks in government offices, domestic servants, employees of government, employees of hotels and restaurants (not clerks), janitors, laborers (not specified), and messengers. The omitted groups clearly leave the total figure an underestimate.

The second was 658,512 employees taken from among the 1,191,238 engaged in trade and transportation, and is probably the most accurate of the three subtotals. Of the 81 categories given in the census 26 have been used: agents; apprentices in stores; boatmen and watermen; bookkeepers in stores; canalmen; clerks in stores; clerks in banks; those in express companies, in insurance companies, in railroad offices, and in telegraph companies; employees of trading companies; employees of banks (not clerks), and the same in express companies, insurance companies, railroad companies, street railroad companies, and telegraph offices; laborers; newspaper carriers; porters; sailors; salesmen and saleswomen; steamboat men; stewards; and toll-gate keepers. In addition, I included 40,000 of the 120,756 "draymen, hackmen, teamsters, &c." No peddlers, tradesmen, or company officials were included.

The third heading gave 2,644,655 wage earners out of 2,707,421 engaged in manufactures, mining, and mechanical industries. The inclusion of such categories as butchers and blacksmiths necessarily makes this figure an overestimate. I used all but eight of the 172 classes. Omitted were: manufacturers, officials of manufacturing companies, officials of mining companies, patent-medicine makers, builders and contractors, card makers, daguerreotypists, and railroad builders and contractors.

The white-collar class was readily identified in both sets of figures. Six groups were selected from the 1940 revised data: the agents and messengers of express companies, salesmen and saleswomen, telegraph operators, all public service employees but soldiers and laborers (two groups), and "clerical occupations." In the 1870 census clerks and salesmen were clearly listed.

A final note of warning: the data of this appendix are presented solely to demonstrate the method by which the conclusions of Chapter 1 were reached. Despite their apparent precision, the figures offered here are *less* accurate and reliable than rough estimates generally employed in the text.

Sex and Nativity Groupings
Among Industrial Wage Earners

The distribution of women in the labor force is clearly given in *Comparative Occupation Statistics* (pp. 122–9). The number of women in each of the groups selected as wage earning (see Appendix A) are listed in this revision of the 1870 data. None of the categories which created problems of judgment there involved any significant number of women except laundry workers, who were omitted.

The following table indicates the number of women in each group and the percentage *of that group* (not of all gainfully employed) who were women.

WOMEN WAGE EARNERS, 1870

EMPLOYMENT STATUS	NUMBER	PER CENT OF WOMEN
Nonagricultural wage earners	1,281,691	25.8
White-collar employees	11,471	0.3
Domestic employees	901,954	87.3
TOTAL WHITE-COLLAR AND DOMESTIC	913,425	64.3
Industrial wage earners	386,266	10.4
Agricultural wage earners	430,085	11.6
Total wage earners	1,711,776	19.7

454 / BEYOND EQUALITY

Domestic servants and white-collar workers account for 7 per cent of agricultural working women. Manufacture of clothing accounted for 310,394 women, or 81.6 per cent of female industrial wage earners.

Ethnic divisions among industrial workers cannot be given as precisely as those of sex, because *Comparative Occupation Statistics* contains no data on the subject. My only recourse, therefore, was to use the data derived from *Ninth Census,* Vol. I, pp. 674–85 and 704–15, where the members of each occupation group are listed according to nativity. This approach involves problems, some of which are insoluble. First, I have concluded on the basis of the 1940 revisions that there were 3,546,300 industrial wage earners in all. The 1870 data, however, yielded 4,082,821 such workers. Many individuals were reclassified to reckon the 1940 figures, including some whole groups, like turpentine laborers.

Nevertheless, the problem can be rendered manageable, at least for the purpose of rough estimates. From the 1870 figures there emerge the following numbers of industrial wage earners: U.S.–born, 2,614,896; German-born, 430,578; Irish-born 558,420; and English- and Welsh-born, 172,001. Since the total is too large, it is likely (not necessary) that each group is too large. The difference between the total from which these figures are taken and the total reckoned from the 1940 revision is 536,521. This difference must be accounted for within the figures already given in 1870, for of the 419,028 Southerners who were not counted at that time, only 32,111 were in manufacturing. The rest were farm and domestic laborers, who do not concern us in this problem. Within the 1870 data, however, were 1,031,666 "laborers, (not specified)," of whom the 1940 revision allotted 59.7 per cent to agriculture (616,527). By working with this group alone, therefore, I can come within 80,006 of the 3,546,300 needed to make the 1870 and 1940 figures commensurate. Under the circumstances, that is the best that can be done.

One more assumption has to be made. Since there is no way of knowing how many of each nativity group classed as "laborers, (not specified)" ended up in a farm category and how many in industry, the safest approach is to subtract 59.7

per cent of the members of that class in each ethnic group from the total of industrial wage earners of that group. For example, 359,800 U.S.–born (59.7 per cent of 602,075) would be taken from 2,614,896, to leave 2,255,096 industrial wage earners (U.S.–born). The following table presents the results:

INDUSTRIAL WAGE EARNERS,
BY NATIVITY, 1870

BIRTHPLACE	NUMBER	PER CENT OF TOTAL
United States	2,255,096	65.1
Germany	372,950	10.8
Ireland	421,451	12.2
England and Wales	158,894	4.6
TOTAL	3,208,391	92.7

There were 35 occupational categories in the 1870 census that showed foreign-born majorities. Their total membership was only 307,148, of which 182,572 (59.4 per cent) were immigrants. These groups were: bakers, bleachers and dyers, brewers and maltsters, bronze workers, candle and soap makers, carpetbag makers, cigar makers, copper workers, fertilizer-establishment operatives, file makers and grinders, fur workers, gas works employees, gilders, glue makers, hair cleaners and dressers, linen mill operatives, macaroni makers, marble and stone cutters, miners (almost half the total), morocco dressers, oilcloth makers, oil refinery operatives, piano makers, plaster molders, print works operatives, quarry-men, quartz and stamp mill laborers, rag pickers, salt makers, ship riggers, starch makers, steam-boiler makers, sugar refiners, upholsterers, and wire makers.

Finally, the proportions of foreign and native born among the whole group of nonagricultural employees can be estimated fairly by combining 1940 and 1870 figures. Starting with the estimate of 2,255,096 American-born industrial wage earners just calculated, I have added 259,177 white-collar workers and 729,180 domestics whom the 1870 figures show to have been native born. In addition, I assume all 38,317 Southern domestics and 25,000 of the 32,111 Southern manufacturing workers who appeared for the first time in the 1940 count to have been native born. Adding all these figures gives a total of 3,306,770 native-born nonagricultural wage earners, or 66.6 per cent of the total.

National Trade Unions and the N.L.U.

Thirty-four national and international trade unions were functioning at some point or other during the series of labor congresses which constituted the life of the National Labor Union and the Industrial Congress. Their names are listed below together with their dates of origin, where known, and the dates of the labor congresses at which delegates holding credentials directly from the national union or the president of the union, or both, participated. Organizations which disappeared and were replaced by a second national union in the same field are bracketed with their successors.

UNION

	1866
National Typographical Union (1850)	
Iron Molders' I.U. (1859)	
Machinists' and Blacksmiths' I.U. (1859)	
American Miners' Association (1861) Miners' National Association (1873)	
Sons of Vulcan (1862)	
National Telegraphic Union (1863) Telegraphers' Protective League (1868)	
Brotherhood of Locomotive Engineers (1863)	
Ship Carpenters' and Caulkers' I.U. (1864)	
Cigar Makers' I.U. (1864)	
N.U. of Journeyman Curriers (1864)	
Plasterers' N.U. (1864, again 1871)	
Iron and Steel Heaters' I.U. (1865, again 1872)	
Coachmakers' I.U. (1865)	X
Dry Goods Clerks' Early Closing Ass'n. (1865)	
Tailors I.U. (1865)	
Carpenters' and Joiners' I.U. (1865)	
Bricklayers' I.U. (1865)	X
Journeyman Painters' I.U. (1865, again 1871)	
Stationary Engineers' N.U. (1866?)	
Mule Spinners' N.U. (1866)	
Knights of St. Crispin (1867)	
Conductors' Brotherhood (1868)	
Workingmen's Benevolent Association (1868)	
Wool Hat Finishers' N.U. (1869)	
Daughters of St. Crispin (1869)	
Coopers' I.U. (1870)	
Morocco Dressers' N.U. (1870)	
American Bricklayers' N.U. (1871)	
N.U. of Woodworking Mechanics (1872)	
Sons of Adam (cloth cutters) (1872)	
Brotherhood of Locomotive Firemen (1873)	
Rollers', Roughers', Catchers', and Hookers', N.U. (1873)	

LABOR CONGRESSES REPRESENTED

1867	1868	1869	1870	1871	1872	1873	1874	1875
X	X	X	X					X
X	X	X	X			X	X	
	X	X				X	X	
							X	
X						X		
X								
X	X	X				X	X	
X								
						X		
X								
X	X	X						
X	X	X						
X	X							
		X	X			X		
							X	
		X	X	X		X		X
					X	X	X	
						X		

Five of these unions were represented at one or more national labor congresses by delegates holding credentials from subordinate locals of that union. These organizations and the congresses at which they were represented are listed below.

Union	1866
American Miners' Association	X
Journeymen Painters' I.U.	X
N.U. of Journeymen Curriers	X
Daughters of St. Crispin	
N.U. of Woodworking Mechanics[1]	

[1] I.e., unions which entered the National Union at its formation in 1872.

LABOR CONGRESSES REPRESENTED

1867	1868	1869	1870	1871	1872	1873	1874	1875
X	X		X			X		
X	X	X						
	X							
			X					
X	X	X						

Labor Reformers of the
Period 1860 to 1875

The sample used in Chapter 5 is made up of the working-men listed in this appendix. The following abbreviations are used in the listing: A.F. of L., American Federation of Labor; A.M.A., American Miners' Association; C.M.I.U., Cigar Makers' International Union; D.A., District Assembly (of the Knights of Labor); F.O.O.T. and L.U., Federation of Organized Trades and Labor Unions; G.L.P., Greenback-Labor party; I.C., Industrial Congress; I.M.I.U., Iron Molders' International Union; I.W.A., International Workingmen's Association; K. of L., Knights of Labor; K.O.S.C., Knights of St. Crispin; L.R.P., Labor Reform party; M. and B.I.U., Machinists' and Blacksmiths' International Union; M.N.A., Miners' National Association; N.L.U., National Labor Union; N.T.U., National (later International) Typographical Union; S.L.P., Socialist Labor party; T.A., city trades' assembly; U.M.W.A., United Mine Workers of America; W.B.A., Work-ingmen's Benevolent Association (later Miners' and Laborers' Benevolent Association).

Thomas A. Armstrong. Printer, born Steubenville, Ohio, son of a tailor. A founder of *National Labor Tribune* in 1874. In

Pittsburgh T.A. and K. of L.; G.L.P. candidate for governor, 1882. Died 1888.

James J. Ayers. President, Workingmen's Convention of California, 1867. In late 1870's an officer and gubernatorial candidate of Workingmen's Party.

Theodore H. Banks. Painter, president, New York City Painters' Union; officer of Workingmen's Union; member of Central Committee I.W.A. in 1871.

Ralph Beaumont. Born England, 1844, son of wool spinner. Came to U.S. at age four, became shoemaker, leader of Utica, N.Y., K.O.S.C.; journalist in 1880's; frequent G.L.P. candidate; Grand Worthy Foreman, K. of L., 1883.

George Blair. Born 1845, leader of a New York City box makers' union from 1863. Executive Committee, I.C., 1874. By 1883 owner of box factory, leader in New York K. of L.

Robert Blissert. Born England, 1843. To U.S. in 1867 after participating in London tailors' strike. Prominent in I.W.A.; K. of L., 1881-3; a founder of New York Central Labor Union.

Friedrich Bolte. German-born cigar packer. Secretary, I.W.A. Section 1; after split, secretary, I.W.A. Federal Council (Marxist).

Robert Bower. English woolen mill hand. Head of Lawrence Amalgamated Short Time Committee. In Mass. legislature on L.R.P. ticket, 1869. Subsequently editor of Lawrence *Journal;* employed at Boston customs house.

Peter Cady. Born Schenectady, 1842. Founder, Utica Cigar Makers' Union, 1863; Secretary, C.M.I.U., 1872.

Alexander P. Callow. Charter member, Pittsburgh Typographical Union, 1851. President of union, frequent delegate to N.T.U. Mayor, Allegheny City, 1873-4.

Andrew C. Cameron. Born Scotland, 1836, son of printer. N.T.U. leader in Chicago; editor, *Workingman's Advocate,* 1864-80. Then edited technical trade journals. Died 1890.

Conrad Carl. Bavaria-born, came to U.S. 1854. Prominent among German tailors in New York City. Member I.W.A. Section 1; elected to General Council, 1872. Expelled in 1873; journalist and Republican until death in 1890.

Albert A. Carlton. Born Lynn, Mass., 1847. Shoemaker, entering K.O.S.C. after 1864-5 army service. In early 1880's headed D.A. 30, K. of L.

Isaac Cline. Born N.J., 1835. Became glass blower in Pittsburgh in 1852. In army, 1861–5. Represented Window Glass Blowers' Union at N.L.U., 1866. Chaired founding convention, F.O.O.T. and L.U. Leader, K. of L. Local Assembly 300.

Charles W. Colburn. Born Rome, N.Y., 1824. Printer, founder New York Typographical Union No. 6, 1849; active there until death in 1890. Proofreader and compositor for New York *Sun* after 1874.

Jennie Collins. 1828–87. Born Amoskeag, N.H., as girl worked in cotton mills and as vest maker. Prominent agitator among working women, 1865 on. In New England Labor Reform League.

Patrick A. Collins. (See Chapter 5, pp. 212–13.)

William Cook. Born Philadelphia, 1822. Tailor, founding father, K. of L.; headed his assembly well into 1880's.

Samuel P. Cummings (often spelled *Cummins*). Lynn shoemaker, leader Massachusetts K.O.S.C. At founding convention F.O.O.T. and L.U., 1881.

Hugh Dalton. Born Ireland, 1839. To U.S. 1841. Printer, with New York *Daily News* 1868–98. President, Typographical Union No. 6, 1873–7. Active in National L.R.P., 1872.

Simon Dereure. French shoemaker's leader, official of Paris Commune. Escaped to U.S. to serve on General Council I.W.A., 1872–3.

John Devlin. Born Pennsylvania farm, 1845. Wounded in war, failed as grocer in 1870's; moved to Detroit to work as painter. Secretary of city's T.A., prominent in K. of L. in 1880's. In legislature as Democrat. Appointed U.S. consul in Windsor, Ontario, 1885.

Thomas M. Dolan. Detroit cigar maker. Michigan vice-president, N.L.U., 1866. In K. of L., contested Powderly's office, 1889. Headed Detroit T.A., 1890.

Frederick F. Dougherty. Born Boston, 1848. In army during war. Secretary, Boston Cigar Makers' Local, 1867; leader of K. of L. cigar makers, 1880's.

John Douglass. Born Indiana, Pa. Officer, N.T.U. locals in Memphis, Pittsburgh, and Boston, 1860's through 1880's.

John O. Edwards. Welsh-born Grand Master, Sons of Vulcan, 1868–71. Represented Covington, Ky., lodge at 1873 I.C.

Christopher Evans. Born England, 1841. Coal miner, to U.S., 1869. M.N.A. founding convention, 1873; early leader U.M.W.A.; secretary, A.F. of L. 1889–94. Still salaried U.M.W.A. officer, 1920.

John M. Farquhar. (See Chapter 5, p. 213.)

John Fehrenbatch. (See Chapter 5, p. 210.)

Martin A. Foran. (See Chapter 5, pp. 214–15.)

Henry George. Detroit Eight Hour League. N.L.U., 1866. Became mill owner.

Richard E. Gormley. Born Boston, 1848. Bricklayer, member of Boston union, 1866 on. President, Boston Amalgamated Building Trades' Council, 1888.

Richard Griffith. Born Wales, 1827. Cabin boy, then in U.S. Marines, 1848–57. Boot crimper, Milwaukee and Chicago; leader, K.O.S.C. 1869–70; national officer, K. of L., 1880–3.

Edward Grosse. German printer and Lassallean. I.W.A. Central Committee, 1871. New York legislature, early 1880's.

W. H. Harden. Born Charlestown, Mass., 1843. In army, 1861–4. Shoemaker, officer of Stoneham K.O.S.C.; officer, K. of L. and Lasters' Union, 1880–7.

John A. Heenan. Born Ireland, 1836. Cigar maker in Albany, active in Catholic youth organizations. Vice-president, C.M.I.U., 1872.

James Madison Hilsee. Born Philadelphia, 1821, son of tailor. Founder, K. of L.; active in order into mid-1880's.

John Hinchcliffe. (See Chapter 5, p. 217.)

Richard Hinchcliffe. Brother of John, born England, 1831. Methodist, spokesman for Massachusetts textile workers; active in N.L.U. Died 1875.

Miles Humphreys. (See Chapter 5, p. 211.)

John James. Born Scotland, 1839. Miner from childhood, active in Scottish unions. Miner, then grocer in Braidwood, Ill. Temperance leader. Elected secretary, M.N.A., 1873. Died 1903.

John Jarrett. Born England, 1843. Iron puddler, active in unions in England and U.S. between 1861 and 1872, when he crossed the Atlantic twice. President, Sons of Vulcan, 1873, then of Amalgamated Iron and Steel Workers; chairman, F.O.O.T. and L.U., 1881–3.

William J. Jessup. (See Chapter 4, pp. 163–4.)

Thomas P. Jones. Born Wales. Active in Scottish unions before coming to U.S. in 1862. President, National Iron Heaters' Union, 1872. I.C. executive, 1873.

John J. Junio. President, C.M.I.U., 1867. In 1877, G.L.P. unsuccessful candidate for N.Y. secretary of state.

Patrick Keady. (See Chapter 5, pp. 210–11.)

Robert W. Keen. Born Pennsylvania, 1832. Son of tailor. Wounded at Fredericksburg during war. Founder, K. of L.; leader through 1880's.

Alexander M. Kenady. Printer. Came to California with New York regiment during Mexican War. Helped found San Francisco Typographical Union, 1853. President, San Francisco T.A., 1865–6.

Joseph S. Kennedy. Born Philadelphia, 1821. Tailor and founder, K. of L. Officer in K. of L. 1869–79.

Conrad Kuhn (often spelled *Kuhm*). Leader, German Cigar Makers' Union in New York City; president, *Arbeiter-Union;* first vice-president, N.L.U., 1870.

Frank Lawler. (See Chapter 5, p. 214.)

Samuel L. Leffingwell. Born in Ohio, served in Mexican and Civil wars. Printer, led Cincinnati union, 1850's; Indianapolis union, 1870's. Prominent in K. of L. and F.O.O.T. and L.U., 1880's.

Augusta Lewis Troup. Educated at Manhattanville Convent of the Sacred Heart, learned printing through S. B. Anthony; founder, Women's Typographical Union No. 1; corresponding secretary, N.T.U. in 1870. Married Alexander Troup.

Henry C. Lucker. German leader in New York of Tailors' International Union. Interim president, N.L.U., 1869.

Homer L. McGaw. Born Ohio, 1845. Printer, served in army. As bank cashier in Pittsburgh, unionized bookkeepers and salesmen. In 1880's led Pittsburgh area K. of L. and directed order's national insurance program.

Robert McKechnie. Born Ireland, 1834. Son of Scottish soldier. Printer, came to U.S. 1854, served in army 1861–3. Leader of New York printers; president, N.T.U., 1866–8. Died 1893.

Daniel McLaughlin. Born Scotland, 1830. Officer of Scottish Miners' Association. Illinois leader, M.N.A., 1873–6. On K. of

L. Executive Board, 1880. Twice mayor of Braidwood; legislator for G.L.P. Vice-president, A.F. of L., 1888.

Hugh McLaughlin. Born Ireland, 1831. Joined Sons of Vulcan in 1863; president, 1871–3. Elected to Illinois legislature, 1872.

William J. McLaughlin. From Ashland, Mass., when he served as Grand Sir Knight of the K.O.S.C., 1868–71. On N.L.U. Executive Committee, 1869–71.

George E. McNeill. Born Amesbury, Mass., 1836. Leader, Boston Eight Hour League, International Labor Union, and K. of L. deputy chief, Mass., B.L.S., 1869–74. Prominent writer and Boston leader in A.F. of L. Died 1894.

George A. R. McNeir. Born Annapolis, Md., *c.* 1840, father was Maryland state printer. Became printer in Washington, D.C.; member Columbia Typographical Union No. 101 until 1915; president, 1867. Led 101 into N.T.U.

Robert Calvin Macauley. Born Ireland, 1840, Scotch ancestry. Twice had own tailoring firm, once as partner of Uriah Stephens; usually worked as foreman. Founder, K. of L.

Matthew Maguire. Born New York City, 1850, of Irish parents. Machinist, national officer, M. and B.I.U. in early 1870's. Active in K. of L. in 1880's; joined S.L.P., elected on its ticket to Patterson, N.J., Board of Aldermen.

William Mooney. Member M.N.A. Elected Illinois legislature as Independent from Will Co. Author of 1875 mine safety act.

John W. Morgan. (See Chapter 5, p. 211.)

William H. Noerr. Born Missouri, 1836. Leader of St. Louis Cigar Makers' Union since 1863. President, C.M.I.U., 1872.

Daniel D. Olive. Born London, England, 1838. Member, Leavenworth, Kansas, Cigar Makers' Union after 1864. First vice-president, C.M.I.U., 1872.

John Parker. English-born leader, W.B.A. Founded *Anthracite Monitor.*

Joseph F. Patterson. Secretary W.B.A. in 1870's. Blacklisted after 1875 Long Strike, later became Pottsville lawyer and historian of W.B.A.

Alfred W. Phelps. Born New Haven, Conn., 1819. Head, New Haven Carpenters' and Joiners' Union and T.A. Officer,

N.L.U., 1866–70. In Conn. legislature, 1867–8. President, Carpenters' and Joiners' National Union, 1868.

Thomas Phillips. (See Chapter 5, pp. 221–2.)

John R. Pike. (See Chapter 5, pp. 216–17.)

John Pollock. Born northern Ireland, 1839. Raised in Scottish mining towns. Officer in Stark Co., Ohio, A.M.A., 1864–5, founder of M.N.A., its vice-president, 1875. Employee of Ohio B.L.S., 1902.

William D. Robinson. Born Richford, New York, 1826. Locomotive engineer; president, Brotherhood of the Footboard, 1863–4. Expelled, then re-emerged as leader in 1873–4.

Edward H. Rogers. (See Chapter 5, 200–10.)

Frank Roney. Born Ireland, 1841. Iron molder, leader of I.M.I.U. and N.L.U. in Omaha, Nebraska, late 1860's. Most prominent figure in California labor, 1880's. Died 1925.

Andrew Roy. Born Scotland, 1834. Coal miner and Owenite. Served in Union army, becoming mining engineer after Civil War. Prominent in founding M.N.A., drafting Ohio mine safety legislation, directing state B.L.S.

Walton Rutledge. Born England, 1835. Coal miner, St. Clair Co., Ill., M.N.A.; county mine inspector, 1874–84, then state inspector.

Arsène Sauva. French-born tailor, fought in Union army, then returned to France and fought for Paris Commune. Returned to U.S. to lead French sections of I.W.A. in New York.

Robert Schilling. Born Saxony, 1843. Served in Union army, then joined Coopers' Union; national vice-president, 1871. President, I.C., 1873–5. General organizer K. of L. in 1880's.

Edward Schlaeger (often spelled *Schlegel*). German-born Lassallean, leader of Chicago *Arbeiter-Verein* and close associate of Cameron on *Workingman's Advocate* in 1860's.

John Siney. Born Ireland, 1830, raised in Lancashire cotton mills. Led British brickmakers' union seven years; came to U.S., organized W.B.A.; then in 1870's, the M.N.A. Prominent in Pa. G.L.P. Died 1879.

H. W. Smith. Born Wales, 1854. In Mahoning Valley strike 1872–3, organizer for K. of L. after 1874. In 1880's led Nat. Fed. of Miners and Mine Laborers; in 1890's became assistant in Ohio B.L.S.

Karl Speyer. Born Germany, 1845. Leader of New York's furniture workers, on I.W.A. General Council. In 1880's edited Brotherhood of Carpenters' journal.

Uriah S. Stephens. Born Cape May, N.J., 1821, educated to Baptist ministry, became tailor in 1840's. Active Republican in 1850's. First head K. of L. Ran unsuccessfully for Congress on G.L.P. ticket, 1878. Died 1882.

John Sterritt. Born Mass., 1844. Leader of Omaha cigar makers in 1860's. National officer, C.M.I.U., 1871–2.

James H. Stillman. Born Plymouth, Mass., 1843. Shoemaker, active in K.O.S.C. and Sovereigns of Industry. In army, 1861–5. In 1880's officer of Lasters' Protective Union and D.A. 30, K. of L.

William H. Sylvis. (See Chapter 5, pp. 223–9.)

Richard F. Trevellick. (See Chapter 5, pp. 222–3.)

Alexander Troup. Prominent printer in Boston, New York, and New Haven, secretary-treasurer, N.T.U., 1866–8; vice-president, N.L.U. Published *Daily Union* in New Haven after 1872. Twice elected to Conn. legislature.

Fred Turner. Born England, 1846. Gold beater, organized his craft in Philadelphia for K. of L., 1873. National leader of Knights through 1880's.

August Vogt. Born Germany, *c.* 1830. Shoemaker, member Cologne Communist League. Worked with Lassalle in early 1860's, then leader in New York I.W.A. Section 6.

H. J. Walls. Iron molders' leader from Philadelphia. Secretary, I.M.I.U., late 1860's and early 1870's. First commissioner, Ohio B.L.S.

John F. Welsh. (See Chapter 5, pp. 211–12.)

William West. Land reformer, prominent in New York mechanics' organizations in 1850's. Became policeman, then clerk in law office. Spokesman for I.W.A. Section 12.

James L. Wright. Born Ireland, 1816. Tailor, manager of large Philadelphia clothing firm until 1859, then garment cutter. Treasurer, Philadelphia T.A. in 1863. Founding father, K. of L. State G.L.P. candidate, 1877.

Bibliography

I. SOURCE MATERIALS

A. *Manuscript Collections*

The Adams Papers. Microfilm, copyright Massachusetts Historical Society, 1958.

John A. Andrew Papers. Massachusetts Historical Society.

Fritz and Mathilde Anneke Papers. State Historical Society of Wisconsin.

Edward A. Atkinson Papers. Massachusetts Historical Society.

Alexander H. Bullock Papers. American Antiquarian Society.

Benjamin F. Butler Papers. Manuscript Division, Library of Congress.

Alexander Campbell Collection. Chicago Historical Society.

Patrick A. Collins Papers. Bapst Library, Boston College.

John Covode Papers. Western Pennsylvania Historical Society.

Caroline H. Dall Papers. Massachusetts Historical Society.

Dana Family Papers. Massachusetts Historical Society.

Edward Daniels Papers. State Historical Society of Wisconsin.

David Davis Papers. Chicago Historical Society.

Henry L. Dawes Papers. Manuscript Division, Library of Congress.

Fall River Iron Works Papers. Baker Library, Harvard University.

Stephen S. and Abby Kelley Foster Papers. American Antiquarian Society.

Patrick R. Guiney Papers. Dinand Library, College of the Holy Cross.

Hamilton Manufacturing Company Papers. Baker Library, Harvard University.

Ezra H. Heywood Papers. Joseph A. Labadie Collection, University of Michigan.

International Workingmen's Association Papers. State Historical Society of Wisconsin.

Joseph A. Labadie Collection. University of Michigan.

Labor Collection. State Historical Society of Wisconsin.

Amos A. Lawrence Papers. Massachusetts Historical Society.

Lynn Lasters' Union Papers. Baker Library, Harvard University.

Matthew MacDonald Political Scrapbook, 1870–1871. Western Pennsylvania Historical Society.

Oliver Iron and Steel Papers. Archives of Industrial Society, University of Pittsburgh.

Thomas Phillips Papers. State Historical Society of Wisconsin.

Edward H. Rogers Papers. State Historical Society of Wisconsin.

John Samuel Papers. State Historical Society of Wisconsin.

Thaddeus Sheldon Papers. Darlington Room, University of Pittsburgh.

Ira Steward Papers. State Historical Society of Wisconsin.

Thomas Tinker Letters. State Historical Society of Wisconsin.

Vincent Tonkin Lumber Papers. Archives of Industrial Society, University of Pittsburgh.

Richard F. Trevellick Papers. Joseph A. Labadie Collection, University of Michigan.

U.S. Congress, Senate, 40th Cong., 2d Sess., Committee on Finance files. National Archives.

U.S. Congress, Senate, 40th Cong., 2d Sess., Committee on Naval Affairs files. National Archives.

Josiah Warren Papers. Joseph A. Labadie Collection, University of Michigan.

B. Government Publications

Massachusetts Bureau of Statistics of Labor: *Report of the Bureau of Statistics of Labor.* 1870.

————: *Report of the Bureau of Statistics of Labor.* 1871.

————: *Third Annual Report of the Bureau of Statistics of Labor.* 1872.

————: *Fourth Annual Report of the Bureau of Statistics of Labor.* 1873.

Massachusetts House of Representatives: *Report of Commissioners on the Hours of Labor.* House Doc., 1867, No. 44.

————: *Report of the Joint Special Committee on the Apprentice System, to whom was referred the Order of March 8th, instructing the Committee to inquire as to the propriety of reducing the hours of labor.* House Doc., 1865, No. 259.

————: *Report of the Special Commission on the Hours of Labor and the Condition and Prospects of the Industrial Classes.* House Doc., 1866, No. 98.

New York Bureau of Statistics of Labor: *Eighth Annual Report of the Bureau of Statistics of Labor of the State of New York, for the Year 1890.*

Ohio Bureau of Labor Statistics: *First Annual Report of the Bureau of Labor Statistics . . . for the Year 1877.*

————: *Second Annual Report of the Bureau of Labor Statistics . . . for the Year 1878.*

————: *Third Annual Report of the Bureau of Labor Statistics . . . for the Year 1879.*

Pennsylvania Archives. Fourth Series, Volume VIII. Papers of the Governors, 1858–1871.

Pennsylvania Archives. Fourth Series, Volume IX. Papers of the Governors, 1871–1883.

Pennsylvania Bureau of Industrial Statistics: *First Annual Report of the Bureau of Statistics of Labor and Agriculture . . . 1872–3.*

————: *Second Annual Report of the Bureau of Statistics of Pennsylvania . . . 1873–4.*

————: *Annual Report of the Secretary of Internal Affairs of the Commonwealth of Pennsylvania. Part III, Industrial Statistics. Volume VII, 1878–9.*

————: *Annual Report of the Secretary of Internal Affairs of the Commonwealth of Pennsylvania. Part III, Industrial Statistics. Volume IX, 1880–1881.*

————: *Annual Report of the Secretary of Internal Affairs of the Commonwealth of Pennsylvania. Part III, Industrial Statistics. Volume XV, 1887.*

United Kingdom Parliament: *Second Report of the Commissioners Appointed to Inquire into the Organization and Rules of Trades Unions and Other Associations.* Parliamentary Sessional Papers, 1867, xxxii. c3893.

————: *Fourth Report of the Commissioners Appointed to Inquire into the Organization and Rules of Trades Unions and Other Associations.* Parliamentary Sessional Papers, 1867, xxxii. c3952.

United States Bureau of the Census: *Historical Statistics of the United States, 1789–1945.* 1949.

————: *Sixteenth Census of the United States: 1940. Population. Comparative Occupation Statistics for the United States, 1870–1940.* 1943.

United States Census Office: *Report on the Factory System of the United States,* by Carroll Wright. 1884.

————: *Statistical Atlas of the United States Based on the Results of the Census of 1870,* compiled by Francis A. Walker. 1874.

————: *The Statistics of the Population of the United States. Ninth Census.* 3 vols. 1872.

United States Commissioner of Labor: *Third Annual Report of the Commissioner of Labor, 1887. Strikes and Lockouts.* 1888.

United States Congress: *Report of the Joint Committee on Reconstruction at the First Session Thirty-Ninth Congress.* 1866.

————: *Reports of the United States Commissioners to the Paris Universal Exposition, 1867.* 5 vols. 1870.

United States Congress, House of Representatives: *Foreign Emigration.* House Rept. 56. 38th Cong., 1st Sess. 1864.

————: *Hours of Labor for Mechanics and Laborers.* House Rept. 1267. 52d Cong., 1st Sess. 1892.

————: *Letter from the Secretary of the Treasury in Answer to a Resolution of the House in Relation to the Decisions of the Second Comptroller of the Treasury.* House Exec. Doc. 72. 43d Cong., 1st ess. 1874.

————: *Preliminary Report on the Eighth Census.* House Exec. Doc. 116. 37th Cong., 2d Sess. 1862.

————: *Report of the Commissioner of Immigration for the Year Ending September 30, 1867.* House Exec. Doc. 18. 40th Cong., 2d Sess. 1867.

United States Congress, Senate: *A Compendium of the Ninth Census.* Senate Document. 42d Cong., 2d Sess. 1872.

————: *Letter of the Secretary of the Navy, July 17, 1868.* Senate Exec. Doc. 76. 40th Cong., 2d Sess. 1868.

————: *Report of the Committee of the Senate upon the Relations between Labor and Capital.* 5 vols. 1885.

————: *Report of the Joint Special Committee to Investigate Chinese Immigration.* Senate Rept. 689. 44th Cong., 2d Sess. 1877.

————: *Report on the Condition of Woman and Child Wage-Earners in the United States in 19 Volumes.* Senate Doc. 645. 61st Cong., 2d Sess. 1910.

————: *Report to Accompany Bill S. No. 217.* Senate Rept. 117. 40th Cong., 2d Sess. 1868.

————: *Wholesale Prices, Wages, and Transportation. Report by Mr. Aldrich, from the Committee on Finance, March 3, 1893.* 4 parts. Senate Rept. 1394. 52d Cong., 2d Sess. 1893.

United States Department of Justice: *Official Opinions of the Attorneys General of the United States, Advising the President and Heads of Departments in Relation to their Official Duties, and Expounding the Constitution, Treaties with Foreign Governments and with Indian Tribes, and the Public Laws of the Country.* Edited by J. Hubley Ashton. Vols. XII–XIV. 1870 ff.

United States Department of Labor, Bureau of Labor Statistics: *History of Wages in the United States from Colonial Times to 1928.* Bulletin of the United States Bureau of Labor Statistics, No. 499. 1929.

United States War Department: *The War of the Rebellion: A Compilation of the Official Records of the Union and Confederate Armies.* 1900.

C. Proceedings

American Federation of Labor: *Report of Proceedings of the Eighteenth Annual Convention of the American Federation of Labor.* n.p.; 1898.

Colored Men of America: *Proceedings of the National Convention of the Colored Men of America, Held in Washington, D.C., on January 13, 14, 15, and 16, 1869.* Washington, D.C.; 1869.

Democratic Party: *Official Proceedings of the National Democratic Convention, Held at New York, July 4–9, 1868.* Boston; 1868.

Iron Molders' International Union: *Proceedings of the Fifth Annual Session of the Iron Molders' International Union, in Convention*

Assembled, at Buffalo, N.Y., January 6, 1864. Philadelphia; 1864.

————: *Proceedings of the Sixth Annual Session of the Iron Molders' International Union, in Convention Assembled, at Chicago, Ill., January 4, 1865.* Philadelphia: 1865.

————: *Proceedings of the Eighth Annual Session of the Iron Molders' International Union, in Convention Assembled, at Boston, Mass., January 2, 1867.* Philadelphia; 1867.

————: *Neunte Sitzung der Eisen-Eiker Internationalen Union, in Convention zusammengetreten zu Toronto, Canada, am 8. Juli 1868.* N.p.; n.d.

International Workingmen's Association: *Proceedings of the First Congress of the American International Workingmen's Association, Held in Philadelphia, Pa., July 9 and 10, 1872.* New York; 1872.

National Labor Union: *Proceedings of the Second Session of the National Labor Union, in Convention Assembled, at New York City, Sept. 21, 1868.* Philadelphia; 1868.

National Typographical Union: *Report of Proceedings of the Fifteenth Annual Session of the National Typographical Union, Held in the City of Memphis, Tenn., June 3, 4, 5, 6 and 7, 1867.* New York; 1867.

————: *Report of Proceedings of the Sixteenth Annual Session of the National Typographical Union, Held in Washington, D.C., June 1, 2, 3, 4 and 5, 1868.* New York; 1868.

————: *Report of Proceedings of the Seventeenth Annual Session of the National Typographical Union, Held in Albany, N.Y., June 7, 8, 9, 10 and 11, 1869.* Cincinnati; 1869.

————: *Report of Proceedings of the Eighteenth Annual Session of the International Typographical Union, Held in Cincinnati, Ohio, June 6, 7, 8, 9 and 10, 1870.* Philadelphia; 1870.

————: *Report of Proceedings of the Nineteenth Annual Session of the International Typographical Union, Held in Baltimore, Md., June 5, 6, 7 and 8, 1871.* Philadelphia: 1871.

Pennsylvania Constitutional Convention: *Debates of the Convention to Amend the Constitution of Pennsylvania.* 9 vols. Harrisburg; 1873.

Peace Convention: *Proceedings of the Great Peace Convention, Held in the City of New York, June 3d, 1863.* New York; 1863.

Republican Party: *Proceedings of the National Union Republican Convention, Held at Chicago, May 20 and 21, 1868.* Chicago; 1868.

D. Published Collections of Letters and Documents

Butler, Benjamin F.: *Private and Official Correspondence of Gen. Benjamin F. Butler during the Period of the Civil War.* 5 vols. Norwood, Mass.: The Plimpton Press; 1917.

Commager, Henry S.: *Documents of American History.* 2 vols. New York: F. S. Crofts & Co.; 1947.

Commons, John R. *et al.*: *A Documentary History of American Industrial Society.* 10 vols. Cleveland: Arthur H. Clark Co.; 1910–11.

Conway, Allan, editor: *The Welsh in America. Letters from the Immigrants.* Minneapolis: University of Minnesota Press; 1961.

Davis, John G.: "Some Letters to John G. Davis, 1857–1860." *Indiana Magazine of History*, Vol. XXIV (Sept. 1928), pp. 201–14.

Devoy, John: *Devoy's Post Bag, 1871–1928.* Edited by William O'Brien and Desmond Ryan. 2 vols. Dublin: C. J. Fallon; 1948.

Fleming, Walter L.: *Documentary History of Reconstruction: Political, Military, Social, Religious, Educational & Industrial, 1865 to the Present Time.* 2 vols. Cleveland: The A. H. Clark Co.; 1906, 1907.

Guilday, Rev. Peter, editor: *The National Pastorals of the American Hierarchy (1792–1919).* Washington, D.C.: National Catholic Welfare Council; 1923.

Heinzen, Karl: *Teutscher Radikalismus in Amerika. Ausgewählte Abhandlungen, Kritiken und Aphorismen aus den Jahren 1854–1879.* Edited by Karl Schmemann. 3 vols. Milwaukee: Freidenker Publishing Co.; 1890–8.

Higginson, Thomas Wentworth: *Letters and Journals of Thomas Wentworth Higginson, 1846–1906.* Edited by Mary Thatcher Higginson. Boston and New York: Houghton Mifflin Co.; 1921.

International Workingmen's Association: *Documents of the First International. The General Council of the First International, 1864–1865. The London Conference 1865. Minutes.* Moscow: Foreign Languages Publishing House; 1964.

————: *La Première Internationale. Recueil de documents publié sous la direction de Jacques Freymond.* 2 vols. Geneva: Institut Universitaire de Hautes Études Internationales; 1962.

Lassalle, Ferdinand: *Nachgelassene Briefe und Schriften.* Edited by Gustav Mayer. 5 vols. Stuttgart and Berlin: Deutsche Verlags-Anstalt; 1921–5.

Lincoln, Abraham: *The Collected Works of Abraham Lincoln.* Edited by Roy P. Basler. 8 vols. New Brunswick, N.J.: Rutgers University Press; 1953.

Marx, Karl and Frederick Engels: *Letters to Americans, 1848–1895. A Selection.* Translated and edited by Leonard E. Mins. New York: International Publishers; 1953.

———: *Selected Correspondence, 1846–1895. Karl Marx and Frederick Engels.* Edited by V. Adoratsky. New York: International Publishers; 1942.

Motley, John Lothrop: *The Correspondence of John Lothrop Motley.* Edited by George William Curtis. 3 vols. New York and London: Harper & Brothers; 1900.

Phillips, Wendell: *Speeches, Lectures, and Letters.* Boston: Lee and Shepard; 1891.

Richardson, James D., editor: *A Compilation of the Messages and Papers of the Presidents, 1789–1908.* 11 vols. Washington, D.C.: Government Printing Office; 1909.

Sumner, Charles: *Charles Sumner, His Complete Works.* 20 vols. Boston: Lee and Shepard; 1883.

Tilden, Samuel J.: *Letters and Literary Memorials of Samuel J. Tilden.* Edited by John Bigelow. 2 vols. New York and London: Harper & Brothers; 1908.

U.S. Works Progress Administration in Ohio: *Annals of Cleveland, 1818–1935, A Digest and Index of the Newspaper Record of Events and Opinions.* Cleveland: multigraphed by the Cleveland W.P.A. Project 16492; 1937.

E. Autobiographies, Memoirs, and Diaries

Bates, Edward: *The Diary of Edward Bates, 1859–1866.* Edited by Howard K. Beale. U.S. Congress, 71st Cong., 3d Sess., House Doc. 818. 1933.

Bausum, Daniel: "Personal Reminiscences of Sergeant Daniel F. Bausum, Co. K, 48th Regt., Penna. Vol. Inf., 1861–1865." *Publications of the Schuylkill County Historical Society.* Vol. IV, pp. 240–9.

Blaine, James G.: *Twenty Years of Congress: from Lincoln to Garfield. With a Review of the Events which Led to the Political Revolution of 1860.* 2 vols. Norwich, Conn.: Henry Bill Publishing Co.; 1884–6.

Boutwell, George S.: *Reminiscences of Sixty Years in Public Affairs.* 2 vols. New York: McClure, Phillips & Co.; 1902.

Buchanan, Joseph R.: *The Story of a Labor Agitator*. New York: The Outlook Co.; 1903.

Butler, Benjamin F.: *Butler's Book*. Boston: A. M. Thayer & Co.; 1892.

Carnegie, Andrew: *Autobiography of Andrew Carnegie*. Boston and New York: Houghton Mifflin Company; 1920.

Channell, G.W.: "Port Carbon and Her People." *Publications of the Schuylkill County Historical Society*. Vol. IV, pp. 156–66.

Chase, Salmon P.: *Annual Report of the American Historical Association for the Year 1902. Volume II. Sixth Report of Historical Manuscripts Commission: With Diary and Correspondence of Salmon P. Chase*. Washington, D.C.: Government Printing Office; 1903.

Cluseret, General [Gustave-Paul]: "My Connection with Fenianism." *Fraser's Magazine*, New Series VI (July 1872), pp. 31–46.

Derr, Charles F.: "The Derr Foundry." *Publications of the Schuylkill County Historical Society*. Vol. IV, pp. 213–32.

Devoy, John: *Recollections of an Irish Rebel*. New York: Chas. D. Young Co.; 1929.

Gladden, Washington: *Recollections*. Boston and New York: Houghton Mifflin Company; 1909.

Gompers, Samuel: *Seventy Years of Life and Labor*. 2 vols. New York: E. P. Dutton & Company; 1925.

Greeley, Horace: *Recollections of a Busy Life*. New York: J. B. Ford & Co.; 1868.

Higginson, Thomas Wentworth: *Cheerful Yesterdays*. Boston and New York: Houghton Mifflin Company; 1898.

Hoar, George Frisbie: *Autobiography of Seventy Years*. 2 vols. New York: Charles Scribner's Sons; 1903.

Ingalls, Joshua King: *Reminiscences of an Octogenarian in the Fields of Industrial and Social Reform*. Elmira, N.Y.: M. L. Holbrook & Co.; 1897.

Johnson, William Henry: *Autobiography of Dr. William Henry Johnson*. Albany, N.Y.: Argus Company; 1900.

Julian, George W.: *Political Recollections, 1840–1872*. Chicago: McClurg & Company; 1884.

McClure, Alexander K.: *Old Time Notes of Pennsylvania*. 2 vols. Philadelphia: J. C. Winston Company; 1905.

O'Leary, John: *Recollections of Fenians and Fenianism*. 2 vols. London: Downey & Co.; 1896.

Patterson, Joseph F.: "After the W.B.A." *Publications of the Schuylkill County Historical Society*. Vol. IV, pp. 168–84.

———: "Old W.B.A. Days." *Publications of the Schuylkill County Historical Society.* Vol. II, pp. 355–84.

———: "Reminiscences of John Maguire after Fifty Years of Mining." *Publications of the Schuylkill County Historical Society.* Vol. IV, pp. 305–36.

Powderly, Terence V.: "A Man and a Stone: The Same Being a Little Journey with John Siney." *United Mine Workers' Journal,* May 11, 1916, pp. 6–7; May 18, 1916, pp. 8, 25; May 25, 1916, pp. 8, 25.

———: *The Path I Trod. The Autobiography of Terence V. Powderly.* Edited by Harry J. Carman, Henry David, and Paul N. Guthrie. New York: Columbia University Press; 1940.

———: *Thirty Years of Labor, 1859–1889.* Columbus, Ohio: Excelsior Publishing House; 1889.

Robinson, Harriet H.: "Early Factory Labor in New England." *Fourteenth Annual Report of the* [Massachusetts] *Bureau of Statistics of Labor.* Boston: Wright & Potter Printing Co.; 1883.

———: *Loom and Spindle, or Life among the Early Mill Girls.* Introduction by Carroll D. Wright. New York and Boston: T. Y. Crowell & Company; 1898.

Rogers, Edward H.: "The Auto-Biography of Edward H. Rogers of Chelsea, Mass., Reformer in Religion, Education, and Labor." Unpublished manuscript in Edward H. Rogers Papers.

———: "Reminiscences." Unpublished manuscript in Edward H. Rogers Papers.

Roney, Frank: *Frank Roney, Irish Rebel and California Labor Leader.* Edited by Ira B. Cross. Berkeley, Cal.: University of California Press; 1931.

Sherman, John: *Recollections of Forty Years in the House, Senate, and Cabinet.* 2 vols. New York: The Werner Company; 1895.

Smart, W. G. H.: "Reminiscences of the Boston Labor Movement of the Early Seventies." *Labor Leader,* March 6, 1897.

Stearns, Frank Preston: *Cambridge Sketches.* Philadelphia and London: J. B. Lippincott Co.; 1905.

[Stoddard, William Osborn]: *The Volcano under the City. By a Volunteer Special.* New York: Fords, Howard, and Hulbert; 1887.

[Trumbull, Matthew Mark]: *Wheelbarrow. Articles and Discussions on the Labor Question.* Chicago: Open Court Publishing Co.; 1894.

Vizetelly, Ernest Alfred: *My Adventures in the Commune, Paris, 1871.* New York: Duffield & Company; 1914.

Warmoth, Henry Clay: *War, Politics and Reconstruction: Stormy Days in Louisiana.* New York: The Macmillan Co.; 1930.

Wilson, John: *Memories of a Labour Leader. The Autobiography of John Wilson, J.P., M.P.* London: J. F. Unwin; 1910.

F. Books, Articles, and Pamphlets by Contemporaries

[Adams, Charles Francis, Jr.]: "The Butler Canvass." *North American Review,* Vol. CXIV (Jan. 1872), pp. 147–70.

Atkinson, Edward A.: *Labor and Capital Allies Not Enemies.* New York: Harper & Brothers; 1879.

Aveling, Edward and Eleanor Marx: *The Labour Movement in America.* London: Swann, Sonnenschein, Lowry & Co.; 1888.

Bagenal, Philip H.: *The American Irish and Their Influence on Irish Politics.* Boston: Roberts Brothers; 1882.

Baldwin, Elmer: *History of LaSalle County, Illinois.* Chicago: Rand, McNally & Co.; 1877.

Barnes, William H.: *The Fortieth Congress of the United States: Historical and Biographical.* 2 vols. New York: G. E. Perine; 1869.

Berkey, William A.: *The Money Question. The Legal Tender Paper Monetary System of the United States.* Grand Rapids, Mich.: W. W. Hart, printer; 1876.

Brandreth, George A.: *Speech of Hon. Geo. A. Brandreth, in Favor of the "Eight Hours Bill." Delivered in the Assembly of the State of New York, at Albany, March 15, 1866.* Albany: Weed, Parsons Co.; 1866.

[Burn, James D.]: *Three Years among the Working Classes in the United States during the War.* London: Smith, Elder and Co.; 1865.

[Cameron, Adam S.]: *The Eight Hour Question.* N.p., n.d.

Campbell, Alexander: *The True American System of Finance; The Rights of Labor and Capital, and the Common Sense Way of Doing Justice to the Soldiers and their Families. No Banks: Greenbacks the Exclusive Currency.* Chicago: Evening Journal Book and Job Print; 1864.

Carey, Henry C.: *Reconstruction: Industrial, Financial and Political, Letters to the Hon. Henry Wilson, Senator from Massachusetts.* Philadelphia: Collins, printer; 1867.

———: *Report for the Committee on Industrial Interests and Labor.* In *Debates of the Convention to Amend the Constitution of Pennsylvania.* Vol. V, pp. 470–81.

———: *The Way to Outdo England without Fighting Her. Letters to the Hon. Schuyler Colfax on the Paper, the Iron, the Farmer's,* the Railroad, and the Currency Questions. Philadelphia: Henry Carey Baird; 1865.

————: *A Memoir of Stephen Colwell.* Philadelphia: H. C. Baird; 1871.

————: *Miscellaneous Works of Henry C. Carey, Ll.D. With a Memoir by Dr. William Elder.* Philadelphia: Henry Carey Baird & Co.; 1895.

Central Working Men's Society of Pittsburgh and Environs: *Hurrah! for the Working Men of New York!* Pittsburgh; 1872.

Chamberlin, Everett: *The Struggle of '72, or History of the Republican Party.* Chicago: Union Publishing Company; 1872.

Civil Rights. The Hibernian Riot and the "Insurrection of the Capitalists." A History of Important Events in New York, in the Midsummer of 1871. New York: Baker & Goodwin, printers; 1871.

Clemenceau, Georges: *American Reconstruction, 1865–1870, and the Impeachment of President Johnson.* Translated by Margaret MacVeagh. Edited by Fernand Baldensperger. New York: The Dial Press; 1928.

"Coal in the United States." *Hunt's Merchants' Magazine and Commercial Review,* Vol. LIV (June 1866), pp. 418–23.

Cooley, Thomas M.: *A Treatise on the Constitutional Limitations which Rest upon the Legislative Power of the States of the American Union.* Boston: Little, Brown, and Company; 1868.

Cooper, Peter: *Ideas for a Science of Good Government in Addresses, Letters and Articles on a Strictly National Currency, Tariff and Civil Service.* New York: Trow's Printing and Bookbinding Company; 1883.

Crawford, Jay Boyd: *The Crédit Mobilier of America: Its Origin and History, Its Work of Constructing the Union Pacific Railroad and the Relation of Members of Congress Therewith.* Boston: C. W. Calkins & Co.; 1880.

Dawes, Henry L.: *Speech of Hon. Henry L. Dawes, of Massachusetts. Delivered in the House of Representatives, May 3, 1872.* Washington, D.C.: F. & J. Rives & Geo. A. Bailey; 1872.

Dean, Henry Clay: *Crimes of the Civil War and Curse of the Funding System.* Baltimore: Innes & Company; 1868.

Declaration of Sentiments and Constitution of the New-England Labor-Reform League. Boston: Office of "Weekly American Workman"; 1869.

"The Eight Hour Strikes." *Hunt's Merchants' Magazine and Commercial Review,* Vol. LIX (Aug. 1868), pp. 91–4.

Foran, Martin A.: *The Other Side. A Social Study Based on Fact.* Washington, D.C.: Gray & Clarkson; 1886.

Forney, John W.: *Life and Military Career of Winfield Scott Hancock.* Philadelphia: Hubbard Bros.; 1880.

Godkin, Edwin L.: "Classes in Politics." *Nation,* Vol. IV (June 27, 1867), pp. 519–20.

——: "Co-operation." *North American Review,* Vol. CVI (Jan. 1868), pp. 150–75.

——: "The Danger of Playing Tricks with the Labor Question." *Nation,* Vol. XV (Sept. 5, 1872), p. 148.

——: "The Democrats and the Public Debt." *Nation,* Vol. V (Sept. 5, 1867), pp. 190–1.

——: "The Eight Hour Movement." *Nation,* Vol. I (Oct. 26, 1865), pp. 517–18; Vol. I (Nov. 16, 1865), pp. 615–16.

——: "General Butler's Ethics." *Nation,* Vol. V (Sept. 12, 1867), pp. 210–11.

——: "The Government and the Eight-Hour Movement." *Nation,* Vol. I (Dec. 21, 1865), pp. 775–6.

——: "How Protection Affects Labor." *Nation,* Vol. XII (May 25, 1871), pp. 352–3.

——: "Labor and Politics." *Nation,* Vol. XIV (June 13, 1872), pp. 386–7.

——: "The Labor Crisis." *North American Review,* Vol. CV (July 1867), pp. 177–213.

——: "Legislation and Social Science." *Journal of Social Science,* III (1871), 115–32.

——: "Lessons of the Butler Canvass." *Nation,* Vol. XIII (Oct. 5, 1871), p. 221.

——: "The National Bank Currency." *Nation,* Vol. V (Nov. 14, 1867), pp. 394–5.

——: " 'Radicals' and 'Conservatives'." *Nation,* Vol. XIII (July 13, 1871), p. 21.

——: "Real Nature of Legal Tenders." *Nation,* Vol. V (Sept. 5, 1867), pp. 234–5.

——: "Rich Men in Politics." *Nation,* Vol. XIII (Nov. 16, 1871), pp. 316–17.

——: "True Radicalism." *Nation,* Vol. V (July 18, 1867), pp. 50–1.

——: "Wages against Co-operation." *Nation,* Vol. V (Aug. 8, 1867), pp. 111–12.

——: "The Working-Men and the Politicians." *Nation,* Vol. V (July 4, 1867), pp. 11–12.

Gould, Benjamin A.: *Investigations in the Military and Anthro-*

pological Statistics of American Soldiers. New York: Hurd and Houghton; 1869.

Granier de Cassagnac, Adolphe: *History of the Working and Burgher Classes.* Translated by Ben. E. Green. Philadelphia: Claxton, Remsen & Haffelfinger; 1871.

Green, Benjamin Edwards: *Letter and Remarks, by Ben. E. Green, Solicitor and General Manager of Branches of the American Industrial Agency. National Labor Congress, Baltimore, Md., August 20, 1866.* New York: Benj. D. Benson; 1866.

————: "William Sylvis." *The Revolution,* Vol. I (July 2, 1868), p. 405.

Green, Duff: *Facts and Suggestions, Biographical, Historical, Financial and Political, Addressed to the People of the United States.* New York: Richardson & Co.; 1866.

Gryzanovski, E.: "On the International Workingmen's Association; Its Origin, Doctrines and Ethics." *North American Review,* Vol. CXIV (April 1872), pp. 309–76.

Gunton, George: *Principles of Social Economics Inductively Considered and Practically Applied with Criticisms on Current Theories.* New York: G. P. Putnam's Sons; 1891.

————: *Wealth and Progress: A Critical Examination of the Labor Problem.* Seventh edition. New York: D. Appleton and Company; 1887.

Hazard, Rowland G.: *The Crédit Mobilier of America. A Paper Read before the Rhode Island Historical Society, Tuesday Evening, February 22, 1881.* Providence, R.I.: Sidney S. Rider; 1881.

————: *Economics and Politics: A Series of Papers upon Public Questions Written on Various Occasions from 1840 to 1885.* Edited by Caroline Hazard. Cambridge: The Riverside Press; 1889.

————: "Hours of Labor." *North American Review,* Vol. CII (Jan. 1866), pp. 195–209.

Headley, J. T.: *The Great Riots of New York, 1712 to 1873. Including a Full and Complete Account of the Four Days' Draft Riot of 1863.* New York: E. B. Treat; 1873.

Heywood, Ezra H.: *The Labor Party: A Speech Delivered before the Labor Reform League of Worcester, Mass.* New York: Journeymen Printers' Co-operative Association; 1868.

[Hicks, Obadiah]: *Life of Richard F. Trevellick, The Labor Orator, or the Harbinger of the Eight-Hour System.* Joliet, Ill.: J. E. Williams & Co.; 1896.

Hill, Adams Sherman: "The Chicago Convention." *North American Review*, Vol. CVII (July 1868), pp. 167–86.

Hill, Hamilton Andrews: "The Relations of the Business Men of the United States to the National Legislation." *Journal of Social Science*, III (1871), 148–68.

Hinckley, Frederic A.: *The Just Demand of Labor, A More Equal Distribution of Wealth*. Boston: American Workman Print.; 1871.

———: *The Philosophy of the Labor Movement*. Boston: George H. Ellis, printer; 1874.

Hinton, Richard J.: "John Bright at Home." *Galaxy*, Vol. V (March 1868), pp. 288–96.

———: "Organization of Labor: Its Aggressive Phases." *Atlantic Monthly*, Vol. XXVII (May 1871), pp. 544–59.

———: "The Race for Commercial Supremacy in Asia." *Galaxy*, Vol. VIII (Aug. 1869), pp. 180–94.

———: "A Talk with Mr. Burlingame about China." *Galaxy*, Vol. VI (Nov. 1868), pp. 613–23.

"Is Labor a Curse?" *Galaxy*, Vol. VI (Oct. 1868), pp. 537–48.

Jelley, S. M.: *The Voice of Labor*. Philadelphia and Chicago: H. J. Smith & Co.; 1888.

Jewell, J. Grey: *Among Our Sailors*. New York: Harper & Brothers; 1874.

[Johnson, Reverdy]: *A Further Consideration of the Dangerous Condition of the Country, The Causes which Have Led to It, and the Duty of the People. By a Marylander*. Baltimore: Sun Job Printing Establishment; 1867.

Johnson, Samuel: *Labor Parties and Labor Reform*. Boston: Cochrane Printer; 1871.

Kapp, Friedrich: *Immigration and the Commissioners of Emigration of the State of New York*. New York: The Nation Press; 1870.

Kelley, Oliver Hudson: *Origin and Progress of the Order of the Patrons of Husbandry in the United States; A History from 1866 to 1873*. Philadelphia: J. A. Wagenseller; 1875.

Kelley, William D.: *Reasons for Abandoning the Theory of Free Trade, and Adopting the Principle of Protection to American Industry*. Philadelphia: Henry Carey Baird; 1872.

Kellogg, Edward: *Labor and Other Capital: The Rights of Each Secured and the Wrongs of Both Eradicated. OR, an Exposition of the Cause Why Few Are Wealthy and Many Poor, And the Delineation of a System, Which, Without Infringing the Rights of Property, Will Give to Labor Its Just Reward*. New York: by the author; 1849.

————: *A New Monetary System: The Only Means of Securing the Respective Rights of Labor and Property, and of Protecting the Public from Financial Revulsions.* Edited by Mary Kellogg Putnam. Fourth edition. New York: Kiggins, Tooker & Co.; 1868.

"L.": "Imperialism in America." *Galaxy*, Vol. VIII (Nov. 1869), pp. 656–66.

"Labor Congresses at Home and Abroad." *Hunt's Merchants' Magazine and Commercial Review*, Vol. LIX (Oct. 1868), pp. 292–5.

Lassalle, Ferdinand: *The Workingman's Programme (Arbeiter Program)*. London: The Modern Press; 1884.

"Law and Labor." *Galaxy*, Vol. VI (Oct. 1868), pp. 566–7.

"The London Financial Panic—Its Causes and Effects." *Hunt's Merchants' Magazine and Commercial Review*, Vol. LIV (June 1866), pp. 413–17.

Magwire, John: *Response of the Hon. John Magwire, to a Resolution of the National Labor Council, Touching the Distribution of the Public Lands and Giving His Views of a Just System of American Finance.* St. Louis: John J. Daly & Co.; 1874.

Marx, Karl: *Capital: A Critique of Political Economy.* 3 vols. Chicago: Charles H. Kerr & Company; 1906–9.

————: *Civil War in France.* New York: International Publishers; 1933.

Masquerier, Lewis: *Sociology: Or, The Reconstruction of Society, Government, and Property, upon the Principles of Equality, the Perpetuity, and the Individuality of the Private Ownership of Life, Person, Government, Homestead and the Whole Product of Labor, by Organizing All Nations into Townships of Self-Governed Homestead Democracies—Self-Employed in Farming and Mechanism, Giving All the Liberty and Happiness to be Found on Earth.* New York: by the author; 1877.

McNeill, George E.: *Argument on the Hours of Labor. Delivered before the Labor Committee of the Massachusetts Legislature.* New York; n.d.

————: *The Eight Hour Primer. Eight Hour Series, No. 1.* Washington, D.C.: American Federation of Labor; 1907.

————: *The Labor Movement: the Problem of To-day.* New York: The M. W. Hazen Co.; 1887.

McPherson, Edward: *Hand-Book of Politics for 1872.* Washington, D.C.: Philip & Solomons; 1872.

————: *The Political History of the United States of America during the Period of Reconstruction.* Washington, D.C.: Solomons & Chapman; 1875.

Merchants, Farmers & Mechanics' Savings Bank, Chicago: *The Labor Question. Extracts, Magazine Articles, and Observations Relating to Social Science & Political Economy As Bearing upon the Subjects of Labor, Trades Unions, Co-operative Societies, and Model Houses and Cottages, in Europe, Great Britain and America.* Chicago: A. Worden & Co.; 1867.

Meyers, John F.: *The Republican Party the Workingman's Friend.* n.p.; n.d.

Moran, Charles: *Labor and Capital.* New York; 1869.

Mulford, Elisha: *The Nation: The Foundations of Civil Order and Political Life in the United States.* Boston: Houghton Mifflin & Co.; 1870.

Motley, John Lothrop: *Four Questions for the People, At the Presidential Election: Address of John Lothrop Motley before the Parker Fraternity, at the Music Hall, October 20, 1868.* Boston: Ticknor and Fields; 1868.

Nason, Elias: *A Gazeteer of Massachusetts.* Boston: B. B. Russell; 1874.

———: *The Life and Public Services of Henry Wilson.* Boston: D. Lothrop & Company; 1881.

National Labor Union: *The Address of the National Labor Congress to the Workingmen of the United States.* Chicago: Hazlitt and Quinton, printers; 1867.

———: *Address of the National Labor Union to the People of the United States, on Money, Land and other Subjects of National Importance.* Chicago: Workingman's Advocate Printers; 1870.

Noyes, John Humphrey: *History of American Socialisms.* Philadelphia: J. B. Lippincott & Co.; 1870.

O'Donovan Rossa, Jeremiah: *In Senate, before Committee on Privileges and Elections, in the Matter of Petition of Jeremiah O'Donovan Rossa, for Seat as Senator from Fourth Senate District, State of New York. Petition and Statement of Claimant, December 30th, 1871, and February 7th, 1872.* New York: E. Sackett Wells, Stationer; 1872.

———: *O'Donovan Rossa's Prison Life.* New York: American News Company; 1874.

Oliphant, Laurence: *On the Present State of Political Parties in America.* Edinburgh and London: William Blackwood and Sons; 1866.

Oliver, Henry K.: "Landmarks in the History of Labor." Unpublished manuscript in Joseph A. Labadie Collection.

"Our Working Classes." *New-York Times*, Feb. 22, Feb. 24, March 2, March 5, March 17, March 24, 1869.

Parton, James: "Our Roman Catholic Brethren." *Atlantic Monthly*, Vol. XXI (April 1868), pp. 432–51; Vol. XXI (May 1868), pp. 556–74.

————: "Pittsburgh." *Atlantic Monthly*, Vol. XXI (Jan. 1868), pp. 17–36.

The Past and Present of LaSalle County, Illinois. Chicago: H. F. Kett & Co.; 1877.

Pinkerton, Allan: *Strikers, Communists, Tramps and Detectives.* New York: G. W. Carleton & Co.; 1878.

Pittsburgh and Allegheny County Almanac, Being a Business Directory . . . for 1867. Pittsburgh: Woods & Co.; 1867.

Pomeroy, "Brick" [Marcus Mills]: *Soliloquies of the Bondholder, The Poor Farmer, The Soldier's Widow, The Political Preacher, The Poor Mechanic, The Freed Negro, The "Radical" Congressman, The Returned Soldier, and Other Political Articles.* New York: Van Evrie, Horton & Company; 1866.

Penny, Virginia: *Five Hundred Employments Adapted to Women.* Philadelphia; 1868.

Poore, Ben: Perley: *Congressional Directory for the Second Session of the Fortieth Congress of the United States.* Washington, D.C.: U.S. Government Printing Office; 1868.

Preble, Commodore George Henry: *History of the Boston Navy Yard in Charlestown, Mass., from 1797 to 1875, with an Historical Introduction and Appendix.* Washington, D.C.: Film Microcopies of Records in the National Archives: No. 118; 1947.

Provisional Federal Council of the I.W.A. in North America: *Appeal to the Workingmen of America.* N.p.; 1872.

Pumpelly, Raphael: "Our Impending Chinese Problem." *Galaxy*, Vol. VIII (July 1869), pp. 22–33.

Reade, Charles: "Put Yourself in His Place." *Galaxy*, Vol. VIII (March 1869), pp. 309 ff.

The Republican Candidate for Vice President on the Eight-Hour Law. N.p.; 1872.

Ricketson, Daniel: *The History of New Bedford.* New Bedford; 1858.

Robinson, William S. ("Warrington"): "General Butler's Campaign in Massachusetts." *Atlantic Monthly*, Vol. XXVIII (Dec. 1871), pp. 742–50.

————: *"Warrington" Pen-Portraits: A Collection of Personal and*

Political Reminiscences from 1848 to 1876, from the Writings of William S. Robinson. Boston: Edited and published by Mrs. W. S. Robinson; 1877.

Rogers, Edward H.: *Is It Expedient to Form a Political Party in the Interest of Labor?* Chelsea, Mass.; 1869.

————: *Reasons for Believing that the People Will Use Leisure Wisely. With a Statement of the Character of the Eight-Hour Movement. By a Workingman.* Boston: Voice Printing and Publishing Co.; 1866.

Saint-Simon, Claude Henri Comte de: *The Doctrine of Saint-Simon: An Exposition. First Year, 1828–1829.* Translated and edited by George C. Iggers. Boston: Beacon Press; 1958.

Spaulding, Elbridge Gerry: *History of the Legal Tender Paper Money Issued during the Great Rebellion. Being a Loan without Interest and a National Currency.* Buffalo: Express Printing Company; 1869.

Steward, Ira: "Poverty." *Fourth Annual Report of the* [Massachusetts] *Bureau of Statistics of Labor.* Boston: Wright and Potter State Printers; 1873.

————: *The Meaning of the Eight Hour Movement.* Boston: by the author; 1868.

————: *A Reduction of Hours Is an Increase of Wages.* Boston: Labor Reform Association; 1865.

————: "Theory of Wages." Unpublished manuscript. State Historical Society of Wisconsin.

————: "Wages and Wealth." Unpublished manuscript. State Historical Society of Wisconsin.

————: "Wealth and Progress." Unpublished manuscript. State Historical Society of Wisconsin.

Sully, Richard: "Capital, Labor, and Co-operation." *Hunt's Merchants' Magazine and Commercial Review,* Vol. LVIII (April 1868), pp. 249–56.

Swinton, John: *The New Issue. The Chinese-American Question.* New York: American News Company; 1870.

Sylvis, James C.: *The Life, Speeches, Labors and Essays of William H. Sylvis, Late President of the Iron-Moulders' International Union; and also of the National Labor Union.* Philadelphia: Claxton, Remsen & Haffelfinger; 1872.

"Three Typical Workingmen." *Atlantic Monthly,* Vol. XVII (Dec. 1878), pp. 717–27.

Tocqueville, Alexis de: *Democracy in America.* Translated by Henry Reeve. New York: G. Dearborn & Co.; 1838.

Tourgée, Albion: *A Fool's Errand. By One of the Fools.* New York: Fords, Howard, & Hulbert; 1879.

Tousey, Sinclair: *A Business Man's Views of Public Matters.* New York: American News Company; 1865.

————: *Indices of Public Opinion, 1860–1870.* New York: Printed for private circulation; 1871.

Trowbridge, J. T.: "A Carpet-Bagger in Pennsylvania." *Atlantic Monthly,* Vol. XXIII (April 1869), pp. 449 ff.

Twombly, Rev. Alexander S.: *A Thanksgiving Plea for Free Labor, North and South.* Albany, N.Y.: J. Munsell; 1864.

Walker, Amasa: "Legal Interference with the Hours of Labor." *Lippincott's Magazine of Literature, Science and Education,* Vol. II (Nov. 1868), pp. 527–33.

Ward, Cyrenus Osborne: *The Ancient Lowly. A History of the Ancient Working People, from the Earliest Known Period to the Adoption of Christianity by Constantine.* 2 vols. Washington, D.C.: Press of the Craftsman; 1889–1900.

————: *The New Idea. Universal Co-operation and Theories of Future Government.* New York: Cosmopolitan Publishing Company; n.d.

Wilder, Daniel W.: *The Annals of Kansas.* Topeka: Geo. W. Martin; 1875.

Wilkes, George: *The Internationale: Its Principles and Purposes. Being a Sequel to the Defense of the Commune.* New York; 1871.

Winn, Gen. Albert Mayer: *Address of Gen. A. M. Winn, President of the Mechanics' State Council of California, Delivered before the Council, the Eight Hour Associations, and the United Mechanics.* San Francisco; 1870.

Woods, George B.: "The New York Convention." *North American Review,* Vol. CCXXI (Oct. 1868), pp. 445–65.

Woolsey, T. D.: "Nature and Sphere of Police Power." *Journal of Social Science,* III (1871), 97–114.

Wright, Hendrick B.: *A Practical Treatise on Labor.* New York: G. W. Carlton & Co.; 1871.

Young, Edward: *Labor in Europe and America.* Philadelphia: S. A. George & Co.; 1875.

II. SECONDARY MATERIALS

A. Reference Works

American Annual Cyclopaedia and Register of Important Events. New York: D. Appleton and Company; 1860–72.

Appleton's Cyclopaedia of American Biography. Edited by James Grant Wilson and John Fiske. 8 vols. New York: D. Appleton and Company; 1900.

Biographical and Portrait Encyclopedia of Schuylkill County, Pennsylvania. Edited by Henry W. Ruoff and Samuel T. Wiley. Philadelphia: Rush, West & Co.; 1893.

Biographical Directory of the American Congress, 1774–1949. U.S. Congress. 81st Cong., 2d Sess. House Doc. 607. 1950.

Burnham, W. Dean: *Presidential Ballots, 1836–1892.* Baltimore: Johns Hopkins Press; 1955.

Dictionary of American Biography. Edited by Allen Johnson and Dumas Malone. 22 vols. New York: Charles Scribner's Sons; 1937.

Encyclopedia of Pennsylvania Biography. Edited by John W. Jordan and others. 31 vols. New York: Lewis Historical Publishing Co.; 1914–63.

The Encyclopedia of Social Reform. Edited by William D. Bliss. New York and London: Funk & Wagnalls; 1897.

Independent Order Knights of Labor: *Official Historical Hand-Book.* Jersey City, N.J.: A. Datz; 1898.

B. Unpublished Doctoral Dissertations and Other Manuscripts

Boyd, David A.: "The Labor Movement of Detroit." Unpublished manuscript. Joseph A. Labadie Collection.

Degler, Carl Neumann: "Labor in the Economy and Politics of New York City, 1850–1860; A Study of the Impact of Early Industrialism." Unpublished doctoral dissertation, Columbia University, 1952. University Microfilms, No. 4174.

James, Edward Topping: "American Labor and Political Action, 1865–1896: The Knights of Labor and Its Predecessors." Unpublished doctoral dissertation, Harvard University, 1954.

Engberg, George B.: "Labor in the Lake States Lumber Industry, 1830–1930." Unpublished doctoral dissertation, University of Minnesota, 1949.

————: "The Rise of Organized Labor in Minnesota, 1850–1890." Unpublished Master's thesis, University of Minnesota, 1939.

Greene, Victor R.: "The Molly Maguire Conspiracy in the Pennsylvania Anthracite Region, 1862–1879." Unpublished Master's thesis, University of Rochester, 1959.

Hall, John Philip: "The Gentle Craft: A Narrative of Yankee Shoemakers." Unpublished doctoral dissertation, Columbia University, 1953. University Microfilms, No. 6629.

Kent, Raymond Patrick: "The Development of Industrial Unionism in the American Iron and Steel Industry." Unpublished doctoral dissertation, University of Pittsburgh, 1938.

Kernaghan, Harold: "History of the Typographical Unions of Northern California." Unpublished manuscript in possession of the author.

Kerr, Allen Humphreys: "The Mayors and Recorders of Pittsburgh, 1816–1951: Their Lives and Somewhat of Their Times." Unpublished manuscript, Historical Society of Western Pennsylvania.

Killeen, Charles Edward: "John Siney: The Pioneer in American Industrial Unionism and Industrial Government." Unpublished doctoral dissertation, University of Wisconsin, 1942.

Lucey, Reverend W. A.: "How Strange Has Been My Fortune. The Civil War Letters of Patrick R. Guiney, Colonel of the Massachusetts Ninth." Unpublished manuscript in possession of the author.

Mavrinac, Harry Charles: "Labor Organization in the Iron and Steel Industry in the Pittsburgh District, 1870–1890, with Special Reference to William Martin." Unpublished Master's thesis, University of Pittsburgh, 1956.

Montgomery, David: "Labor and the Radical Republicans: A Study of the Revival of the American Labor Movement, 1864–1868." Unpublished doctoral dissertation, University of Minnesota, 1962.

O'Hare, Sister M. Jeanne d'Arc, C.S.J.: "The Public Career of Patrick Andrew Collins." Unpublished doctoral dissertation, Boston College, 1959.

Ricker, Ralph R.: "The Greenback-Labor Movement in Pennsylvania." Unpublished doctoral dissertation, Pennsylvania State University, 1955.

Rolland, Siegfried B.: "The Detroit Labor Press 1839–1889." Unpublished Master's thesis, Wayne State University, 1946.

C. Books and Articles

Alexander, Thomas B.: "Persistent Whiggery in the Confederate South, 1860–1877." *Journal of Southern History,* Vol. XXVII (Aug. 1961), pp. 305–29.

Allen, James S.: *Reconstruction. The Battle for Democracy.* New York: International Publishers; 1937.

Allison, Robert: "Early History of Coal Mining and Mining Machinery in Schuylkill County." *Publications of the Schuylkill County Historical Society.* Vol. IV, pp. 134–55.

Anthony, Katherine: *Susan B. Anthony: Her Personal History and Her Era.* Garden City, N.Y.: Doubleday & Co.; 1954.

Austin, George Lowell: *The Life and Times of Wendell Phillips.* New edition. Boston: Lee and Shepard; 1901.

Barclay, Thomas S.: *The Liberal Republican Movement in Missouri, 1865–1871.* Columbia, Mo.: State Historical Society of Missouri; 1926.

Bartlett, Irving H.: *Wendell Phillips; Brahmin Radical.* Boston: Beacon Press; 1961.

Bates, Harry C.: *Bricklayers' Century of Craftsmanship.* Washington, D.C.: Bricklayers', Masons' and Plasterers' International Union; 1955.

Beale, Howard K.: *The Critical Year, A Study of Andrew Johnson and Reconstruction.* New York: Harcourt, Brace and Company; 1930.

———: "The Tariff and Reconstruction." *American Historical Review,* Vol. XXXV (Jan. 1930), pp. 276–94.

Beard, Charles A. and Mary R.: *The Rise of American Civilization.* 2 vols. New York: The Macmillan Company; 1927.

Beath, Robert B.: *History of the Grand Army of the Republic.* New York: Bryan, Taylor & Co.; 1889.

Beck, James A.: "The Old Fifth Ward of Pittsburgh." *Western Pennsylvania Historical Magazine,* XXVIII (1945), 111–26.

Beckner, Earl R.: *A History of Labor Legislation in Illinois.* Chicago: University of Chicago Press; 1929.

Belden, Thomas Graham and Marva Robins: *So Fell the Angels.* Boston and Toronto: Little, Brown; 1956.

Benson, Lee: *The Concept of Jacksonian Democracy: New York as a Test Case.* Princeton: Princeton University Press; 1961.

Bernstein, Samuel: *The First International in America.* New York: Augustus M. Kelly; 1962.

Berthoff, Rowland Tappan: *British Immigrants in Industrial America, 1790–1950.* Cambridge: Harvard University Press; 1953.

———: "The Social Order of the Anthracite Region, 1825–1902." *Pennsylvania Magazine of History and Biography,* Vol. LXXIX (July 1965), pp. 261–91.

Bettersworth, John K.: *Confederate Mississippi.* Baton Rouge: Louisiana State University Press; 1943.

Billington, Ray Allen: *The Protestant Crusade, 1800–1860. A Study of the Origins of American Nativism.* New York: The Macmillan Company; 1938.

Bimba, Anthony: *The Molly Maguires.* New York: International Publishers; 1932.

Binkley, Robert C.: *Realism and Nationalism, 1852–1871.* New York and London: Harper & Brothers; 1935.

Blodgett, Geoffrey T.: "The Mind of a Boston Mugwump." *Mississippi Valley Historical Review,* Vol. XLVIII (March 1962), pp. 614–34.

Bowen, Croswell: *The Elegant Oakey.* New York: Oxford University Press; 1956.

Bradley, Erwin S.: *The Triumph of Militant Republicanism, A Study of Pennsylvania and Presidential Politics, 1860–1872.* Philadelphia: University of Pennsylvania Press; 1964.

Brodie, Fawn M.: *Thaddeus Stevens, Scourge of the South.* New York: Norton Co.; 1959.

Broehl, Wayne G., Jr.: *The Molly Maguires.* Cambridge: Harvard University Press; 1964.

Brock, W. R.: *An American Crisis: Congress and Reconstruction, 1865–1867.* London: St. Martin's Press; 1963.

Brown, Ira V.: "William D. Kelley and Radical Reconstruction." *Pennsylvania Magazine of History and Biography,* Vol. LXXXV (July 1961), pp. 316–29.

Browne, Henry J.: *The Catholic Church and the Knights of Labor.* Washington, D.C.: Catholic University of America Press; 1949.

Bruchey, Stuart: *The Roots of American Economic Growth, 1607–1861. An Essay in Social Causation.* New York and Evanston: Harper & Row; 1965.

Brummer, Sidney David: *Political History of New York State during the Period of the Civil War.* New York: Columbia University Studies in History, Economics, and Public Law, Vol. XXXIX, No. 2; 1911.

Burke, William Maxwell: *History and Functions of Central Labor Unions.* New York: Columbia University Studies in History, Economics, and Public Law, Vol. XII, No. 1; 1899.

Cahill, Marion C.: *Shorter Hours: A Study of the Movement since the Civil War.* New York: Columbia University Studies in History, Economics, and Public Law, No. 380; 1932.

Cale, Edgar Barclay: *The Organization of Labor in Philadelphia, 1850–1870.* Philadelphia: University of Pennsylvania Press; 1940.

Carlton, Frank T.: "Ephemeral Labor Movements, 1866–1889." *Popular Science Monthly,* Vol. LXXXV (Nov. 1914), pp. 487–503.

Carter, Hodding: *The Angry Scar. The Story of Reconstruction.* Garden City, N.Y.: Doubleday & Co.; 1959.

Catton, Bruce: *This Hallowed Ground. The Story of the Union Side of the Civil War.* New York: Doubleday & Co.; 1956.

Clark, Victor S.: "Manufacturing Development during the Civil War." *The Military Historian and Economist,* Vol. III (April 1918), pp. 92–100.

Clarkson, J. Dunsmore: *Labour and Nationalism in Ireland.* New York: Columbia University Studies in History, Economics, and Public Law, Vol. CXX, No. 266; 1925.

Coben, Stanley: "Northeastern Business and Radical Reconstruction: A Re-examination." *Mississippi Valley Historical Review,* Vol. XLVI (July 1959), pp. 67–90.

Cochran, Thomas C.: "Did the Civil War Retard Industrialization?" *Mississippi Valley Historical Review,* Vol. XLVIII (Sept. 1961), pp. 197–210.

Cole, Arthur C.: *The Era of the Civil War, 1848–1870. The Centennial History of Illinois,* edited by Clarence W. Alvord. Vol. III. Springfield: Centennial Commission; 1919.

———: *The Irrepressible Conflict, 1850–1865.* New York: Macmillan Company; 1934.

Cole, Donald B.: *Immigrant City: Lawrence, Massachusetts, 1845–1921.* Chapel Hill: University of North Carolina Press; 1963.

Coleman, Charles H.: *The Election of 1868; the Democratic Effort to Regain Control.* New York: Columbia University Press; 1933.

Coleman, J. Walter: *The Molly Maguire Riots; Industrial Conflicts in the Pennsylvania Coal Region.* Richmond: Garrett and Massie; 1936.

Commons, John R. *et al.*: *History of Labour in the United States.* 4 vols. New York: The Macmillan Company; 1918–35.

———: "Horace Greeley and the Working Class Origins of the Republican Party." *Political Science Quarterly,* Vol. XXIV (Sept. 1909), pp. 468–88.

Coulter, E. Merton: *The South during Reconstruction, 1865–1877.* Baton Rouge: Louisiana State University Press; 1947.

———: *William G. Brownlow, Fighting Parson of the Southern Highlands.* Chapel Hill: University of North Carolina Press; 1937.

Cox, LaWanda and John H.: "Andrew Johnson and His Ghost Writers: An Analysis of the Freedman's Bureau and Civil Rights Veto Messages." *Mississippi Valley Historical Review,* Vol. XLVIII (Dec. 1961), pp. 460–79.

———: *Politics, Principle, and Prejudice 1865–1866: Dilemma of Reconstruction America.* New York: The Free Press of Glencoe; 1963.

Creamer, Daniel: "Recruiting Contract Laborers for the Amoskeag Mills." *Journal of Economic History,* Vol. I (May 1941), pp. 42–56.

Cross, Ira B.: *A History of the Labor Movement in California.* Berkeley: University of California Press; 1935.

Curtis, Francis: *The Republican Party. A History of Its Fifty Years' Existence and a Record of Its Measures and Leaders, 1854–1904.* 2 vols. New York and London: G. P. Putnam's Sons; 1904.

Darwen, M. F.: *One Moral Standard for All. Extracts from the Lives of Victoria Claflin Woodhull, Now Mrs. John Biddulph Martin, and Tennessee Claflin, Now Lady Cook.* New York: Calhoun Press; n.d.

Davis, Winfield J.: *History of Political Conventions in California, 1849–1892.* Sacramento: California State Library; 1893.

Dearing, Mary R.: *Veterans in Politics. The Story of the G.A.R.* Baton Rouge: Louisiana State University Press; 1952.

Deibler, Frederick Shipp: *The Amalgamated Wood Workers' International Union of America.* Madison: Bulletin of the University of Wisconsin, Economics and Political Science Series, Vol. VII; 1912.

Destler, Chester McArthur: *American Radicalism, 1865–1901. Essays and Documents.* New London: Connecticut College Monographs; 1946.

Dewey, Davis Rich: *Financial History of the United States.* Seventh edition. New York: Longmans, Green and Co.; 1920.

Donald, David: *Lincoln Reconsidered. Essays on the Civil War Era.* Second edition. New York: Vintage Books; 1961.

Dorfman, Joseph: *The Economic Mind in American Civilization.* 5 vols. New York: The Viking Press; 1946–9.

Douglas, Dorothy: "Ira Steward on Consumption and Unemployment." *Journal of Political Economy,* Vol. XL (August 1932), pp. 532–43.

Du Bois, W. E. Burghardt: *Black Reconstruction in America, 1860–1880.* New York: Harcourt, Brace and Company; 1935.

———: *The Philadelphia Negro, A Social Study.* Philadelphia: University of Pennsylvania Series in Political Economy and Public Law, No. 14; 1899.

Dunning, William A.: "More Light on Andrew Johnson." *American Historical Review,* Vol. XI (April 1906), pp. 574–94.

————: *Reconstruction, Political and Economic 1865–1877*. New York: Harper & Brothers; 1907.

Economic Change in the Civil War Era. Proceedings of a Conference on American Economic Institutional Change, 1850–1873, and the Impact of the Civil War, Held March 12–14, 1964. Edited by David T. Gilchrist and W. David Lewis. Greenville, Del.: Eleutherian Mills–Hagley Foundation; 1965.

Eiselen, Malcolm Rogers: *The Rise of Pennsylvania Protectionism.* Philadelphia: University of Pennsylvania Press; 1932.

Eliot, Samuel A., editor: *Heralds of a Liberal Faith.* 3 vols. Boston: American Unitarian Association; 1910.

Ely, Richard T.: *The Labor Movement in America.* New York: Thomas Y. Crowell & Co.; 1886.

Engberg, George B.: "Lumber and Labor in the Lake States." *Minnesota History,* Vol. XXXVI (March 1959), pp. 153–66.

Erickson, Charlotte: *American Industry and the European Immigrant, 1860–1885.* Cambridge: Harvard University Press; 1957.

Ernst, Robert: *Immigrant Life in New York City, 1825–1863.* New York: King's Crown Press; 1949.

Evans, Chris: *History of United Mine Workers of America from the year 1860 to 1890.* 2 vols. Indianapolis: United Mine Workers of America; 1918–20.

Evans, George Heberton, Jr.: *Business Incorporations in the United States, 1800–1943.* New York: National Bureau of Economic Research; 1948.

Faulkner, Harold U.: *American Economic History.* Sixth edition. New York: Harper & Brothers; 1949.

Faust, Albert Bernhardt: *The German Element in the United States.* 2 vols. Boston and New York: Houghton, Mifflin Company; 1909.

Fessenden, Francis: *Life and Public Services of William Pitt Fessenden.* 2 vols. Boston and New York: Houghton, Mifflin Company; 1907.

Fine, Sidney: *Laissez Faire and the General-Welfare State, A Study of Conflict in American Thought, 1865–1901.* Ann Arbor: University of Michigan Press; 1956.

Fitch, John Andrews: *The Steel Workers.* New York: Charities Publication Committee, Russell Sage Foundation; 1910.

Fite, Emerson D.: *Social and Industrial Conditions in the North During the Civil War.* New York: The Macmillan Company; 1910.

Foner, Philip S.: *Business and Slavery.* Chapel Hill: University of North Carolina Press; 1941.

————: *History of the Labor Movement in the United States.* 4 vols. New York: International Publishers; 1947–65.

————: *The Life and Writings of Frederick Douglass.* 4 vols. New York: International Publishers; 1950–5.

————: *Morale Education in the American Army; War for Independence, War of 1812, Civil War.* New York: International Publishers; 1944.

Foster, Charles G.: "The Amalgamated Association of Iron and Steel Workers." *Annual Report of the Secretary of Internal Affairs of the Commonwealth of Pennsylvania. Part III, Industrial Statistics. Volume XV, 1887.* Pp. G 1–27.

Foulke, William Dudley: *Life of Oliver P. Morton.* 2 vols. Indianapolis and Kansas City: Bowen-Merrill Company; 1899.

Freemantle, Anne, editor: *The Papal Encyclicals in Their Historical Context.* New York: G. P. Putnam's Sons; 1956.

Fuller, George N., editor: *Michigan, A Centennial History of the State and Its People.* 5 vols. Chicago: Lewis Publishing Company; 1939.

Gallman, Robert E.: "Commodity Output, 1839–1899." *Trends in the American Economy in the Nineteenth Century.* Conference on Research in Income and Wealth, Studies in Income and Wealth, Vol. 24, pp. 13–67. Princeton; 1960.

Gates, Paul Wallace: *Fifty Million Acres: Conflicts over Kansas Land Policy, 1854–1890.* Ithaca, N.Y.: Cornell University Press; 1954.

Gavett, Thomas W.: *Development of the Labor Movement in Milwaukee.* Madison and Milwaukee: University of Wisconsin Press; 1965.

Gibson, Florence E.: *The Attitudes of the New York Irish toward State and National Affairs, 1848–1892.* New York: Columbia University Press; 1951.

Glazer, Sidney: "The Michigan Labor Movement." *Michigan Historical Magazine.* Vol. XXIX (Jan.–March 1945), pp. 73–82.

Goodstein, Anita Shafer: "Labor Relations in the Saginaw Valley Lumber Industry, 1865–1885." *Bulletin of the Business Historical Society*, XXVII (1953), 193–221.

Gray, Wood: *The Hidden Civil War: The Story of the Copperheads.* New York: Viking Press; 1942.

Greene, Evarts Boutell: "Some Aspects of Politics in the Middle West, 1860–1872." *Proceedings of the State Historical Society of Wisconsin, 1911*, pp. 60–76.

Gregory, Frances W. and Irene D. Neu: "The American Industrial Elite in the 1870's." *Men in Business, Essays in the History of*

Entrepreneurship. Edited by William Miller. Cambridge: Harvard University Press; 1952.

Grimes, Alan Pendleton: *The Political Liberalism of the New York Nation, 1865–1932.* Chapel Hill: University of North Carolina Press; 1953.

Grob, Gerald N.: "Organized Labor and the Negro Worker, 1865–1900." *Labor History,* Vol. I (Spring 1960), pp. 164–76.

———: "Reform Unionism: The National Labor Union." *Journal of Economic History,* Vol. XIV (Spring 1954), pp. 126–42.

———: *Workers and Utopia: A Study of Ideological Conflict in the American Labor Movement, 1865–1900.* Evanston, Ill.: Northwestern University; 1961.

Grossman, Jonathan: "Co-operative Foundries." *New York History,* XXIV (1943), 196–210.

———: *William Sylvis, Pioneer of American Labor.* New York: Columbia University Studies in History, Economics, and Public Law, No. 516; 1945.

Guilday, Peter: *A History of the Councils of Baltimore (1791–1884).* New York: Macmillan Company; 1932.

Gutman, Herbert G.: "The Braidwood Lockout of 1874." *Journal of the Illinois State Historical Society,* Vol. LIII (Spring 1960), pp. 5–28.

———: "The Tompkins Square 'Riot' in New York City on January 13, 1874." *Labor History,* Vol. VI (Winter 1965), pp. 44–70.

———: "Two Lockouts in Pennsylvania, 1873–1874." *Pennsylvania Magazine of History and Biography,* Vol. LXXXIII (July 1959), pp. 307–26.

———: "The Worker's Search for Power, Labor in the Gilded Age." *The Gilded Age, A Reappraisal.* Edited by H. Wayne Morgan. Syracuse: Syracuse University Press; 1963.

Habakkuk, H. J.: *American and British Technology in the Nineteenth Century: The Search for Labour-Saving Inventions.* Cambridge: At the University Press; 1962.

Hale, William H.: *Horace Greeley, Voice of the People.* New York: Harper; 1950.

Hall, John Philip: "The Knights of St. Crispin in Massachusetts, 1869–1878." *Journal of Economic History,* Vol. XVIII (June 1957), pp. 161–75.

Hammond, Bray: "The North's Empty Purse, 1861–1862." *American Historical Review,* Vol. LXVII (Oct. 1961), pp. 1–18.

Handlin, Oscar: *Boston's Immigrants: A Study in Acculturation.* Revised and enlarged edition. Cambridge: Belknap Press of Harvard University Press; 1959.

————: *The Uprooted: The Epic Story of the Great Migrations that Made the American People.* Boston: Little, Brown; 1951.

Hansen, Marcus Lee: *The Atlantic Migration, 1607–1860.* Cambridge: Harvard University Press; 1940.

Harper, Ida Husted: *The Life and Work of Susan B. Anthony.* 3 vols. Indianapolis and Kansas City: Bowen-Merrill Company; 1899–1908.

Harrington, Fred Harvey: *Fighting Politician, Major General N. P. Banks.* Philadelphia: University of Pennsylvania Press; 1948.

Harrison, Royden: "The British Labour Movement and the International in 1864." *The Socialist Register, 1964,* edited by Ralph Miliband and John Saville, pp. 293–308. New York: Monthly Review Press; 1964.

Hays, Samuel P.: *The Response to Industrialism, 1885–1914.* Chicago: University of Chicago Press; 1957.

Hesseltine, William B.: *Ulysses S. Grant, Politician.* New York: Dodd, Mead & Company; 1935.

Higham, John: *Strangers in the Land: Patterns of American Nativism, 1860–1925.* New York: Atheneum; 1963.

Hillquit, Morris: *History of Socialism in the United States.* New York: Funk & Wagnalls Company; 1903.

Hirschfeld, Charles: *Baltimore, 1870–1900: Studies in Social History.* Baltimore: Johns Hopkins University Studies in Historical and Political Science, Series LIX, No. 2; 1941.

Hofstadter, Richard: *The Age of Reform, From Bryan to F.D.R.* New York: Alfred A. Knopf; 1955.

————: *The American Political Tradition and the Men Who Made It.* New York: Alfred A. Knopf; 1948.

Hoxie, Robert Franklin: *Trade Unionism in the United States.* New York: D. Appleton & Company; 1917.

Hudson, Frederic: *Journalism in the United States, from 1690 to 1872.* New York: Harper & Brothers; 1873.

Hugins, Walter A.: *Jacksonian Democracy and the Working Class: A Study of the New York Workingmen's Movement, 1829–1837.* Stanford, Cal.: Stanford Studies in History, Economics, and Political Science, Vol. XIX; 1960.

Hutchinson, William T.: *Cyrus Hall McCormick.* 2 vols. New York and London: The Century Co.; 1930–5.

Hyman, Harold Melvin: *Era of the Oath, Northern Loyalty Tests during the Civil War and Reconstruction.* Philadelphia: University of Pennsylvania Press; 1954.

Jellison, Charles A.: *Fessenden of Maine, Civil War Senator.* Syracuse: Syracuse University Press; 1962.

Jones, Fred Mitchell: *Middlemen in the Domestic Trade of the United States, 1800–1860.* Urbana, Ill.: University of Illinois Press; 1937.

Josephson, Matthew: *The Politicos, 1865–1896.* New York: Harcourt, Brace and Company; 1938.

———: *The Robber Barons, The Great American Capitalists, 1861–1901.* New York: Harcourt, Brace and Company; 1934.

Joyaux, Georges J.: "French Language Press in the Upper Mississippi and Great Lakes Areas." *Mid-America,* Vol. XLIII (Oct. 1961), pp. 242–59.

Karson, Marc: *American Labor Unions and Politics, 1900–1918.* Carbondale, Ill.: Southern Illinois University Press; 1958.

Kaufmann, Wilhelm: *Die Deutschen im amerikanischen Bürgerkriege (Sezessionskrieg 1861–1865).* München and Berlin: R. Oldenbourg; 1911.

Kennedy, Charles J.: "Commuter Services in the Boston Area, 1835–1860." *Business History Review,* Vol. XXXVI (Summer 1962), pp. 153–70.

Kent, Frank Richardson: *The Story of Maryland Politics.* Baltimore: Thomas and Evans Printing Co.; 1911.

Kerr, Clark and others: *Industrialism and Industrial Man: the Problems of Labor and Management in Economic Growth.* Second edition. New York: Oxford University Press; 1964.

Keynes, John Maynard: *The General Theory of Employment Interest and Money.* New York: Macmillan Company; 1935.

King, Willard L.: *Lincoln's Manager: David Davis.* Cambridge: Harvard University Press; 1960.

Kingsbury, Susan M., editor: *Labor Laws and Their Enforcement, with Special Reference to Massachusetts.* New York: Longmans, Green, and Co.; 1911.

Kirkland, Edward Chase: *Dream and Thought in the Business Community, 1860–1900.* Ithaca, N.Y.: Cornell University Press; 1956.

———: *Industry Comes of Age. Business, Labor, and Public Policy 1860–1897.* New York: Holt, Rinehart and Winston; 1961.

Klement, Frank: " 'Brick' Pomeroy: Copperhead and Curmudgeon." *Wisconsin Magazine of History,* Vol. XXXV (Winter 1951), pp. 106–13, 156–7.

Kugler, Israel: "The Trade Union Career of Susan B. Anthony." *Labor History,* Vol. II (Winter 1961), pp. 90–100.

Lee, Brother Basil Leo, F.S.C.: *Discontent in New York City, 1861–1865*. Washington, D.C.: Catholic University of America Press; 1943.

Leiby, James: *Carroll Wright and Labor Reform: The Origin of Labor Statistics*. Cambridge: Harvard University Press; 1960.

Lescohier, Don D.: *The Knights of St. Crispin, 1867–1874*. Madison: Bulletin of the University of Wisconsin, Economics and Political Science Series, Vol. VII; 1910.

Lofton, Williston H.: "Abolition· and Labor." *Journal of Negro History*, Vol. XXXIII (July 1948), pp. 249–83.

————: "Northern Labor and the Negro during the Civil War." *Journal of Negro History*, Vol. XXXIV (July 1949), pp. 251–73.

Logan, H. A.: "Labor Costs and Labor Standards." *Labor in Canadian-American Relations*. Edited by H. A. Innis. Toronto: Ryerson Press; 1937.

Lomask, Milton: *Andrew Johnson, President on Trial*. New York: Farrar, Straus; 1960.

Lonn, Ella: *Foreigners in the Union Army and Navy*. Baton Rouge: Louisiana State University Press; 1951.

Lutz, Alma: *Susan B. Anthony, Rebel, Crusader, Humanitarian*. Boston: Beacon Press; 1959.

Macdonald, Fergus: *The Catholic Church and the Secret Societies in the United States*. New York: United States Catholic Historical Society; 1946.

Madison, Charles A.: *American Labor Leaders, Personalities and Forces in the Labor Movement*. New York: Harper & Brothers; 1950.

Man, Albon P., Jr.: "Labor Competition and the New York Draft Riots of 1863." *Journal of Negro History*, Vol. XXXVI (Oct. 1951), pp. 375–405.

Mandelbaum, Seymour J.: *Boss Tweed's New York*. New York: John Wiley & Sons; 1965.

Matison, Sumner Eliot: "The Labor Movement and the Negro during Reconstruction." *Journal of Negro History*, Vol. XXXIII (Oct. 1948), pp. 426–68.

Mayer, George H.: *The Republican Party, 1854–1964*. New York: Oxford University Press; 1964.

McCabe, David A.: *The Standard Rate in American Trade Unions*. Baltimore: Johns Hopkins University Studies in Historical and Political Science, Series XXX, No. 2; 1912.

McGuire, James K., editor: *The Democratic Party of the State of New York*. 3 vols. New York: United States History Company; 1905.

McKitrick, Eric L.: *Andrew Johnson and Reconstruction*. Chicago: University of Chicago Press; 1960.

McPherson, James M.: "Grant or Greeley? The Abolitionist Dilemma in the Election of 1872." *American Historical Review*, Vol. LXXI (Oct. 1965), pp. 43–61.

————: *The Negro's Civil War. How American Negroes Felt and Acted during the War for the Union*. New York: Random House; 1965.

————: *The Struggle for Equality; Abolitionists and the Negro in the Civil War and Reconstruction*. Princeton: Princeton University Press; 1964.

Merk, Frederick: "The Labor Movement in Wisconsin during the Civil War." *Proceedings of the State Historical Society of Wisconsin at Its Sixty-Second Annual Meeting Held October 22, 1914*, pp. 168–91. Madison; 1915.

Merriam, George S.: *The Life and Times of Samuel Bowles*. 2 vols. New York: The Century Co.; 1885.

Merrill, Horace Samuel: *Bourbon Democracy of the Middle West, 1865–1896*. Baton Rouge: Louisiana State University Press; 1953.

Merrill, Louis Taylor: *General Benjamin F. Butler and the Campaign of 1868*. Chicago: Private edition; 1939.

Miller, Clarence Lee: *The States of the Old Northwest and the Tariff, 1865–1888*. Emporia, Kan.: Emporia Gazette Press; 1929.

Mitchell, Wesley C.: *A History of the Greenbacks, with Special Reference to the Economic Consequences of Their Issue: 1862–1865*. Chicago: University of Chicago Press; 1903.

Montgomery, David: "Radical Republicanism in Pennsylvania, 1866–1873." *Pennsylvania Magazine of History and Biography*, Vol. LXXXV (Oct. 1961), pp. 439–57.

Moses, John: *Illinois, Historical and Statistical*. 2 vols. Chicago: Fergus Printing Company; 1889–92.

Mott, Frank Luther: *A History of American Magazines*. 4 vols. Cambridge: Belknap Press of Harvard University Press; 1957.

Myers, Gustavus: *The History of Tammany Hall*. Second edition. New York: Boni & Liveright; 1917.

Nevins, Allan: *Abram S. Hewitt, with Some Account of Peter Cooper*. New York and London: Harper & Brothers; 1935.

————: *The Emergence of Modern America 1865–1878*. New York: Macmillan Company; 1927.

————: *Hamilton Fish: The Inner History of the Grant Administration*. 2 vols. New York: Dodd, Mead, & Company; 1936.

———: *The War for the Union.* 2 vols. New York: Scribner; 1959–60.

Nolen, Russell M.: "The Labor Movement in St. Louis from 1860 to 1890." *Missouri Historical Review,* Vol. XXXIV (Jan. 1940), pp. 157–81.

Nye, Russel B.: *George Bancroft, Brahmin Rebel.* New York: Alfred A. Knopf; 1944.

Oberholtzer, Ellis Paxson: *Jay Cooke, Financier of the Civil War.* 2 vols. Philadelphia: G. W. Jacobs & Co.; 1907.

Obermann, Karl: *Joseph Weydemeyer, Pioneer of American Socialism.* New York: International Publishers; 1947.

100 Years as a Chartered Union, 1852–1952: History of Pittsburgh Typographical Union No. 7. N.p.; n.d.

Osterweis, Rollin G.: *Three Centuries of New Haven, 1638–1938.* New Haven: Yale University Press; 1953.

Ozanne, Robert: "Union-Management Relations: McCormick Harvesting Machine Company, 1862–1886." *Labor History,* Vol. IV (Spring 1963), pp. 132–60.

Parrington, Vernon L.: *Main Currents in American Thought: An Interpretation of American Literature from the Beginnings to 1920.* 3 vols. New York: Harcourt, Brace and Company; 1927–30.

Pelling, Henry: *A History of British Trade Unionism.* Harmondsworth: Penguin Books; 1963.

Perlman, Selig: *A History of Trade Unionism in the United States.* New York: The Macmillan Company; 1922.

———: *A Theory of the Labor Movement.* New York: The Macmillan Company; 1928.

Persons, Charles E.: "The Early History of Factory Legislation in Massachusetts: From 1825 to the Passage of the Ten Hour Law in 1874." *Labor Laws and Their Enforcement, with Special Reference to Massachusetts.* Edited by Susan M. Kingsbury. New York: Longmans, Green, and Company; 1911.

Pierce, Bessie Louise: *A History of Chicago.* 3 vols. New York: Alfred A. Knopf; 1937–40.

Ping Chiu: *Chinese Labor in California, 1850–1880. An Economic Study.* Madison: State Historical Society of Wisconsin; 1963.

Pratt, John W.: "Boss Tweed's Public Welfare Program." *New York Historical Society Quarterly,* Vol. XLV (Oct. 1961), pp. 396–411.

Redlich, Fritz: *History of American Business Leaders, A Series of Studies. Volume I. Theory, Iron and Steel, Iron Ore Mining.* Ann Arbor: Edwards Brothers; 1940.

Rhodes, James Ford: *History of the United States from the Compromise of 1850 to the Final Restoration of Home Rule at the South in 1877.* 5 vols. New York: Harper & Brothers; 1893–1904.

Richardson, Reed C.: *Labor Leader, 1860's.* Ithaca, N.Y.: New York State School of Industrial and Labor Relations, Cornell University, Bulletin 31; 1961.

Riddle, A. G.: *The Life of Benjamin F. Wade.* Cleveland: William W. Williams; 1886.

Robbins, Edwin Clyde: *Railway Conductors, A Study in Organized Labor.* New York: Columbia University Studies in History, Economics and Public Law, No. 148; 1914.

Robinson, Jesse S.: *The Amalgamated Association of Iron, Steel and Tin Workers.* Baltimore: Johns Hopkins University Studies in Historical and Political Science, Series XXXVIII, No. 2; 1920.

Roche, John P.: '"Entrepreneurial Liberty and the Fourteenth Amendment." *Labor History,* Vol. IV (Winter 1963), pp. 3–31.

Roseboom, Eugene H.: *The Civil War Era, 1850–1873. The History of the State of Ohio,* edited by Carl Wittke. Vol. IV. Columbus: Ohio State Archaeological and Historical Society; 1944.

Ross, Earle Dudley: *The Liberal Republican Movement.* New York: Henry Holt and Co.; 1919.

Roy, Andrew: *A History of the Coal Miners of the United States.* Columbus: J. L. Trauger Printing Company; n.d.

Rudé, George: *The Crowd in History: A Study of Popular Disturbances in France and England, 1730–1848.* New York: John Wiley & Sons; 1964.

Rudolph, Frederick: "Chinamen in Yankeedom: Anti-Unionism in Massachusetts in 1870." *American Historical Review,* Vol. LIII (Oct. 1947), pp. 1–29.

Russ, William A., Jr.: "The Failure to Reunite Methodism after the Civil War." *Susquehanna University Studies,* I, 8–16. Selingrove, Pa.: Susquehanna University; 1936.

———: "The Influence of the Methodist Press upon Radical Reconstruction (1865–1868)." *Susquehanna University Studies,* II, 51–62. Selingrove, Pa.: Susquehanna University; 1937.

Sachs, Emanie: *"The Terrible Siren": Victoria Woodhull (1838–1927).* New York: Harper & Brothers; 1928.

Schlegel, Marvin Wilson: *Ruler of the Reading: The Life of Franklin B. Gowen, 1836–1889.* Harrisburg: Archives Publishing Company of Pennsylvania; 1947.

Schlüter, Hermann: *Die Anfänge der deutschen Arbeiterbewegung in Amerika.* Stuttgart: J. H. W. Dietz; 1907.

————: *The Brewing Industry and the Brewery Workers' Movement in America.* Cincinnati: International Union of United Brewery Workmen of America; 1910.

————: *Die Internationale in Amerika: Ein Beitrag zur Geschichte der Arbeiter-Bewegung in den Vereinigten Staaten.* Chicago: Deutsche Sprachgruppe der Sozialist. Partei der Ver. Staaten; 1918.

————: *Lincoln, Labor and Slavery: A Chapter from the Social History of America.* New York: Socialist Literature Co.; 1913.

Schrier, Arnold: *Ireland and the American Emigration 1850–1900.* Minneapolis: University of Minnesota Press; 1958.

Schultz, Theodore W.: "Human Wealth and Economic Growth." *The Humanist,* Vol. XIX (March–April 1959), pp. 71–81.

Seibold, George G.: *Historical Sketch of Columbia Typographical Union Number One Hundred and One (Known as Columbia Typographical Society from 1815 to 1867).* Washington, D.C.: National Capital Press; 1915.

Sellers, Charles G.: "Who Were the Southern Whigs?" *American Historical Review,* Vol. LIX (Jan. 1954), pp. 335–46.

Shalloo, Jeremiah Patrick: *Private Police: With Special Reference to Pennsylvania.* Philadelphia: American Academy of Political and Social Science; 1933.

Shannon, William V.: *The American Irish.* New York: The Macmillan Company; 1963.

Shapiro, Samuel: "'Aristocracy, Mud, and Vituperation': The Butler-Dana Campaign in Essex County in 1868." *New England Quarterly,* Vol. XXXI (Sept. 1958), pp. 340–60.

Sharkey, Robert P.: *Money, Class, and Party: An Economic Study of Civil War and Reconstruction.* Baltimore: Johns Hopkins University Studies in Historical and Political Science, Series LXXVII, No. 2; 1959.

Sherwin, Oscar: *Prophet of Liberty; the Life and Times of Wendell Phillips.* New York: Bookman Associates; 1958.

Shipley, Max L.: "The Background and Legal Aspects of the Pendleton Plan." *Mississippi Valley Historical Review,* Vol. XXIV (Dec. 1937), pp. 329–40.

Shugg, Roger W.: *Origins of Class Struggle in Louisiana. A Social History of White Farmers and Laborers during Slavery and After.* Baton Rouge: Louisiana State University Press; 1939.

Siebert, P. W.: "Old Bayardstown." *Western Pennsylvania Historical Magazine,* IX (1926), 90–103.

Simkins, Francis Butler: *A History of the South.* Third edition. New York: Alfred A. Knopf; 1963.

Smith, Timothy L.: *Revivalism and Social Reform in Mid-Nineteenth Century America*. New York and Nashville: Abingdon Press; 1957.

Smith, Willard H.: *Schuyler Colfax, The Changing Fortunes of a Political Idol*. Indianapolis: Indiana Historical Bureau; 1952.

Sorge, Friedrich A.: "Die Arbeiterbewegung in den Vereinigten Staaten, 1860–1866." *Die Neue Zeit*, IX, 2 Band (1890–1), 397–406, 438–42.

———: "Die Arbeiterbewegung in den Vereinigten Staaten, 1866–1876." *Die Neue Zeit*, X, 1 Band (1891–2), 69–76, 110–18, 172–9, 206–16, 388–98.

Stampp, Kenneth M.: *And the War Came, The North and the Secession Crisis, 1860–1861*. Baton Rouge: Louisiana State University Press; 1950.

———: *The Era of Reconstruction, 1865–1877*. New York: Alfred A. Knopf; 1965.

Stanton, Elizabeth Cady, Susan B. Anthony, and Matilda Joslyn Gage: *History of Woman Suffrage*. 3 vols. New York: Fowler & Wells; 1881–7.

Stevens, George A.: *New York Typographical Union No. 6. Study of a Modern Trade Union and Its Predecessors*. Albany: New York State Department of Labor; 1913.

Sullivan, William A.: *The Industrial Worker in Pennsylvania, 1800–1840*. Harrisburg: Pennsylvania Historical and Museum Commission; 1955.

Tarbell, Ida M.: *The Tariff in Our Times*. New York: Macmillan Co.; 1911.

Taussig, F. W.: *The Tariff History of the United States*. Fifth edition. New York: G. P. Putnam's Sons; 1910.

Taylor, George Rogers: "American Economic Growth Before 1840: An Exploratory Essay." *Journal of Economic History*, Vol. XXIV (Dec. 1964), pp. 427–44.

———: "The National Economy Before and After the Civil War." *Economic Change in the Civil War Era*. Edited by David T. Gilchrist and W. David Lewis. Greenville, Del.: Eleutherian Mills-Hagley Foundation; 1965.

———: *The Transportation Revolution, 1815–1860*. New York: Holt, Rinehart and Winston; 1962.

Todes, Charlotte: *William H. Sylvis and the National Labor Union*. New York: International Publishers; 1942.

Toole, Robert C.: "Anti-Monopoly League of 1866 v. LaCrosse Packet Company Et Al." *Mid-America*, Vol. XLIII (Oct. 1961), pp. 211–25.

Trefousse, Hans Louis: *Ben Butler: The South Called Him Beast.* New York: Twayne Publishers; 1957.

———: *Benjamin Franklin Wade, Radical Republican from Ohio.* New York: Twayne Publishers; 1963.

Tracy, George A.: *History of the Typographical Union.* Indianapolis: International Typographical Union; 1913.

Ulman, Lloyd: *The Rise of the National Trade Union: The Development and Significance of Its Structure, Governing Institutions, and Economic Policies.* Cambridge: Harvard University Press; 1955.

Ulriksson, Vidkunn: *The Telegraphers: Their Craft and Their Unions.* Washington, D.C.: Public Affairs Press; 1953.

Unger, Irwin: "Business Men and Specie Resumption." *Political Science Quarterly,* Vol. LXXIV (March 1959), pp. 46–70.

———: *The Greenback Era, A Social and Political History of American Finance, 1865–1879.* Princeton: Princeton University Press; 1964.

Van Deusen, Glyndon G.: *Horace Greeley, Nineteenth Century Crusader.* Philadelphia: University of Pennsylvania Press; 1953.

Ware, Norman J.: "The History of Labor Interaction." *Labor in Canadian-American Relations.* Edited by H. A. Innis. Toronto: Ryerson Press; 1937.

———: *The Industrial Worker, 1840–1860; the Reaction of American Industrial Society to the Advance of the Industrial Revolution.* Boston and New York: Houghton Mifflin Company; 1924.

———: *The Labor Movement in the United States 1860–1895: A Study in Democracy.* New York and London: D. Appleton and Company; 1929.

Wesley, Charles H.: *Negro Labor in the United States, 1850–1925; A Study in American Economic History.* New York: Vanguard Press; 1927.

Wharton, Vernon Lane: *The Negro in Mississippi, 1865–1890.* Chapel Hill: University of North Carolina Press; 1947.

Wieck, Edward A.: *The American Miners' Association: A Record of the Origin of Coal Miners' Unions in the United States.* New York: Russel Sage Foundation; 1940.

Williams, T. Harry: *Lincoln and the Radicals.* Madison: University of Wisconsin Press; 1941.

Williamson, Harold Francis: *Edward Atkinson, The Biography of an American Liberal, 1827–1905.* Boston: Old Corner Book Store; 1934.

Wittke, Carl: *The Utopian Communist: A Biography of Wilhelm*

Weitling, Nineteenth Century Reformer. Baton Rouge: Louisiana State University Press; 1950.

Wolfe, F. E.: *Admission to American Trade Unions*. Baltimore: Johns Hopkins University Studies in Historical and Political Science, Series XXX, No. 3; 1912.

Woodburn, James Albert: *The Life of Thaddeus Stevens*. Indianapolis: Bobbs-Merrill Company; 1913.

Woodley, Thomas Frederick: *The Great Leveler: The Life of Thaddeus Stevens*. New York: Stackpole Sons; 1937.

Woolfolk, George Ruble: *The Cotton Regency: The Northern Merchants and Reconstruction, 1865–1880*. New York: Bookman Associates; 1958.

Yearley, Clifton K., Jr.: *Britons in American Labor: A History of the Influence of the United Kingdom Immigrants on American Labor, 1820–1914*. Baltimore: Johns Hopkins University Studies in Historical and Political Science, Series LXXV, No. 1; 1957.

———: *Enterprise and Anthracite: Economics and Democracy in Schuylkill County, 1820–1875*. Baltimore: Johns Hopkins University Studies in Historical and Political Science, Series LXXIX, No. 1; 1961.

———: "Richard Trevellick: Labor Agitator." *Michigan History Magazine*, Vol. XXXIX (Dec. 1955), pp. 423–44.

Yearns, Wilfred Buck: *The Confederate Congress*. Athens: University of Georgia Press; 1960.

Zahler, Helene Sara: *Eastern Workingmen and National Land Policy, 1829–1862*. Columbia University Studies in the History of American Agriculture Number 7. New York: Columbia University Press; 1941.

Zornow, William Frank: *Lincoln and the Party Divided*. Norman: University of Oklahoma Press; 1954.

Index

A Note About the Author

David Montgomery was born in Wayne, Pennsylvania, in 1927. He was graduated from Swarthmore College (Phi Beta Kappa) in 1950 and received his M.A. (1960) and Ph.D. (1962) from the University of Minnesota. Between 1951 and 1960 he worked as a machinist in New York City and St. Paul, Minnesota. He taught at Hamline University in 1962–3 and is now assistant professor of history at the University of Pittsburgh.